USHER
iBT TOEFL
FINAL TEST
READING

어셔 iBT 토플 파이널 테스트 리딩

어셔 어학 연구소

USHER
iBT TOEFL FINAL TEST
READING
어셔 iBT 토플 파이널 테스트 리딩

초판 1쇄 발행 · 2012년 5월 1일
개정 10쇄 발행 · 2020년 3월 1일
개정증보판 3쇄 발행 · 2020년 3월 1일
개정증보판 5쇄 발행 · 2024년 9월 1일

지은이 · 어셔토플연구소
펴낸곳 · (주)어셔 어학연구소
펴낸이 · 어셔 어학연구소 출판팀
주   소 · 서울시 서초구 잠원로3길 40 태남빌딩 2층 어셔 어학 연구소
전   화 · 02)595-5679
홈페이지 · www.usher.co.kr
ISBN . 979-11-85317-04-5

정   가 · 26,000원

저작권자 · ⓒ2018, 어셔 어학연구소

이 책 및 mp3 내용의 저작권은 저자에게 있습니다.
서면에 의한 저자와 출판사의 허락없이 내용의 일부 혹은 전부를 인용하거나, 발췌하는 것을 금합니다.
COPYRIGHT ⓒ 2018 by Usher Language Research Institute
All rights reserved including the rights of reproduction In whole or part in any form Printed in Korea

PREFACE I

본 토플 교재는 iBT 토플을 공부하는 학생들의 다음과 같은 요청에서 제작 동기를 찾습니다.

▶ 최신 iBT 토플 실전 경향 반영
과거 토플 형태인 PBT뿐만 아니라, CBT를 지나 새롭게 만들어진 형태인 iBT 토플 시험에서조차 처음 국내에서 시행된 2006년 9월 이후로 많은 변화가 있었습니다. 하지만 토플 시험을 위한 영어 원서의 경우에는 초기 iBT시험 형태가 완전히 모습을 드러내기 전 토플 시험 주관사인 ETS의 시험 방향 발표만을 듣고 만든 형태인데다가 시험이 어느 정도 윤곽을 잡은 뒤 만들어낸 초기 형태의 문제지들 역시 최근 변화된 ETS의 흐름을 읽지 못해 반영하지 못한 부분이 많기에 최근 추세에 따른 문제지를 제작하였습니다.

▶ 토플 고득점 취득을 위한 최상의 난이도
iBT 토플의 최근 변화 중 가장 큰 부분은 토플 시험 지문의 난이도와 문제수준의 변화입니다. 과거 초기의 iBT 토플 시험은 지문 내용이 최근의 토플보다 단순한 형태이나 최근의 토플 리딩과 리스닝의 본문 주제 및 내용들은 일반 상식 선에서 풀 수 없는 독특한 내용들을 수렴하고 있기 때문에 대충 추측해서 접근하면 틀리게 본문 내용을 구성해 두었습니다. 아울러 문제 역시 과거의 문제들은 본문 내용이 오답 아니면 정답으로 쉽게 구별 되었다면, 최근의 iBT 토플은 본문 내용 중 분명 맞는 말이 있더라도 질문에서 묻는 말이 아니라면, 정답 처리되지 않도록 하고 있습니다. 이런 부분들을 포함한, 다양한 토픽 등 과거의 문제들과는 다른 차이점을 성실히 반영하였습니다. 토플 시험에서 고득점을 원하는 학생들이 원하는 문제지는 자신에게 자신감을 주는 문제지 라기 보다는 실제 시험 중 최상의 난이도를 원하는 경우가 많고 실제로 이러한 자세는 문제풀이 과정이나 실제 시험을 대할 때 상당한 긍정적 효과를 낳습니다. 이에 본 iBT 토플 교재는 고득점을 위한 분명한 목적을 담았습니다.

▶ 오답 패턴 정리
50년 이상 문제만 내온 ETS가 토플 문제를 낼 때도 반드시 오답 패턴이 있기에 이런 부분을 집중 분석하여 오답에 낚이지 않고 정답을 채택할 수 있도록 하였습니다. 실수가 생길 때마다 반드시 검토하여 어떤 패턴에 본인이 취약한지 파악하여 같은 실수의 반복을 피할 수 있게 하였습니다.

▶ 토플 독학하기 쉬운 교재
상황이 여의치 않아 토플 학원을 다니지 않고, 토플독학하는 학생들이 가장 힘들어 하는 부분이 해설지 부분에서 왜 답이 되고 아닌지에 대한 설명을 보통 정답만 불러주거나, 별 도움이 되지 않는 정답 이유만을 적고 끝나는 경우가 많습니다. 이에 본 교재는 혼자 공부하는 학생들을 위해 정답이 되는 부분에 대한 설명은 기본으로 하고 이외에 정답의 근거가 되는 부분이 본문에 어디에 위치해 있는지와 오답의 경우에도 왜 오답이 되는지에 대한 이유까지 구체적으로 해설해 두었습니다. 적극적인 문제 해결 의지만 가지고 있다면 효과를 극대화 할 수 있을 것입니다.

마지막으로, 본 교재를 가지고 토플을 준비하면서 생기는 다양한 문제 토론과 궁금증 및 토플 전반에 대한 궁금증 해소는 토플 사이트 usherin.usher.co.kr를 이용하시면 큰 효과를 기대할 수 있을 것입니다.

PREFACE II

학생들이 가장 많이 하는 질문을 서문에서 정리해 볼까 합니다.

질문1. 토플 시험 성적표를 보니, 독해, 듣기, 쓰기, 말하기 네 부분으로 되어있던데 어떤 과목부터 해야 할까요?

유학생들의 현지에서의 학업을 위한 준비여부를 파악하기 위해 만들어진 시험인 토플에서의 독해부분은 수능 영어나, 비즈니스 영 어인 토익 등과 비교해서 볼 때 어휘나, 문장의 복잡성 등이 아무래도 어려운 경향이 있습니다.

많은 학생들이 TOEFL LISTENING(토플 리스닝)을 먼저 걱정하곤 하는데, 이런 학생들에게 스크립트를 주고 문제를 풀어보라고 했 을 때 파악되는 것은 결국 못 들어서가 아닌 기초적인 독해조차 안돼서 못하는 경우가 많습니다.

뿐만 아니라 TOEFL WRITING(토플 라이팅)에 대해서라면 무언가를 창작하고 싶다면 모방이 우선입니다. 글을 쓸 때도 마찬가지로 모방의 대상은 글을 읽는 것이기에 쓰기보다는 당연히 독해가 우선입니다.

나아가 천천히 생각하며 문장조차 만들어 내지 못하는 학생들이 짧은 순간 문장을 만드는 것은 물론 발음과 엑센트와 억양까지 신경 써가며 해야 하는 TOEFL SPEAKING(토플 스피킹)은 더욱 더 설명하기 힘든 일입니다.

이런 점에서 이 iBT 토플 책을 보시는 여러분들은, 다음 순서를 꼭 기억해 주시기 바랍니다.

토플 단어암기 ⟶ 문법 (문장보기) ⟶ 독해 ⟶ 듣기, 쓰기, 말하기.

혹시, 외국 생활이 먼저인 학생들은 (요즘 많은 중·고등학교 생활을 영어권 국가에서 한 학생들) 듣기, 쓰기, 말하기가 더 편할 수도 있을 것입니다. 하지만 만약 토플시험을 즉시 봐서 점수를 넘길 수 없는 학생이라면, 결국(인정하기 싫겠지만, 외국 나가서 학교 다니며 기본 되는 영어실력을 충분히 쌓지 않아서 성적을 따지 못하는 경우라고 해도 틀린 말은 아닐 것입니다. 이런 경우 다른 과목에 비해서 귀찮은 토플 단어암기와 독해, 특히 주로 문제가 나는 어려운 문장을 보는 것에 취약할 것이고 이는 해외에서 살았었다는 이유만으로 어느 정도 해결되는 듣기나 말하기와는 달리 별도의 노력이 필요한 부분이므로 국내에서 새로이 공부하는 학생들과 크게 달라질것 없이, 위의 순서대로「토플 단어암기 ⟶ 문법 (문장보기) ⟶ 독해」라는 순서는 따라야 할 것입니다.

이 토플 교재를 보시기 전의 여러분은 꼭 단어 암기는 기본으로 되어있어야 하며 문장도 기본적인 틀은 잡혀 있는 상태이어야 할 것입니다. 꼭 순서를 기억해서 공부해 주시기 바랍니다.

질문2. 문제 풀 때, 시간이 모자라요….

TOEFL(토플) 시험 섹션 이름에서 알 수 있듯이, 토플 리딩과 리스닝은 정확히 (READING/LISTENING COMPREHENSION)입니다. 묻고자 하는 것이 단순한 읽고 들을 수 있느냐(READING/LISTENING)가 아닌, 이해(COMPREHENSION)를 했느냐를 파악하는데 초점을 맞췄습니다.

단어와 문법이라는 기본이 닦여있다는 가정하에 독해력을 향상시키기 위해서는,
"빨리보다는 먼저 정확히"에 초점을 맞춰 주시기 바랍니다. 점수는 이 두 가지가 잘되면 자연히 따라오게 됩니다.

많은 학생들이 얘기합니다. 시간이 모자라서 문제를 풀지 못한다고…. 하지만, 이런 학생들에게 시간을 아무리 줘도 네 개의 선택지 중에서 두 개는 제끼더라도 결국 둘 중에 하나를 선택할 때는 여지없이 오답을 찍는 경우가 많습니다. 이유는 간단히 문장 해석이 정확히 되지 않으니 이런 어려움을 50년 동안 알고 있는 ETS가 낸 오답패턴을 결국 벗어나지 못해 답을 선택할 수 없는 것입니다.

그러므로 우선은 많은 문제를 풀지 못하더라도 푼 문제는 다 맞힌다는 생각으로 먼저 임해주시기 바랍니다. 만약 10문제 중 다 풀고도 시간이 모자라지 않지만 5문제 밖에 못 맞힌 학생과 시간이 없어 5문제 밖에 못 풀었지만 5문제를 다 맞힌 두 학생이 있다면 발전 가능성은 후자 쪽에 더 많습니다. 정확성을 키운 학생은 하던 방식대로 조금만 더 반복하면 시간은 자연히 줄지만 전자의 학생의 경우에는 실력 자체를 늘리는 일을 해야 하므로 문제해결이 훨씬 어렵습니다.

그러므로, 꼭 「정확성 ⟶ 속도 ⟶ 그리고 토플 점수」를 기대하시기 바랍니다.

Q3. 본문 읽고, 문제 푸는 게 나을까요? vs 문제 풀며 본문을 읽는 게 나을까요?

두 방법 모두 장단점이 있습니다. 결론부터 실력을 기준으로 설명한다면, 대체로 전자는 실력이 있는 학생들이 푸는 방법이고, 후자는 실력이 약한 학생들이 쓰는 방법인 경우가 많습니다.

	본문 읽고 문제풀기	문제 풀며 본문 읽기 (*32p 따라가며 풀기 참조)
실력기준	실력 있는 학생들이 할 수 있습니다	실력이 약한 학생들이 점수 내려할 때 잘 쓰는 방법입니다
장점	대체로 어려운 문제인 Summary, Infer, Purpose를 잘 풀 수 있습니다	대체로 쉬운 문제인 Fact를 잘 푸는 경향이 있습니다.
단점	덤벙대다 오히려 쉬운 문제인 Fact 문제를 잘 틀리는 경향이 있습니다.	실력이 되지 않아 어려운 문제인 Infer, Purpose, Summary 문제를 잘 풀지 못합니다
보완방법	문단정리 + 답근거 꼼꼼히 하는 연습을 많이 합니다.	문단정리 + 답근거 꼼꼼히 하는 것은 당연하고, 이러한 학생들의 문제는 실력이므로, 실력을 키워야 합니다. 많은 문제를 푸는 것보다 적은 지문이더라도 정확히 반복적으로 읽어서 읽는 실력 자체를 많이 늘릴 수 있도록 합니다.
공통점	* 외우지 않은 이상 단어 문제는 둘 다 어려울 수도, 쉬울 수도 있습니다. * 30점 중 25점까지 맞는 것은 둘 다 할 수 있습니다. 하지만, 그 점수가 한계로 굳어지는 경향이 있습니다.	
결론	결국 25점을 넘어 30점으로 가기 위해서는 기초 실력 쌓는 것은 당연하고, 꼼꼼하게 풀어서 실수를 줄이는 것도 해야 하기에 두 가지를 합칠 수 있는 상황이 되어야 합니다. 즉, 문제를 다 풀고 5분 정도 남아서 미심쩍은 문제들은 다시 한 번 훑어볼 수 있도록 만들 수 있어야 합니다. (정확도 + 속도 둘 다 가질 것)	

토플은 어려운 시험이 아닙니다. 간단히 한글로 해석해주고 풀어보라고 했는데도 못풀만큼 내용이 어렵거나, 문제를 꼬아서 수험생을 힘들게 하는 시험이 아닙니다. 그저 해석이 되지 않고 이해가 되지 않아 힘들어한다고 해도 과언이 아닙니다. 그러므로 토플 공부 순서는 문제를 많이 풀려고 하지 말고, 본문 이해를 정확히 하는 연습을 우선하시기 바랍니다. 그림자를 잡아서 움직이려 하지 말고, 그림자를 만드는 몸을 움직이시기 바랍니다.

질문4. 독해 공부할 때, 꼭 해야 하는 것은 무엇일까요?

긴장감있는 문제풀이 + (문제 푼 직후의 확실한 분석, 즉) 정확한 해석 + 문단정리 + 답근거는 필수사항입니다.

문제를 풀 때, 정신 놓고 편안히 풀면 36분이면 풀 두 지문을 두 시간이 넘게 풀고도 실수는 실수대로 많이 하곤 합니다. 게다가 실제 토플 시험을 준비하는 입장에서는 전혀 도움이 되지 않습니다. 아울러, 해설지는 그저 문제의 답을 적어두고 해석만을 적어둔 것이 아닙니다. 여러분이 iBT 토플 공부하는 과정 중 꼭 해야 할 내용들을 체크해 놓은 것이므로 답근거와 문단정리를 한 후 해설지에 서 꼭 두 가지를 비교해 보시기 바랍니다.

아직 스스로 생각할 때 실력이 모자라다고 생각되는 학생의 경우에는 위의 내용을 충분히 따른 후 그 외에 본문을 씹어먹는다는 생각으로 분해 분석해야 합니다. 그러기 위해서는

틀린 문제를 왜 틀렸는지 분석 후, 단어 찾는 것은 당연하고 구문암기, 열 번 읽기 등을 통한 적용까지 마쳐야 합니다.

질문5. 시험이 얼마 안 남았어요. 가장 빨리 독해 점수를 올릴 수 있는 방법은 무엇일까요?

시험이 급박한 학생들이 가장 많이 하는 질문입니다. 이 질문은 두 가지로 나눠서 생각해봐야 합니다. 실력이 충분히 쌓은 경우와 그렇지 못한 경우.

실력이 충분치 못한 경우에는 답이 없습니다. 해석도, 내용 이해도 안되는 상대에시 이해를 묻는 시험문제를 풀 수 있다고 말할 수 없는 것은 당연할 것입니다. 하지만 실력은 기본이 된다는 가정하에서는 마무리 방법으로서 두가지를 해 볼만합니다.

1. 모니터 적응

대부분의 경우 학생들이 공부할 때는 종이로 공부를 하던 버릇이 있어서 모니터로, 특히나 모국어가 아닌 영어의 경우에는 더욱 더 문제가 될 경우가 적지 않습니다. 권하는 내용은 실제 시험을 보기 전, 모의고사를 두세 번 더 보는 것으로 실제 점수를 5점까지 끌어 올린 경우를 드물지 않게 보곤 합니다. 나름 자신이 있는 분들께 권해 드립니다.

2. 오답 정리

본인이 푼 문제지를 다 모아서 틀린 문제유형을 파악하고, 본인이 자주 낚이는 패턴을 분석해 보면, 본인만의 독특한 실수를 찾을 수 있습니다. 이것은 같은 반에서 공부했다고, 같은 수준이라고, 틀리는 문제가 같지는 않기 때문에 가르쳐 주는 선생님도 주변의 친구들도 심지어는 본인도 모르고 지나치는 경우가 많습니다. 하지만 당연히 풀어놓은 문제지가 없는 학생들의 경우에는 파악할 "재료"가 없기 때문에 시도조차 기대할 수는 없습니다. 실제점수로 대략 3점 내지 5점 정도까지도 올릴 수 있습니다. 이때 주의 할 것은 **실수를 줄이도록 노력**하는 것입니다. 더 나은 기술, 더 나은 실력보다는 내가 어이없이 한 실수만 줄여도 이 정도의 점수 향상 폭은 충분히 가능합니다.

사설이 많이 길지만 장황한 문제지의 장점에 대한 설명보다는 당장 문제지를 선택해야 하는 학생들이 궁금해 할 내용들로 서문을 채웠습니다. 본 문제지는 이런 생각을 바탕으로 만들었기에 학생들에게 어떤 모습으로든 도움이 될 것이라 생각합니다. 하지만 그저 안다는 점과 아는 것을 행하는 점은 전혀 다른 문제입니다. 마지막으로 잘 해야 하는 점은 지금까지 설명한 것을 잘 실행하는 것입니다. 꼭 실행해서 좋은 결과를 이루시기 바랍니다.

어셔 어학연구소

TABLE OF CONTENTS

USHER
USHER iBT TOEFL **FINAL TEST** READING
어셔 iBT 토플 파이널 테스트 리딩

Introduction

1. 본 iBT 토플 교재만의 특징 … 8
2. 본 iBT 토플 교재의 구성(공부 순서에 따른 정리) … 10
3. 계획표 짤 준비 … 16
4. 실력별 학습 계획 … 18
5. 토플 리딩 학습방법 및 순서 … 20
6. iBT TOEFL(iBT 토플) 소개 … 24
7. iBT TOEFL READING (iBT 토플 리딩) 소개 … 26
8. READING STRATEGIES(유형별 전략) … 31

문제집

TOEFL TEST 01(토플테스트01) … 45
Method of Measuring Bats' Age … 47
Tracing Language Diversification … 51

TOEFL TEST 02(토플테스트02) … 59
Earth's Atmosphere … 61
The Effects of Light on Flowering … 65

TOEFL TEST 03(토플테스트03) … 73
Naturalistic Painting … 75
Two Types of Evolutionary Theories … 79

TOEFL TEST 04(토플테스트04) … 87
Griffith and Transformation … 89
Maximilian Weber and His Influence … 93

TOEFL TEST 05(토플테스트05) … 101
Pasteur and The Origin of Life … 103
Early Research on Air … 107

TOEFL TEST 06(토플테스트06) … 115
Photography as an Art … 117
How and Why Birds Learn to Sing … 121

TOEFL TEST 07(토플테스트07) … 129
Functions of Roots … 131
History of The Patent Law … 135

TOEFL TEST 08(토플테스트08) … 143
Communication of Ants … 145
Calculating the Age of Earth … 149

TOEFL TEST 09(토플테스트09) … 157
Identifying Playful Behavior in Children … 159
Sentinel Behavior in Meerkats … 163

해설집

TOEFL TEST 01(토플테스트01)
답안 & 문제 유형 분석표 … 287
TEST 1 해석 및 해설 … 288
단어/구문 정리 … 172
묶기 … 210
열번읽기 … 248

TOEFL TEST 02(토플테스트02)
답안 & 문제 유형 분석표 … 305
TEST 2 해석 및 해설 … 306
단어/구문 정리 … 176
묶기 … 214
열번읽기 … 252

TOEFL TEST 03(토플테스트03)
답안 & 문제 유형 분석표 … 323
TEST 3 해석 및 해설 … 324
단어/구문 정리 … 180
묶기 … 218
열번읽기 … 256

TOEFL TEST 04(토플테스트04)
답안 & 문제 유형 분석표 … 341
TEST 4 해석 및 해설 … 342
단어/구문 정리 … 184
묶기 … 222
열번읽기 … 260

TOEFL TEST 05(토플테스트05)
답안 & 문제 유형 분석표 … 359
TEST 5 해석 및 해설 … 360
단어/구문 정리 … 188
묶기 … 226
열번읽기 … 264

TOEFL TEST 06(토플테스트06)
답안 & 문제 유형 분석표 … 377
TEST 6 해석 및 해설 … 378
단어/구문 정리 … 192
묶기 … 230
열번읽기 … 268

TOEFL TEST 07(토플테스트07)
답안 & 문제 유형 분석표 … 395
TEST 7 해석 및 해설 … 396
단어/구문 정리 … 196
묶기 … 234
열번읽기 … 272

TOEFL TEST 08(토플테스트08)
답안 & 문제 유형 분석표 … 413
TEST 8 해석 및 해설 … 414
단어/구문 정리 … 200
묶기 … 238
열번읽기 … 276

TOEFL TEST 09(토플테스트09)
답안 & 문제 유형 분석표 … 431
TEST 9 해석 및 해설 … 432
단어/구문 정리 … 204
묶기 … 242
열번읽기 … 280

부록

부록 … 448
부록해설집 … 467

별도 구매 서비스 소개 … 488

본 iBT 토플 교재의 특징

USHER iBT TOEFL FINAL TEST READING (어셔 iBT 토플 파이널 테스트 리딩)

1 실제 iBT 토플 시험과 가장 유사한 실전서

최신 바뀐 본문 반영 최신 출제 경향을 반영하여 학생들이 어려워하는 과학 주제는 물론 인문, 사회, 역사, 인물 등 지문의 다양화 및 상향된 난이도를 반영하였으며, 각 분야별 빈도를 참고하여 내용을 구성하였습니다.

최신 경향, 문제 반영 문제 역시 좀더 어려워진 최신 경향에 맞게 하였기에 효과적인 iBT토플 리딩 시험을 공략하기에 좋은 점을 모아두었습니다.

2 토플 고득점 달성을 위한 최종 점검을 위한 실전서

최상의 난이도 실제 iBT 토플 시험장에서 당황하지 않도록 하기 위해 난이도를 최상으로 하였으며 지문과 문제 구성 역시 최상의 난이도로 하였습니다.

유형별 제시전략 각 문제 별 유형 전략을 제시하여 기본 실력을 전제로 가장 빠르고 효과적인 문제 접근을 가능케 하였습니다.

3 자세한 한 iBT 토플 공부방법 설명

공부방법 설명 대부분의 여타 토플 교재들이 소홀히 하고 있는 해석에만 초점을 맞춘 것이 아닌 학생들이 공부하는 방법 자체를 설명해 두었습니다.

방법 활용 이를 잘 활용하기 위해 서문과 독해 학습방법, 독해 문제 풀이 전략(오답패턴) 부분을 잘 활용해 주시기 바랍니다.

4 토플 독학하기 쉽게 설명된 해설서 (토플학원에 못다니는 학생들을 위한 추천서)

답근거 찾기 정확한 지문 해석은 물론, 해설 시에도 정답만을 짚어주는 기존의 해설서의 방식을 탈피하여, 답근거를 명확히 하는 연습을 할 수 있도록, 본문과 오답에 각각 답이 되는 이유와, 틀린 이유를 표시해 두었습니다. 토플 독학을 하는 학생들에게 큰 도움이 되도록 하였습니다.

해설서 활용법 꼭 먼저 문제를 풀고, 고민한 후, 정답지의 내용과 하나하나 비교하며 확인하시기 바랍니다

5 체계적인 학습관리

일정표 스스로의 실력과 여건에 맞는 일정표를 작성하여 목표를 갖고 토플 공부에 임하여 더 좋은 결과를 가질 수 있도록 하였습니다.

리딩전략 모든 ETS문제는 정답과 오답을 만드는데 패턴이 있습니다. 이런 패턴들을 모아 정리하였습니다. 본인이 공부 중에 자꾸 틀리는 문제가 있다면, 그 문제의 오답 패턴 중 어떤 것 때문인지를 파악하여 빠른 효과를 기대할 수 있도록 하였습니다.

수준별 학습 학생 별로 공부를 해 본 학생과 해보지 않은 학생들간의 공부 법에 차이를 두어 본 토플책에 설명해 두었습니다. 목표를 어디까지 잡아야 할지를 잘 파악해서 무리한 계획을 세워, 중도 포기하는 일이 없도록 추천 계획표를 잘 이용하시기 바랍니다.

본 iBT 토플 교재의 구성

USHER iBT TOEFL FINAL TEST READING (어셔 iBT 토플 파이널 테스트 리딩)

문제집(뒷부분)

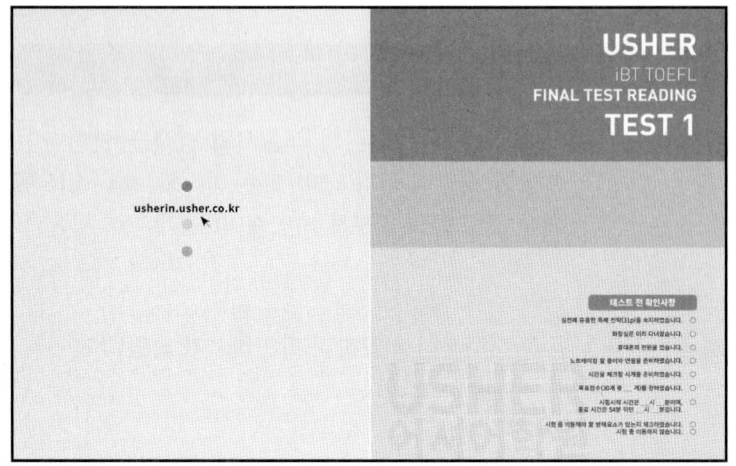

1. 시험 전 준비 사항

토플 시험 시작 전 시험 칠 수 있는 환경인지 여부부터 파악하기 위해, 준비사항을 적어놓았습니다. 토플 어학원에선 담당 매니저 선생님들이 챙겨주시지만, 혼자 공부할 때는 중간에 끊김이 생길 수 있으므로 특히 주의해서 지켜주시기 바랍니다.

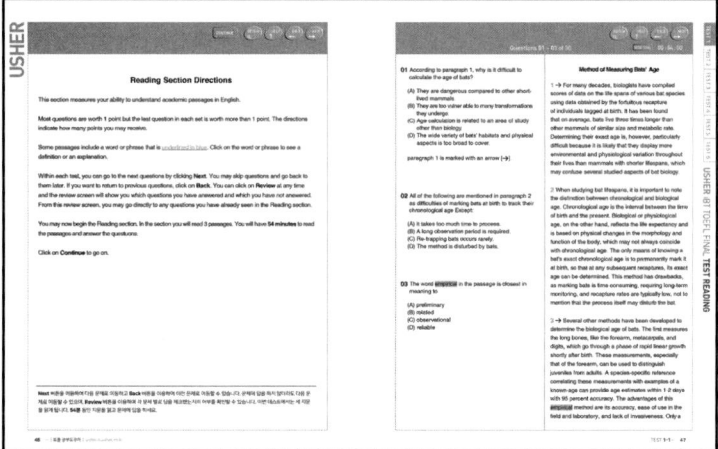

2. Test

실전 감각유지 및 실제 iBT 토플 시험에서의 확실한 효과를 위해서 9회분의 문제를 구성하였습니다. 실제 시험과 같은 형식의 문제지로 주의해서 문제를 풀어주시기 바랍니다.

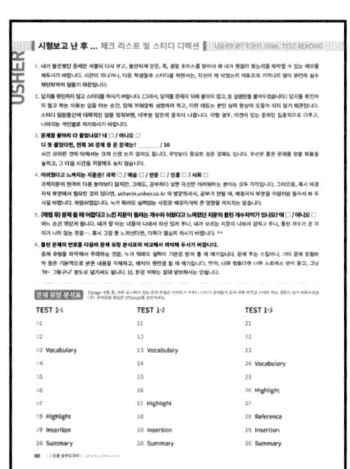
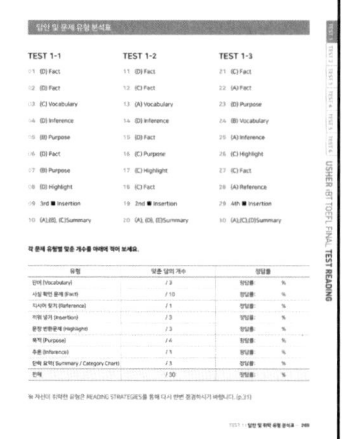

3. 시험 직후 체크 리스트 + 문제 유형 분석
(나의 취약점 분석)

iBT 토플 시험 직후 주의 사항과, 단순한 채점이 아닌, 스스로의 문제점을 점검할 수 있도록 만들어놓은 유형 분석표를 만들어 놓았습니다. 답을 먼저 확인하지 말고, 작은 책의 제일 뒤의 시험 직후의 디렉션대로, 우선 스스로 어려웠던 문제가 무엇이었는지, 나를 혼란스럽게 한 부분과 이유를 체크와, (가능하다면, 정답없이 스터디를 하는) 방법을 통해 스스로 문제가 무엇인지 꼭 점검해 주시기 바랍니다.

(공부 순서에 따라서 정리하였습니다)

| 토플 공부도우미 | usherin.usher.co.kr |

해설서(앞부분)

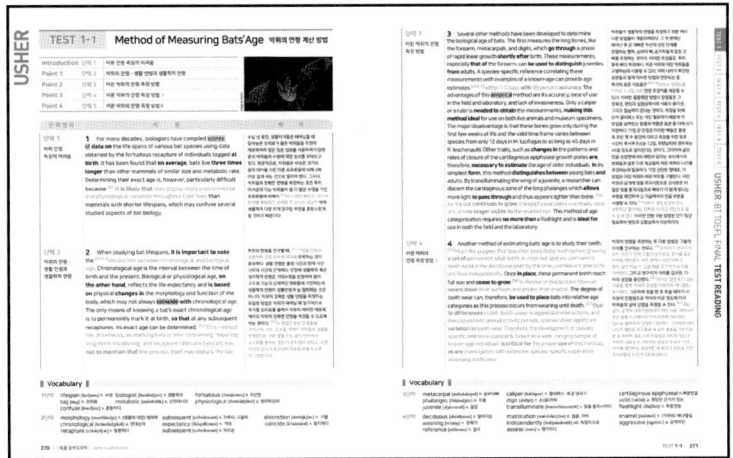

4. 정답 및 해석 + 해설

매회 문제를 푼 뒤, 이를 정확히 알기 위해 해석과 자세한 해설, 지문의 구조, 토플 단어정리뿐만 아니라, 토플 독학하시는 분들을 위해 문제 초이스 내에 오답이유 표시 및 본문에 정답 근거 등의 공부 편의성을 위한 부가 내용을 넣었습니다.

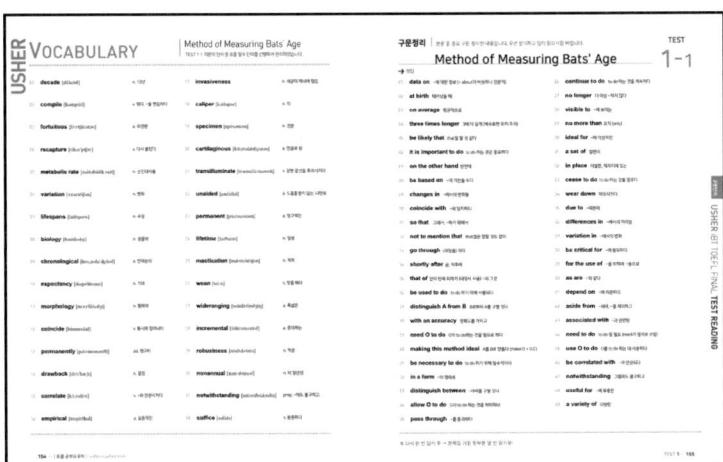

5. VOCABULARY + 구문정리

본문에 나온 토플 단어 정리와 구문을 각각 한페이지씩 정리해 두었습니다. 열번 읽기 위해서는 필히 단어와 구문암기를 먼저 한 후 넘어가시기 바랍니다.

문제집(뒷부분)

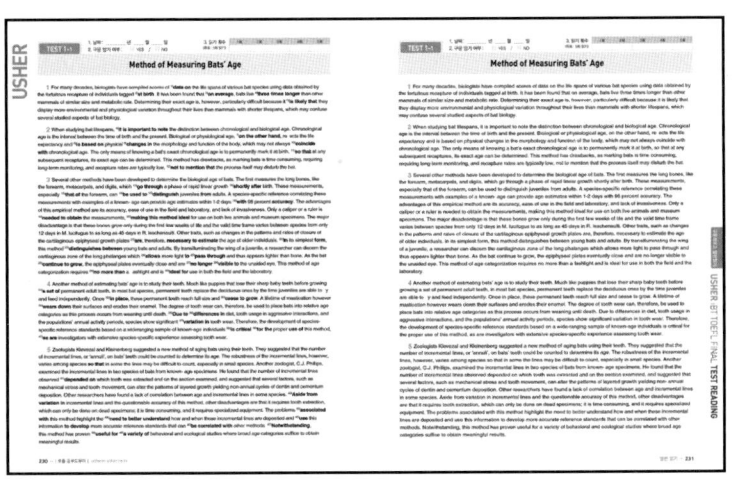

6. 열 번 읽기

문제지 맨 뒤에는 간단한 정답과 더불어, 각 본문만 주요 구문 표시만을 해두어 반복할 수 있도록 추가페이지를 만들었습니다. 그냥 버리지 말고, 꼭 들고 다니면서 반복적으로 읽어두시기 바랍니다.

본 iBT 토플 교재 구성 ··· 11

이외, 본책에 대한 좀 더 자세한 설명 (해설서 전반부 - 앞부분)

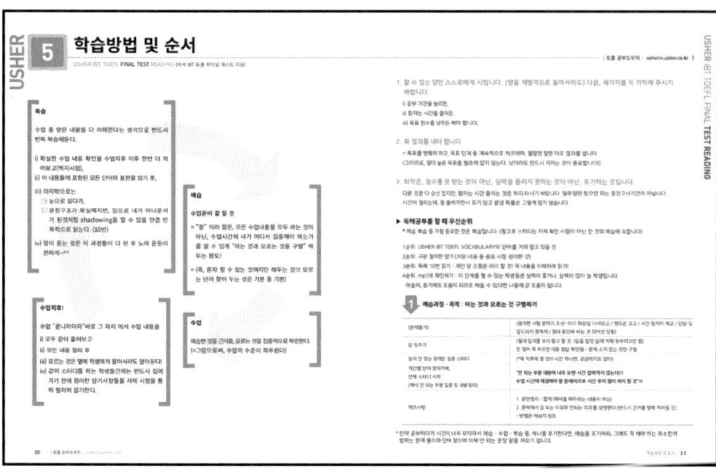

7. 학습방법

학생들의 토플 독해 실력 향상을 위해 특별히 학습 방법을 자세히 적어두었습니다. 각각의 이유를 읽고 납득 후, 따라 주시기 바랍니다.

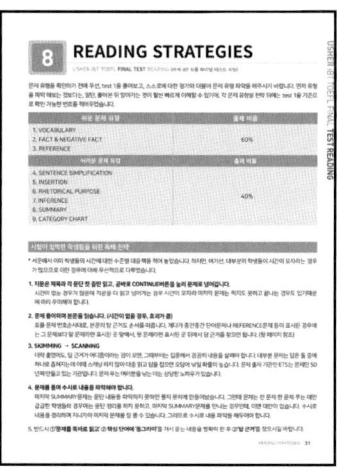

8. READING STRATEGIES

토플 독해문제 풀이에 있어서 가장 좋은 전략은 철저히 본문을 이해할 수 있는 실력 만들기입니다. 이점은 분명히 하되, 어느 정도 실력이 있는 학생들(대략 25점 이상)을 위해 리딩 문제 구성과 각 문제 유형에 따른 전략을 적어 두었습니다. 문제가 묻는 대상과, 오답패턴을 주의해서 보면, 큰 도움이 될 것입니다.

해석·해설 추가설명

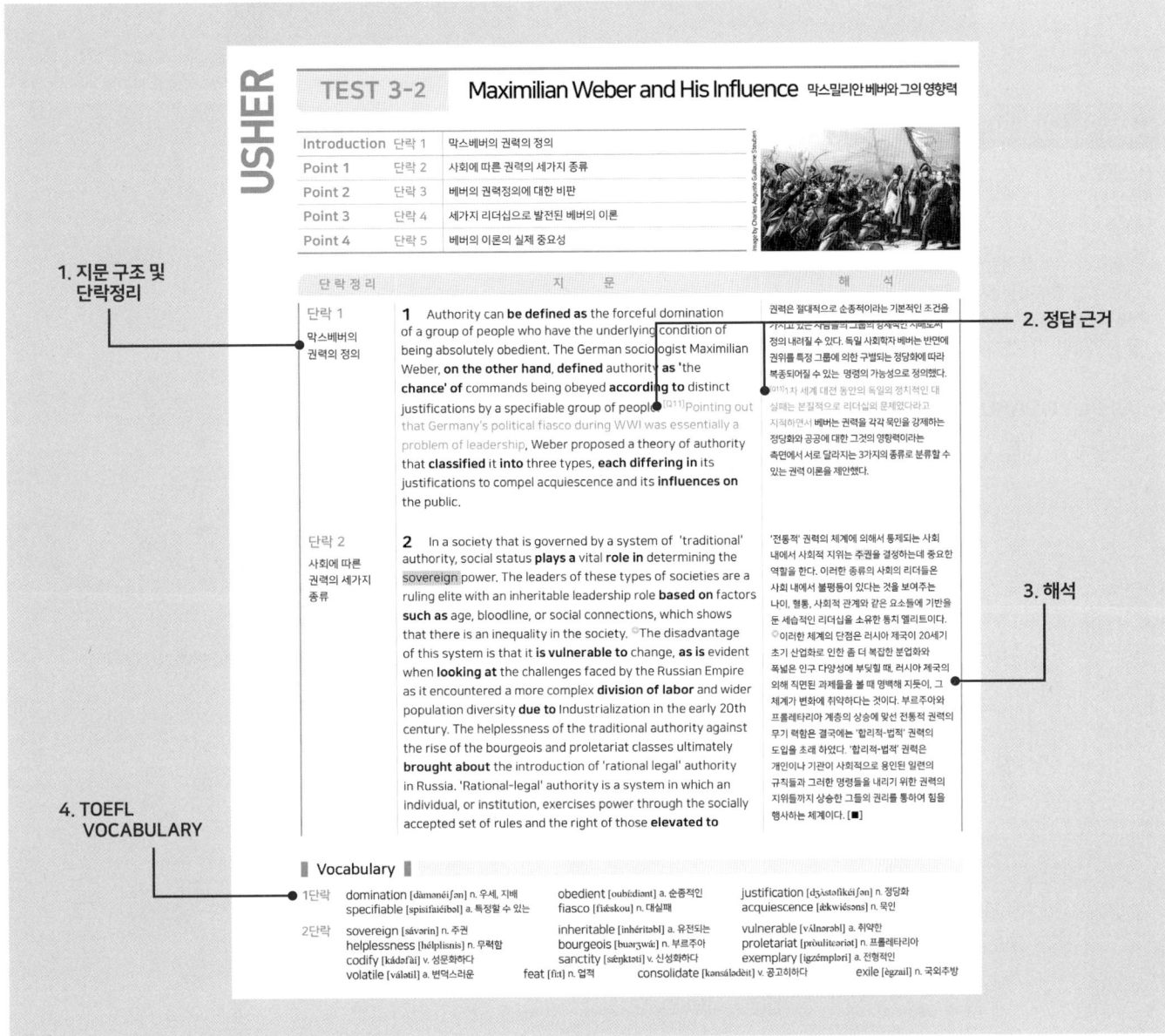

1. 지문 구조 및 단락정리

단락의 내용을 알아볼 수 있도록 도표화한 내용정리를 제공하였습니다.
내용정리와 더불어 제공한 사진을 보시면서 내용을 충분히 이해하시기 바랍니다.

2. 정답 근거

모든 문제는 정답근거가 없이는 문제를 만들지 않습니다. 꼭 정답 근거를 찾아가며 문제 푸는 버릇을 들이시기 바랍니다.
그냥 감으로 '어딘가에서..' 라는 식의 답 근거 제공은 ETS가 쉽게 엮어버리는 오답채택 확률을 높일 뿐입니다.
꼭 본인이 답 근거라고 지목한 부분과 답지의 부분이 맞는지 파악하는 습관을 들이시길 바랍니다.

3. 해석

지문 이해를 위해선 꼭 필요한 내용입니다. 하지만, 문장 해석에 급급해서 내용을 놓치는 일이 없도록 주의해서 '되감기'를 많이해 두시기 바랍니다.

참고로 되감기라 함은...

i) 문장
ii) 문단
iii) 글

전체에서 두루 쓰이는 방법으로,
긴 문장일 경우에는 문장 내에서,
문단의 경우에는 문장과 문장 사이의 전개를,
글 전체라면, 각 문단별의 연결 관계를 생각하며 읽는 것을 말합니다.

4. TOEFL VOCABULARY (토플 단어)

독해할 때 사전 찾는 불편을 덜 수 있도록 지문에서 사용된 단어의 뜻과 발음을 제시하였습니다.

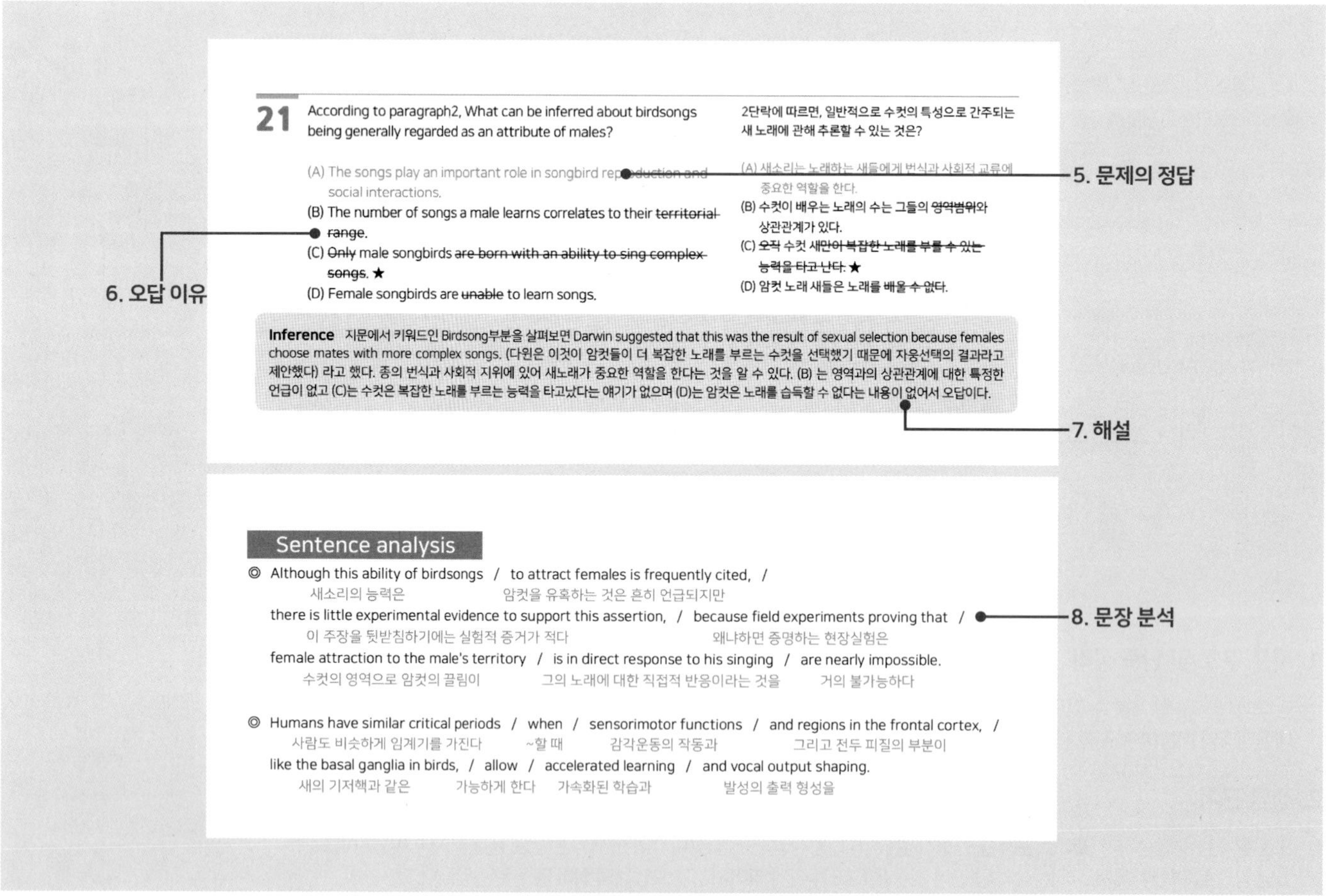

---

21 According to paragraph2, What can be inferred about birdsongs being generally regarded as an attribute of males?

(A) The songs play an important role in songbird reproduction and social interactions.
(B) The number of songs a male learns correlates to their territorial range.
(C) Only male songbirds are born with an ability to sing complex songs. ★
(D) Female songbirds are unable to learn songs.

2단락에 따르면, 일반적으로 수컷의 특성으로 간주되는 새 노래에 관해 추론할 수 있는 것은?

(A) 새소리는 노래하는 새들에게 번식과 사회적 교류에 중요한 역할을 한다.
(B) 수컷이 배우는 노래의 수는 그들의 영역범위와 상관관계가 있다.
(C) 오직 수컷 새만이 복잡한 노래를 부를 수 있는 능력을 타고 난다. ★
(D) 암컷 노래 새들은 노래를 배울 수 없다.

— 5. 문제의 정답

6. 오답 이유 —

Inference 지문에서 키워드인 Birdsong부분을 살펴보면 Darwin suggested that this was the result of sexual selection because females choose mates with more complex songs. (다윈은 이것이 암컷들이 더 복잡한 노래를 부르는 수컷을 선택했기 때문에 자웅선택의 결과라고 제안했다) 라고 했다. 종의 번식과 사회적 지위에 있어 새노래가 중요한 역할을 한다는 것을 알 수 있다. (B) 는 영역과의 상관관계에 대한 특정한 언급이 없고 (C)는 수컷은 복잡한 노래를 부르는 능력을 타고났다는 얘기가 없으며 (D)는 암컷은 노래를 습득할 수 없다는 내용이 없어서 오답이다.

— 7. 해설

Sentence analysis

◎ Although this ability of birdsongs / to attract females is frequently cited, /
　새소리의 능력은　　　　　　암컷을 유혹하는 것은 흔히 언급되지만
there is little experimental evidence to support this assertion, / because field experiments proving that /
　이 주장을 뒷받침하기에는 실험적 증거가 적다　　　　　　왜냐하면 증명하는 현장실험은
female attraction to the male's territory / is in direct response to his singing / are nearly impossible.
　수컷의 영역으로 암컷의 끌림이　　　그의 노래에 대한 직접적 반응이라는 것을　거의 불가능하다

◎ Humans have similar critical periods / when / sensorimotor functions / and regions in the frontal cortex, /
　사람도 비슷하게 임계기를 가진다　　～할 때　　감각운동의 작동과　　　　그리고 전두 피질의 부분이
like the basal ganglia in birds, / allow / accelerated learning / and vocal output shaping.
　새의 기저핵과 같은　　　가능하게 한다　가속화된 학습과　　　발성의 출력 형성을

— 8. 문장 분석

5. 문제의 정답

문제의 정답에 색을 넣어 표시해 쉽게 알 수 있도록 하였고, 옆의 해석 부분과 가급적 찾기 쉽도록 위치를 맞추어 두었습니다.

6. 오답 이유

일반 문제지들이 정답 근거만 제시하는 것에 반해, USHER iBT TOEFL FINAL TEST READING(어셔 iBT 토플 파이널테스트 리딩) 에서는, 오답의 이유도 밝혀 두어 혼자 공부하는 토플 독학생들에게 도움이 될 수 있도록 하였습니다.

7. 해설

답이 되는 이유와 오답 이유를 좀더 필요로 하는 학생들을 위해, 하나하나 풀어 더욱더 자세히 설명해 두었습니다. 하지만, 만약 정답 근거와 오답 표시를 보고 금방 이해가 간다면 굳이 다 읽으실 필요는 없습니다.

8. 문장 분석

본문 중 내용이나 구조가 어려운 문장을 별도로 끊어 해석하기를 보여 줌으로서 학생들의 실력 향상을 도울 수 있도록 하였습니다.

계획표 짤 준비

USHER iBT TOEFL FINAL TEST READING (어셔 iBT 토플 파이널 테스트 리딩)

1. 난 왜 토플 공부 할까? = 토플 점수 따서 뭐할까? Know-why

많은 학생들이 주로 고민하는 것은 늘 know-how에 대한 연구입니다. 물론 효율적인 토플 공부방법 참 중요합니다. 하지만, 그보다 먼저 해야 할 것은 과연 내가 왜 이 짓(?!!!)을 하고 있는가를 분명히 하는 것입니다. 즉, 다른 말로 목적이 뚜렷해야 한다는 뜻입니다. 공부하는 다수의 학생들이 공부하면서 매우 지겨워 하는 이유는 간단히 아직 내가 왜 해야 하는지가 명확하지 않기 때문입니다. 당장 4개월 뒤 외국에 공부하러 나가야 한다거나, 외국으로 이민수속을 준비하고 있고 2개월 뒤 비행기표를 끊어놓은 상황 또는 국내에서라면 과외자리를 얻기 위해선 보여줄 점수가 필요하다면 당장 써먹어야 한다는 생각 때문에 하루하루를 정말 꽉꽉 채워서 공부할 수 밖에 없습니다. 하지만, 배워봐야 언제 써먹을까 싶은 학생들에게, 특히나 공부의 목적이 단순히 점수를 위해서라면 대부분 공부할 때의 목적은 저 먼 나라의 이야기처럼 별 관심도 없습니다. (물론 중요하지 않다는 것은 아닙니다) 이런 상황이라면 공부하다 가 도중에 그만두기 딱 입니다. 싫다면? 이유부터 생각해 봅시다

< 나는 토플공부해서 (　　) 점 따면, (　　) 하겠다 >

2. 위의 목표에서 (　) 달 내에라는 말은 뺐습니다. 이유는 누구나 공부를 질질 끌면서 하기는 싫어합니다.

하지만, 그렇다고 내 능력은 생각지도 않고 시간 계획을 짜버리면 중간에 포기하기 쉽습니다. 남들은 1→2→3→4→5 단계를 가는 것이 정석이라고들 할 때, 왠지 나는 1→3→5로 갈 수 있을 것 같은 근거 없는 자신감? 이런 계획은 수시로 고칠 일만 더 만들 뿐 별로 도움 되진 않습니다.

지금은 시간을 생각하지 마십시오. 일단 샘플로 해보고 시간 계산해도 늦지 않습니다.

그리고 다음 단계도 생각하지 마십시오. 단어, 문법, 독해, 듣기, 쓰기, 말하기 어느 하나 다 안 중요한 것이 없다고 생각하는 순간, 무리한 계획을 세우게 되고, 그 후엔 스스로 질려 포기하기 쉽습니다.

하지만, 확실한 것은 지금 앞 단계를 확실히 끝내면 다음 단계로의 과정이 자연스레 이뤄진다는 점이고, 지금 확실치 않게 해두면, 두고두고 발목 잡는 일이 된다는 점입니다.

3. 현재 나의 공부를 방해하는 요소 파악 - 뇌구조 놀이.

다들 익숙한 놀이이지만, 정말 잘 이용하는 것이 어려운 이유는 오직 한가지 솔직하지 못해서입니다.
솔직하게 적어보십시오.

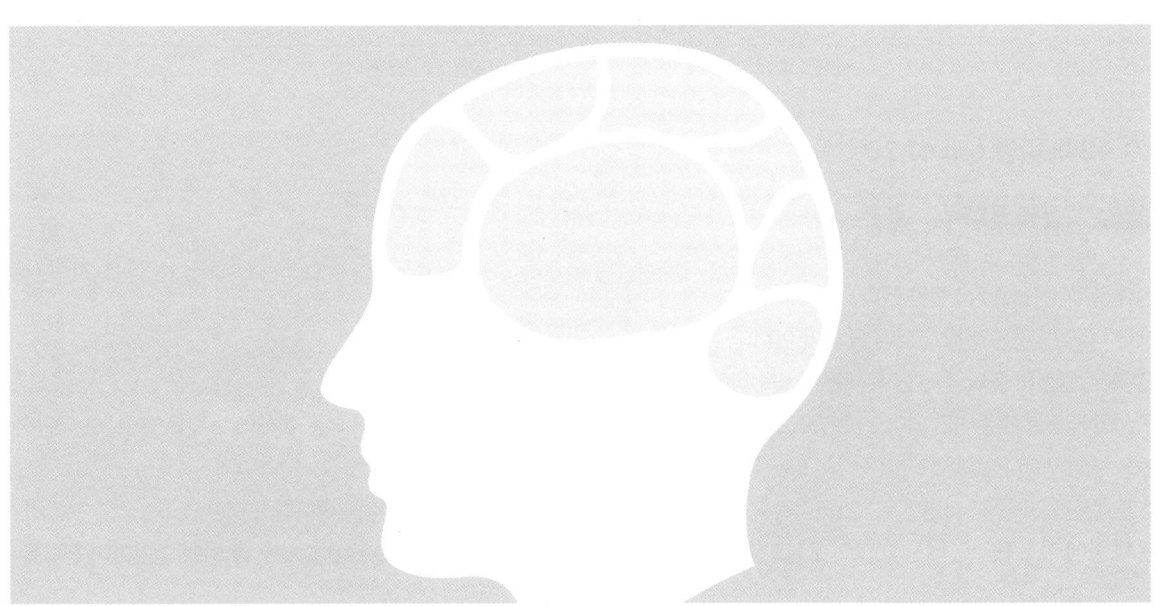

4. 1번부터 3번까지의 내용들을 정리하고 나서 이제 본격적인 스스로의 공부방법을 짜보십시오.

실력별 학습 계획

USHER iBT TOEFL FINAL TEST READING (어셔 iBT 토플 파이널 테스트 리딩)

Test 1을 푼 뒤, 본인의 실력에 맞는 계획표를 다음을 참고해서 짜서 실행시키시기 바랍니다.

1. 맞은 개수 18개 이상 out of 20

목표 - 매일 1회 (2지문씩 푼다)

- 다 맞겠다는 생각으로 푼다.
- 매일 정해진 지문을 각각 17분씩 35분 동안 푼다.
- 매일매일 꾸준히 2지문을 소화하되, 꼭 확실히 짚고 넘어간다.
- 채점한 후 틀린 문제를 꼭 확인한 뒤, 실수를 줄이려 노력한다.
- 주로 틀리는 문제 패턴이 무엇인지 꼭 알아내서 다음 시험에선 같은 실수 반복을 피할 수 있도록 한다.
- 단어, 구문 등의 정리는 거의 끝났어야 하므로, 간단히 빠진 것 몇 개 정도는 챙겨두자.

1주	1일차	2일차	3일차	4일차	5일차
	지문 2	지문 4	지문 6	지문 8	지문 10
	Out of 18	Out of 18	Out of 18	Out of 18	Out of 18
2주	6일차	7일차	8일차	9일차	
	지문 12	지문 14	지문 16	지문 18	
	Out of 18	Out of 18	Out of 18	Out of 18	

2. 맞은 개수 18개 미만 out of 20

목표 - 매일 1 지문씩 푼다

- 매일 정해진 1지문을 17분 동안 푼다.
- 시간 내에 다 푸는 것은 아직 염두에 둘 때가 아니다.
  그저 편하게, 열심히 풀되, 풀었던 문제는 다 맞힌다는 생각으로 진지할 필요는 있다.
- 아직은 시험에 충분한 준비가 되어있지 않으므로, 반드시 문제보다는 본문에 초점을 맞추어 본문 이해에 노력을 하고, 모든 단어와 구문 등은 반드시 암기한다.
- 채점한 후 틀린 문제를 꼭 확인한 뒤, (스터디가 가능하다면, 스터디를 통해서 확인 후) 실수를 줄이려 노력한다.
- 틀린 문제 중에 기초적인 단어 등이 많이 포함되어 있다면, 무조건 USHER iBT TOEFL VOCABULARY 를 병행 암기하며 진도를 나가야 한다.
- 아직 시간계산 등의 어려움이 극복되지 않았을 것이고, 다 풀기도 빠듯할 것이지만, 시험 시간 동안 최선을 다하는 자세를 가져야 한다.

- 매일매일 꾸준히 1지문을 소화하되, 꼭 확실히 짚고 넘어간다.
- 아직 중간중간 처리되지 않는 문장, 단어, 구문 등은 필히 꼭 챙겨서 다음 시험에선 같은 실수 반복하지 않게 하여야 한다.
- 아직, 기본 실력 부분에서 밀리는 것이므로, 반복적으로 읽는 것을 게을리하지 않는다.
- 문제의 실수 여부보다는 실력 자체에 초점을 맞춰 노력한다.
- 아무리 시간이 많이 걸려도, 풀었던 문제지는 꼭 반복적으로 읽는 것을 많이 하여야 실력 향상을 이룰 수 있다.

1주	1일차	2일차	3일차	4일차	5일차	6일차
	지문 1 Out of 18	지문 2 Out of 18	지문 3 Out of 18	지문 4 Out of 18	지문 5 Out of 18	지문 6 Out of 18
2주	7일차	8일차	9일차	10일차	11일차	12일차
	지문 7 Out of 18	지문 8 Out of 18	지문 9 Out of 18	지문 10 Out of 18	지문 11 Out of 18	지문 12 Out of 18
3주	13일차	14일차	15일차	16일차	17일차	18일차
	지문 13 Out of 18	지문 14 Out of 18	지문 15 Out of 18	지문 16 Out of 18	지문 17 Out of 18	지문 18 Out of 18

학습방법 및 순서

USHER iBT TOEFL FINAL TEST READING (어셔 iBT 토플 파이널 테스트 리딩)

복습

수업 중 얻은 내용을 다 이해한다는 생각으로 반드시 반복 복습해둔다.

i) 확실한 수업 내용 확인을 수업직후 이후 한번 더 적어보고(백지시험),
ii) 이 내용들에 포함된 모든 단어와 표현을 암기 후,
iii) 마지막으로는
   ㉠ 눈으로 읽다가,
   ㉡ 문장구조가 확실해지면, 입으로 내가 아나운서가 된것처럼 shadowing을 할 수 있을 만큼 반복적으로 읽는다. (10번)
iv) 많이 듣는 것은 이 과정들이 다 된 후 노래 듣듯이 편하게~^^

예습

수업준비 잘 할 것

= "잘" 이라 함은, 모든 수업내용을 모두 아는 것이 아닌, 수업시간에 내가 어디서 집중해야 하는가를 알 수 있게 "아는 것과 모르는 것을 구별" 해두는 정도!

= (즉, 혼자 할 수 있는 것까지만 해두는 것!!! 모르는 단어 찾아 두는 것은 기본 중 기본)

수업직후!

수업 "끝나자마자"바로 그 자리에서 수업 내용을

i) 모두 같이 훑어보고
ii) 모든 내용 정리 후
iii) 모르는 것은 옆에 학생에게 물어서라도 알아둔다!
iv) 같이 스터디를 하는 학생들간에는 반드시 집에 가기 전에 정리한 암기사항들을 자체 시험을 통해 철저히 암기한다.

수업

예습한 것을 근거로, 모르는 것을 집중적으로 확인한다. (=그럼으로써, 수업의 수준이 좌우된다)

1. 할 수 있는 양만 스스로에게 시킵니다. (양을 개별적으로 줄여서라도) 다음, 세가지를 꼭 기억해 주시기 바랍니다.

　i) 공부 기간을 늘리든,
　ii) 잠자는 시간을 줄이든,
　iii) 목표 점수를 낮추든 해야 합니다.

2. 꼭 결과를 내야 합니다

　= 목표를 명확히 하고, 목표 단계 중 계속적으로 체크하며, 월말엔 말한 대로 결과를 냅니다.
　(그러므로, 절대 높은 목표를 월초에 잡지 않는다. 낮더라도 반드시 지키는 것이 중요합니다!)

3. 최악은, 점수를 못 받는 것이 아닌, 실력을 올리지 못하는 것이 아닌, 포기하는 것입니다.

　다른 것은 다 승산 있지만, 잠자는 시간 줄이는 것은 하지 마시기 바랍니다. 일주일만 참으면 되는 중간고사기간이 아닙니다.
　시간이 걸리는데, 잠 줄여가면서 포기 않고 끝낼 확률은 그렇게 많지 않습니다.

▶ 독해공부를 할 때 우선순위

　* 예습 복습 중 가장 중요한 것은 복습입니다. (참고로 스터디는 자체 확인 시험이 아닌 한 것의 예습에 속합니다)

　1순위. USHER iBT TOEFL VOCABULARY의 단어를 거의 알고 있을 것.
　2순위. 구문 철저한 암기 (지문 내용 중 중요 사항 정리한 것)
　3순위. 독해 10번 읽기 - 개인 양 조절은 미리 할 것! 꼭 내용을 이해하며 읽기!
　4순위. mp3로 확인하기 - 이 단계를 할 수 있는 학생들은 실력이 좋거나, 실력이 많이 늘 학생입니다.
　　아울러, 듣기에도 도움이 되므로 해둘 수 있다면 나중에 큰 도움이 됩니다.

 예습과정 - 목적 : 아는 것과 모르는 것 구별하기

(문제풀기)	(엄격한 시험 분위기 조성- 미리 화장실 다녀오고 / 핸드폰 끄고 / 시간 철저히 재고 / 잡담 및 엎드리지 못하게 / 절대 중간에 쉬는 것 있어선 안됨)
답 맞추기	(절대 답지를 보지 말고 할 것. (답을 알면 답에 끼워 맞추려고만 함) 한 명이 쭉 부르면 대충 정답 확인됨 - 문제 소지 있는 것만 구별
답이 안 맞는 문제만 집중 스터디	(*꼭 직후에 할 것!!! 시간 지나면, 궁금하지도 않다)
개인별 단어 찾아가며, 전체 스터디 시작 (해석 안 되는 부분 집중 및 내용정리)	"안 되는 부분 때문에 너무 오랜 시간 잡아먹지 않는다!!! 수업 시간에 해결해야 할 문제이므로 시간 투자 많이 하지 말 것"₩
체크사항	1. 문단정리 - 짧게 (해석을 해두라는 내용이 아님) 2. 문제에서 답 되는 이유와 안되는 이유를 설명한다 (반드시 근거를 옆에 적어둘 것) 　- 방법은 해설지 참조

* 만약 공부하다가 시간이 너무 모자라서 예습 - 수업 - 복습 중, 하나를 포기한다면, 예습을 포기하되, 그래도 꼭 해야 하는 최소한의 범위는 문제 풀이와 단어 찾으며 이해 안 되는 문장 밑줄 쳐오기 입니다.

2. 수업 중 (독학시 제외)

수업의 질은 철저하게 학생들이 예습을 얼마나 잘 해두었나에 달려있다 해도 과언이 아닙니다. 꼭 앞의 과정을 잘 정리해서 확실히 챙겨두시기 바랍니다. 특히, 궁금해서 밑줄 쳐둔 부분 등은 집중해서 잘 처리해 주시기 바랍니다.

단, 우선문장 해석 및 내용 정리위주로 하되, 문제 푸는 나름의 요령은 어느 정도 실력에 신경 쓸 것

3. 수업 직후 (독학 시 제외)

수업시간에 적은 내용은 즉시 **확인+정리** 해야 합니다.
보통 수업시간 50분 분량을 한번 훑어보는데 걸리는 시간은 많지 않습니다.
잘 집중했다면, 한번 다 보고, 화장실 다녀와도 될 만큼이니까, 꼭 해두시기 바랍니다.
한번 귀찮은 5분을 투자하면, 집에 가서 한 시간은 아낄 수 있고,
덤으로, 공부하는 것이 그렇게 어렵지만은 않다는 걸 알게 될 겁니다.

* 방법

스터디 그룹 조원 중 한 명이 처음부터 중요 내용이라고 짚어준 내용을 훑어 나갈 때, 나머지 조원들은 틀리거나 빠진 내용들을 채워주며 정리하면 됩니다. 시간은 5분 내외면 충분합니다.

** 학생들이 문장은 이해를 하되, 글 내용(문단)을 모르고 가는 경우가 많으므로, 반드시 간단히 문단 정리할 때, 내가 이해한 것인지 꼭 스스로를 의심하며 읽어야 합니다. 가끔씩은 스터디 때, 또는 수업시간에 선생님이 정리해준 내용을 스스로 이해한 걸로 착각하고 넘어가는 학생들이 많습니다. (READING **COMPREHENSION**임을 명심!!)

4. * 복습

i) 단어 및 구문 암기 퀴즈 (스스로라도 해야 합니다 - 시험은 인간이 만든 가장 완벽한 시스템!!!) (***백지시험)
ii) 10번 읽기 (열 번 읽고, usherin.usher.co.kr > 난 오늘 흔적에 mp3 녹음해서 기록 남기기)
iii) mp3확인 (들으면서 다 알아 들어야 합니다. 이게 쉬운 것이 아니므로 안된다고 실망은 하지 말되, 되도록 노력해 보시기 바랍니다)

예습 - 수업 - 복습 중에서 **가장 중요한 것은 복습입니다.**
밥상 잘 차려놓고 먹지 않는 사람처럼, 예습 수업만 잘 준비하고 복습하지 않는 **"짓"** 은 하지 마시기 바랍니다.

▶ 복습 부분에 대한 재강조

1.1. 백지시험 (반드시 암기 후 읽기!)

누구나 시험 보는 것은 싫어합니다.
하지만, 시험은 인간이 만든 가장 좋은 확인 방법입니다. 본인이 안다고 생각했던 내용들도 정작 확인 시에는 잘 모르고 있다는 점을 파악할 일이 있을 것입니다. 이런 경우, 스스로 문제점이 있다고 생각할 일이 아니고, 원래 공부과정 중 하나로서 당연하게 받아들이되, 분발해서 모자란 부분을 잘 채워 나갈 수 있도록 하는 방법으로서 스스로 체크하는 시험을 권해드립니다.

*시험 방법

각 지문 별로, 해석하다가 막히는 부분은 단어 아니면, 구문에서 막혔을 것입니다.
이런 경우, 혼자 공부할 경우에는, 시험지를 우선 작성해서 여러 장 복사해 놓거나, 여러 명이 같이 할 경우에는 한 명씩 돌아가면서 시험을 봐서 90% 이상 맞지 못하면, 통과시키지 않는 연습을 미리 해두면, 그날 부분은 확실한 복습을 하게 될 것입니다.

다시 한번!! 예습, 수업, 복습 중에서 가장 중요한 것은 복습이라는 점을 기억해 두시기 바랍니다. 그저 수업 시간에 앉아있었다는 사실만으로, 노트에 적어놓았다는 사실만으로는 실력이 늘지 않습니다. 어떻게든, 그 내용들을 잘 정리해서 써먹을 수 있을 만큼 만들어 두어야 진짜 본인 실력이 되는 것입니다.

1.2. 10번 읽기

다시 한번, 반드시 **암기 후 읽어야 합니다.** '읽다 보면 암기 되겠지...' 란 생각은 통하지 않습니다.

앞선 백지 시험을 다 마쳤을 경우에서 멈추면, 외운 것을 적용할 수 있다고 장담할 수 있는 상황은 아닙니다. 결국, 자연스레 독해를 해둬야 문제가 해결될 수 있는데, 문제는 늘 같은 내용이 같은 문장 형태로 나오지 않는다는 사실입니다. 그렇다고, 막연히 그냥 어떻게 되겠지. 라는 생각으로 손을 놓으면 안되고, 꼭 수업나간 지문을 반복적으로 읽으시기 바랍니다. 이때, 주의할 것은 그냥 소리 내서 읽으라는 말이 아닙니다. 꼭 내용을 이해하면서 해석하고, 문단 문단마다 꼭 내용을 정리하면서 읽으셔야 합니다. 그냥 소리 내서 읽기만 하거나, 문장 문장해석만을 할 경우에는 많이 읽었더라도 이해 실력을 높이는 데는 도움이 되지 않습니다. 토플이 원하는 것은 READING이 아닌, COMPREHENSION입니다.!!!

*방법

처음 읽을 때는 상당히 긴 시간이 걸릴 것입니다. 보통 iBT지문 750자 내외를 기준으로 30분에서 한 시간 이상이 걸리기도 합니다. (단어를 다 외우고 구문을 다 외웠음에도) 하지만, 이건 본인의 실력이 나쁜게 아닌 원래 정상적인 일입니다. 그리고 두 번째 읽을 때도 크게 차이가 나지는 않을 것입니다. 하지만, 세 번째 네 번째로 가면 갈수록 속도도 이해도도 높아지는 것을 느낄 수 있을 것입니다. 읽으면서 수시로 스스로에게 물어보시기 바랍니다. '이 지문을 2주 뒤 갑자기 읽어도 자신 있게 읽을 수 있을까?' 자신 있을 경우에만, 다음 공부로 넘어가시기 바랍니다. 바를 정(正)자를 지문 상단에 체크하면서 읽으시고, 소요되는 시간도 같이 체크해보시기 바랍니다. 항상 긴장하고 점검하며 공부해야 집중력도 유지됩니다. 보통 이렇게 되는 데는 최소 5번은 읽어야 자신감이 생길 것이고, 보수적으로 내용에 따라 열 번을 각오하고 읽으시는 것을 권해드립니다.

스스로 준비가 충분히 되어있는지를 테스트 할 때는, 공부가 끝난 다음날 문제지의 제일 뒤에 있는 지문만을 **모아놓은 '열번읽기' 를 펴고 읽었을 때**, 막힘없이 잘 이해가 될 만큼 읽히면 일차통과입니다.

이후, 주말마다 메모 없는 책 뒤 부분만을 펴고 확인을 반복하시기 바랍니다. 확실히 굳히는 방법이기도 하며, 새로운 내용들이 보이기도 할 것입니다.

1.3. mp3 확인

보통 한국학생들은 읽기에 집중해서 공부를 해왔기 때문에, 듣는 것은 상당히 하지 못하는 경우가 많습니다.

이런 토플 네 과목 성적표를 봤을 때 쉽게 확인할 수 있습니다.

- 리딩 25점 / 리스닝 15점 / 스피킹 17점 / 라이팅 21점.

이런 경우 학생들에게 리스닝 스크립트를 주고 문제를 풀게 하면 곧잘 풀곤 합니다.

이유는 간단합니다. 많이 안 들어서... 하지만, 그냥 무조건 듣는 것 보다 내용이 있는 글들을 많이 들어야 하는데, 리스닝 공부를 할 때도 결국 강의 내용을 다 해석한 후, 문제확인 후, 일일이 해석하고 글을 분석한 후 많이 듣는 것인데, 이는 앞서 반복적으로 읽은 독해 지문에서 한 것과 별반 다르지 않습니다. (물론, 독해 지문이 듣기 지문보다 문어체이기 때문에 조금 어렵긴 하지만, 기본적으로 독해 지문을 듣고 이해하는 학생들이 듣기 지문을 이해하기 어려워지지 않습니다) 열 번 읽기가 다 되었으면, 길거리를 걸으며, 지하철에서, 쉬는 시간 등 짬짬이 수시로 mp3를 들으며 내용들과 구문들을 상기시키시기 바랍니다.

참고로, 성우가 불러주는 속도는 상당히 빠르게 느껴지실 것입니다. 이는, 보통 학생들이 750자의 토플 리딩 지문을 **읽는데 7분내지 10분 이상을** 쓰는 반면 성우들이 **읽어주는 속도는 5분에서 6분** 사이이기 때문에 당연히 빠르게 느껴지는 것입니다. 하지만, 여러분이 양보해서는 안될 이유는, 여러분은 이미 이 지문 문제를 풀었고, (수업을 했으며) 복습도 했고, 열 번씩이나 읽었기에, 이 속도로 못 들을 이유는 없습니다. 만약 따라가지 못한다면, 열 번 읽기 연습이 덜 되어있거나, 기본적인 듣기 실력이 상당히 약해서일 것이므로, 결국 많이 들으면서 해결해야 할 문제이므로 앞서 말한 대로 반복적으로 듣는 것을 실천하시기 바랍니다.

iBT TOEFL (iBT 토플) 시험 소개

USHER iBT TOEFL INTERMEDIATE TEST LISTENING (어셔 iBT 토플 인터미디어트 테스트 리스닝)

iBT TOEFL (iBT 토플)이란?

TOEFL(Test of English as a Foreign Language)이란 주로 영어권 국가의 대학교에 진학하는 외국인 학생의 영어실력을 평가하기 위하여 만들어진 시험입니다. 현재 TOEFL (토플)은 iBT(internet-Based Test) TOEFL이라 불리며, PBT(Paper-Based Test) 와 CBT(Computer-Based Test)를 거쳐 채택된 3세대 시험방식입니다. 읽기, 듣기, 말하기, 쓰기의 다양한 분야의 영어실력을 보기 때문에 현재 세계적으로 가장 공신력 있는 영어시험으로 자리잡았습니다.

iBT TOEFL (iBT 토플) 구성

시험순서	지문 개수	시간	세부사항	만점
Reading (상대평가)	Passage 2개 (700단어 X 2개)	35분	**Passage 당** 17분 30초 10문제	30점
Listening (상대평가)	Conversation 1개 Lecture 1개	36분	문제풀이시간 7분	30점
	Conversation 1개 Lecture 2개		문제풀이시간 10분	
Speaking (절대평가)	Independent 1개 Intergrated 3개	16분 내외	-	30점
Writing (절대평가)	Intergrated 1개 Discussion 1개	29분	-	30점
	총 약 2시간 (116분)			총점 120점

꼭 알아두세요!

접수	시험일정이 나오면 접수 가능 * Late fee(응시 7일 전 시험 신청 시) 40$추가	
비용	시험	- 미화 $ 220 (원화결제 가능)
	취소한 성적 복원	- 미화 $ 20
	성적 전송	- 미화 $ 20 (1개 기관당)
	일자 변경	- 미화 $ 60
	재채점	- 미화 $ 80 (1개 section당: 성적 불신시 speaking, writing만 가능)

시험	3일에 1번 수/토/일 가능
시험장소	전국 27개 도시에 있는 Test Center 및 세계 각국의 ETS Test Center (안양, 아산, 부천, 부산, 천안, 청주, 춘천, 대구, 대전, 고성, 고양, 군포, 광주, 경기, 경주, 경산, 화성, 인천, 제주, 전주, 진주, 오산, 포천, 성남, 서울, 울산, 용인 등 27개 도시 - 토플 시험장에 대한 자세한 정보는 usherin.usher.co.kr 참조)
준비물	토플 web site에 등록되어 있는 신분증 지참
성적 발표일	리딩 리스닝은 시험 직후, 스피킹 라이팅은 최소 6일 ~ 최대 14일
성적 유효기간	2년
토플 시험 등록 취소	시험 등록 후 7일 까지 : 전액환불 시험 등록 후 8일 이후 : 금액의 50% 환불 시험보기 4일전 : 금액의 50% 환불 콜센터에 전화하거나 홈페이지에서 취소 (e-mail로는 불가능)

시험장에서

1.	시험절차	시험장에 도착하면 여권 확인 후, 성적표에 나올 사진을 찍고 감독관의 안내에 따라 순서대로 시험을 시작한다.
2.	필기도구	연필과 종이는 감독관이 나누어주므로 따로 필요가 없고, 부족하면 얼마든지 더 달라고 할 수 있다. 다만, Section 시작 전에 종이에 필기할 경우, 부정행위로 간주될 수 있으므로 각별히 주의하자.
3.	헤드폰 음량	시험 도중 언제든지 조절할 수 있다.
4.	마이크 음량	시험 시작 직후와 Speaking Section 직전에 조절할 수 있다.
5.	휴식시간	없음
6.	주의사항	각 응시자마다 시험 진행 시간이 다르기 때문에, 내가 Listening이나 Writing Section을 풀고 있을 때, 다른 사람의 목소리가 방해가 되는 경우가 많으니 염두해 두자.

iBT TOEFL READING 소개

USHER iBT TOEFL FINAL TEST READING (어셔 iBT 토플 파이널 테스트 리딩)

iBT READING 영역에서는 유학을 나갔을 때, 학생들이 학교생활, 즉, 수업을 따라가는데 필요한 가장 기초적인 수준의 읽기 능력여부를 파악하는데 목적이 있습니다. 그러므로, 다양한 분야의 지문이 있지만, 꼭 배경 지식을 요구하지는 않으므로 시작부터 너무 겁먹을 필요는 없습니다. 하지만, 18분 이내에 1지문을 푸는 것을 대다수의 시험보는 학생들은 힘들어 하므로, 정확하고 빠른 독해 능력은 문제 푸는데 있어 핵심적인 부분이다. 여기서 중요한 것은 정확이 먼저이고 빠름은 다음순서라는 사실은꼭 기억해야 합니다.

iBT READING 구성

총 지문 개수는 2개의 지문으로 구성되어 있습니다.
시험 시간도 35분으로 줄었습니다.

iBT READING 특징

- **NOTE TAKING**이 허용된다
- 지문에 제목이 주어진다.
- 전문용어 등은 뜻을 알려주는 **GLOSSARY**기능이 있다.

GLOSSARY

blood poisoning caused by pathogenic microorganisms and their toxic products in the bloodstream.

iBT READING 문제 유형 분석

난이도	문제 유형	문제 유형 설명	배점	지문당 문항 수
쉬움 (기본점수 약 50% 차지함)	VOCABULARY	유의어 찾기	1점	1~2개
	FACT & NEGATIVE FACT	지문 내용과 맞거나, 틀린 내용 찾기	1점	3~5개
	REFERENCE	지시어가 가리키는 대상 찾기	1점	0~1개
어려움 (변별력 목적 약 50% 차지함)	SENTENCE SIMPLICATION	문장 PARAPHRASE	1점	1개
	INSERTION	논리에 맞게 문장 끼워 넣기	1점	1개
	RHETORICAL PURPOSE	작가가 글속에 내용을 넣은 이유 찾기	1점	1~2개
	INFEREMCE	제공된 정보로 내용 추론하기	1점	1~2개
	SUMMARY	문단 정리	2점	둘 중 선택적으로 하나만 나옴. 하지만, 주로 SUMMARY가 많이 남
	CATEGORY CHART	문단 속 정보를 알맞게 정렬하기	2~3점	

- 현재 풀고 있는 문제의 위치와, 시간확인 및 뒤로 돌아갈 수 있는 기능들이 우측 상단에 있다. (아래 그림 참조)

iBT READING 화면 구성

화면 상단 우측에 시험 진행 사항을 알려주는 부분이 있다. Question 14 of 20

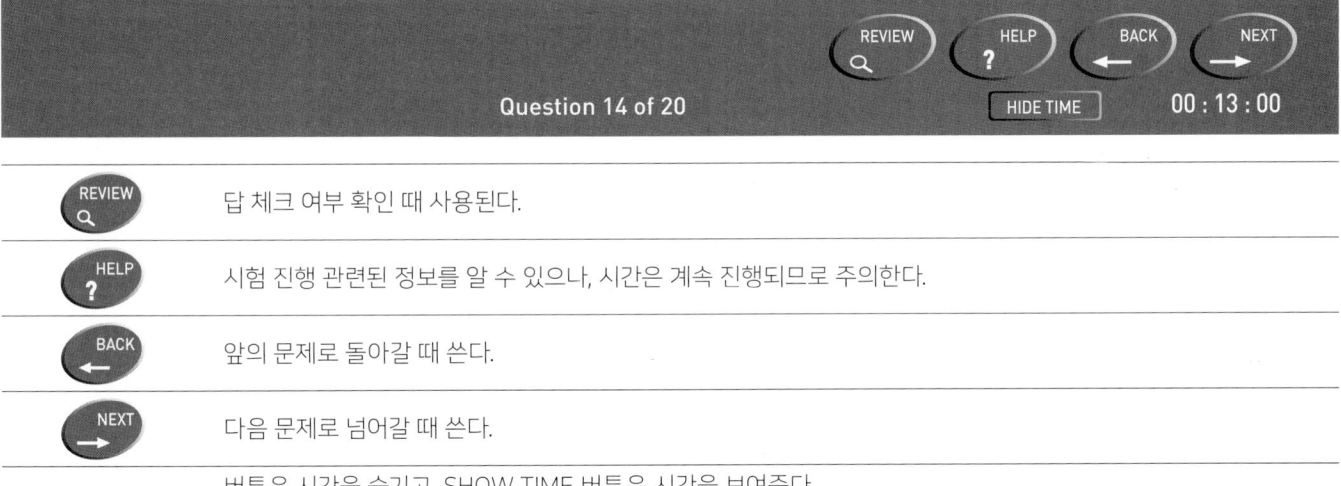

REVIEW	답 체크 여부 확인 때 사용된다.
HELP	시험 진행 관련된 정보를 알 수 있으나, 시간은 계속 진행되므로 주의한다.
BACK	앞의 문제로 돌아갈 때 쓴다.
NEXT	다음 문제로 넘어갈 때 쓴다.
HIDE TIME	버튼은 시간을 숨기고, SHOW TIME 버튼은 시간을 보여준다. 00:13:00 남은 시간을 보여줌
VIEW NEXT	마지막 문제인 SUMMARY 문제나 CATEGORY CHART문제를 풀 때 보여주는데, 이 버튼을 누르면, 지문전체를 보여주고, VIEW QUESTION버튼을 누르면 다시 문제가 있는 화면으로 돌아간다.

READING DIRECTION 화면

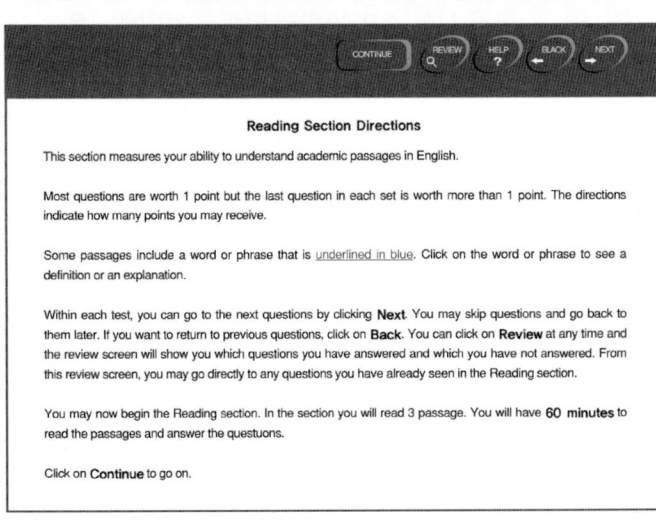

리딩 시험 진행방식을 설명해준다.

USHER

지문 화면

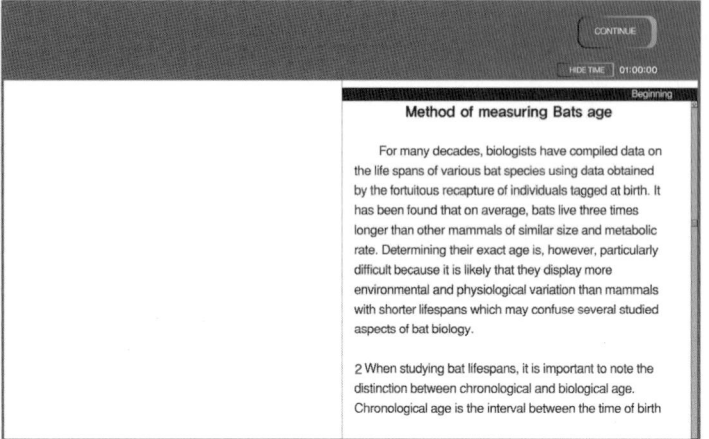

처음엔 문제없이 지문만 보여주는 화면이 있는데, 이때 스크롤을 내려 지문 전체를 봐야만 CONTINUE 버튼을 눌러 본 문제로 넘어갈 수 있다.

지문과 문제

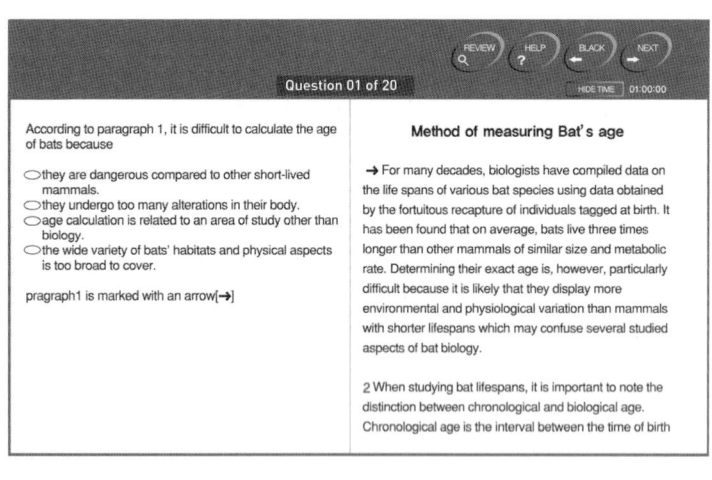

문제로 넘어가면, 문제는 왼쪽에, 지문은 오른쪽에 한 문제씩 보여지며, 우측 상단의 NEXT 버튼을 누르면 다음 문제로 넘어간다. 가끔 본문 속의 파란색 밑줄은 용어해설을 보여줄 때 쓰이며, 누르면 좌측 화면 하단에 나타난다.

SUMMARY 문제 화면

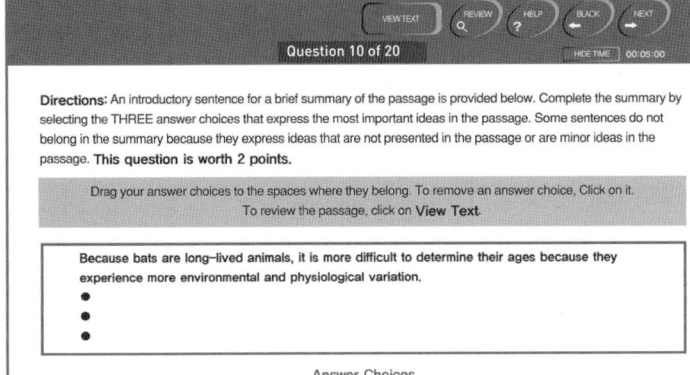

SUMMARY 문제가 나올 때는 화면 속엔 지문없이 문제만 전체 화면으로 보인다. 이때 상단의 VIEW TEXT버튼을 누르면 지문만 다시 보여 주며, 다시 문제를 보고 싶을 땐, VIEW QUESTION버튼을 누르면 다시 돌아갈 수 있다 답을 선택하는 방법은 초이스에 있는 보기를 박스 안에 드래그해서 놓으면 되고, 답을 바꿀 때는 보기를 한번 더 클릭하면 정답자리에서 없어진다

CATEGORY 문제 화면

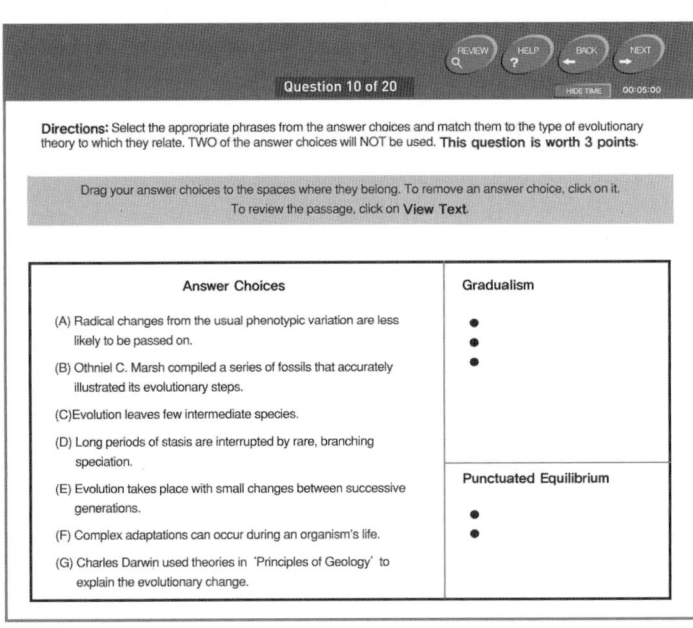

SUMMARY 문제와 같은 화면과 같은 답 선택 방법이 사용된다.

REVIEW 화면

REVIEW버튼을 누르면 현재 풀고 있는 문제 목록이 나타나고, 각 문제 별로 답을 체크했는지 여부가 다음 세가지로 보여진다.
- **ANSWERED** - 문제 답을 하고 넘어간 경우
- **NOT ANSWERED** - 문제 답 체크하지 않고 넘어간 경우
- **NOT SEEN** - 문제를 아직 보지 않은 경우

문제를 클릭하면, 해당 문제가 색깔표시 되고, 이때 우측 상단의 **GO TO QUESTION** 버튼을 누르면 해당 문제로 이동된다.
REVIEW버튼을 누르기 전 화면으로 갈 땐 **RETURN** 버튼을 누르면 된다.

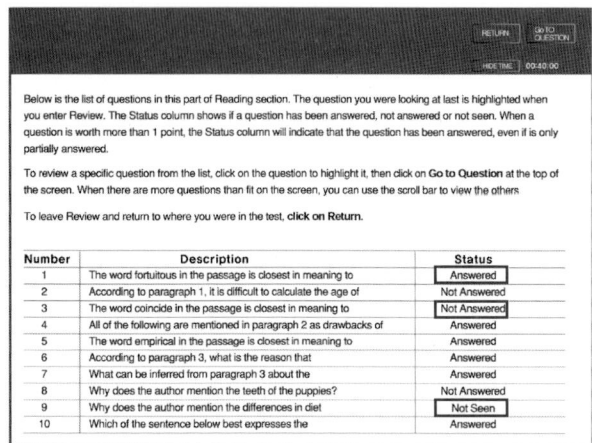

한 개의 파트가 끝났을 때 나오는 화면

각 파트가 끝나면 **Review** 버튼을 이용해 시간을 활용하라는것과 **Continue** 버튼을 눌러 다음 파트로 넘어가면 이전 파트로 돌아올 수 없다는 내용의 디렉션 화면이 주어진다.

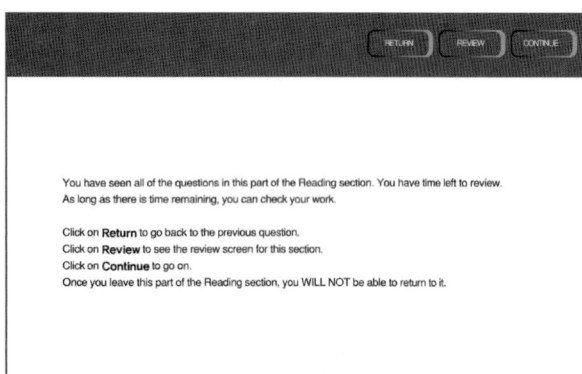

READING STRATEGIES

USHER iBT TOEFL FINAL TEST READING (어셔 iBT 토플 파이널 테스트 리딩)

문제 유형을 확인하기 전에 우선, test 1을 풀어보고, 스스로에 대한 평가와 더불어 문제 유형 파악을 해주시기 바랍니다. 먼저 유형을 파악 해보는 것보다는, 일단, 풀어본 뒤 알아가는 것이 훨씬 빠르게 이해할 수 있기에, 각 문제 유형별 전략 뒤에는 test 1을 기준으로 확인 가능한 번호를 적어두었습니다.

쉬운 문제 유형	출제 비율
1. VOCABULARY 2. FACT & NEGATIVE FACT 3. REFERENCE	50%

어려운 문제 유형	출제 비율
4. SENTENCE SIMPLIFICATION 5. INSERTION 6. RHETORICAL PURPOSE 7. INFERENCE 8. SUMMARY 9. CATEGORY CHART	50%

시험이 임박한 학생들을 위한 독해 전략

* 서문에서 이미 학생들의 시간에 대한 수준별 대응책을 적어 놓았습니다. 하지만, 여기선, 대부분의 학생들이 시간이 모자라는 경우가 많으므로 이런 경우에 대해 우선적으로 다루었습니다.

1. 지문은 제목과 각 문단 첫 줄만 읽고, 곧바로 CONTINUE버튼을 눌러 문제로 넘어갑니다.
　시간이 없는 경우가 많은데 지문을 다 읽고 넘어가는 경우 시간이 모자라 마지막 문제는 찍지도 못하고 끝나는 경우도 있기때문에 미리 주의해야 합니다.

2. 문제 풀이하며 본문을 읽습니다. (시간이 없을 경우, 효과가 큼)
　토플 문제 번호순서대로, 본문의 답 근거도 순서를 따릅니다. 게다가 중간중간 단어문제나 REFERENCE문제 등이 표시된 경우에는 그 문제보다 앞 문제라면 표시된 곳 앞에서, 뒷 문제라면 표시된 곳 뒤에서 답 근거를 찾으면 됩니다. (뒷 페이지 참조)

3. SKIMMING → SCANNING
　대략 훑었어도, 답 근거가 어디쯤이라는 감이 오면, 그때부터는 집중해서 꼼꼼히 내용을 살펴야 합니다. 대부분 문제는 답은 둘 중에 하나로 좁혀지는데 이때 스캐닝 하지 않아 대충 읽고 답을 잡으면 오답에 낚일 확률이 높습니다. 문제 출제 기관인 ETS는 문제만 50년째 만들고 있는 기관입니다. 문제 푸는 여러분을 낚는 데는 상당한 노하우가 있습니다.

4. 문제를 풀며 수시로 내용을 파악해야 합니다.
　마지막 SUMMARY문제는 문단 내용을 파악하지 못하면 풀지 못하게 만들어놨습니다. 그런데 문제는 한 문제 한 문제 푸는 데만 급급한 학생들의 경우에는 문단 정리를 하지 못하고, 마지막 SUMMARY문제를 만나는 경우인데, 이땐 대안이 없습니다. 수시로 내용을 정리하며 지나가야 마지막 문제를 잘 풀 수 있습니다. 그러므로 수시로 내용 파악을 해두어야 합니다.

5. 반드시 ①'문제를 똑바로 읽고' ② 핵심 단어에 '동그라미'를 쳐서 묻는 내용을 명확히 한 후 ③'답 근거'를 찾으시길 바랍니다.

*따라가면서 푼다는 말은....

1. **Fact**
2. **Infer**
3. Purpose
4. **Fact**
5. Vocab
6. Sentence simplification
7. **Negative fact**
8. Vocab
9. **Insert**
10. **Summary**

위의 ▇▇▇▇ 에 해당하는 문제들은 모두 힌트를 줄 수 있는 내용들입니다.

1. VOCABULARY - 유의어 찾기 문제

▶ 질문 형태

The word "_____" in the passage is closest in meaning to

The phrase "_____" in the passage is closet in meaning to

▶ 오답 패턴 (학생들이 잘 낚이는 경우 모음)
- 선택지 중 두 개의 단어가 모두 사전의 동의어에 있을 경우 (난이도 상)
- 선택지 중 어떤 단어도 사전의 동의어에 없을 경우 (난이도 상)
- 넣어봤을 때, 말은 되지만, 유의어는 아닌 경우
- 단어랑 스펠링이 비슷한 경우

▶ 핵심 전략

- 무조건 시험장 들어가기 전에 단어 책 한 권은 끝내고 들어가야 합니다. USHER iBT TOEFL VOCABULARY를 마친 후라면 80%는 처리가 가능합니다.

- 단어 문제는 무조건 시간을 벌어주는 문제유형입니다.
  즉, 완전 쉬워서 딱 보고 답이 나왔기 때문에 시간을 벌어주거나, 완전 어렵게 나와서 고민해야 될 상황에서는 절대 고민하지 않고 그냥 콱 찍고 지나가야 합니다. 단어 문제가 어려울 때는 아무리 봐도 어차피 답을 정확히 잡을 수는 없습니다. 본인을 믿고 빨리 체크하고 다음 문제에서 승부를 거는 것이 더 낫습니다.
  그러므로 어려우나 쉬우나, 무조건 단어 문제에서는 시간을 벌어야 하고, 고민하지 않아야 합니다. 단, 아무리 쉬운 문제라도 꼭 문장에 넣어보고 대입 후 체크하도록 함을 잊어서는 안됩니다.

- 만약 단어 문제가 어렵게 난다면, 둘 중 하나입니다. 동의어가 선택지중에서 두 개가 있거나,
  동의어 전혀 없을 때
  이땐, 문맥을 봐서 가장 알맞은 답을 찾아야 합니다.
  단어의 뉘앙스를 정확히 알고 있어야 알 수 있는 문제이므로 앞서 적은 대로 시간을 많이 들이지 않도록 합니다.

- 꼭 집어 넣어서 재확인을 해야 합니다.
  아무리 동의어라도 문맥상 여러 개의 뜻 중에서 다른 의미로 사용될 수 있기 때문에 반드시 확인을 해봐야 합니다.

2. FACT & NEGATIVE FACT - 지문의 세부 정보를 맞게 적었거나 틀리게 적은 경우를 찾아내는 문제

▶ 질문 형태

- Fact
  According to paragraph #, which of the following is true of (about) _____?
  According to paragraph #, _____?
  According to paragraph #, what / when / where / why / how _____?
- Negative fact
  According to paragraph #, all of the following are true of _____ EXCEPT
  According to paragraph #, all of the following statements about _____ EXCEPT
  According to paragraph #, which of the following is NOT true of _____ ?

▶ 오답 패턴 (학생들이 잘 낚이는 경우 모음)

- 해석이 안될 경우 (난이도 상)
- 투 클릭(Two click) 문제 (정답 개수로 난이도 중)
- 단어만 사용하고 지문과 무관한 내용
- 언급 안된 내용이 그럴싸하게 적힌 경우
- "EXCEPT"문제는 꼭 똑바로 묻는대로 대답할 것
  (아닌 것 고르라는 얘기는 오답 세 개는 모두 본문에서 맞단 얘기! → 틀린 것 3개를 먼저 배제시켜서 잡는게 확실합니다)
- 상식으로 접근할 경우
- 반만 맞고 반은 틀린 경우 (특히 틀린 부분이 뒷부분일 경우, 학생들은 앞만 보고 답으로 선택하는 경우 주의할 것)
- 본문과 반대 내용을 적어둘 때 (은근히 혼동됨)

▶ 핵심 전략

- 문제에서 **핵심 되는 단어**를 본문에서 빨리 찾습니다.
  모든 문제를 풀 때는 질문을 잘 읽어야 합니다. 알면서도 틀리는 경우가 많음은 한국어로 내는 시험이나 토플시험이나 마찬가지입니다. 그러므로, 질문에서 묻는 내용 중 핵심이 되는 단어를 재빨리 지문에서 찾아야 답 근거를 정확히 찾을 수 있습니다. 평상시 문제 풀고 스터디 할 때 조원들과 답 근거 찾기를 열심히 해둔 학생이라면 절대 어렵게 푸는 문제는 아닙니다.

- 지문에서 찾은 내용을 PARAPHRASE한 것을 찾습니다.
  토플시험에는 이런 말이 있습니다. 듣기시험에선 들은 단어가 많은 선택지를 답으로 찍고, 독해시험에선 본문에 서 본 단어가 많은 선택지는 피하십시오. 극단적이긴 하지만, 전혀 틀린 말은 아닙니다. 즉, 본문의 내용을 다른 단어로 바꿔서 정답을 내곤 하기 때문에 정보 전달은 올바로 하되, 표현은 모두 바뀌어져 있는 경우가 대부분입니다. 그리고 NEGATIVE FACT의 경우에는 지문과 내용이 다르거나, 언급되어 있지 않는 보기가 정답입니다.

- 너무 강한 표현은 주의해서 봅니다. (절대 답이 안되는 것은 아닙니다)
  예) never, only.

3. REFERENCE - 지문 속의 음영 표시된 지시어가 가리키는 단어가 무엇인지 찾는 문제

▶ 질문 형태

The word "_____" in the passage refers to

The phrase "_____" in the passage refers to

▶ 오답 패턴 (학생들이 잘 낚이는 경우 모음)
- 정답과 (단수 복수의) 수가 일치되는 주변의 명사를 미끼로 쓸 때
- 앞의 내용 중 혼동될만한 내용을 미리 던져두는 경우

▶ 핵심 전략 (앞문장의 주어나 목적어일 가능성이 크다)

- 평상시 문장을 읽을 때, 인칭대명사 it, they, their나 지시대명사 this, that, those, 그리고 부정대명사 some, others가 무엇을 가리키는지를 늘 확인하며 표시하는 버릇이 필요합니다.

- 답은 앞 문장 또는 같은 문장 앞일 확률이 높습니다.
  지시어가 가리키는 단어는 문장의 뒤, 그리고 두 문장 이상 떨어진 앞 문장에선 찾지 않습니다.

- 답을 찾았다 싶어도 꼭 다시 바뀐 단어로 **집어넣어 보고** 확인합니다.
  자연스러운지 확인하지 않고 찍으면 틀릴 수 있습니다. 쉬운 문제유형이므로 실수하지 않도록 해야 합니다.

4. SENTENCE SIMPLIFICATION
- 본문에서 음영 표시된 한문장의 내용을 그대로 담고 있는 또 다른 문장을 찾아내는 문제

▶ 질문 형태
Which of the sentences below best expresses the essential information in the highlighted sentence in the passage? Incorrect choices change the meaning in important ways or leave out essential information.

▶ 오답 패턴 (학생들이 잘 낚이는 경우 모음)
- 일단, 어려운 문장구조이거나, 내용이 복잡하거나, 단어가 어려운 경우라는 것 자체
- 내용 중 일부를 생략하는 경우 (마이너로서 내용은 맞지만, 답이 안됨) (난이도 상)
- 내용은 그럴싸하나 순서나, 인과 등을 반대로 엮는 경우 (난이도 상)
- 논리적으로 비약하는 경우
- 상식으로 내용을 엮은 경우
- 일부는 맞고 일부는 틀린 경우

▶ 핵심 전략
- **평상시 문법부분이 강해야 합니다.**
  토플문제의 출제포인트는 뭐든 중간에 막히는 문장입니다. 쉽게 잘 해석되는 부분에서는 문제 출제를 않습니다. 특히나 Sentence Simplification 스타일의 문제는 작정하고 어려운 문장을 문제로 만든 것입니다. 그러므로, 평상시 대충 내용만 파악하는 독해 습관을 가진 학생들에겐 난감할 수 있는 유형입니다.

- **내용을 잘게 자릅니다. → 꼭 수렴시킵니다.**
  문장 속에서 다루고 있는 내용들을 잘게 자른 후, 그 내용들을 어떻게든 수렴시켜야 답이 됩니다. 문제 내용과 다르게 적는 오답 스타일은 쉽게 낸 것입니다. 이런 것은 당연히 오답처리 할 수 있어야 하고, 이보다 더 주의 할 것은 아무리 맞는 내용을 적었다 하더라도 생략된 것은 답이 아닙니다. 그러므로 꼭 잘게 자른 후, 그 내용들을다 포함하였는지 꼼꼼히 따져봐야 합니다.

5. INSERTION - 지문에서 빠진 문장을 알맞은 위치에 넣는 유형

▶ 질문 형태

Look at the four squares [■] that indicate where the following sentence could be added to the passage.

삽입문장

Where would the sentence best fit? Click on a square [■] to add the sentence to the passage.
(문제가 뜨면 지문에 4개의 ■가 뜨고 그 중에 하나를 찍으면 문장이 삽입이 됩니다)

▶ 오답 패턴 (학생들이 잘 낚이는 경우 모음)
- 덩어리에서 작은 내용으로 넘어가는 경우 (난이도 상)
- 답이 잘 보이지 않을 때는 끼워넣기 뒤의 문장에서 관련성 있는 단어가 있는지 찾아볼 것. (예 - test 4-9번)
- 중복되는 단어, 지시어 또는 연결어 없이 내용으로만 연결되는 문장 (난이도 상)
- 연결어로 연결되는 경우 (예 - however, moreover, thus) (이어지는 내용은 틀리지만 연결어 보고 단순 선택)
- 지시어나 중복되는 단어로 연결되는 경우 (예 - this, that, 중복단어)
- for example이 끼워넣을 문장에 나오면 앞에 내용보다 뒤에 내용이 훨씬 더 구체적입니다.

▶ 핵심 전략
- 일단 제시된 끼워 넣을 문장을 읽습니다.
- 끼워 넣을 문장 중 IT, THIS, THAT 등 지시어가 나오면 쉬운 문제입니다.
  이런 문제는 지시어가 가리키는 단어를 앞 문장에서 찾을 수 있기만 하면 됩니다. 그러므로 쉽게 풀 수 있는 유형입니다.
  in fact, indeed가 나오면 끼워넣기 문장은 앞의 문장의 반복입니다. 즉, 같은 내용을 포함한 (약간은 더 클수도 있는) 내용이 끼워넣을 문장앞에 와야 합니다.
- 끼워 넣을 문장 중, HOWEVER, MOREOVER, ALSO, THEREFORE 등 연결단어가 나오면 쉬운 문제입니다. 연결어 역시, 내용을 매끄럽게 이어주기 위해 도움을 주는 단어이므로 이런 단어가 있을 땐 앞뒤 문장의 논리가 매끄러운 곳만 찾아내면 되기에 쉬운 문제입니다.
- 영어마인드로서 항상 덩어리를 먼저 얘기하고, 구체적인 예를 드는 스타일의 문제라면 어려운 문제입니다.
  원어민들은 항상 결론을 던지고 예를 드는 경우가 많습니다.
  하지만, 한글은 예를 들고 결론을 얘기해도 문제되지 않습니다. 예를 들면,
  I) 한국 학생들은 공부를 열심히 한다는 점을 알 수 있습니다.
  지하철에서도, 버스에서도, 도서관에서도, 복도에서도 늘 공부하는 학생들을 많이 만났기 때문입니다.
  II) 지하철에서도, 버스에서도, 도서관에서도, 복도에서도 늘 공부하는 한국 학생들을 많이 만났습니다.
  그렇기 때문에, 한국 학생들은 공부를 열심히 한다는 점을 알 수 있습니다.
  답은 I)으로 해야 합니다. 이유는 한국어처럼, 두괄식, 미괄식, 병렬식, 수미 상관 등의 다양한 글 전개 방법을 취하는 것과 달리, 영어에서는 항상 결론을 먼저 던져놓는 두괄식 형태의 글 전개가 많기 때문입니다.
  한국 학생들에게, 위 두 가지에서 무엇이 맞냐고 묻는다면, 답하지 못하는 경우가 많습니다. 해석해 주고 풀라고 해도 헤매는 유일한 문제 스타일이 될 수 있는 유형이므로 꼭 전제를 먼저 인식해야 합니다.

"덩어리 → 구체적 내용"
- 답을 체크하기 전에 꼭 문장에 넣어보고 확인합니다. 특히 끼워넣은 뒤, 뒤에 나오는 지시어 it이나 this들을 설명할 수 있어야 합니다.

6. RHETORICAL PURPOSE - 글쓴이가 글 속의 내용을 넣은 이유 찾기

▶ 질문 형태

The phrase"_____"in the passage refers to the explanation why
In paragraph #, what is the author's main purpose in the discussion of _____?
Why does the author mention
In paragraph #, why does the author mention _____ ?
Why does the author include a description of _____ ?

▶ 오답 패턴 (학생들이 잘 낚이는 경우 모음)

- 문단 (paragraph) 전체가 큰 (passage) 전체에서 하는 기능을 물을 때 (난이도 상)
  (문단 정리가 있어야 함 = 서머리 문제)
- 가끔 어려운 문장을 섞은 부분에서 내는 경우 (난이도 상)
- 사실은 맞지만, 묻는 말에 대한 답이 아닌 경우 - 예) 결과를 묻는 질문에 과정은 오답 (난이도 상)
- 예의 특징으로서는 맞으나, 언급 이유는 아닌 경우 (난이도 상)
- 단어만 나열하고 딴소리 한 경우
- 상식으로 접근하는 경우
- 언급 없는 경우

▶ 핵심 전략

- **문제를 똑바로 읽습니다**
  학생들이 가장 잘 하는 건 달을 보라고 가리켰건만, 달은 안보고 손가락만 보는 경우입니다.
  예를 들어, 국가의 기능이 약하면 국민들이 자구책을 찾습니다. 그 예로는 소말리아 해적과 같이 무정부 상태에서는 잔학하게 활동하는 해적무리들을 우리는 신문지상에서 종종 보곤 합니다. 라는 글에서 왜 해적을 언급했느냐 에 대해 보기에는, =
  A) 무정부 상태에서의 해적들은 잔학하게 활동 할 수도 있다는 점을 인식시키기 위하여
  B) 무정부 상태에서 국가의 기능이 약할 경우 일어날수 있는 예를 들기 위하여
  답은 당연히 B) 입니다. 하지만, A)를 찍는 경우는 해적이라는 단어의 임팩트와, 본문에서 분명히 해적들이 잔학 하게 활동한다는 내용이 있었기 때문입니다. 하지만, 절대 잊어서는 안 될 일이 질문이 묻는 말에 대답하는 것입니다. 왜 해적을 언급 했느냐 이지, 해적들에 대해 맞는 것을 고르라는 것이 아니므로, 주의해야 합니다

- 문제에서 언급한 부분만 읽지 말고 **앞부분 또는 뒷부분을 꼭 읽습니다.**
  문제에서 언급한 부분만 읽는 것은 앞서 예를든 것처럼, **예의 특징에 현혹되기 쉽기** 때문입니다.
  꼭 앞부분을 읽어서 흐름상 왜 그 얘기를 집어 넣었는지를 생각해봐야 합니다.

- 문제에 제시된 표현의 기능을 생각해봅니다. **(특히 argue와 explain의 차이를 분명히 구분합니다)**
  다음과 같은 말들이 주로 보기에 나옵니다.
  설명하기 위해서 / 예를 들기 위해서 / 비교, 대조하기 위해서 / 강조하기 위해서 / 주장하기 위해서 / 증명하기 위해서… 등

- 보기 내용을 끝까지 읽습니다.
  앞부분은 맞는 것 같지만, **뒤에서** 지문과 틀린 얘기로 **살짝 뒤트는** 경우가 있습니다.
  그러므로 마지막까지 다 읽고 지문과의 일치성을 꼭 파악하여야 합니다.

7. INFERENCE - 지문에서 콕 집어 얘기하지 않았지만, 충분히 추론할 수 있는 내용 찾기

▶ **질문 형태**

Which of the following can be inferred from paragraph # about _____?
It can be inferred from the discussion in paragraph # that _____
What can be inferred from paragraph # about _____?

▶ **오답 패턴 (학생들이 잘 낚이는 경우 모음)**
- 어려운 문장을 잘못 해석한 경우, 잘못 해석한 것이 꼭 선택지에 있음 (난이도 상)
- 비약 (난이도 상) * infer문제는 원래 본문에 fact문제처럼 직접적인 답 근거는 없지만, 그렇다고 비약해서는 안됨
- 언급 없는 경우
- 상식으로 푼 경우,
- 단어만 사용하고 딴소리 한 경우
- 반대 사실 언급
- 반은 맞고 반은 틀린 경우

▶ **핵심 전략**

- **문제의 키워드를 본문에서 찾습니다.**
  FACT 문제에서처럼 문제에서 묻는 핵심적인 키워드를 찾아야 한다는 공통점은 있으나, 대체로 FACT 문제보다는 고민하게 만드는 문장에서 문제를 내는 경우가 많아, 많은 학생들이 어려워하는 문제 유형입니다. 기본 실력이 되어야 하므로, 문장을 읽다가 막힌다 싶으면 그곳이 INFERENCE 문제가 출제될 확률이 높은 곳입니다. 근본적으로 이해가 되지 않으면 풀리지 않으므로 기본 실력이 중요시 되는 유형입니다.

- **지문에서 근거를 꼭 찾을 것**
  문장을 근거로 하든, 문단을 근거로 하든, 결국 항상 본문에 근거를 두고 있으므로, 반드시 지문 내용 중 내용을 연결 지어 답을 찾아야 합니다.

- **상식이나 비약으로 문제를 풀지 않습니다.**
  꼭 주의해야 할 점은 상식이나 비약, 또는 혼자 소설을 써가며 문제를 푸는 경우입니다. 다시 한번, 꼭 본문에서 답 근거를 짚어낼 수 있어야 합니다.

8. SUMMARY - 지문 내용 중 문단 정리를 잘 한 것을 선택하는 문제

▶ **질문 형태**

Directions: An introductory sentence for a brief summary of the passage is provided below. Complete the summary by selecting the THREE answer choices that express the most important ideas in the passage. Some sentences do not belong in the summary because they express ideas that are not presented in thepassage or are minor ideas in the passage. **This question is worth 2 points.**

Drag your answer choices to the spaces where they belong.
To remove an answer choice, click on it. To review the passage, click **View Text**.

Introductory sentence
-
-
-

(A)	(D)
(B)	(E)
(C)	(F)

▶ **오답 패턴 (학생들이 잘 낚이는 경우 모음)**
- 너무 디테일한 내용은 맞아도 답이 아님, 단락급의 덩치가 있는 내용정리이어야 함(난이도 상)
- 상식으로 푼 경우
- 반만 맞고 반은 틀린 경우 (앞부분은 맞았다고 답으로 하면 안됨), 끝까지 다 잘 읽어보고 답을 고를 것
- 전혀 다른 말을 단어만 섞어서 하는 경우
- 완전히 틀린 내용

▶ **핵심 전략 (≒ Fact 문제 처럼)**
- 오답부터 제낍니다. (정답 3개를 먼저 잡기가 더 어렵습니다)

- 박스 안의 INTRODUCTORY SENTENCE는 참고만 하고, 문단 급 내용을 고릅니다.
  답이라고 체크할 수 있기 위해선, 그 답이라고 생각한 문단이 과연 몇 문단을 아우를 수 있는지 꼭 생각해봐야 합니다. 즉, 정답들은 모두 몇 문단 내용이라고 짚을 수 있어야 합니다.

- 본문 내용과 맞아도 답이 아닐 수 있습니다.
  문단 급의 내용을 다뤄야 하므로, 비록 본문에서 언급한 맞는 내용이라 하더라도, 너무 디테일해서 틀릴 수도 있음을 주의해야 합니다. 즉, 맞아도(?) 맞지 않을 수(!!!) 있음을 주의해야 합니다.

9. CATEGORY CHART - CATEGORY화 시킬 수 있는 내용일 경우, 맞는 내용들을 짝지어 넣기

▶ 질문 형태

Directions: Complete the table below by selecting three answer choices that are characteristics of and two answer choices that are characteristics of _____ . **This question is worth 3 points.**

Drag your answer choices to the spaces where they belong.
To remove an answer choice, click on it. To review the passage, click View Text.

Answer choice	Category 1
(A)	•
(B)	•
(C)	•
(D)	**Category 2**
(E)	•
(F)	•
(G)	•

▶ 오답 패턴 (학생들이 잘 낚이는 경우 모음)

FACT 문제를 지문 전반에서 짝짓기로 냈다고 생각하면 편합니다. 그러므로 FACT 문제와 오답 패턴도 상당히 유사합니다. 그러므로 성가시게 시간이 상당히 많이 걸립니다. (다행히 서머리 문제가 많이 나오고 이 유형의 문제는 드물게 나옵니다)

- 해석이 안될 경우 (난이도 상)
- 단어만 사용하고 지문과 무관한 내용
- 언급 안된 내용을 그럴싸하게 적힌 경우
- 상식으로 접근할 경우
- 반만 맞고 반은 틀린 경우 (특히 틀린 부분이 뒷부분일 경우, 학생들은 앞만 보고 답으로 선택하는 경우 주의할 것)
- 본문과 반대 내용을 적어둘 때 (은근히 혼동됨)

▶ 핵심 전략 (≒ Fact 문제 처럼)

- 우선 대부분의 마지막 문제는 SUMMARY가 나오므로 **이 유형의 문제는 많이 나오지 않습니다.**
- 하지만 만약 나온다면 시간을 많이 잡아먹는 유형입니다.
  그러므로 본문을 읽을 때 왠지 유형화 시킬 수 있는 본문내용이라면 미리부터 지문에서 확인하기 쉽도록 비슷한 내용이라 생각되는 것들을 노트테이킹 해놓을 필요가 있습니다.
- 내용이 일치하는지를 꼭 재검토합니다.
  기억으로 문제를 풀면 틀리기 쉬운 문제유형입니다. 비록 시간은 많이 잡아 먹지만 FACT 문제처럼 꼼꼼히만 시간을 가지고 보면 어려운 문제만은 아닙니다. 하지만, 시간이 없어서 또는 귀찮아서라는 이유로 확인하지 않으면 틀릴 확률이 상당히 높은 문제유형 입니다. 주의해야 합니다.

usherin.usher.co.kr

USHER

iBT TOEFL
FINAL TEST
READING | 문제집

어셔 iBT 토플 파이널 테스트 리딩 문제집

어셔 어학 연구소

usherin.usher.co.kr

USHER

iBT TOEFL
FINAL TEST READING
TEST 1

테스트 전 확인사항

실전에 유용한 독해 전략(31p)을 숙지하였습니다. ○

화장실은 미리 다녀왔습니다. ○

휴대폰의 전원을 껐습니다. ○

노트테이킹 할 종이와 연필을 준비하였습니다. ○

시간을 체크할 시계를 준비하였습니다. ○

목표점수(20개 중 ___ 개)를 정하였습니다. ○

시험시작 시간은 ___ 시 ___ 분이며, ○
종료 시간은 35분 뒤인 ___ 시 ___ 분입니다.

시험 중 이동해야 할 방해요소가 있는지 체크하였습니다. ○
시험 중 이동하지 않습니다. ○

Reading Section Directions

This section measures your ability to understand academic passages in English.

Most questions are worth 1 point but the last question in each set is worth more than 1 point. The directions indicate how many points you may receive.

Some passages include a word or phrase that is underlined in blue. Click on the word or phrase to see a definition or an explanation.

Within each test, you can go to the next questions by clicking **Next**. You may skip questions and go back to them later. If you want to return to previous questions, click on **Back**. You can click on **Review** at any time and the review screen will show you which questions you have answered and which you have not answered. From this review screen, you may go directly to any questions you have already seen in the Reading section.

You may now begin the Reading section. In the section you will read 2 passages. You will have **35 minutes** to read the passages and answer the questuons.

Click on **Continue** to go on.

Next 버튼을 이용하여 다음 문제로 이동하고 **Back** 버튼을 이용하여 이전 문제로 이동할 수 있습니다. 문제에 답을 하지 않더라도 다음 문제로 이동할 수 있으며, **Review** 버튼을 이용하여 각 문제 별로 답을 체크했는지의 여부를 확인할 수 있습니다. 이번 테스트에서는 세 지문을 읽게 됩니다. **35분** 동안 지문을 읽고 문제에 답을 하세요.

Method of Measuring Bats' Age

1 → For many decades, biologists have compiled scores of data on the life spans of various bat species using data obtained by the fortuitous recapture of individuals tagged at birth. It has been found that on average, bats live three times longer than other mammals of similar size and metabolic rate. Determining their exact age is, however, particularly difficult because it is likely that they display more environmental and physiological variation throughout their lives than mammals with shorter lifespans, which may confuse several studied aspects of bat biology.

2 When studying bat lifespans, it is important to note the distinction between chronological and biological age. Chronological age is the interval between the time of birth and the present. Biological or physiological age, on the other hand, reflects the life expectancy and is based on physical changes in the morphology and function of the body, which may not always coincide with chronological age. The only means of knowing a bat's exact chronological age is to permanently mark it at birth, so that at any subsequent recaptures, its exact age can be determined. This method has drawbacks, as marking bats is time consuming, requiring long-term monitoring, and recapture rates are typically low, not to mention that the process itself may disturb the bat.

3 → Several other methods have been developed to determine the biological age of bats. The first measures the long bones, like the forearm, metacarpals, and digits, which go through a phase of rapid linear growth shortly after birth. These measurements, especially that of the forearm, can be used to distinguish juveniles from adults. A species-specific reference correlating these measurements with examples of a known-age can provide age estimates within 1-2 days with 95 percent accuracy. The advantages of this empirical method are its accuracy, ease of use in the field and laboratory, and lack of invasiveness. Only a

---

01 According to paragraph 1, why is it difficult to calculate the age of bats?

(A) They are dangerous compared to other short-lived mammals.
(B) They are too vulner able to many transformations they undergo.
(C) Age calculation is related to an area of study other than biology.
(D) The wide variety of bats' habitats and physical aspects is too broad to cover.

paragraph 1 is marked with an arrow [→].

02 All of the following are mentioned in paragraph 2 as difficulties of marking bats at birth to track their chronological age Except:

(A) It takes too much time to process.
(B) A long observation period is required.
(C) Re-trapping bats occurs rarely.
(D) The method is disturbed by bats.

03 The word empirical in the passage is closest in meaning to

(A) preliminary
(B) related
(C) observational
(D) reliable

04 What can be inferred from paragraph 3 about the cartilaginous epiphyseal plate?

(A) It is the easiest external physical characteristic for accurately measuring bats' age throughout its lifetime.
(B) It is possible to determine the adult bat's age by looking at its mineralized bone tissue.
(C) Changes in the pattern and rate of closure happen due to linear growth in adult long bones.
(D) Light can no longer penetrate it because it shuts as the bat gets older.

05 In paragraph 4, why does the author mention the teeth of puppies?

(A) To show that dogs' ages can also be measured through their teeth
(B) To show the similarity of the growth of teeth with bats
(C) To illustrate the high degree of accuracy of age measurement using teeth
(D) To support the claim that dogs live longer than bats due to their healthy teeth

06 According to paragraph 4, what is true about bat's teeth?

(A) The age of bats can be determined by the degree at which their teeth are angled regularly.
(B) Bats experience continuous tooth growth until death.
(C) Through their size, it is possible to know the bat's exact age.
(D) When bats become adults, they will have more blunt teeth.

paragraph 4 is marked with an arrow [→]

caliper or a ruler is needed to obtain the measurements, making this method ideal for use on both live animals and museum specimens. The major disadvantage is that these bones grow only during the first few weeks of life and the valid time frame varies between species from only 12 days in M. lucifugus to as long as 45 days in R. leschenaulti. Other traits, such as changes in the patterns and rates of closure of the cartilaginous epiphyseal growth plates are, therefore, necessary to estimate the age of older individuals. In its simplest form, this method distinguishes between young bats and adults. By transilluminating the wing of a juvenile, a researcher can discern the cartilaginous zone of the long phalanges which allows more light to pass through and thus appears lighter than bone. As the bat continues to grow, the epiphyseal plates eventually close and are no longer visible to the unaided eye. This method of age categorization requires no more than a flashlight and is ideal for use in both the field and the laboratory.

4 → Another method of estimating bats' age is to study their teeth. Much like puppies that lose their sharp baby teeth before growing a set of permanent adult teeth, in most bat species, permanent teeth replace the deciduous ones by the time juveniles are able to fly and feed independently. Once in place, these permanent teeth reach full size and cease to grow. A lifetime of mastication however wears down their surfaces and erodes their enamel. The degree of tooth wear can, therefore, be used to place bats into relative age categories as this process occurs from weaning until death. Due to differences in diet, tooth usage in aggressive interactions, and the populations' xannual activity periods, species show significant variation in tooth wear. Therefore, the development of species-specific reference standards based on a wide-ranging sample of known-age individuals is critical for the proper use of this method, as are investigators with extensive species-specific experience assessing tooth wear.

07 Why does the author mention the differences in diet, tooth usage in aggressive interactions, and populations' annual activity periods?

(A) To illustrate the bats' life cycle as they grow older
(B) To give some reasons that a species-specific reference standard was required to determine bats' ages
(C) To provide evidence that adult bats live in wild habitats
(D) To show the main seasons in which adult bats' teeth are worn.

08 Which of the sentences below best expresses the essential information in the highlighted sentence in the passage? Incorrect choices change the meaning in important ways or leave out essential information.

(A) The variety of biological studies gave insight into the methods of using teeth to determine the age of bats.
(B) The teeth of bats provided substantial information to the researchers studying methods of determining their age.
(C) There was abundant scientific research that gave significant outcomes regardless of the help of a broad reference.
(D) In various studies, where an approximate age range is sufficient, scientists have found tooth measurements to be valid forms of age determination in bats.

5 Zoologists Klevezal and Kleinenberg suggested a new method of aging bats using their teeth. They suggested that the number of incremental lines, or 'annuli,' on bat's teeth could be counted to determine its age. The robustness of the incremental lines, however, varies among species so that in some the lines may be difficult to count, especially in small species. Another zoologist, C.J. Phillips, examined the incremental lines in two species of bats from known-age specimens. [■] He found that the number of incremental lines observed depended on which tooth was extracted and on the section examined, and suggested that several factors, such as mechanical stress and tooth movement, can alter the patterns of layered growth yielding non- annual cycles of dentin and cementum deposition. [■] Other researchers have found a lack of correlation between age and incremental lines in some species. [■] The problems associated with this method highlight the need to better understand how and when these incremental lines are deposited and use this information to develop more accurate reference standards that can be correlated with other methods. [■] <mark>Notwithstanding, this method has proven useful for a variety of behavioral and ecological studies where broad age categories suffice to obtain meaningful results.</mark>

09 Look at the four squares [■] that indicate where the following sentence could be added to the passage.

Aside from variation in incremental lines and the questionable accuracy of this method, other disadvantages are that it requires tooth extraction, which can only be done on dead specimens, it is time consuming, and it requires specialized equipment.

Where would the sentence best fit?

Click on a square [■] to add the sentence to the passage.

10 Directions: An introductory sentence for a brief summary of the passage is provided below. Complete the summary by selecting the THREE answer choices that express the most important ideas in the passage. Some sentences do not belong in the summary because they express ideas that are not presented in the passage or are minor ideas in the passage. **This question is worth 2 points.**

Drag your answer choices to the spaces where they belong. To remove an answer choice, click on it. To review the passage, click on **View Text**.

> **Because bats are long-lived animals, it is more difficult to determine their ages because they experience more environmental and physiological variation.**
>
> ●
> ●
> ●

Answer Choices

(A) The age of bats can be categorized in two separate ways which measure different aspects of a bat's life span.

(B) While impractical for most stages of a bat's life, physical measurements and observations in juvenile bats' age can provide reliable calculations of its age.

(C) Many scientists argued that adult bats' age can be measured by their teeth, but there are drawbacks and inaccuracies in the methods

(D) People can determine puppies' age through examining their teeth, which is the same as a theory that scientists suggested.

(E) Chronological age of juvenile bats is easier to find because their teeth are not eroded like those of adult bats.

(F) Using long bones and the cartilaginous epiphyseal plates for measuring ages can be done on adult bats with no teeth.

11 According to paragraph 2, which of the following is true about backward reconstruction?

(A) It allows the derivation of new vocabulary from previous language forms.
(B) It is a technique that has been used for thousands of years.
(C) It is used to create a new language from ancient languages.
(D) It enables revival of pre-existing words.

paragraph 2 is marked with an arrow [→].

12 According to paragraph 3, Muslim and Hindu laws were

(A) only accessible to the Indian people.
(B) similar to that of Greek and Latin.
(C) both originally written in Sanskrit.
(D) further developed by William Jones.

paragraph 3 is marked with an arrow [→].

13 The word affinity is closest in meaning to

(A) resemblance
(B) understanding
(C) affection
(D) superiority

Tracing Language Diversification

1 Linguists study language relationships to find their similarities and differences. One way to find and chart these is to look for inter-language sound shifts over time. These are slight alternations in words between related subfamily languages since their origin. From these linguists can deduce a connection between them through sound shifts.

2 → The technique used to record sound shifts and consonant hardening is called backward reconstruction. This technique takes humanity's linguistic family tree back thousands of years. Using it, scholars infer vocabulary from previous languages. It may even be possible to go further and re-create the preceding languages.

3 → Linguist Sir William Jones was an early researcher into language diversification. He made unrivalled contributions to linguistic scholarship, promoting an understanding of and appreciation for Asian languages and cultures. Having arrived in Calcutta as a Bengal Supreme Court judge, he studied Sanskrit in order to approach Muslim and Hindu laws in their original form. He found grammatical roots corresponding to classical European languages. From this, he developed the idea of a common language source. In 'The Sanskrit Language', he wrote of Sanskrit's resemblance to Greek and Latin, which led him to suggest that they not only had a common root but were also related to other European languages. He stated: The Sanskrit language, whatever be its antiquity, is of a wonderful structure; more perfect than the Greek, more copious than the Latin, and more exquisitely refined than either, yet bearing to both of them a stronger affinity, both in the roots of verbs and the forms of grammar, than could possibly have been produced by accident; so strong indeed, that no philologer could examine them all three, without believing them to have sprung from some common source, which, perhaps, no longer exists.

14 According to paragraph 3, it can be inferred from William Jones's quote that a philologer

(A) would not be able to find the same root for three languages.
(B) would not understand why Sanskrit is more advanced than the others.
(C) would not believe the fact that the three languages no longer exist.
(D) would not doubt William Jones's hypothesis of language.

15 According to paragraph 4, the rural inhabitants did not welcome Grimm because

(A) he asked them personal questions about their taxes.
(B) he was better educated than they were.
(C) he bothered them by requesting to tell him stories.
(D) he was thought to work for the government.

paragraph 4 is marked with an arrow [→].

16 Why does the author mention the Hard consonants?

(A) To show how the same word can be transformed differently
(B) To exemplify the letters shared by languages in the same subfamily
(C) To explain the theory of language change that Grimm suggested
(D) To emphasize that softer consonant words are found in old languages

4 → Another major linguistic contributor was Jacob Grimm. During the nineteenth century, he sought to scientifically prove that sound shifts showed relationships between languages. Grimm sought rare unchanged words throughout the German countryside to clarify the history of the German language. Unfortunately, rural Germans presumed that a 'linguistics researcher' was just a new way for the government to figure out how much property tax they owed. [■] To entice people to speak freely, Grimm asked them to tell him stories, which he faithfully recorded. His primary interest was not initially the stories themselves but any exotic vocabulary they happened to use. [■] Grimm, however, did get what he wanted word-wise. [■] In the stories, he noticed an evolutionary pattern of Germanic languages which pointed to a change that had taken place long ago. [■] He explained that related languages have similar, but not identical consonants, which had undergone predictable changes over time. Hard consonants such as the v and t in German word vater, softened into the Dutch vader and the English father. Using Grimm's theory, linguists realized that consonants would become harder as they went 'backwards' toward the original language.

5 → From Jones' and Grimm's theories, linguists came up with the first major linguistic hypothesis: the existence of a common ancestral language called Proto-Indo-European which transformed into ancient Latin, Greek, and Sanskrit. This single language links modern languages around the world. Study of this language has helped identify that, although they share only a few similarities, both Slavonic and Germanic are sub-branches of a common ancestral language. Several research tasks naturally followed this hypothesis. First, the vocabulary of the proposed ancestral language needed to be reconstructed, before the hearth of the language could be located. After this, the routes of dispersion needed to be traced. Finally, the ways of life of those who spoke and spread the language needed to be established.

17 Which of the sentences below best expresses the essential information in the highlighted sentence in the passage? Incorrect choices change the meaning in important ways or leave out essential information.

(A) Because languages were able to be spread by relocation diffusion, it allowed people to freely move to another place with no difficulty.
(B) Relocation diffusion, which is caused by people moving to different places, makes languages complicated to track.
(C) Languages do not simply spread by people remaining stationary ; the process is complicated by relocation diffusion, which is done when people move around.
(D) Human mobility has made the study of language difficult for language was diffused not by fixed population but by relocation diffusion.

18 According to paragraph 7, convergence makes the study of language difficult because

(A) it changes a language into two different languages.
(B) it allows relocation diffusion to take place.
(C) it makes an exception to a rule of relocation diffusion.
(D) it uses the unreliable rules of reconstruction.

paragraph 7 is marked with an arrow [→].

6 → Nineteenth century linguist August Schleicher described language families as the branches of a tree. He suggested that new languages form through language divergence, when a language breaks down and fragments into dialects and then into discrete tongues due to separation of speakers. This can be seen in Spanish and Portuguese and is now happening with Quebecois French. Due to geographical separation, Parisian French and Quebecois French started to differ after the colonial era. Now the pronunciation and vocabulary use of the two places differ greatly. These new languages become the leaves on the tree. Through backward reconstruction, linguists can find how languages branches fit together. Tracing backward far enough, they can find the hearth of a language.

7 → Finding this hearth is a daunting task, as reconstructing even a small branch is complicated. A complicating factor is that with human mobility, languages did not merely diffuse through static populations; they also spread by relocation diffusion. If people with different languages have consistent spatial interaction, language convergence can take place, collapsing two languages into one. This creates problems for researchers because the reconstruction rules sometimes do not apply and can be unreliable.

19 Look at the four squares [■] that indicate where the following sentence could be added to the passage.

What he ended up with was a fascinating body of folklore which he and his brother Wilhelm published as Grimms' Fairy Tales.

Where would the sentence best fit?

Click on a square [■] to add the sentence to the passage.

20 Directions: An introductory sentence for a brief summary of the passage is provided below. Complete the summary by selecting the THREE answer choices that express the most important ideas in the passage. Some sentences do not belong in the summary because they express ideas that are not presented in the passage or are minor ideas in the passage. **This question is worth 2 points**.

Drag your answer choices to the spaces where they belong. To remove an answer choice, click on it. To review the passage, click on **View Text**.

For hundreds of years, linguists have studied languages and tracked their changes.

-
-
-

Answer Choices

(A) In order to study the language of the past, scholars use a technique to track sound shifts and hardening of consonants.

(B) Linguists use backward reconstruction to infer new words from previous forms of a language.

(C) Sir William Jones mastered multiple languages at an early age and also mastered Sanskrit in order to learn the law.

(D) The results from different studies on two linguistic hypotheses had similarities which implied the existence of a common source of language.

(E) The Proto-Indo-European language has split into many languages through the divergence process but convergence has made it hard to find its hearth.

(F) William Jones and Jacob Grimm focused on fairytales to use the resources to decipher the ancient texts.

RETURN　REVIEW　CONTINUE

You have seen all of the questions in this part of the Reading section. You have time left to review. As long as there is time remaining, you can check your work.

Click on **Return** to go back to the previous question.
Click on **Review** to see the review screen for this section.
Click on **Continue** to go on.
Once you leave this part of the Reading section, you **WILL NOT** be able to return to it.

이제 Reading Section이 끝났습니다.
Countinue 버튼을 누르면 다시 문제를 검토할 수 없으므로 유의하세요.

시험보고 난 후 ... 체크 리스트 및 스터디 디렉션 — USHER iBT TOEFL FINAL TEST READING

1. 내가 불안했던 문제만 재빨리 다시 보고, 불안하게 만든, 즉, 경쟁 초이스를 찾아서 왜 내가 헷갈려 했는지를 파악할 수 있는 메모를 해두시기 바랍니다. 시간이 지나거나, 다른 학생들과 스터디를 하면서는, 자신이 왜 낚였는지 이유조차 기억나지 않아 본인의 실수 패턴파악이 힘들기 때문입니다.

2. 답지를 확인하지 않고 스터디를 하시기 바랍니다. (그래서, 답지를 문제지 뒤에 붙이지 않고, 본 설명만을 붙여두었습니다.) 답지를 확인하지 않고 하는 이유는 답을 아는 순간, 답에 끼워맞춰 설명하려 하고, 이런 태도는 본인 실력 향상에 도움이 되지 않기 때문입니다. 스터디 팀원들간에 대략적인 답을 맞춰보면, 대부분 답안의 윤곽이 나옵니다. 이럴 경우, 이견이 있는 문제만 집중적으로 다루고, 나머지는 개인별로 처리하시기 바랍니다.

3. 문제를 끝까지 다 풀었나요? 네 □ / 아니오 □
   다 못 풀었다면, 전체 20 문제 중 푼 문제는? _____ / 20
   시간 모자란 것에 대해서는 크게 신경 쓰지 않아도 됩니다. 무엇보다 중요한 것은 정확도 입니다. 우선은 푼 문제를 맞출 확률을 높이고, 그 다음 시간을 걱정해도 늦지 않습니다.

4. 어려웠다고 느껴지는 지문은? 과학 □ / 예술 □ / 인문 □ / 인물 □ / 사회 □
   과학지문이 현격히 다른 분야보다 많지만, 그래도, 공부하다 보면 자신만 어려워하는 분야는 모두 각각입니다. 그러므로, 혹시 배경지식 부분에서 필요한 것이 있다면, usherin.usher.co.kr 에 방문하셔서, 공부가 안될 때, 배경지식 부분을 쉬엄쉬엄 들러서 봐 두시길 바랍니다. 쉬엄쉬엄입니다. 누가 뭐래도 실력있는 사람은 배경지식이 큰 영향을 끼치지는 않습니다.

5. (채점 후) 문제 풀 때 어렵다고 느낀 지문이 틀리는 개수와 쉬웠다고 느껴졌던 지문의 틀린 개수차이가 있나요? 예 □ / 아니오 □
   어느 순간 깨닫게 됩니다. 내가 잘 아는 내용이 나와서 자신 있게 푸나, 내가 모르는 지문이 나와서 겁먹고 푸나, 틀린 개수가 큰 차이가 나지 않는 것을…. 혹시 그걸 못 느끼신다면, 더욱더 열심히 하시기 바랍니다. ^^

6. 틀린 문제의 번호를 다음의 문제 유형 분석표와 비교해서 파악해 두시기 바랍니다.
   문제 유형을 파악해서 주의하는 것은, 누가 뭐래도 실력이 기본은 받쳐 줄 때 얘기입니다. 문제 푸는 스킬이나, 기타 문제 유형파악 등은 기본적으로 본문 내용을 이해하고, 해석이 웬만큼 될 때 얘기입니다. 만약, 너무 힘들다면 너무 스트레스 받지 말고, 그냥 '아~ 그렇구나' 정도로 넘기셔도 됩니다. 단, 본문 이해는 절대 양보해서는 안됩니다.

문제 유형 분석표 — 31page 내용 중, 아래 표시되어 있는 문제 유형은 파악하기 쉬우나 나머지 문제들의 문제 유형 파악은 어려워 하는 경향이 있어 비워두었습니다. 문제유형 정답은 287page를 참조하세요.

TEST 1-1

01
02
03 Vocabulary
04
05
06
07
08 Highlight
09 Insertion
10 Summary

TEST 1-2

11
12
13 Vocabulary
14
15
16
17 Highlight
18
19 Insertion
20 Summary

이름: Test 1

1

TEST번호	시험날짜	실제토플/모의토플 총점	RC	틀린갯수/전체갯수	LC	틀린갯수/전체갯수	SP	WR
tpo				/		/		
tpo				/		/		
tpo				/		/		
tpo				/		/		
tpo				/		/		
tpo				/		/		

2

RC			
첫 번째 지문 중 틀린 개수			

Topic1 제목:

문제유형	틀린갯수/전체갯수	실력으로 틀린 문제	실수로 틀린 문제
Voca 문제	/		
Fact 문제	/		
Reference 문제	/		
Purpose 문제	/		
Infer 문제	/		
Highlight 문제	/		
Insertion 문제	/		
Summary 문제	/		

→ 문제 유형 구분이 어려울 경우 물어봐주세요

RC			
첫 번째 지문 중 틀린 개수			

Topic1 제목:

문제유형	틀린갯수/전체갯수	실력으로 틀린 문제	실수로 틀린 문제
Voca 문제	/		
Fact 문제	/		
Reference 문제	/		
Purpose 문제	/		
Infer 문제	/		
Highlight 문제	/		
Insertion 문제	/		
Summary 문제	/		

→ 문제 유형 구분이 어려울 경우 물어봐주세요

3

오늘의 결론

내가 주의해야할 실수 패턴	내가 늘려야할 실력	내가 하고싶은 말(질문)

※ 순서대로 따라서 적어주세요.

| 문제구별 *tip*

Fact와 Purpose의 가장 큰 구별방법

· **Fact** 문제 : Except, true, Not true
· **Purpose** 문제 : why mention, in order to, what is the purpose

why는 Fact문제 일수도 있습니다.

usherin.usher.co.kr

USHER

iBT TOEFL
FINAL TEST READING
TEST 2

답안 및 취약 유형 분석표
해석·해설

테스트 전 확인사항

실전에 유용한 독해 전략(31p)을 숙지하였습니다. ○
화장실은 미리 다녀왔습니다. ○
휴대폰의 전원을 껐습니다. ○
노트테이킹 할 종이와 연필을 준비하였습니다. ○
시간을 체크할 시계를 준비하였습니다. ○
목표점수(20개 중 ___ 개)를 정하였습니다. ○
시험시작 시간은 ___시 ___분이며,
종료 시간은 35분 뒤인 ___시 ___분입니다. ○
시험 중 이동해야 할 방해요소가 있는지 체크하였습니다. ○
시험 중 이동하지 않습니다. ○

Reading Section Directions

This section measures your ability to understand academic passages in English.

Most questions are worth 1 point but the last question in each set is worth more than 1 point. The directions indicate how many points you may receive.

Some passages include a word or phrase that is underlined in blue. Click on the word or phrase to see a definition or an explanation.

Within each test, you can go to the next questions by clicking **Next**. You may skip questions and go back to them later. If you want to return to previous questions, click on **Back**. You can click on **Review** at any time and the review screen will show you which questions you have answered and which you have not answered. From this review screen, you may go directly to any questions you have already seen in the Reading section.

You may now begin the Reading section. In the section you will read 2 passages. You will have **35 minutes** to read the passages and answer the questuons.

Click on **Continue** to go on.

Next 버튼을 이용하여 다음 문제로 이동하고 **Back** 버튼을 이용하여 이전 문제로 이동할 수 있습니다. 문제에 답을 하지 않더라도 다음 문제로 이동할 수 있으며, **Review** 버튼을 이용하여 각 문제 별로 답을 체크했는지의 여부를 확인할 수 있습니다. 이번 테스트에서는 세 지문을 읽게 됩니다. **35분** 동안 지문을 읽고 문제에 답을 하세요.

Earth's Atmosphere

1 → The Earth's atmosphere consists mainly of heavy gases like nitrogen, but lacks light gases such as hydrogen and helium. This is odd, because nitrogen is known to be the seventh most abundant element in the universe, whereas hydrogen is the most common, which begs the question of why hydrogen is no longer abundant in Earth's atmosphere. Earth, currently the only planet known to support life, has an atmosphere distinguishable from others in the solar system, due to being composed of byproducts of life, such as oxygen. This distinction can be seen in the changes observed through studies done by a series of scientists, which have ultimately classified Earth's atmosphere into three stages of evolution: primordial atmosphere, secondary atmosphere, and the addition of oxygen.

2 → Initially, light gases were abundant in Earth's primordial atmosphere, but gradually started to decline. This can be explained through 'Jeans escape', a classical form of thermal escape based on Maxwell's Distribution that prescribes that the kinetic energy distribution of molecules is dependent on the mass and velocity of the molecule. From this, one can conclude that the bigger the molecule, the lower its average velocity at a given temperature, which makes escape more unlikely. Furthermore, the greater the mass of the planet, the higher the required escape velocity; which ultimately results in less escaping molecules. Thus, giant planets with high gravity possess higher concentrations of light gases such as hydrogen and helium, which are rare in the inner planet's atmospheres. [■] The distance from the star also affects molecular velocity; the closer the planet, the hotter the atmosphere becomes, leading to higher molecular velocity and higher escape rates. [■] This is how Saturn's relatively small moon, Titan, keeps its atmosphere. [■] Even though its gravitational pull is lower than that of Earth, its cooler temperature allows it to hold on to its atmosphere. [■]

---

01 According to paragraph 1, which of the following is true about Earth?

(A) It currently has three different atmospheres: the primordial atmosphere, secondary atmosphere and the addition of oxygen.
(B) Nitrogen is most dominant in its atmosphere due to it being a byproduct of life.
(C) The ratio of the components in its atmosphere is different from that of the universe.
(D) Nitrogen is the seventh most abundant element on Earth.

paragraph 1 is marked with an arrow [→].

02 What is the significance of Titan mentioned in paragraph 2?

(A) It exemplifies how the distance from the Sun affects the atmosphere of an object despite the effects of its gravity.
(B) It is a relatively small moon that is an example of an object that is far from the Sun.
(C) It is far away from the Sun and hence sustains a ring structure through low temperatures.
(D) It shows that 'Jeans escape' may not be enough to preserve its atmosphere.

03 In paragraph 3, why does the author mention that light gases are not found in Earth's atmosphere?

(A) To emphasize the fact that the gases escaped from the Earth's atmosphere
(B) To point out that hydrogen is the most common element in the universe, but is no longer common in the Earth's atmosphere
(C) To support the idea that light gases once existed as a component of the Earth's atmosphere
(D) To point out one of the reasons nitrogen became dominant in the atmosphere

04 The word volatile in the passage is closest in meaning to

(A) flammable
(B) evaporable
(C) mixable
(D) condensable

05 According to paragraph 3, what can be inferred about nitrogen?

(A) Nitrogen is stable and does not react with other elements easily.
(B) Nitrogen becomes stable as a part of a crystal lattice and doesn't bond with other elements.
(C) Nitrogen is the most common element in the Earth's crust.
(D) Nitrogen was originally frozen, but filled the atmosphere after volcanic eruptions cause temperatures to rise.

paragraph 3 is marked with an arrow [→].

3 → Scientists believe that as light gases escaped from Earth's atmosphere, nitrogen began constituting a larger part of it after volcanic eruptions spewed gases, ultimately forming the main component of the secondary atmosphere. Three primary reasons why only nitrogen filled the environment are that it is volatile even at low temperatures, unreactive with the materials that make up the earth's crust, and very stable in the presence of solar radiation. In contrast to more abundant elements which are major components of Earth's crust, nitrogen is not stable as a part of a crystal lattice, and will not bond with the others to form the terrestrial earth; it, instead, remains a gas. Unlike nitrogen, other elements are unstable and easily react with each other in the atmosphere as well as break down when exposed to solar radiation. Thus, over time, nitrogen built up in the atmosphere to a much greater extent than other elements.

4 → One theory introducing the presence of atmospheric oxygen is the Gaia theory. It is believed by scientists that the primordial atmosphere of Earth did not contain oxygen and that the appearance of this gas required the evolution of photosynthetic life forms, such as early cyanobacteria and later single-celled algae, which emerged as the earth cooled and the gaseous water condensed and formed oceans. As a result of photosynthesis, molecular oxygen built up to the present level, which appears to have been relatively stable for several billion years. If this level were even slightly higher, then the earth's biomass would be combustible, leading to extensive explosions and forest fires, severely damaging earth's ecosystem. The Gaia theory, thus, suggests that there is a planetary, homeostatic control over the oxygen concentration in the atmosphere that balances the ratio of organisms producing oxygen to those consuming it.

5 However, some argue that the amount of oxygen collected in the Earth's atmosphere cannot be accounted for entirely by cyanobacteria. They believe that the theory is not adequate because it can only

06 Which of the sentences below best expresses the essential information in the highlighted sentence in the passage? Incorrect choices change the meaning in important ways or leave out essential information.

(A) Due to the appearance of photosynthetic life forms, the primordial atmosphere did not contain any oxygen.
(B) Photosynthesis, a crucial process which bacteria and plants use to produce energy from sunlight and water, is the main reason oxygen was not present in the primordial atmosphere.
(C) Scientists think that without photosynthetic life forms such as cyanobacteria and algae, the primitive atmosphere could not have acquired oxygen.
(D) Oxygen gas was one of the important compounds which algae and bacteria used to thrive in primordial atmosphere.

07 According to paragraph 4, which of the following is true according to the Gaia theory?

(A) The oxygen levels of Earth have gone through several fluctuations over the past billions of years.
(B) If nitrogen concentrations in the atmosphere were higher, the earth's biomass would be combustible.
(C) A balance between oxygen producers and consumers controls the amount of atmospheric oxygen.
(D) It explains the evolution of photosynthetic life forms such as cyanobacteria and single-celled algae.

paragraph 4 is marked with an arrow [→].

08 The word it in paragraph 5 refers to

(A) theory
(B) atmosphere
(C) oxygen
(D) earth

account for 1 percent to 10 percent concentration levels, while today's atmosphere contains 21 percent. Thus, a second theory called the planetary atmosphere tectonic machine theory was developed. The theory posits that all of earth's oxygen came from not life forms, but the ocean, near the tectonic plates where magma is released and water comes into contact with temperatures over 2000°C. The super-heated water is then converted into hydrogen and oxygen. The oxygen bubbles then oxygenate the ocean, and are released into the atmosphere when they reach the surface. This oxygen in the atmosphere is then shielded from being fully lost to space by the ozone and the earth's magnetic field.

09 Look at the four squares [■] that indicate where the following sentence could be added to the passage.

Neptune's moon, Triton, being attached to the farthest planet from the sun, is also, in this way, able to retain a non-negligible nitrogenous atmosphere due to the extreme temperatures at the edge of the solar system.

Where would the sentence best fit?

Click on a square [■] to add the sentence to the passage.

10 Directions: An introductory sentence for a brief summary of the passage is provided below. Complete the summary by selecting the THREE answer choices that express the most important ideas in the passage. Some sentences do not belong in the summary because they express ideas that are not presented in the passage or are minor ideas in the passage. **This question is worth 2 points.**

Drag your answer choices to the spaces where they belong. To remove an answer choice, click on it.
To review the passage, click on **View Text**.

The atmosphere of earth has gone through many different phases.

-
-
-

Answer Choices

(A) Nitrogen was spread through Earth's atmosphere without reacting with other compounds to form compounds, but remained a gas.

(B) Even though its gravitational force is lower than that of Earth, Titan keeps its atmosphere.

(C) Light gases were able to escape from the Earth's atmosphere because its molecular velocity was fast enough to overcome the pull the Earth's gravity.

(D) A theory explains that under the ocean, at the location of the tectonic plates, tremendously hot magma boils water and releases its oxygen.

(E) According to the Gaia Theory, the appearance of photosynthetic life forms started to consume molecular oxygen in the primordial atmosphere.

(F) The availability of atmospheric oxygen is a critically important environmental factor for most of Earth's species and for many ecological processes.

11 According to paragraph 1, what can be inferred about slower-growing plants with healthy leaves?

(A) The area in which they are growing is favorable to them.
(B) They receive insufficient levels of energy to initiate photosynthesis.
(C) Their thin, long stems are not strong enough to support the entire plant.
(D) Their leaves lack the ability to convert carbon dioxide into organic compounds.

paragraph 1 is marked with an arrow [→].

12 Which of the sentences below best expresses the essential information in the highlighted sentence in the passage? Incorrect choices change the meaning in important ways or leave out essential information.

(A) When exposed to inadequate sunlight, plants grow shorter internodes which have longer and thinner stems to search for sources of light.
(B) Sunlight-deprived plants will grow taller stems with longer internodes more quickly than those with adequate sunlight as they search for a new light source.
(C) Plants that are exposed to enough sunlight grow thinner and longer stems with fewer internodes compared to plants that do not have adequate sunlight.
(D) Plants that have not received enough sunlight will continue to rapidly produce longer but thinner and fewer stems, that search for light.

The Effects of Light on Flowering

1 Plant growth and development are controlled by interactions between environmental factors and inner developmental processes. Amongst the diverse environmental factors, light plays the most essential role, affecting plants in various ways, from their growth and ability to produce energy to their bloom time. For example, in the absence of sufficient light, plants exhibit a unique growth pattern called etiolation. These plants will produce thinner and longer stems with longer internodes to reach a faint light source or to find one, in a much more rapid way than those exposed to adequate sunlight. A plant suffering from etiolation will also produce fewer leaves.

2 → Perhaps the most interesting influence light has on plants is on their flowering patterns. The blossoming of flowers in plants is an intricate and delicate process which has evolved to suit plants' different environments. To maximize the probability of their seeds being successfully dispersed, plants use environmental factors to determine the current season. Some of these factors, like temperature and water availability, can fluctuate heavily. An unusually cool summer or unexpected rain outside the monsoon seasons would confuse the plants. Fortunately, plants can also use the length of day as a cue. Length of day is perhaps the most reliable indicator of the season because it is controlled by the angle of Earth's rotation, which is unaltered by terrestrial events. Longer days always indicate springtime and the coming of summer while shorter days are only possible during autumn and winter.

3 → Depending on their reaction to the length of the day, species of plants are traditionally categorized into three groups: the long-day, the short-day and day-neutral plants. A day-neutral plant produces flowers as soon as it has sufficiently grown and developed, regardless of the length of the day. The traditional

13 According to paragraph 3, which of the following is true about the flowering of plants?

(A) The flowering of plants is strictly controlled by their exposure to light in various durations.
(B) The flowering of plants, whether short-day or long-day, does not depend on the amount of time that they are exposed to light.
(C) The day-neutral plants flower in response to the length of the daytime, hence they mainly flower in the summer.
(D) The spinach, a long-day plant, requires long nights, a minimum of eleven hours of darkness, in order to produce flowers.

paragraph 2 is marked with an arrow [→].

14 The author mentions humans in the passage in order to

(A) Point out that the biological clock of humans is poorly understood
(B) Explain that humans are also organisms and a part of nature
(C) Illustrate how widespread the internal biological clock is in nature
(D) Suggest that plants' light detection methods are similar to those of humans

15 According to paragraph 4, what role does phytochrome play in a plant's flowering?

(A) Stimulating growth and development in the plant's leaves
(B) Resetting the biological clock of a plant by way of light detection
(C) Keeping track of the length of nighttime in the absence of external signals
(D) Reacting to cellular changes in the plant caused by light

paragraph 4 is marked with an arrow [→].

names of long-day and short-day plants are, however, better described as short-night and long-night plants since it is the duration of continuous darkness rather than the day length which controls flowering. Long-night plants produce flowers during times when there is more than a specified duration of continuous darkness. Conversely, short-night plants require periods of darkness to be less than a specified period. The threshold for the length of darkness of both long-night and short-night plants differ by species. The duration of this is called the critical photoperiod. For example, spinach, a short-night plant, only produces flowers when exposed to less-than-eleven-hour intervals of darkness. Spinach's critical photoperiod is, therefore, eleven hours.

4 → Compared to their flowering behavior, the actual method used by plants to distinguish daytime from nighttime is not well understood. So far, botanists have discovered that plants utilize an internal clock and a light-detecting pigment called phytochrome in order to measure the length of uninterrupted darkness. The internal biological clock is used to measure the length of time the plant has spent without light. It works as a timer that starts ticking when the light goes out, and resets when it returns. This clock is found in almost all organisms, including humans, yet is poorly understood. There is, however, a better grasp of the phytochrome. Phytochrome is a pigment found in plants which has the ability to detect light and bring about cellular change when it is present. One such cellular change is the resetting of the internal clock that measures the length of continuous darkness.

5 → This mechanism is quite sensitive; many species of long-night plants that have their darkness interrupted for even a minute or two with either sunlight or artificial light may not flower. [■] It was found that red light shone on a plant during the night is perceived by the plant and the plant resets its biological clock. [■] But the same plant does not reset its clock when exposed

16 The word it in the passage refers to
(A) ability
(B) phytochrome
(C) light
(D) pigment

17 According to paragraph 6, all of the following statements about the alleged characteristics of florigen are true EXCEPT
(A) Florigen may be a number of collaborative compounds
(B) Florigen has the ability to travel from one part of a plant to another
(C) The release of florigen stimulates flower buds to begin producing flowers
(D) Scientists' level of understanding of florigen has recently improved to match the understanding of phytochrome

18 The word subjected to in the passage is closest in meaning to
(A) exposed to
(B) removed from
(C) uncovered by
(D) weakened by

to far-red light (light with a longer wavelength than red light), and therefore it produces flowers. [■] This is not because phytochrome cannot detect far-red light, but because it reacts to the two types of light differently. [■]

6 → The discovery of what internal factors actually signal plants to flower in response to light has overarching potential in biology and agriculture, which makes it an intriguing topic of study. Experiments conducted on cockleburs, a family of long-night plants that require more than eight hours of darkness to flower, revealed that despite their strong sensitivity to light exposure, if even a single leaf of the cocklebur experiences a long night, while the rest of the plant is subjected to short nights, it still produced flowers. This experiment suggested that a flowering factor is sent from the leaves to the flower buds when the flowering conditions for the plants are met. So far scientists have not found this factor, but the most widely accepted notion is that interactions among multiple, as yet unidentified plant hormones or other compounds, referred to as florigen, trigger flowering.

19 Look at the four squares [■] that indicate where the following sentence could be added to the passage.

This effect, however, does not occur with all types of light.

Where would the sentence best fit?

Click on a square [■] to add the sentence to the passage.

20 Directions: An introductory sentence for a brief summary of the passage is provided below. Complete the summary by selecting the THREE answer choices that express the most important ideas in the passage. Some sentences do not belong in the summary because they express ideas that are not presented in the passage or are minor ideas in the passage. **This question is worth 2 points.**

Drag your answer choices to the spaces where they belong. To remove an answer choice, click on it. To review the passage, click on **View Text**.

The plants show different reactions to light, which is an essential factor of growth.

-
-
-

Answer Choices

(A) Long-day plants and short-day plants produce flowers depending on the duration of uninterrupted darkness, while day-neutral plants are unaffected by the length of exposure to light and darkness.

(B) Cockleburs are a family of long-night plants which scientists have used to learn about plants' flowering in different lighting conditions.

(C) Long-day, short-day and day-neutral plants all require different intervals of continuous darkness while also maintaining certain temperature levels.

(D) Plants use a biological internal clock and the pigment phytochrome, which reacts to specific types of light, to measure the length of time without light.

(E) Although not enough information has been uncovered regarding the internal processes in initiating flower production in plants, it is proposed that the signal can travel from the leaf to the bud.

(F) The ability of a plant's flower to absorb light is influenced by a variety of factors including temperature and water availability.

| RETURN | REVIEW | CONTINUE |

You have seen all of the questions in this part of the Reading section. You have time left to review. As long as there is time remaining, you can check your work.

Click on **Return** to go back to the previous question.
Click on **Review** to see the review screen for this section.
Click on **Continue** to go on.
Once you leave this part of the Reading section, you **WILL NOT** be able to return to it.

이제 Reading Section이 끝났습니다.
Countinue 버튼을 누르면 다시 문제를 검토할 수 없으므로 유의하세요.

시험보고 난 후 ... 체크 리스트 및 스터디 디렉션 | USHER iBT TOEFL FINAL TEST READING

1. 내가 불안했던 문제만 재빨리 다시 보고, 불안하게 만든, 즉, 경쟁 초이스를 찾아서 왜 내가 헷갈려 했는지를 파악할 수 있는 메모를 해두시기 바랍니다. 시간이 지나거나, 다른 학생들과 스터디를 하면서는, 자신이 왜 낚였는지 이유조차 기억나지 않아 본인의 실수 패턴파악이 힘들기 때문입니다.

2. 답지를 확인하지 않고 스터디를 하시기 바랍니다. (그래서, 답지를 문제지 뒤에 붙이지 않고, 본 설명만을 붙여두었습니다.) 답지를 확인하지 않고 하는 이유는 답을 아는 순간, 답에 끼워맞춰 설명하려 하고, 이런 태도는 본인 실력 향상에 도움이 되지 않기 때문입니다. 스터디 팀원들간에 대략적인 답을 맞춰보면, 대부분 답안의 윤곽이 나옵니다. 이럴 경우, 이견이 있는 문제만 집중적으로 다루고, 나머지는 개인별로 처리하시기 바랍니다.

3. 문제를 끝까지 다 풀었나요? 네 □ / 아니오 □
   다 못 풀었다면, 전체 20 문제 중 푼 문제는? _____ / 20
   시간 모자란 것에 대해서는 크게 신경 쓰지 않아도 됩니다. 무엇보다 중요한 것은 정확도 입니다. 우선은 풀 문제를 맞출 확률을 높이고, 그 다음 시간을 걱정해도 늦지 않습니다.

4. 어려웠다고 느껴지는 지문은? 과학 □ / 예술 □ / 인문 □ / 인물 □ / 사회 □
   과학지문이 현격히 다른 분야보다 많지만, 그래도, 공부하다 보면 자신만 어려워하는 분야는 모두 각각입니다. 그러므로, 혹시 배경지식 부분에서 필요한 것이 있다면, usherin.usher.co.kr 에 방문하셔서, 공부가 안될 때, 배경지식 부분을 쉬엄쉬엄 들러서 봐 두시길 바랍니다. 쉬엄쉬엄입니다. 누가 뭐래도 실력있는 사람은 배경지식이 큰 영향을 끼치지는 않습니다.

5. (채점 후) 문제 풀 때 어렵다고 느낀 지문이 틀리는 개수와 쉬웠다고 느껴졌던 지문의 틀린 개수차이가 있나요? 예 □ / 아니오 □
   어느 순간 깨닫게 됩니다. 내가 잘 아는 내용이 나와서 자신 있게 푸나, 내가 모르는 지문이 나와서 겁먹고 푸나, 틀린 개수가 큰 차이가 나지 않는 것을…. 혹시 그걸 못 느끼신다면, 더욱더 열심히 하시기 바랍니다. ^^

6. 틀린 문제의 번호를 다음의 문제 유형 분석표와 비교해서 파악해 두시기 바랍니다.
   문제 유형을 파악해서 주의하는 것은, 누가 뭐래도 실력이 기본은 받쳐 줄 때 얘기입니다. 문제 푸는 스킬이나, 기타 문제 유형파악 등은 기본적으로 본문 내용을 이해하고, 해석이 웬만큼 될 때 얘기입니다. 만약, 너무 힘들다면 너무 스트레스 받지 말고, 그냥 '아~ 그렇구나' 정도로 넘기셔도 됩니다. 단, 본문 이해는 절대 양보해서는 안됩니다.

문제 유형 분석표
31page 내용 중, 아래 표시되어 있는 문제 유형은 파악하기 쉬우나 나머지 문제들의 문제 유형 파악은 어려워 하는 경향이 있어 비워두었습니다. 문제유형 정답은 305page를 참조하세요.

TEST 2-1

01
02
03
04 Vocabulary
05
06 Highlight
07
08 Reference
09 Insertion
10 Summary

TEST 2-2

11
12 Highlight
13
14
15
16 Reference
17
18 Vocabulary
19 Insertion
20 Summary

이름:

Test 2

1

TEST번호	시험날짜	실제토플/모의토플 총점	RC	틀린갯수/전체갯수	LC	틀린갯수/전체갯수	SP	WR
tpo				/		/		
tpo				/		/		
tpo				/		/		
tpo				/		/		
tpo				/		/		
tpo				/		/		

2

RC

Topic 1 제목:

문제유형	틀린갯수/전체갯수	실력으로 틀린 문제	실수로 틀린 문제
Voca 문제	/		
Fact 문제	/		
Reference 문제	/		
Purpose 문제	/		
Infer 문제	/		
Highlight 문제	/		
Insertion 문제	/		
Summary 문제	/		

첫 번째 지문 중 틀린 개수

→ 문제 유형 구분이 어려울 경우 물어보세요

RC

Topic 1 제목:

문제유형	틀린갯수/전체갯수	실력으로 틀린 문제	실수로 틀린 문제
Voca 문제	/		
Fact 문제	/		
Reference 문제	/		
Purpose 문제	/		
Infer 문제	/		
Highlight 문제	/		
Insertion 문제	/		
Summary 문제	/		

첫 번째 지문 중 틀린 개수

→ 문제 유형 구분이 어려울 경우 물어보세요

3

오늘의 결론

내가 주의해야할 실수 패턴	내가 놀려야할 실력	내가 하고싶은 말 (질문)

※ 순서대로 따라서 적어주세요.

| 문제구별 tip

Fact와 Purpose의 가장 큰 구별방법

- **Fact** 문제 : Except, true, Not true
- **Purpose** 문제 : why mention, in order to, what is the purpose

why는 **Fact**문제 일수도 있습니다.

usherin.usher.co.kr

USHER

iBT TOEFL
FINAL TEST READING
TEST 3

답안 및 취약 유형 분석표
해석·해설

테스트 전 확인사항

실전에 유용한 독해 전략(31p)을 숙지하였습니다. ○
화장실은 미리 다녀왔습니다. ○
휴대폰의 전원을 껐습니다. ○
노트테이킹 할 종이와 연필을 준비하였습니다. ○
시간을 체크할 시계를 준비하였습니다. ○
목표점수(20개 중 ___ 개)를 정하였습니다. ○
시험시작 시간은 ___시 ___분이며,
종료 시간은 35분 뒤인 ___시 ___분입니다. ○
시험 중 이동해야 할 방해요소가 있는지 체크하였습니다. ○
시험 중 이동하지 않습니다. ○

Reading Section Directions

This section measures your ability to understand academic passages in English.

Most questions are worth 1 point but the last question in each set is worth more than 1 point. The directions indicate how many points you may receive.

Some passages include a word or phrase that is underlined in blue. Click on the word or phrase to see a definition or an explanation.

Within each test, you can go to the next questions by clicking **Next**. You may skip questions and go back to them later. If you want to return to previous questions, click on **Back**. You can click on **Review** at any time and the review screen will show you which questions you have answered and which you have not answered. From this review screen, you may go directly to any questions you have already seen in the Reading section.

You may now begin the Reading section. In the section you will read 2 passages. You will have **35 minutes** to read the passages and answer the questuons.

Click on **Continue** to go on.

Next 버튼을 이용하여 다음 문제로 이동하고 **Back** 버튼을 이용하여 이전 문제로 이동할 수 있습니다. 문제에 답을 하지 않더라도 다음 문제로 이동할 수 있으며, **Review** 버튼을 이용하여 각 문제 별로 답을 체크했는지의 여부를 확인할 수 있습니다. 이번 테스트에서는 세 지문을 읽게 됩니다. **35분** 동안 지문을 읽고 문제에 답을 하세요.

01 According to paragraph 2, why did naturalistic painting become a competitive style of painting?

(A) There were too many painters of naturalistic style that only those who made a name for themselves could be remembered by the public.
(B) Naturalistic painters started to mimic the painting competition of Parrhasius and Zeuxis.
(C) The artistic achievement of naturalistic painting was easier to measure than that of other styles of painting.
(D) The mastery of a brushstroke, which was largely subjective, was a criterion for evaluation.

paragraph 2 is marked with an arrow [→].

02 Which of the following is true about Parrhasius and his style according to paragraph 2?

(A) Parrhasius' parents started training him to be an artist at an early age.
(B) Parrhasius was known for being attentive to the foundations of his painting.
(C) Parrhasius began his career as a sketch artist but eventually turned to naturalistic painting.
(D) Parrhasius was criticized by his rival because the sketches of his paintings were too elaborate.

Naturalistic Painting

1 → The civilization of Ancient Greece, which lasted from the 8th century to the mid-1st century BC, had a lasting cultural influence over such a huge area, and over such powerful empires that it is often considered the underpinning of Western culture. Historians have discovered that even paintings from Ancient Greece had a strong influence on art in remote parts of Europe for millennia to come. One such artistic influence was the movement known as naturalism. Naturalistic painters aspire to depict the world's natural objects, people and unadorned scenery as realistically as possible. Their paintings are characterized by meticulous detail and near-perfect symmetry. In simple terms, naturalistic artists strive to create realistic paintings hardly distinguishable from actual photographs. This movement originated in Ancient Greece and spread through Europe to the Netherlands, where it continuously evolved.

2 → In Ancient Greece, the early naturalistic painters tended to put more emphasis on skill than on creativity, and painters of Greece would often compare their works to see which was more 'realistic'. While the artists' creativity was largely subjective, a brushstroke was an objective means of assessment. As a result, naturalistic painting became a competitive style of painting, as shown by the legendary painting competition of Parrhasius and Zeuxis, two of the greatest painters of the 5th century BC. Parrhasius, who was born in the city of Ephesus and lived in Athens, had distinguished himself as an extraordinary artist at a young age. Often, those who witnessed the initial stages of his paintings mistook him for a sketch artist, an artist who completes his work using only a pencil or pastel. His works were so great that they were preserved as study aids for painters that came after him. His rival Zeuxis was born in the Southern Italian city of Heraclea, and was widely renowned in the artistic scene of the time. At the peak of their

03 The word attained in the passage is closest in meaning to

(A) required
(B) retained
(C) awarded
(D) achieved

04 Why does the author mention Netherlands painters Adriaen van der Spelt and Frans van Mieris?

(A) To show that painters in The Netherlands were inherited and developed the ideals of the naturalist movement.
(B) To show how naturalist paintings evolved into more symbolic modern paintings.
(C) To show that critics were unwilling to accept paintings that displayed symbolism.
(D) To show that later painters had much more talent than the earlier naturalistic painters.

05 What do the insects around the flower of Parrhasius' Curtains in paragraph 3 signify?

(A) The beauty and perfection of affluence are easily lost.
(B) Flowers, which make their owners wealthy, would be destroyed by insects.
(C) Happiness and comfort are associated with the rich.
(D) The poverty-stricken members of the society are attracted to the rich.

careers, a contest was staged to determine the greater of the two. At the competition, Zeuxis revealed a painting of grapes which was realistic enough to fool nearby birds. Absorbed in a sense of achievement, he confidently asked Parrhasius to pull aside the curtains and reveal his painting, only to be told that the curtains themselves were his painted work. Zeuxis was confounded by this and exclaimed "I have deceived the birds, but Parrhasius has deceived Zeuxis." Parrhasius' painting later became known as 'Parrhasius' Curtain' and he attained the title of the best naturalistic painter of the time, gaining even more fame and respect. He was even asked to paint murals for the Capitol of Rome by city officials.

3 Millenniums later, Adriaen van der Spelt and Frans van Mieris, painters from Netherlands, led a movement that challenged the original principles of naturalism. Their paintings portrayed objects and acts that interested them, with little regard for whether they resembled the natural world. For example, they painted a lily in the center of Parrhasius' Curtain with insects around it. The lily served no naturalistic purpose, but with it the painting gained scores of symbolic meaning. Critics and fellow artists were awakened to the ideas of naturalist painting, surprised and awed at the same time. The lily represented wealth and property while the insects around the flower illustrated how the flower could be robbed of its nectar and left to die in a matter of days. The painting was lauded for its combination of symbolism and realistic insights. This led critics to begin questioning whether 'art' was defined by how well a natural object is depicted, or by how well it is embellished and enhanced. [■] This became more pronounced as technological progress and development led to the emergence of cameras and professional photography. [■] Clearly, the new artistic photographs captured naturalistic images much more easily than paintings. [■] While an intricate and time-consuming process in the past, re-creating nature on paper became only a matter of the click of a shutter. [■]

06 According to paragraph 4, what is the significance of coloring the lily in red?
- (A) It acts as evidence of the claim that the artist unknowingly puts down his personality into his works.
- (B) It is an example of a way the artist intentionally expresses himself in the painting.
- (C) It was a way for the artist to bring attention to Parrhasius' painting and remind others of the founding philosophy of naturalism.
- (D) By painting the lily in its most common color, the painting was improved to better portray the real world.

paragraph 4 is marked with an arrow [→].

07 Why does the author mention Jean Auguste Dominique Ingres in paragraph 4?
- (A) To explain the modernized form of the naturalist movement through one of the strongest opponents of naturalism.
- (B) To indicate the role French painters had in the development of naturalistic painting
- (C) To describe an argument against the statement that naturalistic paintings do contain the artist's intention
- (D) To show that painters can unknowingly make mistakes on their finished works

08 Which of the sentences below best expresses the essential information in the highlighted sentence in the passage? Incorrect choices change the meaning in important ways or leave out essential information.
- (A) Because naturalism was not well accepted throughout history, it could not play an important part in the past, present, and future of art.
- (B) Because naturalism is an essential part of the history of art, it is slowly losing its reputation among critics.
- (C) The naturalistic style of painting influenced the development of art in the past and will continue to impact artists in the future.
- (D) There was a growing dissent of naturalism, but the influences of naturalism which span from the past to future are irrefutable.

4 → As art entered the modern era, the common belief became that painting to resemble nature as closely as possible is not really art, but rather an act of duplication. There have not only been convincing arguments which support this claim, but also several credible arguments that oppose it. One modern artist, for instance, added his touch to Adriaen van der Spelt and Frans van Mieris' painting by coloring the lily bright red. The red lily, the artist explained, represented passion and supported the assertion that art should express the artist's mind. According to him, an artist must deliberately convey his vision through various methods, such as the use of color and brushstroke. On the other hand, the French Neoclassical painter Jean Auguste Dominique Ingres, pointed out that regardless of what or how an artist paints, the painter unintentionally leaves traces of himself in the work. Ingres believed that the painter would subconsciously make different choices according to his mood, such as using harsher brushstrokes when feeling angry, or passionate colors when in love, all inadvertently. With all things considered, despite the fact that it was decreasing in popularity and was occasionally criticized, the naturalistic style of painting has played a major role in the history of art and will continue to do so in the future.

09 Look at the four squares [■] that indicate where the following sentence could be added to the passage.

Initially, photography was used to capture and record subjects of scientific interest, but it quickly turned into a new art form.

Where would the sentence best fit?

Click on a square [■] to add the sentence to the passage.

10 Directions: An introductory sentence for a brief summary of the passage is provided below. Complete the summary by selecting the THREE answer choices that express the most important ideas in the passage. Some sentences do not belong in the summary because they express ideas that are not presented in the passage or are minor ideas in the passage. **This question is worth 2 points.**

Drag your answer choices to the spaces where they belong. To remove an answer choice, click on it. To review the passage, click on **View Text**.

Naturalistic painting is a style of painting in which the artist emulates natural subjects as closely as possible.

-
-
-

Answer Choices

(A) For a certain period of time, naturalism was a competitive art form.

(B) Naturalism emerged in theater and literature as a reaction to naturalistic painting in the 19th century.

(C) Technological improvements and the movement towards symbolism has led opponents of naturalistic painting to argue that naturalism cannot be considered artistic.

(D) In a contest to select the best naturalistic painter, Zeuxis' painting fooled nearby birds and Parrhasius's Curtains fooled Zeuxis.

(E) Symbolism in painting was frowned upon by many when it was first introduced in Netherlands.

(F) Naturalistic artists have helped shape the history of art and will likely continue to be an essential part of art.

Two Types of Evolutionary Theories

1 Evolution occurs as populations adjust to habitat change with those experiencing the best genetic adaptations surviving and passing on their genes. These phenotypic changes in populations are common to all organisms and affect every species, no matter what ecosystem. There are two prevailing, non-mutually exclusive theories of evolution today, gradualism and punctuated equilibrium, which differ in the speed at which evolutionary changes occur.

2 → One of the early proponents of complete gradualism was Charles Darwin whose 'Origin of Species' adopted Charles Lyell's 'Principles of Geology' to suggest gradualism occurs in a slow manner with only small intergenerational changes. As Lyell proposed, sudden changes cannot be assumed to occur as they are not presently observed and thus cannot be assumed to have occurred in the past. Darwin also felt that extreme deviations from the usual phenotypic variation would be more likely to be selected against. The most famous historical model supporting the idea of complete gradualism was the evolution of the modern horse from the fox-sized, forest-dwelling Hyracotherium. Over time, paleozoologists pieced together the gradual evolution of the horse in a more complete way than any other modern animal. They traced the lineage from early ancestors with splayed toes for walking on the soft, moist grounds of primeval forests, to the longer legged, faster species which grazed on the firm grassy steppes and were able to outrun predators and eventually to the modern hoofed horse. Paleontologist Othniel C. Marsh was so sure of this theory of gradual equine evolution that he put together a series of fossils showing it in 1870. The fact that these fossils displayed successive adaptations was held as an example of gradualism until 100 years later, when it was shown they were not, in fact, even successive members of a single line of descent, let alone stages of an unbroken, gradually evolving lineage.

---

11 According to paragraph 2, on what grounds did Darwin insist that an occurrence which cannot be observed today could not have happened in the past?

(A) He theorized that the evolutionary process must occur gradually, not abruptly.
(B) Cladogenesis, which breaks stasis, cannot be proven scientifically.
(C) Phenotypic variation would be selected against from extreme variation.
(D) He thought Lyell's principles of methodology should be adopted to biology as well.

paragraph 2 is marked with an arrow [→].

12 According to paragraph 2, all of the following affected horses evolution EXCEPT:

(A) The firmer steppe meant they no longer needed wide-toed feet.
(B) Early horses migrated from the primeval forest because their feet had evolved into hooves.
(C) Soft, moist grounds gave less pressure to horse's feet.
(D) Adaptations which occurred on the steppes helped early horses to evade predation.

13 Which of the following statements is true about horses according to paragraph 2?

(A) They are a good example of gradualism.
(B) The evolutionary history of horses was inaccurate.
(C) Fossils of the horse's ancestors were abundant.
(D) Their fossils are evidence of punctuated equilibrium.

14 The word envisaged in the passage is closest in meaning to

(A) visualized
(B) dreamed
(C) publicized
(D) confirmed

15 According to paragraph 4, how does habitat tracking possibly explain the periods of apparent stasis in the fossil record?

(A) Populations migrate to favorable environments where they can flourish exclusively.
(B) Flying insects or sea-dwellers with limited ranges of movement did not show signs of evolution.
(C) Habitat tracking can only occur in populations that evolve through punctuated equilibrium.
(D) Populations are unlikely to change if they keep moving to favorable places for their survival.

paragraph 4 is marked with an arrow [→].

16 Which of the following claims about habitat tracking can be inferred from paragraph 4?

(A) It is required before evolution or extinction can occur.
(B) It is the most common reaction to habitat change in mobile organisms.
(C) Extinction is followed immediately by it most of the time.
(D) Populations usually return to their original environment.

3 → Scientists studying fossils noted that the evolution of some species was nearly 'mapped out,' while others had a few, very different species along the evolutionary course, with few or no intermediary fossils. They envisaged that this second group's evolution must have occurred rapidly to produce a great change over a short period. They reasoned that there had to be another evolutionary method that was quicker and left fewer intermediate species, thus the idea of punctuated equilibrium was formed. The theory of punctuated equilibrium states that most sexually-reproducing species will remain in an extended state of little evolutionary change between generations, called stasis, which is broken up by rare, rapid events of branching speciation called cladogenesis when they split into two distinct species. They pointed out that for most species, there was a sudden appearance in the geologic record with no evidence of substantial, gradual changes. Darwin had noted this problem also, but ascribed it to imperfections in the fossil record rather than catastrophism and progressive creationism, or supernatural creation, while privately noting on the margin of his essay, "Better begin with this: If species really, after catastrophes, created in showers world over, my theory false."

4 → While these theories vary widely on their methods of evolution, both show major adaptations over time whereby a population becomes better suited to its habitat. [■] These successive intergenerational changes occur in all species and are one of the basic phenomena of biology. [■] From this one can see that adaptation is not just a matter of visible traits, complex adaptations to changes can occur during an organism's life. [■] These reactions to habitat change happen in three major ways, either exclusively or in succession. [■] The most basic adaptation to change is to simply move to a locale that better suits the organism. This response, typical of organisms that have wide spheres of movement such as flying insects or sea-dwellers, is called habitat tracking, and is one explanation put forth

17 What is the main purpose of this passage?

(A) To explain why scientists cannot agree on which theory of evolution is the most accurate.
(B) To compare and contrast two theories of the process of evolution
(C) To emphasize that punctuated equilibrium has rendered gradualism obsolete
(D) To show the similarities between two dominant theories

18 Which of the sentences below best expresses the essential information in the highlighted sentence in the passage? Incorrect choices change the meaning in important ways or leave out essential information.

(A) Punctuated equilibrium says that evolution happens through cladogenesis in sexually reproducing species which usually display few changes between generations.
(B) While remaining in an extended state or little evolutionary change between generations is called stasis, splitting into two distinct species with huge change is called cladogenesis.
(C) Punctuated equilibrium explains that species evolve through cladogenesis, an uncommon event in which a species splits into two distinct species in a short period of time.
(D) The splitting into two distinct sexually-reproducing species of punctuated equilibrium was a means to explain the lack of change between generations that Darwin mentioned.

for the periods of apparent stasis in the fossil record. The term genetic change, on the other hand, pertains to changes in the population when natural selection acts on the genetic variations of a population. These mutations, which may be physical features or adjusted physiological activity, create genetic variations that lead to differing characteristics in offspring and, consequently, a population better genetically adapted to its environment. The third, and most dramatic, change that can occur to resident populations is extinction, or the demise of a population that was unable to properly adapt to change.

5 Whether by gradualism or punctuated equilibrium, a species must always adapt to its changing habitat, as it is now clear that habitats and biota are constantly changing and the process of adaptation is never complete.

19 Look at the four squares [■] that indicate where the following sentence could be added to the passage.

Even creatures which have very simple bodily structures, like internal parasites, are highly adapted to their specific environments.

Where would the sentence best fit?

Click on a square [■] to add the sentence to the passage.

20 Directions: Select the appropriate phrases from the answer choices and match them to the type of evolutionary theory to which they relate. TWO of the answer choices will NOT be used. **This question is worth 3 points.**

Drag your answer choices to the spaces where they belong. To remove an answer choice, click on it. To review the passage, click on **View Text**.

Answer Choices

(A) Radical changes from the usual phenotypic variation are less likely to be passed on.

(B) Othniel C. Marsh compiled a series of fossils that accurately illustrated its evolutionary steps.

(C) Evolution leaves few intermediate species.

(D) Long periods of stasis are interrupted by rare, branching speciation.

(E) Evolution takes place with small changes between successive generations.

(F) Complex adaptations can occur during an organism's life.

(G) Charles Darwin used theories in 'Principles of Geology' to explain the evolutionary change.

Gradualism
-
-
-

Punctuated Equilibrium
-
-

You have seen all of the questions in this part of the Reading section. You have time left to review. As long as there is time remaining, you can check your work.

Click on **Return** to go back to the previous question.
Click on **Review** to see the review screen for this section.
Click on **Continue** to go on.
Once you leave this part of the Reading section, you **WILL NOT** be able to return to it.

이제 Reading Section이 끝났습니다.
Countinue 버튼을 누르면 다시 문제를 검토할 수 없으므로 유의하세요.

시험보고 난 후 ... 체크 리스트 및 스터디 디렉션   USHER iBT TOEFL FINAL TEST READING

1. 내가 불안했던 문제만 재빨리 다시 보고, 불안하게 만든, 즉, 경쟁 초이스를 찾아서 왜 내가 헷갈려 했는지를 파악할 수 있는 메모를 해두시기 바랍니다. 시간이 지나거나, 다른 학생들과 스터디를 하면서는, 자신이 왜 낚였는지 이유조차 기억나지 않아 본인의 실수 패턴파악이 힘들기 때문입니다.

2. 답지를 확인하지 않고 스터디를 하시기 바랍니다. (그래서, 답지를 문제지 뒤에 붙이지 않고, 본 설명만을 붙여두었습니다.) 답지를 확인하지 않고 하는 이유는 답을 아는 순간, 답에 끼워맞춰 설명하려 하고, 이런 태도는 본인 실력 향상에 도움이 되지 않기 때문입니다. 스터디 팀원들간에 대략적인 답을 맞춰보면, 대부분 답안의 윤곽이 나옵니다. 이럴 경우, 이견이 있는 문제만 집중적으로 다루고, 나머지는 개인별로 처리하시기 바랍니다.

3. 문제를 끝까지 다 풀었나요? 네 □ / 아니오 □
   다 못 풀었다면, 전체 20 문제 중 푼 문제는? _____ / 20
   시간 모자란 것에 대해서는 크게 신경 쓰지 않아도 됩니다. 무엇보다 중요한 것은 정확도 입니다. 우선은 푼 문제를 맞출 확률을 높이고, 그 다음 시간을 걱정해도 늦지 않습니다.

4. 어려웠다고 느껴지는 지문은? 과학 □ / 예술 □ / 인문 □ / 인물 □ / 사회 □
   과학지문이 현격히 다른 분야보다 많지만, 그래도, 공부하다 보면 자신만 어려워하는 분야는 모두 각각입니다. 그러므로, 혹시 배경지식 부분에서 필요한 것이 있다면, usherin.usher.co.kr 에 방문하셔서, 공부가 안될 때, 배경지식 부분을 쉬엄쉬엄 들러서 봐 두시길 바랍니다. 쉬엄쉬엄입니다. 누가 뭐래도 실력있는 사람은 배경지식이 큰 영향을 끼치지는 않습니다.

5. (채점 후) 문제 풀 때 어렵다고 느낀 지문이 틀리는 개수와 쉬웠다고 느껴졌던 지문의 틀린 개수차이가 있나요? 예 □ / 아니오 □
   어느 순간 깨닫게 됩니다. 내가 잘 아는 내용이 나와서 자신 있게 푸나, 내가 모르는 지문이 나와서 겁먹고 푸나, 틀린 개수가 큰 차이가 나지 않는 것을…. 혹시 그걸 못 느끼신다면, 더욱더 열심히 하시기 바랍니다. ^^

6. 틀린 문제의 번호를 다음의 문제 유형 분석표와 비교해서 파악해 두시기 바랍니다.
   문제 유형을 파악해서 주의하는 것은, 누가 뭐래도 실력이 기본은 받쳐 줄 때 얘기입니다. 문제 푸는 스킬이나, 기타 문제 유형파악 등은 기본적으로 본문 내용을 이해하고, 해석이 웬만큼 될 때 얘기입니다. 만약, 너무 힘들다면 너무 스트레스 받지 말고, 그냥 '아~ 그렇구나' 정도로 넘기셔도 됩니다. 단, 본문 이해는 절대 양보해서는 안됩니다.

문제 유형 분석표
31page 내용 중, 아래 표시되어 있는 문제 유형은 파악하기 쉬우나 나머지 문제들의 문제 유형 파악은 어려워 하는 경향이 있어 비워두었습니다. 문제유형 정답은 323page를 참조하세요.

TEST 3-1	TEST 3-2
01	11
02	12
03 Vocabulary	13
04	14 Vocabulary
05	15
06	16
07	17
08 Highlight	18 Highlight
09 Insertion	19 Insertion
10 Summary	20 Category Chart

이름: *Test 3*

1

TEST번호	시험날짜	실제토플/모의토플 총점	RC	틀린갯수/전체갯수	LC	틀린갯수/전체갯수	SP	WR
tpo		/		/		/		
tpo		/		/		/		
tpo		/		/		/		
tpo		/		/		/		
tpo		/		/		/		
tpo		/		/		/		

2

RC

Topic 1 제목:

문제유형	틀린갯수/전체갯수	실력으로 틀린 문제	실수로 틀린 문제
Voca 문제	/		
Fact 문제	/		
Reference 문제	/		
Purpose 문제	/		
Infer 문제	/		
Highlight 문제	/		
Insertion 문제	/		
Summary 문제	/		

첫 번째 지문 중 틀린 개수 → 문제 유형 구분이 어려우면 풀어보세요

RC

Topic 1 제목:

문제유형	틀린갯수/전체갯수	실력으로 틀린 문제	실수로 틀린 문제
Voca 문제	/		
Fact 문제	/		
Reference 문제	/		
Purpose 문제	/		
Infer 문제	/		
Highlight 문제	/		
Insertion 문제	/		
Summary 문제	/		

첫 번째 지문 중 틀린 개수 → 문제 유형 구분이 어려우면 풀어보세요

3

오늘의 결론

내가 주의해야할 실수 패턴	내가 늘려야할 실력	내가 하고싶은 말(질문)

※ 순서대로 따라서 적어주세요.

| 문제구별 tip

Fact와 Purpose 문제 구별방법

- **Fact** 문제: Except, true, Not true
- **Purpose** 문제: why mention, in order to, what is the purpose

why는 **Fact** 문제 일수도 있습니다.

usherin.usher.co.kr

USHER

iBT TOEFL
FINAL TEST READING
TEST 4

테스트 전 확인사항

- 실전에 유용한 독해 전략(31p)을 숙지하였습니다. ○
- 화장실은 미리 다녀왔습니다. ○
- 휴대폰의 전원을 껐습니다. ○
- 노트테이킹 할 종이와 연필을 준비하였습니다. ○
- 시간을 체크할 시계를 준비하였습니다. ○
- 목표점수(20개 중 ___개)를 정하였습니다. ○
- 시험시작 시간은 ___시 ___분이며, 종료 시간은 35분 뒤인 ___시 ___분입니다. ○
- 시험 중 이동해야 할 방해요소가 있는지 체크하였습니다. ○
- 시험 중 이동하지 않습니다. ○

Reading Section Directions

This section measures your ability to understand academic passages in English.

Most questions are worth 1 point but the last question in each set is worth more than 1 point. The directions indicate how many points you may receive.

Some passages include a word or phrase that is underlined in blue. Click on the word or phrase to see a definition or an explanation.

Within each test, you can go to the next questions by clicking **Next**. You may skip questions and go back to them later. If you want to return to previous questions, click on **Back**. You can click on **Review** at any time and the review screen will show you which questions you have answered and which you have not answered. From this review screen, you may go directly to any questions you have already seen in the Reading section.

You may now begin the Reading section. In the section you will read 2 passages. You will have **35 minutes** to read the passages and answer the questuons.

Click on **Continue** to go on.

Next 버튼을 이용하여 다음 문제로 이동하고 **Back** 버튼을 이용하여 이전 문제로 이동할 수 있습니다. 문제에 답을 하지 않더라도 다음 문제로 이동할 수 있으며, **Review** 버튼을 이용하여 각 문제 별로 답을 체크했는지의 여부를 확인할 수 있습니다. 이번 테스트에서는 세 지문을 읽게 됩니다. **35분** 동안 지문을 읽고 문제에 답을 하세요.

Griffith and Transformation

1 The 19th century Romantic Movement reshaped science by opening new avenues of research that were unheard of under the Enlightenment's classical approaches. Major breakthroughs, such as Darwin's theory of evolution, were developed during this period, along with advances in physics, non-Euclidean geometry and organic chemistry. During this time, science became a major source for increasing humankind's knowledge. During the 19th and 20th centuries, the practice of science became much more professionally institutionalized than it had been. One of the great breakthroughs in biology is attributed to Frederick Griffith of the British Ministry of Health. Griffith undertook one of the most pivotal experiments of the era, which tried to establish a more precise scientific understanding by typing, or classifying, pneumococci bacteria samples in order to find overarching patterns so as to clarify the epidemiology of lobar pneumonia, an infectious lung disorder.

2 He also sought to improve the understanding of the pathology of pneumococci on the individual by testing them on mice. Pneumococci generally have two forms, smooth and rough. Smooth pneumococci, denoted by S, are encapsulated and more virulent; this form was shown to result in pneumonia and death of the mice within days of being injected. Their capsules are slippery polysaccharide coatings that allow the bacteria to evade phagocytosis from the host's immune cells. On the other hand, the rough form, R, lacks a capsule and was considered non-infective. In Griffith's experiment, as expected, when mice were injected with S that had been killed by heat, it failed to cause illness despite being the virulent strain. Surprisingly, however, Griffith observed pneumonia and death when live R were injected alongside large amounts of heat-killed S; this was generally unexpected, since R, the only live bacteria in the experiment, were avirulent. During necropsy, Griffith found that the live R had developed capsules and morphed into S, then retained

---

01 The word overarching in the passage is closest in meaning to

(A) encompassing
(B) bending
(C) clear
(D) overwhelming

02 What is important about the fact that pneumococci generally have two forms?

(A) It proves Griffith's hypothesis that bacteria of the same species display different phenotypes.
(B) It suggests that some forms of bacteria have beneficial effects on organisms.
(C) It is the reason that Griffith refused to experiment on bacteria.
(D) It is a fundamental characteristic that allowed Griffith to produce his significant results.

03 According to paragraph 2, which of the following statements regarding the R and S pneumococcus is true?

(A) S form of pneumococci usually does not cause any harm in animals because they have smooth exteriors
(B) The smooth polysaccharide-coated cell wall of S are able to fight the host's immune cells and consume them
(C) The immune system is unable to defeat pneumococci because S can effectively slip away from the immune cells
(D) The R type is known to be the same pneumococci that causes other illnesses in the host's body

04 Which of the following can be inferred from paragraph 2 about the bacteria used in Griffith's experiments?

(A) The R pneumococcus can steal the capsule of the dead S.
(B) The S pneumococcus has slippery cell walls that can destroy immune cells.
(C) Introduction of sufficient loads of either type of pneumococcus bacteria can lead to infection.
(D) An R pneumococcus that has transformed into S remains in its new form until it is surrounded by large amounts of R.

05 Which of the sentences below best expresses the essential information in the highlighted sentence in the passage? Incorrect choices change the meaning in important ways or leave out essential information.

(A) Bacteriologists and physicians thought that unfit bacteria died through competition, and bacteria could, only be replicated through sharing particular genes seen in previous generations.
(B) There was a belief among biologists that bacteria kill each other for better habitats and that they multiplied asexually.
(C) Replication of bacteria was known to occur within pneumococci because they fight each other to multiply.
(D) Bacteriologists believed that bacteria come from a previous generation of the same strain which survived massive competition.

this phenotype over successive generations. Griffith hypothesized that a transforming principle-derived from the killed S-had helped transform the R into S. He also reported that heavy loads of live R alone could also transform into S. Griffith, however, noted that the addition of heat-killed S bacteria made this transformation much more likely.

3 Griffith had previously held, along with most bacteriologists, that bacteria's forms were essentially fixed and unchangeable. They held that each strain had emerged from, and was genetically similar to their progenitor, through an evolutionary lineage determined by Darwinian natural selection resulting in the death of unfit bacterial cells. Besides this implicit belief that bacterial strains could be extinguished through competition, many bacteriologists and physicians believed that any particular strain of bacteria had necessarily multiplied from previous, genetically-related strains. Griffith's findings, though generally neglected after the initial contention against them subsided, revealed that his original supposition was incorrect by showing that bacteria are able to acquire genes without the need for reproducing as well. He summarized his work as such: "The results of the experiments on enhancement of virulence and on transformation of type are discussed and their significance in regard to questions of epidemiology is indicated."

4 → An American medical researcher named Oswald Avery with colleagues Macleod and McCarty furthered Griffith's 1927 findings regarding the mysteries of inheritance. [■] Being driven to prove Griffith's theory, Avery continued to work on adjusting previous techniques even after he retired in 1943. [■] To do this, the cellular structures of the S strain bacteria were first removed, and then their proteins were removed through the use of protease enzyme treatments. [■] Finally, the cellular remainders were placed in a dish containing R strain bacteria. [■] The R strain bacteria transformed, meaning that proteins did not carry the virulent genes. Then the remainder of the S strain

06 What was the importance of Griffith's findings according to paragraph 3?

(A) They were accepted by the scientific community soon after Griffith's death.
(B) They proved that unfit bacterial cells face death or even extinction.
(C) They showed that bacteria follow Darwinian natural selection.
(D) They proved that bacteria are one exception that only partially follows lineage determined by Darwinian selection.

07 According to paragraph 4, under which of the following circumstances will the phenotype of R pneumococcus most likely change?

(A) DNA-removed S pneumococci are mixed with intact R pneumococci.
(B) The non-infective R type is solely injected
(C) A small amount of live, untreated R pneumococcus are present.
(D) Remains after the use of protease enzymes are present.

paragraph 4 is marked with an arrow [→].

08 What is the purpose of mentioning Joshua Lederberg in paragraph 5?

(A) To show that Avery's research into bacteria was flawed.
(B) To illustrate that Griffith's findings led to other experiments with significant results.
(C) To show that the Nobel Prize was won through more advanced research on bacteria.
(D) To disprove Griffith's findings from his experiments on bacteria.

bacteria had their DNA removed by being treated with deoxyribonuclease. When they were treated in this manner, the R strain bacteria resisted transformation, proving that DNA was the transforming factor of pneumococci.

5 Over time, more advanced discoveries have been made through the findings of Griffith and Avery. Joshua Lederberg's discoveries concerning genetic recombination and the organization of the bacterial genetic material are a prime example of this continuation. Inspired by previous discoveries, Lederberg, in 1944, started to think about genetic experimentations on bacteria despite the fact that there was still no consensus on whether bacteria even had genes or not. He showed that bacteria could reproduce sexually and substantiated the hypothesis by proving that they are endowed with genetic systems akin to those of higher-level organisms, thus opening a new realm for scientists to study the genetic basis of life and winning the 1958 Nobel Prize in Physiology or Medicine. During his speech, he stated that former researchers and their laboratories provided the historical platform of modern DNA research.

09 Look at the four squares [■] that indicate where the following sentence could be added to the passage.

By using techniques to remove bacteria's organic compounds, scientists could observe that if the R-strain bacteria still transformed, it would mean that the materials removed were not the carrier of the transformation gene.

Where would the sentence best fit?

Click on a square [■] to add the sentence to the passage.

10 Directions: An introductory sentence for a brief summary of the passage is provided below. Complete the summary by selecting the THREE answer choices that express the most important ideas in the passage. Some sentences do not belong in the summary because they express ideas that are not presented in the passage or are minor ideas in the passage. **This question is worth 2 points.**

Drag your answer choices to the spaces where they belong. To remove an answer choice, click on it. To review the passage, click on **View Text**.

Griffith's work influenced science for years to come.

-
-
-

Answer Choices

(A) All scientific discoveries including areas of chemistry, physics, and biology can be attributed to the Romantic movement of the 19th century.

(B) The ability of R-type pneumococci to convert to S-type proved that there was a transforming factor that did not follow Darwinian evolution.

(C) Oswald Avery worked subsequently to Griffith in order to find the cause of inheritance and was able to find that DNA was the transforming factor of pneumococci.

(D) Scientists were intrigued by the ability of the R-type pneumococci to shed their capsules to become S-type, depending on the environment.

(E) Joshua Lederberg was able to prove that bacteria were equipped with generic systems due to prior research from former bacteriologists.

(F) Bacteriologists originally believed that the form of a bacterium was unchangeable and was determined by the ancestral line from which they had descended.

11 According to paragraph 1, what can be inferred about the background of the development of Weber's theory?

(A) He found the systematic classification termed by leaders around the world in terms of succession and transition of country with regards to authority.
(B) He argued against the fact that the traditional definition of authority be further categorized in three ways.
(C) He realized the importance of authority and its immense effects on society.
(D) He wanted to find a way to take over Germany's leadership after WWI.

paragraph 1 is marked with an arrow [→].

12 The word sovereign in the passage is closest in meaning to

(A) reigning
(B) dependent
(C) minimal
(D) coarse

13 The author mentions with no regard to personal attributes in order to

(A) demonstrate that an office holder must impose influence on the office.
(B) show that once the office holder loses power they leave office.
(C) explain that the extent of power of an office holder is limited by the rules.
(D) highlight that the authority acquires its power due to individual characteristics.

Maximilian Weber and His Influence

1 → Authority can be defined as the forceful domination of a group of people who have the underlying condition of being absolutely obedient. The German sociologist Maximilian Weber, on the other hand, defined authority as 'the chance' of commands being obeyed according to distinct justifications by a specifiable group of people. Pointing out that Germany's political fiasco during WWI was essentially a problem of leadership, Weber proposed a theory of authority that classified it into three types, each differing in its justifications to compel acquiescence and its influences on the public.

2 In a society that is governed by a system of 'traditional' authority, social status plays a vital role in determining the sovereign power. The leaders of these types of societies are a ruling elite with an inheritable leadership role based on factors such as age, bloodline, or social connections, which shows that there is an inequality in the society. The disadvantage of this system is that it is vulnerable to change, as is evident when looking at the challenges faced by the Russian Empire as it encountered a more complex division of labor and wider population diversity due to Industrialization in the early 20th century. The helplessness of the traditional authority against the rise of the bourgeois and proletariat classes ultimately brought about the introduction of rational-legal authority in Russia. 'Rational-legal' authority is a system in which an individual, or institution, exercises power through the socially accepted set of rules and the right of those elevated to positions of authority to issue such commands. [■] Power is held by the office itself, with no regard to the personal attributes of the office holder, and it is limited by the official codified rules which state the extent of the office's power. [■] 'Rational-Legal' authority fosters financial stability and technological development because the rights of individuals act as the law, guaranteeing their property and investments. [■] 'Charismatic' authority can exist under 'traditional'

14 In paragraph 2, it refers to

(A) The office holder
(B) The office
(C) The power
(D) The character

15 Why is Napoleon Bonaparte a good example of a charismatic leader according to paragraph 2?

(A) He brought dramatic changes to his followers.
(B) His authority lasted longer than the other types.
(C) He took over a complex country with a strong division of labor.
(D) His authority fell at an unexpected rate.

16 According to paragraph 4, in what aspect does charismatic authority resemble transformational leaders?

(A) They both derive their power from a foundation of social standings such as age, class, experience, and gender.
(B) They are ideal leaders who follow long-established obligations and deal with their citizens according to the law.
(C) They both have different points-of-view and are extremely influenitial to their followers.
(D) They are both based on the fact that the leader changes to adapt to the followers' needs and social systems.

paragraph 4 is marked with an arrow [→].

or 'rational-legal' authorities systems when power is gained through widespread devotion to the exceptional sanctity, heroism, or a specific exemplary characteristic of a person. [■] According to Weber, this form of authority is extremely volatile and dynamic as charisma eventually recedes after it has entered the permanent routine of social interaction, which can result in the sudden collapse of its power. For example, Napoleon Bonaparte gained his fame through his military feats, immediately consolidating absolute political power over France and reforming the country. His defeat during the Napoleonic Wars, however, resulted in the abrupt end of his reign as emperor and the beginning of his exile.

3 Although Weber's theory has strongly influenced the aspects of sociology that deal with leadership, scholars have pointed out two flaws in it. First, they believed that the standardization of a variety of concepts of authority and Weber's theoretical notion of an 'iron cage', in which the increased rationalization of modern life causes individuals to be driven purely by objective, rather than by values, was an oversimplified, limited idea of authority. Furthermore, they posit that he failed to distinguish between reigning and governing, with governing requiring a positive change in society whereas reigning does not.

4 → Despite these objections, Weber's theory of authority influenced modern sociology and brought about the development of three new models of leadership in the late 20th century. The theory behind 'transformational' leadership is that leaders can make radical changes in their followers' thoughts and actions and exploit the order of their needs and aims to satisfy the greater need, which is, in turn, closely aligned with the followers' internal motivational factors. The leaders who Weber would have classified as having charismatic authority are, therefore, transformational, since they approach things from entirely different perspectives. In contrast, individuals that can be

17 Which of the sentences below best expresses the essential information in the highlighted sentence in the passage? Incorrect choices change the meaning in important ways or leave out essential information.

(A) Transactional leaders formulate closer relationships based on rewards and punishment creating a more intimate bond than transformational leaders.
(B) Transactional leaders negotiate with those being led while transformational leaders emphasize the individual needs.
(C) Transactional leaders aim to satisfy the needs of individuals, whereas transformational leaders control people with rewards and punishment.
(D) Transactional and transformational leaders both create strong bonds with their followers to gratify their intrinsic needs.

18 What is true about the characteristics of the transactional leaders?

(A) Transactional leaders rest their ideology on satisfying follower's needs.
(B) They are in power because the followers accept the validity of their leadership based on the mutaul benefits.
(C) They are those that permit the decisions to be carried out by the followers.
(D) They are proactive and form new expectations in their followers.

described as 'rational-legal' leaders can also be seen as 'transactional' leaders, as they are effective in using their knowledge to achieve results, based on the hypothesis that followers are motivated through a system of 'quid pro quo' or 'give and take'. The differing qualities of the two leadership types can be simply stated as: 'transactional' leaders form mutual bonds with people through reward and punishment, while, in contrast, 'transformational' leaders seek to gratify the intrinsic needs of the individual. The third form, 'laissez-faire' leadership, is characterized by a completely permissive leader who does not contribute to making decisions, which produces groups that often lack direction, and may lead to anarchy, but offer their followers many opportunities to make their own decisions.

5 Weber stressed that the importance of theories of authority is not to label, or classify, prevalent forms of leadership in history, but rather to show how the state of authority transits from one type to another. His precise intention led to scholars viewing his theory as a hierarchical development order, and it is now considered more of a theory on social evolution.

Questions 19 ~ 20 of 20

19 Look at the four squares [■] that indicate where the following sentence could be added to the passage.

It, however, does not automatically lead to economic stability or scientific development.

Where would the sentence best fit?

Click on a square [■] to add the sentence to the passage.

20 Directions: An introductory sentence for a brief summary of the passage is provided below. Complete the summary by selecting the THREE answer choices that express the most important ideas in the passage. Some sentences do not belong in the summary because they express ideas that are not presented in the passage or are minor ideas in the passage. **This question is worth 2 points.**

Drag your answer choices to the spaces where they belong. To remove an answer choice, click on it. To review the passage, click on **View Text**.

> **Weber came up with a theory that states different reasons and motivations for obedience to authority, having subsequent influence.**
>
> ●
> ●
> ●

Answer Choices

(A) Weber's theory discusses the inept leaders around the world in order to categorize them into his theory.

(B) Weber categorized leadership based on how authority was gained and held in a society.

(C) Laissez-faire leaders are those that exercise the minimum influence on the group that the person imposes control of.

(D) Weber's theory on authority influenced the development of three styles of leadership, which differ based upon the leaders' relationship formed with the followers.

(E) Critics of Weber's theory argue that it limits the variables in society and does not have a clear measure to discern reigning from governing.

(F) Weber wanted to emphasize the role of values in individuals' actions in the increased rationalization of modern life by developing the concept of 'iron cage'.

| | RETURN | REVIEW | CONTINUE |

You have seen all of the questions in this part of the Reading section. You have time left to review. As long as there is time remaining, you can check your work.

Click on **Return** to go back to the previous question.
Click on **Review** to see the review screen for this section.
Click on **Continue** to go on.
Once you leave this part of the Reading section, you **WILL NOT** be able to return to it.

이제 Reading Section이 끝났습니다.
Countinue 버튼을 누르면 다시 문제를 검토할 수 없으므로 유의하세요.

시험보고 난 후 ... 체크 리스트 및 스터디 디렉션 — USHER iBT TOEFL FINAL TEST READING

1. 내가 불안했던 문제만 재빨리 다시 보고, 불안하게 만든, 즉, 경쟁 초이스를 찾아서 왜 내가 헷갈려 했는지를 파악할 수 있는 메모를 해두시기 바랍니다. 시간이 지나거나, 다른 학생들과 스터디를 하면서는, 자신이 왜 낚였는지 이유조차 기억나지 않아 본인의 실수 패턴파악이 힘들기 때문입니다.

2. 답지를 확인하지 않고 스터디를 하시기 바랍니다. (그래서, 답지를 문제지 뒤에 붙이지 않고, 본 설명만을 붙여두었습니다.) 답지를 확인하지 않고 하는 이유는 답을 아는 순간, 답에 끼워맞춰 설명하려 하고, 이런 태도는 본인 실력 향상에 도움이 되지 않기 때문입니다. 스터디 팀원들간에 대략적인 답을 맞춰보면, 대부분 답안의 윤곽이 나옵니다. 이럴 경우, 이견이 있는 문제만 집중적으로 다루고, 나머지는 개인별로 처리하시기 바랍니다.

3. 문제를 끝까지 다 풀었나요? 네 □ / 아니오 □
   다 못 풀었다면, 전체 20 문제 중 푼 문제는? _____ / 20
   시간 모자란 것에 대해서는 크게 신경 쓰지 않아도 됩니다. 무엇보다 중요한 것은 정확도 입니다. 우선은 풀은 문제를 맞출 확률을 높이고, 그 다음 시간을 걱정해도 늦지 않습니다.

4. 어려웠다고 느껴지는 지문은? 과학 □ / 예술 □ / 인문 □ / 인물 □ / 사회 □
   과학지문이 현격히 다른 분야보다 많지만, 그래도, 공부하다 보면 자신만 어려워하는 분야는 모두 각각입니다. 그러므로, 혹시 배경지식 부분에서 필요한 것이 있다면, usherin.usher.co.kr 에 방문하셔서, 공부가 안될 때, 배경지식 부분을 쉬엄쉬엄 들러서 봐 두시길 바랍니다. 쉬엄쉬엄입니다. 누가 뭐래도 실력있는 사람은 배경지식이 큰 영향을 끼치지는 않습니다.

5. (채점 후) 문제 풀 때 어렵다고 느낀 지문이 틀리는 개수와 쉬웠다고 느껴졌던 지문의 틀린 개수차이가 있나요? 예 □ / 아니오 □
   어느 순간 깨닫게 됩니다. 내가 잘 아는 내용이 나와서 자신 있게 푸나, 내가 모르는 지문이 나와서 겁먹고 푸나, 틀린 개수가 큰 차이가 나지 않는 것을…. 혹시 그걸 못 느끼신다면, 더욱더 열심히 하시기 바랍니다. ^^

6. 틀린 문제의 번호를 다음의 문제 유형 분석표와 비교해서 파악해 두시기 바랍니다.
   문제 유형을 파악해서 주의하는 것은, 누가 뭐래도 실력이 기본은 받쳐 줄 때 얘기입니다. 문제 푸는 스킬이나, 기타 문제 유형파악 등은 기본적으로 본문 내용을 이해하고, 해석이 웬만큼 될 때 얘기입니다. 만약, 너무 힘들다면 너무 스트레스 받지 말고, 그냥 '아~ 그렇구나' 정도로 넘기셔도 됩니다. 단, 본문 이해는 절대 양보해서는 안됩니다.

문제 유형 분석표 31page 내용 중, 아래 표시되어 있는 문제 유형은 파악하기 쉬우나 나머지 문제들의 문제 유형 파악은 어려워 하는 경향이 있어 비워두었습니다. 문제유형 정답은 341page를 참조하세요.

TEST 4-1

01 Vocabulary
02
03
04
05 Highlight
06
07
08
09 Insertion
10 Summary

TEST 4-2

11
12 Vocabulary
13
14 Reference
15
16
17 Highlight
18
19 Insertion
20 Summary

이름: Test 4

1

TEST번호	시험날짜	실제토플/모의토플 총점	RC	틀린갯수/전체갯수	LC	틀린갯수/전체갯수	SP	WR
tpo				/		/		
tpo				/		/		
tpo				/		/		
tpo				/		/		
tpo				/		/		
tpo				/		/		

2

RC — Topic 1 제목:

첫 번째 지문 중 틀린 개수	문제유형	틀린갯수/전체갯수	실력으로 틀린 문제	실수로 틀린 문제
	Voca 문제	/		
	Fact 문제	/		
	Reference 문제	/		
	Purpose 문제	/		
	Infer 문제	/		
	Highlight 문제	/		
	Insertion 문제	/		
	Summary 문제	/		

→ 문제유형 중 틀린 부분이 경향성을 통하는지

RC — Topic 1 제목:

첫 번째 지문 중 틀린 개수	문제유형	틀린갯수/전체갯수	실력으로 틀린 문제	실수로 틀린 문제
	Voca 문제	/		
	Fact 문제	/		
	Reference 문제	/		
	Purpose 문제	/		
	Infer 문제	/		
	Highlight 문제	/		
	Insertion 문제	/		
	Summary 문제	/		

→ 문제유형 중 틀린 부분이 경향성을 통하는지

3 오늘의 결론

내가 주의해야할 실수 패턴	내가 늘려야할 실력	내가 하고싶은 말 (질문)

※ 순서대로 따라서 적어주세요.

| 문제구별 tip

Fact와 Purpose의 가장 큰 구별방법

· **Fact** 문제: Except, true, Not true
· **Purpose** 문제: why mention, in order to, what is the purpose

why는 Fact문제 일수도 있습니다.

usherin.usher.co.kr

USHER

iBT TOEFL
FINAL TEST READING
TEST 5

테스트 전 확인사항

실전에 유용한 독해 전략(31p)을 숙지하였습니다. ○
화장실은 미리 다녀왔습니다. ○
휴대폰의 전원을 껐습니다. ○
노트테이킹 할 종이와 연필을 준비하였습니다. ○
시간을 체크할 시계를 준비하였습니다. ○
목표점수(20개 중 ___ 개)를 정하였습니다. ○
시험시작 시간은 ___시 ___분이며,
종료 시간은 35분 뒤인 ___시 ___분입니다. ○
시험 중 이동해야 할 방해요소가 있는지 체크하였습니다. ○
시험 중 이동하지 않습니다. ○

Reading Section Directions

This section measures your ability to understand academic passages in English.

Most questions are worth 1 point but the last question in each set is worth more than 1 point. The directions indicate how many points you may receive.

Some passages include a word or phrase that is underlined in blue. Click on the word or phrase to see a definition or an explanation.

Within each test, you can go to the next questions by clicking **Next**. You may skip questions and go back to them later. If you want to return to previous questions, click on **Back**. You can click on **Review** at any time and the review screen will show you which questions you have answered and which you have not answered. From this review screen, you may go directly to any questions you have already seen in the Reading section.

You may now begin the Reading section. In the section you will read 2 passages. You will have **35 minutes** to read the passages and answer the questuons.

Click on **Continue** to go on.

Next 버튼을 이용하여 다음 문제로 이동하고 **Back** 버튼을 이용하여 이전 문제로 이동할 수 있습니다. 문제에 답을 하지 않더라도 다음 문제로 이동할 수 있으며, **Review** 버튼을 이용하여 각 문제 별로 답을 체크했는지의 여부를 확인할 수 있습니다. 이번 테스트에서는 세 지문을 읽게 됩니다. **35분** 동안 지문을 읽고 문제에 답을 하세요.

Pasteur and the The Origin of Life

1 Logical and methodical scientists sometimes, ironically, blindly adhere to spuriously hypothesized assertions. For instance, Aristotle hypothesized that flies were the result of spontaneous generation in rotting materials and that microorganisms could appear naturally. Scientists believed these theories for nearly two millennia. These errant theories led them to believe that the bacteria required for fermentation were naturally generated without any external stimuli. Scientist Louis Pasteur, however, skeptical of spontaneous generation, successfully falsified the long-held theory.

2 → Pasteur proposed the new theory of biogenesis, claiming that the natural generation of bacteria was preposterous, and that fermentation required the introduction of the necessary bacteria. In order to prove this, he conducted two experiments. In the first, a glass filled with meat broth, which would have fermented in open air, was placed in a sealed box that was completely sterile and had a filter over its opening. This did not allow anything to enter the glass and as a result there were no signs of fermentation in the glass. This, however, did not convince scientists at the time, because they thought that even if organisms were generated in the glass, they would have expired due to lack of oxygen. Therefore, he conducted a second experiment, the 'swan-neck duct' experiment. In this experiment, he put the broth into a spherical glass with a long curved tube atop it. With this structure, nothing but weightless air could enter. This also yielded no fermentation. In 1864, Pasteur finally announced the results of these and further experiments, demonstrating that life cannot spontaneously arise in areas that have not been exposed to existing life.

3 → Unsurprisingly, Pasteur's experiments were eye-openers, having definitively disproved the antiquated theory of spontaneous generation and giving birth to

---

01 The word spuriously in the passage is closest in meaning to

(A) genuinely
(B) inaccurately
(C) quickly
(D) meticulously

02 Why did author mention spontaneous generation in the first paragraph?

(A) To indicate there were many significant discoveries over two millennia.
(B) To show that Aristotle's theories were often wrong.
(C) To propose Pasteur's new theory and state how it refuted a long held misconception.
(D) To criticize scientists who believed in spontaneous bacterial generation during the previous two millennia.

03 Which of the sentences below best expresses the essential information in the highlighted sentence in the passage? Incorrect choices change the meaning in important ways or leave out essential information.

(A) Biogenesis opposed spontaneous generation, and supported the idea that only living things can give life to other living organisms.
(B) An influx of bacteria is required as evidence of Pasteur's new theory on natural generation of bacteria, which is required in fermentation.
(C) Without bacteria, fermentation cannot occur, and thereby no natural generation is possible.
(D) Pasteur's new theory of biogenesis states that the bacteria that play an important role in fermentation can only be derived from other living organisms, not spontaneous generation.

04 According to paragraph 2, what did Pasteur prove?

(A) Spontaneous generation of bacteria may occur through the addition of substances.
(B) Biogenesis was the cause of spontaneous generation in the fermenting process.
(C) Generation of bacteria cannot be natural and an external source must exist.
(D) Bacteria generation is not the major cause of fermentation.

paragraph 2 is marked with an arrow [→].

05 According to paragraph 3, what can be inferred about Pasteur's experiment?

(A) Although it explained a natural phenomenon at the time, it failed to do the same for the initial rise of life.
(B) Scientists were shocked and wanted to prove that spontaneous generation of life was not possible.
(C) Biogenesis is automatically established when life forms are exposed to a natural environment.
(D) Scientists' rebuttal of the first experiment was weaker than their rebuttal of the second experiment.

biogenesis. Even though he was the first to empirically prove this, he was not the first scientist to propose this type of theory. Scientists Girolamo Fracastoro, Agostino Bassi, and Friedrich Henle had previously suggested various theories which influenced Pasteur's work later. The development of biogenesis, however, left a vacuum in the understanding of how life first arose. As it requires previous forms of life, biogenesis alone could not ultimately explain the origin of life on the early, barren Earth. No notable related theories, however, appeared until 1924, when Alexander Oparin surmised that the presence of oxygen in the atmosphere prevents the synthesis of certain organic compounds that are necessary for the evolution of life. In 'The Origin of Life', he proffered that the type of abiogenesis that Pasteur attacked had in fact occurred once, but no longer could because the conditions found on the early Earth had changed. Oparin felt that an organic 'primeval soup' could be created in an oxygen-free atmosphere due to the effects of sunlight. He hypothesized that 4 billion years ago, the earth's environment met these criteria after volcanic eruptions filled the environment with carbon dioxide, nitrogen, and other gases. Originally he thought that the early atmosphere, in contrast to the Earth's current atmosphere, contained mostly ammonia and methane, but it is likely that most of the atmospheric carbon was carbon dioxide with perhaps some carbon monoxide and nitrogen. In practice these mixtures have many of the same properties as those containing ammonia and methane as long as free oxygen molecules are not present.

4 → [■] These theories were tested in the Miller and Urey experiment which attempted to recreate these hypothetical conditions, and tested for the occurrence of the chemical origins of life. [■] In order to test for the generation of the amino acids, required for protein generation in living cells under primitive Earth's conditions, they required a less hydrogen-rich mixture than the current environment. [■] Their experiments

06 Which of the following is true about biogenesis and abiogenesis according to paragraph 2 and 3?

(A) They contradict each other, but have to be combined to explain spontaneous generation.
(B) They both mention oxygen in different ways to either support life or prevent synthesis of certain organic compounds.
(C) Pasteur thought that they complement each other because abiogenesis theory suggests the possible origin of life and biogenesis supports the reproductive cycle of life.
(D) They are both attributed to the swan neck duct experiments in a way that the experiment showed how life cannot be generated with only oxygen.

07 What is the importance of the primeval soup theory mentioned in paragraph 3?

(A) It attempts to explain the Earth's atmosphere and conditions 4 billion years ago.
(B) It was a theory by Alexander Oparin which attacked Pasteur's findings.
(C) It explains why the Earth's current atmosphere is so different from the past.
(D) It indicates that abiogenesis was possible in the past.

08 According to paragraph 4, why was it necessary to experiment using gases sealed inside interconnected sterile glass tubes and beakers?

(A) It was very complicated to recreate an environment resembling early Earths for Millers experiment.
(B) They hypothesis by Oparin had clear instructions as to how to conduct the experiment.
(C) It was essential that Miller and Urey mimic earths early environment as closely as possible.
(D) The array was the only way to show each process and chemical reaction of earths atmosphere in its early stages.

paragraph 4 is marked with an arrow [→].

used water, methane, ammonia, and hydrogen, sealed inside interconnected sterile glass tubes and beakers, with one half filled with water and another holding two electrodes. [■] The water was boiled to produce evaporation, then the electrodes were fired to simulate lightning through the atmosphere and water vapor, and then it was cooled again to condense the water back into the first beaker in a repetitive cycle. After one week, they observed that 10-15 percent of the carbon was in the form of organic compounds. Two percent of the carbon had formed amino acids, with glycine being the most plentiful. Although nucleic acids were not formed, the 20 common amino acids were formed in various concentrations. This was interesting because amino acids can potentially create the most basic component of most living creatures, namely DNA.

09 Look at the four squares [■] that indicate where the following sentence could be added to the passage.

Specifically, the experiment tested Oparin's hypothesis that conditions on the primitive Earth favored chemical reactions that synthesized organic compounds from inorganic precursors.

Where would the sentence best fit?

Click on a square [■] to add the sentence to the passage.

10 Directions: An introductory sentence for a brief summary of the passage is provided below. Complete the summary by selecting the THREE answer choices that express the most important ideas in the passage. Some sentences do not belong in the passage or they express ideas that are not presented in the passage or are minor ideas in the passage. **This question is worth 2 points.**

Drag your answer choices to the spaces where they belong. To remove an answer choice, click on it. To review the passage, click on **View Text**.

> **In the 19th century, Pasteur questioned Aristotle's long-held assertion on spontaneous generation as he proposed an alternative hypothesis, later leading to more research concerning the origin of life.**
>
> ●
> ●
> ●

Answer Choices

(A) In order to overcome the criticism after his first experiment, Pasteur conducted another experiment, to verify his theory.

(B) Swan-neck duct was one of the most significant discoveries of the era due to its help in Pasteur's experiment.

(C) After Pasteur's experiments proving biogenesis, a theory was suggested to explain the initial appearance of living organisms on Earth from inorganic matter.

(D) Due to Pasteur's experiments, Oparin was able to successfully prove that living organisms could spontaneously form from inorganic matter.

(E) The dominance of ammonia and methane released into the atmosphere made it a favorable place for abiogenesis to occur 4 billion years ago.

(F) The Miller and Urey experiment helped the 'primordial soup' theory gain credibility by succeeding in creating common amino acids.

11 What can be inferred from paragraph 1 about why air was not studied carefully by scholars in earlier times?

(A) Scholars working on the research on air attempted to study many other subjects, resulting in the lack of specialization.
(B) Scientists did not consider studying doing research on the components of air important and only made false assumptions.
(C) Scholars working on individual aspects of the research on air had difficulty unifying air with fire, earth, and water.
(D) Early people had limited skills in breaking down the composition of air.

12 According to paragraph 2, what is Einstein's opinion about Boyle?

(A) He commended Boyle for his meticulous inquisitiveness that never over looked 'natural' phenomena.
(B) He felt that Boyle's accomplishment in the combustion experiment were no longer valid.
(C) He thought that his theories were unnatural.
(D) He thought that Boyle accepted holy phenomena as natural.

Early Research on Air

1 The composition of air has fascinated scientists since early times. According to the ancient Greeks, air was regarded as one of the four elements, which also included fire, earth, and water. It was not, however, precisely studied or correctly understood by many scholars. They generally thought that the air people breathe had the same composition as the gases found in any other part of the universe. Eventually, a few analytical scientists began to question its properties and conducted research to define them, but their studies were limited by the fact that they only sought to study air in the perspective of their specialties. Prior to the seventeenth century, chemists believed that gases were not involved in chemical reactions, and focused on matter in its solid or liquid states: according to them, gases were in the domain of physicists. This trend significantly impeded progress on the study of air.

2 → It was not until the seventeenth century that the understanding of air was seriously pursued by scientists. However, due to the lack of scientific instruments and the need for those beyond the usual tools, their experiments soon faced limitations. For example, Robert Boyle, a British scientist known for Boyle's Law, began a series of experiments to find out the composition of air through combustion. Boyle vacuumed the air out of a jar and showed that neither charcoal nor sulfur burned in the vacuum. Boyle had discovered the very first property of air stating that it is required for a fire to burn. His finding was not, however, recognized by the scientific community of the day because his definition of the component of air responsible for combustion was vague. In addition, most scientists were reportedly more interested in finding the chemical composition of air than in its physical characteristics. Thus, he shifted the focus of his research to air's chemical aspects and in 1659, with continuous effort, discovered that both hydrogen and nitric oxide gases were present in air. Boyle also

13 In to paragraph 3, why does the author mention the definition of air as is exemplified in the encyclopedia?

(A) To indicate that scientists were never able to collect the gases in the air due to its invisibility.
(B) To illustrate that they could not precisely understand what people wanted to know about air.
(C) To argue that physicists and chemists could not agree on the definition of air due to their different points of view.
(D) To show that they could not draw in-depth conclusions about the properties of air.

14 The word rudimentary in the passage is closest in meaning to

(A) primitive
(B) vague
(C) straightforward
(D) ancient

15 Which of the sentences below best expresses the essential information in the highlighted sentence in the passage? Incorrect choices change the meaning in important ways or leave out essential information.

(A) Irritable characteristics of air, such as its ability to diffuse, complicated scientists' measurements of the amount of air used in experiments and other scrutiny of it.
(B) The complicated calculation associated with the amount of air irritated scientists who were exploring the invisibility of air and its ability to diffuse.
(C) Scholars had difficulty seeing air due to its transparency while its propensity to spread made it difficult to determine the amount of air upon which they were experimenting.
(D) Since air cannot be observed through the microscope, scientists could not calculate the amount of air.

tried to revise misconceptions regarding air, such as the popular belief that air had no weight. Years later, Einstein credited Boyle for having a holy curiosity in poorly understood phenomena that others simply accepted as 'natural'. As a result of his persistence, he is now known as the father of chemistry.

3 → Even with all of Boyle's achievements, people's understanding of air was still elementary and more study using advanced laboratory equipment was required. [■] Scientists still struggled to uncover the many unknown properties of air, which were exemplified by the rudimentary definition of air as 'the elastic, invisible mixture of gases that surround the earth' from an eighteenth century encyclopedia. [■] Its invisibility meant that it could not be observed under a microscope and its ability to diffuse quickly proved to be an irritable characteristic to scientists for it complicated calculations measuring the amount of air being experimented upon. [■] Therefore, many prominent physicists investigated air wishing to further their understanding, but they showed little noticeable progress; having no success in isolating even one of the many compounds in air. [■]

4 Luckily, the research on air was significantly advanced by Stephen Hales, an English physiologist and chemist, in the late eighteenth century. In search of the various properties of air and anxious to clearly define it, he gave birth to a new branch in chemistry called pneumatic chemistry. He invented the pneumatic trough to study the physical properties of air and their relation to chemical reactions. The trough was made from household objects such as a hunting gun and a glass vessel. The device measured the amount of gas produced when a substance was heated by measuring the amount of water displaced in the vessel. Hales' pneumatic trough became the basis for experimental instruments that are widely used today. The creativity demonstrated through his improvisation of turning common tools into useful scientific instruments was

16 According to paragraph 3, all of the following are mentioned as a difficulty of a successful research on air EXCEPT:

(A) Its rapid rate of dispersal
(B) Physicists' lack of proper equipment
(C) Its transparent nature
(D) Its ability to mix with other gases

paragraph 3 is marked with an arrow [→].

17 What is the main purpose of paragraph 3?

(A) To show that the discoveries mentioned in paragraph 2 did not satisfy researchers' curiosity
(B) To explain that the eighteenth century encyclopedia had an incorrect definition of air
(C) To differentiate the intention of studies on air done by scientists of different fields
(D) To give a reason for Hales not gaining more recognition

18 What is true about Hales and his invention according to paragraph 4?

(A) The inspiration in constructing the pneumatic trough came from Boyle's vacuum device.
(B) His pneumatic trough guided other scholars who were interested in making experimental tools.
(C) His ingenuity and originality were precursors of the success of pneumatic chemistry.
(D) His research was a basis for the respect physicists had for chemists.

recognized by, and won the praise of, fellow scientists. According to the scientific community, however, Hales deserves more recognition than he received in the past as experiments regarding air were actively held by scientists of various fields using his invention.

5 Despite his tremendous contributions to pneumatic chemistry, Hales passed up the opportunity to study the chemical properties of the various gases, as he was solely interested in studying their concentrations. Scientists that came after him revised his pneumatic trough and proceeded with further experiments. With the efforts of these scientists, the properties of the air have been gradually unveiled. They have even successfully broken down all of the components of atmospheric air and calculated their proportions.

19 Look at the four squares [■] that indicate where the following sentence could be added to the passage.

Additionally, chemists thought that air was out of their scope of research.

Where would the sentence best fit?

Click on a square [■] to add the sentence to the passage.

20 Directions: An introductory sentence for a brief summary of the passage is provided below. Complete the summary by selecting the THREE answer choices that express the most important ideas in the passage. Some sentences do not belong in the summary because they express ideas that are not presented in the passage or are minor ideas in the passage. **This question is worth 2 points.**

Drag your answer choices to the spaces where they belong. To remove an answer choice, click on it. To review the passage, click on **View Text**.

Early research on air was rarely done by many scientists of any field because of their misunderstanding of its composition.

-
-
-

Answer Choices

(A) Research on air as a new area of scientific study progressed modestly because researchers were uninterested in others' field of studies regarding the subject matter.

(B) By the mid-seventeenth century, experiments that were designed to satiate the scientific communities' specific interests were able to unveil a few properties of air.

(C) Robert Boyle's experiment related to combustion led him to invent a trough that was used by other scientists.

(D) The pneumatic trough enabled scientists to study air more effectively and precisely define its properties for others.

(E) As one of the most renowned scholars of his time, Stephen Hales shed light on the chemical properties of various gases.

(F) Boyle's vacuum jar experiment was able to prove that air had no weight, in addition to answering some of the most questioned chemical properties of air.

You have seen all of the questions in this part of the Reading section. You have time left to review. As long as there is time remaining, you can check your work.

Click on **Return** to go back to the previous question.
Click on **Review** to see the review screen for this section.
Click on **Continue** to go on.
Once you leave this part of the Reading section, you **WILL NOT** be able to return to it.

이제 Reading Section이 끝났습니다.
Countinue 버튼을 누르면 다시 문제를 검토할 수 없으므로 유의하세요.

시험보고 난 후 ... 체크 리스트 및 스터디 디렉션 | USHER iBT TOEFL FINAL TEST READING

1. 내가 불안했던 문제만 재빨리 다시 보고, 불안하게 만든, 즉, 경쟁 초이스를 찾아서 왜 내가 헷갈려 했는지를 파악할 수 있는 메모를 해두시기 바랍니다. 시간이 지나가나, 다른 학생들과 스터디를 하면서는, 자신이 왜 낚였는지 이유조차 기억나지 않아 본인의 실수 패턴파악이 힘들기 때문입니다.

2. 답지를 확인하지 않고 스터디를 하시기 바랍니다. (그래서, 답지를 문제지 뒤에 붙이지 않고, 본 설명만을 붙여두었습니다.) 답지를 확인하지 않고 하는 이유는 답을 아는 순간, 답에 끼워맞춰 설명하려 하고, 이런 태도는 본인 실력 향상에 도움이 되지 않기 때문입니다. 스터디 팀원들간에 대략적인 답을 맞춰보면, 대부분 답안의 윤곽이 나옵니다. 이럴 경우, 이견이 있는 문제만 집중적으로 다루고, 나머지는 개인별로 처리하시기 바랍니다.

3. 문제를 끝까지 다 풀었나요? 네 □ / 아니오 □
   다 못 풀었다면, 전체 20 문제 중 푼 문제는? _____ / 20
   시간 모자란 것에 대해서는 크게 신경 쓰지 않아도 됩니다. 무엇보다 중요한 것은 정확도 입니다. 우선은 푼 문제를 맞출 확률을 높이고, 그 다음 시간을 걱정해도 늦지 않습니다.

4. 어려웠다고 느껴지는 지문은? 과학 □ / 예술 □ / 인문 □ / 인물 □ / 사회 □
   과학지문이 현격히 다른 분야보다 많지만, 그래도, 공부하다 보면 자신만 어려워하는 분야는 모두 각각입니다. 그러므로, 혹시 배경지식 부분에서 필요한 것이 있다면, usherin.usher.co.kr 에 방문하셔서, 공부가 안될 때, 배경지식 부분을 쉬엄쉬엄 들러서 봐 두시길 바랍니다. 쉬엄쉬엄입니다. 누가 뭐래도 실력있는 사람은 배경지식이 큰 영향을 끼치지는 않습니다.

5. (채점 후) 문제 풀 때 어렵다고 느낀 지문이 틀리는 개수와 쉬웠다고 느껴졌던 지문의 틀린 개수차이가 있나요? 예 □ / 아니오 □
   어느 순간 깨닫게 됩니다. 내가 잘 아는 내용이 나와서 자신 있게 푸나, 내가 모르는 지문이 나와서 겁먹고 푸나, 틀린 개수가 큰 차이가 나지 않는 것을…. 혹시 그걸 못 느끼신다면, 더욱더 열심히 하시기 바랍니다. ^^

6. 틀린 문제의 번호를 다음의 문제 유형 분석표와 비교해서 파악해 두시기 바랍니다.
   문제 유형을 파악해서 주의하는 것은, 누가 뭐래도 실력이 기본은 받쳐 줄 때 얘기입니다. 문제 푸는 스킬이나, 기타 문제 유형파악 등은 기본적으로 본문 내용을 이해하고, 해석이 웬만큼 될 때 얘기입니다. 만약, 너무 힘들다면 너무 스트레스 받지 말고, 그냥 '아~ 그렇구나' 정도로 넘기셔도 됩니다. 단, 본문 이해는 절대 양보해서는 안됩니다.

문제 유형 분석표 31page 내용 중, 아래 표시되어 있는 문제 유형은 파악하기 쉬우나 나머지 문제들의 문제 유형 파악은 어려워 하는 경향이 있어 비워두었습니다. 문제유형 정답은 359page를 참조하세요.

TEST 5-1

01 Vocabulary
02
03 Highlight
04
05
06
07
08
09 Insertion
10 Summary

TEST 5-2

11
12
13
14 Vocabulary
15 Highlight
16
17
18
19 Insertion
20 Summary

이름: Test 5

1

TEST번호	시험날짜	실제토플/모의토플 총점	RC	틀린갯수/전체갯수	LC	틀린갯수/전체갯수	SP	WR
tpo				/		/		
tpo				/		/		
tpo				/		/		
tpo				/		/		
tpo				/		/		
tpo				/		/		

2

RC — 첫 번째 지문 중 틀린 개수

Topic 1 제목 :

문제유형	틀린갯수/전체갯수	실력으로 틀린 문제	실수로 틀린 문제
Voca 문제	/		
Fact 문제	/		
Reference 문제	/		
Purpose 문제	/		
Infer 문제	/		
Highlight 문제	/		
Insertion 문제	/		
Summary 문제	/		

→ 문제 유형 구분이 어려울 경우 물어보세요

RC — 첫 번째 지문 중 틀린 개수

Topic 1 제목 :

문제유형	틀린갯수/전체갯수	실력으로 틀린 문제	실수로 틀린 문제
Voca 문제	/		
Fact 문제	/		
Reference 문제	/		
Purpose 문제	/		
Infer 문제	/		
Highlight 문제	/		
Insertion 문제	/		
Summary 문제	/		

→ 문제 유형 구분이 어려울 경우 물어보세요

3

오늘의 결론

내가 주의해야할 실수 패턴	내가 늘려야할 실력	내가 하고싶은 말(잔문)

※ 순서대로 따라서 적어주세요.

| 문제구별 tip

Fact와 Purpose의 가장 큰 구별방법

- **Fact 문제**: Except, true, Not true
- **Purpose 문제**: why mention, in order to, what is the purpose

why는 Fact문제 일수도 있습니다.

usherin.usher.co.kr

# USHER

iBT TOEFL
FINAL TEST READING
TEST 6

테스트 전 확인사항

실전에 유용한 독해 전략(31p)을 숙지하였습니다. ○
화장실은 미리 다녀왔습니다. ○
휴대폰의 전원을 껐습니다. ○
노트테이킹 할 종이와 연필을 준비하였습니다. ○
시간을 체크할 시계를 준비하였습니다. ○
목표점수(20개 중 ___개)를 정하였습니다. ○
시험시작 시간은 ___시 ___분이며,
종료 시간은 35분 뒤인 ___시 ___분입니다. ○
시험 중 이동해야 할 방해요소가 있는지 체크하였습니다. ○
시험 중 이동하지 않습니다. ○

Reading Section Directions

This section measures your ability to understand academic passages in English.

Most questions are worth 1 point but the last question in each set is worth more than 1 point. The directions indicate how many points you may receive.

Some passages include a word or phrase that is underlined in blue. Click on the word or phrase to see a definition or an explanation.

Within each test, you can go to the next questions by clicking **Next**. You may skip questions and go back to them later. If you want to return to previous questions, click on **Back**. You can click on **Review** at any time and the review screen will show you which questions you have answered and which you have not answered. From this review screen, you may go directly to any questions you have already seen in the Reading section.

You may now begin the Reading section. In the section you will read 2 passages. You will have **35 minutes** to read the passages and answer the questuons.

Click on **Continue** to go on.

Next 버튼을 이용하여 다음 문제로 이동하고 **Back** 버튼을 이용하여 이전 문제로 이동할 수 있습니다. 문제에 답을 하지 않더라도 다음 문제로 이동할 수 있으며, **Review** 버튼을 이용하여 각 문제 별로 답을 체크했는지의 여부를 확인할 수 있습니다. 이번 테스트에서는 세 지문을 읽게 됩니다. **35분** 동안 지문을 읽고 문제에 답을 하세요.

01 According to paragraph 1, the following were the ideas of those opposing photography as art EXCEPT

(A) It was too simple a process compared to real art, such as drawings.
(B) Photographers were seen as technicians who operated the camera to make pictures.
(C) A camera is just a lifeless piece of metal until a photographer uses it.
(D) It did not satisfy all three components needed to be considered art.

paragraph 1 is marked with an arrow [→].

02 What is the importance of Mark Chamberlain's views according to paragraph 1?

(A) They demonstrate a view of an artist from back when photography was first discovered.
(B) They exemplify how a camera can be seen as just a tool, like a paintbrush.
(C) They show many artists viewed the camera in relation to art.
(D) They explain what was meant by photographers being technicians who produced artwork.

03 The word novel in the passage is closest in meaning to

(A) fiction
(B) innovative
(C) chronicle
(D) peculiar

Photography as an Art

1 → Three components are required for a work to be considered artistic: artist, medium, and artwork, the idea being that an artist manifests artwork through the medium. Since the camera's invention, photography has struggled to convince many that it falls within this definition. The opposition recognizes the medium and work as artful, but not the photographers' role as artist. They see them as technicians who 'operate the medium' to produce works instead of as artists, who, they claim, take time to complete works, poring over them. The photographer's ability to capture an image with a simple click was thus unequal, and photography was a process unequal to art. Photographer Mark Chamberlain disagreed with this, stating that "in the hands of an artist, the camera is only another tool," which can become an extension of the eye if properly utilized, but is a lifeless piece of metal otherwise. He contended that releasing the shutter may only take a second, but timing and framing are crucial, and the photographer has to find perfect lighting and conditions.

2 → Chamberlain was not the only photographer to fight denigration of photography. Earlier, between 1851 and 1862, famous photographers such as Antoine Claudet, Andre Disderi, and William Lake Price published articles in professional journals attempting to analyze the aesthetic similarities and differences between graphic works and photographs and to convince readers that photography was actually an art. Their points of view were summed up in a piece in the 1862 Photographic Journal addressing whether photography should be hung in the Fine Arts or Industrial Section of the International Exposition. The author observed that the question is not whether photography is fine art per se, but whether it is capable of artistic expression in the hands of an artist. This point-of-view was echoed in the Catalogue of the 1859 Salon of Photography by French naturalist

04 According to paragraph 3, Pictorialism

(A) was popular amongst artists in the 20th century, when photography was first invented.
(B) imitated the styles of paintings of that time to be more art-like.
(C) was later also termed fine art photography, which then later played an important role in advancing causes.
(D) was a series of procedures for making pictures look less familiar.

05 Which of the sentences below best expresses the essential information in the highlighted sentence in the passage? Incorrect choices change the meaning in important ways or leave out essential information.

(A) Alfred Stieglitz produced a series of fifteen photographs called 'Camera Work' to help promote Pictorialism, and this helped make photography an art.
(B) 'Camera Work' began the movement of Pictorialism, and when all fifteen of Stieglitz's photographs were sold by Albright Gallery, photography officially became accepted by artists as an art.
(C) 'Camera Work' by Alfred Stieglitz helped further progress the movement, and when a gallery bought fifteen photographs, photography could be more confidently called art.
(D) Alfred Stieglitz's 'Camera Work,' played the biggest role in promoting the movement, when the Albright Gallery bought its fifteen photographs in order to use it as an example of artistic photography.

Louis Figuier. He and other scientists were convinced that artistic expression and taste would be improved by photography, just as the general quality of life benefits from applied science. They, like Chamberlain, considered the lens a new tool, like the pencil or brush, which conveys the feelings of the photographer, and photography is, therefore, an art.

3 → Later, photographers, in an effort to compete with high art, focused on still-lifes, allegorical costumes, genre scenes and composite images. However, as the novel idea of capturing images began to wear off, people began to question whether the camera's images were too accurate and detailed. To overcome this literalism, photographers used inferior optical elements, smeared lenses, kicked tripods, or blurred their black-and-white prints. As a result, pictorialism, an aesthetic movement imitating contemporary painting styles and techniques, was born. This movement which originated in Britain reached its height in the 20th century and had a strong influence on American photography in its later phases. One of the most important promoters of this movement was the journal 'Camera Work' published by Alfred Stieglitz, whose sale of fifteen photographs to the Albright Gallery solidified photography's status as an art in the United States.

4 With the rise and fall of pictorialism, struggles over artistic nature and the quest to determine what truly constituted art raged on for over a century. In hindsight, many conclude that photographic art is at its best when capturing the real world, and least inspiring when emulating other art forms. The unique power of photography is its disposition to form the varies of textural experience and the contrasts in lighting, rather than narrative content, regardless of whether the images were considered documents or art.

5 Recognizing this, some photographers began producing prints of artistic masterpieces for both their

06 In paragraph 5, what is the author's purpose of mentioning that what was once rejected as being too real had become indispensable in terms of historical preservation?

(A) To explain an ironic situation regarding photography
(B) To point out the photographers who adamantly fought for photography as an art form
(C) To support the idea that fine art can be enjoyed by an exclusive group of people
(D) To stress photography's profound ability to resemble reality

07 The word This in the passage refers to

(A) art
(B) photography
(C) heritage
(D) preservation

08 What can be inferred from paragraph 6 about photography's radical expansion?

(A) The radical expansion is attributed solely to artistic photographers who fought for the name 'artists' about two decades ago.
(B) Photography is now accepted as art, but has transcended it to influence other aspects of people's life and society as a whole.
(C) The radical expansion of photography has led to privacy concerns.
(D) Photography has gone from not being considered an art form to dominating the art world.

commercial and the general population's cultural benefit. Since then, photographs have been the most significant supplier of visual artifacts to the masses, revolutionizing public access to the art heritage of the world. What was once rejected as being too real had become indispensable in terms of historical preservation. This was a welcomed advantage of photography since it was believed that familiarity with classical art would not only lift people's spirit, but also improve their taste.

6 Today, there is little doubt that photography is a fine art. [■] This shows that photography has stood its ground and found its place in the art world. [■] In recent decades, photography's potential has radically expanded. [■] Aside from the traditional two-dimensional, modest-sized black-and-white photographs, photographs now display various shapes, colors, and formats, to provide information, make statements, sell products, or analyze events. [■] The development of new technology and aesthetic theories combined with the enhanced role of photography as a marketable commodity has influenced the way the medium is now used and perceived. This expanded role of photography is the result of a rich history tied to developments in technology, art, and society.

09 Look at the four squares [■] that indicate where the following sentence could be added to the passage.

Every well-known, respected fine-art museum has a section dedicated solely to photographic art; and there are a number of museums and galleries dedicated specifically to photography.

Where would the sentence best fit?

Click on a square [■] to add the sentence to the passage.

10 Directions: An introductory sentence for a brief summary of the passage is provided below. Complete the summary by selecting the THREE answer choices that express the most important ideas in the passage. Some sentences do not belong in the summary because they express ideas that are not presented in the passage or are minor ideas in the passage. **This question is worth 2 points.**

Drag your answer choices to the spaces where they belong. To remove an answer choice, click on it. To review the passage, click on **View Text.**

The status of photography as an art form has been debated for hundreds of years.

-
-
-

Answer Choices

(A) With the invention of the camera, the debate about photography being considered an art came into question.

(B) Mark Chamberlain is a photographer that supported the view that photographers should be considered artists and foresaw that photography holds greater good for mankind just like applied sciences.

(C) Photographers in the 19th century worked to formalize their status as artists, not mere practitioners of cameras who only push the shutter button.

(D) Pictorialism is still considered predominant in the area of art up to day because of its superiority.

(E) The Pictorialism movement emerged as photographers continued to struggle to have the idea that taking photographs was a process that was as demanding as creating pieces of fine art accepted.

(F) Photographic art is best at producing lifelike images and its power has allowed it to change and expand its role in society.

11 According to paragraph 2, what can be inferred about birdsongs being generally regarded as an attribute of males?

(A) The songs play an important role in songbird reproduction and social interactions.
(B) The number of songs a male learns correlates to their territorial range
(C) Only male songbirds are born with an ability to sing complex songs
(D) Female songbirds are unable to learn songs.

paragraph 2 is marked with an arrow [→].

12 The word assortment in the passage is closest in meaning to

(A) collection
(B) segment
(C) style
(D) adaptation

13 According to paragraph 2, which of the following responses occurs in male birds of the surrounding territory when a male bird is removed and a prerecorded song is played in a territory?

(A) They are discouraged from encroaching on the territory by the singing.
(B) They place territorial markers in the vacated territory.
(C) They are more frightened by the pre-recorded song than by the real one.
(D) They sing louder to compete with the recorded song.

How and Why Birds Learn to Sing

1 Beautifully complex birdsongs have inspired our greatest poets and composers, and aroused the curiosity of biologists. They wondered how and why such an elaborate communication form developed among birds. One of the many who struggled to answer these questions was Darwin who was clearly influenced by these intricate songs as he developed the theory of sexual selection. Since then biologists from many disciplines have found birdsongs to be fascinating and productive research subjects.

2 → Birdsongs, generally regarded as an attribute of males, are in some rare species produced by females with complexity comparable to those of males. In general though, male songbirds are the sources of these complex songs. Darwin suggested that this was the result of sexual selection because females choose mates with more complex songs. Although this ability of birdsongs to attract females is frequently cited, there is little experimental evidence to support this assertion because field experiments proving that female attraction to the male's territory is in direct response to his singing are nearly impossible. One experiment on pair formation of flycatchers, however, came close to doing so. Male dummies were positioned near nest-boxes with automatic traps; some played a tape-recorded song from loudspeakers, while others remained silent. Even when their positions were switched to control external variables, 90 percent of females were caught in nest-box traps of 'singing' dummies, showing that a male's song attracts mates. Further, females of some species prefer males with more varied songs, so these males quickly add to their repertoires. The diverse assortments of songs may indicate an older male with access to better resources or proven longevity and survival skills, both good traits to pass on to offspring. Experiments have also shown that songs act as territorial markers. House Wrens, for example, respond aggressively to recordings of

14 Why does the author mention the tutor adult White-crowned Sparrow in paragraph 3?

(A) To describe the steps in the rearing of White-crowned Sparrows
(B) To explain why some White-crowned Sparrow nestlings developed abnormal songs
(C) To introduce a song-learning characteristic of one type of birdsong learning
(D) To demonstrate how nestlings of a bird species can be raised by adults of different species

15 Which of the sentences below best expresses the essential information in the highlighted sentence in the passage? Incorrect choices change the meaning in important ways or leave out essential information.

(A) Sparrow nestlings were trained to learn a song in its entirety even though scientists only played short overlapping sections of it to them.
(B) Scientists have taught young sparrows to sing complete songs by overlapping segment of different adult sparrows, which was more effective than playing the entire song.
(C) The overlapping segments of a tune were placed in the incorrect melodic order by the baby sparrows that the scientists had trained.
(D) The sparrows that were exposed to many segments of adult sparrows' songs could be taught by scientists to learn a full melody.

other males' songs, sometimes even attacking the speaker. Researchers have also shown that removing male birds from their territories but broadcasting their songs prevented neighboring males from entering their territories, showing that the songs warned others to keep out.

3 → Just as their reasons for singing vary, so do the ways that songbirds learn to sing. Some are born with an innate knowledge of the songs, while others learn them from older birds then add to them to create personalized songs, and still others incorporate auditory stimuli into their repertoire and eventually end up with thousands of variations. Unlike birds with innate abilities to sing, some are extremely susceptible to external sound stimuli when learning songs. Studies of the White-crowned Sparrow show that nestlings raised alone in a laboratory develop an abnormal song. If they are housed with a tutor adult White-crowned Sparrow, however, they will learn proper songs from it. If they are only housed with a Song Sparrow, however, they may learn to sing as a Song Sparrow. Scientists have also taught baby sparrows to sing a complete song by exposing them to overlapping segments of a tune rather than a full melody. This means that the sparrows reassembled segments of a song which were imprinted in their brains, showing that they have the ability to identify and utilize the different song parts presented in the experiment. Other birds, such as Northern Mockingbirds and Brown Thrashers, are adept at mimicking the calls of other species and add to their repertoires throughout their lives, learning around 200 and 2,000 different songs, respectively.

4 → An interesting fact is that birds acquire most of these songs during critical periods of brain development. To do this, they rely on the specialized frontal cortex section of the brain known as the basal ganglia. This section of the brain internalizes sensory experiences and then shapes them into vocal output through sensorimotor learning and integration. [■]

16 According to paragraph 4, which of the following occurs in the basal ganglia after the critical period?

(A) It changes and therefore has a different function than that of humans.
(B) It becomes unable to recognize or integrates different melodies the bird hears.
(C) It is best timely for it to learn and retain the details of a teacher's song.
(D) It becomes relatively less sensitive to perceive and memorize details of a tutor's song.

paragraph 4 is marked with an arrow [→].

17 The experiment mentioned in paragraph 4 suggest that birds whose auditory systems were disturbed

(A) could acquire and develop a new song even in their adulthoods.
(B) developed distortions as well as inaccuracies in their songs.
(C) were able to maintain the perfect version of their songs.
(D) forget their original songs should their plasticity return.

18 In paragraph 4, which of the following plays the most significant role in maintaining the song the bird has acquired?

(A) subsong
(B) sensitive period
(C) auditory feedback
(D) spectral variation

This innate disposition for 'language acquisition' is similar to humans. [■] Humans have critical periods when sensorimotor functions and regions in the frontal cortex, like the basal ganglia in birds, allow accelerated learning and vocal output shaping. [■] It is during these brief periods that birds are best equipped to memorize details of a tutor's song. [■] For the White-crowned Sparrow, this age is between 15 and 50 days, after which learning becomes more difficult. They, therefore, begin practicing singing shortly after leaving the nest, at about three weeks of age. Recalling the sounds they heard during the sensitive period, they match it in their practice singing called the subsong. The subsong becomes louder, more persistent, and structured over time. These corrections eventually result in a perfect copy of the remembered song, which goes through 'crystallization', after which there is little variation. Evidence, however, suggests that auditory feedback is actively used in adulthood to maintain the song's structure. It can be shown that disturbing auditory feedback during adult Zebra Finches' singing caused their song to deteriorate. This 'decrystallization' is a marked loss of the temporal and spectral stereotypy seen in crystallized songs. Once normal feedback is restored, these deviations gradually disappear and the original song returns. Thus, adult birds that do not seem to learn new songs still retain a significant amount of plasticity in their brains.

19 Look at the four squares [■] that indicate where the following sentence could be added to the passage.

Similarly, most songbirds seem to have what is called a 'sensitive period' for song learning.

Where would the sentence best fit?

Click on a square [■] to add the sentence to the passage.

20 Directions: An introductory sentence for a brief summary of the passage is provided below. Complete the summary by selecting the THREE answer choices that express the most important ideas in the passage. Some sentences do not belong in the summary because they express ideas that are not presented in the passage or are minor ideas in the passage. **This question is worth 2 points.**

Drag your answer choices to the spaces where they belong. To remove an answer choice, click on it.
To review the passage, click on **View Text**.

Biologists have developed various theories explaining how and why songbirds sing.

-
-
-

Answer Choices

(A) Bird songs have many communicative functions and have been proven to be used as mating calls and territorial markers.

(B) Primitive birds learned to sing through an intuitive ability, and have evolved since to the point where some species can copy the songs of other birds.

(C) Female birds are attracted to male birds with the ability to sing a variety of songs, as they are reliable indicators of strong survival abilities.

(D) Through the process of crystallization, birds obtain a collection of subsongs during the critical periods, which occurs in early childhood.

(E) The process of learning songs may differ significantly depending on the birds' species and environment.

(F) Nestlings, like humans, are likely to utilize auditory input more effectively than adults whose song development has been finalized.

You have seen all of the questions in this part of the Reading section. You have time left to review.
As long as there is time remaining, you can check your work.

Click on **Return** to go back to the previous question.
Click on **Review** to see the review screen for this section.
Click on **Continue** to go on.
Once you leave this part of the Reading section, you **WILL NOT** be able to return to it.

이제 Reading Section이 끝났습니다.
Countinue 버튼을 누르면 다시 문제를 검토할 수 없으므로 유의하세요.

시험보고 난 후 ... 체크 리스트 및 스터디 디렉션   USHER iBT TOEFL FINAL TEST READING

1. 내가 불안했던 문제만 재빨리 다시 보고, 불안하게 만든, 즉, 경쟁 초이스를 찾아서 왜 내가 헷갈려 했는지를 파악할 수 있는 메모를 해두시기 바랍니다. 시간이 지나거나, 다른 학생들과 스터디를 하면서는, 자신이 왜 낚였는지 이유조차 기억나지 않아 본인의 실수 패턴파악이 힘들기 때문입니다.

2. 답지를 확인하지 않고 스터디를 하시기 바랍니다. (그래서, 답지를 문제지 뒤에 붙이지 않고, 본 설명만을 붙여두었습니다.) 답지를 확인하지 않고 하는 이유는 답을 아는 순간, 답에 끼워맞춰 설명하려 하고, 이런 태도는 본인 실력 향상에 도움이 되지 않기 때문입니다. 스터디 팀원들간에 대략적인 답을 맞춰보면, 대부분 답안의 윤곽이 나옵니다. 이럴 경우, 이견이 있는 문제만 집중적으로 다루고, 나머지는 개인별로 처리하시기 바랍니다.

3. 문제를 끝까지 다 풀었나요? 네 ☐ / 아니오 ☐
   다 못 풀었다면, 전체 20 문제 중 푼 문제는? _____ / 20
   시간 모자란 것에 대해서는 크게 신경 쓰지 않아도 됩니다. 무엇보다 중요한 것은 정확도 입니다. 우선은 풀은 문제를 맞출 확률을 높이고, 그 다음 시간을 걱정해도 늦지 않습니다.

4. 어려웠다고 느껴지는 지문은? 과학 ☐ / 예술 ☐ / 인문 ☐ / 인물 ☐ / 사회 ☐
   과학지문이 현격히 다른 분야보다 많지만, 그래도, 공부하다 보면 자신만 어려워하는 분야는 모두 각각입니다. 그러므로, 혹시 배경 지식 부분에서 필요한 것이 있다면, usherin.usher.co.kr 에 방문하셔서, 공부가 안될 때, 배경지식 부분을 쉬엄쉬엄 들러서 봐 두시길 바랍니다. 쉬엄쉬엄입니다. 누가 뭐래도 실력있는 사람은 배경지식이 큰 영향을 끼치지는 않습니다.

5. (채점 후) 문제 풀 때 어렵다고 느낀 지문이 틀리는 개수와 쉬웠다고 느껴졌던 지문의 틀린 개수차이가 있나요? 예 ☐ / 아니오 ☐
   어느 순간 깨닫게 됩니다. 내가 잘 아는 내용이 나와서 자신 있게 푸나, 내가 모르는 지문이 나와서 겁먹고 푸나, 틀린 개수가 큰 차이가 나지 않는 것을…. 혹시 그걸 못 느끼신다면, 더욱더 열심히 하시기 바랍니다. ^^

6. 틀린 문제의 번호를 다음의 문제 유형 분석표와 비교해서 파악해 두시기 바랍니다.
   문제 유형을 파악해서 주의하는 것은, 누가 뭐래도 실력이 기본은 받쳐 줄 때 얘기입니다. 문제 푸는 스킬이나, 기타 문제 유형파악 등은 기본적으로 본문 내용을 이해하고, 해석이 웬만큼 될 때 얘기입니다. 만약, 너무 힘들다면 너무 스트레스 받지 말고, 그냥 '아~ 그렇구나' 정도로 넘기셔도 됩니다. 단, 본문 이해는 절대 양보해서는 안됩니다.

문제 유형 분석표
31page 내용 중, 아래 표시되어 있는 문제 유형은 파악하기 쉬우나 나머지 문제들의 문제 유형 파악은 어려워 하는 경향이 있어 비워두었습니다. 문제유형 정답은 377page를 참조하세요.

TEST 6-1

01
02
03 Vocabulary
04
05 Highlight
06
07 Reference
08
09 Insertion
10 Summary

TEST 6-2

11
12 Vocabulary
13
14
15 Highlight
16
17
18
19 Insertion
20 Summary

이름: Test 6

1

TEST번호	시험날짜	실제토플/모의토플 총점	RC	틀린갯수/전체갯수	LC	틀린갯수/전체갯수	SP	WR
tpo				/		/		
tpo				/		/		
tpo				/		/		
tpo				/		/		
tpo				/		/		
tpo				/		/		

2

RC — 첫 번째 지문 중 틀린 개수

Topic 1 제목 :

문제유형	틀린갯수/전체갯수	실력으로 틀린 문제	실수로 틀린 문제
Voca 문제	/		
Fact 문제	/		
Reference 문제	/		
Purpose 문제	/		
Infer 문제	/		
Highlight 문제	/		
Insertion 문제	/		
Summary 문제	/		

→ 取약한 유형순으로 틀린 문제 다시 풀어보기

RC — 첫 번째 지문 중 틀린 개수

Topic 1 제목 :

문제유형	틀린갯수/전체갯수	실력으로 틀린 문제	실수로 틀린 문제
Voca 문제	/		
Fact 문제	/		
Reference 문제	/		
Purpose 문제	/		
Infer 문제	/		
Highlight 문제	/		
Insertion 문제	/		
Summary 문제	/		

→ 取약한 유형순으로 틀린 문제 다시 풀어보기

3

오늘의 결론

내가 주의해야할 실수 패턴	내가 늘려야할 실력	내가 하고싶은 말(결론)

※ 순서대로 따라서 적어주세요.

| 문제구별 tip

Fact와 Purpose의 가장 큰 구별방법

· **Fact 문제**: Except, true, Not true
· **Purpose 문제**: why mention, in order to, what is the purpose

why는 Fact문제 일수도 있습니다.

usherin.usher.co.kr

USHER

iBT TOEFL
FINAL TEST READING
TEST 7

테스트 전 확인사항

실전에 유용한 독해 전략(31p)을 숙지하였습니다. ○
화장실은 미리 다녀왔습니다. ○
휴대폰의 전원을 껐습니다. ○
노트테이킹 할 종이와 연필을 준비하였습니다. ○
시간을 체크할 시계를 준비하였습니다. ○
목표점수(20개 중 ___개)를 정하였습니다. ○
시험시작 시간은 ___시 ___분이며, ○
종료 시간은 35분 뒤인 ___시 ___분입니다.
시험 중 이동해야 할 방해요소가 있는지 체크하였습니다. ○
시험 중 이동하지 않습니다. ○

Reading Section Directions

This section measures your ability to understand academic passages in English.

Most questions are worth 1 point but the last question in each set is worth more than 1 point. The directions indicate how many points you may receive.

Some passages include a word or phrase that is underlined in blue. Click on the word or phrase to see a definition or an explanation.

Within each test, you can go to the next questions by clicking **Next**. You may skip questions and go back to them later. If you want to return to previous questions, click on **Back**. You can click on **Review** at any time and the review screen will show you which questions you have answered and which you have not answered. From this review screen, you may go directly to any questions you have already seen in the Reading section.

You may now begin the Reading section. In the section you will read 2 passages. You will have **35 minutes** to read the passages and answer the questuons.

Click on **Continue** to go on.

Next 버튼을 이용하여 다음 문제로 이동하고 **Back** 버튼을 이용하여 이전 문제로 이동할 수 있습니다. 문제에 답을 하지 않더라도 다음 문제로 이동할 수 있으며, **Review** 버튼을 이용하여 각 문제 별로 답을 체크했는지의 여부를 확인할 수 있습니다. 이번 테스트에서는 세 지문을 읽게 됩니다. **35분** 동안 지문을 읽고 문제에 답을 하세요.

01 Why does the author mention bluebell in paragraph 2?

(A) To show how plant footing also prevents erosion
(B) To give an example of a harsh environment in which modified roots store nutrients.
(C) To show one of the crucial functions plants' roots have
(D) To illustrate that plants regrow when conditions improve

02 According to paragraph 3, how do red mangroves survive in their environment?

(A) The roots of the mangrove are able to expel the salt it has absorbed.
(B) The mangrove has roots that separately absorb water and salt.
(C) Lenticels on the prop roots provide oxygen to the subterranean roots.
(D) The salinity of water lessens as it passes through a strainer in the stem.

paragraph 3 is marked with an arrow [→].

Functions of Roots

1 Roots, the water-absorbing organs of a plant, are present on essentially all vascular plants and serve three primary functions: to anchor the plant to a substrate, to absorb nutrients through osmosis, and to store food reserves. They can adapt to carry out these primary functions in ways optimized for different environments.

2 One of the most important functions of root networks is to provide a stable footing for plants so they do not fall over or get swept away. This also provides the secondary benefit of controlling soil erosion around the plant's base. In addition to this, many plants like the carrot and turnip also store nutrients in modified roots. Roots of plants such as the bluebell store so much energy that they act as perennating organs allowing the plant to survive harsh conditions such as drought, frigid winters, or light deficiency. They do this by allowing the exposed part of the plant to die down and storing as much energy as possible for regrowth when conditions improve.

3 → For plants which are constantly exposed to harsh environments, such as salt water swamps, survival is more challenging due to the lack of basic necessities. The deeper roots of most plants die because of the lack of oxygen under the waterlogged soil, leading to the plant's slow death. Mangrove roots, however, are well-suited to the region. The red mangrove, a tropical tree which colonizes coastlines and brackish water between the northern and southern latitudes of 25 degrees, can often be found on the water's edge. These are distinguished from other mangroves by the prominent prop roots extending into the water from high up on their stems. They thrive in the highly saline habitats by not relying on traditional roots growing under the substrate. Instead, it is assumed, lenticels, or pores, on their prop roots act as conduits for supplying oxygen for respiration to the subterranean roots. Unlike most

03 Which of the sentences below best expresses the essential information in the highlighted sentence in the passage? Incorrect choices change the meaning in important ways or leave out essential information.

(A) The restricted amount of nutrients plants need results in a direct competition between plants to take as many nutrients as they can.
(B) When there is a scarcity of nutrients, plants grow near each other, competing for limited nutrients.
(C) The amount of plant necessities may be limited if plants grow too close to one another, leading to competition between the plants.
(D) Plants save the limited amount of nutrients through a fierce competition with other plants that are located near them.

04 According to paragraph 4, what can be inferred about the strangler figs?

(A) It grows relatively slowly until it begins competing with its host.
(B) It penetrates the host tree to find the nutrients it requires.
(C) It harms the host plant in the process of growing downward to reach the soil.
(D) It steals the host's nutrients by strangling its trunk.

paragraph 4 is marked with an arrow [→].

05 The word secrete in the passage is closest in meaning to

(A) promote
(B) discharge
(C) conceal
(D) exploit

---

plants, their roots also enable them to obtain freshwater from highly saline water sources through non-metabolic ultra-filtration, using negative pressure inside the root to draw freshwater in through a membrane too fine for salt to pass through, in a process called reverse-osmosis.

4 → Unlike the mangroves, however, most plants exist in environments filled with other plants leading to a competition-filled bio-diverse habitat. To triumph over competition, plants use various methods such as root adaptations to attain the necessary nutrients, water, sunlight, and territory. If the plants are grown in close proximity, there may be a limited amount of these essential nutrients, resulting in a head-to-head competition for as large a share as possible. One of the ways they do this is by adapting. One example of this is the dark, competition-filled forest floor where strangler figs have adapted roots that snake down the trunk of a host tree or dangle from its branches as aerial roots enabling it to live in the tree branches. When they reach the ground, however, they dig in and grow more rapidly, fighting the host for nutrients. This root network surrounds the host and intertwines around it. As they grow thicker they squeeze the trunk of the host and cut off its flow of nutrients. Eventually the host dies from strangulation, insufficient sunlight and root competition, and the strangler fig stands on its own.

5 → Some plants also compete using chemical methods. The roots of these plants secrete chemical compounds known as root exudates. Through the exudation of a variety of compounds, they regulate the microbial content of nearby soil, cope with herbivores, alter the physical and chemical make-up of the soil, and inhibit the growth of competing plants. [■] Chemical-mediated plant-plant interference, or allelopathy, is one mechanism plants use to gain an advantage over their competitors. [■] In research conducted by biologists from a chemical company, it was found that a plant called lemon bottlebrush excreted an allelopathic chemical called leptospermone. [■] One day, they noted

06 According to paragraph 5, which of the following is NOT a characteristic of exudates?

(A) They can cause changes in the soil conditions.
(B) They encourage competitiveness with other species.
(C) They can hinder the growth of other plants.
(D) They control nearby microorganism colonies.

paragraph 5 is marked with an arrow [→].

07 According to paragraph 5, why does the author mention the research conducted by biologists from a chemical company?

(A) To prove the existence of the herbicidal compound
(B) To describe how allelopathy can affect bushes and nearby plants
(C) To explain why lemon bottlebrush excretes leptospermone
(D) To provide an example of a plant that use allelopathy

08 What is true about lemon bottlebrush bushes according to paragraph 5?

(A) Lemon bottlebrush bush exudates are not practically useable because of their strong herbicidal effect.
(B) Usually many plants can live under the bushes despite their allelopathy.
(C) The soil surrounding them is much different than the soil under nearby bushes.
(D) Lemon bottlebrush bushes in their original form can be used as a selective herbicide for corn crops.

that under certain bushes, such as lemon bottlebrush, other plants only rarely grew. By collecting samples of the soil under the bush, they were able to extract many chemicals from the plants, one of which was identified as an herbicide. [■] While it did have herbicidal effects, the amount required for effective crop coverage was too high to be practical. Leptospermone was, therefore, reworked into thousands of compounds, with several being effective but too toxic, environmentally persistent or non-selective. Mesotrione, the final compound they created could, however, be used as a selective herbicide for corn crops.

09 Look at the four squares [■] that indicate where the following sentence could be added to the passage.

It also has important implications for agriculture where its effects may be beneficial, as in the case of natural weed control, or detrimental, when chemicals produced by plants affect the growth of crops.

Where would the sentence best fit?

Click on a square [■] to add the sentence to the passage.

10 Directions: An introductory sentence for a brief summary of the passage is provided below. Complete the summary by selecting the THREE answer choices that express the most important ideas in the passage. Some sentences do not belong in the summary because they express ideas that are not presented in the passage or are minor ideas in the passage. **This question is worth 2 points.**

Drag your answer choices to the spaces where they belong. To remove an answer choice, click on it. To review the passage, click on **View Text**.

Plants are able to adapt to harsh environments when their roots can carry out primary roles through specialization.

- ●
- ●
- ●

Answer Choices

(A) Plants that are subjected to unfavorable conditions develop unique roots that help the plant overcome such circumstances.

(B) When roots are exposed to unfavorable environments, such as saline water, they utilize nutrients that they have stored in the roots.

(C) Some plants produce chemical compounds that are too toxic for other plants and herbivores that feed on the plants.

(D) Some plants like the strangler fig grows on other trees with roots exposed in the air.

(E) To physically compete against nearby plants for nutrients, plants utilize their roots.

(F) Chemicals exuded by some plants can affect the growth of other plants and are used by humans.

11 What does the word it in paragraph 1 refer to?

(A) individual
(B) state
(C) idea
(D) invention

12 Which of the following is true about the Renaissance period according to paragraph 1?

(A) There were many more talented inventors worth protecting in the Renaissance period.
(B) During the Renaissance period people started to recognize the importance of the talent and achievements of the individual.
(C) Because of rigid structures and hierarchies of the Renaissance period, people decided to utilize more inventions.
(D) Talented inventors of the Renaissance period were eager to share their novel products.

13 Which of the sentences below best expresses the essential information in the highlighted sentence in the passage? Incorrect choices change the meaning in important ways or leave out essential information.

(A) Efforts in making a systemized way of protecting inventors' rights started with the Venetian Senate's 1474 Act, which took 10 years to establish this prohibition of producing devices similar to an already invented one, because each inventor had to report his device to the council.
(B) The Venetian Senate's 1474 Act is the first standardized implementation of a patent law in that as long as an original, completed device was reported to the council, it prohibited anyone from producing a device similar to the patented one without the consent of the inventor for a given period.
(C) The inventors reported their products to the council, prompting the Venetian Senate's 1474 Act which prohibited reproduction of such devices without authorization by the inventor.
(D) The systemized protection of inventors' rights is considered to have started with the Venetian Senate's 1474 Act, which required that anyone who produces a device similar to a patented one report it to the council.

History of The Patent Law

1 The State's protection of a person's right to utilize and control the utilization of an invention, be it a machine or a unique method of production, was not prevalent until the Renaissance period. As a result, in the Middle Ages, one would have had to hide the fact that one had invented a novel product in order to keep it. This lack of protection from the state has been attributed to rigid social structures and hierarchies that ignored the talent of the individual inventor.

2 This changed when the first systemic mechanism for protecting an inventor's rights to monopoly was introduced by a 1474 Act of the Venetian Senate, which prohibited the production of a device conforming to a patented one without the authorization of the inventor for 10 years, provided the inventor had recorded the innovation with the council. This system differed from the modern one in that it required the inventor to produce a completed, working device. In other words, the inventor had to report a device that could be used immediately and was societally useful. However, it still laid out all the major features of modern patent law, such as requiring the device to be officially registered, 'useful' to the society, 'not previously made in this state', and providing a fixed term of exclusivity.

3 Even before the Venetian Senate's act of 1474, isolated monopolies were granted in Europe. For example, in England the monarchs would grant letters patent, or 'letters that lie open', to people in their graces, granting them a monopoly to produce or provide specific goods and services. This tradition of granting monopolies eventually led to the term 'patents' we use today. It was not, however, until the Venetian Act that the standardized process of granting patents occurred. Britain, influenced by this new concept, eventually implemented such a system as a kind of mercantilist instrument to attract emigrants with skills that could possibly aid British industry with the

14 Which statement regarding modern patent systems is supported by paragraph 2?

(A) The modern system allows for the registration of devices that may not yet be suitable for real life use.
(B) The first patent system allowed for the endowment of patents to the same kind of inventions as the modern system.
(C) The modern system does not appreciate 'complete' and 'perfect' devices that are ready for use right away.
(D) The modern system allows monopolization of 10 years for inventions.

15 What is implied in paragraph 3 about Britain at around the time a patent system was introduced?

(A) Britain was one of the most attractive states for emigrants to go to due to the invention of the first patent system.
(B) The increased rate of immigration caused by the introduction of the patent system improved England's faltering economy.
(C) Britain did not have a population skilled and technically proficient enough to develop as fast as the government wanted.
(D) The patent system, as a mercantilist instrument, significantly drained England's economy as many emigrants flooded in.

guarantee of exclusive monopoly, after the significant economic drain caused by the War of the Roses. By the early 17th century, patents had become royal favors to subjects of loyalty or wealth, with monopolies being granted on products and services such as running ale-houses. This led to inefficiency and left room for the corruption that brought about the Statute of Monopolies of 1624, which required courts to outlaw all monopolies but those based on true inventive intentions. When the Industrial Revolution spurred an explosive number of new inventions, patents became an increasingly important component of the socioeconomic machine. This era marks a change in the perception of the role of patents in society, in that they were no longer given only for the introduction of a new finished product, but also for the introduction of technological know-how or processes.

4 → Along with many other British legal concepts, the patent system was introduced in the United States during the colonial period between 1640 and 1776. Initially, each of the 13 colonies formed their own patent systems, which led to disputes, such as identifying the true inventor of the steamboat, as different inventors were registered in the patent archives of two colonies. These problems continued to arise even after the United States' independence. The government, therefore, sought to solve this problem and the 1789 Constitutional Convention imbedded a national patent system in the constitution itself. [■] The result was Article I, Section 8 of the Constitution which authorized Congress to selectively endow individual authors and inventors with 'exclusive rights to their writings and discoveries'. [■] Samuel Hopkins received the first United States federal patent in 1790 for a process that derived potash from wood ashes. [■] The United States patent system grew to its full, modern status with the 1836 revision that introduced a formal system of examination by appointed, professional examiners.[■] Since then, patents have rapidly become an important thread of the American economic

16 According to paragraph 4, why was the patent law an important aspect of the Constitutional Convention of 1789?

(A) It allowed each of the 13 states to enact its own patent law.
(B) It classified the steamboat to have been invented by two different people.
(C) It added an American characteristic to a legal concept imported from Great Britain.
(D) It made a national patent system so as to avoid confusion between states.

paragraph 4 is marked with an arrow [→].

17 The word exclusive in the passage is closest in meaning to?

(A) unshared
(B) partial
(C) noble
(D) unprecedented

18 Why is the United States patent system considered to have reached full maturity in 1836 according to paragraph 4?

(A) Because the patent system had evolved from an already efficient mechanism.
(B) Because an established protocol of examination was introduced.
(C) Because the patent system did not have an important impact on the economic system of America any more.
(D) Because the system was revised so that the government could appoint certain inventors.

fabric, despite the fact that the process' effectiveness is still debated.

5 Throughout history the concept of protecting one's rights to one's own creations has advanced along with the burgeoning capitalist, industrial world economy, which is increasingly dependent on new technological advancements. Despite changes in the patent systems over time, the principal idea that the inventor must contribute in some way to the state, or society, through novel, useful inventions has remained.

19 Look at the four squares [■] that indicate where the following sentence could be added to the passage.

Therefore, not only was the patent law nationalized, but also the process of granting patents standardized.

Where would the sentence best fit?

Click on a square [■] to add the sentence to the passage.

20 Directions: An introductory sentence for a brief summary of the passage is provided below. Complete the summary by selecting the THREE answer choices that express the most important ideas in the passage. Some sentences do not belong in the summary because they express ideas that are not presented in the passage or are minor ideas in the passage. **This question is worth 2 points.**

Drag your answer choices to the spaces where they belong. To remove an answer choice, click on it. To review the passage, click on **View Text**.

The law of patents has gone through dramatic changes.

-
-
-

Answer Choices

(A) The first patent law to properly protect an individual's right to manufacture a newly established invention was enacted in 1474 by the Venetian Senate.

(B) The Venetian Senate's 1474 Act allowed the monopolization of a device for 10 years.

(C) Letters patent were issued before the Venetian Senate's Act of 1474 and influenced the systemized implementation of patent law.

(D) The United States patent law matured because monarchs granted patent holder a monopoly to produce or provide specific goods and services.

(E) The Industrial Revolution marked a major change in the patent system, as the British patent office began issuing patents from both products and technological knowledge.

(F) The American patent law was nationalized and the process of granting patents standardized when the principles of individuals' rights to their creations was included and revised in the constitution.

You have seen all of the questions in this part of the Reading section. You have time left to review. As long as there is time remaining, you can check your work.

Click on **Return** to go back to the previous question.
Click on **Review** to see the review screen for this section.
Click on **Continue** to go on.
Once you leave this part of the Reading section, you **WILL NOT** be able to return to it.

이제 Reading Section이 끝났습니다.
Countinue 버튼을 누르면 다시 문제를 검토할 수없으므로 유의하세요.

시험보고 난 후 ... 체크 리스트 및 스터디 디렉션 | USHER iBT TOEFL FINAL TEST READING

1. 내가 불안했던 문제만 재빨리 다시 보고, 불안하게 만든, 즉, 경쟁 초이스를 찾아서 왜 내가 헷갈려 했는지를 파악할 수 있는 메모를 해두시기 바랍니다. 시간이 지나거나, 다른 학생들과 스터디를 하면서는, 자신이 왜 낚였는지 이유조차 기억나지 않아 본인의 실수 패턴파악이 힘들기 때문입니다.

2. 답지를 확인하지 않고 스터디를 하시기 바랍니다. (그래서, 답지를 문제지 뒤에 붙이지 않고, 본 설명만을 붙여두었습니다.) 답지를 확인하지 않고 하는 이유는 답을 아는 순간, 답에 끼워맞춰 설명하려 하고, 이런 태도는 본인 실력 향상에 도움이 되지 않기 때문입니다. 스터디 팀원들간에 대략적인 답을 맞춰보면, 대부분 답안의 윤곽이 나옵니다. 이럴 경우, 이견이 있는 문제만 집중적으로 다루고, 나머지는 개인별로 처리하시기 바랍니다.

3. 문제를 끝까지 다 풀었나요? 네 □ / 아니오 □
   다 못 풀었다면, 전체 20 문제 중 푼 문제는? _____ / 20
   시간 모자란 것에 대해서는 크게 신경 쓰지 않아도 됩니다. 무엇보다 중요한 것은 정확도 입니다. 우선은 풀은 문제를 맞출 확률을 높이고, 그 다음 시간을 걱정해도 늦지 않습니다.

4. 어려웠다고 느껴지는 지문은? 과학 □ / 예술 □ / 인문 □ / 인물 □ / 사회 □
   과학지문이 현격히 다른 분야보다 많지만, 그래도, 공부하다 보면 자신만 어려워하는 분야는 모두 각각입니다. 그러므로, 혹시 배경 지식 부분에서 필요한 것이 있다면, usherin.usher.co.kr 에 방문하셔서, 공부가 안될 때, 배경지식 부분을 쉬엄쉬엄 들러서 봐 두시길 바랍니다. 쉬엄쉬엄입니다. 누가 뭐래도 실력있는 사람은 배경지식이 큰 영향을 끼치지는 않습니다.

5. (채점 후) 문제 풀 때 어렵다고 느낀 지문이 틀리는 개수와 쉬웠다고 느껴졌던 지문의 틀린 개수차이가 있나요? 예 □ / 아니오 □
   어느 순간 깨닫게 됩니다. 내가 잘 아는 내용이 나와서 자신 있게 푸나, 내가 모르는 지문이 나와서 겁먹고 푸나, 틀린 개수가 큰 차이가 나지 않는 것을…. 혹시 그걸 못 느끼신다면, 더욱더 열심히 하시기 바랍니다. ^^

6. 틀린 문제의 번호를 다음의 문제 유형 분석표와 비교해서 파악해 두시기 바랍니다.
   문제 유형을 파악해서 주의하는 것은, 누가 뭐래도 실력이 기본은 받쳐 줄 때 얘기입니다. 문제 푸는 스킬이나, 기타 문제 유형파악 등은 기본적으로 본문 내용을 이해하고, 해석이 웬만큼 될 때 얘기입니다. 만약, 너무 힘들다면 너무 스트레스 받지 말고, 그냥 '아~ 그렇구나' 정도로 넘기셔도 됩니다. 단, 본문 이해는 절대 양보해서는 안됩니다.

문제 유형 분석표 31page 내용 중, 아래 표시되어 있는 문제 유형은 파악하기 쉬우나 나머지 문제들의 문제 유형 파악은 어려워 하는 경향이 있어 비워두었습니다. 문제유형 정답은 395page를 참조하세요.

TEST 7-1

01
02
03 Highlight
04
05 Vocabulary
06
07
08
09 Insertion
10 Summary

TEST 7-2

11 Reference
12
13 Highlight
14
15
16
17 Vocabulary
18
19 Insertion
20 Summary

이름: Test7

1

TEST번호	시험날짜	실제토플/모의토플 총점	RC	틀린갯수/전체갯수	LC	틀린갯수/전체갯수	SP	WR
tpo		/		/		/		
tpo		/		/		/		
tpo		/		/		/		
tpo		/		/		/		
tpo		/		/		/		
tpo		/		/		/		

2

RC

첫 번째 지문 중 틀린 개수

Topic1 제목:

문제유형	틀린갯수 / 전체갯수	실력으로 틀린 문제	실수로 틀린 문제
Voca 문제	/		
Fact 문제	/		
Reference 문제	/		
Purpose 문제	/		
Infer 문제	/		
Highlight 문제	/		
Insertion 문제	/		
Summary 문제	/		

→ 문제 유형 구분이 어려울 경우 풀이보세요

RC

첫 번째 지문 중 틀린 개수

Topic1 제목:

문제유형	틀린갯수 / 전체갯수	실력으로 틀린 문제	실수로 틀린 문제
Voca 문제	/		
Fact 문제	/		
Reference 문제	/		
Purpose 문제	/		
Infer 문제	/		
Highlight 문제	/		
Insertion 문제	/		
Summary 문제	/		

→ 문제 유형 구분이 어려울 경우 풀이보세요

3

오늘의 결론

내가 주의해야할 실수 패턴	내가 늘려야할 실력	내가 하고싶은 말(질문)

※ 순서대로 따라서 적어주세요.

| 문제구별 tip

Fact와 Purpose의 가장 큰 구별방법

- **Fact** 문제: Except, true, Not true
- **Purpose** 문제: why mention, in order to, what is the purpose

why는 Fact문제 일수도 있습니다.

usherin.usher.co.kr

USHER

iBT TOEFL
FINAL TEST READING
TEST 8

테스트 전 확인사항

- 실전에 유용한 독해 전략(31p)을 숙지하였습니다. ○
- 화장실은 미리 다녀왔습니다. ○
- 휴대폰의 전원을 껐습니다. ○
- 노트테이킹 할 종이와 연필을 준비하였습니다. ○
- 시간을 체크할 시계를 준비하였습니다. ○
- 목표점수(20개 중 ___ 개)를 정하였습니다. ○
- 시험시작 시간은 ___시 ___분이며, 종료 시간은 35분 뒤인 ___시 ___분입니다. ○
- 시험 중 이동해야 할 방해요소가 있는지 체크하였습니다. ○
- 시험 중 이동하지 않습니다. ○

Reading Section Directions

This section measures your ability to understand academic passages in English.

Most questions are worth 1 point but the last question in each set is worth more than 1 point. The directions indicate how many points you may receive.

Some passages include a word or phrase that is underlined in blue. Click on the word or phrase to see a definition or an explanation.

Within each test, you can go to the next questions by clicking **Next**. You may skip questions and go back to them later. If you want to return to previous questions, click on **Back**. You can click on **Review** at any time and the review screen will show you which questions you have answered and which you have not answered. From this review screen, you may go directly to any questions you have already seen in the Reading section.

You may now begin the Reading section. In the section you will read 2 passages. You will have **35 minutes** to read the passages and answer the questuons.

Click on **Continue** to go on.

Next 버튼을 이용하여 다음 문제로 이동하고 **Back** 버튼을 이용하여 이전 문제로 이동할 수 있습니다. 문제에 답을 하지 않더라도 다음 문제로 이동할 수 있으며, **Review** 버튼을 이용하여 각 문제 별로 답을 체크했는지의 여부를 확인할 수 있습니다. 이번 테스트에서는 세 지문을 읽게 됩니다. **35분** 동안 지문을 읽고 문제에 답을 하세요.

Communication of Ants

1 Ants have several advantages over solitary insects such as increased system reliability and division of labor. The major advantage, however, is the communication among members. This allows the colony to regulate its foraging activity and retain a memory of previously rewarding locations. To do this, ants rely on chemical signals called pheromones. When foragers find a successful foraging site, they deposit a trail of pheromones on their return to the nest. This trail gains strength as more and more workers add more pheromones to it.

2 → Unlike the traditional views on ant pheromone trails, recent studies have shown that distinct roles are assigned to different pheromones, as can be illustrated by the differences in the pheromones produced by the poison and pygidial glands of Malaysian ponerine army ants. The poison glands of these ants contain two pheromone components, one eliciting a strong, short-term attraction to prey targets and another guiding workers from foraging sites back to the colony. These pheromone trails are highly volatile, lasting only a few minutes, to ensure that ants are not attracted to sites long after the prey has been collected. The pygidial gland, on the other hand, produces a longer-lasting trail pheromone that guides workers back to the trail network of the colony. These pheromones act as the 'bread crumbs' in the tale of 'Hansel and Gretel', allowing the ants to maintain their spatial organization and helping them forage in an organized manner which enables the rapid transport of food to the colony.

3 → [■] Furthermore, in Pharaoh's ant, research has shown distinct, short-lived and long-lived attractive-trail pheromone effects, as well as a short-lived repellent pheromone. [■] In contrast to most ant pheromones, the long-lived trails of Pharaoh's ants can persist for several days, allowing the trail network to be explored for a longer period of time. [■] Sections of the network leading to food are reinforced with the short-lived trail

---

01 According to paragraph 2, what can be inferred about the traditional view of ant pheromone trails?

(A) The communicational methods of ants were thought to be simple.
(B) The long-lasting and short-lasting attraction pheromones were believed to attract nearby ants for a long period of time.
(C) The trail pheromones were thought to be secretions from a single gland that poisoned and repelled other insects.
(D) The pygidial and poison glands were believed to secrete harmful pheromones that capture prey.

paragraph 2 is marked with an arrow [→].

02 According to paragraph 2, why does the 'attraction pheromone' last only for a short period of time?

(A) To provide protection from predators to ants when foraging
(B) To prevent foragers from going to sites after prey is completely acquired
(C) To guide the foragers back to their colony
(D) To attract as many foragers as possible to capture certain prey

03 In paragraph 2, the author mentioned the tale of Hansel and Gretel in order to

(A) provide an analogy to explain a phenomenon that occurs in ants.
(B) show how ants foraged for bread crumbs in the tale.
(C) demonstrate that pheromones are as volatile as Hansel and Gretel's situation.
(D) show that ants enable the rapid transport of food to the colony.

04 Which of the sentences below best expresses the essential information in the highlighted sentence in the passage? Incorrect choices change the meaning in important ways or leave out essential information.

(A) A forager uses an extensive amount of pheromones when locating prey which attracts nearby foragers to help it when returning to its colony.
(B) Foragers release a large amount of pheromones when they detect another forager that has located prey, attracting other by stridulating, which in turn causes the poison gland to produce a pheromone trail.
(C) Ants return to the colony rapidly when they detect stridulation and pheromones, creating clear trailing system to the prey.
(D) By stridulating when it has found prey, a foraging ant draws in other members in the area which leads to an increase in the pheromone markers, allowing rapid collection.

05 According to paragraph 4, what is true about stridulating by ants?

(A) The sounds they produced by stridulating deters other foraging insects from approaching their prey items.
(B) Ants begin stridulating when they find a prey item so that ants in the area can hear it and join them in bringing the prey item back to the nest.
(C) The volume of the stridulating is determined by the quality of the food item the ants are foraging.
(D) Stridulating in the nest gives the worker ants information about nearby prey items.

pheromone, and the repellent pheromone is placed immediately after non-rewarding trails. [■] These three scents seem to work complementarily.

4 → Foraging ants also utilize tactile communication methods, such as vibration to communicate a wider repertoire of messages that promote the organization of the colony's foraging system. Desert ants, for example, rub their abdominal areas together to make sounds. Although ants do not have auditory organs, they can perceive these messages by sensing the vibration of the ground with their legs. When a worker locates a large prey item, such as a dead insect, it makes sharp sounds to attract workers in the area, through a process called stridulating, that encourages nearby workers to release pheromones over longer distances, causing rapid recruitment to the prey item, thereby retrieving it significantly faster. Furthermore, in leaf-cutting ants, recruitment behavior changes in relation to the quality of food. In order to test what causes different levels of sound to be created, researchers presented ants with leaves of different qualities - tender leaves, tough leaves, sugar-coated tough leaves, and acid-coated leaves - and then noted the proportion of workers that stridulated as they cut through the different leaves. The results clearly showed that the workers stridulated most strongly when cutting through leaves of a good quality or attractiveness, with the most stridulation occurring while cutting tender or sugar-coated leaves as opposed to the other leaves.

5 → This pheromone system may seem unique, but other communal insects, such as honeybees, have also developed advanced communication systems. Unlike ants honeybees use discernible movements like the 'waggle dances' to communicate complex concepts such as the approximate distance and directions to food sources. Returning foragers also perform tremble dances to recruit receiver bees to collect their nectar. A further difference is that honeybees individually remember their rewarding foraging sites and return

06 In paragraph 5, the author mentions the 'waggle dances' in order to

(A) show that honeybees have one of the most sophisticated forms of communication.
(B) contrast the ant's communication methods with that of another communal insect.
(C) explain how animals which cannot produce pheromones can use chemical methods of communications.
(D) provide an example of how the ant's communication methods are more based on the physical methods.

07 What is true about ants according to paragraph 5?

(A) They increase the efficiency of their foraging by allowing themselves to share information collectively.
(B) There are many undiscovered communication movements, that ants use to communicate with one another.
(C) Their ability to remember rewarding foraging sites is similar to that of honeybees.
(D) Ants individually recall the sites where their prey objects have been detected and return to them.

08 The word discernible in the passage is closest in meaning to

(A) meaningful
(B) creative
(C) perceptible
(D) predictable

to them. 'Trail-following' ants, on the other hand, are bound to the externally encoded group memory of their pheromone trails. These trails ensure that a channel of communication is always open and allows them to continually react and exchange information whilst foraging without needing to return to their nest, unlike the honeybees. This ability to constantly locate productive foraging sites is probably the most important reason for insects to communicate.

09 Look at the four squares [■] that indicate where the following sentence could be added to the passage.

In other words, the long-lived attractive pheromone acts as a memory, the short-lived attractive pheromone marks out routes to current food sources, and the short-lived repellent pheromone is a no entry signal to unrewarding branches of rewarding trail sections.

Where would the sentence best fit?

Click on a square [■] to add the sentence to the passage.

10 Directions: An introductory sentence for a brief summary of the passage is provided below. Complete the summary by selecting the THREE answer choices that express the most important ideas in the passage. Some sentences do not belong in the summary because they express ideas that are not presented in the passage or are minor ideas in the passage. **This question is worth 2 points.**

Drag your answer choices to the spaces where they belong. To remove an answer choice, click on it.
To review the passage, click on **View Text.**

Ants employ various chemical and physical methods when communicating with each other.

-
-
-

Answer Choices

(A) Ants utilize tactile methods of communication to complement the wide range of messages that they communicate through their chemical trails.

(B) The poison gland of ants secretes a short-term pheromone, which plays significant roles of attracting foragers from its colony while repelling those of other species.

(C) Foraging involves wide varieties of pheromones and stridulations in order to communicate both direction and distance of food sources.

(D) Ants can communicate through hearing the sounds created by using their abdominal body parts while foraging.

(E) Other communal insects have physical methods of communicating information which differ from those of ants.

(F) Ants have glands that secrete chemical pheromones for the purpose of communicating with one another during foraging activities.

11 Which of the sentences below best expresses the essential information in the highlighted sentence in the passage? Incorrect choices change the meaning in important ways or leave out essential information.

(A) Buffon's experiment underestimated Earth's age since iron, which was the major component he used to make his figure, cooled much faster than crystals and other rock components.
(B) The age of Earth was not what Buffon calculated as his research using the globe model was limited to one of the many constituents of Earth.
(C) As crystals and other rock components cool relatively faster than iron, experiment that Buffon conducted with globe-like figure underestimated the age of Earth.
(D) Buffon miscalculated the age of Earth with his globe-figure and then focused on the cooling rate of iron.

12 The word they in paragraph 3 refers to

(A) oceans
(B) rivers
(C) salts
(D) methods

Calculating the Age of Earth

1 → Religion was the only source of historical and scientific knowledge, such as the age of Earth, until the mid-eighteenth century. After this time, scientists began more openly questioning the formation of Earth, and while studying the different rock layers of it, they recognized that it had gone through various changes over a period of time. The scientists proposed a number of theories and methods that had inaccurate results due to lack of understanding of the Earth and heavy speculation. As the scientific method and logical reasoning developed within the scientific community, scholars were motivated to conduct more precise and scientific research.

2 In 1779, a French scientist, Comte de Buffon, attempted the first calculation of Earth's age by experimentation. Based on Earth's internal heat and rate of cooling, Buffon's approach utilized a small globe-like figure that resembled Earth in composition. He measured the cooling rate of the figure tested at his laboratory and calculated the age of Earth to be 75,000 years. The result completely underestimated the age of Earth as Buffon, from his globe figure, mainly focused on the cooling rate of iron, an element which cools much quicker than crystals and other rock components. The true significance of his study, however, was that it dared to break away from previous methods that derived Earth's age without experimentation.

3 → Later, others attempted to measure Earth's age, but their methods were just as inadequate. Edmund Halley, for example, based his estimation on the simple concept of the salinity of the ocean. He surmised that since rivers continuously dragged salt components from land to the oceans, increasing their salinity, the time they took to reach present salinity-levels will give an approximate timeframe for Earth's formation. Just like the previous conjectures, Halley's method was not a viable way of measuring Earth's age, as it

13 According to paragraph 3, how did Edmund Halley determine the age of Earth?

(A) He calculated the salinity of the ocean water at his time and compared it with that of the rivers.
(B) He constructed a model of the complex systems of rivers and oceans to precisely show the age of Earth.
(C) He computed a formula which showed how long it takes for the salinity of the oceans to reach the present levels.
(D) He complicated the simple courses of the ocean's salinity and used his understanding of the structure in determining the age.

paragraph 3 is marked with an arrow [→].

14 The word viscous in the passage is closest in meaning to

(A) scorching
(B) thick
(C) overflowing
(D) salient

15 According to paragraph 4, what was the problem with William Thomson's calculations?

(A) The law of physics he used in the calculation had fundamental flaws which distorted the results.
(B) He neglected the fact that the core of Earth was the main energy source during the primitive stage of Earth.
(C) The rate of cooling that is seen in Earth's core and the nebula is different.
(D) Thomson was not aware of a variable that affected the temperature of the Earth.

paragraph 4 is marked with an arrow [→].

oversimplified the complex salinification process and failed to take into account plate tectonics and undersea volcanic eruptions that continuously add salt to the ocean.

4 → Since then, measurements of physical properties have been used to estimate the age of Earth using the laws of physics. William Thomson, the forerunning supporter of these physical measurements, believed that during Earth's primitive stage, it was a sphere of hot molten rock held together by gravity and the only conceivable source of heat energy was the nebula. By estimating the rate at which heat dissipated from the nebula, scientists could determine the time necessary for Earth to cool from the molten ball of rock to its present state. Through this method, the age of Earth was calculated to be 20 to 40 million years. He had, however, neglected an important variable: the viscous fluid mantle that played an influential role in the circulation of heat energy within the Earth.

5 → Scientists calculated Earth's age with even more precision after the arrival of radiometric dating. It allowed them to derive the absolute age of rock using its components. First developed by Ernest Rutherford and enhanced by Arthur Holmes, radiometric dating is a technique based on the spontaneous decay of different naturally occurring radioactive isotopes found in rocks. These initial parent isotopes are unstable and break down into more stable daughter isotopes. This break down occurs according to an isotope's individual rate of decay, or 'decay constant,' regardless of the physical or chemical conditions it is exposed to. Scientists, therefore, do not have to be concerned with other variables since the rate of isotope transformation is almost invariable. Radiometric dating allows scientists to calculate the time that has elapsed since the formation of rocks by measuring the ratio of parent to daughter isotopes in them. [■] Radiometric testing shows Earth to be around 4.5 billion years, the most widely accepted age of Earth today.

16 According to paragraph 5, what can be inferred about the process of isotopes decaying in rocks?

(A) When a large number of parent isotopes are present in a rock, it indicates that there will be more rapid decay.
(B) After an isotope breaks down, daughter isotopes are removed from the rock.
(C) All isotopes decay at the same rate, known as the decay constant.
(D) Rocks with more parent isotopes are relatively younger than those with more daughter isotopes.

paragraph 5 is marked with an arrow [→].

17 According to paragraph 5, which of the following is true about the radiometric dating method?

(A) Despite its accuracy in dating, it is not regarded as a useful method for determining Earth's age.
(B) It makes use of rock elements that remain relatively constant over a long period of time.
(C) It measures a property that behaves in a predictable manner, deriving reliable results.
(D) Because their rates of decay are invariable, isotopes cannot be used as a variable.

18 What is the author's main argument in paragraph 6?

(A) To refute the accuracy of radiometric dating method with the support from a group of scientists.
(B) To defend radiometric dating as the most precise method of determining the earth's age at present
(C) To point out that the radiometric dating method should be enhanced by other scientific research
(D) To suggest that there are some controversies on the validity of radiometric dating method

6 [■] Still, there are controversies over the age of the earth as a minor group of scientists argues that Earth is less than 4.5 billion years. These people believe that the earth is 'young', only about 6,000 to 10,000 years old. [■] Stressing that the ratio of parent to daughter isotopes when the rock was created is unknown, they challenge the validity of scientifically-accepted radiometric methods. They further claim that some parent or daughter isotopes may be added from external sources. [■] Although there is evidence for variability in radiometric dating, Arthur Holmes used a variety of isotopes to obtain sufficient data and derived a precise result. Therefore, many regard these refutations to be implausible and until further scientific research produces a more accurate result, 4.5 billion years will continue to be considered the approximate age of the Earth.

19 Look at the four squares [■] that indicate where the following sentence could be added to the passage.

These issues of initial ratio of isotopes spotlight a flaw within radiometric dating method

Where would the sentence best fit?

Click on a square [■] to add the sentence to the passage.

20 Directions: an introductory sentence for a brief summary of the passage is provided below. Complete the summary by selecting the THREE answer choices that express the most important ideas in the passage. Some sentences do not belong in the summary because they express ideas that are not presented in the passage or are minor ideas in the passage. **This question is worth 2 points.**

Drag your answer choices to the spaces where they belong. To remove an answer choice, click on it.
To review the passage, click on **View Text.**

> The challenge of figuring out the age of Earth has been undertaken by many scientists since the nineteenth century.
>
> ●
> ●
> ●

Answer Choices

(A) Using a small globe figure, Buffon was able to obtain a reasonable age of Earth.

(B) Early attempts to calculate the age of Earth were thwarted by inaccurate understandings of its physical composition and environmental systems.

(C) The law of thermodynamics was utilized by Thomson, but he neglected a major area of thermodynamic heat circulation.

(D) William Thomson's attempt to apply the laws of physics to calculate Earth's age was widely accepted by scientists despite its limitations.

(E) Radiometric dating through counting the parent and daughter isotopes present is the most accurate method of age determination known to scientists.

(F) As radioactive isotopes decay at different rates, radiometric dating method is not the best means to determine the age of Earth.

You have seen all of the questions in this part of the Reading section. You have time left to review. As long as there is time remaining, you can check your work.

Click on **Return** to go back to the previous question.
Click on **Review** to see the review screen for this section.
Click on **Continue** to go on.
Once you leave this part of the Reading section, you **WILL NOT** be able to return to it.

이제 Reading Section이 끝났습니다.
Countinue 버튼을 누르면 다시 문제를 검토할 수 없으므로 유의하세요.

시험보고 난 후 ... 체크 리스트 및 스터디 디렉션 | USHER iBT TOEFL FINAL TEST READING

1. 내가 불안했던 문제만 재빨리 다시 보고, 불안하게 만든, 즉, 경쟁 초이스를 찾아서 왜 내가 헷갈려 했는지를 파악할 수 있는 메모를 해두시기 바랍니다. 시간이 지나거나, 다른 학생들과 스터디를 하면서는, 자신이 왜 낚였는지 이유조차 기억나지 않아 본인의 실수 패턴파악이 힘들기 때문입니다.

2. 답지를 확인하지 않고 스터디를 하시기 바랍니다. (그래서, 답지를 문제지 뒤에 붙이지 않고, 본 설명만을 붙여두었습니다.) 답지를 확인하지 않고 하는 이유는 답을 아는 순간, 답에 끼워맞춰 설명하려 하고, 이런 태도는 본인 실력 향상에 도움이 되지 않기 때문입니다. 스터디 팀원들간에 대략적인 답을 맞춰보면, 대부분 답안의 윤곽이 나옵니다. 이럴 경우, 이견이 있는 문제만 집중적으로 다루고, 나머지는 개인별로 처리하시기 바랍니다.

3. 문제를 끝까지 다 풀었나요? 네 □ / 아니오 □
   다 못 풀었다면, 전체 20 문제 중 푼 문제는? _____ / 20
   시간 모자란 것에 대해서는 크게 신경 쓰지 않아도 됩니다. 무엇보다 중요한 것은 정확도 입니다. 우선은 풀 문제를 맞출 확률을 높이고, 그 다음 시간을 걱정해도 늦지 않습니다.

4. 어려웠다고 느껴지는 지문은? 과학 □ / 예술 □ / 인문 □ / 인물 □ / 사회 □
   과학지문이 현격히 다른 분야보다 많지만, 그래도, 공부하다 보면 자신만 어려워하는 분야는 모두 각각입니다. 그러므로, 혹시 배경지식 부분에서 필요한 것이 있다면, usherin.usher.co.kr 에 방문하셔서, 공부가 안될 때, 배경지식 부분을 쉬엄쉬엄 들러서 봐 두시길 바랍니다. 쉬엄쉬엄입니다. 누가 뭐래도 실력있는 사람은 배경지식이 큰 영향을 끼치지는 않습니다.

5. (채점 후) 문제 풀 때 어렵다고 느낀 지문이 틀리는 개수와 쉬웠다고 느껴졌던 지문의 틀린 개수차이가 있나요? 예 □ / 아니오 □
   어느 순간 깨닫게 됩니다. 내가 잘 아는 내용이 나와서 자신 있게 푸나, 내가 모르는 지문이 나와서 겁먹고 푸나, 틀린 개수가 큰 차이가 나지 않는 것을…. 혹시 그걸 못 느끼신다면, 더욱더 열심히 하시기 바랍니다. ^^

6. 틀린 문제의 번호를 다음의 문제 유형 분석표와 비교해서 파악해 두시기 바랍니다.
   문제 유형을 파악해서 주의하는 것은, 누가 뭐래도 실력이 기본은 받쳐 줄 때 얘기입니다. 문제 푸는 스킬이나, 기타 문제 유형파악 등은 기본적으로 본문 내용을 이해하고, 해석이 웬만큼 될 때 얘기입니다. 만약, 너무 힘들다면 너무 스트레스 받지 말고, 그냥 '아~ 그렇구나' 정도로 넘기셔도 됩니다. 단, 본문 이해는 절대 양보해서는 안됩니다.

문제 유형 분석표   31page 내용 중, 아래 표시되어 있는 문제 유형은 파악하기 쉬우나 나머지 문제들의 문제 유형 파악은 어려워 하는 경향이 있어 비워두었습니다. 문제유형 정답은 413page를 참조하세요.

TEST 8-1

01
02
03
04 Highlight
05
06
07
08 Vocabulary
09 Insertion
10 Summary

TEST 8-2

11 Highlight
12 Reference
13
14 Vocabulary
15
16
17
18
19 Insertion
20 Summary

이름: Test 8

1

TEST번호	시험날짜	실제토플/모의토플 총점	RC	틀린갯수/전체갯수	LC	틀린갯수/전체갯수	SP	WR
tpo				/		/		
tpo				/		/		
tpo				/		/		
tpo				/		/		
tpo				/		/		
tpo				/		/		

2

RC

첫 번째 지문 중 틀린 개수:

Topic 1 제목 :

문제유형	틀린갯수/전체갯수	실력으로 틀린 문제	실수로 틀린 문제
Voca 문제	/		
Fact 문제	/		
Reference 문제	/		
Purpose 문제	/		
Infer 문제	/		
Highlight 문제	/		
Insertion 문제	/		
Summary 문제	/		

→ 문제 유형 구분이 어려울 경우 풀어보세요

RC

첫 번째 지문 중 틀린 개수:

Topic 1 제목 :

문제유형	틀린갯수/전체갯수	실력으로 틀린 문제	실수로 틀린 문제
Voca 문제	/		
Fact 문제	/		
Reference 문제	/		
Purpose 문제	/		
Infer 문제	/		
Highlight 문제	/		
Insertion 문제	/		
Summary 문제	/		

→ 문제 유형 구분이 어려울 경우 풀어보세요

3

오늘의 결론

내가 주의해야할 실수 패턴	내가 늘려야할 실력	내가 하고싶은 말(질문)

※ 순서대로 따라서 적어주세요.

| 문제구별 tip

Fact와 Purpose의 가장 큰 구별법

- **Fact 문제**: Except, true, Not true
- **Purpose 문제**: why mention, in order to, what is the purpose

why는 Fact문제 일수도 있습니다.

usherin.usher.co.kr

USHER

iBT TOEFL
FINAL TEST READING
TEST 9

테스트 전 확인사항

실전에 유용한 독해 전략(31p)을 숙지하였습니다. ○

화장실은 미리 다녀왔습니다. ○

휴대폰의 전원을 껐습니다. ○

노트테이킹 할 종이와 연필을 준비하였습니다. ○

시간을 체크할 시계를 준비하였습니다. ○

목표점수(20개 중 ___개)를 정하였습니다. ○

시험시작 시간은 ___시 ___분이며,
종료 시간은 35분 뒤인 ___시 ___분입니다. ○

시험 중 이동해야 할 방해요소가 있는지 체크하였습니다. ○
시험 중 이동하지 않습니다. ○

Reading Section Directions

This section measures your ability to understand academic passages in English.

Most questions are worth 1 point but the last question in each set is worth more than 1 point. The directions indicate how many points you may receive.

Some passages include a word or phrase that is <u>underlined in blue</u>. Click on the word or phrase to see a definition or an explanation.

Within each test, you can go to the next questions by clicking **Next**. You may skip questions and go back to them later. If you want to return to previous questions, click on **Back**. You can click on **Review** at any time and the review screen will show you which questions you have answered and which you have not answered. From this review screen, you may go directly to any questions you have already seen in the Reading section.

You may now begin the Reading section. In the section you will read 2 passages. You will have **35 minutes** to read the passages and answer the questuons.

Click on **Continue** to go on.

Next 버튼을 이용하여 다음 문제로 이동하고 **Back** 버튼을 이용하여 이전 문제로 이동할 수 있습니다. 문제에 답을 하지 않더라도 다음 문제로 이동할 수 있으며, **Review** 버튼을 이용하여 각 문제 별로 답을 체크했는지의 여부를 확인할 수 있습니다. 이번 테스트에서는 세 지문을 읽게 됩니다. **35분** 동안 지문을 읽고 문제에 답을 하세요.

Identifying Playful Behavior in Children

1 → Play, usually associated with children, comes in many forms in both humans and other animals. Even with such prevalence, its definition, function and forms are often misunderstood. This may be because play evolves both with age and over time. For example, most people recognize that a toddler's frolicking is play, but not that engaging in sport activities by adults is another form. Moreover, the way play has changed over time is also ignored. One such major change is the decrease in usage of imagination since computers and video games have begun to create virtual worlds for children, when compared to the past when they had only wooden toys and dolls with which to play. With such major changes happening, one cannot predict what form it will take next, only that it will continue to exist. Due to these changes and the lack of an apparent distinction between playful and non-playful behaviors sociologists have continuously tried to form a complete definition of play, with three having gained widespread acceptance: the functional, the structural, and the criterion approaches.

2 → Anthropologist Donald Symons, after observing African monkeys, developed the first of these in 1978. He defined play as an act that has neither a clear benefit, nor external goal. Following this, acts like learning are not considered play because their benefits are readily noticeable. Similarly, eating and working are not considered play because their purposes are specific and obvious. Although Symons' definition was intended for the monkeys that he studied, it soon became evident to other scholars that his definition, which came to be known as the functional approach, could likewise be applied to play in humans. Applying his approach to further studies has shown that although there are benefits to playful behavior, its long-term consequences are unclear. An easy way to see this is to look at common playground toys, like the jungle gym. While children enjoy climbing, hanging

---

01 According to paragraph 1, all of the following statements are true of playful behavior EXCEPT:

(A) Members of species other than humans also partake in playful behavior.
(B) Children today are less obliged to use their imagination in play because of technology.
(C) Wooden toys are no longer played with, because only video games are considered to be fun playthings now.
(D) Although their perception of play is different from that of children, adults also enjoy playful behavior.

Paragraph 1 is marked with an arrow [→].

02 Why does the author mention that one cannot predict what form it will take next, only that it will continue to exist?

(A) To suggest that the evolution of play will continue in unknown ways in the future
(B) To suggest the futility of people's attempts at predicting the future
(C) To suggest that humans' preference for types of play is predictable
(D) To illustrate that the distinction between play and non-play will get more obscure in the future

03 Which of the sentences below best expresses the essential information in the highlighted sentence in the passage? Incorrect choices change the meaning in important ways or leave out essential information.

(A) After the similarity was discovered between humans and monkeys, sociologists believed that Symons functional approach could be applied to humans.
(B) Scientists agreed that the functional approach could also be applied to humans even though Symons produced the definition for monkeys.
(C) Because his peers thought that the functional approach for monkeys was exceptional, Symons was encouraged to create a definition for humans as well.
(D) Even though Symons definition would be inadequate to be applied to humans, other scholars believed that it worked just as well for monkeys.

04 What is the main problem with the functional approach according to paragraph 3?

(A) It will wrongly categorize many acts because it does not consider the conditions under which the action was performed.
(B) Its definition of playful behavior is at odds with that of the structural approach.
(C) It does not take into account that sometimes play occurs without laughter.
(D) It disregards the fact that individuals of different ages have varying views on what they consider to be playful.

05 According to paragraph 3, all of the following are identified as playful behavior by the structural approach EXCEPT:

(A) Laughing while running with friends towards a tree on a hill
(B) Climbing up the slippery slope and then walking down the stairs of a slide
(C) Kicking and splashing large amounts of water in a shallow pool
(D) Punching and pushing other children to take their toys

Paragraph 3 is marked with an arrow [→].

and swinging on the metal labyrinth, the ultimate goal of these activities is not known, and neither is the actions' ability to supply the child with food, clothing, or shelter. Further, it is unclear whether time spent on the playground fulfills the child's education, health, or other basic needs at all, and it is, thus, considered playful behavior under this approach.

3 → The functional approach, however, does not account for the many non-playful actions without immediately obvious purposes, or for playful behavior that seems to serve a purpose, such as running. While running is often a playful behavior, if a person was running towards shelter to hide from the rain, it would have a clear purpose, and therefore not qualify as functionalistic play. In cases such as this, the structural approach can be used. The structural approach identifies specific behaviors that are associated with play or with the playful execution of actions. When studying an action using this approach, one begins by identifying any characteristics that often only occur during playtime, like laughter or playful squabbling, such as a push or a light punch. Secondly, the structural approach looks for repeated, fragmented, exaggerated, and or re-ordered actions. For example, climbing stairs has a clear end and goal, but if the child repeats it by quickly climbing up and down the stairs, fragments the climb by climbing up only half-way, exaggerates it by jumping two stairs at a time, or re-orders it by climbing them backwards, then under the structural approach the child is considered to be performing playful behavior.

4 When studying play, it became evident that the two approaches were not mutually exclusive, but that the factors that they used to identify behavior were dissimilar. Thus, in 1980, Krasnor and Pepler suggested a third method, called the criterion approach. It combined ideas from the other approaches into four criteria for identifying playful behavior. The first criterion, positive effect, refers to the enjoyment that comes from doing playful behavior.

06 By stating that the approaches are not mutually exclusive, the author means that

(A) Some actions covered by one approach might also be covered by the other.
(B) If one theory is true, then the other must be false.
(C) Childrens actions are covered by one or two of the approaches.
(D) The two approaches are similar in the way they classify behavior.

07 The word intrinsic in passage is closest in meaning to

(A) intriguing
(B) intricate
(C) innate
(D) integral

08 What can be inferred from paragraph 4 about the methods of identifying playful behavior?

(A) The structural approach is the method that the majority of sociologists agree is most reliable.
(B) Krasnor and Pepler were successful in making an absolute definition of playful behavior by establishing the criterion approach.
(C) The criterion approach is liable to misclassify many non-play activities as play.
(D) If an act is classified as play by one or more of the criteria, then one must consider the act as playful.

The second, non-literality, is the imaginative aspect of playing, which encompasses acts such as pretending and placing oneself in fictitious perspectives for the purpose of play. The third, intrinsic motivation, means that the behavior is done of one's own accord and not due to social pressure. Finally, flexibility covers the characteristics described by the structural approach. [■] While meeting one criterion is sufficient to define a behavior as being playful, when the behavior meets more than one criteria, one may be more certain that the behavior is playful. [■] Confusing as it may be, one must understand that the criterion approach was not developed to create a one-sentence definition for play, as many behaviors that are undoubtedly non-playful will fall within one or more of the criterion. [■] So, while the criterion approach may not be used to definitively distinguish between activities that are play and those that are not, it plays a significant role in helping sociologists understand how humans recognize play. [■]

09 Look at the four squares [■] that indicate where the following sentence could be added to the passage.

Instead, the approach defines which factors an everyday observer uses as a basis for determining if an action is playful.

Where would the sentence best fit?

Click on a square [■] to add the sentence to the passage.

10 Directions: An introductory sentence for a brief summary of the passage is provided below. Complete the summary by selecting the THREE answer choices that express the most important ideas in the passage. Some sentences do not belong in the summary because they express ideas that are not presented in the passage or are minor ideas in the passage. **This question is worth 2 points.**

Drag your answer choices to the spaces where they belong. To remove an answer choice, click on it. To review the passage, click on **View Text**.

Studies of playful behavior have yielded different approaches to understand its characteristics.

-
-
-

Answer Choices

(A) The criterion approach helps explain how playful behavior is detected, but it is still incomplete in terms of defining play itself.

(B) Even after several promising attempts throughout history, sociologists agreed that an exact definition for playful behavior is unachievable.

(C) The functional approach, established by Donald Symons, proposes that all activities without apparent reason or obvious end should be considered playful.

(D) The criterion approach borrows ideas used in the structural approach and improves it to directly oppose the functional approach.

(E) An activity can be scanned for specific characteristics which the structural approach lists to determine the nature of the activity.

(F) A child using the equipment found on a playground exemplifies playful behavior described by the functional approach.

Sentinel Behavior in Meerkats

1 → Meerkats are small, mongoose-like mammals that live in the Kalahari Desert of Southern Africa. Being primarily insectivores, they feed on beetles and scorpions buried underground, which they locate using their strong sense of smell. Unfortunately, when the meerkat lowers its head to search out prey under grasses, it limits its own range of sight by a significant amount. As a result they are extremely vulnerable to airborne predators such as hawks and owls. To ensure that they can reach the safety of their bolt-holes before being snatched up by birds, meerkats forage in packs and partake in what is known as sentinel behavior. As the term suggests, one meerkat in the group acts as a sentinel and does not look for food like the rest, but rather stands upright on its hind legs to gain a wider field of view with which it scans the surrounding area for possible predators and other threats to the community. When it senses danger approaching, the sentinel barks loudly to warn the others of the danger. Many scientists questioned this phenomenon because the revealing stance and loud vocalization were thought to expose the meerkat to an increased risk of predation.

2 → The motivations behind this behavior have been attributed to kin selection, the evolutionary strategy that favors the reproductive success of an organism's relatives over one's own survival. In Belding's ground squirrels, individuals sound an alarm at the approach of a predator, warning its nearby relatives and thereby benefitting the population. This explanation gained credibility because research revealed that, like Belding's squirrels, meerkat communities are composed mostly of family members. In a typical community of meerkats, about 70 percent of its members are related to the dominant female. In their authoritarian societies, the alpha female rarely tolerates offspring from anyone other than herself. Therefore, if the sentinel is able to protect one of its

---

11 In paragraph 1, why does the author mention that they feed on beetles and scorpions buried underground?

(A) To explain the reason for their vulnerability against predators
(B) To show how they survive in a hazardous and arid environment
(C) To provide an example of a type of prey available in Southern Africa
(D) To point out an adaptation that has emerged as a response to airborne predation

12 Select the TWO answer choices According to paragraph 1, what are the methods utilized by meerkats to avoid predation? **To receive credit, you must select TWO answers.**

(A) They utilize bolt-holes to hide from predators.
(B) They stay under the grass to hide from birds.
(C) They bark loudly to scare away the oncoming predator.
(D) They form groups when hunting for prey.

paragraph 1 is marked with an arrow [→].

13 Which of the sentences below best expresses the essential information in the highlighted sentence in the passage? Incorrect choices change the meaning in important ways or leave out essential information.

(A) A sentineling meerkat stands upright to gain a panoramic view of its environment, so it can forage for prey more easily and anticipate predators and other threats more accurately.
(B) A meerkat scans the surrounding area more keenly in order to spot danger, by getting up on its back legs and acting as a sentinel, rather than looking for food with the rest of the group.
(C) Because of the dangers of predators, a meerkat stands on its back legs, which allows it a better view of the surrounding area, so it can forage faster while the rest do not.
(D) When a meerkat has finished foraging for food, it begins to act as the sentinel to protect its community, getting up on its hind legs and scanning the area for predators.

14 According to paragraph 1, why was sentinel behavior thought to be disadvantageous?

(A) It warns the predator of where the meerkat group is.
(B) It allows the meerkat to sense danger and warn the group.
(C) It helps the predators locate the sentinel meerkat.
(D) It encourages the predator to prey on meerkats over other species.

15 According to paragraph 2, all of the following statements are true of a meerkat community EXCEPT:

(A) The relatives of a single meerkat comprises the majority of the community.
(B) It is usually headed by one individual.
(C) About a quarter of nieces and nephews remain in the community until death.
(D) Meerkats of a community benefit from one another.

16 The word substantiated in the passage is closest in meaning to

(A) argued
(B) disproved
(C) authorized
(D) confirmed

siblings, it ensures passing on 50 percent of its own genes, or 25 percent for saving a niece or nephew. This follows the gene selection theory, postulating that individuals are genetically programmed to proliferate their DNA. In addition, if the sentinel allows other group members to spend less time scanning and more time foraging, they will be able to catch more prey, which will also increase the survivability of the group.

3 A variant theory was that in order to protect their kin, meerkats demonstrated reciprocal altruism, an act that benefits another at the expense of one's own interest. If the receiver's benefit outweighs the cost of the altruist, and if the receiver is expected to also become the altruist, then evolutionarily the entire group profits from the behavior. This can be seen in various animals such as fish and birds, as well as in close relatives of the meerkat, the banded mongoose. Their pups cooperate in creating annoying chirps to beg for food from their chaperones, which are assigned to individual pups. When one chaperone was removed from the group, the corresponding pup would stop crying. This in turn caused the rest of the pups to increase the volume of their crying, which induces the adults to bring more food, benefitting the quiet pup. Scientists tested for two conditions that had been laid out by the developed, mature definition of reciprocal altruism to determine if this was what the meerkats were in fact doing: a systematic method of deciding individuals' duty as sentinels, and a unified punishment for those who abandon their duties as a sentinel. But observations substantiated that there was neither a particular order nor any sort of punishment. Moreover, the dedication and the length of time that a meerkat displayed sentinel behavior were consistent regardless of the number of non-relatives in the group.

4 → Later scientists questioned the theory, proposing that sentinel behavior was actually a selfish anti-predator behavior. The proposition was that, contrary to popular belief, standing guard would increase the

17 What is the main purpose of paragraph 3?

(A) To give examples of studies conducted in an attempt to support the hypothesis mentioned in the previous paragraph
(B) To introduce a theory that is related to the one mentioned in the previous paragraph, which is then challenged in the next paragraph
(C) To point out evidence for the proposition that is described in the following paragraph
(D) To provide an explanation of how a behavior mentioned in the previous paragraph is carried out

18 According to paragraph 4, why were lone meerkats observed?

(A) To demonstrate that they were just as likely to flee from predators as meerkats in communities
(B) To confirm that sentinel behavior was performed for the protection of the meerkat's own interest
(C) To study sentinel behavior more closely than could be done with a large group of meerkats
(D) To prove that they have more time to spend foraging compared to meerkats in a group

paragraph 4 is marked with an arrow [→].

sentinel's own chances for survival. To find evidence for this claim, a team of scientists set out to observe sentinel behavior in lone meerkats. They confirmed that solitary meerkats first focused on foraging, then returned to the sentinel stance once their hunger was satiated. [■] This strengthened the anti-predator hypothesis. [■] The next question to answer was whether sentineling meerkats had better chances of survival than those who were not standing guard when attacked by a predator. [■] Of a total of 2,000 hours of observation, not a single meerkat that was standing guard at the moment of attack was caught because they chose positions that were safer when sentineling than foraging. [■] The conclusion was that meerkats stand guard to protect themselves from predators, but they forage in groups because then they can invest more time hunting for food and put trust in the sentinels to warn them of any signs of danger.

19 Look at the four squares [■] that indicate where the following sentence could be added to the passage.

Further, they never wandered more than five meters away from at least one of their group's bolt-holes.

Where would the sentence best fit?

Click on a square [■] to add the sentence to the passage.

20 Directions: An introductory sentence for a brief summary of the passage is provided below. Complete the summary by selecting the THREE answer choices that express the most important ideas in the passage. Some sentences do not belong in the summary because they express ideas that are not presented in the passage or are minor ideas in the passage. **This question is worth 2 points.**

Drag your answer choices to the spaces where they belong. To remove an answer choice, click on it. To review the passage, click on **View Text.**

Meerkats are known to exhibit sentinel behavior to increase their community's chance of escape from predators.

-
-
-

Answer Choices

(A) Sentinelling is thought to be the result of evolution, which selected the meerkat behavior that allowed improved proliferation of their DNA.

(B) Meerkats are thought to be the only animal to partake in actions that put the interests of their relatives ahead of its own, like the Belding's ground squirrels.

(C) Scientists deduced that, despite being a close relative of the meerkats, the banded mongoose's sentinel behavior could not be explained by reciprocal altruism.

(D) Research on the studies of meerkat behavior demonstrated their unselfish devotion to the welfare of others.

(E) Backed up by research results, proponents of the selfish anti-predator theory asserted that meerkats were acting as sentinels on their own behalf.

(F) During the 2,000-hour observation, scientists could not figure why not a single meerkat that was standing guard at the moment of attack was caught.

You have seen all of the questions in this part of the Reading section. You have time left to review. As long as there is time remaining, you can check your work.

Click on **Return** to go back to the previous question.
Click on **Review** to see the review screen for this section.
Click on **Continue** to go on.
Once you leave this part of the Reading section, you **WILL NOT** be able to return to it.

이제 Reading Section이 끝났습니다.
Countinue 버튼을 누르면 다시 문제를 검토할 수없으므로 유의하세요.

시험보고 난 후 ... 체크 리스트 및 스터디 디렉션 — USHER iBT TOEFL FINAL TEST READING

1. 내가 불안했던 문제만 재빨리 다시 보고, 불안하게 만든, 즉, 경쟁 초이스를 찾아서 왜 내가 헷갈려 했는지를 파악할 수 있는 메모를 해두시기 바랍니다. 시간이 지나거나, 다른 학생들과 스터디를 하면서는, 자신이 왜 낚였는지 이유조차 기억나지 않아 본인의 실수 패턴파악이 힘들기 때문입니다.

2. 답지를 확인하지 않고 스터디를 하시기 바랍니다. (그래서, 답지를 문제지 뒤에 붙이지 않고, 본 설명만을 붙여두었습니다.) 답지를 확인하지 않고 하는 이유는 답을 아는 순간, 답에 끼워맞춰 설명하려 하고, 이런 태도는 본인 실력 향상에 도움이 되지 않기 때문입니다. 스터디 팀원들간에 대략적인 답을 맞춰보면, 대부분 답안의 윤곽이 나옵니다. 이럴 경우, 이견이 있는 문제만 집중적으로 다루고, 나머지는 개인별로 처리하시기 바랍니다.

3. 문제를 끝까지 다 풀었나요? 네 □ / 아니오 □

   다 못 풀었다면, 전체 20 문제 중 푼 문제는? _____ / 20

   시간 모자란 것에 대해서는 크게 신경 쓰지 않아도 됩니다. 무엇보다 중요한 것은 정확도 입니다. 우선은 푼 문제를 맞출 확률을 높이고, 그 다음 시간을 걱정해도 늦지 않습니다.

4. 어려웠다고 느껴지는 지문은? 과학 □ / 예술 □ / 인문 □ / 인물 □ / 사회 □

   과학지문이 현격히 다른 분야보다 많지만, 그래도, 공부하다 보면 자신만 어려워하는 분야는 모두 각각입니다. 그러므로, 혹시 배경지식 부분에서 필요한 것이 있다면, usherin.usher.co.kr 에 방문하셔서, 공부가 안될 때, 배경지식 부분을 쉬엄쉬엄 들어서 봐 두시길 바랍니다. 쉬엄쉬엄입니다. 누가 뭐래도 실력있는 사람은 배경지식이 큰 영향을 끼치지는 않습니다.

5. (채점 후) 문제 풀 때 어렵다고 느낀 지문이 틀리는 개수와 쉬웠다고 느껴졌던 지문의 틀린 개수차이가 있나요? 예 □ / 아니오 □

   어느 순간 깨닫게 됩니다. 내가 잘 아는 내용이 나와서 자신 있게 푸나, 내가 모르는 지문이 나와서 겁먹고 푸나, 틀린 개수가 큰 차이가 나지 않는 것을…. 혹시 그걸 못 느끼신다면, 더욱더 열심히 하시기 바랍니다. ^^

6. 틀린 문제의 번호를 다음의 문제 유형 분석표와 비교해서 파악해 두시기 바랍니다.

   문제 유형을 파악해서 주의하는 것은, 누가 뭐래도 실력이 기본은 받쳐 줄 때 얘기입니다. 문제 푸는 스킬이나, 기타 문제 유형파악 등은 기본적으로 본문 내용을 이해하고, 해석이 웬만큼 될 때 얘기입니다. 만약, 너무 힘들다면 너무 스트레스 받지 말고, 그냥 '아~ 그렇구나' 정도로 넘기셔도 됩니다. 단, 본문 이해는 절대 양보해서는 안됩니다.

문제 유형 분석표 — 31page 내용 중, 아래 표시되어 있는 문제 유형은 파악하기 쉬우나 나머지 문제들의 문제 유형 파악은 어려워 하는 경향이 있어 비워두었습니다. 문제유형 정답은 431page를 참조하세요.

TEST 9-1

01
02
03 Highlight
04
05
06
07 Vocabulary
08
09 Insertion
10 Summary

TEST 9-2

11
12
13 Highlight
14
15
16 Vocabulary
17
18
19 Insertion
20 Summary

이름: Test 9

1

TEST번호	시험날짜	실제토플/모의토플 총점	RC	틀린갯수/전체갯수	LC	틀린갯수/전체갯수	SP	WR
tpo				/		/		
tpo				/		/		
tpo				/		/		
tpo				/		/		
tpo				/		/		
tpo				/		/		

2

RC

첫 번째 지문 중 틀린 개수

Topic 1 제목:

문제유형	틀린갯수/전체갯수	실력으로 틀린 문제	실수로 틀린 문제
Voca 문제	/		
Fact 문제	/		
Reference 문제	/		
Purpose 문제	/		
Infer 문제	/		
Highlight 문제	/		
Insertion 문제	/		
Summary 문제	/		

문제유형 구분이 어려울 경우 물어보세요

RC

첫 번째 지문 중 틀린 개수

Topic 1 제목:

문제유형	틀린갯수/전체갯수	실력으로 틀린 문제	실수로 틀린 문제
Voca 문제	/		
Fact 문제	/		
Reference 문제	/		
Purpose 문제	/		
Infer 문제	/		
Highlight 문제	/		
Insertion 문제	/		
Summary 문제	/		

경향주어를 풀은 통라오 문제유형 유형 틀린리

3

오늘의 결론

내가 주의해야할 실수 패턴	내가 늘려야할 실력	내가 하고싶은 말(결심)

※순서대로 따라서 적어주세요.

|문제구별 *tip*

Fact와 Purpose의 가장 큰 구별방법

- **Fact** 문제: Except, true, Not true
- **Purpose** 문제: why mention, in order to, what is the purpose

why는 Fact문제 일수도 있습니다.

Fact와 Purpose의 가장 큰 구별방법

usherin.usher.co.kr

USHER

iBT TOEFL
FINAL TEST READING
구문단어

USHER VOCABULARY

Method of Measuring Bats' Age
TEST 1-1 지문의 단어 중 토플 필수 단어를 선별하여 정리하였습니다.

01	**decade** [dékeid]	n. 10년
02	**compile** [kəmpáil]	v. 엮다, ~을 편집하다
03	**fortuitous** [fɔ:rtjú:ətəs]	a. 우연한
04	**recapture** [rikæ'ptʃər]	v. 다시 붙잡다
05	**metabolic rate** [mètəbɑ́lik reit]	n. 신진대사율
06	**variation** [vɛəriéiʃən]	n. 변화
07	**lifespans** [laifspæn]	n. 수명
08	**biology** [baiɑ́lədʒi]	n. 생물학
09	**chronological** [kra,nəla'dʒikəl]	a. 연대순의
10	**expectancy** [ikspéktənsi]	n. 기대
11	**morphology** [mɔ:rfɑ́lədʒi]	n. 형태학
12	**coincide** [kòuinsáid]	v. 동시에 일어나다
13	**permanently** [pə́:rmənəntli]	ad. 영구히
14	**drawback** [drɔ'bæ,k]	n. 결점
15	**correlate** [kɔ́:rəlèit]	v. ~와 연관시키다
16	**empirical** [impírikəl]	a. 실증적인
17	**invasiveness**	n. 세균이 체내에 침입
18	**caliper** [kǽləpər]	n. 자
19	**specimen** [spésəmən]	n. 견본
20	**cartilaginous** [kɑ̀:rtəlǽdʒənəs]	a. 연골로 된
21	**transilluminate** [trænsilú:məneit]	v. 강한 광선을 투과시키다
22	**unaided** [ʌnéidid]	a. 도움을 받지 않는, 나만의
23	**permanent** [pə́:rmənənt]	a. 영구적인
24	**lifetime** [laiftaim]	n. 일생
25	**mastication** [mæ̀stəkéiʃən]	n. 저작
26	**wean** [wi:n]	v. 젖을 떼다
27	**wideranging** [wáidréindʒiŋ]	a. 폭넓은
28	**incremental** [ínkrəmentəl]	a. 증대하는
29	**robustness** [roubʌstnis]	n. 억셈
30	**nonannual** [nan-ǽnjuəl]	n. 비 일년생
31	**notwithstanding** [nɑ̀twiðstǽndiŋ]	prep. ~에도 불구하고
32	**suffice** [səfáis]	v. 충분하다

구문정리

Method of Measuring Bats' Age

TEST 1-1

→ 정답

01 **data on** ~에 대한 정보 (= about과 비슷하나 전문적)
02 **at birth** 태어났을 때
03 **on average** 평균적으로
04 **three times longer** 3배 더 길게 (배수표현 위치 주의)
05 **be likely that** that절 할 것 같다
06 **it is important to do** to do 하는 것은 중요하다
07 **on the other hand** 반면에
08 **be based on** ~에 기반을 두다
09 **changes in** ~에서의 변화들
10 **coincide with** ~와 일치하다
11 **so that** 그래서, ~하기 위해서
12 **not to mention that** that절은 말할 것도 없이
13 **go through** (과정을) 겪다
14 **shortly after** 곧, 직후에
15 **that of** 단어 반복 피하기 (대명사 사용) ~의 그것
16 **be used to do** to do 하기 위해 사용되다
17 **distinguish A from B** B로부터 A를 구별 짓다
18 **with an accuracy** 정확도를 가지고
19 **need O to do** O가 to do하는 것을 필요로 하다
20 **making this method ideal** A를 B로 만들다 (make O + O.C)
21 **be necessary to do** to do 하기 위해 필수이다
22 **in a form** ~의 형태로
23 **distinguish between** ~사이를 구별 짓다
24 **allow O to do** O가 to do 하는 것을 허락하다
25 **pass through** ~를 통과하다

26 **continue to do** to do 하는 것을 계속하다
27 **no longer** 더 이상 ~하지 않다
28 **visible to** ~에 보이는
29 **no more than** 오직 (only)
30 **ideal for** ~에 이상적인
31 **a set of** 일련의
32 **in place** 적절한, 제자리에 있는
33 **cease to do** to do 하는 것을 멈추다
34 **wear down** 마모시키다
35 **due to** ~때문에
36 **differences in** ~에서의 차이점
37 **variation in** ~에서의 변화
38 **be critical for** ~에 중요하다
39 **for the use of** ~을 위하여, ~용으로
40 **as are** ~와 같다
41 **depend on** ~에 의존하다
42 **aside from** ~외에, ~을 제외하고
43 **associated with** ~과 관련된
44 **need to do** to do 할 필요 (need가 명사로 쓰임)
45 **use O to do** O를 to do 하는 데 사용하다
46 **be correlated with** ~과 연관되다
47 **notwithstanding** 그럼에도 불구하고
48 **useful for** ~에 유용한
49 **a variety of** 다양한

※ 다시 한 번 암기 후 → 문제집 가장 뒷부분 열 번 읽기로!

USHER VOCABULARY

Tracing Language Diversification

TEST 1-2 지문의 단어 중 토플 필수 단어를 선별하여 정리하였습니다.

01	**alternation** [ɔ:ltərnéiʃən, æl-]	n. 교체
02	**subfamily** [sʌbfǽməli]	n. 아과
03	**consonant** [kánsənənt]	n. 자음
04	**hardening** [hɑ́:rdniŋ]	n. 경화
05	**backward** [bǽkwərd]	a. 뒤쪽으로의, 뒤의
06	**reconstruction** [ri,kənstrə'kʃən]	n. 복원
07	**linguistic** [liŋgwístik]	a. 언어학의
08	**scholar** [skάlər]	n. 학자
09	**preceding** [prisí:diŋ]	a. 이전의
10	**diversification** [divə̀:rsəfikéiʃən]	n. 다양성
11	**unrivaled** [ənrai'vəld]	a. 비할 데 없는
12	**contribution** [kὰntrəbjú:ʃən]	n. 기부금
13	**promote** [prəmóut]	v. 촉진하다
14	**appreciation** [əprì:ʃiéiʃən]	n. 감탄
15	**grammatical** [grəmǽtikəl]	a. 문법의
16	**corresponding** [kɔ̀:rəspándiŋ]	a. ~에 해당하는
17	**resemblance** [rizémbləns]	n. 유사함, 닮음
18	**antiquity** [æntíkwəti]	n. 고대, 유물
19	**copious** [kóupiəs]	a. 엄청난
20	**exquisitely** [ikskwízitli]	ad. 절묘하게
21	**bearing** [béəriŋ]	n. 영향
22	**affinity** [əfínəti]	n. 공통점
23	**philologer** [filάlədʒi]	n. 문헌학자
24	**contributor** [kəntríbjutər]	n. 공헌자
25	**scientifically** [sàiəntífikli]	ad. 과학적으로
26	**presume** [prizú:m]	v. 추정하다
27	**linguistics** [liŋgwístiks]	n. 언어학
28	**researcher** [risə́:rtʃər]	n. 연구원
29	**wordwise**	말에 관하여
30	**evolutionary** [èvəlú:ʃənèri]	a. 진화의, 점진적인
31	**undergo** [ə,ndərgou']	v. 겪다
32	**predictable** [pridíktəbl]	a. 예측할 수 있는
33	**existence** [igzístəns]	n. 존재
34	**ancestral** [ænséstrəl]	a. 조상의
35	**hypothesis** [haipάθəsis]	n. 가설
36	**reconstruct** [ri,kənstrə'kt]	v. ~을 재건하다
37	**divergence** [divə́:rdʒəns]	n. 분기, 일탈
38	**fragment** [frǽgmənt]	n. 조각, 파편
39	**dialect** [dáiəlèkt]	n. 방언
40	**discrete** [diskrí:t]	a. 별개의
41	**geographical** [dʒì:əgrǽfikəl]	a. 지리학적인
42	**colonial era** [kəlóuniəl érə]	n. 식민지 시대
43	**daunting** [dɔ́:ntiŋ]	a. 벅찬, 힘든
44	**static** [stǽtik]	a. 고정된
45	**relocation** [rilou'kei'ʃən]	n. 이주
46	**consistent** [kənsístənt]	a. 한결같은
47	**spatial** [spéiʃəl]	a. 공간의
48	**interaction** [i,ntəræ'kʃən]	n. 상호작용
49	**convergence** [kənvə́:rdʒəns]	n. 집중성
50	**unreliable** [ə,nrilai'əbəl]	a. 믿을 수 없는

구문정리
본문 중 중요 구문 정리한 내용입니다. 우선 암기하고 많이 읽으시길 바랍니다.

TEST 1-2

Tracing Language Diversification

→ 정답

01 **way to do** to do 하는 방법

02 **look for** ~를 찾다

03 **over time** 시간이 지나면서

04 **used to do** to do 하기 위해 사용된

05 **be called** ~라 불리다 (call + O + O.C)

06 **infer A from B** A를 B로부터 추론하다

07 **to go further** 진주어(말하는 내용에 있어) - 나아가다

08 **researcher into** ~에 대한(관련된) 조사관

09 **make contributions to** ~에 공헌을 하다

10 **arrive in** ~에 도착하다

11 **in order to do** to do 하기 위해

12 **in a form** ~의 형태로

13 **corresponding to** ~에 상응하는

14 **write of** ~에 관해 쓰다 (특정주제에 관해)

15 **resemblance to** ~에 대한 유사점

16 **lead O to do** O를 to do하도록 이끌다

17 **not only A but (also) B** A뿐만 아니라 B도

18 **be related to** ~와 관련되다

19 **whatever be** 무엇이든지간에

20 **be of** ~에 속하다

21 **bear affinity to A in B** A와 B라는 점에서 공통점을 가지다. (= have similarity to A in B)

22 **by accident** 우연히

23 **so 원인 that 결과** so해서 (원인) that절 (결과) 하다

24 **believe O to do** O가 to do 하는 것을 믿다

25 **no longer** 더 이상 ~ 않다

26 **seek to do** to do 하는 것을 추구하다

27 **way (for 의미상 주어) to do** to do 하는 방법 (for 의미상 주어)

28 **figure out** 알아내다

29 **entice O to do** O가 to do 하도록 유혹하다

30 **ask O to do** O가 to do 하도록 요청하다

31 **not A but B** A가 아니라 B이다

32 **happen to do** 우연히 to do 하게 되다

33 **end up with** 결국 ~하게 되다

34 **point to** ~을 나타내다

35 **take place** 발생하다

36 **come up with** ~을 생각해내다

37 **transform into** ~으로 변형되다

38 **need to be done** be done 될 필요가 있다

39 **fragment into** ~으로 나누어지다

40 **start to do** to do 하기 시작하다

※ 다시 한 번 암기 후 → 문제집 가장 뒷부분 열 번 읽기로!

USHER VOCABULARY

Earth's Atmosphere
TEST 2-1 지문의 단어 중 토플 필수 단어를 선별하여 정리하였습니다.

01	**nitrogen** [náitrədʒən]	n. 질소
02	**hydrogen** [háidrədʒən]	n. 수소
03	**helium** [híːliəm]	n. 헬륨
04	**odd** [ad]	a. 이상한
05	**currently** [kə́ːrəntli]	ad. 지금
06	**distinguishable** [distíŋgwiʃəbl]	a. 구별할 수 있는
07	**oxygen** [ɑ́ksidʒen]	n. 산소
08	**distinction** [distíŋkʃən]	n. 차이
09	**ultimately** [ʌ́ltəmətli]	ad. 궁극적으로
10	**classified** [klǽsəfàid]	a. 정보가 기밀의
11	**primordial** [praimɔ́ːrdiəl]	a. 태고의
12	**secondary** [sékəndèri]	a. 이차적인
13	**initially** [iníʃəli]	ad. 처음에
14	**gradually** [grǽdʒuəli]	ad. 서서히
15	**thermal** [θə́ːrməl]	a. 열의
16	**prescribe** [priskráib]	v. 규정하다
17	**kinetic** [kinétik]	a. 운동의
18	**molecule** [mɑ́ləkjùːl]	n. 분자
19	**conclude** [kənklúːd]	v. 결론을 내다
20	**possess** [pəzés]	v. 소유하다
21	**gravitational** [grævətéiʃənl]	a. 중력의
22	**non-negligible** [nan-néglidʒəbl]	a. 무시할 수 없는
23	**consititue** [kɑ́nstətjùːt]	v. ~을 구성하다
24	**eruption** [irʌ́pʃən]	n. 폭발
25	**spew** [spjuː]	v. 뿜어져 나오다
26	**form** [fɔːrm]	v. 형성하다
27	**component** [kəmpóunənt]	n. 구성 요소
28	**volatile** [vɑ́lətil]	a. 휘발성의
29	**unreactive**	n. 화학 반응을 일으키지 않는
30	**presence** [prézns]	n. 존재
31	**radiation** [rèidiéiʃən]	n. 방사선
32	**contrast** [kəntrǽst]	n. 대조
33	**terrestrial** [təréstriəl]	a. 지구의
34	**atmospheric** [ætməsférik]	a. 대기의
35	**single-celled**	a. 단세포의
36	**algae** [ǽldʒiː]	n. 해조류
37	**emerge** [imə́ːrdʒ]	v. 떠오르다
38	**gaseous** [gǽsiəs]	a. 기체의
39	**condensed** [kəndénst]	a. 응축된
40	**slightly** [sláitli]	ad. 약간
41	**biomass** [báioumæs]	n. 생물량
42	**combustible** [kəmbʌ́stəbl]	a. 가연성인
43	**ecosystem** [iˈkousiˌstəm]	n. 생태계
44	**planetary** [plǽnətèri]	a. 행성의
45	**concentration** [kɑ̀nsəntréiʃən]	n. 정신 집중
46	**adequate** [ǽdikwət]	a. 충분한
47	**tectonic** [tektɑ́nik]	a. 구조상의
48	**posit** [pɑ́zit]	v. 가정하다
49	**magma** [mǽgmə]	n. 마그마
50	**super-heated**	a. 과열된
51	**oxygenate** [ɑ́ksidʒənèit]	v. 산소를 공급하다
52	**ozone** [óuzoun]	n. 오존
53	**magnetic** [mægnétik]	a. 자석 같은

구문정리
본문 중 중요 구문 정리한 내용입니다. 우선 암기하고 많이 읽으시길 바랍니다.

Earth's Atmosphere

TEST 2-1

→ 정답

01 **consist of** ~으로 구성되다 (=be composed of)
02 **be known to do** to do 하는 것으로 알려져 있다
03 **the seventh most abundant** 7번째로 가장 풍부한
04 **beg the question** 질문을 하게 만든다
05 **no longer** 더 이상 ~않다
06 **distinguishable from** ~으로부터 구별되는
07 **composed of** ~으로 구성된
08 **a series of** 일련의
09 **classify A into B** A를 B로 분류하다
10 **start to do** to do 하기 시작하다
11 **based on** ~에 기반을 둔
12 **dependent on** ~에 의존적인
13 **the ~er, the ~er** ~할수록, ~하다
14 **at a temperature** ~의 온도에서
15 **result in** ~을 초래하다
16 **leading to** ~을 초래하는
17 **that of** 명사 반복 피하기 대명사 that
18 **allow O to do** O로 하여금 to do 하는 것을 허락하다
19 **hold on to** ~를 고수하다, 지키다
20 **be attached to** ~에 부착되다
21 **in this way** 이런 방법에서
22 **be able to do** to do 할 수 있다
23 **at the edge of** ~의 가장자리에서
24 **escape from** ~으로부터 탈출하다
25 **begin v-ing** v~ing 하기 시작하다
26 **unreactive with** ~과 반응을 일으키지 않는
27 **in the presence of** ~가 있을 때
28 **in contrast to** ~과는 대조적으로
29 **bond with** ~과의 유대를 형성하다
30 **react with** ~과 반응하다
31 **A as well as B** B뿐만 아니라 A도
32 **exposed to** ~에 노출된
33 **over time** 시간이 지나면서
34 **to an extent** ~의 정도까지
35 **as a result of** ~의 결과로서
36 **to a level** ~의 수준까지
37 **appear to do** to do 하는 것처럼 보이다
38 **control over** ~에 대한 통제
39 **ratio of A to B** A와 B의 비율
40 **account for** ~을 설명하다
41 **come into contact with** ~과 접촉하게 되다
42 **be converted into** ~으로 전환되다
43 **be released into** ~으로 발산되다
44 **be shielded from** ~으로부터 보호되다
45 **lost to** ~로의 손실

※ 다시 한 번 암기 후 → 문제집 가장 뒷부분 열 번 읽기로!

USHER VOCABULARY

The Effects of Light on Flowering
TEST 2-2 지문의 단어 중 토플 필수 단어를 선별하여 정리하였습니다.

01	interaction [iˌntəræˈkʃən]	n. 상호작용
02	environmental [invàiərənméntl]	a. 환경의
03	diverse [divə́:rs]	a. 다양한
04	essential [isénʃəl]	a. 필수적인
05	bloom [blu:m]	v. 개화하다
06	sufficient [səfíʃənt]	a. 충분한
07	stem [stem]	n. 줄기
08	internode [íntərnòud]	n. 마디와 마디 사이
09	expose [èkspouzéi]	v. 드러내다
10	adequate [ǽdikwət]	a. 충분한
11	intricate [íntrikət]	a. 복잡한
12	delicate [délikət]	a. 섬세한
13	maximize [mǽksəmàiz]	v. 극대화하다
14	probability [prɑ̀bəbíləti]	n. 가능성
15	dispersed [dispə́:rs]	a. 분산된
16	fluctuate [flʌ́ktʃuèit]	v. 변동을 거듭하다
17	unexpected [ˌənikspeˈktid]	a. 예기치 않은
18	monsoon [mansú:n]	n. 우기
19	cue [kju:]	n. 신호
20	reliable [riláiəbl]	a. 믿을 수 있는
21	indicator [índikèitər]	n. 지표
22	unaltered [ənɔˈltərd]	a. 바뀌지 않는
23	terrestrial [təréstriəl]	a. 지구의
24	regardless of	prep. ~와 관계없이
25	traditional [trədíʃənl]	a. 전통의
26	botanist [bɑ́tənist]	n. 식물학자
27	pigment [ˈpɪgmənt]	n. 색소
28	uninterrupted [əˌnintərəˈptid]	a. 연속된, 중단되지 않은
29	biological [bàiəlɑ́dʒikəl]	a. 생물학의
30	organism [ɔ́:rgənìzm]	n. 유기체
31	including [inklú:diŋ]	prep. ~을 포함하여
32	poorly [púərli]	ad. 저조하게
33	cellular [séljulər]	a. 세포의
34	measure [méʒər]	v. 측정하다
35	mechanism [mékənìzm]	n. 기계장치
36	artificial [ɑ̀:rtəfíʃəl]	a. 인공의
37	perceive [pərsí:v]	v. 감지하다
38	overarching [ouˈvərˌrtʃiŋ]	a. 대단히 중요한, 전반에 걸친
39	intriguing [intrí:giŋ]	a. 아주 흥미로운
40	reveal [riví:l]	v. 드러내다
41	exposure [ikspóuʒər]	n. 노출
42	hormone [hɔ́:rmòun]	n. 호르몬
43	trigger [trígər]	v. 촉발하다, 시작하다

구문정리
본문 중 중요 구문 정리한 내용입니다. 우선 암기하고 많이 읽으시길 바랍니다.

The Effects of Light on Flowering

TEST **2-2**

→ 정답

01 **amongst (=among)** ~중에서

02 **play a role** 역할을 하다

03 **in ways** ~방법으로

04 **ability to do** to do하는 능력

05 **produce A to B** A를 B에 제공하다

06 **in the absence of** ~이 없을 때에

07 **called** ~라고 불리는

08 **exposed to** ~에 노출된

09 **suffer from** ~로 고통 받다

10 **use A to do** A를 to do 하는데 사용하다

11 **use A as B** A를 B로서 사용하다

12 **depend on** ~에 의지하다

13 **as soon as** ~하자마자, 곧

14 **regardless of** ~에 상관없이

15 **describe as** ~로써 묘사하다

16 **require A to do** A가 to do 하는 것을 요구하다

17 **compared to ~** ~와 비교해 보았을 때

18 **so far** 지금까지

19 **in order to** ~하기 위해서

20 **work as** ~로써 일하다

21 **bring about** 야기하다, 초래하다

22 **either A or B** A나 B 둘 중 하나

23 **shine on** ~을 비추다

24 **not A but B** A가 아니라 B

25 **react to** ~에 반응하다

26 **make A B** A를 B로 만들다

27 **sensitivity to** ~에 대한 민감한

28 **be subjected to** ~의 대상이다, ~을 받다

29 **send from A to B** A에서 B로 보내다

30 **refer to as** ~라고 언급되다

※ 다시 한 번 암기 후 → 문제집 가장 뒷부분 열 번 읽기로!

USHER VOCABULARY

Naturalistic Painting
TEST 3-1 지문의 단어 중 토플 필수 단어를 선별하여 정리하였습니다.

#	Word	Pronunciation	Meaning
01	**underpinning**	[ə'ndərpi,niŋ]	n. 지주
02	**millennia**		n.(pl) 수천 년
03	**artistic**	[a:rtístik]	a. 예술의
04	**movement**	[mú:vmənt]	n. 운동
05	**naturalism**	[nǽtʃərəlìzm]	a. 자연주의
06	**aspire**	[əspáiər]	v. ~을 열망하다
07	**depict**	[dipíkt]	v. ~을 묘사하다
08	**unadorned**	[ʌnədɔ́:rnd]	a. 아무런 꾸밈이 없는
09	**scenery**	[sí:nəri]	n. 배경
10	**realistically**	[rì:əlístikəli]	ad. 현실적으로
11	**meticulous**	[mətíkjuləs]	a. 꼼꼼한, 세심한
12	**strive**	[straiv]	v. 분투하다
13	**realistic**	[rì:əlístik]	a. 현실적인
14	**distinguishable**	[distíŋgwiʃəbl]	a. 구별할 수 있는
15	**spread**	[spred]	v. 퍼지다
16	**assessment**	[əsésmənt]	n. 평가
17	**competitive**	[kəmpétətiv]	a. 경쟁하는
18	**extraordinary**	[ikstrɔ́:rdənèri]	a. 보기드문
19	**stage**	[steidʒ]	n. 단계
20	**preserve**	[prizə́:rv]	v. 보존하다
21	**renown**	[rináun]	a. 유명한
22	**reveal**	[riví:l]	v. ~을 드러내다
23	**achievement**	[ətʃí:vmənt]	n. 업적
24	**confidently**	[kάnfədəntli]	ad. 자신있게
25	**confound**	[kanfáund]	v. ~을 당황하게 하다
26	**exclaim**	[ikskléim]	v. 소리치다
27	**insect**	[ínsekt]	n. 곤충
28	**symbolic**	[simbάlik]	a. 상징적인
29	**awaken**	[əwéikən]	v. 깨우다, 일깨우다
30	**naturalist**	[nǽtʃərəlist]	n. 동식물학자
31	**property**	[prάpərti]	n. 재산
32	**combination**	[kὰmbənéiʃən]	n. 결합
33	**insight**	[ínsàit]	n. 통찰력, 이해
34	**define**	[difáin]	v. ~을 정의하다
35	**embellish**	[imbéliʃ]	v. ~을 꾸미다
36	**intricate**	[íntrikət]	a. 복잡한
37	**duplication**	[djù:plikéiʃən]	n. 복제
38	**convince**	[kənvíns]	v. ~을 납득시키다
39	**argument**	[ά:rgjumənt]	n. 논쟁
40	**credible**	[krédəbl]	a. 믿을 수 있는
41	**assertion**	[əsə́:rʃən]	n. 주장
42	**deliberately**	[dilíbərətli]	ad. 의도적으로
43	**convey**	[kənvéi]	v. ~을 운반하다
44	**unintentionally**		ad. 고의 아니게
45	**subconsciously**		ad. 잠재 의식적으로
46	**inadvertently**	[inədvə́:rtntli]	ad. 무심코
47	**occasionally**	[əkéiʒənəli]	ad. 가끔
48	**criticize**	[krítəsàiz]	v. 비난하다

구문정리

본문 중 중요 구문 정리한 내용입니다. 우선 암기하고 많이 읽으시길 바랍니다.

Naturalistic Painting

TEST 3-1

→ 정답

01	**be considered (to be)** 간주되다(consider + O + O.C)
02	**have an influence on** ~에 영향을 가지다
03	**known as** ~로써 알려진
04	**aspire to do** to do하는 것을 열망하다
05	**as ~ as possible** 가능한 한 ~만큼
06	**in terms** ~한 면에서
07	**strive to do** to do 하려고 분투하다
08	**distinguishable from** ~로 부터 구별할 수 있는
09	**originate in** ~에서 기인하다
10	**tend to do** to do 하는 경향이 있다
11	**put an emphasis on** ~에 대해 강조하다
12	**means of** ~의 수단
13	**as a result** 결과적으로
14	**distinguish oneself as something** (something으로서) 유명인이 되다
15	**mistake A for B** A를 B라고 혼동하다
16	**so 형/부 that** ~해서 that절 하다
17	**be preserved as** ~로 보존되다
18	**aids for** ~의 보조자료
19	**come after** ~을 따라가다
20	**at the peak** ~정점에서
21	**enough to do** to do 하기에 충분한
22	**absorbed in** ~에 열중한
23	**ask O to do** O에게 to do 하도록 요청하다
24	**pull aside** (커튼 등을) 옆으로 걷다
25	**only to do** 결국 to do 했을 뿐이다 (놀라움, 실망)
26	**be confounded by** ~에 의해 혼동되다
27	**become known as** ~로써 알려지게 되다
28	**gaining even more fame and respect** 더많은 명성과 존경을 얻다
29	**with little regard for** ~에 대해 관련이 거의 없이
30	**served no purpose** 소용없다, 도움 되지 않다
31	**scores of** 수많은
32	**be awakened to** ~에 대해 깨우침을 받다(awaken A to B)
33	**at the same time** 동시에
34	**be robbed of** ~을 빼앗기다 (rob A of B)
35	**be left to do** to do 하게 남겨지다 (leave+O+to do)
36	**in a matter of (days / hours / months)** ~동안에
37	**be lauded for** for 때문에 칭송 받다
38	**lead O to do** O가 to do 하도록 이끌다
39	**be defined by** ~에 의해 정의되다
40	**lead to** 초래하다
41	**not only A but also B** A뿐만 아니라 B도
42	**add A to B** A를 B에 더하다
43	**according to** ~에 따르면
44	**on the other hand** 반면에
45	**regardless of** ~에 상관없이
46	**with all things considered** 모든 것을 고려했을 때
47	**despite the fact that** that 절이라는 사실에도 불구하고
48	**decreasing in** ~에서 감소하는
49	**play a major role** 중요한 역할을 하다
50	**continue to do** to do 하는 것을 계속하다

※ 다시 한 번 암기 후 → 문제집 가장 뒷부분 열 번 읽기로!

USHER VOCABULARY

Two Types of Evolutionary Theories
TEST 3-2 지문의 단어 중 토플 필수 단어를 선별하여 정리하였습니다.

01	**habitat** [hǽbitæt]	n. 서식지
02	**genetic** [dʒənétik]	a. 유전학의
03	**adaptation** [ædəptéiʃən]	n. 적응
04	**prevailing** [privéiliŋ]	a. 우세한
05	**exclusive** [iksklú:siv]	a. 독점적인
06	**gradualism** [grǽdʒuəlìzm]	n. 점진주의
07	**punctuate** [pʌ́ŋktʃuèit]	v. 간간이 끼어들다
08	**equilibrium** [ì:kwəlíbriəm]	n. 평형
09	**proponent** [prəpóunənt]	n. 지지자
10	**adopt** [ədɑ́pt]	v. 채택하다, 취하다
11	**deviation** [dì:viéiʃən]	n. 일탈
12	**variation** [vɛəriéiʃən]	n. 변화
13	**lineage** [láinidʒ]	n. 혈통
14	**splay** [splei]	v. 벌리다
15	**primeval** [praimí:vəl]	a. 태고의
16	**legged** [légidʒ, légd]	a. 다리가 있는
17	**graze** [greiz]	v. 풀을 뜯다
18	**grassy** [grǽsi]	a. 풀로 덮인
19	**outrun** [autrə́n]	v. 더 빨리 달리다
20	**hoofed** [huft, hu:ft]	a. 발굽이 있는
21	**paleontologist** [peiliəntɑ́lədʒist]	n. 고생물학자
22	**intermediary** [ìntərmí:dièri]	n. 중재자
23	**envisage** [invízidʒ]	v. 예상하다
24	**reproduce** [ri,prədu's]	v. 생식하다, 번식하다
25	**speciation** [spì:ʃiéiʃən]	n. 종 형성
26	**imperfection** [ìmpərfékʃən]	n. 불완전, 미비점
27	**progressive** [prəgrésiv]	a. 혁신적인
28	**supernatural** [su,pərnæ'tʃərəl]	a. 초자연적인
29	**creation** [kriéiʃən]	n. 창조
30	**privately** [práivitli]	ad. 은밀히
31	**parasite** [pǽrəsàit]	n. 기생 동물
32	**exclusively** [iksklú:sivli]	ad. 배타적으로
33	**sphere** [sfiər]	n. 구
34	**apparent** [əpǽrənt, əpéər-]	a. 분명한
35	**mutation** [mju:téiʃən]	n. 돌연변이
36	**offspring** [ɔ'fspri,ŋ]	n. 자손, 새끼
37	**consequently** [kɑ́nsəkwèntli]	ad. 그 결과
38	**demise** [dimáiz]	n. 죽음, 서거

Two Types of Evolutionary Theories

TEST 3-2

→ 정답

#	표현	뜻
01	**adjust to**	~에 적응하다
02	**those**	those (같은 명사 반복 피하기)
03	**pass on**	~에 넘겨주다
04	**change in**	~에서의 변화
05	**be common to**	~에 일반적이다
06	**no matter what**	무엇이든 간에 (=whatever)
07	**differ in**	~라는 점에서 다르다
08	**at speed**	~한 속도로
09	**one of the**	~중의 하나는
10	**in a manner**	~한 방식으로
11	**assume O to do**	O가 to do 하다고 추정하다
12	**deviation from**	~로부터의 이탈
13	**be likely to do**	to do 할 것 같다
14	**select against**	선택 받지 않다 (opp. = select for)
15	**over time**	시간이 지나면서
16	**piece together**	종합하다, 잇다
17	**in a way**	~한 면 (방법)에서
18	**be sure of**	~에 확신을 가지다
19	**put together**	모으다
20	**let alone**	~은 커녕
21	**split into**	~로 분열되다, 나누다
22	**ascribe A to B**	A를 B의 탓 (덕)으로 돌리다
23	**begin with**	~부터 시작하다
24	**in showers**	~떼로, 많이
25	**world over**	세계에 걸쳐
26	**whereby**	(그것에 의하여) ~하는
27	**suit A to B**	A를 B에 맞추다
28	**not just A, (but) also B**	A뿐 아니라 B도
29	**in succession**	계속하여, 연속하여
30	**typical of**	~의 전형적인
31	**on the other hand**	반면에
32	**pertain to**	~와 관련되다
33	**act on**	~에 작용하다
34	**lead to**	~를 초래하다
35	**adapt to**	~에 적응하다
36	**unable to do**	to do 할 수 없는

※ 다시 한 번 암기 후 → 문제집 가장 뒷부분 열 번 읽기로!

USHER VOCABULARY

Griffith and Transformation
TEST 4-1 지문의 단어 중 토플 필수 단어를 선별하여 정리하였습니다.

01	**reshape** [riʃei'p]	v. 재형성하다, ~의 모양을 고치다
02	**breakthrough** [brei'kθru,]	n. 돌파구
03	**geometry** [dʒiámətri]	n. 기하학
04	**organic** [ɔ:rgǽnik]	a. 유기적인
05	**professionally** [prəféʃənəli]	ad. 전문적으로
06	**institutionalize** [ìnstətjú:ʃənəlàizd]	v. 제도화 하다
07	**pivotal** [pívətl]	a. 중심이 되는
08	**precise** [prisáis]	a. 정확한
09	**overarching** [ou'vərɑ,rtʃiŋ]	a. 대단히 중요한
10	**clarify** [klǽrəfài]	v. 명확하게 하다
11	**pneumonia** [njumóunjə]	n. 폐렴
12	**infectious** [infékʃəs]	a. 전염되는
13	**lung** [lʌŋ]	n. 폐
14	**disorder** [disɔ́:rdər]	n. 병
15	**encapsulated** [inkǽpsjulèitid]	a. 캡슐에 넣어진
16	**virulent** [vírjulənt]	a. 악성의, 치명적인
17	**slippery** [slípəri]	a. 미끄러운
18	**coating** [kóutiŋ]	n. 칠[도금]
19	**alongside** [əlɔ'ŋsai'd]	prep. ~옆에, 나란히
20	**avirulent** [eivírjulənt]	a. 독성이 없는
21	**necropsy** [nékrapsi]	n. 검시, 부검
22	**phenotype** [fí:nətàip]	n. 표현형
23	**hypothesize** [haipάθisàiz]	v. 가설을 세우다
24	**principle** [prínsəpl]	n. 원칙
25	**genetically** [dʒənétikəli]	ad. 유전적으로
26	**progenitor** [proudʒénətər]	n. 조상
27	**unfit** [ənfi't]	a. ~을 할 수 없는
28	**implicit** [implísit]	a. 내포된
29	**strain** [strein]	n. 종류
30	**extinguish** [ikstíŋgwiʃ]	v. ~을 없애다
31	**neglect** [niglékt]	v. 도외시하다, 등한하다
32	**contention** [kənténʃən]	n. 주장
33	**supposition** [sʌpəzíʃən]	n. 추정
34	**enhancement** [inhǽnsmənt]	n. 상승
35	**virulence** [vírjuləns]	n. 독성
36	**significance** [signífikəns]	n. 중요성
37	**colleague** [kάli:g]	n. 동료
38	**regarding** [rigά:rdiŋ]	prep. ~에 관하여
39	**inheritance** [inhérətəns]	n. 유전
40	**enzyme** [énzaim]	n. 효소
41	**experimentation** [ikspèrəmentéiʃən]	n. 실험
42	**substantiate** [səbstǽnʃièit]	v. 입증하다
43	**hypothesis** [haipάθəsis]	n. 가설

구문정리

본문 중 중요 구문 정리한 내용입니다. 우선 암기하고 많이 읽으시길 바랍니다.

Griffith and Transformation

TEST **4-1**

→ 정답

01 **be unheard of** ~에 관해 듣지 못하다
02 **along with** ~에 따라
03 **advance in** ~에서의 진보
04 **attribute A to B** A를 B의 탓으로 돌리다
05 **try to do** to do 하는 것을 시도하다
06 **in order to do** to do 하기 위해
07 **so as to do** to do 하기 위해
08 **seek to do** to do 하는 것을 추구하다
09 **show O to do** O가 to do하는 것을 증명하다 (보여주다)
10 **result in** 결과를 초래하다
11 **allow O to do** O가 to do하는 것을 허락하다
12 **evade from** ~로부터 피하다
13 **on the other hand** 반면에
14 **as expected** 예상된 것처럼
15 **inject A with B** A에게 B를 주입하다
16 **fail to do** to do 하는 것에 실패하다
17 **morph into** ~으로 변형되다
18 **derived from** ~으로부터 기인한, 파생된
19 **transform A into B** A를 B로 변형시키다
20 **hold that** that절이라고 생각하다 (주장하다)
21 **emerge from** ~으로부터 출현하다
22 **similar to** ~과 유사한
23 **contention against** 반대하는 주장 (논쟁)
24 **be able to do** to do 할 수 있다
25 **as such** 그러한 것으로써; 그 자체로서
26 **experiment on** ~에 대한 실험
27 **in regard to** ~에 관하여
28 **regarding** ~에 관하여
29 **drive O to do** O가 to do하게 만들다
30 **continue to do** to do 하는 것을 계속하다
31 **work on** ~에 애쓰다, 공들이다
32 **through the use of** ~의 사용함으로서
33 **have O done** O가 ~되어지게 (done) 하다
34 **treat A with B** B로 A를 처치 (처리)하다
35 **in manner** ~방법으로
36 **over time** 시간이 흐르면서
37 **through the findings of** ~의 발견을 통해
38 **concerning** ~에 관하여
39 **start to do about** ~에 대해 to do 하기 시작하다
40 **experimentation on** ~에의 실험
41 **despite the fact that** that 절이라는 사실에도 불구하고
42 **consensus on** ~에 대한 합의
43 **endow A with B** A에게 B를 부여하다
44 **akin to** ~와 유사한
45 **those of** 앞명사 반복 피하기 those (여기서 systems)

※ 다시 한 번 암기 후 → 문제집 가장 뒷부분 열 번 읽기로!

USHER VOCABULARY

Maximilian Weber and His Influence
TEST 4-2 지문의 단어 중 토플 필수 단어를 선별하여 정리하였습니다.

01	**underlying** [ʌ̀ndərlàiiŋ]	a. 근본적인	18	**volatile** [vάlətil]	a. 불안한, 휘발성의
02	**obedient** [oubíːdiənt]	a. 말을 잘 듣는	19	**recede** [risíːd]	v. 물러나다
03	**sociologist** [sòusiάlədʒist]	n. 사회학자	20	**permanent** [pə́ːrmənənt]	a. 영구적인
04	**fiasco** [fiǽskou]	n. 대실패	21	**defeat** [difíːt]	v. ~을 패배시키다
05	**acquiescence** [ækwiésns]	n. 묵인	22	**abrupt** [əbrʌpt]	a. 갑작스런
06	**sovereign** [sάvərin]	n. 주권, 군주	23	**exile** [égzail]	n. 유배
07	**inheritable** [inhéritəbl]	a. 상속되는	24	**standardization** [stænd-ərdizéiʃən]	n. 표준화
08	**bloodline** [blə'dlai,n]	n. 혈통	25	**theoretical** [θìːərétikəl]	a. 이론의
09	**inequality** [ìnikwάləti]	n. 불평등	26	**rationalization** [ræʃənəlizéiʃən]	n. 합리화
10	**diversity** [divə́ːrsəti]	n. 다양성	27	**oversimplify** [òuvərsímpləfài]	v. 지나치게 단순화하다
11	**elevate** [éləvèit]	v. ~을 승격시키다	28	**radical** [rǽdikəl]	a. 근본적인
12	**stability** [stəbíləti]	n. 안정성	29	**perspective** [pərspéktiv]	n. 관점
13	**guarantee** [gærəntíː]	v. ~을 보장하다	30	**gratify** [grǽtəfài]	v. 만족시키다
14	**investment** [invéstmənt]	n. 투자	31	**intrinsic** [intrínsik]	a. 내재된, 고유한
15	**devotion** [divóuʃən]	n. 헌신, 전념	32	**permissive** [pərmísiv]	a. 관대한
16	**sanctity** [sǽŋktəti]	n. 존엄성	33	**anarchy** [ǽnərki]	n. 무정부 상태
17	**exemplary** [igzémpləri]	a. 모범적인	34	**hierarchical** [hàiərάːrkikəl]	a. 계급에 따른

구문정리
본문 중 중요 구문 정리한 내용입니다. 우선 암기하고 많이 읽으시길 바랍니다.

Maximilian Weber and His Influence

TEST 4-2

→ 정답

01 **define A as B** A를 B라고 정의하다
02 **on the other hand** 반면에
03 **chance of** ~의 가능성 (기회)
04 **according to** ~에 따르면
05 **classify A into B** A를 B로 나누어 분류하다
06 **each differ** 분사의 의미상 주어 each
07 **differ in** ~점에서 다르다
08 **influence on** ~에 대한 영향
09 **play a role in** ~에서 역할을 하다
10 **base on** ~에 기반을 두다
11 **such as** ~와 같은
12 **be vulnerable to** ~에 취약하다
13 **as is** ~와 같이 (관계대명사 as)
14 **look at** ~를 바라보다
15 **division of labor** 분업
16 **due to** ~때문에
17 **bring about** ~을 야기하다
18 **elevate A to B** A를 B로 승진 (승격)시키다
19 **issue commands** 명령을 내리다
20 **with no regard to** ~에 관련없이
21 **act as** ~로서 역할을 하다
22 **lead to** 야기하다
23 **under system** ~의 체계 아래에서
24 **devotion to** ~에 대한 헌신
25 **result in** ~를 초래하다
26 **gain fame** 명성을 얻다
27 **deal with** ~를 다루다
28 **a variety of** 여러가지의
29 **cause O to do** O가 to do 하는 것을 야기하다
30 **rather than** ~라기 보다는
31 **fail to do** to do 하는 것에 실패하다
32 **change in** ~에서의 변화
33 **satisfy need** 수요를 충족시키다
34 **align with** ~에 맞춰 조절하다
35 **classify as** ~로써 분류하다
36 **from perspective** ~의 관점에서
37 **in contrast** 대조적으로
38 **be described as** ~로서 묘사되다
39 **be seen as** ~라고 간주되다
40 **effective in** ~에 유효한
41 **achieve result** 결과를 얻다
42 **based on** ~에 근거를 둔
43 **be stated as** ~로서 언급되다
44 **bond with** ~과의 유대
45 **seek to do** to do 하는 것을 추구하다
46 **needs of** ~의 수요
47 **contribute to** ~에 기여하다
48 **make decisions** 결정하다
49 **opportunity to do** to do 할 기회
50 **stress that** that절을 강조하다
51 **view A as B** A를 B라고 여기다
52 **be considered (to be)** ~로 간주되다
53 **theory on** ~에 관한 이론(on = about)

※ 다시 한 번 암기 후 → 문제집 가장 뒷부분 열 번 읽기로!

USHER VOCABULARY

Pasteur and The Origin of Life
TEST 5-1 지문의 단어 중 토플 필수 단어를 선별하여 정리하였습니다.

#	Word	#	Word
01	**methodical** [məθɑ́dikəl] — a. 체계적인	18	**atop** [ətɑ́p] — a. 꼭대기의
02	**spuriously** — ad. 부정하게	19	**spontaneously** [spantéiniəsli] — ad. 자발적으로
03	**assertion** [əsə́:rʃən] — n. 주장	20	**definitively** [difínətivli] — ad. 결정적으로
04	**spontaneous** [spantéiniəs] — a. 자발적인	21	**disprove** [disprú:v] — v. 틀렸음을 입증하다
05	**rot** [rat] — v. ~을 썩히다	22	**empirically** [impírikəli] — ad. 경험적으로
06	**microorganism** [màikrouɔ́:rgənìzm] — n. 미생물	23	**surmise** [sərmáiz] — v. ~을 추측하다
07	**fermentation** [fə̀:rmentéiʃən] — n. 발효	24	**proffer** [prɑ́fər] — v. ~을 내놓다
08	**stimuli** [sti'mjəlai,] — n.(pl) 자극	25	**primeval** [praimí:vəl] — a. 태고의
09	**skeptical** [sképtikəl] — a. 의심많은	26	**criteria** [kraiti'riə] — n.(pl) 표준
10	**falsify** [fɔ́:lsəfài] — v. 그릇됨[거짓임]을 증명하다 …을 논파[반증] 하다	27	**synthesize** [sínθəsàizd] — v. ~을 합성하다
11	**biogenesis** [bàioudʒénisis] — n. 생물 발생설	28	**inorganic** [ìnɔ:rgǽnik] — a. 무기물의
12	**preposterous** [pripɑ́stərəs] — a. 터무니없는	29	**electrode** [iléktroud] — n. 전극
13	**broth** [brɔ:θ] — n. 맑은 수프	30	**evaporation** [ivæpəréiʃən] — n. 증발
14	**ferment** [fə́:rment] — v. 발효되다, ~을 발효시키다	31	**vapor** [véipər] — n. 증기
15	**sealed** [si:ld] — a. 봉인된	32	**condense** [kəndéns] — v. ~응결되다
16	**sterile** [stéril] — a. 살균한	33	**repetitive** [ripétətiv] — a. 반복적인
17	**spherical** [sférikəl] — a. 구체의	34	**nucleic** [nju:klí:ik] — a. 핵의

구문정리 | 본문 중 중요 구문 정리한 내용입니다. 우선 암기하고 많이 읽으시길 바랍니다.

Pasteur and The Origin of Life

TEST 5-1

→ 정답

01 **adhere to** ~을 고수하다

02 **lead O to do** O가 to do 하도록 이끌다

03 **skeptical of** ~에 비판적인

04 **in order to do** to do 하기 위해

05 **conduct experiment** 실험을 수행하다

06 **fill A with B** A를 B로 채우다

07 **allow O to do** O가 to do하는 것을 허락하다

08 **as a result** 결과적으로

09 **at the time** 당시에

10 **even if** 심지어 ~할지라도 (=even though)

11 **would have p.p.** (추측) ~일지도 모른다

12 **due to lack of** ~의 부족때문에

13 **nothing but** 오직 (=only)

14 **exposed A to B** A를 B에 노출시키다

15 **give birth to** ~을 낳다

16 **in the understanding of** ~의 이해에 대한

17 **necessary for** ~에 필수적인

18 **no longer** 더 이상 ~하지 않다

19 **meet criteria** 기준을 충족시키다

20 **in contrast to** ~과 대조적으로

21 **it is likely that** that절을 할 것 같다

22 **the same as** ~과 같은 종류의

23 **as long as** ~하는 한

24 **attempt to do** to do 하는 것을 시도하다

25 **test for** ~을 실험하다

26 **under condition** ~의 조건 아래에서

27 **in the form of** ~의 형태로

※ 다시 한 번 암기 후 → 문제집 가장 뒷부분 열 번 읽기로!

USHER VOCABULARY

Early Research on Air

TEST 5-2 지문의 단어 중 토플 필수 단어를 선별하여 정리하였습니다.

01	**fascinated** [fǽsənèitid]	a. 매료된		19	**elastic** [ilǽstik]	a. 탄성있는, 고무로 된
02	**precisely** [prisáisli]	ad. 정확하게		20	**encyclopedia** [insàikləpí:diə]	n. 백과사전
03	**properties** [prɑ́pərti]	n. 특징		21	**invisibility** [invìzəbíləti]	n. 눈에 보이지 않음
04	**perspective** [pərspéktiv]	n. 관점		22	**diffuse** [difjú:z]	v. 퍼트리다, 방산하다
05	**impede** [impí:d]	v. 방해하다, 지연시키다		23	**isolate** [áisəlèit]	v. 고립시키다
06	**pursue** [pərsú:]	v. ~을 추구하다		24	**vessel** [vésəl]	n. 용기
07	**instrument** [ínstrəmənt]	n. 기구		25	**displace** [displéis]	v. 대체하다
08	**limitation** [lìmətéiʃən]	n. 제한		26	**experimental** [ikspèrəméntl]	a. 실험적인
09	**combustion** [kəmbʌ́stʃən]	n. 연소		27	**demonstrate** [démənstrèit]	v. ~을 입증하다
10	**vacuum** [vǽkjuəm]	n. 진공		28	**improvisation** [imprɑ̀vəzéiʃən]	n. 즉석에서 한것
11	**definition** [dèfəníʃən]	n. 정의		29	**praise** [preiz]	n. 찬사
12	**component** [kəmpóunənt]	n. 요소		30	**tremendous** [triméndəs]	a. 엄청난
13	**revise** [riváiz]	v. 변경하다		31	**contribution** [kɑ̀ntrəbjú:ʃən]	n. 기부금
14	**misconception** [miskənse'pʃən]	n. 오해		32	**proceed** [prəsí:d]	v. ~진행되다
15	**persistence** [pərsístəns]	n. 지속됨		33	**gradually** [grǽdʒuəli]	ad. 서서히
16	**laboratory** [lǽbərətɔ̀:ri]	n. 연구실		34	**unveil** [ənvei'l]	v. ~을 벗기다
17	**equipment** [ikwípmənt]	n. 도구		35	**proportion** [prəpɔ́:rʃən]	n. 비율, 부분
18	**rudimentary** [rù:dəméntəri]	a. 기본적인				

구문정리
본문 중 중요 구문 정리한 내용입니다. 우선 암기하고 많이 읽으시길 바랍니다.

Early Research on Air

TEST **5-2**

→ 정답

01 **according to** ~에 따르면
02 **be regarded as** ~로서 간주되다
03 **begin to do** to do 하기 시작하다
04 **conduct research** 조사를 수행하다
05 **by the fact that** that절이라는 사실에 의해
06 **seek to do** to do 하는 것을 추구하다
07 **in the perspective of** ~의 관점에서
08 **prior to** ~이전에
09 **be involved in** 연루되다
10 **focus on** ~에 집중하다
11 **in states** 상태에서
12 **in the domain of** ~의 영역에서
13 **it is not until A that** A하고 나서야 비로소 that절 하다
14 **due to the lack of** ~의 부족 때문에
15 **known for** ~로 알려진
16 **neither A nor B** A도 아니고 B도 아닌
17 **for O to do** (to부정사 의미상의 주어) for가 to do 하는 것이
18 **of the day** 당시의
19 **responsible for** ~에 책임있는
20 **in addition** 게다가
21 **be interested in** ~에 관심이 있다
22 **shift A to B** A를 B로 이동시키다
23 **with effort** 노력으로

24 **present in** ~에 존재하는
25 **try to do** to do 하려고 시도하다
26 **regarding** ~에 관하여
27 **credit A for B** A에게 B의 공적을 돌리다
28 **accept as** ~로서 받아들이다
29 **as a result of** ~의 결과로서
30 **be known as** ~라고 알려진다
31 **struggle to do** to do 하려고 분투하다
32 **ability to do** to do 하는 능력
33 **prove to be** ~라고 증명되다
34 **wish to do** to do 하는 것을 희망하다
35 **have no success in** ~에서 성공하지 못하다
36 **research on** ~에 대한 조사
37 **in search of** ~을 찾으면서
38 **anxious to do** to do 하고 싶어하는 (갈망하는)
39 **give birth to** ~를 발생시키다 (낳다)
40 **relation to** ~에 대한 관계
41 **be made from** ~으로부터 만들어지다
42 **win the praise of** ~에 대해 칭찬을 받다
43 **contribution to** ~에 대한 공헌
44 **pass up** 포기하다; 놓치다
45 **opportunity to do** to do 할 기회
46 **come after** ~의 뒤를 쫓다

※ 다시 한 번 암기 후 → 문제집 가장 뒷부분 열 번 읽기로!

USHER VOCABULARY

Photography as an Art
TEST 6-1 지문의 단어 중 토플 필수 단어를 선별하여 정리하였습니다.

#	Word	Pron.	Meaning
01	component	[kəmpóunənt]	n. 요소
02	manifest	[mǽnəfèst]	v. 분명히 나타내다
03	convince	[kənvíns]	v. 납득시키다
04	definition	[dèfəníʃən]	n. 정의
05	pore	[pɔ:r]	v. 숙고하다
06	state	[steit]	v. 서술하다
07	framing	[fréimiŋ]	n. 구성, 뼈대
08	crucial	[krú:ʃəl]	a. 중대한
09	denigration	[dènigréiʃən]	n. 명예훼손
10	aesthetic	[esθétik]	a. 미적인
11	observe	[əbzə́:rv]	v. ~을 관찰하다
12	echo	[ékou]	v. 반향을 일으키다, 회자되다
13	convey	[kənvéi]	v. ~을 전달하다
14	allegorical	[æligɔ́:rikəl]	a. 우화적인
15	genre	[ʒɑ́:nrə; F. ʒɑ:r]	n. 장르
16	scene	[si:n]	n. 장면
17	capture	[kǽptʃər]	v. ~에 담다
18	accurate	[ǽkjurət]	a. 정확한
19	overcome	[ou'vərkə,m]	v. 극복하다
20	inferior	[infíəriər]	a. ~보다 못한
21	optical	[ɑ́ptikəl]	a. 시각적인
22	tripod	[tráipad]	n. 삼각대
23	blur	[blə:r]	v. ~을 흐리다
24	imitate	[ímətèit]	v. 모방하다
25	contemporary	[kəntémpərèri]	a. 동시대의
26	phase	[feiz]	n. 단계
27	promoter	[prəmóutər]	n. 기획자
28	solidify	[səlídəfài]	v. 굳어지다
29	hindsight	[hai'ndsai,t]	n. 뒤늦은 깨달음
30	conclude	[kənklú:d]	v. ~결론을 내리다
31	inspire	[inspáiər]	v. ~를 고무하다
32	emulate	[émjulèit]	v. ~을 모방하다
33	masterpiece	[mǽ'stərpi,s]	n. 걸작
34	artifact	[ɑ́:rtəfækt]	n. 공예품
35	indispensable	[ìndispénsəbl]	a. 필수적인
36	spirit	[spírit]	n. 마음
37	dedicate	[dédikèit]	v. ~에 전념하다
38	solely	[sóulli]	ad. 오로지
39	two-dimensional	[tú:diménʃənl]	a. 2차원의
40	modest-sized	[mɑ́dist-sàizd]	a 적당한 크기의
41	commodity	[kəmɑ́dəti]	n. 상품
42	tie	[tai]	v. ~을 묶다

구문정리
본문 중 중요 구문 정리한 내용입니다. 우선 암기하고 많이 읽으시길 바랍니다.

Photography as an Art

TEST 6-1

→ 정답

01 **for O to do** to 부정사 의미상의 주어 for
02 **be considered (to be)** ~로 간주되다
03 **struggle to do** to do 하려고 분투하다
04 **convince O that** O에게 that절을 설득시키다
05 **fall within** ~에 포함되다
06 **recognize A as B** A를 B라고 인식하다
07 **see A as B** A을 B라고 간주하다
08 **instead of** ~대신에
09 **take time to do** to do 하는데 시간이 걸리다
10 **poring over** 쏟아 붓다
11 **ability to do** to do 하는 능력
12 **unequal to** ~에 동등하지 않는
13 **disagree with** ~에 동의하지 않다
14 **in the hands of** ~의 관리하에
15 **if utilized** 만약 이용된다면
16 **otherwise** 그렇지 않으면
17 **contend that** that절 이하를 강력하게 주장하다
18 **take a second** 시간이 잠시 걸리다
19 **have to do** to do 해야만 한다
20 **attempt to do** to do 하는 것을 시도하다
21 **points of view** 관점
22 **per se**[pəir séi] 그 자체로는
23 **be capable of** ~할 수 있는
24 **benefit from** ~으로부터 혜택을 누리다
25 **applied science** 응용 과학
26 **in an effort to do** to do 하려는 노력으로
27 **compete with** ~와 경쟁하다
28 **focus on** ~에 집중하다
29 **wear off** (차츰) 사라지다, 없어지다
30 **begin to question** 의문을 갖기 시작하다
31 **as a result** 결과적으로
32 **reach its height** 절정에 도달하다
33 **have a strong influence on** ~에 강력한 영향력을 갖다
34 **in phases** 단계적으로, ~한 단계에서
35 **one of** ~중의 하나
36 **solidify one's status as** ~로서 지위를 확고히 하다
37 **rise and fall** 융성과 쇠퇴
38 **struggle over** ~에 대한 분투
39 **rage on** 맹위를 떨치다
40 **in hindsight** 지나고 나서 보니까
41 **disposition to do** ~하려는 성향
42 **contrast in** ~점에서의 대조
43 **regardless of** ~에 상관없이
44 **begin producing** 생산을 시작하다
45 **for one's benefit** ~을 위하여(= in one' favor)
46 **access to** ~로의 접근
47 **in terms of** ~한 면에서, 견지에서
48 **familiarity with** ~와의 친근함
49 **not only A but also B** A뿐만 아니라 B도
50 **dedicate A to B** B에게 A를 헌신시키다
51 **stand its ground** (입장, 주장) 고수하다, 견지하다
52 **aside from** ~외에도
53 **make statement** 진술하다
54 **combine A with B** A와 B를 결합시키다
55 **tie A to B** B에게 A를 묶다

※ 다시 한 번 암기 후 → 문제집 가장 뒷부분 열 번 읽기로!

Vocabulary

How and Why Birds Learn to Sing

TEST 6-2 지문의 단어 중 토플 필수 단어를 선별하여 정리하였습니다.

01	**inspire** [inspáiər]	v. ~를 격려하다
02	**composer** [kəmpóuzər]	n. 작곡자
03	**arouse** [əráuz]	v. ~을 자아내다
04	**elaborate** [ilǽbərət]	a. 정교한
05	**struggle** [strʌgl]	v. ~와 싸우다
06	**intricate** [íntrikət]	a. 복잡한
07	**discipline** [dísəplin]	n. 학문
08	**fascinating** [fǽsənèitiŋ]	a. 매력적인
09	**attribute** [ətríbjuːt]	v. ~의 결과로 보다
10	**complexity** [kəmpléksəti]	n. 복잡성
11	**comparable** [kάmpərəbl]	a. 비슷한
12	**attract** [ətrǽkt]	v. ~끌어들이다
13	**experimental** [ikspèrəméntl]	a. 실험적인
14	**assertion** [əsə́ːrʃən]	n. 주장
15	**pair** [pɛər]	n. 한 쌍
16	**formation** [fɔːrméiʃən]	n. 형성
17	**dummy** [dʌmi]	n. 모형
18	**trap** [træp]	n. 덫
19	**variable** [vέəriəbl]	a. 변하기 쉬운
20	**prefer** [prifə́ːr]	v. ~을 더 좋아하다
21	**repertoire** [répərtwὰːr]	n. 레퍼토리, 상연목록
22	**diverse** [divə́ːrs]	a. 다양한
23	**assortment** [əsɔ́ːrtmənt]	n. 모음
24	**trait** [treit, trei]	n. 특성
25	**offspring** [ɔ́ːfspriŋ]	n. 자손, 새끼
26	**aggressively** [əgrésivli]	ad. 공격적으로
27	**broadcast** [brɔ́ːdkæst]	v. 방송하다, 널리 알리다
28	**incorporate** [inkɔ́ːrpərèit]	v. 포함하다
29	**auditory** [ɔ́ːditɔ̀ːri]	a. 청각의
30	**stimuli** [stímjuləs]	n. (pl) 자극
31	**extremely** [ikstríːmli]	ad. 극도로
32	**susceptible** [səséptəbl]	a. 민감한
33	**abnormal** [æbnɔ́ːrməl]	a. 비정상적인
34	**reassemble** [rìːəsémbl]	v. 재조립하다
35	**adept** [ədépt]	a. 능숙한
36	**mimic** [mímik]	v. 흉내내다
37	**frontal** [frʌntl]	a. 정면의
38	**internalize** [intə́ːrnəlàiz]	v. 내면화 하다
39	**sensory** [sénsəri]	a. 감각의
40	**sensorimotor** [sènsərimóutər]	n. 지각 운동의
41	**integration** [ìntəgréiʃən]	n. 통합
42	**acquisition** [ækwizíʃən]	n. 습득
43	**persistent** [pərsístənt]	a. 끈질긴
44	**crystallization** [krìstəlizéiʃən]	a. 결정화
45	**variation** [vɛəriéiʃən]	n. 변화
46	**disturb** [distə́ːrb]	v. ~을 방해하다
47	**deteriorate** [ditíəriərèit]	v. 악화되다
48	**decrystallization**	n. 재결정
49	**temporal** [témpərəl]	a. 시간의

구문정리

본문 중 중요 구문 정리한 내용입니다. 우선 암기하고 많이 읽으시길 바랍니다.

TEST 6-2

How and Why Birds Learn to Sing

→ 정답

01 **struggle to do** to do하기 위해 분투하다
02 **find O to be O.C** O를 O.C라고 생각하다
03 **regard A as B** A를 B라고 간주하다
04 **comparable to** ~에 비견될 만한
05 **in general** 일반적으로
06 **ability to do** to do 하는 능력
07 **attraction to** ~에 대한 매력
08 **in direct response to** ~에 대한 직접적인 반응으로
09 **come close to doing** 거의 ~하게 되다
10 **add to** ~에 더해지다
11 **pass on to** ~에게 전달하다
12 **act as** ~로서 역할을 하다
13 **respond to** ~에 반응하다
14 **prevent O from ~ing** O를 ~ing 하는 것으로부터 막다
15 **warn O to do** O에게 to do 하도록 경고하다
16 **learn to do** to do 하는 것을 배우다
17 **born with** ~에 타고나다
18 **incorporate A into B** A를 B로 통합하다
19 **end up with** 결국 ~로 되다

20 **with ability** ~능력을 가진
21 **be susceptible to** 영향 받기 쉽다
22 **teach O to do** O에게 to do 하는 것을 가르치다
23 **expose A to B** A를 B에 노출시키다
24 **be adept at** ~에 능숙한
25 **respectively** 각각
26 **rely on** ~에 의존하다
27 **known as** ~로서 알려진
28 **shape A into B** A를 B로 만들다
29 **be similar to** ~과 유사하다
30 **seem to do** to do 하는 것 처럼 보이다
31 **what is called** 이른바, 소위
32 **shortly after** 직후에
33 **over time** 시간이 지나면서
34 **result in** ~를 초래하다
35 **go through** (과정들을) 거치다
36 **cause O to do** O가 to do 하는 것을 야기하다

※ 다시 한 번 암기 후 → 문제집 가장 뒷부분 열 번 읽기로!

USHER VOCABULARY

Functions of Roots
TEST 7-1 지문의 단어 중 토플 필수 단어를 선별하여 정리하였습니다.

#	Word	Pron.	Meaning
01	**vascular**	[væskjulər]	a. 관의
02	**substrate**	[sʌbstreit]	n. 기질
03	**osmosis**	[azmóusis]	n. 삼투현상
04	**optimize**	[áptəmàiz]	v. ~을 적합하게 만들다
05	**stable**	[stéibl]	a. 안정된
06	**erosion**	[iróuʒən]	n. 부식
07	**modify**	[mάdəfài]	v. 수정하다
08	**perennating**	[pérənèit]	a. 다년생의
09	**deficiency**	[difíʃənsi]	n. 결핍
10	**swamp**	[swamp]	n. 늪
11	**necessity**	[nəsésəti]	n. 필요
12	**waterlogged**	[wɔ'tərla,gd]	a. 물을 잔뜩 머금은
13	**colonize**	[kάlənàiz]	v. 이식하다, 이주시키다
14	**coastline**	[kou'stlai,n]	n. 해안지대
15	**brackish**	[brǽkiʃ]	a. 염분이 섞인
16	**prominent**	[prάmənənt]	a. 중요한
17	**saline**	[séilain]	a. 염분이 함유된
18	**habitat**	[hǽbitæt]	n. 서식지
19	**pore**	[pɔ:r]	n. 구멍
20	**conduit**	[kάndwit]	n. 도관
21	**respiration**	[rèspəréiʃən]	n. 호흡
22	**subterranean**	[sʌbtəréiniən]	a. 지하의
23	**membrane**	[mémbrein]	n. 막
24	**bio-diverse**	[báiou-divə́:rs]	a. 생물이 다양한
25	**triumph**	[tráiəmf]	v. 승리하다, 이기다
26	**adaptation**	[ædəptéiʃən]	n. 적응
27	**attain**	[ətéin]	v. 획득하다
28	**proximity**	[praksíməti]	n. 근접
29	**dangle**	[dǽŋgl]	v. 매달리다
30	**aerial**	[ɛ́əriəl]	a. 공중에 걸린, 공기의
31	**intertwine**	[intərtwai'n]	v. 뒤얽히다
32	**squeeze**	[skwi:z]	v. 짜내다
33	**strangulation**	[stræŋgjuléiʃən]	n. 교살
34	**microbial**	[maikróubiəl]	a. 미생물의
35	**herbivore**	[ə́:rbəvɔ̀:r]	n. 초식동물
36	**implication**	[ìmplikéiʃən]	n. 영향
37	**detrimental**	[dètrəméntl]	a. 해로운
38	**excrete**	[ikskrí:t]	v. 분비하다
39	**extract**	[ikstrǽkt]	v. 추출하다
40	**herbicide**	[ə́:rbəsàid]	n. 제초제
41	**coverage**	[kʌ́vəridʒ]	n. 적용범위, 통용범위, 가능범위

구문정리
본문 중 중요 구문 정리한 내용입니다. 우선 암기하고 많이 읽으시길 바랍니다.

Functions of Roots

TEST 7-1

→ 정답

01 **serve function** 역할을 하다
02 **adapt to** ~에 적응하다
03 **carry out function** 기능을 수행하다
04 **in ways** ~한 방법으로
05 **fall over** 중단되다 ; (갑자기) 넘어지다
06 **in addition to** 게다가
07 **allow O to do** O가 to do 하는 것을 허락하다
08 **as ~ as possible** 가능한 ~하게
09 **be exposed to** ~에 노출되다
10 **due to** ~때문에
11 **lead to** ~를 초래하다
12 **be distinguished from** ~와 구별되다
13 **rely on** ~에 의지하다
14 **act as** ~로서 작용하다
15 **enable O to do** O가 to do 하는 것을 가능하게 하다
16 **too ~for O to do** 너무 ~해서 O가 to do 하지 못한다
17 **in a process** 과정에서
18 **fill A with B** A를 B로 채우다
19 **triumph over** ~에 대해 승리하다, 극복하다
20 **in proximity** 근접하여

21 **result in** ~결과로 되다
22 **competition for** ~에 대한 경쟁
23 **cut off** 자르다
24 **die from** ~로(때문에) 죽다
25 **stand on its own** 자립하다
26 **known as** ~로서 알려진
27 **a variety of** 다양한
28 **cope with** ~에 대처하다
29 **gain an advantage over** ~보다 우월한 입장을 차지하다, ~을 능가하다
30 **implication for** ~에의 영향
31 **in the case of** ~의 경우에
32 **conduct research** 연구를 시행하다
33 **extract A from B** A를 B로부터 추출하다
34 **be identified as** ~로서 확인되다
35 **too A to do** to do 하기에 너무 A하다
36 **be reworked into** ~로 재작업되다
37 **be used as** ~로서 사용되다

※ 다시 한 번 암기 후 → 문제집 가장 뒷부분 열 번 읽기로!

Vocabulary

History of The Patent Law
TEST 7-2 지문의 단어 중 토플 필수 단어를 선별하여 정리하였습니다.

01	**prevalent** [prévələnt]	a. 일반적인
02	**hierarchy** [háiərɑ̀:rki]	n. 계급
03	**prohibit** [prouhíbit]	v. ~을 금하다
04	**patent** [pǽtnt]	n. 특허권
05	**exclusivity** [èksklu:sívəti]	n. 고급스러움
06	**monarch** [mɑ́nərk]	n. 군주
07	**implement** [ímpləmənt]	v. ~을 시행하다
08	**instrument** [ínstrəmənt]	n. 기구
09	**emigrant** [émigrənt]	n. 이주민
10	**drain** [drein]	v. 물을 빼내다
11	**inefficiency** [ìnifíʃənsi]	n. 비능률
12	**outlaw** [au'tlɔ,]	v. 불법화하다
13	**spur** [spəːr]	v. 자극하다
14	**increasingly** [inkríːsiŋli]	ad. 점점 더
15	**component** [kəmpóunənt]	n. 요소
16	**perception** [pərsépʃən]	n. 지각
17	**colonial** [kəlóuniəl]	a. 식민지의
18	**dispute** [dispjúːt]	n. 분쟁
19	**steamboat** [sti'mbou,t]	n. 증기선
20	**independence** [ìndipéndəns]	n. 독립
21	**constitutional** [kɑ̀nstətjúːʃənl]	a. 헌법의
22	**imbed** [imbéd]	v. 단단히 박다
23	**constitution** [kɑ̀nstətjúːʃən]	n. 헌법
24	**congress** [kɑ́ŋgris]	n. 의회
25	**discovery** [diskʌ́vəri]	n. 발견
26	**federal** [fédərəl]	a. 연방제의
27	**revision** [rivíʒən]	n. 변경
28	**examiner** [igzǽmənər]	n. 심사위원
29	**fabric** [fǽbrik]	n. 직물
30	**debate** [dibéit]	v. 토의하다
31	**burgeoning** [bə́ːrdʒəniŋ]	a. 급증하는
32	**capitalist** [kǽpitlist]	n. 자본주의자
33	**advancement** [ædvǽnsmənt]	n. 발전
34	**eventually** [ivéntʃuəli]	ad. 결국
35	**introduce** [ìntrədjúːs]	v. ~을 도입하다
36	**society** [səsáiəti]	n. 사회

구문정리 | 본문 중 중요 구문 정리한 내용입니다. 우선 암기하고 많이 읽으시길 바랍니다.

TEST **7-2**

History of The Patent Law

→ 정답

01 **right to do** to do할 권리
02 **be it** ~이든지 (whether 생략)
03 **as a result** 결과적으로
04 **in order to do** to do 하기 위해
05 **protection from** ~으로부터의 보호
06 **be attributed to** ~덕분이다 (attribute A to B)
07 **conform to** ~를 따르다, 순응하다; 일치하다
08 **provided** 만약 ~한다면(= if)
09 **differ from** ~이랑 다르다
10 **in that** that 절이라는 점에서 (접속사)
11 **require O to do** O가 to do 하는 것을 요구하다
12 **in other words** 다시 말해서
13 **have to do** to do 해야만 한다
14 **lay out** 펼치다, 설계하다
15 **such as** ~과 같은
16 **lie open to** ~에게 열려있다
17 **in graces** 은총으로
18 **grant IO DO** IO에게 DO를 수여하다
19 **lead to** ~을 초래하다
20 **not until A that B** A하고 나서야 비로소 B하다
21 **by + 시간** ~까지
22 **monopoly being granted on** ~에 부여되는 독점 (grant monopoly on)

23 **leave room for** ~에 대한 여지를 남기다
24 **bring about** ~을 야기하다
25 **require O to do** O에게 to do 하도록 요구하다
26 **based on** ~에 기반을 둔
27 **change in** ~에서의 변화
28 **no longer** 더 이상 ~하지 않다
29 **along with** ~에 더불어
30 **continue to do** to do 하는 것을 계속하다
31 **seek to do** to do 하는 것을 추구하다
32 **solve problem** 문제를 해결하다
33 **authorize O to do** O가 to do 하는 것을 허락하다
34 **endow A with B** A에게 B를 주다
35 **rights to** ~에 대한 권리
36 **derive A from B** A를 B로부터 끌어내다
37 **grow to status** ~의 위치까지 성장하다 (승격하다)
38 **not only A but also B** A뿐만 아니라 B도
39 **despite the fact that** that절이라는 사실에도 불구하고
40 **dependent on** ~에 의존적인
41 **change in** ~에서의 변화
42 **over time** 시간이 흐르면서
43 **contribute to** 기여하다

※ 다시 한 번 암기 후 → 문제집 가장 뒷부분 열 번 읽기로!

USHER VOCABULARY

Communication of Ants
TEST 8-1 지문의 단어 중 토플 필수 단어를 선별하여 정리하였습니다.

01	**solitary** [sάlətèri]	a. 혼자하는
02	**reliability** [rilàiəbíləti]	n. 확실성
03	**forage** [fɔ́:ridʒ]	v. ~을 찾다
04	**retain** [ritéin]	v. ~을 유지하다
05	**trail** [treil]	n. 자국
06	**gland** [glænd]	n. 샘
07	**component** [kəmpóunənt]	n. 요소
08	**elicit** [ilísit]	v. 끌어내다
09	**attraction** [ətrǽkʃən]	n. 끌림
10	**volatile** [vάlətil]	a. 휘발성의
11	**crumb** [krʌm]	n. 작은 것
12	**tale** [teil]	n. 이야기
13	**spatial** [spéiʃəl]	a. 공간의
14	**enable** [inéibl]	v. ~을 할 수 있게 하다
15	**repellent** [ripélənt]	a. 배지 않는, 물리치는
16	**persist** [pərsíst]	v. 집요하게 계속하다
17	**explore** [iksplɔ́:r]	v. 답사하다
18	**reinforce** [rì:infɔ́:rs]	v. 강화하다
19	**complementarily** [kὰmpləméntərili]	ad. 서로 보완하여
20	**tactile** [tǽktil]	a. 촉각의
21	**repertoire** [répərtwὰ:r]	n. 래퍼토리
22	**abdominal** [æbdάmənl]	a. 복부의
23	**organ** [ɔ́:rgən]	n. 장기
24	**perceive** [pərsí:v]	v. ~을 감지하다
25	**stridulate** [strídʒəlèit]	v. 날카로운 마찰음을 내다; (매미,귀뚜라미 등이)울다
26	**recruitment** [rikrú:tmənt]	n. 모집, 선발
27	**retrieve** [ritrí:v]	v. ~을 되찾다
28	**proportion** [prəpɔ́:rʃən]	n. 비율
29	**attractiveness** [ətrǽktivnis]	n. 끌어 당기는 힘
30	**communal** [kəmjú:nəl]	a. 공동의
31	**discernible** [disə́:rnəbl]	a. 식별가능한
32	**tremble** [trémbl]	v. 떨다, 떨리다
33	**constantly** [kάnstəntli]	ad. 끊임없이

구문정리
본문 중 중요 구문 정리한 내용입니다. 우선 암기하고 많이 읽으시길 바랍니다.

Communication of Ants

TEST 8-1

→ 정답

01	**have advantages over** ~에 비해 장점을 가진다	17	**for +** 시간 ~동안
02	**division of labor** 분업	18	**leading to** ~을 초래하는
03	**allow O to do** O로 하여금 to do 하는 것을 허락하다	19	**in other words** 즉, 다시 말하면
04	**rely on** 의존하다	20	**seem to do** to do 하는 것처럼 보인다
05	**gain strength** 힘을 얻다	21	**encourage O to do** O가 to do 하도록 조장하다
06	**add A to B** A를 B에 더하다	22	**in relation to** ~에 관계하여
07	**views on** ~에 대한 관점들	23	**in order to do** to do 하기 위해
08	**be assigned to** ~에 할당되다	24	**cause O to do** O가 to do 하도록 야기하다
09	**as** (관계대명사 as) ~처럼 ~듯이	25	**present A with B** A에게 B를 제공하다
10	**long after** 오랜 뒤에	26	**as opposed to** ~와는 대조적으로
11	**on the other hand** 반면에	27	**perform dances** 춤을 추다
12	**act as** ~로서 역할을 하다	28	**be bound to** ~과 결속되다
13	**help O do** O로 하여금 do 하게끔 도와주다	29	**need to do** to do 하는 것을 필요로 하다
14	**in a manner** ~한 방법으로	30	**ability to do** to do 하는 능력
15	**A as well as B** B뿐만 아니라 A도	31	**for O to do** (의미상 주어) O가 to do 하는
16	**in contrast to** ~과는 대조적으로		

※ 다시 한 번 암기 후 → 문제집 가장 뒷부분 열 번 읽기로!

USHER VOCABULARY

Calculating the Age of Earth
TEST 8-2 지문의 단어 중 토플 필수 단어를 선별하여 정리하였습니다.

01	**religion** [rilídʒən]	n. 종교
02	**inaccurate** [inǽkjərit]	a. 부정확한
03	**speculation** [spèkjuléiʃən]	n. 추측
04	**precise** [prisáis]	a. 정확한
05	**experimentation** [ikspèrəmentéiʃən]	n. 실험
06	**globe-like** [gloub-laik]	n. 지구 모양의
07	**figure** [fígjər]	n. 모양
08	**resemble** [rizémbl]	v. 닮다, 비슷하다
09	**laboratory** [lǽbərətɔ̀:ri]	n. 실험실
10	**underestimate** [ə'ndəre'stəmei,t]	v. 너무 적게 잡다
11	**inadequate** [inǽdikwət]	a. 불충분한
12	**estimation** [èstəméiʃən]	n. 판단
13	**salinity** [səlínəti]	n. 염분
14	**surmise** [sərmáiz]	v. 추측하다
15	**drag** [drǽg]	v. 끌다
16	**conjecture** [kəndʒéktʃər]	n. 추측
17	**viable** [váiəbl]	a. 실행가능한
18	**oversimplify** [òuvərsímpləfài]	v. ~을 지나치게 단순화하다
19	**measurement** [méʒərmənt]	n. 측정
20	**supporter** [səpɔ́:rtər]	n. 지지자
21	**sphere** [sfiər]	n. 구
22	**conceivable** [kənsí:vəbl]	a. 상상할(믿을) 수 있는
23	**nebula** [nébjələ]	n. 성운(가스와 대기로 이루어진 대규모 성간물질)
24	**estimate** [éstəmèit]	v. 측정하다
25	**dissipate** [dísəpèit]	v. 흩뜨리다
26	**neglect** [niglékt]	v. 간과하다, 무시하다
27	**variable** [véəriəbl]	a. 변동이 심한
28	**viscous** [vískəs]	a. 점성이 있는
29	**fluid** [flú:id]	a. 유동적인
30	**precision** [prisíʒən]	n. 정확성
31	**radiometric** [rèidioumétrik]	a. 방사성의
32	**enhance** [inhǽns]	v. 높이다(항상시키다)
33	**spontaneous** [spantéiniəs]	a. 자발적인
34	**decay** [dikéi]	n. 부패, 부식
35	**isotope** [áisətòup]	n. 동위 원소
36	**unstable** [ənstei'bəl]	a. 불안정한
37	**expose** [èkspouzéi]	v. ~을 노출시키다
38	**invariable** [invéəriəbl]	a. 변함없는
39	**elapse** [ilǽps]	v. 경과하다
40	**ratio** [réiʃou]	n. 비율
41	**controversy** [kántrəvə̀:rsi]	n. 논란
42	**validity** [vəlídəti]	n. 유효함
43	**variability** [vɛəriəbíləti]	n. 가변성
44	**sufficient** [səfíʃənt]	a. 충분한
45	**refutation** [rèfjutéiʃən]	n. 논박, 반박
46	**implausible** [implɔ́:zəbl]	a. 믿기 어려운
47	**accurate** [ǽkjurət]	a. 정확한

구문정리

본문 중 중요 구문 정리한 내용입니다. 우선 암기하고 많이 읽으시길 바랍니다.

Calculating the Age of Earth

TEST 8-2

→ 정답

01 **begin v-ing** v-ing 하기 시작하다

02 **go through** 겪다

03 **a number of** 수많은

04 **due to** ~때문에

05 **be motivated to** to do 하도록 동기부여 되다

06 **conduct research** 조사를 수행하다

07 **based on** ~에 기반한

08 **resemble O in** ~라는 점에서 O를 닮았다

09 **focus on** ~에 집중하다

10 **dare to do** 감히 to do 하다

11 **attempt to do** to do 하는 것을 시도하다

12 **take 시간 to do** to do 하는 것에 시간이 걸리다

13 **reach levels** 수준에 도달하다

14 **fail to do** to do 하는 것에 실패하다

15 **take into account** 고려하다

16 **add A to B** A를 B에 더하다

17 **be used to do** to do 하기 위해 사용되다

18 **held together** 뭉쳐진

19 **at the rate** 속도로

20 **necessary for O to do** for가 to do 하기 위해 필요한

21 **be calculated to be** ~라고 추정되다

22 **play a role in** ~에서 역할을 하다

23 **allow O to do** O가 to do 하는 것을 허락하다

24 **according to** ~에 따라

25 **be concerned with** ~에 관계가 있다

26 **ratio of A to B** A와 B의 비율

27 **controversy over** ~에 대한 논쟁

28 **variability in** ~점에서의 가변성

29 **use O to do** O를 to do 하는데 사용하다

30 **regard A to be B** A를 B라고 간주하다

31 **continue to do** to do 하는 것을 계속하다

※ 다시 한 번 암기 후 → 문제집 가장 뒷부분 열 번 읽기로!

USHER VOCABULARY

Identifying Playful Behavior in Children

TEST 9-1 지문의 단어 중 토플 필수 단어를 선별하여 정리하였습니다.

01	**prevalence** [prévələns]	n. 널리 퍼짐, 유행, 보급
02	**evolve** [iválv]	v. 발달[진전]하다[시키다]
03	**toddler** [tádlər]	n. 걸음마를 배우는 아이
04	**frolick** [frálik]	v. 즐겁게 뛰놀다
05	**engage** [ingéidʒ]	v. 관여하다
06	**moreover** [mɔ:róuvər]	ad. 게다가, 더욱이
07	**virtual** [və́:rtʃuəl]	a. 가상의
08	**predict** [pridíkt]	v. 예측[예견]하다
09	**apparent** [əpǽrənt]	a. 명백한, 분명한
10	**distinction** [distíŋkʃən]	n. 차이[대조]
11	**sociologist** [sòusiálədʒist]	n. 사회학자
12	**continuously** [kəntínjuəsli]	ad. 계속해서, 연속적으로, 끊임없이
13	**acceptance** [ækséptəns]	n. 받아들임[수락]
14	**criterion** [kraitíəriən]	n. 기준
15	**anthropologist** [ænθrəpálədʒist]	n. 인류학자
16	**define** [difáin]	v. 정의하다, 규정하다
17	**intend** [inténd]	v. 의도[작정]하다, (…하려고)
18	**likewise** [láikwàiz]	ad. 똑같이, 비슷하게
19	**labyrinth** [lǽbərìnθ]	n. 미궁
20	**ultimate** [ʌ́ltəmət]	a. 궁극[최종]적인, 최후의
21	**shelter** [ʃéltər]	n. 주거지, 피신
22	**fulfill** [fulfíl]	v. ~을 만족시키다
23	**functionalistic**	a. 실용적인
24	**identify** [aidéntəfài]	v. ~을 확인하다
25	**execution** [èksikjú:ʃən]	n. 실행, 수행
26	**squabble** [skwábl]	v. ~로 옥신각신하다
27	**exaggerate** [igzǽdʒərèit]	v. 과장하다
28	**stair** [stɛər]	n. 계단
29	**fragment** [frǽgmənt]	n. 조각, 파편
30	**backward** [bǽkwərd]	ad. 뒤로
31	**mutually** [mjú:tʃuəli]	ad. 서로, 상호간에
32	**dissimilar** [dissímələr]	a. 같지 않은
33	**encompass** [inkʌ́mpəs]	v. 포함하다
34	**pretend** [priténd]	v. ~인 척하다
35	**fictitious** [fiktíʃəs]	a. 허구의
36	**intrinsic** [intrínsik]	a. 고유한
37	**motivation** [mòutəvéiʃən]	n. 자극
38	**flexibility** [flèksəbíləti]	n. 구부리기 쉬움
39	**sufficient** [səfíʃənt]	a. 충분한
40	**undoubtedly** [ʌndáutidli]	ad. 의심할 여지없이
41	**determine** [ditə́:rmin]	v. ~을 결정하다
42	**definitively** [difínətivli]	ad. 결정적으로
43	**distinguish** [distíŋgwiʃ]	v. 구별하다

구문정리 | 본문 중 중요 구문 정리한 내용입니다. 우선 암기하고 많이 읽으시길 바랍니다.

Identifying Playful Behavior in Children

TEST **9-1**

→ 정답

01 **associated with** ~와 관련된
02 **in forms** ~의 형태로
03 **with prevalence** 만연함과 더불어
04 **engage in** ~에 참여하는
05 **over time** 시간이 지나면서
06 **begin to do** to do 하기 시작하다
07 **compared to** ~와 비교해 봤을 때
08 **take a form** 형태를 취하다
09 **continue to do** to do 하는 것을 계속하다
10 **due to** ~때문에
11 **try to do** to do 것을 시도하다
12 **gain acceptance** 용인을 얻다
13 **define A as B** A를 B라고 정의내리다
14 **neither A nor B** A도 아니고 B도 아닌
15 **be not considered** 간주되지 않는다
16 **come to be known as** ~로써 알려지게 되다
17 **be applied to** ~에 적용되다
18 **way to do** to do 하는 방법
19 **look at** ~을 보다
20 **ability to do** to do 하는 능력
21 **supply A with B** A에게 B를 공급하다
22 **time spent on** ~에 소비된 시간 (spend time on)

23 **at all** (긍정문) 조금이라도
24 **be considered (to be)** (~로) 간주되다
25 **account for** ~을 설명하다
26 **seem to do** to do 하는 것처럼 보이다
27 **serve a purpose** 목적을 수행하다
28 **hide from** ~으로부터 숨다
29 **qualify as** ~로서 자격을 갖추다
30 **in cases** 경우들에서
31 **look for** 찾다
32 **at a time** 한번에
33 **use O to do** O를 to do 하기 위해 사용하다
34 **for the purpose of** ~의 목적을 위해
35 **of one's own accord** 자발적으로
36 **meet criterion** 기준을 충족하다
37 **be certain that** that절을 확신한다
38 **confusing as it may be** 혼란스럽겠지만 (as = although, because)
39 **fall within** 범위에 들어가다
40 **use A as B** A를 B로써 사용하다
41 **those** 대명사 (동어 반복 피하기)
42 **plays a role in** ~에서 역할을 하다

※ 다시 한 번 암기 후 → 문제집 가장 뒷부분 열 번 읽기로!

USHER VOCABULARY

Sentinel Behavior in Meerkats
TEST 9-2 지문의 단어 중 토플 필수 단어를 선별하여 정리하였습니다.

01	**primarily** [praimérəli]	ad. 주로
02	**insectivore** [inséktəvɔ̀:r]	n. 식충 동물
03	**buried** [bérid]	a. 파묻힌
04	**underground** [ə'ndərgrauˌnd]	a. 지하의
05	**extremely** [ikstrí:mli]	ad. 극도로, 극히
06	**vulnerable** [vʌ́lnərəbl]	a. 취약한, 연약한
07	**airborne** [e'rbɔˌrn]	a. 비행중인, 공수의, 공기로 운반되는
08	**snatch up** [snætʃ ʌp]	v. 낚아채다, 손에넣다
09	**sentinel** [séntənəl]	n. 보초병, 감시병
10	**stance** [stæns]	n. 자세, 입장
11	**vocalization** [vòukəli-zéiʃən]	n. 발성
12	**predation** [pridéiʃən]	n. 포식
13	**reproductive** [riˌprədə'ktiv]	a. 생식[번식]의
14	**squirrel** [skwə́:rəl]	n. 다람쥐
15	**dominant** [dámənənt]	a. 우세한, 지배적인
16	**rarely** [réərli]	ad. 드물게, 좀처럼 …하지 않는
17	**tolerate** [tálərèit]	v. 용인하다, 참다, 견디다
18	**sibling** [síbliŋ]	n. 형제자매
19	**postulate** [pástʃulèit]	v. 상정하다
20	**proliferate** [prəlífərèit]	v. 급증하다, 확산되다
21	**forage** [fɔ́(:)ridʒiŋ]	v. 먹이를 찾다
22	**variant** [véəriənt]	n. 변종, 이형
23	**reciprocal** [risíprəkəl]	a. 상호간의
24	**altruist** [ǽltruist]	n. 이타주의자
25	**pup** [pʌp]	n. 새끼
26	**cooperate** [kouápərèit]	v. 협력[합동]하다
27	**chirp** [tʃə:rp]	v. 짹짹[찍찍]거리다
28	**chaperone** [ʃǽpəròun]	n. 보호자[인솔자]
29	**definition** [dèfəníʃən]	n. 의미[정의]
30	**substantiate** [səbstǽnʃièit]	v. 입증하다
31	**consistent** [kənsístənt]	a. 거듭되는, 변함없는
32	**regardless of**	prep. …에 상관없이 [구애받지 않고]
33	**contrary** [kántreri]	a. ~와는 다른[반대되는]
34	**confirm** [kənfə́:rm]	v. 사실임을 보여주다 [확인해 주다]
35	**solitary** [sálətèri]	a. 혼자 하는
36	**satiate** [séiʃièit]	v. 실컷 만족시키다, 물릴[질릴]정도로 주다

구문정리

본문 중 중요 구문 정리한 내용입니다. 우선 암기하고 많이 읽으시길 바랍니다.

Sentinel Behavior in Meerkats

TEST **9-2**

→ 정답

01 **feed on** ~를 먹다 (feed는 먹이다)
02 **search out** ~을 찾다
03 **as a result** 결과적으로
04 **be vulnerable to** ~에 취약한
05 **partake in** ~에 참여하다
06 **be known as** ~로서 알려지다
07 **act as** ~로서 역할을 하다
08 **look for** 찾다
09 **threats to** ~에 대한 위협
10 **warn A of B** A에게 B를 경고하다
11 **expose A to B** A를 B에 노출시키다
12 **be attributed to** ~때문이다
13 **be composed of** ~로 구성되다
14 **be related to** ~와 관련되다
15 **other than** ~외에
16 **in addition** 게다가
17 **allow O to do** O에게 to do 하도록 허락하다
18 **spend 시간 v-ing** v-ing 하는 것에 시간을 쓰다
19 **in order to do** to do 하기 위해
20 **at the expense of** ~을 희생하며
21 **be expected to do** to do 하는 것이 예측되다 (expect O to do)
22 **profit from** ~으로부터 이득을 얻다
23 **A as well as B** B뿐만 아니라 A도

24 **beg for** ~을 간청하다
25 **be assigned to** ~에 배정하다, 할당하다
26 **be removed from** ~으로부터 제거되다
27 **stop v-ing** v-ing 하는 것을 멈추다
28 **in turn** 결과적으로; 차례차례
29 **cause O to do** O가 to do 하도록 야기하다
30 **induce O to do** O가 to do 하도록 유도하다
31 **test for** ~에 대해 테스트 하다
32 **lay out** ~을 펼치다; 계획하다 (= arrange)
33 **if** ~인지 아닌지 (= whether)
34 **in fact** 사실
35 **neither A nor B** A도 아니고 B도 아닌
36 **regardless of** ~에 상관 없이
37 **contrary to** ~에 반해서
38 **set out to do** to do 하기 시작하다 (착수하다)
39 **focus on** ~에 집중하다
40 **question to answer** 대답할 질문
41 **than those** 대명사 (동어반복 피하기)
42 **at the moment of** 그 순간에
43 **protect A from B** A를 B로부터 보호하다
44 **hunt for** ~를 사냥하다
45 **put trust in** ~을 신뢰하다
46 **warn A of B** A에게 B를 경고하다

※ 다시 한 번 암기 후 → 문제집 가장 뒷부분 열 번 읽기로!

usherin.usher.co.kr

USHER

iBT TOEFL
FINAL TEST READING
묶기

TEST 1-1   Method of Measuring Bats' Age

01. (For many decades,) biologists have compiled scores (of data) (on the scores) (of life spans) (of various bat species) using data obtained (by the fortuitous recapture) (of individuals) tagged (at birth.) It has been found [that (on average,) bats live three times longer (than other mammals) (of similar size and metabolic rate.)] Determining their exact age is, however, particularly difficult [because it is likely [that they display more environment physiological variation (throughout their lives) (than mammals) (with shorter lifespans,) [which may confuse several studied aspects (of bat biology.)]]]

02. [When studying bat lifespans,] it is important (to note) the distinction (between chronological and biological age.) Chronological age is the interval (between the time) (of birth and the present.) Biological or physiological age, (on the other hand,) reflects the life expectancy and is based (on physical changes) (in the morphology and function) (of the body,) [which may not always coincide (with chronological age.)] The only means (of knowing) a bat's exact chronological age is (to permanently mark) it (at birth,) so [that (at any subsequent recaptures,) its exact age can be determined.] This method has drawbacks, [as marking bats is time consuming, requiring long-term monitoring, and recapture rates are typically low, not (to mention) [that the process itself may disturb the bat.]]

03. Several other methods have been developed (to determine) the biological age (of bats.) The first measures the long bones, (like the forearm, metacarpals, and digits,) [which go (through a phase) (of rapid linear growth) shortly (after birth.)] These measurements, especially that (of the forearm,) can be used (to distinguish) juveniles (from adults.) A species-specific reference correlating these measurements (with examples) (of a known-age) can provide age estimates (within 1-2 days) (with 95percent accuracy.) The advantages (of this empirical method) are its accuracy, ease (of use) (in the field and laboratory,) and lack (of invasiveness.) Only a caliper or a ruler is needed (to obtain) the measurements, making this method ideal (for use) (on both live animals and museum specimens.) The major disadvantage is [that these bones grow only (during the first few weeks) (of life) and the valid time frame varies (between species) (from only 12 days) (in M. lucifugus) (to as long as 45 days) (in R. leschenaulti.)] Other traits, (such as changes) (in the patterns and rates) (of closure) (of the cartilaginous epiphyseal growth plates) are, therefore, necessary (to estimate) the age (of older individuals.) (In its simplest form,) this method distinguishes (between young bats and adults.) (By transilluminating) the wing (of a juvenile,) a researcher can discern the cartilaginous zone (of the long phalanges) [which allows more light (to pass through) and thus appears lighter (than bone.)] [As the bat continue (to grow,)] the epiphyseal plates eventually close and are no longer visible (to the unaided eye.) This method (of age categorization) requires no more (than a fashlight) and is ideal (for use) (in both the field and the laboratory.)

04. Another method (of estimating) bats' age is (to study) their teeth. Much (like puppies) [that lose their sharp baby teeth (before growing) a set (of permanent adult teeth,) (in most bat species,)] permanent teeth replace the deciduous ones [(by the time) juveniles are able (to fly and feed) independently.] Once (in place,) these permanent teeth reach full size and cease (to grow.) A lifetime (of mastication) however wears down their surfaces and erodes their enamel. The degree (of tooth wear) can, therefore, be used (to place) bats (into relative age categories) [as this process occurs (from weaning) (until death.)] (Due to differences) (in diet,) tooth usage) (in aggressive interactions,) and the populations' annual activity periods), species show significant variation (in tooth wear.)

05. Therefore, the development (of species-specific reference standards) based (on a wide-ranging sample) (of known-age individuals) is critical (for the proper use) (of this method,) [as are investigators (with extensive species-specific experience) assessing tooth wear.] Zoologists Klevezal and Kleinenberg suggested a new method (of aging) bats using their teeth. They suggested [that the number (of incremental lines, or 'annuli,') (on bats' teeth) could be counted (to determine) its age.] The robustness (of the incremental lines,) however, varies (among species) so [that (in some) the lines may be difficult (to count,) especially (in small species.)] Another zoologist, C.J. Phillips, examined the incremental lines (in two species) (of bats) (from known-age specimens.) He found [that the number (of incremental lines) observed depended (on [which tooth was extracted]) and (on the section) examined,] and suggested [that several factors, (such as mechanical stress and tooth movement,) can alter the patterns (of layered growth) yielding non-annual cycles (of dentin and cementum deposition.)] Other researchers have found a lack (of correlation) (between age and incremental lines) (in some species.) (Aside from variation) (in incremental lines and the questionable accuracy) (of this method), other disadvantages are [that it requires tooth extraction, [which can only be done (on dead specimens)], it is time consuming, and it requires specialized equipment]. The problems associated (with this method) highlight the need (to better understand) [how and [when these incremental lines are deposited]] and use this information (to develop) more accurate reference standards [that can be correlated (with other methods.)] Notwithstanding, this method has proven useful (for a variety) (of behavioral and ecological studies) [where broad age categories suffice (to obtain) meaningful results.]

TEST 1-2 Tracing Language Diversification

01. Linguists study language relationships (to find) their similarities and differences. One way (to find and chart) these is (to look) (for inter-language sound shifts) (over time.) These are slight alternations (in words) (between related subfamily languages) (since their origin.) (From these) linguists can deduce a connection (between them) (through sound shifts.)

02. The technique used (to record) sound shifts and consonant hardening is called backward reconstruction. This technique takes humanity's linguistic family tree back thousands (of years.) Using it, scholars infer vocabulary (from previous languages.)

03. It may even be possible (to go) further and re-create) the preceding languages. Linguist Sir William Jones was an early researcher (into language diversification.) He made unrivalled contributions (to linguistic scholarship,) promoting an understanding (of and appreciation (for Asian languages and cultures.)) Having arrived (in Calcutta) (as a Bengal Supreme Court judge,) he studied Sanskrit (in order to approach) Muslim and Hindu laws (in their original form.) He found grammatical roots corresponding (to classical European languages.) (From this,) he developed the idea (of a common language source.) (In The Sanskrit Language,) he wrote (of Sanskrit's resemblance) (to Greek and Latin,) [which led him (to suggest) [that they not only had a common root but were also related (to other European languages.)]] He stated: The Sanskrit language, [whatever be its antiquity], is (of a wonderful structure); more perfect (than the Greek), more copious (than the Latin), and more exquisitely refined (than either), yet bearing (to both) (of them) a stronger affinity, both (in the roots) (of verbs) and the forms) (of grammar), [than could possibly have been produced (by accident); so strong indeed, [that no philologer could examine them all three, (without believing) them (to have sprung) (from some common source), [which, perhaps, no longer exists.]]]

04. Another major linguistic contributor was Jacob Grimm. (During the nineteenth century,) he sought (to scientifically prove) [that sound shifts showed relationships (between languages.)] Grimm sought rare unchanged words (throughout the German countryside) (to clarify) the history (of the German language.) Unfortunately, rural Germans presumed [that a 'linguistics researcher' was just a new way (for the government) (to figure out) [how much property tax they owed.]] (To entice) people (to speak) freely, Grimm asked them (to tell) him stories, [which he faithfully recorded.] His primary interest was not initially the stories themselves but any exotic vocabulary [they happened (to use.)] Grimm, however, did get [what he wanted word-wise.] (In the stories,) he noticed an evolutionary pattern (of Germanic languages) [which pointed (to a change) [that had taken place long ago.]] He explained [that related languages have similar, but not identical consonants, [which had undergone predictable changes (over time.)]] Hard consonants (such as the v and t) (in German word vater,) softened (into the Dutch vader and the English father.) Using Grimm's theory, linguists realized [that consonants would become harder [as they went 'backwards' (toward the original language.)]]

05. (From Jones and Grimm's theories,) linguists came up (with the first major linguistic hypothesis:) the existence (of a common ancestral language) called Proto-Indo-European [which transformed (into ancient Latin, Greek, and Sanskrit)]. This single language links modern languages (around the world.) Study (of this language) has helped identify [that, [although they share only a few similarities,] both Slavonic and Germanic are sub-branches (of a common ancestral language.)] Several research tasks naturally followed this hypothesis. First, the vocabulary (of the proposed ancestral language) needed (to be reconstructed,) [before the hearth (of the language) could be located.] (After this,) the routes (of dispersion) needed (to be traced.) Finally, the ways (of life) (of those) [who spoke and spread the language] needed (to be established.)

06. Nineteenth century linguist August Schleicher described language families (as the branches) (of a tree.) He suggested [that new languages form (through language divergence,) [when a language breaks down and fragments (into dialects) and then (into discrete tongues) (due to separation) (of speakers.)]] This can be seen (in Spanish and Portuguese) and is now happening (with Quebecois French.) (Due to geographical separation,) Parisian French and Quebecois French started (to differ) (after the colonial era.) Now the pronunciation and vocabulary use (of the two places) differ greatly. These new languages become leaves (on the tree.) (Through backward reconstruction,) linguists can find [how languages branches fit together.] Tracing backward far enough, they can find the hearth (of a language.)

07. Finding this hearth is a daunting task, [as reconstructing even a small branch is complicated.] A complicating factor is [that (with human mobility,) languages did not merely diffuse (through static populations;)] they also spread (by relocation diffusion.) [If people (with different languages) have consistent spatial interaction,] language convergence can take place, collapsing two languages (into one.) This creates problems (for researchers) [because the reconstruction rules sometimes do not apply and can be unreliable.]

TEST 2-1 Earth's Atmosphere

01. The Earth's atmosphere consists mainly (of heavy gases) (like nitrogen,) but lacks light gases (such as hydrogen and helium.) This is odd, [because nitrogen is known (to be) the seventh most abundant element (in the universe,) [whereas hydrogen is the most common,]] [which begs the question (of [why hydrogen is no longer abundant (in Earth's atmosphere.)])] Earth, currently the only planet known (to support) life, has an atmosphere distinguishable (from others) (in the solar system,) (due to being composed) (of byproducts) (of life,) (such as oxygen.) This distinction can be seen (in the changes) observed (through studies) done (by a series) (of scientists,) [which have ultimately classified Earth's atmosphere (into three stages) (of evolution:)] primordial atmosphere, secondary atmosphere, and the addition (of oxygen.)

02. Initially, light gases were abundant (in Earth's primordial atmosphere,) but gradually started (to decline.) This can be explained (through 'Jeans escape',) a classical form (of thermal escape) based (on Maxwell's Distribution) [that prescribes [that the kinetic energy distribution (of molecules) is dependent (on the mass and velocity) (of the molecule.)]] (From this,) one can conclude [that the bigger the molecule, the lower its average velocity (at a given temperature,) [which makes escape more unlikely.]] Furthermore, the greater the mass (of the planet,) the higher the required escape velocity; [which ultimately result (in less escaping molecules.)] Thus, giant planets (with high gravity) possess higher concentrations (of light gases) (such as hydrogen and helium,) [which are rare (in the innerplanet's atmospheres.)] The distance (from the star) also affects molecular velocity; the closer the planet, the hotter the atmosphere becomes, leading (to higher molecular velocity and higher escape rates.) This is [how Saturn's relatively small moon, Titan, keeps its atmosphere.] [Even though its gravitational pull is lower (than that) (of Earth,)] its cooler temperature allows it (to hold on) (to its atmosphere.)

03. Scientists believe [that [as light gases escaped (from Earth's atmosphere,)] nitrogen began constituting a larger part (of it) [after volcanic eruptions spewed gases, ultimately forming the main component (of the secondary atmosphere.)]] Three primary reasons [why only nitrogen filled the environment] are [that it is volatile even (at low temperatures,) unreactive (with the materials) [that make up the earth's crust,] and very stable (in the presence) (of solar radiation.)] (In contrast to more abundant elements) [which are major components (of Earth's crust,)] nitrogen is not stable (as a part) (of a crystal lattice,) and will not bond (with the others) (to form) the terrestrial earth; it, instead, remains a gas. (Unlike nitrogen,) other elements are unstable and easily react (with each other) (in the atmosphere) as well as break down [when exposed (to solar radiation.)] Thus, (over time,) nitrogen built up (in the atmosphere) (to a much greater extent) (than other elements.)

04. One theory introducing the presence (of atmospheric oxygen) is the Gaia theory. It is believed (by scientists) [that the primordial atmosphere (of Earth) did not contain oxygen] and [that the appearance (of this gas) required the evolution (of photosynthetic life forms,) (such as early cyanobacteria and later singlecelled algae,) [which emerged [as the earth cooled and the gaseous water condensed and formed oceans.]]] (As a result) (of photosynthesis,) molecular oxygen built up (to the present level,) [which appears (to have been) relatively stable (for several billion years.)] [If this level were even slightly higher,] then the earth's biomass would be combustible, leading (to extensive explosions and forest fires,) severely damaging earth's ecosystem. The Gaia theory, thus, suggests [that there is a planetary, homeostatic control (over the oxygen concentration) (in the atmosphere) [that balances the ratio (of organisms) producing oxygen (to those) consuming it.]]

05. However, some argue [that the amount (of oxygen) collected (in the earth's atmosphere) cannot be accounted for entirely (by cyanobacteria.)] They believe [that the theory is not adequate [because it can only account for 1 percent (to 10 percent concentration levels,) [while today's atmosphere contains 21 percent.]]] Thus, a second theory called the planetary atmosphere tectonic machine theory was developed. The theory posits [that all (of earth's oxygen) came (from not life forms,) but the ocean, (near the tectonic plates) [where magma is released and water comes (into contact) (with temperatures) (over 2000 °C.)]] The super-heated water is then converted (into hydrogen and oxygen.) The oxygen bubbles then oxygenate the ocean, and are released (into the atmosphere) [when they reach the surface.] This oxygen (in the atmosphere) is then shielded (from being fully lost) (to space) (by the ozone and the earth's magnetic field.)

TEST 2-2 The Effects of Light on Flowering

01. Plant growth and development are controlled by interactions between environmental factors and inner developmental processes. Amongst the diverse environmental factors, light plays the most essential role, affecting plants in various ways, from their growth and ability to produce energy to their bloom time. For example, in the absence of sufficient light, plants exhibit a unique growth pattern called etiolation. These plants will produce thinner and longer stems with longer internodes to reach a faint light source or to find one, in a much more rapid way than those exposed to adequate sunlight. A plant suffering from etiolation will also produce fewer leaves.

02. Perhaps the most interesting influence light has on plants is on their flowering patterns. The blossoming of flowers in plants is an intricate and delicate process which has evolved to suit plants different environments. To maximize the probability of their seeds being successfully dispersed, plants use environmental factors to determine the current season. Some of these factors, like temperature and water availability, can fluctuate heavily. An unusually cool summer or unexpected rain outside the monsoon seasons would confuse the plants. Fortunately, plants can also use the length of day as a cue. Length of day is perhaps the most reliable indicator of the season because it is controlled by the angle of Earth's rotation, which is unaltered by terrestrial events. Longer days always indicate springtime and the coming of summer while shorter days are only possible during autumn and winter.

03. Depending on their reaction to the length of the day, species of plants are traditionally categorized into three groups: the long-day, the short-day and day-neutral plants. A day-neutral plant produces flowers as soon as it has sufficiently grown and developed, regardless of the length of the day. The traditional names of long-day and short-day plants are, however, better described as short-night and long-night plants since it is the duration of continuous darkness rather than the day length which controls flowering. Long-night plants produce fowers during times when there is more than a specified duration of continuous darkness. Conversely, short-night plants require periods of darkness to be less than a specified period. The threshold for the length of darkness of both long-night and short-night plants differ by species. The duration of this is called the critical photoperiod. For example, spinach, a shortnight plant, only produces flowers

[when exposed (to less-than-eleven-hour intervals) (of darkness.)] Spinach's critical photoperiod is, therefore, eleven hours.

04. Compared (to their flowering behavior,) the actual method used (by plants) (to distinguish) daytime (from nighttime) is not well understood. So far, botanists have discovered [that plants utilize an internal clock and a light-detecting pigment called phytochrome (in order to measure) the length (of uninterrupted darkness.)] The internal biological clock is used (to measure) the length (of time) [the plant has spent (without light.)] It works (as a timer) [that starts ticking [when the light goes out,] and resets [when it returns.]] This clock is found (in almost all organisms,) (including humans), yet is poorly understood. There is, however, a better grasp (of the phytochrome.) Phytochrome is a pigment found (in plants) [which has the ability (to detect) light and bring about cellular change [when it is present.]] One such cellular change is the resetting (of the internal clock) [that measures the length (of continuous darkness.)]

05. This mechanism is quite sensitive; many species (of long-night plants) [that have their darkness interrupted (for even a minute or two) (with either sunlight or artificial light)] may not flower. It was found [that red light shone (on a plant) (during the night) is perceived (by the plant) and the plant resets its biological clock.] But the same plant does not reset its clock [when exposed (to far-red light) (light (with a longer wavelength) (than red light,))] and therefore it produces fowers. This is not [because phytochrome cannot detect far-red light,] but [because it reacts (to the two types) (of light) differently.]

06. The discovery (of [what internal factors actually signal plants (to flower) (in response) (to light)]) has overarching potential (in biology and agriculture,) [which makes it an intriguing topic (of study.)] Experiments conducted (on cockleburs,) a family (of long-night plants) [that require more than eight hours (of darkness) (to flower,)] revealed [that (despite their strong sensitivity) (to light exposure,) [when even a single leaf (of the cocklebur) experiences a long night [while the rest (of the plant) were subjected (to short nights,)]] it still produced flowers.] This experiment suggested [that a flowering factor is sent (from the leaves) (to the flower buds) [when the flowering conditions (for the plants) are met.]] So far scientists have not found this factor, but the most widely accepted notion is [that interactions (among multiple, as yet unidentified plant hormones or other compounds,) referred to (as florigen,) trigger flowering.]

TEST 3-1 Naturalistic painting

01. The civilization (of Ancient Greece,) [which lasted (from the 8th century) (to the mid-1st century BC,)] had a lasting cultural influence (over such a huge area,) and (over such powerful empires) [that it is often considered the underpinning (of Western culture.)] Historians have discovered [that even paintings (from Ancient Greece) had a strong influence (on art) (in remote parts) (of Europe) (for millennia) (to come.)] One such artistic influence was the movement known (as naturalism.) Naturalistic painters aspire (to depict) the world's natural objects, people and unadorned scenery as realistically [as possible.] Their paintings are characterized (by meticulous detail and near-perfect symmetry.) (In simple terms,) naturalistic artists strive (to create) realistic paintings hardly distinguishable (from actual photographs.) This movement originated (in Ancient Greece) and spread (through Europe) (to the Netherlands,) [where it continuously evolved.]

02. (In Ancient Greece,) the early naturalistic painters tended (to put) more emphasis (on skill) [than (on creativity,)] and painters (of Greece) would often compare their works (to see) [which was more 'realistic'.] [While the artists' creativity was largely subjective,] a brushstroke was an objective means (of assessment.) (As a result,) naturalistic painting became a competitive style (of painting,) [as shown (by the legendary painting competition) (of Parrhasius and Zeuxis,) two (of the greatest painters) (of the 5th century BC.)] Parrhasius, [who was born (in the city) (of Ephesus) and lived (in Athens,)] had distinguished himself (as an extraordinary artist) (at a young age.) Often, those [who witnessed the initial stages (of his paintings)] mistook him (for a sketch artist,) an artist [who completes his work using only a pencil or pastel.] His works were so great [that they were preserved (as study aids) (for painters) [that came (after him.)]] His rival Zeuxis was born (in the Southern Italian city) (of Heraclea,) and was widely renowned (in the artistic scene) (of the time.) (At the peak) (of their careers,) a contest was staged (to determine) the greater (of the two.) (At the competition,) Zeuxis revealed a painting (of grapes) [which was realistic enough (to fool) nearby birds.] Absorbed (in a sense) (of achievement,) he confidently asked Parrhasius (to pull) aside the curtains and reveal) his painting, only (to be told) [that the curtains themselves were his painted work.] Zeuxis was confounded (by this) and exclaimed ["I have deceived the birds, but Parrhasius has deceived Zeuxis."] Parrhasius' painting later became known (as 'Parrhasius' Curtain') and he attained the title (of the best naturalistic painter) (of the time,) gaining even more fame and respect. He was even asked (to paint) murals (for the Capitol of Rome) (by city officials.)

03. Millenniums later, Adriaen van der Spelt and Frans van Mieris, painters from Netherlands, led a movement that challenged the original principles of naturalism. Their paintings portrayed objects and acts that interested them, with little regard for whether they resembled the natural world. For example, they painted a lily in the center of Parrhasius' Curtain with insects around it. The lily served no naturalistic purpose, but with it the painting gained scores of symbolic meaning. Critics and fellow artists were awakened to the ideas of naturalist painting, surprised and awed at the same time. The lily represented wealth and property while the insects around the flower illustrated how the flower could be robbed of its nectar and left to die in a matter of days. The painting was lauded for its combination of symbolism and realistic insights. This led critics to begin questioning whether 'art' was defined by how well a natural object is depicted, or by how well it is embellished and enhanced. This became more pronounced as technological progress and development led to the emergence of cameras and professional photography. Clearly, the new artistic photographs captured naturalistic images much more easily than paintings. While an intricate and time-consuming process in the past, re-creating nature on paper became only a matter of the click of a shutter.

04. As art entered the modern era, the common belief became that painting to resemble nature as closely as possible is not really art, but rather an act of duplication. There have not only been convincing arguments which support this claim, but also several credible arguments that oppose it. One modern artist, for instance, added his touch to Adriaen van der Spelt and Frans van Mieris' painting by coloring the lily bright red. The red lily, the artist explained, represented passion and supported the assertion that art should express the artist's mind. According to him, an artist must deliberately convey his vision through various methods, such as the use of color and brushstroke. On the other hand, the French Neoclassical painter Jean Auguste Dominique Ingres, pointed out that regardless of what or how an artist paints, the painter unintentionally leaves traces of himself in the work. Ingres believed that the painter would subconsciously make different choices according to his mood, such as using harsher brushstrokes when feeling angry, or passionate colors when in love, all inadvertently. With all things considered, despite the fact that it was decreasing in popularity and was occasionally criticized, the naturalistic style of painting has played a major role in the history of art and will continue to do so in the future.

TEST 3-2 Two types of evolutionary theories

01. Evolution occurs [as populations adjust (to habitat change) (with those) experiencing the best genetic adaptations surviving and passing (on their genes.)] These phenotypic changes (in populations) are common (to all organisms) and affect every species, no matter what ecosystem. There are two prevailing, non-mutually exclusive theories (of evolution) today, gradualism and punctuated equilibrium, [which differ (in the speed) [(at which) evolutionary changes occur.]]

02. One (of the early proponents) (of complete gradualism) was Charles Darwin [whose 'Origin of Species' adopted Charles Lyell's 'Principles of Geology' (to suggest) [gradualism occurs (in a slow manner) (with only small intergenerational changes.)]] [As Lyell proposed,] sudden changes cannot be assumed (to occur) [as they are not presently observed] and thus cannot be assumed (to have occurred) (in the past.) Darwin also felt [that extreme deviations (from the usual phenotypic variation) would be more likely (to be selected) against.] The most famous historical model supporting the idea (of complete gradualism) was the evolution (of the modern horse) (from the fox-sized, forest-dwelling Hyracotherium.) (Over time,) paleozoologists pieced together the gradual evolution (of the horse) (in a more complete way) (than any other modern animal.) They traced the lineage (from early ancestors) (with splayed toes) (for walking) (on the soft, moist grounds) (of primeval forests,) (to the longer legged, faster species) [which grazed (on the firm grassy steppes) and were able (to outrun) predators] and eventually (to the modern hoofed horse.) Paleontologist Othniel C. Marsh was so sure (of this theory) (of gradual equine evolution) [that he put together a series (of fossils) showing it (in 1870.)] The fact [that these fossils displayed successive adaptations] was held (as an example) (of gradualism) (until 100 years later,) [when it was shown [they were not, (in fact,) even successive members (of a single line) (of descent,) (let alone stages) (of an unbroken, gradually evolving lineage.)]]

03. Scientists studying fossils noted [that the evolution (of some species) was nearly 'mapped out,' [while others had a few, very different species (along the evolutionary course,) (with few or no intermediary fossils.)]] They envisaged [that this second group's evolution must have occurred rapidly (to produce) a great change (over a short period.)] They reasoned [that there had (to be) another evolutionary method [that was quicker and left fewer intermediate species,]] thus the idea (of punctuated equilibrium) was formed. The theory (of punctuated equilibrium) states [that most sexually-reproducing species will remain (in an extended state) (of little evolutionary change) (between generations,) called stasis, [which is broken up (by rare, rapid events) (of branching speciation) called cladogenesis [when they split (into two distinct species.)]]] They pointed out [that (for most species,) there was a sudden appearance (in the geologic record) (with no evidence) (of substantial, gradual changes.)] Darwin had noted this problem also, but ascribed it (to imperfections) (in the fossil record) rather (than catastrophism and progressive creationism, or supernatural creation,) [while privately noting (on the margin) (of his essay,) "Better begin (with this): [If species really, (after catastrophes,) created (in showers) world over], my theory false."]

04. [While these theories vary widely (on their methods) (of evolution,)] both show major adaptations (over time) [whereby a population becomes better suited (to its habitat.)] These successive intergenerational changes occur (in all species) and are one (of the basic phenomena) (of biology.) (From this) one can see [that adaptation is not just a matter (of visible traits,) complex adaptations (to changes) can occur (during an organism's life.)] These reactions (to habitat change) happen (in three major ways,) either exclusively or (in succession.) The most basic adaptation (to change) is (to simply move) (to a locale) [that better suits the organism.] This response, typical (of organisms) [that have wide spheres (of movement) (such as flying insects or sea-dwellers,)] is called habitat tracking, and is one explanation put forth (for the periods) (of apparent stasis) (in the fossil record.) The term genetic change, (on the other hand,) pertains (to changes) (in the population) [when natural selection acts (on the genetic variations) (of a population.)] These mutations, [which may be physical features or adjusted physiological activity,] create genetic variations [that lead (to differing characteristics) (in offspring) and, consequently, a population better genetically adapted (to its environment.)] The third, and most dramatic, change [that can occur (to resident populations)] is extinction, or the demise (of a population) [that was unable (to properly adapt) (to change.)]

05. [Whether (by gradualism or punctuated equilibrium,)] a species must always adapt (to its changing habitat,) [as it is now clear [that habitats and biota are constantly changing and the process (of adaptation) is never complete.]]

TEST 4-1   Griffith and transformation

01. The 19th century Romantic Movement reshaped science (by opening) new avenues (of research) [that were unheard of (under the Enlightenment's classical approaches.)] Major breakthroughs, (such as Darwin's theory) (of evolution,) were developed (during this period,) (along with advances) (in physics, non-Euclidean geometry and organic chemistry.) (During this time,) science became a major source (for increasing) humankind's knowledge. (During the 19th and 20th centuries,) the practice (of science) became much more professionally institutionalized [than it had been.] One (of the great breakthroughs) (in biology) is attributed (to Frederick Griffith) (of the British Ministry of Health.) Griffith undertook one (of the most pivotal experiments) (of the era,) [which tried (to establish) a more precise scientific understanding (by typing,) or classifying, pneumococci bacteria samples (in order to find) overarching patterns (so as to clarify) the epidemiology (of lobar pneumonia,) an infectious lung disorder.]

02. He also sought (to improve) the understanding (of the pathology) (of pneumococci) (on the individual) (by testing) them (on mice.) Smooth pneumococci, denoted (by S,) are encapsulated and more virulent; this form was shown (to result) (in pneumonia and death) (of the mice) (within days) (of being injected). Their capsules are slippery polysaccharide coatings [that allow the bacteria (to evade) phagocytosis (from the host's immune cells.)] (On the other hand,) the rough form, R, lacks a capsule and was considered non-infective. (In Griffith's experiment,) [as expected,] [when mice were injected (with S) [that had been killed (by heat,)]] it failed (to cause) illness (despite being) the virulent strain. Surprisingly, however, Griffith observed pneumonia and death [when live R were injected (alongside large amounts) (of heat-killed S;)] this was generally unexpected, [since R, the only live bacteria (in the experiment,) were avirulent.] (During necropsy,) Griffith found [that the live R had developed capsules and morphed (into S), then retained this phenotype (over successive generations.)] Griffith hypothesized [that a transforming principle — derived (from the killed S) — had helped transform the R (into S.)] He also reported [that heavy loads (of live R) alone could also transform (into S.)] Griffith, however, noted [that the addition (of heat-killed S bacteria) made this transformation much more likely.]

03. Griffith had previously held, (along with most bacteriologists), [that bacteria's forms were essentially fixed and unchangeable.] They held [that each strain had emerged (from, and was genetically similar (to their progenitor,) (through an evolutionary lineage) determined (by Darwinian natural selection) resulting (in the death) (of unfit bacterial cells.)] (Besides this implicit belief) [that bacterial strains could be extinguished (through competition,)] many bacteriologists and physicians believed [that any particular strain (of bacteria) had necessarily multiplied (from previous, genetically-related strains.)] Griffith's findings, [though generally neglected [after the initial contention (against them) subsided,]] revealed [that his original supposition was incorrect (by showing) [that bacteria are able (to acquire) genes (without the need) (for reproducing) as well.]] He summarized his work (as such:) "The results (of the experiments) (on enhancement) (of virulence) and (on transformation) (of type) are discussed and their significance (in regard to questions) (of epidemiology) is indicated."

04. An American medical researcher named Oswald Avery, (with colleagues Macleod and McCarty) furthered Griffith's 1927 findings (regarding the mysteries) (of inheritance.) Being driven (to prove) Griffith's theory, Avery continued (to work) (on adjusting) previous techniques even [after he retired (in 1943.)] (To do) this, the cellular structures (of the S strain bacteria) were first removed, and then their proteins were removed (through the use) (of protease enzyme treatments.) Finally, the cellular remainders were placed (in a dish) containing R strain bacteria. The R strain bacteria transformed, meaning [that proteins did not carry the virulent genes.] Then the remainder (of the S strain bacteria) had their DNA removed (by being treated) (with deoxyribonuclease.) [When they were treated (in this manner,)] the R strain bacteria resisted transformation, proving [that DNA was the transforming factor (of pneumococci.)]

05. (Over time,) more advanced discoveries have been made (through the findings) (of Griffith and Avery.) Joshua Lederberg's discoveries (concerning genetic recombination and the organization) (of the bacterial genetic material) are a prime example (of this continuation.) Inspired (by previous discoveries,) Lederberg, (in 1944,) started (to think) (about genetic experimentations) (on bacteria) (despite the fact) [that there was still no consensus (on [whether bacteria even had genes or not.]))] He showed [that bacteria could reproduce sexually and substantiated the hypothesis (by proving) [that they are endowed (with genetic systems) akin (to those) (of higher-level organisms,)]] thus opening a new realm (for scientists) (to study) the genetic basis (of life) and winning the 1958 Nobel Prize (in Physiology or Medicine.) (During his speech,) he stated [that former researchers and their laboratories provided the historical platform (of modern DNA research.)]

TEST 4-2 Maximilian Weber and His Influence

01. Authority can be defined (as the forceful domination) (of a group) (of people) [who have the underlying condition (of being) absolutely obedient.] The German sociologist Maximilian Weber, (on the other hand,) defined authority (as 'the chance') (of commands) being obeyed (according to distinct justifications) (by a specifiable group) (of people.) Pointing out [that Germany's political fiasco (during WWI) was essentially a problem (of leadership,)] Weber proposed a theory (of authority) [that classified it (into three types,) each differing (in its justifications) (to compel) acquiescence and its influences (on the public.)]

02. (In a society) [that is governed (by a system) (of 'traditional' authority,)] social status plays a vital role (in determining) the sovereign power. The leaders (of these types) (of societies) are a ruling elite (with an inheritable leadership role) based (on factors) (such as age, bloodline, or social connections,) [which shows [that there is an inequality (in the society.)]] The disadvantage (of this system) is [that it is vulnerable (to change,)] [as is evident [when looking (at the challenges) faced (by the Russian Empire) [as it encountered a more complex division (of labor) and wider population diversity (due to Industrialization) (in the early 20th century.)]]] The helplessness (of the traditional authority) (against the rise) (of the bourgeois and proletariat classes) ultimately brought (about the introduction) (of 'rational-legal' authority) (in Russia.) 'Rational-legal' authority is a system [(in which) an individual, or institution, exercises power (through the socially accepted set) (of rules) and the right) (of those) elevated (to positions) (of authority) (to issue) such commands.] Power is held (by the office) itself, (with no regard) (to the personal attributes) (of the office holder,) and it is limited (by the official codified rules) [which state the extent (of the office's power.)] 'Rational-Legal' authority fosters financial stability and technological development [because the rights (of individuals) act (as the law,) guaranteeing their property and investments.] 'Charismatic' authority can exist (under 'traditional' or 'rational-legal' authorities systems) [when power is gained (through widespread devotion) (to the exceptional sanctity, heroism, or a specific exemplary characteristic) (of a person.)] (According to Weber,) this form (of authority) is extremely volatile and dynamic [as charisma eventually recedes [after it has entered the permanent routine (of social interaction,) [which can result (in the sudden collapse) (of its power.)]]] (For example,) Napoleon Bonaparte gained his fame (through his military feats,) immediately consolidating absolute political power (over France) and reforming the country. His defeat (during the Napoleonic Wars,) however, resulted (in the abrupt end) (of his reign) (as emperor) and the beginning) (of his exile.)

03. [Although Weber's theory has strongly influenced the aspects (of sociology) [that deal (with leadership,)]] scholars have pointed out two faws (in it.) First, they believed [that the standardization (of a variety) (of concepts) (of authority) and Weber's theoretical notion (of an 'iron cage',) [(in which) the increased rationalization (of modern life) causes individuals (to be driven) purely (by objective,) rather [than (by values,)]] was an oversimplified, limited idea (of authority.)] Furthermore, they posit [that he failed (to distinguish) (between reigning and governing,)] (with governing) requiring a positive change (in society) [whereas reigning does not.]

04. (Despite these objections,) Weber's theory (of authority) influenced modern sociology and brought (about the development) (of three new models) (of leadership) (in the late 20th century.) The theory (behind 'transformational' leadership) is [that leaders can make radical changes (in their followers' thoughts and actions) and exploit the order (of their needs)] and aims (to satisfy) the greater need, [which is, (in turn,) closely aligned (with the followers' internal motivational factors.)] The leaders [who Weber would have classified (as having) charismatic authority] are, therefore, transformational, [since they approach things (from entirely different perspectives.)] (In contrast,) individuals [that can be described (as 'rational-legal' leaders)] can also be seen (as 'transactional' leaders,) [as they are effective (in using) their knowledge (to achieve) results, based (on the hypothesis) [that followers are motivated (through a system) (of 'quid pro quo' - or 'give and take'.)]] The differing qualities (of the two leadership types) can be simply stated as: 'transactional' leaders form mutual bonds (with people) (through reward and punishment,) [while, (in contrast,) 'transformational' leaders seek (to gratify) the intrinsic needs (of the individual.)] The third form, 'laissez-faire' leadership, is characterized (by a completely permissive leader) [who does not contribute (to making) decisions, [which produces groups [that often lack direction], and may lead (to anarchy,) but offer their followers many opportunities (to make) their own decisions.]]

05. Weber stressed [that the importance (of theories) (of authority) is not (to label,) or classify,) prevalent forms (of leadership) (in history,) but rather (to show) [how the state (of authority) transits (from one type) (to another.)]] His precise intention led (to scholars) viewing his theory (as a hierarchical development order,) and it is now considered more (of a theory) (on social evolution.)

TEST 5-1 Pasteur and origin of life

01. Logical and methodical scientists sometimes, ironically, blindly adhere to spuriously hypothesized assertions. For instance, Aristotle hypothesized that flies were the result of spontaneous generation in rotting materials and that microorganisms could appear naturally. Scientists believed these theories for nearly two millennia. These errant theories led them to believe that the bacteria required for fermentation were naturally generated without any external stimuli. Scientist Louis Pasteur, however, skeptical of spontaneous generation, successfully falsified the long-held theory.

02. Pasteur proposed the new theory of biogenesis, claiming that the natural generation of bacteria was preposterous, and that fermentation required the introduction of the necessary bacteria. In order to prove this, he conducted two experiments. In the first, a glass filled with meat broth, which would have fermented in open air, was placed in a sealed box that was completely sterile and had a filter over its opening. This did not allow anything to enter the glass and as a result there were no signs of fermentation in the glass. This, however, did not convince scientists at the time, because they thought that even if organisms were generated in the glass, they would have expired due to lack of oxygen. Therefore, he conducted a second experiment, the 'swan-neck duct' experiment. In this experiment, he put the broth into a spherical glass with a long curved tube atop it. With this structure, nothing but weightless air could enter. This also yielded no fermentation. In 1864, Pasteur finally announced the results of these and further experiments, demonstrating that life cannot spontaneously arise in areas that have not been exposed to existing life.

03. Unsurprisingly, Pasteur's experiments were eye-openers, having definitively disproved the antiquated theory of spontaneous generation and giving birth to biogenesis. Even though he was the first to empirically prove this, he was not the first scientist to propose this type of theory. Scientists Girolamo Fracastoro, Agostino Bassi, and Friedrich Henle had previously suggested various theories which influenced Pasteur's work later. The development of biogenesis, however, left a vacuum in the understanding of how life first arose. As it requires previous forms of life, biogenesis alone could not ultimately explain the origin of life on the early, barren Earth. No notable related theories, however, appeared until 1924, when Alexander Oparin surmised that the presence of oxygen in the atmosphere prevents the synthesis of certain organic compounds that are necessary for the evolution of life. In 'The Origin of Life,' he proffered that the type of abiogenesis that Pasteur attacked

had (in fact) occurred once, but no longer could [because the conditions found (on the early Earth) had changed.]] Oparin felt [that an organic 'primeval soup' could be created (in an oxygen-free atmosphere) (due to the effects) (of sunlight.)] He hypothesized [that 4 billion years ago, the earth's environment met these criteria [after volcanic eruptions filled the environment (with carbon dioxide, nitrogen, and other gases.)]] Originally he thought [that the early atmosphere, (in contrast to the Earth's current atmosphere,) contained mostly ammonia and methane], but it is likely [that most (of the atmospheric carbon) was carbon dioxide (with perhaps some carbon monoxide and nitrogen.)] (In practice) these mixtures have many (of the same properties) (as those) containing ammonia and methane as long [as free oxygen molecules are not present.]

04. These theories were tested (in the Miller and Urey experiment) [which attempted (to recreate) these hypothetical conditions,] and tested (for the occurrence) (of the chemical origins) (of life.) (In order to test) (for the generation) (of the amino acids,) required (for protein generation) (in living cells) (under primitive Earth's conditions,) they required a less hydrogen-rich mixture (than the current environment.) Their experiments used water, methane, ammonia, and hydrogen, sealed (inside interconnected sterile glass tubes and beakers,) (with one) half filled (with water) and another) holding two electrodes. The water was boiled (to produce) evaporation, then the electrodes were fired (to simulate) lightning (through the atmosphere and water vapor,) and then it was cooled again (to condense) the water back (into the first beaker) (in a repetitive cycle.) (After one week,) they observed [that 10~15 percent (of the carbon) was (in the form) (of organic compounds.)] Two percent (of the carbon) had formed amino acids, (with glycine) being the most plentiful. [Although nucleic acids were not formed,] the 20 common amino acids were formed (in various concentrations.) This was interesting [because amino acids can potentially create the most basic component (of most living creatures,) namely DNA.]

TEST 5-2 Early Research on Air

01. The composition (of air) has fascinated scientists (since early times.) (According to the ancient Greeks,) air was regarded (as one) (of the four elements,) [which also included fire, earth, and water.] It was not, however, precisely studied or correctly understood (by many scholars.) They generally thought [that the air [people breathe] had the same composition (as the gases) found (in any other part) (of the universe.)] Eventually, a few analytical scientists began (to question) its properties and conducted research (to define) them but their studies were limited (by the fact) [that they only sought (to study) air (in the perspective) (of their specialties.)] (Prior to the seventeenth century,) chemists believed [that gases were not involved (in chemical reactions,)] and focused (on matter) (in its solid or liquid states:) (according to them,) gases were (in the domain) (of physicists.) This trend significantly impeded progress (on the study) (of air.)

02. It was (not until the seventeenth century) [that the understanding (of air) was seriously pursued (by scientists.)] However, (due to the lack) (of scientific instruments) and the need) (for those) (beyond the usual tools,) their experiments soon faced limitations. (For example,) Robert Boyle, a British scientist known (for Boyle's Law,) began a series (of experiments) (to find out) the composition (of air) (through combustion.) Boyle vacuumed the air (out of a jar) and showed [that neither charcoal nor sulfur burned (in the vacuum.)] Boyle had discovered the very first property (of air) stating [that it is required (for a fire) (to burn.)] His finding was not, however, recognized (by the scientific community) (of the day) [because his definition (of the component) (of air) responsible (for combustion) was vague.] (In addition,) most scientists were reportedly more interested (in finding) the chemical composition (of air) [than (in its physical characteristics.)] Thus, he shifted the focus (of his research) (to air's chemical aspects) and (in 1659,) (with continuous effort,) discovered [that both hydrogen and nitric oxide gases were present (in air.)] Boyle also tried (to revise) misconceptions (regarding air,) (such as the popular belief) [that air had no weight.] Years later, Einstein credited Boyle (for having) a holy curiosity (in poorly understood phenomena) [that others simply accepted (as 'natural')] (As a result) (of his persistence,) he is now known (as the father) (of chemistry.)

03. Even (with all) (of Boyle's achievements,) people's understanding (of air) was still elementary and more study using advanced laboratory equipment was required. Scientists still struggled (to uncover) the many unknown properties (of air,) [which were exemplified (by the rudimentary definition) (of air) (as 'the elastic, invisible mixture) (of gases) [that surround the earth' (from an eighteenth century encyclopedia.)]]

Its invisibility meant [that it could not be observed (under a microscope)] and its ability (to diffuse) quickly proved (to be) an irritable characteristic (to scientists) for it complicated calculations measuring the amount (of air) being experimented upon. Therefore, many prominent physicists investigated air wishing (to further) their understanding, but they showed little noticeable progress; having no success (in isolating) even one (of the many compounds) (in air.)

04. Luckily, the research (on air) was significantly advanced (by Stephen Hales,) an English physiologist and chemist, (in the late eighteenth century.) (In search) (of the various properties) (of air) and anxious (to clearly define) it, he gave birth (to a new branch) (in chemistry) called pneumatic chemistry. He invented the pneumatic trough (to study) the physical properties (of air) and their relation (to chemical reactions.) The trough was made (from household objects) (such as a hunting gun and a glass vessel.) The device measured the amount (of gas) produced [when a substance was heated] (by measuring) the amount (of water) displaced (in the vessel.) Hales' pneumatic trough became the basis (for experimental instruments) [that are widely used today.] The creativity demonstrated (through his improvisation) (of turning) common tools (into useful scientific instruments) was recognized (by, and won the praise (of, fellow scientists.)) (According to the scientific community,) however, Hales deserves more recognition [than he received (in the past)] [as experiments (regarding air) were actively held (by scientists) (of various fields) using his invention.]

05. (Despite his tremendous contributions) (to pneumatic chemistry,) Hales passed up the opportunity (to study) the chemical properties (of the various gases,) [as he was solely interested (in studying) their concentrations.] Scientists [that came (after him)] revised his pneumatic trough and proceeded (with further experiments.) (With the efforts) (of these scientists,) the properties (of the air) have been gradually unveiled. They have even successfully broken down all (of the components) (of atmospheric air) and calculated their proportion.

TEST 6-1 Photography as an Art

01. Three components are required for a work to be considered artistic: artist, medium, and artwork, the idea being that an artist manifests artwork through the medium. Since the camera's invention, photography has struggled to convince many that it falls within this definition. The opposition recognizes the medium and work as artful, but not the photographers' role as artist. They see them as technicians who 'operate the medium' to produce works instead of as artists, who, they claim, take time to complete works, poring over them. The photographer's ability to capture an image with a simple click was thus unequal, and photography was a process unequal to art. Photographer Mark Chamberlain disagreed with this, stating that 'in the hands of an artist, the camera is only another tool', which can become an extension of the eye if properly utilized, but is a lifeless piece of metal otherwise. He contended that releasing the shutter may only take a second, but timing and framing are crucial, and the photographer has to find perfect lighting and conditions.

02. Chamberlain was not the only photographer to fight denigration of photography. Earlier, between 1851 and 1862, famous photographers such as Antoine Claudet, Andre Disderi, and William Lake Price published articles in professional journals attempting to analyze the aesthetic similarities and differences between graphic works and photographs and to convince readers that photography was actually an art. Their points of view were summed up in a piece in the 1862 Photographic Journal addressing whether photography should be hung in the Fine Arts or Industrial Section of the International Exposition. The author observed that the question is not whether photography is fine art per se, but whether it is capable of artistic expression in the hands of an artist. Their point-of-view was echoed in the Catalogue of the 1859 Salon of Photography by French naturalist Louis Figuier. He and other scientists were convinced that artistic expression and taste would be improved by photography, just as the general quality of life benefits from applied science. They, like Chamberlain, considered the lens a new tool, like the pencil or brush, which conveys the feelings of the photographer, and photography is, therefore, an art.

03. Later, photographers, in an effort to compete with high art, focused on still-lifes, allegorical costumes, genre scenes and composite images. However, as the novel idea of capturing images began to wear off, people began to question whether the camera's images were too accurate and

detailed.] (To overcome) this literalism, photographers used inferior optical elements, smeared lenses, kicked tripods, or blurred their black-and-white prints. (As a result,) pictorialism, an aesthetic movement imitating contemporary painting styles and techniques, was born. This movement [which originated (in Britain)] reached its height (in the 20th century) and had a strong influence (on American photography) (in its later phases.) One (of the most important promoters) (of this movement) was the journal 'Camera Work' published (by Alfred Stieglitz,) [whose sale (of fifteen photographs) (to the Albright Gallery) solidified photography's status (as an art) (in the United States.)]

04. (With the rise and fall) (of pictorialism,) struggles (over artistic nature) and the quest (to determine) [what truly constituted art] raged on (for over a century.) (In hindsight,) many conclude [that photographic art is (at its best) [when capturing the real world,] and least inspiring) [when emulating other art forms.]] The unique power (of photography) is its disposition (to form) the varieties (of textural experience) and the contrasts (in lighting,) rather (than narrative content,) (regardless of [whether the images were considered documents or art.])

05. Recognizing this, some photographers began producing prints (of artistic masterpieces) (for both their commercial and the general population's cultural benefit.) (Since then,) photographs have been the most significant supplier (of visual artifacts) (to the masses,) revolutionizing public access (to the art heritage) (of the world.) [What was once rejected (as being) too real] had become indispensable (in terms) (of historical preservation.) This was a welcomed advantage (of photography) [since it was believed [that familiarity (with classical art) would not only lift people's spirit, but also improve their taste.]]

06. Today, there is little doubt [that photography is a fine art.] This shows [that photography has stood its ground and found its place (in the art world.)] (In recent decades,) photography's potential has radically expanded. (Aside from the traditional two-dimensional, modest-sized black-and-white photographs,) photographs now display various shapes, colors, and formats, (to provide) information, make) statements, sell) products, or analyze) events. The development (of new technology and aesthetic theories) combined (with the enhanced role) (of photography) (as a marketable commodity) has influenced the way [the medium is now used and perceived.] This expanded role (of photography) is the result (of a rich history) tied (to developments) (in technology, art, and society.)

TEST 6-2 How and why birds learn to sing

01. Beautifully complex birdsongs have inspired our greatest poets and composers, and aroused the curiosity (of biologists.) They wondered [how and [why such an elaborate communication form developed (among birds.)]] One (of the many) [who struggled (to answer) these questions] was Darwin [who was clearly influenced (by these intricate songs) [as he developed the theory (of sexual selection.)]] (Since then) biologists (from many disciplines) have found birdsongs (to be) fascinating and productive research subjects.

02. Birdsongs, generally regarded (as an attribute) (of males,) are (in some rare species) produced (by females) (with complexity) comparable (to those) (of males.) (In general) though, male songbirds are the sources (of these complex songs.) Darwin suggested [that this was the result (of sexual selection) [because females choose mates (with more complex songs.)]] [Although this ability (of birdsongs) (to attract) females is frequently cited,] there is little experimental evidence (to support) this assertion [because field experiments proving [that female attraction (to the male's territory) is (in direct response) (to his singing)] are nearly impossible.] One experiment (on pair formation) (of flycatchers,) however, came close (to doing) so. Male dummies were positioned (near nest-boxes) (with automatic traps;) some played a tape-recorded song (from loudspeakers,) [while others remained silent.] Even [when their positions were switched (to control) external variables,] 90 percent (of females) were caught (in nest-box traps) (of 'singing' dummies,) showing [that a male's song attracts mates.] Further, females (of some species) prefer males (with more varied songs,) so these males quickly add (to their repertoires.) The diverse assortments (of songs) may indicate an older male (with access) (to better resources or proven longevity and survival skills,) both good traits (to pass on) (to offspring.) Experiments have also shown [that songs act (as territorial markers.)] House Wrens, (for example,) respond aggressively (to recordings) (of other males songs,) sometimes even attacking the speaker. Researchers have also shown [that removing male birds (from their territories) but broadcasting their songs prevented neighboring males (from entering) their territories, showing [that the songs warned others (to keep out.)]]

03. Just [as their reasons (for singing) vary,] so do the ways [that songbirds learn (to sing)]. Some are born (with an innate knowledge) (of the songs,) [while others learn them (from older birds) then add (to them) (to create) personalized songs,] and still others incorporate auditory stimuli (into their repertoire) and eventually end up (with thousands) (of variations.) (Unlike birds) (with innate abilities) (to sing,)

some are extremely susceptible (to external sound stimuli) [when learning songs.] Studies (of the White-crowned Sparrow) show [that nestlings raised alone (in a laboratory) develop an abnormal song.] [If they are housed (with a tutor adult White-crowned Sparrow,)] however, they will learn proper songs (from it.) [If they are only housed (with a Song Sparrow,)] however, they may learn (to sing) (as a Song Sparrow.) Scientists have also taught baby sparrows (to sing) a complete song (by exposing) them (to overlapping segments) (of a tune) rather (than a full melody.) This means [that the sparrows reassembled segments (of a song) [which were imprinted (in their brains,)] showing [that they have the ability (to identify and utilize) the different song parts presented (in the experiment.)]] Other birds, (such as Northern Mockingbirds and Brown Thrashers,) are adept (at mimicking) the calls (of other species) and add (to their repertoires) (throughout their lives,) learning around 200 and 2,000 different songs, respectively.

04. An interesting fact is [that birds acquire most (of these songs) (during critical periods) (of brain development.)] (To do) this, they rely (on the specialized frontal cortex section) (of the brain) known (as the basal ganglia.) This section (of the brain) internalizes sensory experiences and then shapes them (into vocal output) (through sensorimotor learning and integration.) This innate disposition (for 'language acquisition') is similar (to humans.) Humans have critical periods [when sensorimotor functions and regions (in the frontal cortex,) (like the basal ganglia) (in birds,) allow accelerated learning and vocal output shaping.] It is (during these brief periods) [that birds are best equipped (to memorize) details (of a tutor's song.)] (For the White-crowned Sparrow,) this age is (between 15 and 50 days), [(after which) learning becomes more difficult.] They, therefore, begin practicing singing shortly (after leaving) the nest, (at about three weeks) (of age.) Recalling the sounds [they heard (during the sensitive period,)] they match it (in their practice singing) called the subsong. The subsong becomes louder, more persistent, and structured (over time.) These corrections eventually result (in a perfect copy) (of the remembered song,) [which goes (through 'crystallization,') [(after which) there is little variation.]] Evidence, however, suggests [that auditory feedback is actively used (in adulthood) (to maintain) the song's structure.] It can be shown [that disturbing auditory feedback (during adult Zebra Finches' singing) caused their song (to deteriorate.)] This 'decrystallization' is a marked loss (of the temporal and spectral stereotypy) seen (in crystallized songs.) [Once normal feedback is restored,] these deviations gradually disappear and the original song returns. Thus, adult birds [that do not seem (to learn) new songs] still retain a significant amount (of plasticity) (in their brains.)

TEST 7-1 Functions of Roots

01. Roots, the water-absorbing organs (of a plant,) are present (on essentially all vascular plants) and serve three primary functions: (to anchor) the plant (to a substrate,) (to absorb) nutrients (through osmosis), and (to store) food reserves. They can adapt (to carry out) these primary functions (in ways) optimized (for different environments.)

02. One (of the most important functions) (of root networks) is (to provide) a stable footing (for plants) so they do not fall over or get swept away. This also provides the secondary benefit (of controlling) soil erosion (around the plant's base.) (In addition to this,) many plants (like the carrot and turnip) also store nutrients (in modified roots.) Roots (of plants) (such as the bluebell) store so much energy [that they act (as perennating organs) allowing the plant (to survive) harsh conditions (such as drought, frigid winters, or light deficiency.)] They do this (by allowing) the exposed part (of the plant) (to die down) and storing) as much energy [as possible] (for regrowth) [when conditions improve.]

03. (For plants) [which are constantly exposed (to harsh environments,) (such as salt water swamps,)] survival is more challenging (due to the lack) (of basic necessities.) The deeper roots (of most plants) die (because of the lack) (of oxygen) (under the waterlogged soil,) leading (to the plant's slow death.) Mangrove roots, however, are well-suited (to the region.) The red mangrove, a tropical tree [which colonizes coastlines and brackish water (between the northern and southern latitudes) (of 25 degrees,)] can often be found (on the water's edge.) These are distinguished (from other mangroves) (by the prominent prop roots) extending (into the water) (from high up) (on their stems.) They thrive (in the highly saline habitats) (by not relying) (on traditional roots) growing (under the substrate.) Instead, it is assumed, [lenticels, or pores, (on their prop roots) act (as conduits) (for supplying) oxygen (for respiration) (to the subterranean roots.)] (Unlike most plants,) its roots also enable them (to obtain) freshwater (from highly saline water sources) (through non-metabolic ultra-filtration,) using negative pressure (inside the root) (to draw) freshwater in (through a membrane) too fine (for salt) (to pass through,) (in a process) called reverse-osmosis.

04. (Unlike the mangroves,) however, most plants exist (in environments) filled (with other plants) leading (to a competition-filled bio-diverse habitat.) (To triumph) (over competition,) plants use various methods (such as root adaptations) (to attain) the necessary nutrients, water, sunlight, and territory. [If the plants are grown (in close proximity,)] there may be a limited amount (of these essential nutrients,) resulting (in a head-to-head competition) (for as large a share) [as possible.] One (of the ways) [they do this] is (by adapting.) One example (of this) is the dark, competition-filled forest floor, [where strangler figs have adapted roots [that snake down the trunk (of a host tree) or dangle (from its branches) (as aerial roots) enabling it (to live) (in the tree branches.)]] [When they reach the ground,] however, they dig in and grow more rapidly, fighting the host (for nutrients.) This root network surrounds the host and intertwines (around it.) [As they grow thicker] they squeeze the trunk (of the host) and cut off its flow (of nutrients.) Eventually the host dies (from strangulation, insufficient sunlight and root competition,) and the strangler fig stands (on its own.)

05. Some plants also compete using chemical methods. The roots (of these plants) secrete chemical compounds known (as root exudates.) (Through the exudation) (of a variety) (of compounds,) they regulate the microbial content (of nearby soil,) cope (with herbivores,) alter the physical and chemical make-up (of the soil,) and inhibit the growth (of competing plants.) Chemical-mediated plant-plant interference, or allelopathy, is one mechanism [plants use (to gain) an advantage (over their competitors.)] (In research) conducted (by biologists) (from a chemical company,) it was found [that a plant called lemon bottlebrush excreted an allelopathic chemical called leptospermone.] One day, they noted [that (under certain bushes,) (such as lemon bottlebrush,) other plants only rarely grew.] (By collecting) samples (of the soil) (under the bush,) they were able (to extract) many chemicals (from the plants,) [one (of which) was identified (as an herbicide.)] [While it did have herbicidal effects,] the amount required (for effective crop coverage) was too high (to be) practical. Leptospermone was, therefore, reworked (into thousands) (of compounds,) (with several) being effective but too toxic, environmentally persistent or non-selective. Mesotrione, the final compound [they created] could, however, be used (as a selective herbicide) (for corn crops.)

TEST 7-2　History of the Patent Law

01. The State's protection (of a person's right) (to utilize and control) the utilization (of an invention,) [be it a machine or a unique method (of production,)] was not prevalent (until the Renaissance period.) (As a result,) (in the Middle Ages,) one would have had (to hide) the fact [that one had invented a novel product] (in order to keep) it. This lack (of protection) (from the state) has been attributed (to rigid social structures and hierarchies) [that ignored the talent (of the individual inventor.)]

02. This changed [when the first systemic mechanism (for protecting) an inventor's rights (to monopoly) was introduced (by a 1474 Act of the Venetian Senate,) [which prohibited the production (of a device) conforming (to a patented one) (without the authorization) (of the inventor) (for 10 years,) [provided the inventor had recorded the innovation (with the council.)]]] This system differed (from the modern one) [in that it required the inventor (to produce) a completed, working device.] (In other words,) the inventor had (to report) a device [that could be used immediately and was societally useful.] However, it still laid out all the major features (of modern patent law,) (such as requiring) the device (to be officially registered,) 'useful' (to the society,) 'not previously made (in this state',) and providing) a fixed term (of exclusivity.)

03. Even (before the Venetian Senate's act) (of 1474,) isolated monopolies were granted (in Europe.) (For example,) (in England) the monarchs would grant letters patent, or 'letters [that lie open',] (to people) (in their graces,) granting them a monopoly (to produce or provide) specific goods and services. This tradition (of granting) monopolies eventually led (to the term 'patents') [we use today.] It was not, however, (until the Venetian Act) [that the standardized process (of granting) patents occurred.] Britain, influenced (by this new concept,) eventually implemented (such a system) (as a kind) (of mercantilist instrument) (to attract) emigrants (with skills) [that could possibly aid Britain's industry (with the guarantee) (of exclusive monopoly,) (after the significant economic drain) caused (by the War of the Roses.)] (By the early 17th century,) patents had become royal favors (to subjects) (of loyalty or wealth,) (with monopolies) being granted (on products and services) (such as running) ale-houses. This led (to inefficiency) and left room (for the corruption) [that brought about the Statute (of Monopolies) (of 1624,) [which required courts (to outlaw) all monopolies (but those) based (on true inventive intentions.)]] [When the Industrial Revolution spurred an explosive number (of new inventions,)] patents became an increasingly important component (of the socioeconomic machine.) This era marks a change (in the perception) (of the role) (of patents) (in society,) [in that they were no longer given only (for the introduction) (of a new finished product,) but also (for the introduction) (of technological know-how or processes.)]

04. (Along with many other British legal concepts,) the patent system was introduced (in the United States) (during the colonial period) (between 1640 and 1776.) Initially, each (of the 13 colonies) formed their own patent systems, [which led (to disputes,) (such as identifying) the true inventor (of the steamboat,) [as different inventors were registered (in the patent archives) (of two colonies.)]] These problems continued (to arise) even (after the United States' independence.) The government, therefore, sought (to solve) this problem and the 1789 Constitutional Convention imbedded a national patent system (in the constitution) itself. The result was Article I, Section 8 (of the Constitution) [which authorized Congress (to selectively endow) individual authors and inventors (with 'exclusive rights) (to their writings and discoveries'.)] Samuel Hopkins received the first United States federal patent (in 1790) (for a process) [that derived potash (from wood ashes.)] The United States patent system grew (to its full, modern status) (with the 1836 revision) introducing a formal system (of examination) (by appointed, professional examiners.) (Since then,) patents have rapidly become an important thread (of the American economic fabric,) (despite the fact) [that the process' effectiveness is still debated.]

05. (Throughout history) the concept (of protecting) one's rights (to one's own creations) has advanced (along with the burgeoning capitalist, industrial world economy,) [which is increasingly dependent (on new technological advancements.)] (Despite changes) (in the patent systems) (over time,) the principal idea [that the inventor must contribute (in some way) (to the state, or society,) (through novel, useful inventions)] has remained.

TEST 8-1 Communication of Ants

01. Ants have several advantages over solitary insects such as increased system reliability and division of labor. The major advantage, however, is the communication among members. This allows the colony to regulate its foraging activity and retain a memory of previously rewarding locations. To do this, ants rely on chemical signals called pheromones. When foragers find a successful foraging site, they deposit a trail of pheromones on their return to the nest. This trail gains strength as more and more workers add more pheromones to it.

02. Unlike the traditional views on ant pheromone trails, recent studies have shown that distinct roles are assigned to different pheromones, as can be illustrated by the differences in the pheromones produced by the poison and pygidial glands of Malaysian ponerine army ants. The poison glands of these ants contain two pheromone components, one eliciting a strong, short-term attraction to prey targets and another guiding workers from foraging sites back to the colony. These pheromone trails are highly volatile, lasting only a few minutes, to ensure that ants are not attracted to sites long after the prey has been collected. The pygidial gland, on the other hand, produces a longer-lasting trail pheromone that guides workers back to the trail network of the colony.

03. These pheromones act as the 'bread crumbs' in the tale of 'Hansel and Gretel,' allowing the ants to maintain their spatial organization and helping them forage in an organized manner which enables the rapid transport of food to the colony. Furthermore, in Pharaoh's ant, research has shown distinct, shortlived and long-lived attractive-trail pheromone effects, as well as a short-lived repellent pheromone. In contrast to most ant pheromones, the long-lived trails of Pharaoh's ants can persist for several days, allowing the trail network to be explored for a longer period of time. Sections of the network leading to food are reinforced with the short-lived trail pheromone, and the repellent pheromone is placed immediately after non-rewarding trails. These three scents seem to work complementarily.

04. Foraging ants also utilize tactile communication methods, such as vibration to communicate a wider repertoire of messages that promote the organization of the colony's foraging system. Desert ants, for example, rub their abdominal areas together to make sounds. Although ants do not have auditory organs, they can still perceive these messages by sensing the vibration of the ground with their legs. When a worker locates a large prey item, such as a dead insect, it makes sharp sounds to attract workers in the area, through a process called stridulating, that encourages nearby workers to release pheromones over longer distances, causing rapid recruitment to the prey item, thereby retrieving it significantly faster. Furthermore, in leaf-cutting ants, recruitment behavior changes in relation to the quality of food. In order to test what causes different levels of sound to be created, researchers presented ants with leaves of different qualities - tender leaves, tough leaves, sugar-coated tough leaves, and acid-coated leaves - and then noted the proportion of workers that stridulated as they cut through the different leaves. The results clearly showed that the workers stridulated most strongly when cutting through leaves of a good quality or attractiveness, with the most stridulation occurring while cutting tender or sugar-coated leaves as opposed to the other leaves.

05. This pheromone system may seem unique, but other communal insects, such as honeybees, have also developed advanced communication systems. Unlike ants honeybees use discernible movements (like the 'waggle dances') to communicate complex concepts (such as the approximate distance and directions) to food sources. Returning foragers also perform tremble dances, to recruit receiver bees to collect their nectar. A further difference is that honeybees individually remember their rewarding foraging sites and return to them. 'Trail-following' ants, on the other hand, are bound to the externally encoded group memory of their pheromone trails. These trails ensure that a channel of communication is always open and allows them to continually react and exchange information whilst foraging without needing to return to the nest, unlike the honeybees. This ability to constantly locate productive foraging sites is probably the most important reason for insects to communicate.

TEST 8-2 Calculating age of the earth

01. Religion was the only source (of historical and scientific knowledge,) (such as the age) (of Earth,) (until the mid-eighteenth century.) (After this time,) scientists began more openly questioning the formation (of Earth,) and [while studying the different rock layers (of it,)] they recognized [that it had gone (through various changes) (over a period) (of time.)] The scientists proposed a number (of theories and methods) [that had inaccurate results (due to lack) (of understanding) (of the Earth) and heavy speculation.)] [As the scientific method and logical reasoning developed (within the scientific community,)] scholars were motivated (to conduct) more precise and scientific research.

02. (In 1779,) a French scientist, Comte de Buffon, attempted the first calculation (of Earth's age) (by experimentation.) Based (on Earth's internal heat and rate) (of cooling,) Buffon's approach utilized a small globe-like figure [that resembled Earth (in composition.)] He measured the cooling rate (of the figure) tested (at his laboratory) and calculated the age (of Earth) (to be) 75,000 years. The result completely underestimated the age (of Earth) [as Buffon, (from his globe figure,) mainly focused (on the cooling rate) (of iron), an element [which cools much quicker (than crystals and other rock components.)]] The true significance (of his study,) however, was [that it dared (to break away) (from previous methods) [that derived Earth's age (without experimentation.)]]

03. Later, others attempted (to measure) Earth's age, but their methods were just (as inadequate.) Edmund Halley, (for example,) based his estimation (on the simple concept) (of the salinity) (of the ocean.) He surmised [that [since rivers continuously dragged salt components (from land) (to the oceans,) increasing their salinity,] the time [they took (to reach) present salinity-levels] will give an approximate timeframe (for Earth's formation.)] Just (like the previous conjectures,) Halley's method was not a viable way (of measuring) Earth's age, [as it oversimplified the complex salinification process and failed (to take into account) plate tectonics and undersea volcanic eruptions [that continuously add salt (to the ocean.)]]

04. (Since then,) measurements (of physical properties) have been used (to estimate) the age (of Earth) using the laws (of physics.) William Thomson, the forerunning supporter (of these physical measurements,) believed [that (during Earth's primitive stage,) it was a sphere (of hot molten rock) held together by gravity and the only conceivable source of heat energy was the nebula. By estimating the rate at which heat dissipated from the nebula, scientists could determine the time necessary for Earth to cool from the molten ball of rock to its present state. Through this method, the age of Earth was calculated to be 20 to 40 million years. He had, however, neglected an important variable: the viscous fluid mantle that play an influential role in the circulation of heat energy within the Earth.

05.   Scientists calculated Earth's age with even more precision after the arrival of the radiometric dating. It allowed them to derive the absolute age of rock using its elements. First developed by Ernest Rutherford and enhanced by Arthur Holmes, radiometric dating is a technique based on the spontaneous decay of naturally occurring radioactive isotopes found in rocks. These initial parent isotopes are unstable and break down into more stable daughter isotopes. This break down occurs according to an isotope's individual rate of decay, or 'decay constant', regardless of the physical or chemical condition it is exposed to. Scientists, therefore, do not have to be concerned with other variables since the rate of isotope transformation is almost invariable. Radiometric dating allows scientists to calculate the time that has elapsed since the formation of rocks by measuring the ratio of parent to daughter isotopes in them. Radiometric testing shows Earth to be around 4.5 billion years, the most widely accepted age of Earth today.

06.   Still, there are controversies over the age of the earth as a minor group of scientists argues that Earth is less than 4.5 billion years. These people believe that the earth is 'young', only about 6,000 to 10,000 years old. Stressing that the ratio of parent to daughter isotopes when the rock was created is unknown, they challenge the validity of scientifically-accepted radiometric methods. They further claim that some parent or daughter isotopes may be added from external sources. Although there is evidence for variability in radiometric dating, Arthur Holmes used a variety of isotopes to obtain sufficient data and derived a precise result. Therefore, many regard these refutations to be implausible and until further scientific research produces a more accurate result, 4.5 billion years will continue to be considered the approximate age of the Earth.

TEST 9-1   Identifying Playful Behavior in Children

01. Play, usually associated with children, comes in many forms in both humans and other animals. Even with such prevalence, its definition, function and forms are often misunderstood. This may be because play evolves both with age and over time. For example, most people recognize that a toddler's frolicking is play, but not that engaging in sport activities by adults is another form. Moreover, the way play has changed over time is also ignored. One such major change is the decrease in usage of imagination since computers and video games have begun to create virtual worlds for children, when compared to the past when they had only wooden toys and dolls with which to play. With such major changes happening, one cannot predict what form it will take next, only that it will continue to exist. Due to these changes and the lack of an apparent distinction between playful and non-playful behaviors, sociologists have continuously tried to form a complete definition of play, with three having gained widespread acceptance: the functional, the structural, and the criterion approaches.

02. Anthropologist Donald Symons, after observing African monkeys, developed the first of these in 1978. He defined play as an act that has neither a clear benefit, nor external goal. Following this, acts like learning are not considered play because their benefits are readily noticeable. Similarly, eating and working are not considered play because their purposes are specific and obvious. Although Symons' definition was intended for the monkeys that he studied, it soon became evident to other scholars that his definition, which came to be known as the functional approach, could likewise be applied to play in humans. Applying his approach to further studies has shown that although there are benefits to playful behavior, its long-term consequences are unclear. An easy way to see this is to look at common playground toys, like the jungle gym. While children enjoy climbing, hanging and swinging on the metal labyrinth, the ultimate goal of these activities is not known, and neither is the actions' ability to supply the child with food, clothing, or shelter. Further, it is unclear whether time spent on the playground fulfills the child's education, health, or other basic needs at all, and it is, thus, considered playful behavior under this approach.

03. The functional approach, however, does not account for the many non-playful actions without immediately obvious purposes, or for playful behavior that seems to serve a purpose, such as running. While running is often a playful behavior, if a person was running towards shelter to hide

(from the rain,)] it would have a clear purpose, and therefore not qualify (as functionalistic play.) (In cases) (such as this,) the structural approach can be used. The structural approach identifies specific behaviors [that are associated (with play) or (with the playful execution) (of actions.)] [When studying an action using this approach,] one begins (by identifying) any characteristics [that often only occur (during playtime,) (like laughter or playful squabbling,) (such as a push or a light punch.)] Secondly, the structural approach looks (for repeated, fragmented, exaggerated, or re-ordered actions.) (For example,) climbing stairs has a clear end and goal, but [if the child repeats it (by quickly climbing) up and down the stairs, fragments the climb (by climbing up) only half-way, exaggerates it (by jumping) two stairs (at a time,) or re-orders it (by climbing) them backwards,] then (under the structural approach) the child is considered (to be performing) playful behavior.

04. [When studying play,] it became evident [that the two approaches were not mutually exclusive,] but [that the factors [that they used (to identify) behavior] were dissimilar.] Thus, (in 1980,) Krasnor and Pepler suggested a third method, called the criterion approach. It combined ideas (from the other approaches) (into four criteria) (for identifying) playful behavior. The first criterion, positive effect, refers to the enjoyment [that comes (from doing) playful behavior.] The second, non-literality, is the imaginative aspect (of playing,) [which encompasses acts (such as pretending and placing) oneself (in fictitious perspectives) (for the purpose) (of play.)] The third, intrinsic motivation, means [that the behavior is done (of one's own accord) and not (due to social pressure.)] Finally, flexibility covers the characteristics described (by the structural approach.) [While meeting one criterion is sufficient (to define) a behavior (as being) playful,] [when the behavior meets more (than one criterion,)] one may be more certain [that the behavior is playful.] Confusing] [as it may be, one must understand [that the criterion approach was not developed (to create) a one-sentence definition (for play,)] [as many behaviors [that are undoubtedly non-playful] will fall (within one or more) (of the criterion.)] So, [while the criterion approach may not be used (to definitively distinguish) (between activities) [that are play] and those) [that are not,]] it plays a significant role (in helping) sociologists understand [how humans recognize play.]

TEST 9-2 Sentinel Behavior in Meerkats

01. Meerkats are small, mongoose-like mammals that live in the Kalahari Desert of Southern Africa. Being primarily insectivores, they feed on beetles and scorpions buried underground, which they locate using their strong sense of smell. Unfortunately, when the meerkat lowers its head to search out prey under grasses, it significantly limits its own range of sight by a significant amount. As a result they are extremely vulnerable to airborne predators such as hawks and owls. To ensure that they can reach the safety of their bolt-holes before being snatched up by birds, meerkats forage in packs and partake in what is known as sentinel behavior. As the term suggests, one meerkat in the group acts as a sentinel and does not look for food like the rest, but rather stands upright on its hind legs to gain a wider field of view with which it scans the surrounding area for possible predators and other threats to the community. When it senses danger approaching, the sentinel barks loudly to warn the others of the danger. Many scientists questioned this phenomenon because the revealing stance and loud vocalization was thought to expose the meerkat to an increased risk of predation.

02. The motivations behind this behavior have been attributed to kin selection, the evolutionary strategy that favors the reproductive success of an organism's relatives over one's own survival. In Belding's ground squirrels, individuals sound an alarm at the approach of a predator, warning its nearby relatives and thereby benefitting the population. This explanation gained credibility because research revealed that, like Belding's squirrels, meerkat communities are composed mostly of family members. In a typical community of meerkats, about 70% of its members are related to the dominant female. In their authoritarian societies, the alpha female rarely tolerates offspring from anyone other than herself. Therefore, if the sentinel is able to protect one of its siblings, it ensures passing on 50% of its own genes, or 25% for saving a niece or nephew. This follows the gene selection theory, postulating that individuals are genetically programmed to proliferate their DNA. In addition, if the sentinel allows other group members to spend less time scanning and more time foraging, they will be able to catch more prey, which will also increase the survivability of the group.

03. A variant theory was [that (in order to protect) their kin, meerkats demonstrated reciprocal altruism, an act [that benefits another (at the expense) (of one's own interest.)]] [If the receiver's benefit outweighs the cost (of the altruist,)] and [if the receiver is expected (to also become) the altruist,] then evolutionarily the entire group profits (from the behavior.) This can be seen (in various animals) (such as fish and birds,) as well as (in close relatives) (of the meerkat,) the banded mongoose. Their pups cooperate (in creating) annoying chirps (to beg) (for food) (from their chaperones,) [which are assigned (to individual pups.)] [When one chaperone was removed (from the group,)] the corresponding pup would stop crying. This (in turn) caused the rest (of the pups) (to increase) the volume (of their crying,) [which induces the adults (to bring) more food, benefitting the quiet pup.] Scientists tested (for two conditions) [that had been laid out (by the developed, mature definition) (of reciprocal altruism) (to determine) [if this was [what the meerkats were (in fact) doing:]]] a systematic method (of deciding) individuals' duty (as sentinels,) and a unified punishment (for those) [who abandon their duties (as a sentinel.)] But observations substantiated [that there was neither a particular order nor any sort (of punishment.)] Moreover, the dedication and the length (of time) [that a meerkat displayed sentinel behavior] were consistent (regardless of the number) (of non-relatives) (in the group.)

04. Later scientists questioned the theory, proposing [that sentinel behavior was a selfish anti-predator behavior.] The proposition was [that, contrary (to popular belief,) standing guard would increase the sentinel's own chances (for survival.)] (To find) evidence (for this claim,) a team of scientists set out (to observe) sentinel behavior (in lone meerkats.) They confirmed [that solitary meerkats first focused (on foraging,) then returned (to the sentinel stance) [once their hunger was satiated.]] This strengthened the anti-predator hypothesis. The next question (to answer) was [whether sentineling meerkats had better chances (of survival) (than those) [who were not standing guard] [when attacked (by a predator.)]] (Of a total) (of 2,000 hours) (of observation,) not a single meerkat [that was standing guard (at the moment) (of attack)] was caught [because they chose positions [that were safer [when sentineling] [than foraging.]]] The conclusion was [that meerkats stand guard (to protect) themselves (from predators,)] but they forage (in groups) [because then they can invest more time hunting (for food) and put trust (in the sentinels) (to warn) them (of any signs) (of danger.)]

usherin.usher.co.kr

USHER

iBT TOEFL
FINAL TEST READING
구문 외우고 · 열번 읽기

단계별

1 정확히 구문 암기!

2 하나하나 철저히 적용!

3 확실히 적용할 줄 알면 7분내 지문 읽기!

Method of Measuring Bats' Age

1 For many decades, biologists have compiled scores of [1)]**data on** the life spans of various bat species using data obtained by the fortuitous recapture of individuals tagged [2)]**at birth**. It has been found that [3)]**on average**, bats live [4)]**three times longer** than other mammals of similar size and metabolic rate. Determining their exact age is, however, particularly difficult because it [5)]**is likely that** they display more environmental and physiological variation throughout their lives than mammals with shorter lifespans, which may confuse several studied aspects of bat biology.

2 When studying bat lifespans, [6)]**it is important to note** the distinction between chronological and biological age. Chronological age is the interval between the time of birth and the present. Biological or physiological age, [7)]**on the other hand**, reflects the life expectancy and [8)]**is based on** physical [9)]**changes in** the morphology and function of the body, which may not always [10)]**coincide with** chronological age. The only means of knowing a bat's exact chronological age is to permanently mark it at birth, [11)]**so that** at any subsequent recaptures, its exact age can be determined. This method has drawbacks, as marking bats is time consuming, requiring long-term monitoring, and recapture rates are typically low, [12)]**not to mention that** the process itself may disturb the bat.

3 Several other methods have been developed to determine the biological age of bats. The first measures the long bones, like the forearm, metacarpals, and digits, which [13)]**go through** a phase of rapid linear growth [14)]**shortly after** birth. These measurements, especially [15)]**that of** the forearm, can [16)]**be used to** [17)]**distinguish** juveniles **from** adults. A species-specific reference correlating these measurements with examples of a known- age can provide age estimates within 1-2 days [18)]**with** 95 percent **accuracy**. The advantages of this empirical method are its accuracy, ease of use in the field and laboratory, and lack of invasiveness. Only a caliper or a ruler is [19)]**needed to obtain** the measurements, [20)]**making this method ideal** for use on both live animals and museum specimens. The major disadvantage is that these bones grow only during the first few weeks of life and the valid time frame varies between species from only 12 days in M. lucifugus to as long as 45 days in R. leschenaulti. Other traits, such as changes in the patterns and rates of closure of the cartilaginous epiphyseal growth plates [21)]**are**, therefore, **necessary to estimate** the age of older individuals. [22)]**In its simplest form**, this method [23)]**distinguishes between** young bats and adults. By transilluminating the wing of a juvenile, a researcher can discern the cartilaginous zone of the long phalanges which [24)]**allows** more light **to** [25)]**pass through** and thus appears lighter than bone. As the bat [26)]**continue to grow**, the epiphyseal plates eventually close and are [27)]**no longer** [28)]**visible to** the unaided eye. This method of age categorization requires [29)]**no more than** a flashlight and is [30)]**ideal for** use in both the field and the laboratory.

4 Another method of estimating bats' age is to study their teeth. Much like puppies that lose their sharp baby teeth before growing [31)]**a set of** permanent adult teeth, in most bat species, permanent teeth replace the deciduous ones by the time juveniles are able to fly and feed independently. Once [32)]**in place**, these permanent teeth reach full size and [33)]**cease to grow**. A lifetime of mastication however [34)]**wears down** their surfaces and erodes their enamel. The degree of tooth wear can, therefore, be used to place bats into relative age categories as this process occurs from weaning until death. [35)]**Due to** [36)]**differences in** diet, tooth usage in aggressive interactions, and the populations' annual activity periods, species show significant [37)]**variation in** tooth wear. Therefore, the development of species-specific reference standards based on a wideranging sample of known-age individuals [38)]**is critical** [39)]**for the** proper **use of** this method, [40)]**as are** investigators with extensive species-specific experience assessing tooth wear.

5 Zoologists Klevezal and Kleinenberg suggested a new method of aging bats using their teeth. They suggested that the number of incremental lines, or 'annuli', on bats' teeth could be counted to determine its age. The robustness of the incremental lines, however, varies among species **so that** in some the lines may be difficult to count, especially in small species. Another zoologist, C.J. Phillips, examined the incremental lines in two species of bats from known- age specimens. He found that the number of incremental lines observed [41)]**depended on** which tooth was extracted and on the section examined, and suggested that several factors, such as mechanical stress and tooth movement, can alter the patterns of layered growth yielding non-annual cycles of dentin and cementum deposition. Other researchers have found a lack of correlation between age and incremental lines in some species. [42)]**Aside from variation in** incremental lines and the questionable accuracy of this method, other disadvantages are that it requires tooth extraction, which can only be done on dead specimens; it is time consuming, and it requires specialized equipment. The problems [43)]**associated with** this method highlight the [44)]**need to better understand** how and when these incremental lines are deposited and [45)]**use** this information **to develop** more accurate reference standards that can [46)]**be correlated with** other methods. [47)]**Notwithstanding**, this method has proven [48)]**useful for** [49)]**a variety of** behavioral and ecological studies where broad age categories suffice to obtain meaningful results.

Method of Measuring Bats' Age

1 For many decades, biologists have compiled scores of data on the life spans of various bat species using data obtained by the fortuitous recapture of individuals tagged at birth. It has been found that on average, bats live three times longer than other mammals of similar size and metabolic rate. Determining their exact age is, however, particularly difficult because it is likely that they display more environmental and physiological variation throughout their lives than mammals with shorter lifespans, which may confuse several studied aspects of bat biology.

2 When studying bat lifespans, it is important to note the distinction between chronological and biological age. Chronological age is the interval between the time of birth and the present. Biological or physiological age, on the other hand, reflects the life expectancy and is based on physical changes in the morphology and function of the body, which may not always coincide with chronological age. The only means of knowing a bat's exact chronological age is to permanently mark it at birth, so that at any subsequent recaptures, its exact age can be determined. This method has drawbacks, as marking bats is time consuming, requiring long-term monitoring, and recapture rates are typically low, not to mention that the process itself may disturb the bat.

3 Several other methods have been developed to determine the biological age of bats. The first measures the long bones, like the forearm, metacarpals, and digits, which go through a phase of rapid linear growth shortly after birth. These measurements, especially that of the forearm, can be used to distinguish juveniles from adults. A species-specific reference correlating these measurements with examples of a known- age can provide age estimates within 1-2 days with 95 percent accuracy. The advantages of this empirical method are its accuracy, ease of use in the field and laboratory, and lack of invasiveness. Only a caliper or a ruler is needed to obtain the measurements, making this method ideal for use on both live animals and museum specimens. The major disadvantage is that these bones grow only during the first few weeks of life and the valid time frame varies between species from only 12 days in M. lucifugus to as long as 45 days in R. leschenaulti. Other traits, such as changes in the patterns and rates of closure of the cartilaginous epiphyseal growth plates are, therefore, necessary to estimate the age of older individuals. In its simplest form, this method distinguishes between young bats and adults. By transilluminating the wing of a juvenile, a researcher can discern the cartilaginous zone of the long phalanges which allows more light to pass through and thus appears lighter than bone. As the bat continue to grow, the epiphyseal plates eventually close and are no longer visible to the unaided eye. This method of age categorization requires no more than a fashlight and is ideal for use in both the field and the laboratory.

4 Another method of estimating bats' age is to study their teeth. Much like puppies that lose their sharp baby teeth before growing a set of permanent adult teeth, in most bat species, permanent teeth replace the deciduous ones by the time juveniles are able to fly and feed independently. Once in place, these permanent teeth reach full size and cease to grow. A lifetime of mastication however wears down their surfaces and erodes their enamel. The degree of tooth wear can, therefore, be used to place bats into relative age categories as this process occurs from weaning until death. Due to differences in diet, tooth usage in aggressive interactions, and the populations' annual activity periods, species show significant variation in tooth wear. Therefore, the development of species-specific reference standards based on a wide-ranging sample of known-age individuals is critical for the proper use of this method, as are investigators with extensive species-specific experience assessing tooth wear.

5 Zoologists Klevezal and Kleinenberg suggested a new method of aging bats using their teeth. They suggested that the number of incremental lines, or 'annuli', on bats' teeth could be counted to determine its age. The robustness of the incremental lines, however, varies among species so that in some the lines may be difficult to count, especially in small species. Another zoologist, C.J. Phillips, examined the incremental lines in two species of bats from known- age specimens. He found that the number of incremental lines observed depended on which tooth was extracted and on the section examined, and suggested that several factors, such as mechanical stress and tooth movement, can alter the patterns of layered growth yielding non- annual cycles of dentin and cementum deposition. Other researchers have found a lack of correlation between age and incremental lines in some species. Aside from variation in incremental lines and the questionable accuracy of this method, other disadvantages are that it requires tooth extraction, which can only be done on dead specimens; it is time consuming, and it requires specialized equipment. The problems associated with this method highlight the need to better understand how and when these incremental lines are deposited and use this information to develop more accurate reference standards that can be correlated with other methods. Notwithstanding, this method has proven useful for a variety of behavioral and ecological studies where broad age categories suffice to obtain meaningful results.

Tracing Language Diversification

1 Linguists study language relationships to find their similarities and differences. One ¹⁾**way to find** and chart these is to ²⁾**look for** inter-language sound shifts ³⁾**over time**. These are slight alternations in words between related subfamily languages since their origin. From these linguists can deduce a connection between them through sound shifts.

2 The technique ⁴⁾**used to record** sound shifts and consonant hardening ⁵⁾**is called** backward reconstruction. This technique takes humanity's linguistic family tree back thousands of years. Using it, scholars ⁶⁾**infer** vocabulary **from** previous languages. It may even be possible ⁷⁾**to go further** and re-create the preceding languages.

3 Linguist Sir William Jones was an early ⁸⁾**researcher into** language diversification. He ⁹⁾**made** unrivalled **contributions to** linguistic scholarship, promoting an understanding of and appreciation for Asian languages and cultures. Having ¹⁰⁾**arrived in** Calcutta as a Bengal Supreme Court judge, he studied Sanskrit ¹¹⁾**in order to approach** Muslim and Hindu laws ¹²⁾**in their original form**. He found grammatical roots ¹³⁾**corresponding to** classical European languages. From this, he developed the idea of a common language source. In The Sanskrit Language, he ¹⁴⁾**wrote of** Sanskrit's ¹⁵⁾**resemblance to** Greek and Latin, which ¹⁶⁾**led** him **to suggest** that they ¹⁷⁾**not only** had a common root **but** ¹⁸⁾**were also related to** other European languages. He stated: The Sanskrit language, ¹⁹⁾**whatever be** its antiquity, ²⁰⁾**is of** a wonderful structure; more perfect than the Greek, more copious than the Latin, and more exquisitely refined than either, yet ²¹⁾**bearing to** both of them a stronger **affinity**, both **in** the roots of verbs and the forms of grammar, than could possibly have been produced ²²⁾**by accident**; ²³⁾**so** strong indeed, **that** no philologer could examine them all three, without ²⁴⁾**believing** them **to have** sprung from some common source, which, perhaps, ²⁵⁾**no longer** exists.

4 Another major linguistic contributor was Jacob Grimm. During the nineteenth century, he ²⁶⁾**sought to** scientifically **prove** that sound shifts showed relationships between languages. Grimm sought rare unchanged words throughout the German countryside to clarify the history of the German language. Unfortunately, rural Germans presumed that a 'linguistics researcher' was just a new ²⁷⁾**way for** the government **to** ²⁸⁾**figure out** how much property tax they owed. To ²⁹⁾**entice** people **to speak** freely, Grimm ³⁰⁾**asked** them **to tell** him stories, which he faithfully recorded. His primary interest was ³¹⁾**not** initially the stories themselves **but** any exotic vocabulary they ³²⁾**happened to use**. What he ³³⁾**ended up with** was a fascinating body of folklore which he and his brother Wilhelm published as Grimms' Fairy Tales. Grimm, however, did get what he wanted word-wise. In the stories, he noticed an evolutionary pattern of Germanic languages which ³⁴⁾**pointed to** a change that had ³⁵⁾**taken place** long ago. He explained that related languages have similar, but not identical consonants, which had undergone predictable changes over time. Hard consonants such as the v and t in German word vater, softened into the Dutch vader and the English father. Using Grimm's theory, linguists realized that consonants would become harder as they went 'backwards' toward the original language.

5 From Jones' and Grimm's theories, linguists ³⁶⁾**came up with** the first major linguistic hypothesis: the existence of a common ancestral language called Proto-Indo-European which ³⁷⁾**transformed into** ancient Latin, Greek, and Sanskrit. This single language links modern languages around the world. Study of this language has helped identify that, although they share only a few similarities, both Slavonic and Germanic are sub-branches of a common ancestral language. Several research tasks naturally followed this hypothesis. First, the vocabulary of the proposed ancestral language ³⁸⁾**needed to be reconstructed**, before the hearth of the language could be located. After this, the routes of dispersion needed to be traced. Finally, the ways of life of those who spoke and spread the language needed to be established.

6 Nineteenth century linguist August Schleicher described language families as the branches of a tree. He suggested that new languages form through language divergence, when a language breaks down and ³⁹⁾**fragments into** dialects and then into discrete tongues due to separation of speakers. This can be seen in Spanish and Portuguese and is now happening with Quebecois French. Due to geographical separation, Parisian French and Quebecois French ⁴⁰⁾**started to differ** after the colonial era. Now the pronunciation and vocabulary use of the two places differ greatly. These new languages become leaves on the tree. Through backward reconstruction, linguists can find how languages branches fit together. Tracing backward far enough, they can find the hearth of a language.

7 Finding this hearth is a daunting task, as reconstructing even a small branch is complicated. A complicating factor is that with human mobility, languages did not merely diffuse through static populations; they also spread by relocation diffusion. If people with different languages have consistent spatial interaction, language convergence can take place, collapsing two languages into one. This creates problems for researchers because the reconstruction rules sometimes do not apply and can be unreliable.

Tracing Language Diversification

1 Linguists study language relationships to find their similarities and differences. One way to find and chart these is to look for inter-language sound shifts over time. These are slight alternations in words between related subfamily languages since their origin. From these linguists can deduce a connection between them through sound shifts.

2 The technique used to record sound shifts and consonant hardening is called backward reconstruction. This technique takes humanity's linguistic family tree back thousands of years. Using it, scholars infer vocabulary from previous languages. It may even be possible to go further and re-create the preceding languages.

3 Linguist Sir William Jones was an early researcher into language diversification. He made unrivalled contributions to linguistic scholarship, promoting an understanding of and appreciation for Asian languages and cultures. Having arrived in Calcutta as a Bengal Supreme Court judge, he studied Sanskrit in order to approach Muslim and Hindu laws in their original form. He found grammatical roots corresponding to classical European languages. From this, he developed the idea of a common language source. In The Sanskrit Language, he wrote of Sanskrit's resemblance to Greek and Latin, which led him to suggest that they not only had a common root but were also related to other European languages. He stated: The Sanskrit language, whatever be its antiquity, is of a wonderful structure; more perfect than the Greek, more copious than the Latin, and more exquisitely refined than either, yet bearing to both of them a stronger affinity, both in the roots of verbs and the forms of grammar, than could possibly have been produced by accident; so strong indeed, that no philologer could examine them all three, without believing them to have sprung from some common source, which, perhaps, no longer exists.

4 Another major linguistic contributor was Jacob Grimm. During the nineteenth century, he sought to scientifically prove that sound shifts showed relationships between languages. Grimm sought rare unchanged words throughout the German countryside to clarify the history of the German language. Unfortunately, rural Germans presumed that a 'linguistics researcher' was just a new way for the government to figure out how much property tax they owed. To entice people to speak freely, Grimm asked them to tell him stories, which he faithfully recorded. His primary interest was not initially the stories themselves but any exotic vocabulary they happened to use. What he ended up with was a fascinating body of folklore which he and his brother Wilhelm published as Grimms' Fairy Tales. Grimm, however, did get what he wanted word-wise. In the stories, he noticed an evolutionary pattern of Germanic languages which pointed to a change that had taken place long ago. He explained that related languages have similar, but not identical consonants, which had undergone predictable changes over time. Hard consonants such as the v and t in German word vater, softened into the Dutch vader and the English father. Using Grimm's theory, linguists realized that consonants would become harder as they went 'backwards' toward the original language.

5 From Jones' and Grimm's theories, linguists came up with the first major linguistic hypothesis: the existence of a common ancestral language called Proto-Indo-European which transformed into ancient Latin, Greek, and Sanskrit. This single language links modern languages around the world. Study of this language has helped identify that, although they share only a few similarities, both Slavonic and Germanic are sub-branches of a common ancestral language. Several research tasks naturally followed this hypothesis. First, the vocabulary of the proposed ancestral language needed to be reconstructed, before the hearth of the language could be located. After this, the routes of dispersion needed to be traced. Finally, the ways of life of those who spoke and spread the language needed to be established.

6 Nineteenth century linguist August Schleicher described language families as the branches of a tree. He suggested that new languages form through language divergence, when a language breaks down and fragments into dialects and then into discrete tongues due to separation of speakers. This can be seen in Spanish and Portuguese and is now happening with Quebecois French. Due to geographical separation, Parisian French and Quebecois French started to differ after the colonial era. Now the pronunciation and vocabulary use of the two places differ greatly. These new languages become leaves on the tree. Through backward reconstruction, linguists can find how languages branches fit together. Tracing backward far enough, they can find the hearth of a language.

7 Finding this hearth is a daunting task, as reconstructing even a small branch is complicated. A complicating factor is that with human mobility, languages did not merely diffuse through static populations; they also spread by relocation diffusion. If people with different languages have consistent spatial interaction, language convergence can take place, collapsing two languages into one. This creates problems for researchers because the reconstruction rules sometimes do not apply and can be unreliable.

Earth's Atmosphere

1 The Earth's atmosphere ¹⁾**consists** mainly **of** heavy gases like nitrogen, but lacks light gases such as hydrogen and helium. This is odd, because nitrogen ²⁾**is known to be** ³⁾**the seventh most abundant** element in the universe, whereas hydrogen is the most common, which ⁴⁾**begs the question** of why hydrogen is ⁵⁾**no longer** abundant in Earth's atmosphere. Earth, currently the only planet known to support life, has an atmosphere ⁶⁾**distinguishable from** others in the solar system, due to being ⁷⁾**composed of** byproducts of life, such as oxygen. This distinction can be seen in the changes observed through studies done by ⁸⁾**a series of** scientists, which have ultimately ⁹⁾**classified** Earth's atmosphere **into** three stages of evolution: primordial atmosphere, secondary atmosphere, and the addition of oxygen.

2 Initially, light gases were abundant in Earth's primordial atmosphere, but gradually ¹⁰⁾**started to decline**. This can be explained through 'Jeans escape', a classical form of thermal escape ¹¹⁾**based on** Maxwell's Distribution that prescribes that the kinetic energy distribution of molecules is ¹²⁾**dependent on** the mass and velocity of the molecule. From this, one can conclude that ¹³⁾**the bigger** the molecule, **the lower** its average velocity ¹⁴⁾**at a** given **temperature**, which makes escape more unlikely. Furthermore, **the greater** the mass of the planet, **the higher** the required escape velocity; which ultimately ¹⁵⁾**result in** less escaping molecules. Thus, giant planets with high gravity possess higher concentrations of light gases such as hydrogen and helium, which are rare in the inner planet's atmospheres. The distance from the star also affects molecular velocity; **the closer** the planet, **the hotter** the atmosphere becomes, ¹⁶⁾**leading to** higher molecular velocity and higher escape rates. This is how Saturn's relatively small moon, Titan, keeps its atmosphere. Even though its gravitational pull is lower than ¹⁷⁾**that of** Earth, its cooler temperature ¹⁸⁾**allows it to** ¹⁹⁾**hold on to** its atmosphere. Neptune's moon, Triton, ²⁰⁾**being attached to** the farthest planet from the sun, is also, ²¹⁾**in this way**, ²²⁾**able to retain** a non-negligible nitrogenous atmosphere due to the extreme temperatures ²³⁾**at the edge of** the solar system.

3 Scientists believe that as light gases ²⁴⁾**escaped from** Earth's atmosphere, nitrogen ²⁵⁾**began constituting** a larger part of it after volcanic eruptions spewed gases, ultimately forming the main component of the secondary atmosphere. Three primary reasons why only nitrogen filled the environment are that it is volatile even **at low temperatures**, ²⁶⁾**unreactive with** the materials that make up the earth's crust, and very stable ²⁷⁾**in the presence of** solar radiation. ²⁸⁾**In contrast to** more abundant elements which are major components of Earth's crust, nitrogen is not stable as a part of a crystal lattice, and will not ²⁹⁾**bond with** the others to form the terrestrial earth; it, instead, remains a gas. Unlike nitrogen, other elements are unstable and easily ³⁰⁾**react with** each other in the atmosphere ³¹⁾**as well as** break down when ³²⁾**exposed to** solar radiation. Thus, ³³⁾**over time**, nitrogen built up in the atmosphere ³⁴⁾**to a** much greater **extent** than other elements.

4 One theory introducing the presence of atmospheric oxygen is the Gaia theory. It is believed by scientists that the primordial atmosphere of Earth did not contain oxygen and that the appearance of this gas required the evolution of photosynthetic life forms, such as early cyanobacteria and later single-celled algae, which emerged as the earth cooled and the gaseous water condensed and formed oceans. ³⁵⁾**As a result of** photosynthesis, molecular oxygen built up ³⁶⁾**to** the present **level**, which ³⁷⁾**appears to** have been relatively stable for several billion years. If this level were even slightly higher, then the earth's biomass would be combustible, leading to extensive explosions and forest fires, severely damaging earth's ecosystem. The Gaia theory, thus, suggests that there is a planetary, homeostatic ³⁸⁾**control over** the oxygen concentration in the atmosphere that balances the ³⁹⁾**ratio of** organisms producing oxygen **to those** consuming it.

5 However, some argue that the amount of oxygen collected in the earth's atmosphere cannot be accounted for entirely by cyanobacteria. They believe that the theory is not adequate because it can only ⁴⁰⁾**account for** 1 percent to 10 percent concentration levels, while today's atmosphere contains 21 percent. Thus, a second theory called the planetary atmosphere tectonic machine theory was developed. The theory posits that all of earth's oxygen came from not life forms, but the ocean, near the tectonic plates where magma is released and water ⁴¹⁾**comes into contact with** temperatures over 2000°C. The super-heated water ⁴²⁾**is then converted into** hydrogen and oxygen. The oxygen bubbles then oxygenate the ocean, and ⁴³⁾**are released into** the atmosphere when they reach the surface. This oxygen in the atmosphere ⁴⁴⁾**is then shielded from** being fully ⁴⁵⁾**lost to** space by the ozone and the earth's magnetic field.

Earth's Atmosphere

1 The Earth's atmosphere consists mainly of heavy gases like nitrogen, but lacks light gases such as hydrogen and helium. This is odd, because nitrogen is known to be the seventh most abundant element in the universe, whereas hydrogen is the most common, which begs the question of why hydrogen is no longer abundant in Earth's atmosphere. Earth, currently the only planet known to support life, has an atmosphere distinguishable from others in the solar system, due to being composed of byproducts of life, such as oxygen. This distinction can be seen in the changes observed through studies done by a series of scientists, which have ultimately classified Earth's atmosphere into three stages of evolution: primordial atmosphere, secondary atmosphere, and the addition of oxygen.

2 Initially, light gases were abundant in Earth's primordial atmosphere, but gradually started to decline. This can be explained through 'Jeans escape', a classical form of thermal escape based on Maxwell's Distribution that prescribes that the kinetic energy distribution of molecules is dependent on the mass and velocity of the molecule. From this, one can conclude that the bigger the molecule, the lower its average velocity at a given temperature, which makes escape more unlikely. Furthermore, the greater the mass of the planet, the higher the required escape velocity; which ultimately result in less escaping molecules. Thus, giant planets with high gravity possess higher concentrations of light gases such as hydrogen and helium, which are rare in the inner planet's atmospheres. The distance from the star also affects molecular velocity; the closer the planet, the hotter the atmosphere becomes, leading to higher molecular velocity and higher escape rates. This is how Saturn's relatively small moon, Titan, keeps its atmosphere. Even though its gravitational pull is lower than that of Earth, its cooler temperature allows it to hold on to its atmosphere. Neptune's moon, Triton, being attached to the farthest planet from the sun, is also, in this way, able to retain a non-negligible nitrogenous atmosphere due to the extreme temperatures at the edge of the solar system.

3 Scientists believe that as light gases escaped from Earth's atmosphere, nitrogen began constituting a larger part of it after volcanic eruptions spewed gases, ultimately forming the main component of the secondary atmosphere. Three primary reasons why only nitrogen filled the environment are that it is volatile even at low temperatures, unreactive with the materials that make up the earth's crust, and very stable in the presence of solar radiation. In contrast to more abundant elements which are major components of Earth's crust, nitrogen is not stable as a part of a crystal lattice, and will not bond with the others to form the terrestrial earth; it, instead, remains a gas. Unlike nitrogen, other elements are unstable and easily react with each other in the atmosphere as well as break down when exposed to solar radiation. Thus, over time, nitrogen built up in the atmosphere to a much greater extent than other elements.

4 One theory introducing the presence of atmospheric oxygen is the Gaia theory. It is believed by scientists that the primordial atmosphere of Earth did not contain oxygen and that the appearance of this gas required the evolution of photosynthetic life forms, such as early cyanobacteria and later single-celled algae, which emerged as the earth cooled and the gaseous water condensed and formed oceans. As a result of photosynthesis, molecular oxygen built up to the present level, which appears to have been relatively stable for several billion years. If this level were even slightly higher, then the earth's biomass would be combustible, leading to extensive explosions and forest fires, severely damaging earth's ecosystem. The Gaia theory, thus, suggests that there is a planetary, homeostatic control over the oxygen concentration in the atmosphere that balances the ratio of organisms producing oxygen to those consuming it.

5 However, some argue that the amount of oxygen collected in the earth's atmosphere cannot be accounted for entirely by cyanobacteria. They believe that the theory is not adequate because it can only account for 1 percent to 10 percent concentration levels, while today's atmosphere contains 21 percent. Thus, a second theory called the planetary atmosphere tectonic machine theory was developed. The theory posits that all of earth's oxygen came from not life forms, but the ocean, near the tectonic plates where magma is released and water comes into contact with temperatures over 2000°C. The superheated water is then converted into hydrogen and oxygen. The oxygen bubbles then oxygenate the ocean, and are released into the atmosphere when they reach the surface. This oxygen in the atmosphere is then shielded from being fully lost to space by the ozone and the earth's magnetic field.

The Effects of Light on Flowering

1 Plant growth and development are controlled by interactions between environmental factors and inner developmental processes. ¹⁾**Amongst** the diverse environmental factors, light ²⁾**plays** the most essential **role**, affecting plants ³⁾**in** various **ways**, **from** their growth and ⁴⁾**ability to** ⁵⁾**produce** energy **to** their bloom time. For example, ⁶⁾**in the absence of** sufficient light, plants exhibit a unique growth pattern ⁷⁾**called** etiolation. These plants will produce thinner and longer stems with longer internodes to reach a faint light source or to find one, **in** a much more rapid **way** than those ⁸⁾**exposed to** adequate sunlight. A plant ⁹⁾**suffering from** etiolation will also produce fewer leaves.

2 Perhaps the most interesting influence light has on plants is on their flowering patterns. The blossoming of flowers in plants is an intricate and delicate process which has evolved to suit plants' different environments. To maximize the probability of their seeds being successfully dispersed, plants ¹⁰⁾**use** environmental factors **to determine** the current season. Some of these factors, like temperature and water availability, can fluctuate heavily. An unusually cool summer or unexpected rain outside the monsoon seasons would confuse the plants. Fortunately, plants can also ¹¹⁾**use** the length of day **as** a cue. Length of day is perhaps the most reliable indicator of the season because it is controlled by the angle of Earth's rotation, which is unaltered by terrestrial events. Longer days always indicate springtime and the coming of summer while shorter days are only possible during autumn and winter.

3 ¹²⁾**Depending on** their reaction to the length of the day, species of plants are traditionally categorized into three groups: the long-day, the short-day and day-neutral plants. A day-neutral plant produces flowers ¹³⁾**as soon as** it has sufficiently grown and developed, ¹⁴⁾**regardless of** the length of the day. The traditional names of long-day and short-day plants are, however, better ¹⁵⁾**described as** short-night and long-night plants since it is the duration of continuous darkness **rather than** the day length which controls flowering. Long-night plants produce flowers during times when there is more than a specified duration of continuous darkness. Conversely, short-night plants ¹⁶⁾**require** periods of darkness **to be** less than a specified period. The threshold for the length of darkness of both long-night and short-night plants differ by species. The duration of this **is called** the critical photoperiod. For example, spinach, a short-night plant, only produces flowers when **exposed to** less-than-eleven-hour intervals of darkness. Spinach's critical photoperiod is, therefore, eleven hours.

4 ¹⁷⁾**Compared to** their flowering behavior, the actual method **used** by plants **to distinguish** daytime from nighttime is not well understood. ¹⁸⁾**So far**, botanists have discovered that plants utilize an internal clock and a light-detecting pigment **called** phytochrome ¹⁹⁾**in order to** measure the length of uninterrupted darkness. The internal biological clock **is used to measure** the length of time the plant has spent without light. It ²⁰⁾**works as** a timer that starts ticking when the light goes out, and resets when it returns. This clock is found in almost all organisms, including humans, yet is poorly understood. There is, however, a better grasp of the phytochrome. Phytochrome is a pigment found in plants which has the **ability to detect** light and ²¹⁾**bring about** cellular change when it is present. One such cellular change is the resetting of the internal clock that measures the length of continuous darkness.

5 This mechanism is quite sensitive; many species of long-night plants that have their darkness interrupted for even a minute or two with ²²⁾**either** sunlight **or** artificial light may not flower. This effect however does not occur with all types of light. It was found that red light ²³⁾**shone on** a plant during the night is perceived by the plant and the plant resets its biological clock. But the same plant does not reset its clock when **exposed to** far-red light (light with a longer wavelength than red light), and therefore it produces flowers. This is ²⁴⁾**not** because phytochrome cannot detect far-red light, **but** because it ²⁵⁾**reacts to** the two types of light differently.

6 The discovery of what internal factors actually signal plants to flower **in response to** light has overarching potential in biology and agriculture, which ²⁶⁾**makes** it an intriguing topic of study. Experiments conducted on cockleburs, a family of long-night plants that **require** more than eight hours of darkness **to flower**, revealed that despite their strong ²⁷⁾**sensitivity to** light exposure, if even a single leaf of the cocklebur experiences a long night, while the rest of the plant is ²⁸⁾**subjected to** short nights, it still produced flowers. This experiment suggested that a flowering factor ²⁹⁾**is sent from** the leaves **to** the flower buds when the flowering conditions for the plants are met. **So far** scientists have not found this factor, but the most widely accepted notion is that interactions among multiple, as yet unidentified plant hormones or other compounds, ³⁰⁾**referred to as** florigen, trigger flowering.

The Effects of Light on Flowering

1 Plant growth and development are controlled by interactions between environmental factors and inner developmental processes. Amongst the diverse environmental factors, light plays the most essential role, affecting plants in various ways, from their growth and ability to produce energy to their bloom time. For example, in the absence of sufficient light, plants exhibit a unique growth pattern called etiolation. These plants will produce thinner and longer stems with longer internodes to reach a faint light source or to find one, in a much more rapid way than those exposed to adequate sunlight. A plant suffering from etiolation will also produce fewer leaves.

2 Perhaps the most interesting influence light has on plants is on their flowering patterns. The blossoming of flowers in plants is an intricate and delicate process which has evolved to suit plants' different environments. To maximize the probability of their seeds being successfully dispersed, plants use environmental factors to determine the current season. Some of these factors, like temperature and water availability, can fluctuate heavily. An unusually cool summer or unexpected rain outside the monsoon seasons would confuse the plants. Fortunately, plants can also use the length of day as a cue. Length of day is perhaps the most reliable indicator of the season because it is controlled by the angle of Earth's rotation, which is unaltered by terrestrial events. Longer days always indicate springtime and the coming of summer while shorter days are only possible during autumn and winter.

3 Depending on their reaction to the length of the day, species of plants are traditionally categorized into three groups: the long-day, the short-day and day-neutral plants. A day-neutral plant produces flowers as soon as it has sufficiently grown and developed, regardless of the length of the day. The traditional names of long-day and short-day plants are, however, better described as short-night and long-night plants since it is the duration of continuous darkness rather than the day length which controls flowering. Long-night plants produce flowers during times when there is more than a specified duration of continuous darkness. Conversely, short-night plants require periods of darkness to be less than a specified period. The threshold for the length of darkness of both long-night and short-night plants differ by species. The duration of this is called the critical photoperiod. For example, spinach, a short-night plant, only produces flowers when exposed to less-than-eleven-hour intervals of darkness. Spinach's critical photoperiod is, therefore, eleven hours.

4 Compared to their flowering behavior, the actual method used by plants to distinguish daytime from nighttime is not well understood. So far, botanists have discovered that plants utilize an internal clock and a light-detecting pigment called phytochrome in order to measure the length of uninterrupted darkness. The internal biological clock is used to measure the length of time the plant has spent without light. It works as a timer that starts ticking when the light goes out, and resets when it returns. This clock is found in almost all organisms, including humans, yet is poorly understood. There is, however, a better grasp of the phytochrome. Phytochrome is a pigment found in plants which has the ability to detect light and bring about cellular change when it is present. One such cellular change is the resetting of the internal clock that measures the length of continuous darkness.

5 This mechanism is quite sensitive; many species of long-night plants that have their darkness interrupted for even a minute or two with either sunlight or artificial light may not flower. This effect however does not occur with all types of light. It was found that red light shone on a plant during the night is perceived by the plant and the plant resets its biological clock. But the same plant does not reset its clock when exposed to far-red light (light with a longer wavelength than red light), and therefore it produces flowers. This is not because phytochrome cannot detect far-red light, but because it reacts to the two types of light differently.

6 The discovery of what internal factors actually signal plants to flower in response to light has overarching potential in biology and agriculture, which makes it an intriguing topic of study. Experiments conducted on cockleburs, a family of long-night plants that require more than eight hours of darkness to flower, revealed that despite their strong sensitivity to light exposure, if even a single leaf of the cocklebur experiences a long night, while the rest of the plant is subjected to short nights, it still produced flowers. This experiment suggested that a flowering factor is sent from the leaves to the flower buds when the flowering conditions for the plants are met. So far scientists have not found this factor, but the most widely accepted notion is that interactions among multiple, as yet unidentified plant hormones or other compounds, referred to as florigen, trigger flowering.

Naturalistic Painting

1 The civilization of Ancient Greece, which lasted from the 8th century to the mid-1st century BC, had a lasting cultural influence over such a huge area, and over such powerful empires that it ¹⁾**is** often **considered** the underpinning of Western culture. Historians have discovered that even paintings from Ancient Greece ²⁾**had a** strong **influence on** art in remote parts of Europe for millennia to come. One such artistic influence was the movement ³⁾**known as** naturalism. Naturalistic painters ⁴⁾**aspire to** depict the world's natural objects, people and unadorned scenery ⁵⁾**as** realistically **as possible**. Their paintings are characterized by meticulous detail and near-perfect symmetry. ⁶⁾**In** simple **terms**, naturalistic artists ⁷⁾**strive to create** realistic paintings hardly ⁸⁾**distinguishable from** actual photographs. This movement ⁹⁾**originated in** Ancient Greece and spread through Europe to the Netherlands, where it continuously evolved.

2 In Ancient Greece, the early naturalistic painters ¹⁰⁾**tended to** ¹¹⁾**put** more **emphasis on** skill than **on** creativity, and painters of Greece would often compare their works to see which was more 'realistic'. While the artists' creativity was largely subjective, a brushstroke was an objective ¹²⁾**means of** assessment. ¹³⁾**As a result**, naturalistic painting became a competitive style of painting, as shown by the legendary painting competition of Parrhasius and Zeuxis, two of the greatest painters of the 5th century BC. Parrhasius, who was born in the city of Ephesus and lived in Athens, had ¹⁴⁾**distinguished** himself **as** an extraordinary artist at a young age. Often, those who witnessed the initial stages of his paintings ¹⁵⁾**mistook** him **for** a sketch artist, an artist who completes his work using only a pencil or pastel. His works were ¹⁶⁾**so** great **that** they ¹⁷⁾**were preserved as** study ¹⁸⁾**aids for** painters that ¹⁹⁾**came after** him. His rival Zeuxis was born in the Southern Italian city of Heraclea, and was widely renowned in the artistic scene of the time. ²⁰⁾**At the peak** of their careers, a contest was staged to determine the greater of the two. At the competition, Zeuxis revealed a painting of grapes which was realistic ²¹⁾**enough to fool** nearby birds. ²²⁾**Absorbed in** a sense of achievement, he confidently ²³⁾**asked** Parrhasius **to** ²⁴⁾**pull aside** the curtains and reveal his painting, ²⁵⁾**only to be told** that the curtains themselves were his painted work. Zeuxis ²⁶⁾**was confounded by** this and exclaimed "I have deceived the birds, but Parrhasius has deceived Zeuxis" Parrhasius' painting later ²⁷⁾**became known as** 'Parrhasius' Curtain' and he attained the title of the best naturalistic painter of the time, ²⁸⁾**gaining even more fame and respect**. He **was** even **asked to paint** murals for the Capitol of Rome by city officials.

3 Millenniums later, Adriaen van der Spelt and Frans van Mieris, painters from Netherlands, led a movement that challenged the original principles of naturalism. Their paintings portrayed objects and acts that interested them, ²⁹⁾**with little regard for** whether they resembled the natural world. For example, they painted a lily in the center of Parrhasius' Curtain with insects around it. The lily ³⁰⁾**served no** naturalistic **purpose**, but with it the painting gained ³¹⁾**scores of** symbolic meaning. Critics and fellow artists ³²⁾**were awakened to** the ideas of naturalist painting, surprised and awed ³³⁾**at the same time**. The lily represented wealth and property while the insects around the flower illustrated how the flower could ³⁴⁾**be robbed of** its nectar and ³⁵⁾**left to die** ³⁶⁾**in a matter of days**. The painting ³⁷⁾**was lauded for** its combination of symbolism and realistic insights. This ³⁸⁾**led** critics **to begin** questioning whether 'art' ³⁹⁾**was defined by** how well a natural object is depicted, or by how well it is embellished and enhanced. This became more pronounced as technological progress and development ⁴⁰⁾**led to** the emergence of cameras and professional photography. Initially, photography was used to capture and record subjects of scientific interest, but it quickly turned into a new art form. Clearly, the new artistic photographs captured naturalistic images much more easily than paintings. While an intricate and time-consuming process in the past, re-creating nature on paper became only a matter of the click of a shutter.

4 As art entered the modern era, the common belief became that painting to resemble nature **as** closely **as possible** is not really art, but rather an act of duplication. There have ⁴¹⁾**not only** been convincing arguments which support this claim, **but also** several credible arguments that oppose it. One modern artist, for instance, ⁴²⁾**added** his touch **to** Adriaen van der Spelt and Frans van Mieris' painting by coloring the lily bright red. The red lily, the artist explained, represented passion and supported the assertion that art should express the artist's mind. ⁴³⁾**According to** him, an artist must deliberately convey his vision through various methods, such as the use of color and brushstroke. ⁴⁴⁾**On the other hand**, the French Neoclassical painter Jean Auguste Dominique Ingres, pointed out that ⁴⁵⁾**regardless of** what or how an artist paints, the painter unintentionally leaves traces of himself in the work. Ingres believed that the painter would subconsciously make different choices **according to** his mood, such as using harsher brushstrokes when feeling angry, or passionate colors **when in love**, all inadvertently. ⁴⁶⁾**With all things considered**, ⁴⁷⁾**despite the fact that** it was ⁴⁸⁾**decreasing in** popularity and was occasionally criticized, the naturalistic style of painting has ⁴⁹⁾**played a major role in** the history of art and will ⁵⁰⁾**continue to do** so **in the future**.

Naturalistic Painting

1 The civilization of Ancient Greece, which lasted from the 8th century to the mid-1st century BC, had a lasting cultural influence over such a huge area, and over such powerful empires that it is often considered the underpinning of Western culture. Historians have discovered that even paintings from Ancient Greece had a strong influence on art in remote parts of Europe for millennia to come. One such artistic influence was the movement known as naturalism. Naturalistic painters aspire to depict the world's natural objects, people and unadorned scenery as realistically as possible. Their paintings are characterized by meticulous detail and near-perfect symmetry. In simple terms, naturalistic artists strive to create realistic paintings hardly distinguishable from actual photographs. This movement originated in Ancient Greece and spread through Europe to the Netherlands, where it continuously evolved.

2 In Ancient Greece, the early naturalistic painters tended to put more emphasis on skill than on creativity, and painters of Greece would often compare their works to see which was more 'realistic'. While the artists' creativity was largely subjective, a brushstroke was an objective means of assessment. As a result, naturalistic painting became a competitive style of painting, as shown by the legendary painting competition of Parrhasius and Zeuxis, two of the greatest painters of the 5th century BC. Parrhasius, who was born in the city of Ephesus and lived in Athens, had distinguished himself as an extraordinary artist at a young age. Often, those who witnessed the initial stages of his paintings mistook him for a sketch artist, an artist who completes his work using only a pencil or pastel. His works were so great that they were preserved as study aids for painters that came after him. His rival Zeuxis was born in the Southern Italian city of Heraclea, and was widely renowned in the artistic scene of the time. At the peak of their careers, a contest was staged to determine the greater of the two. At the competition, Zeuxis revealed a painting of grapes which was realistic enough to fool nearby birds. Absorbed in a sense of achievement, he confidently asked Parrhasius to pull aside the curtains and reveal his painting, only to be told that the curtains themselves were his painted work. Zeuxis was confounded by this and exclaimed "I have deceived the birds, but Parrhasius has deceived Zeuxis" Parrhasius' painting later became known as 'Parrhasius' Curtain' and he attained the title of the best naturalistic painter of the time, gaining even more fame and respect. He was even asked to paint murals for the Capitol of Rome by city officials.

3 Millenniums later, Adriaen van der Spelt and Frans van Mieris, painters from Netherlands, led a movement that challenged the original principles of naturalism. Their paintings portrayed objects and acts that interested them, with little regard for whether they resembled the natural world. For example, they painted a lily in the center of Parrhasius' Curtain with insects around it. The lily served no naturalistic purpose, but with it the painting gained scores of symbolic meaning. Critics and fellow artists were awakened to the ideas of naturalist painting, surprised and awed at the same time. The lily represented wealth and property while the insects around the flower illustrated how the flower could be robbed of its nectar and left to die in a matter of days. The painting was lauded for its combination of symbolism and realistic insights. This led critics to begin questioning whether 'art' was defined by how well a natural object is depicted, or by how well it is embellished and enhanced. This became more pronounced as technological progress and development led to the emergence of cameras and professional photography. Initially, photography was used to capture and record subjects of scientific interest, but it quickly turned into a new art form. Clearly, the new artistic photographs captured naturalistic images much more easily than paintings. While an intricate and time-consuming process in the past, re-creating nature on paper became only a matter of the click of a shutter.

4 As art entered the modern era, the common belief became that painting to resemble nature as closely as possible is not really art, but rather an act of duplication. There have not only been convincing arguments which support this claim, but also several credible arguments that oppose it. One modern artist, for instance, added his touch to Adriaen van der Spelt and Frans van Mieris' painting by coloring the lily bright red. The red lily, the artist explained, represented passion and supported the assertion that art should express the artist's mind. According to him, an artist must deliberately convey his vision through various methods, such as the use of color and brushstroke. On the other hand, the French Neoclassical painter Jean Auguste Dominique Ingres, pointed out that regardless of what or how an artist paints, the painter unintentionally leaves traces of himself in the work. Ingres believed that the painter would subconsciously make different choices according to his mood, such as using harsher brushstrokes when feeling angry, or passionate colors when in love, all inadvertently. With all things considered, despite the fact that it was decreasing in popularity and was occasionally criticized, the naturalistic style of painting has played a major role in the history of art and will continue to do so in the future.

Two Types of Evolutionary Theories

1 Evolution occurs as populations [1)]**adjust to** habitat change with [2)]**those experiencing** the best genetic adaptations surviving and [3)]**passing on** their genes. These phenotypic [4)]**changes in** populations [5)]**are common to** all organisms and affect every species, [6)]**no matter what** ecosystem. There are two prevailing, non-mutually exclusive theories of evolution today, gradualism and punctuated equilibrium, which [7)]**differ in** the [8)]**speed at which** evolutionary changes occur.

2 [9)]**One of the** early proponents of complete gradualism was Charles Darwin whose 'Origin of Species' adopted Charles Lyell's 'Principles of Geology' to suggest gradualism occurs [10)]**in a** slow **manner** with only small intergenerational changes. As Lyell proposed, sudden changes cannot [11)]**be assumed to occur** as they are not presently observed and thus cannot **be assumed to have occurred** in the past. Darwin also felt that extreme [12)]**deviations from** the usual phenotypic variation would [13)]**be** more **likely to be** [14)]**selected against**. The most famous historical model supporting the idea of complete gradualism was the evolution of the modern horse from the fox-sized, forest-dwelling Hyracotherium. [15)]**Over time**, paleozoologists [16)]**pieced together** the gradual evolution of the horse [17)]**in a** more complete **way** than any other modern animal. They traced the lineage from early ancestors with splayed toes for walking on the soft, moist grounds of primeval forests, to the longer legged, faster species which grazed on the firm grassy steppes and were able to outrun predators and eventually to the modern hoofed horse. Paleontologist Othniel C. Marsh [18)]**was so sure of** this theory of gradual equine evolution **that** he [19)]**put together** a series of fossils showing it in 1870. The fact that these fossils displayed successive adaptations was held as an example of gradualism until 100 years later, when it was shown they were not, in fact, even successive members of a single line of descent, [20)]**let alone** stages of an unbroken, gradually evolving lineage.

3 Scientists studying fossils noted that the evolution of some species was nearly 'mapped out,' while others had a few, very different species along the evolutionary course, with few or no intermediary fossils. They envisaged that this second group's evolution must have occurred rapidly to produce a great change over a short period. They reasoned that there had to be another evolutionary method that was quicker and left fewer intermediate species, thus the idea of punctuated equilibrium was formed. The theory of punctuated equilibrium states that most sexually-reproducing species will remain in an extended state of little evolutionary change between generations, called stasis, which is broken up by rare, rapid events of branching speciation called cladogenesis when they [21)]**split into** two distinct species. They pointed out that for most species, there was a sudden appearance in the geologic record with no evidence of substantial, gradual changes. Darwin had noted this problem also, but [22)]**ascribed** it **to** imperfections in the fossil record rather than catastrophism and progressive creationism, or supernatural creation, while privately noting on the margin of his essay, "Better [23)]**begin with** this: If species really, after catastrophes, created [24)]**in showers** [25)]**world over**, my theory false."

4 While these theories vary widely on their methods of evolution, both show major adaptations **over time** [26)]**whereby** a population becomes better [27)]**suited to** its habitat. These successive intergenerational changes occur in all species and are one of the basic phenomena of biology. Even creatures which have very simple bodily structures, like internal parasites, are highly adapted to their specific environments. From this one can see that adaptation is [28)]**not just** a matter of visible traits, complex adaptations to changes can occur during an organism's life. These reactions to habitat change happen in three major ways, either exclusively or [29)]**in succession**. The most basic adaptation to change is to simply move to a locale that better suits the organism. This response, [30)]**typical of** organisms that have wide spheres of movement such as flying insects or seadwellers, is called habitat tracking, and is one explanation **put forth** for the periods of apparent stasis in the fossil record. The term genetic change, [31)]**on the other hand**, [32)]**pertains to** changes in the population when natural selection [33)]**acts on** the genetic variations of a population. These mutations, which may be physical features or adjusted physiological activity, create genetic variations that [34)]**lead to** differing characteristics in offspring and, consequently, a population better genetically [35)]**adapted to** its environment. The third, and most dramatic, change that can occur to resident populations is extinction, or the demise of a population that was [36)]**unable to** properly **adapt to** change.

5 Whether by gradualism or punctuated equilibrium, a species must always **adapt to** its changing habitat, as it is now clear that habitats and biota are constantly changing and the process of adaptation is never complete.

Two Types of Evolutionary Theories

1 Evolution occurs as populations adjust to habitat change with those experiencing the best genetic adaptations surviving and passing on their genes. These phenotypic changes in populations are common to all organisms and affect every species, no matter what ecosystem. There are two prevailing, non-mutually exclusive theories of evolution today, gradualism and punctuated equilibrium, which differ in the speed at which evolutionary changes occur.

2 One of the early proponents of complete gradualism was Charles Darwin whose 'Origin of Species' adopted Charles Lyell's 'Principles of Geology' to suggest gradualism occurs in a slow manner with only small intergenerational changes. As Lyell proposed, sudden changes cannot be assumed to occur as they are not presently observed and thus cannot be assumed to have occurred in the past. Darwin also felt that extreme deviations from the usual phenotypic variation would be more likely to be selected against. The most famous historical model supporting the idea of complete gradualism was the evolution of the modern horse from the fox-sized, forest-dwelling Hyracotherium. Over time, paleozoologists pieced together the gradual evolution of the horse in a more complete way than any other modern animal. They traced the lineage from early ancestors with splayed toes for walking on the soft, moist grounds of primeval forests, to the longer legged, faster species which grazed on the firm grassy steppes and were able to outrun predators and eventually to the modern hoofed horse. Paleontologist Othniel C. Marsh was so sure of this theory of gradual equine evolution that he put together a series of fossils showing it in 1870. The fact that these fossils displayed successive adaptations was held as an example of gradualism until 100 years later, when it was shown they were not, in fact, even successive members of a single line of descent, let alone stages of an unbroken, gradually evolving lineage.

3 Scientists studying fossils noted that the evolution of some species was nearly 'mapped out,' while others had a few, very different species along the evolutionary course, with few or no intermediary fossils. They envisaged that this second group's evolution must have occurred rapidly to produce a great change over a short period. They reasoned that there had to be another evolutionary method that was quicker and left fewer intermediate species, thus the idea of punctuated equilibrium was formed. The theory of punctuated equilibrium states that most sexually-reproducing species will remain in an extended state of little evolutionary change between generations, called stasis, which is broken up by rare, rapid events of branching speciation called cladogenesis when they split into two distinct species. They pointed out that for most species, there was a sudden appearance in the geologic record with no evidence of substantial, gradual changes. Darwin had noted this problem also, but ascribed it to imperfections in the fossil record rather than catastrophism and progressive creationism, or supernatural creation, while privately noting on the margin of his essay, "Better begin with this: If species really, after catastrophes, created in showers world over, my theory false."

4 While these theories vary widely on their methods of evolution, both show major adaptations over time whereby a population becomes better suited to its habitat. These successive intergenerational changes occur in all species and are one of the basic phenomena of biology. Even creatures which have very simple bodily structures, like internal parasites, are highly adapted to their specific environments. From this one can see that adaptation is not just a matter of visible traits, complex adaptations to changes can occur during an organism's life. These reactions to habitat change happen in three major ways, either exclusively or in succession. The most basic adaptation to change is to simply move to a locale that better suits the organism. This response, typical of organisms that have wide spheres of movement such as flying insects or sea-dwellers, is called habitat tracking, and is one explanation put forth for the periods of apparent stasis in the fossil record. The term genetic change, on the other hand, pertains to changes in the population when natural selection acts on the genetic variations of a population. These mutations, which may be physical features or adjusted physiological activity, create genetic variations that lead to differing characteristics in offspring and, consequently, a population better genetically adapted to its environment. The third, and most dramatic, change that can occur to resident populations is extinction, or the demise of a population that was unable to properly adapt to change.

5 Whether by gradualism or punctuated equilibrium, a species must always adapt to its changing habitat, as it is now clear that habitats and biota are constantly changing and the process of adaptation is never complete.

Griffith and Transformation

1 The 19th century Romantic Movement reshaped science by opening new avenues of research that [1)]**were unheard of** under the Enlightenment's classical approaches. Major breakthroughs, such as Darwin's theory of evolution, were developed during this period, [2)]**along with** [3)]**advances in** physics, non-Euclidean geometry and organic chemistry. During this time, science became a major source for increasing humankind's knowledge. During the 19th and 20th centuries, the practice of science became much more professionally institutionalized than it had been. One of the great breakthroughs in biology [4)]**is attributed to** Frederick Griffith of the British Ministry of Health. Griffith undertook one of the most pivotal experiments of the era, which [5)]**tried to establish** a more precise scientific understanding by typing, or classifying, pneumococci bacteria samples [6)]**in order to find** overarching patterns [7)]**so as to clarify** the epidemiology of lobar pneumonia, an infectious lung disorder.

2 He also [8)]**sought to improve** the understanding of the pathology of pneumococci on the individual by testing them on mice. Smooth pneumococci, denoted by S, are encapsulated and more virulent; this form [9)]**was shown to** [10)]**result in** pneumonia and death of the mice within days of being injected. Their capsules are slippery polysaccharide coatings that [11)]**allow** the bacteria **to** [12)]**evade** phagocytosis **from** the host's immune cells. [13)]**On the other hand**, the rough form, R, lacks a capsule and was considered non-infective. In Griffith's experiment, [14)]**as expected**, when mice [15)]**were injected with** S that had been killed by heat, it [16)]**failed to cause** illness despite being the virulent strain. Surprisingly, however, Griffith observed pneumonia and death when live R were injected alongside large amounts of heat-killed S; this was generally unexpected, since R, the only live bacteria in the experiment, were avirulent. During necropsy, Griffith found that the live R had developed capsules and [17)]**morphed into** S, then retained this phenotype over successive generations. Griffith hypothesized that a transforming principle-[18)]**derived from** the killed S-had helped [19)]**transform** the R **into** S. He also reported that heavy loads of live R alone could also **transform into** S. Griffith, however, noted that the addition of heat-killed S bacteria made this transformation much more likely.

3 Griffith had previously held, along with most bacteriologists, that bacteria's forms were essentially fixed and unchangeable. They [20)]**held that** each strain had [21)]**emerged from**, and was genetically [22)]**similar to** their progenitor, through an evolutionary lineage determined by Darwinian natural selection **resulting in** the death of unfit bacterial cells. Besides this implicit belief that bacterial strains could be extinguished through competition, many bacteriologists and physicians believed that any particular strain of bacteria had necessarily multiplied from previous, genetically-related strains. Griffith's findings, though generally neglected after the initial [23)]**contention against** them subsided, revealed that his original supposition was incorrect by showing that bacteria [24)]**are able to acquire** genes without the need for reproducing as well. He summarized his work [25)]**as such**: "The results of the [26)]**experiments on** enhancement of virulence and **on** transformation of type are discussed and their significance [27)]**in regard to** questions of epidemiology is indicated."

4 An American medical researcher named Oswald Avery, with colleagues Macleod and McCarty furthered Griffith's 1927 findings [28)]**regarding** the mysteries of inheritance. [29)]**Being driven to prove** Griffith's theory, Avery [30)]**continued to** [31)]**work on** adjusting previous techniques even after he retired in 1943. By using techniques to remove bacteria's organic compounds, scientists could observe that if the R-strain bacteria still transformed, it would mean that the materials removed were not the carrier of the transformation gene. To do this, the cellular structures of the S strain bacteria were first removed, and then their proteins were removed [32)]**through the use of** protease enzyme treatments. Finally, the cellular remainders were placed in a dish containing R strain bacteria. The R strain bacteria transformed, meaning that proteins did not carry the virulent genes. Then the remainder of the S strain bacteria [33)]**had** their DNA **removed by** [34)]**being treated with** deoxyribonuclease. When they were treated [35)]**in** this **manner**, the R strain bacteria resisted transformation, proving that DNA was the transforming factor of pneumococci.

5 [36)]**Over time**, more advanced discoveries have been made [37)]**through the findings of** Griffith and Avery. Joshua Lederberg's discoveries [38)]**concerning** genetic recombination and the organization of the bacterial genetic material are a prime example of this continuation. Inspired by previous discoveries, Lederberg, in 1944, [39)]**started to think about** genetic [40)]**experimentations on** bacteria [41)]**despite the fact that** there was still no [42)]**consensus on** whether bacteria even had genes or not. He showed that bacteria could reproduce sexually and substantiated the hypothesis by proving that they [43)]**are endowed with** genetic systems [44)]**akin to** [45)]**those of** higher-level organisms, thus opening a new realm for scientists to study the genetic basis of life and winning the 1958 Nobel Prize in Physiology or Medicine. During his speech, he stated that former researchers and their laboratories provided the historical platform of modern DNA research.

Griffith and Transformation

1 The 19th century Romantic Movement reshaped science by opening new avenues of research that were unheard of under the Enlightenment's classical approaches. Major breakthroughs, such as Darwin's theory of evolution, were developed during this period, along with advances in physics, non-Euclidean geometry and organic chemistry. During this time, science became a major source for increasing humankind's knowledge. During the 19th and 20th centuries, the practice of science became much more professionally institutionalized than it had been. One of the great breakthroughs in biology is attributed to Frederick Griffith of the British Ministry of Health. Griffith undertook one of the most pivotal experiments of the era, which tried to establish a more precise scientific understanding by typing, or classifying, pneumococci bacteria samples in order to find overarching patterns so as to clarify the epidemiology of lobar pneumonia, an infectious lung disorder.

2 He also sought to improve the understanding of the pathology of pneumococci on the individual by testing them on mice. Smooth pneumococci, denoted by S, are encapsulated and more virulent; this form was shown to result in pneumonia and death of the mice within days of being injected. Their capsules are slippery polysaccharide coatings that allow the bacteria to evade phagocytosis from the host's immune cells. On the other hand, the rough form, R, lacks a capsule and was considered non-infective. In Griffith's experiment, as expected, when mice were injected with S that had been killed by heat, it failed to cause illness despite being the virulent strain. Surprisingly, however, Griffith observed pneumonia and death when live R were injected alongside large amounts of heat-killed S; this was generally unexpected, since R, the only live bacteria in the experiment, were avirulent. During necropsy, Griffith found that the live R had developed capsules and morphed into S, then retained this phenotype over successive generations. Griffith hypothesized that a transforming principle-derived from the killed S-had helped transform the R into S. He also reported that heavy loads of live R alone could also transform into S. Griffith, however, noted that the addition of heat-killed S bacteria made this transformation much more likely.

3 Griffith had previously held, along with most bacteriologists, that bacteria's forms were essentially fixed and unchangeable. They held that each strain had emerged from, and was genetically similar to their progenitor, through an evolutionary lineage determined by Darwinian natural selection resulting in the death of unfit bacterial cells. Besides this implicit belief that bacterial strains could be extinguished through competition, many bacteriologists and physicians believed that any particular strain of bacteria had necessarily multiplied from previous, genetically-related strains. Griffith's findings, though generally neglected after the initial contention against them subsided, revealed that his original supposition was incorrect by showing that bacteria are able to acquire genes without the need for reproducing as well. He summarized his work as such: "The results of the experiments on enhancement of virulence and on transformation of type are discussed and their significance in regard to questions of epidemiology is indicated."

4 An American medical researcher named Oswald Avery, with colleagues Macleod and McCarty furthered Griffith's 1927 findings regarding the mysteries of inheritance. Being driven to prove Griffith's theory, Avery continued to work on adjusting previous techniques even after he retired in 1943. By using techniques to remove bacteria's organic compounds, scientists could observe that if the R-strain bacteria still transformed, it would mean that the materials removed were not the carrier of the transformation gene. To do this, the cellular structures of the S strain bacteria were first removed, and then their proteins were removed through the use of protease enzyme treatments. Finally, the cellular remainders were placed in a dish containing R strain bacteria. The R strain bacteria transformed, meaning that proteins did not carry the virulent genes. Then the remainder of the S strain bacteria had their DNA removed by being treated with deoxyribonuclease. When they were treated in this manner, the R strain bacteria resisted transformation, proving that DNA was the transforming factor of pneumococci.

5 Over time, more advanced discoveries have been made through the findings of Griffith and Avery. Joshua Lederberg's discoveries concerning genetic recombination and the organization of the bacterial genetic material are a prime example of this continuation. Inspired by previous discoveries, Lederberg, in 1944, started to think about genetic experimentations on bacteria despite the fact that there was still no consensus on whether bacteria even had genes or not. He showed that bacteria could reproduce sexually and substantiated the hypothesis by proving that they are endowed with genetic systems akin to those of higher-level organisms, thus opening a new realm for scientists to study the genetic basis of life and winning the 1958 Nobel Prize in Physiology or Medicine. During his speech, he stated that former researchers and their laboratories provided the historical platform of modern DNA research.

Maximilian Weber and His Influence

1 Authority can [1)]**be defined as** the forceful domination of a group of people who have the underlying condition of being absolutely obedient. The German sociologist Maximilian Weber, [2)]**on the other hand**, **defined authority as** 'the [3)]**chance**' of commands being obeyed [4)]**according to** distinct justifications by a specifiable group of people. Pointing out that Germany's political fiasco during WWI was essentially a problem of leadership, Weber proposed a theory of authority that [5)]**classified** it **into** three types, [6)]**each** [7)]**differing in** its justifications to compel acquiescence and its [8)]**influences on** the public.

2 In a society that is governed by a system of 'traditional' authority, social status [9)]**plays a** vital **role in** determining the sovereign power. The leaders of these types of societies are a ruling elite with an inheritable leadership role [10)]**based on** factors [11)]**such as** age, bloodline, or social connections, which shows that there is an inequality in the society. The disadvantage of this system is that it [12)]**is vulnerable** to change, [13)]**as is** evident when [14)]**looking at** the challenges faced by the Russian Empire as it encountered a more complex [15)]**division of labor** and wider population diversity [16)]**due to** Industrialization in the early 20th century. The helplessness of the traditional authority against the rise of the bourgeois and proletariat classes ultimately [17)]**brought about** the introduction of 'rational-legal' authority in Russia. 'Rational-legal' authority is a system in which an individual, or institution, exercises power through the socially accepted set of rules and the right of those [18)] **elevated to** positions of authority to [19)]**issue** such **commands**. Power is held by the office itself, [20)]**with no regard to** the personal attributes of the office holder, and it is limited by the official codified rules which state the extent of the office's power. 'Rational-Legal' authority fosters financial stability and technological development because the rights of individuals [21)]**act as** the law, guaranteeing their property and investments. It, however, does not automatically [22)]**lead to** economic stability or scientific development. 'Charismatic' authority can exist [23)]**under** 'traditional' or 'rational-legal' authorities **systems** when power is gained through widespread [24)]**devotion to** the exceptional sanctity, heroism, or a specific exemplary characteristic of a person. **According to** Weber, this form of authority is extremely volatile and dynamic as charisma eventually recedes after it has entered the permanent routine of social interaction, which can [25)]**result in** the sudden collapse of its power. For example, Napoleon Bonaparte [26)]**gained** his **fame** through his military feats, immediately consolidating absolute political power over France and reforming the country. His defeat during the Napoleonic Wars, however, **resulted in** the abrupt end of his reign as emperor and the beginning of his exile.

3 Although Weber's theory has strongly influenced the aspects of sociology that [27)]**deal with** leadership, scholars have pointed out two flaws in it. First, they believed that the standardization of [28)]**a variety of** concepts of authority and Weber's theoretical notion of an 'iron cage', in which the increased rationalization of modern life [29)]**causes** individuals **to be driven** purely by objective, [30)]**rather than** by values, was an oversimplified, limited idea of authority. Furthermore, they posit that he [31)]**failed to distinguish** between reigning and governing, with governing requiring a positive change in society whereas reigning does not.

4 Despite these objections, Weber's theory of authority influenced modern sociology and **brought about** the development of three new models of leadership in the late 20th century. The theory behind 'transformational' leadership is that leaders can make radical [32)]**changes in** their followers' thoughts and actions and exploit the order of their needs and aims to [33)]**satisfy** the greater **need**, which is, in turn, closely [34)]**aligned with** the followers' internal motivational factors. The leaders who Weber would have [35)]**classified as** having charismatic authority are, therefore, transformational, since they approach things [36)]**from** entirely different **perspectives**. [37)]**In contrast**, individuals that can [38)]**be described as** 'rational-legal' leaders can also [39)]**be seen as** 'transactional' leaders, as they are [40)]**effective in** using their knowledge to [41)]**achieve results**, [42)]**based on** the hypothesis that followers are motivated through a system of 'quid pro quo' or 'give and take'. The differing qualities of the two leadership types can [43)]**be simply stated as**: 'transactional' leaders form mutual [44)]**bonds with** people through reward and punishment, while, in contrast, 'transformational' leaders [45)]**seek to gratify** the intrinsic [46)]**needs of** the individual. The third form, 'laissez-faire' leadership, is characterized by a completely permissive leader who does not [47)]**contribute to** [48)]**making decisions**, which produces groups that often lack direction, and may **lead to** anarchy, but offer their followers many [49)]**opportunities to make** their own decisions.

5 Weber [50)]**stressed that** the importance of theories of authority is not to label, or classify, prevalent forms of leadership in history, but rather to show how the state of authority transits from one type to another. His precise intention led to scholars [51)]**viewing** his theory **as** a hierarchical development order, and it [52)]**is now considered** more of a [53)]**theory on** social evolution.

Maximilian Weber and His Influence

1 Authority can be defined as the forceful domination of a group of people who have the underlying condition of being absolutely obedient. The German sociologist Maximilian Weber, on the other hand, defined authority as 'the chance' of commands being obeyed according to distinct justifications by a specifiable group of people. Pointing out that Germany's political fiasco during WWI was essentially a problem of leadership, Weber proposed a theory of authority that classified it into three types, each differing in its justifications to compel acquiescence and its influences on the public.

2 In a society that is governed by a system of 'traditional' authority, social status plays a vital role in determining the sovereign power. The leaders of these types of societies are a ruling elite with an inheritable leadership role based on factors such as age, bloodline, or social connections, which shows that there is an inequality in the society. The disadvantage of this system is that it is vulnerable to change, as is evident when looking at the challenges faced by the Russian Empire as it encountered a more complex division of labor and wider population diversity due to Industrialization in the early 20th century. The helplessness of the traditional authority against the rise of the bourgeois and proletariat classes ultimately brought about the introduction of 'rational-legal' authority in Russia. 'Rational-legal' authority is a system in which an individual, or institution, exercises power through the socially accepted set of rules and the right of those elevated to positions of authority to issue such commands. Power is held by the office itself, with no regard to the personal attributes of the office holder, and it is limited by the official codified rules which state the extent of the office's power. 'Rational-Legal' authority fosters financial stability and technological development because the rights of individuals act as the law, guaranteeing their property and investments. It, however, does not automatically lead to economic stability or scientific development. 'Charismatic' authority can exist under 'traditional' or 'rational-legal' authorities systems when power is gained through widespread devotion to the exceptional sanctity, heroism, or a specific exemplary characteristic of a person. According to Weber, this form of authority is extremely volatile and dynamic as charisma eventually recedes after it has entered the permanent routine of social interaction, which can result in the sudden collapse of its power. For example, Napoleon Bonaparte gained his fame through his military feats, immediately consolidating absolute political power over France and reforming the country. His defeat during the Napoleonic Wars, however, resulted in the abrupt end of his reign as emperor and the beginning of his exile.

3 Although Weber's theory has strongly influenced the aspects of sociology that deal with leadership, scholars have pointed out two flaws in it. First, they believed that the standardization of a variety of concepts of authority and Weber's theoretical notion of an 'iron cage', in which the increased rationalization of modern life causes individuals to be driven purely by objective, rather than by values, was an oversimplified, limited idea of authority. Furthermore, they posit that he failed to distinguish between reigning and governing, with governing requiring a positive change in society whereas reigning does not.

4 Despite these objections, Weber's theory of authority influenced modern sociology and brought about the development of three new models of leadership in the late 20th century. The theory behind 'transformational' leadership is that leaders can make radical changes in their followers' thoughts and actions and exploit the order of their needs and aims to satisfy the greater need, which is, in turn, closely aligned with the followers' internal motivational factors. The leaders who Weber would have classified as having charismatic authority are, therefore, transformational, since they approach things from entirely different perspectives. In contrast, individuals that can be described as 'rational-legal' leaders can also be seen as 'transactional' leaders, as they are effective in using their knowledge to achieve results, based on the hypothesis that followers are motivated through a system of 'quid pro quo' or 'give and take'. The differing qualities of the two leadership types can be simply stated as: 'transactional' leaders form mutual bonds with people through reward and punishment, while, in contrast, 'transformational' leaders seek to gratify the intrinsic needs of the individual. The third form, 'laissez-faire' leadership, is characterized by a completely permissive leader who does not contribute to making decisions, which produces groups that often lack direction, and may lead to anarchy, but offer their followers many opportunities to make their own decisions.

5 Weber stressed that the importance of theories of authority is not to label, or classify, prevalent forms of leadership in history, but rather to show how the state of authority transits from one type to another. His precise intention led to scholars viewing his theory as a hierarchical development order, and it is now considered more of a theory on social evolution.

Pasteur and The Origin of Life

1 Logical and methodical scientists sometimes, ironically, blindly [1)]**adhere to** spuriously hypothesized assertions. For instance, Aristotle hypothesized that flies were the result of spontaneous generation in rotting materials and that microorganisms could appear naturally. Scientists believed these theories for nearly two millennia. These errant theories [2)]**led** them **to believe** that the bacteria required for fermentation were naturally generated without any external stimuli. Scientist Louis Pasteur, however, [3)]**skeptical of** spontaneous generation, successfully falsified the long-held theory.

2 Pasteur proposed the new theory of biogenesis, claiming that the natural generation of bacteria was preposterous, and that fermentation required the introduction of the necessary bacteria. [4)]**In order to prove** this, he [5)]**conducted** two **experiments**. In the first, a glass [6)]**filled with** meat broth, which would have fermented in open air, was placed in a sealed box that was completely sterile and had a filter over its opening. This did not [7)]**allow** anything **to enter** the glass and [8)]**as a result** there were no signs of fermentation in the glass. This, however, did not convince scientists [9)]**at the time**, because they thought that [10)]**even if** organisms were generated in the glass, they [11)]**would have expired** [12)]**due to lack of** oxygen. Therefore, he conducted a second experiment, the 'swan-neck duct' experiment. In this experiment, he put the broth into a spherical glass with a long curved tube atop it. With this structure, [13)]**nothing but** weightless air could enter. This also yielded no fermentation. In 1864, Pasteur finally announced the results of these and further experiments, demonstrating that life cannot spontaneously arise in areas that have not [14)]**been exposed to** existing life.

3 Unsurprisingly, Pasteur's experiments were eye-openers, having definitively disproved the antiquated theory of spontaneous generation and [15)]**giving birth to** biogenesis. Even though he was the first to empirically prove this, he was not the first scientist to propose this type of theory. Scientists Girolamo Fracastoro, Agostino Bassi, and Friedrich Henle had previously suggested various theories which influenced Pasteur's work later. The development of biogenesis, however, left a vacuum [16)]**in the understanding of** how life first arose. As it requires previous forms of life, biogenesis alone could not ultimately explain the origin of life on the early, barren Earth. No notable related theories, however, appeared until 1924, when Alexander Oparin surmised that the presence of oxygen in the atmosphere prevents the synthesis of certain organic compounds that are [17)]**necessary for** the evolution of life. In 'The Origin of Life', he proffered that the type of abiogenesis that Pasteur attacked had in fact occurred once, but [18)]**no longer** could because the conditions found on the early Earth had changed. Oparin felt that an organic 'primeval soup' could be created in an oxygen-free atmosphere due to the effects of sunlight. He hypothesized that 4 billion years ago, the earth's environment [19)]**met** these **criteria** after volcanic eruptions filled the environment with carbon dioxide, nitrogen, and other gases. Originally he thought that the early atmosphere, [20)]**in contrast to** the Earth's current atmosphere, contained mostly ammonia and methane, but [21)]**it is likely that** most of the atmospheric carbon was carbon dioxide with perhaps some carbon monoxide and nitrogen. In practice these mixtures have many of [22)]**the same** properties **as** those containing ammonia and methane [23)]**as long as** free oxygen molecules are not present.

4 These theories were tested in the Miller and Urey experiment which [24)]**attempted to recreate** these hypothetical conditions, and [25)]**tested for** the occurrence of the chemical origins of life. Specifically, the experiment tested Oparin's hypothesis that conditions on the primitive Earth favored chemical reactions that synthesized organic compounds from inorganic precursors. **In order to** test for the generation of the amino acids, required for protein generation in living cells [26)]**under** primitive Earth's **conditions**, they required a less hydrogen-rich mixture than the current environment. Their experiments used water, methane, ammonia, and hydrogen, sealed inside interconnected sterile glass tubes and beakers, with one half **filled with** water and another holding two electrodes. The water was boiled to produce evaporation, then the electrodes were fired to simulate lightning through the atmosphere and water vapor, and then it was cooled again to condense the water back into the first beaker in a repetitive cycle. After one week, they observed that 10-15 percent of the carbon was [27)]**in the form of** organic compounds. Two percent of the carbon had formed amino acids, with glycine being the most plentiful. Although nucleic acids were not formed, the 20 common amino acids were formed in various concentrations. This was interesting because amino acids can potentially create the most basic component of most living creatures namely DNA.

Pasteur and The Origin of Life

1 Logical and methodical scientists sometimes, ironically, blindly adhere to spuriously hypothesized assertions. For instance, Aristotle hypothesized that flies were the result of spontaneous generation in rotting materials and that microorganisms could appear naturally. Scientists believed these theories for nearly two millennia. These errant theories led them to believe that the bacteria required for fermentation were naturally generated without any external stimuli. Scientist Louis Pasteur, however, skeptical of spontaneous generation, successfully falsified the long-held theory.

2 Pasteur proposed the new theory of biogenesis, claiming that the natural generation of bacteria was preposterous, and that fermentation required the introduction of the necessary bacteria. In order to prove this, he conducted two experiments. In the first, a glass filled with meat broth, which would have fermented in open air, was placed in a sealed box that was completely sterile and had a filter over its opening. This did not allow anything to enter the glass and as a result there were no signs of fermentation in the glass. This, however, did not convince scientists at the time, because they thought that even if organisms were generated in the glass, they would have expired due to lack of oxygen. Therefore, he conducted a second experiment, the 'swan-neck duct' experiment. In this experiment, he put the broth into a spherical glass with a long curved tube atop it. With this structure, nothing but weightless air could enter. This also yielded no fermentation. In 1864, Pasteur finally announced the results of these and further experiments, demonstrating that life cannot spontaneously arise in areas that have not been exposed to existing life.

3 Unsurprisingly, Pasteur's experiments were eye-openers, having definitively disproved the antiquated theory of spontaneous generation and giving birth to biogenesis. Even though he was the first to empirically prove this, he was not the first scientist to propose this type of theory. Scientists Girolamo Fracastoro, Agostino Bassi, and Friedrich Henle had previously suggested various theories which influenced Pasteur's work later. The development of biogenesis, however, left a vacuum in the understanding of how life first arose. As it requires previous forms of life, biogenesis alone could not ultimately explain the origin of life on the early, barren Earth. No notable related theories, however, appeared until 1924, when Alexander Oparin surmised that the presence of oxygen in the atmosphere prevents the synthesis of certain organic compounds that are necessary for the evolution of life. In 'The Origin of Life', he proffered that the type of abiogenesis that Pasteur attacked had in fact occurred once, but no longer could because the conditions found on the early Earth had changed. Oparin felt that an organic 'primeval soup' could be created in an oxygen-free atmosphere due to the effects of sunlight. He hypothesized that 4 billion years ago, the earth's environment met these criteria after volcanic eruptions filled the environment with carbon dioxide, nitrogen, and other gases. Originally he thought that the early atmosphere, in contrast to the Earth's current atmosphere, contained mostly ammonia and methane, but it is likely that most of the atmospheric carbon was carbon dioxide with perhaps some carbon monoxide and nitrogen. In practice these mixtures have many of the same properties as those containing ammonia and methane as long as free oxygen molecules are not present.

4 These theories were tested in the Miller and Urey experiment which attempted to recreate these hypothetical conditions, and tested for the occurrence of the chemical origins of life. Specifically, the experiment tested Oparin's hypothesis that conditions on the primitive Earth favored chemical reactions that synthesized organic compounds from inorganic precursors. In order to test for the generation of the amino acids, required for protein generation in living cells under primitive Earth's conditions, they required a less hydrogen-rich mixture than the current environment. Their experiments used water, methane, ammonia, and hydrogen, sealed inside interconnected sterile glass tubes and beakers, with one half filled with water and another holding two electrodes. The water was boiled to produce evaporation, then the electrodes were fired to simulate lightning through the atmosphere and water vapor, and then it was cooled again to condense the water back into the first beaker in a repetitive cycle. After one week, they observed that 10-15 percent of the carbon was in the form of organic compounds. Two percent of the carbon had formed amino acids, with glycine being the most plentiful. Although nucleic acids were not formed, the 20 common amino acids were formed in various concentrations. This was interesting because amino acids can potentially create the most basic component of most living creatures namely DNA.

Early Research on Air

1 The composition of air has fascinated scientists since early times. [1]**According to** the ancient Greeks, air [2]**was regarded as** one of the four elements, which also included fire, earth, and water. It was not, however, precisely studied or correctly understood by many scholars. They generally thought that the air people breathe had the same composition as the gases found in any other part of the universe. Eventually, a few analytical scientists [3]**began to question** its properties and [4]**conducted research** to define them, but their studies were limited [5]**by the fact that** they only [6]**sought to study** air [7]**in the perspective of** their specialties. [8]**Prior to** the seventeenth century, chemists believed that gases [9]**were not involved in** chemical reactions, and [10]**focused on** matter [11]**in** its solid or liquid **states: according to** them, gases were [12]**in the domain of** physicists. This trend significantly impeded progress on the study of air.

2 [13]**It was not until** the seventeenth century **that** the understanding of air was seriously pursued by scientists. However, [14]**due to the lack of** scientific instruments and the need for those beyond the usual tools, their experiments soon faced limitations. For example, Robert Boyle, a British scientist [15]**known for** Boyle's Law, began a series of experiments to find out the composition of air through combustion. Boyle vacuumed the air out of a jar and showed that [16]**neither** charcoal **nor** sulfur burned in the vacuum. Boyle had discovered the very first property of air stating that it [17]**is required for a fire to burn**. His finding was not, however, recognized by the scientific community [18]**of the day** because his definition of the component of air [19]**responsible for** combustion was vague. [20]**In addition**, most scientists [21]**were reportedly more interested in** finding the chemical composition of air than in its physical characteristics. Thus, he [22]**shifted** the focus of his research **to** air's chemical aspects and in 1659, [23]**with** continuous **effort**, discovered that both hydrogen and nitric oxide gases were [24]**present in** air. Boyle also [25]**tried to revise** misconceptions [26]**regarding** air, such as the popular belief that air had no weight. Years later, Einstein [27]**credited** Boyle **for** having a holy curiosity in poorly understood phenomena that others simply [28]**accepted as** 'natural'. [29]**As a result of** his persistence, he [30]**is** now **known as** the father of chemistry.

3 Even with all of Boyle's achievements, people's understanding of air was still elementary and more study using advanced laboratory equipment was required. Scientists still [31]**struggled to uncover** the many unknown properties of air, which were exemplified by the rudimentary definition of air as 'the elastic, invisible mixture of gases that surround the earth' from an eighteenth century encyclopedia. Its invisibility meant that it could not be observed under a microscope and its [32]**ability to diffuse** quickly [33]**proved to be** an irritable characteristic to scientists for it complicated calculations measuring the amount of air being experimented upon. Additionally, chemists thought that air was out of their scope of research. Therefore, many prominent physicists investigated air [34]**wishing to further** their understanding, but they showed little noticeable progress; [35]**having no success in** isolating even one of the many compounds in air.

4 Luckily, the [36]**research on** air was significantly advanced by Stephen Hales, an English physiologist and chemist, in the late eighteenth century. [37]**In search of** the various properties of air and [38]**anxious to** clearly define it, he [39]**gave birth to** a new branch in chemistry called pneumatic chemistry. He invented the pneumatic trough to study the physical properties of air and their [40]**relation to** chemical reactions. The trough [41]**was made from** household objects such as a hunting gun and a glass vessel. The device measured the amount of gas produced when a substance was heated by measuring the amount of water displaced in the vessel. Hales' pneumatic trough became the basis for experimental instruments that are widely used today. The creativity demonstrated through his improvisation of turning common tools into useful scientific instruments was recognized by, and [42]**won the praise of**, fellow scientists. **According to** the scientific community, however, Hales deserves more recognition than he received in the past as experiments **regarding** air were actively held by scientists of various fields using his invention.

5 Despite his tremendous [43]**contributions to** pneumatic chemistry, Hales [44]**passed up** the [45]**opportunity to study** the chemical properties of the various gases, as he was solely interested in studying their concentrations. Scientists that [46]**came after** him revised his pneumatic trough and proceeded with further experiments. With the efforts of these scientists, the properties of the air have been gradually unveiled. They have even successfully broken down all of the components of atmospheric air and calculated their proportions.

Early Research on Air

1 The composition of air has fascinated scientists since early times. According to the ancient Greeks, air was regarded as one of the four elements, which also included fire, earth, and water. It was not, however, precisely studied or correctly understood by many scholars. They generally thought that the air people breathe had the same composition as the gases found in any other part of the universe. Eventually, a few analytical scientists began to question its properties and conducted research to define them, but their studies were limited by the fact that they only sought to study air in the perspective of their specialties. Prior to the seventeenth century, chemists believed that gases were not involved in chemical reactions, and focused on matter in its solid or liquid states: according to them, gases were in the domain of physicists. This trend significantly impeded progress on the study of air.

2 It was not until the seventeenth century that the understanding of air was seriously pursued by scientists. However, due to the lack of scientific instruments and the need for those beyond the usual tools, their experiments soon faced limitations. For example, Robert Boyle, a British scientist known for Boyle's Law, began a series of experiments to find out the composition of air through combustion. Boyle vacuumed the air out of a jar and showed that neither charcoal nor sulfur burned in the vacuum. Boyle had discovered the very first property of air stating that it is required for a fire to burn. His finding was not, however, recognized by the scientific community of the day because his definition of the component of air responsible for combustion was vague. In addition, most scientists were reportedly more interested in finding the chemical composition of air than in its physical characteristics. Thus, he shifted the focus of his research to air's chemical aspects and in 1659, with continuous effort, discovered that both hydrogen and nitric oxide gases were present in air. Boyle also tried to revise misconceptions regarding air, such as the popular belief that air had no weight. Years later, Einstein credited Boyle for having a holy curiosity in poorly understood phenomena that others simply accepted as 'natural'. As a result of his persistence, he is now known as the father of chemistry.

3 Even with all of Boyle's achievements, people's understanding of air was still elementary and more study using advanced laboratory equipment was required. Scientists still struggled to uncover the many unknown properties of air, which were exemplified by the rudimentary definition of air as 'the elastic, invisible mixture of gases that surround the earth' from an eighteenth century encyclopedia. Its invisibility meant that it could not be observed under a microscope and its ability to diffuse quickly proved to be an irritable characteristic to scientists for it complicated calculations measuring the amount of air being experimented upon. Additionally, chemists thought that air was out of their scope of research. Therefore, many prominent physicists investigated air wishing to further their understanding, but they showed little noticeable progress; having no success in isolating even one of the many compounds in air.

4 Luckily, the research on air was significantly advanced by Stephen Hales, an English physiologist and chemist, in the late eighteenth century. In search of the various properties of air and anxious to clearly define it, he gave birth to a new branch in chemistry called pneumatic chemistry. He invented the pneumatic trough to study the physical properties of air and their relation to chemical reactions. The trough was made from household objects such as a hunting gun and a glass vessel. The device measured the amount of gas produced when a substance was heated by measuring the amount of water displaced in the vessel. Hales' pneumatic trough became the basis for experimental instruments that are widely used today. The creativity demonstrated through his improvisation of turning common tools into useful scientific instruments was recognized by, and won the praise of, fellow scientists. According to the scientific community, however, Hales deserves more recognition than he received in the past as experiments regarding air were actively held by scientists of various fields using his invention.

5 Despite his tremendous contributions to pneumatic chemistry, Hales passed up the opportunity to study the chemical properties of the various gases, as he was solely interested in studying their concentrations. Scientists that came after him revised his pneumatic trough and proceeded with further experiments. With the efforts of these scientists, the properties of the air have been gradually unveiled. They have even successfully broken down all of the components of atmospheric air and calculated their proportions.

Photography as an Art

1 Three components are required [1)]**for a work to** [2)]**be considered** artistic: artist, medium, and artwork, the idea being that an artist manifests artwork through the medium. Since the camera's invention, photography has [3)]**struggled to** [4)]**convince many that** it [5)]**falls within** this definition. The opposition [6)]**recognizes** the medium and work **as** artful, but not the photographers' role as artist. They [7)]**see** them **as** technicians who 'operate the medium' to produce works [8)]**instead of** as artists, who, they claim, [9)]**take time to complete** works, [10)]**poring over** them. The photographer's [11)]**ability to capture** an image with a simple click was thus unequal, and photography was a process [12)]**unequal to** art. Photographer Mark Chamberlain [13)]**disagreed with** this, stating that "[14)]**in the hands of** an artist, the camera is only another tool," which can become an extension of the eye [15)] **if** properly **utilized**, but is a lifeless piece of metal [16)]**otherwise**. He [17)]**contended that** releasing the shutter may only [18)]**take a second**, but timing and framing are crucial, and the photographer [19)]**has to find** perfect lighting and conditions.

2 Chamberlain was not the only photographer to fight denigration of photography. Earlier, between 1851 and 1862, famous photographers such as Antoine Claudet, Andre Disderi, and William Lake Price published articles in professional journals [20)] **attempting to analyze** the aesthetic similarities and differences between graphic works and photographs and to convince readers that photography was actually an art. Their [21)]**points of view** were summed up in a piece in the 1862 Photographic Journal addressing whether photography should be hung in the Fine Arts or Industrial Section of the International Exposition. The author observed that the question is not whether photography is fine art [22)]**per se**, but whether it [23)]**is capable of** artistic expression in the hands of an artist. Their **point-of-view** was echoed in the Catalogue of the 1859 Salon of Photography by French naturalist Louis Figuier. He and other scientists **were convinced** that artistic expression and taste would be improved by photography, just as the general quality of life [24)]**benefits from** [25)]**applied science**. They, like Chamberlain, **considered the lens a new tool**, like the pencil or brush, which conveys the feelings of the photographer, and photography is, therefore, an art.

3 Later, photographers, [26)]**in an effort to** [27)]**compete with** high art, [28)]**focused on** still-lifes, allegorical costumes, genre scenes and composite images. However, as the novel idea of capturing images [29)]**began to wear off**, people [30)]**began to question** whether the camera's images were too accurate and detailed. To overcome this literalism, photographers used inferior optical elements, smeared lenses, kicked tripods, or blurred their black-and-white prints. [31)]**As a result**, pictorialism, an aesthetic movement imitating contemporary painting styles and techniques, was born. This movement which originated in Britain [32)]**reached its height** in the 20th century and [33)]**had a strong influence on** American photography [34)]**in its later phases**. [35)]**One of** the most important promoters of this movement was the journal 'Camera Work' published by Alfred Stieglitz, whose sale of fifteen photographs to the Albright Gallery [36)]**solidified** photography's **status as** an art in the United States.

4 With the [37)]**rise and fall** of pictorialism, [38)]**struggles over** artistic nature and the quest to determine what truly constitued art [39)]**raged on** for over a century. [40)]**In hindsight**, many conclude that photographic art is at its best when capturing the real world, and least inspiring when emulating other art forms. The unique power of photography is its [41)]**disposition to form** the varies of textural experience and the [42)]**contrasts in** lighting, rather than narrative content, [43)]**regardless of** whether the images **were considered** documents or art.

5 Recognizing this, some photographers [44)]**began producing** prints of artistic masterpieces [45)]**for** both their commercial and the general population's cultural **benefit**. Since then, photographs have been the most significant supplier of visual artifacts to the masses, revolutionizing public [46)]**access to** the art heritage of the world. What was once rejected as being too real had become indispensable [47)]**in terms of** historical preservation. This was a welcomed advantage of photography since it was believed that [48)]**familiarity with** classical art would [49)]**not only** lift people's spirit, **but also** improve their taste.

6 Today, there is little doubt that photography is a fine art. Every well-known, respected fine-art museum has a section [50)]**dedicated** solely **to** photographic art; and there are a number of museums and galleries dedicated specifically to photography. This shows that photography has [51)]**stood its ground** and found its place in the art world. In recent decades, photography's potential has radically expanded. [52)]**Aside from** the traditional two-dimensional, modest-sized black-and-white photographs, photographs now display various shapes, colors, and formats, to provide information, [53)]**make statements**, sell products, or analyze events. The development of new technology and aesthetic theories [54)]**combined with** the enhanced role of photography as a marketable commodity has influenced the way the medium is now used and perceived. This expanded role of photography is the result of a rich history [55)]**tied to** developments in technology, art, and society.

Photography as an Art

1 Three components are required for a work to be considered artistic: artist, medium, and artwork, the idea being that an artist manifests artwork through the medium. Since the camera's invention, photography has struggled to convince many that it falls within this definition. The opposition recognizes the medium and work as artful, but not the photographers' role as artist. They see them as technicians who 'operate the medium' to produce works instead of as artists, who, they claim, take time to complete works, poring over them. The photographer's ability to capture an image with a simple click was thus unequal, and photography was a process unequal to art. Photographer Mark Chamberlain disagreed with this, stating that "in the hands of an artist, the camera is only another tool," which can become an extension of the eye if properly utilized, but is a lifeless piece of metal otherwise. He contended that releasing the shutter may only take a second, but timing and framing are crucial, and the photographer has to find perfect lighting and conditions.

2 Chamberlain was not the only photographer to fight denigration of photography. Earlier, between 1851 and 1862, famous photographers such as Antoine Claudet, Andre Disderi, and William Lake Price published articles in professional journals attempting to analyze the aesthetic similarities and differences between graphic works and photographs and to convince readers that photography was actually an art. Their points of view were summed up in a piece in the 1862 Photographic Journal addressing whether photography should be hung in the Fine Arts or Industrial Section of the International Exposition. The author observed that the question is not whether photography is fine art per se, but whether it is capable of artistic expression in the hands of an artist. Their point-of-view was echoed in the Catalogue of the 1859 Salon of Photography by French naturalist Louis Figuier. He and other scientists were convinced that artistic expression and taste would be improved by photography, just as the general quality of life benefits from applied science. They, like Chamberlain, considered the lens a new tool, like the pencil or brush, which conveys the feelings of the photographer, and photography is, therefore, an art.

3 Later, photographers, in an effort to compete with high art, focused on still-lifes, allegorical costumes, genre scenes and composite images. However, as the novel idea of capturing images began to wear off, people began to question whether the camera's images were too accurate and detailed. To overcome this literalism, photographers used inferior optical elements, smeared lenses, kicked tripods, or blurred their black-and-white prints. As a result, pictorialism, an aesthetic movement imitating contemporary painting styles and techniques, was born. This movement which originated in Britain reached its height in the 20th century and had a strong influence on American photography in its later phases. One of the most important promoters of this movement was the journal 'Camera Work' published by Alfred Stieglitz, whose sale of fifteen photographs to the Albright Gallery solidified photography's status as an art in the United States.

4 With the rise and fall of pictorialism, struggles over artistic nature and the quest to determine what truly constituted art raged on for over a century. In hindsight, many conclude that photographic art is at its best when capturing the real world, and least inspiring when emulating other art forms. The unique power of photography is its disposition to form the varies of textural experience and the contrasts in lighting, rather than narrative content, regardless of whether the images were considered documents or art.

5 Recognizing this, some photographers began producing prints of artistic masterpieces for both their commercial and the general population's cultural benefit. Since then, photographs have been the most significant supplier of visual artifacts to the masses, revolutionizing public access to the art heritage of the world. What was once rejected as being too real had become indispensable in terms of historical preservation. This was a welcomed advantage of photography since it was believed that familiarity with classical art would not only lift people's spirit, but also improve their taste.

6 Today, there is little doubt that photography is a fine art. Every well-known, respected fine-art museum has a section dedicated solely to photographic art; and there are a number of museums and galleries dedicated specifically to photography. This shows that photography has stood its ground and found its place in the art world. In recent decades, photography's potential has radically expanded. Aside from the traditional two-dimensional, modest-sized black-and-white photographs, photographs now display various shapes, colors, and formats, to provide information, make statements, sell products, or analyze events. The development of new technology and aesthetic theories combined with the enhanced role of photography as a marketable commodity has influenced the way the medium is now used and perceived. This expanded role of photography is the result of a rich history tied to developments in technology, art, and society.

How and Why Birds Learn to Sing

1 Beautifully complex birdsongs have inspired our greatest poets and composers, and aroused the curiosity of biologists. They wondered how and why such an elaborate communication form developed among birds. One of the many who [1)]**struggled to answer** these questions was Darwin who was clearly influenced by these intricate songs as he developed the theory of sexual selection. Since then biologists from many disciplines have [2)]**found** birdsongs **to be** fascinating and productive research subjects.

2 Birdsongs, generally [3)]**regarded as** an attribute of males, are in some rare species produced by females with complexity [4)]**comparable to** those of males. [5)]**In general** though, male songbirds are the sources of these complex songs. Darwin suggested that this was the result of sexual selection because females choose mates with more complex songs. Although this [6)]**ability** of birdsongs **to attract** females is frequently cited, there is little experimental evidence to support this assertion because field experiments proving that female [7)]**attraction to** the male's territory is [8)]**in direct response to** his singing are nearly impossible. One experiment on pair formation of flycatchers, however, [9)]**came close to doing** so. Male dummies were positioned near nest-boxes with automatic traps; some played a tape-recorded song from loudspeakers, while others remained silent. Even when their positions were switched to control external variables, 90 percent of females were caught in nest-box traps of 'singing' dummies, showing that a male's song attracts mates. Further, females of some species prefer males with more varied songs, so these males quickly [10)]**add to** their repertoires. The diverse assortments of songs may indicate an older male with access to better resources or proven longevity and survival skills, both good traits to [11)]**pass on to** offspring. Experiments have also shown that songs [12)]**act as** territorial markers. House Wrens, for example, [13)]**respond** aggressively **to** recordings of other males' songs, sometimes even attacking the speaker. Researchers have also shown that removing male birds from their territories but broadcasting their songs [14)]**prevented** neighboring males **from entering** their territories, showing that the songs [15)]**warned** others **to keep out**.

3 Just as their reasons for singing vary, so do the ways that songbirds [16)]**learn to sing**. Some are [17)]**born with** an innate knowledge of the songs, while others learn them from older birds then add to them to create personalized songs, and still others [18)]**incorporate** auditory stimuli **into** their repertoire and eventually [19)]**end up with** thousands of variations. Unlike birds [20)]**with** innate **abilities to sing**, some [21)]**are** extremely **susceptible to** external sound stimuli when learning songs. Studies of the White-crowned Sparrow show that nestlings raised alone in a laboratory develop an abnormal song. If they are housed with a tutor adult White-crowned Sparrow, however, they will learn proper songs from it. If they are only housed with a Song Sparrow, however, they may learn to sing as a Song Sparrow. Scientists have also [22)]**taught** baby sparrows **to sing** a complete song by [23)]**exposing** them **to** overlapping segments of a tune rather than a full melody. This means that the sparrows reassembled segments of a song which were imprinted in their brains, showing that they have the **ability to identify and utilize** the different song parts presented in the experiment. Other birds, such as Northern Mockingbirds and Brown Thrashers, [24)]**are adept at** mimicking the calls of other species and add to their repertoires throughout their lives, learning around 200 and 2,000 different songs, [25)]**respectively**.

4 An interesting fact is that birds acquire most of these songs during critical periods of brain development. To do this, they [26)]**rely on** the specialized frontal cortex section of the brain [27)]**known as** the basal ganglia. This section of the brain internalizes sensory experiences and then [28)]**shapes** them **into** vocal output through sensorimotor learning and integration. This innate disposition for 'language acquisition' [29)]**is similar to** humans. Humans have critical periods when sensorimotor functions and regions in the frontal cortex, like the basal ganglia in birds, allow accelerated learning and vocal output shaping. Similarly, most songbirds [30)]**seem to have** [31)]**what is called** a 'sensitive period' for song learning. It is during these brief periods that birds are best equipped to memorize details of a tutor's song. For the White-crowned Sparrow, this age is between 15 and 50 days, after which learning becomes more difficult. They, therefore, begin practicing singing [32)]**shortly after** leaving the nest, at about three weeks of age. Recalling the sounds they heard during the sensitive period, they match it in their practice singing called the subsong. The subsong becomes louder, more persistent, and structured [33)]**over time**. These corrections eventually [34)]**result in** a perfect copy of the remembered song, which [35)]**goes through** 'crystallization,' after which there is little variation. Evidence, however, suggests that auditory feedback is actively used in adulthood to maintain the song's structure. It can be shown that disturbing auditory feedback during adult Zebra Finches' singing [36)]**caused** their song **to deteriorate**. This 'decrystallization' is a marked loss of the temporal and spectral stereotypy seen in crystallized songs. Once normal feedback is restored, these deviations gradually disappear and the original song returns. Thus, adult birds that do not seem to learn new songs still retain a significant amount of plasticity in their brains.

How and Why Birds Learn to Sing

1 Beautifully complex birdsongs have inspired our greatest poets and composers, and aroused the curiosity of biologists. They wondered how and why such an elaborate communication form developed among birds. One of the many who struggled to answer these questions was Darwin who was clearly influenced by these intricate songs as he developed the theory of sexual selection. Since then biologists from many disciplines have found birdsongs to be fascinating and productive research subjects.

2 Birdsongs, generally regarded as an attribute of males, are in some rare species produced by females with complexity comparable to those of males. In general though, male songbirds are the sources of these complex songs. Darwin suggested that this was the result of sexual selection because females choose mates with more complex songs. Although this ability of birdsongs to attract females is frequently cited, there is little experimental evidence to support this assertion because field experiments proving that female attraction to the male's territory is in direct response to his singing are nearly impossible. One experiment on pair formation of flycatchers, however, came close to doing so. Male dummies were positioned near nest-boxes with automatic traps; some played a tape-recorded song from loudspeakers, while others remained silent. Even when their positions were switched to control external variables, 90 percent of females were caught in nest-box traps of 'singing' dummies, showing that a male's song attracts mates. Further, females of some species prefer males with more varied songs, so these males quickly add to their repertoires. The diverse assortments of songs may indicate an older male with access to better resources or proven longevity and survival skills, both good traits to pass on to offspring. Experiments have also shown that songs act as territorial markers. House Wrens, for example, respond aggressively to recordings of other males' songs, sometimes even attacking the speaker. Researchers have also shown that removing male birds from their territories but broadcasting their songs prevented neighboring males from entering their territories, showing that the songs warned others to keep out.

3 Just as their reasons for singing vary, so do the ways that songbirds learn to sing. Some are born with an innate knowledge of the songs, while others learn them from older birds then add to them to create personalized songs, and still others incorporate auditory stimuli into their repertoire and eventually end up with thousands of variations. Unlike birds with innate abilities to sing, some are extremely susceptible to external sound stimuli when learning songs. Studies of the White-crowned Sparrow show that nestlings raised alone in a laboratory develop an abnormal song. If they are housed with a tutor adult White-crowned Sparrow, however, they will learn proper songs from it. If they are only housed with a Song Sparrow, however, they may learn to sing as a Song Sparrow. Scientists have also taught baby sparrows to sing a complete song by exposing them to overlapping segments of a tune rather than a full melody. This means that the sparrows reassembled segments of a song which were imprinted in their brains, showing that they have the ability to identify and utilize the different song parts presented in the experiment. Other birds, such as Northern Mockingbirds and Brown Thrashers, are adept at mimicking the calls of other species and add to their repertoires throughout their lives, learning around 200 and 2,000 different songs, respectively.

4 An interesting fact is that birds acquire most of these songs during critical periods of brain development. To do this, they rely on the specialized frontal cortex section of the brain known as the basal ganglia. This section of the brain internalizes sensory experiences and then shapes them into vocal output through sensorimotor learning and integration. This innate disposition for 'language acquisition' is similar to humans. Humans have critical periods when sensorimotor functions and regions in the frontal cortex, like the basal ganglia in birds, allow accelerated learning and vocal output shaping. Similarly, most songbirds seem to have what is called a 'sensitive period' for song learning. It is during these brief periods that birds are best equipped to memorize details of a tutor's song. For the White-crowned Sparrow, this age is between 15 and 50 days, after which learning becomes more difficult. They, therefore, begin practicing singing shortly after leaving the nest, at about three weeks of age. Recalling the sounds they heard during the sensitive period, they match it in their practice singing called the subsong. The subsong becomes louder, more persistent, and structured over time. These corrections eventually result in a perfect copy of the remembered song, which goes through 'crystallization,' after which there is little variation. Evidence, however, suggests that auditory feedback is actively used in adulthood to maintain the song's structure. It can be shown that disturbing auditory feedback during adult Zebra Finches' singing caused their song to deteriorate. This 'decrystallization' is a marked loss of the temporal and spectral stereotypy seen in crystallized songs. Once normal feedback is restored, these deviations gradually disappear and the original song returns. Thus, adult birds that do not seem to learn new songs still retain a significant amount of plasticity in their brains.

Functions of Roots

1 Roots, the water-absorbing organs of a plant, are present on essentially all vascular plants and [1)]**serve** three primary **functions**: to anchor the plant to a substrate, to absorb nutrients through osmosis, and to store food reserves. They can [2)]**adapt to** [3)]**carry out** these primary **functions** [4)]**in ways** optimized for different environments.

2 One of the most important functions of root networks is to provide a stable footing for plants so they do not [5)]**fall over** or get swept away. This also provides the secondary benefit of controlling soil erosion around the plant's base. [6)]**In addition to** this, many plants like the carrot and turnip also store nutrients in modified roots. Roots of plants such as the bluebell store so much energy that they act as perennating organs [7)]**allowing** the plant **to survive** harsh conditions such as drought, frigid winters, or light deficiency. They do this by **allowing** the exposed part of the plant **to** die down and storing [8)]**as** much energy **as possible** for regrowth when conditions improve.

3 For plants which [9)]**are** constantly **exposed to** harsh environments, such as salt water swamps, survival is more challenging [10)]**due to** the lack of basic necessities. The deeper roots of most plants die because of the lack of oxygen under the waterlogged soil, [11)]**leading to** the plant's slow death. Mangrove roots, however, are well-suited to the region. The red mangrove, a tropical tree which colonizes coastlines and brackish water between the northern and southern latitudes of 25 degrees, can often be found on the water's edge. These [12)]**are distinguished from** other mangroves by the prominent prop roots extending into the water from high up on their stems. They thrive in the highly saline habitats by not [13)]**relying on** traditional roots growing under the substrate. Instead, it is assumed, lenticels, or pores, on their prop roots [14)]**act as** conduits for supplying oxygen for respiration to the subterranean roots. Unlike most plants, its roots also [15)]**enable** them **to obtain** freshwater from highly saline water sources through non-metabolic ultra-filtration, using negative pressure inside the root to draw freshwater in through a membrane [16)]**too fine for salt to pass through**, [17)]**in a process** called reverse-osmosis.

4 Unlike the mangroves, however, most plants exist in environments [18)]**filled with** other plants **leading to** a competition-filled bio-diverse habitat. To [19)]**triumph over** competition, plants use various methods such as root adaptations to attain the necessary nutrients, water, sunlight, and territory. If the plants are grown [20)]**in** close **proximity**, there may be a limited amount of these essential nutrients, [21)]**resulting in** a head-to-head [22)]**competition for** as large a share as possible. One of the ways they do this is by adapting. One example of this is the dark, competition-filled forest floor where strangler figs have adapted roots that snake down the trunk of a host tree or dangle from its branches as aerial roots enabling it to live in the tree branches. When they reach the ground, however, they dig in and grow more rapidly, fighting the host for nutrients. This root network surrounds the host and intertwines around it. As they grow thicker they squeeze the trunk of the host and [23)]**cut off** its flow of nutrients. Eventually the host [24)]**dies from** strangulation, insufficient sunlight and root competition, and the strangler fig [25)]**stands on its own**.

5 Some plants also compete using chemical methods. The roots of these plants secrete chemical compounds [26)]**known as** root exudates. Through the exudation of [27)]**a variety of** compounds, they regulate the microbial content of nearby soil, [28)]**cope with** herbivores, alter the physical and chemical make-up of the soil, and inhibit the growth of competing plants. Chemical-mediated plant-plant interference, or allelopathy, is one mechanism plants use to [29)]**gain an advantage over** their competitors. It also has important [30)]**implications for** agriculture where its effects may be beneficial, as [31)]**in the case of** natural weed control, or detrimental, when chemicals produced by plants affect the growth of crops. In [32)]**research conducted by** biologists from a chemical company, it was found that a plant called lemon bottlebrush excreted an allelopathic chemical called leptospermone. One day, they noted that under certain bushes, such as lemon bottlebrush, other plants only rarely grew. By collecting samples of the soil under the bush, they were able to [33)]**extract** many chemicals **from** the plants, one of which [34)]**was identified as** an herbicide. While it did have herbicidal effects, the amount required for effective crop coverage was [35)]**too** high **to** be practical. Leptospermone [36)]**was**, therefore, **reworked into** thousands of compounds, with several being effective but too toxic, environmentally persistent or non-selective. Mesotrione, the final compound they created could, however, [37)]**be used as** a selective herbicide for corn crops.

Functions of Roots

1 Roots, the water-absorbing organs of a plant, are present on essentially all vascular plants and serve three primary functions: to anchor the plant to a substrate, to absorb nutrients through osmosis, and to store food reserves. They can adapt to carry out these primary functions in ways optimized for different environments.

2 One of the most important functions of root networks is to provide a stable footing for plants so they do not fall over or get swept away. This also provides the secondary benefit of controlling soil erosion around the plant's base. In addition to this, many plants like the carrot and turnip also store nutrients in modified roots. Roots of plants such as the bluebell store so much energy that they act as perennating organs allowing the plant to survive harsh conditions such as drought, frigid winters, or light deficiency. They do this by allowing the exposed part of the plant to die down and storing as much energy as possible for regrowth when conditions improve.

3 For plants which are constantly exposed to harsh environments, such as salt water swamps, survival is more challenging due to the lack of basic necessities. The deeper roots of most plants die because of the lack of oxygen under the waterlogged soil, leading to the plant's slow death. Mangrove roots, however, are well-suited to the region. The red mangrove, a tropical tree which colonizes coastlines and brackish water between the northern and southern latitudes of 25 degrees, can often be found on the water's edge. These are distinguished from other mangroves by the prominent prop roots extending into the water from high up on their stems. They thrive in the highly saline habitats by not relying on traditional roots growing under the substrate. Instead, it is assumed, lenticels, or pores, on their prop roots act as conduits for supplying oxygen for respiration to the subterranean roots. Unlike most plants, its roots also enable them to obtain freshwater from highly saline water sources through non-metabolic ultra-filtration, using negative pressure inside the root to draw freshwater in through a membrane too fine for salt to pass through, in a process called reverse-osmosis.

4 Unlike the mangroves, however, most plants exist in environments filled with other plants leading to a competition-filled bio-diverse habitat. To triumph over competition, plants use various methods such as root adaptations to attain the necessary nutrients, water, sunlight, and territory. If the plants are grown in close proximity, there may be a limited amount of these essential nutrients, resulting in a head-to-head competition for as large a share as possible. One of the ways they do this is by adapting. One example of this is the dark, competition-filled forest floor where strangler figs have adapted roots that snake down the trunk of a host tree or dangle from its branches as aerial roots enabling it to live in the tree branches. When they reach the ground, however, they dig in and grow more rapidly, fighting the host for nutrients. This root network surrounds the host and intertwines around it. As they grow thicker they squeeze the trunk of the host and cut off its flow of nutrients. Eventually the host dies from strangulation, insufficient sunlight and root competition, and the strangler fig stands on its own.

5 Some plants also compete using chemical methods. The roots of these plants secrete chemical compounds known as root exudates. Through the exudation of a variety of compounds, they regulate the microbial content of nearby soil, cope with herbivores, alter the physical and chemical make-up of the soil, and inhibit the growth of competing plants. Chemical-mediated plant-plant interference, or allelopathy, is one mechanism plants use to gain an advantage over their competitors. It also has important implications for agriculture where its effects may be beneficial, as in the case of natural weed control, or detrimental, when chemicals produced by plants affect the growth of crops. In research conducted by biologists from a chemical company, it was found that a plant called lemon bottlebrush excreted an allelopathic chemical called leptospermone. One day, they noted that under certain bushes, such as lemon bottlebrush, other plants only rarely grew. By collecting samples of the soil under the bush, they were able to extract many chemicals from the plants, one of which was identified as an herbicide. While it did have herbicidal effects, the amount required for effective crop coverage was too high to be practical. Leptospermone was, therefore, reworked into thousands of compounds, with several being effective but too toxic, environmentally persistent or non-selective. Mesotrione, the final compound they created could, however, be used as a selective herbicide for corn crops.

History of The Patent Law

1 The State's protection of a person's [1)]**right to utilize and control** the utilization of an invention, [2)]**be it** a machine or a unique method of production, was not prevalent until the Renaissance period. [3)]**As a result**, in the Middle Ages, one would have had to hide the fact that one had invented a novel product [4)]**in order to keep** it. This lack of [5)]**protection from** the state has [6)]**been attributed to** rigid social structures and hierarchies that ignored the talent of the individual inventor.

2 This changed when the first systemic mechanism for protecting an inventor's rights to monopoly was introduced by a 1474 Act of the Venetian Senate, which prohibited the production of a device [7)]**conforming to** a patented one without the authorization of the inventor for 10 years, [8)]**provided** the inventor had recorded the innovation with the council. This system [9)]**differed from** the modern one [10)]**in that** it [11)]**required** the inventor **to produce** a completed, working device. [12)]**In other words**, the inventor [13)]**had to report** a device that could be used immediately and was societally useful. However, it still [14)]**laid out** all the major features of modern patent law, [15)]**such as** requiring the device to be officially registered, 'useful' to the society, 'not previously made in this state', and providing a fixed term of exclusivity.

3 Even before the Venetian Senate's act of 1474, isolated monopolies were granted in Europe. For example, in England the monarchs would grant letters patent, or 'letters that [16)]**lie open**', to people [17)]**in their graces**, [18)]**granting them a monopoly** to produce or provide specific goods and services. This tradition of granting monopolies eventually [19)]**led to** the term 'patents' we use today. It was [20)]**not**, however, **until** the Venetian Act **that** the standardized process of granting patents occurred. Britain, influenced by this new concept, eventually implemented such a system as a kind of mercantilist instrument to attract emigrants with skills that could possibly aid Britain's industry with the guarantee of exclusive monopoly, after the significant economic drain caused by the War of the Roses. [21)]**By** the early 17th century, patents had become royal favors to subjects of loyalty or wealth, with [22)]**monopolies being granted on** products and services **such as** running ale-houses. This led to inefficiency and [23)]**left room for** the corruption that [24)]**brought about** the Statute of Monopolies of 1624, which [25)]**required courts to outlaw** all monopolies but [26)]**those based on** true inventive intentions. When the Industrial Revolution spurred an explosive number of new inventions, patents became an increasingly important component of the socioeconomic machine. This era marks a [27)]**change in** the perception of the role of patents in society, in that they were [28)]**no longer** given only for the introduction of a new finished product, but also for the introduction of technological know-how or processes.

4 [29)]**Along with** many other British legal concepts, the patent system was introduced in the United States during the colonial period between 1640 and 1776. Initially, each of the 13 colonies formed their own patent systems, which **led to** disputes, **such as** identifying the true inventor of the steamboat, as different inventors were registered in the patent archives of two colonies. These problems [30)]**continued to arise** even after the United States' independence. The government, therefore, [31)]**sought to** [32)]**solve this problem** and the 1789 Constitutional Convention imbedded a national patent system in the constitution itself. The result was Article I, Section 8 of the Constitution which [33)]**authroized** Congress **to** selectively [34)]**endow** individual authors and inventors **with** 'exclusive [35)]**rights to** their writings and discoveries'. Samuel Hopkins received the first United States federal patent in 1790 for a process that [36)]**derived** potash **from** wood ashes. The United States patent system [37)]**grew to** its full, modern **status** with the 1836 revision introducing a formal system of examination by appointed, professional examiners. Therefore, [38)]**not only** was the patent law nationalized, **but also** the process of granting patents standardized. Since then, patents have rapidly become an important thread of the American economic fabric, [39)]**despite the fact that** the process' effectiveness is still debated.

5 Throughout history the concept of protecting one's rights to one's own creations has advanced **along with** the burgeoning capitalist, industrial world economy, which is increasingly [40)]**dependent on** new technological advancements. Despite [41)]**changes in** the patent systems [42)]**over time**, the principal idea that the inventor must [43)]**contribute** in some way **to** the state, or society, through novel, useful inventions has remained.

History of The Patent Law

1 The State's protection of a person's right to utilize and control the utilization of an invention, be it a machine or a unique method of production, was not prevalent until the Renaissance period. As a result, in the Middle Ages, one would have had to hide the fact that one had invented a novel product in order to keep it. This lack of protection from the state has been attributed to rigid social structures and hierarchies that ignored the talent of the individual inventor.

2 This changed when the first systemic mechanism for protecting an inventor's rights to monopoly was introduced by a 1474 Act of the Venetian Senate, which prohibited the production of a device conforming to a patented one without the authorization of the inventor for 10 years, provided the inventor had recorded the innovation with the council. This system differed from the modern one in that it required the inventor to produce a completed, working device. In other words, the inventor had to report a device that could be used immediately and was societally useful. However, it still laid out all the major features of modern patent law, such as requiring the device to be officially registered, 'useful' to the society, 'not previously made in this state', and providing a fixed term of exclusivity.

3 Even before the Venetian Senate's act of 1474, isolated monopolies were granted in Europe. For example, in England the monarchs would grant letters patent, or 'letters that lie open', to people in their graces, granting them a monopoly to produce or provide specific goods and services. This tradition of granting monopolies eventually led to the term 'patents' we use today. It was not, however, until the Venetian Act that the standardized process of granting patents occurred. Britain, influenced by this new concept, eventually implemented such a system as a kind of mercantilist instrument to attract emigrants with skills that could possibly aid Britain's industry with the guarantee of exclusive monopoly, after the significant economic drain caused by the War of the Roses. By the early 17th century, patents had become royal favors to subjects of loyalty or wealth, with monopolies being granted on products and services such as running ale-houses. This led to inefficiency and left room for the corruption that brought about the Statute of Monopolies of 1624, which required courts to outlaw all monopolies but those based on true inventive intentions. When the Industrial Revolution spurred an explosive number of new inventions, patents became an increasingly important component of the socioeconomic machine. This era marks a change in the perception of the role of patents in society, in that they were no longer given only for the introduction of a new finished product, but also for the introduction of technological know-how or processes.

4 Along with many other British legal concepts, the patent system was introduced in the United States during the colonial period between 1640 and 1776. Initially, each of the 13 colonies formed their own patent systems, which led to disputes, such as identifying the true inventor of the steamboat, as different inventors were registered in the patent archives of two colonies. These problems continued to arise even after the United States' independence. The government, therefore, sought to solve this problem and the 1789 Constitutional Convention imbedded a national patent system in the constitution itself. The result was Article I, Section 8 of the Constitution which authroized Congress to selectively endow individual authors and inventors with 'exclusive rights to their writings and discoveries'. Samuel Hopkins received the first United States federal patent in 1790 for a process that derived potash from wood ashes. The United States patent system grew to its full, modern status with the 1836 revision introducing a formal system of examination by appointed, professional examiners. Therefore, not only was the patent law nationalized, but also the process of granting patents standardized. Since then, patents have rapidly become an important thread of the American economic fabric, despite the fact that the process' effectiveness is still debated.

5 Throughout history the concept of protecting one's rights to one's own creations has advanced along with the burgeoning capitalist, industrial world economy, which is increasingly dependent on new technological advancements. Despite changes in the patent systems over time, the principal idea that the inventor must contribute in some way to the state, or society, through novel, useful inventions has remained.

Communication of Ants

1 Ants [1)]**have** several **advantages over** solitary insects such as increased system reliability and [2)]**division of labor**. The major advantage, however, is the communication among members. This [3)]**allows** the colony **to regulate** its foraging activity and retain a memory of previously rewarding locations. To do this, ants [4)]**rely on** chemical signals called pheromones. When foragers find a successful foraging site, they deposit a trail of pheromones on their return to the nest. This trail [5)]**gains strength** as more and more workers [6)]**add** more pheromones **to it**.

2 Unlike the traditional [7)]**views on** ant pheromone trails, recent studies have shown that distinct roles [8)]**are assigned to** different pheromones, [9)]**as** can be illustrated by the differences in the pheromones produced by the poison and pygidial glands of Malaysian ponerine army ants. The poison glands of these ants contain two pheromone components, one eliciting a strong, short-term attraction to prey targets and another guiding workers from foraging sites back to the colony. These pheromone trails are highly volatile, lasting only a few minutes, to ensure that ants are not attracted to sites [10)]**long after** the prey has been collected. The pygidial gland, [11)]**on the other hand**, produces a longer-lasting trail pheromone that guides workers back to the trail network of the colony. These pheromones [12)]**act as** the 'bread crumbs' in the tale of 'Hansel and Gretel', **allowing the ants to maintain** their spatial organization and [13)]**helping** them **forage** [14)]**in an** organized **manner** which enables the rapid transport of food to the colony.

3 Furthermore, in Pharaoh's ant, research has shown distinct, short-lived and long-lived attractive-trail pheromone effects, [15)]**as well as** a short-lived repellent pheromone. [16)]**In contrast to** most ant pheromones, the long-lived trails of Pharaoh's ants can persist [17)]**for** several days, **allowing** the trail network **to be explored** for a longer period of time. Sections of the network [18)]**leading to** food are reinforced with the short-lived trail pheromone, and the repellent pheromone is placed immediately after non-rewarding trails. [19)]**In other words**, the long-lived attractive pheromone acts as a memory, the short-lived attractive pheromone marks out routes to current food sources, and the short-lived repellent pheromone is a no entry signal to unrewarding branches of rewarding trail sections. These three scents [20)]**seem to work** complementarily.

4 Foraging ants also utilize tactile communication methods, such as vibration to communicate a wider repertoire of messages that promote the organization of the colony's foraging system. Desert ants, for example, rub their abdominal areas together to make sounds. Although ants do not have auditory organs, they can still perceive these messages by sensing the vibration of the ground with their legs. When a worker locates a large prey item, such as a dead insect, it makes sharp sounds to attract workers in the area, through a process called stridulating, that [21)]**encourages** nearby workers **to release** pheromones over longer distances, causing rapid recruitment to the prey item, thereby retrieving it significantly faster. Furthermore, in leaf-cutting ants, recruitment behavior changes [22)]**in relation to** the quality of food. [23)]**In order to test** what [24)]**causes** different levels of sound **to be created**, researchers [25)]**presented** ants **with** leaves of different qualities - tender leaves, tough leaves, sugar-coated tough leaves, and acid-coated leaves - and then noted the proportion of workers that stridulated as they cut through the different leaves. The results clearly showed that the workers stridulated most strongly when cutting through leaves of a good quality or attractiveness, with the most stridulation occurring while cutting tender or sugar-coated leaves [26)]**as opposed to** the other leaves.

5 This pheromone system may seem unique, but other communal insects, such as honeybees, have also developed advanced communication systems. Unlike ants honeybees use discernible movements like the 'waggle dance' to communicate complex concepts such as the approximate distance and directions to food sources. Returning foragers also [27)]**perform** tremble **dances**, to recuit receiver bees to collect their nectar. A further difference is that honeybees individually remember their rewarding foraging sites and return to them. 'Trail-following' ants, **on the other hand**, [28)]**are bound to** the externally encoded group memory of their pheromone trails. These trails ensure that a channel of communication is always open and **allows** them **to** continually react and exchange information whilst foraging without [29)]**needing to return** to their nest, unlike the honeybees. This [30)]**ability to** constantly **locate** productive foraging sites is probably the most important reason [31)]**for insects to communicate**.

Communication of Ants

1 Ants have several advantages over solitary insects such as increased system reliability and division of labor. The major advantage, however, is the communication among members. This allows the colony to regulate its foraging activity and retain a memory of previously rewarding locations. To do this, ants rely on chemical signals called pheromones. When foragers find a successful foraging site, they deposit a trail of pheromones on their return to the nest. This trail gains strength as more and more workers add more pheromones to it.

2 Unlike the traditional views on ant pheromone trails, recent studies have shown that distinct roles are assigned to different pheromones, as can be illustrated by the differences in the pheromones produced by the poison and pygidial glands of Malaysian ponerine army ants. The poison glands of these ants contain two pheromone components, one eliciting a strong, short-term attraction to prey targets and another guiding workers from foraging sites back to the colony. These pheromone trails are highly volatile, lasting only a few minutes, to ensure that ants are not attracted to sites long after the prey has been collected. The pygidial gland, on the other hand, produces a longer-lasting trail pheromone that guides workers back to the trail network of the colony. These pheromones act as the 'bread crumbs' in the tale of 'Hansel and Gretel', allowing the ants to maintain their spatial organization and helping them forage in an organized manner which enables the rapid transport of food to the colony.

3 Furthermore, in Pharaoh's ant, research has shown distinct, short-lived and long-lived attractive-trail pheromone effects, as well as a short-lived repellent pheromone. In contrast to most ant pheromones, the long-lived trails of Pharaoh's ants can persist for several days, allowing the trail network to be explored for a longer period of time. Sections of the network leading to food are reinforced with the short-lived trail pheromone, and the repellent pheromone is placed immediately after non-rewarding trails. In other words, the long-lived attractive pheromone acts as a memory, the short-lived attractive pheromone marks out routes to current food sources, and the short-lived repellent pheromone is a no entry signal to unrewarding branches of rewarding trail sections. These three scents seem to work complementarily.

4 Foraging ants also utilize tactile communication methods, such as vibration to communicate a wider repertoire of messages that promote the organization of the colony's foraging system. Desert ants, for example, rub their abdominal areas together to make sounds. Although ants do not have auditory organs, they can still perceive these messages by sensing the vibration of the ground with their legs. When a worker locates a large prey item, such as a dead insect, it makes sharp sounds to attract workers in the area, through a process called stridulating, that encourages nearby workers to release pheromones over longer distances, causing rapid recruitment to the prey item, thereby retrieving it significantly faster. Furthermore, in leaf-cutting ants, recruitment behavior changes in relation to the quality of food. In order to test what causes different levels of sound to be created, researchers presented ants with leaves of different qualities - tender leaves, tough leaves, sugar-coated tough leaves, and acid-coated leaves - and then noted the proportion of workers that stridulated as they cut through the different leaves. The results clearly showed that the workers stridulated most strongly when cutting through leaves of a good quality or attractiveness, with the most stridulation occurring while cutting tender or sugar-coated leaves as opposed to the other leaves.

5 This pheromone system may seem unique, but other communal insects, such as honeybees, have also developed advanced communication systems. Unlike ants honeybees use discernible movements like the 'waggle dance' to communicate complex concepts such as the approximate distance and directions to food sources. Returning foragers also perform tremble dances, to recuit receiver bees to collect their nectar. A further difference is that honeybees individually remember their rewarding foraging sites and return to them. 'Trail-following' ants, on the other hand, are bound to the externally encoded group memory of their pheromone trails. These trails ensure that a channel of communication is always open and allows them to continually react and exchange information whilst foraging without needing to return to their nest, unlike the honeybees. This ability to constantly locate productive foraging sites is probably the most important reason for insects to communicate.

Calculating the Age of Earth

1 Religion was the only source of historical and scientific knowledge, such as the age of Earth, until the mid-eighteenth century. After this time, scientists [1)]**began** more openly **questioning** the formation of Earth, and while studying the different rock layers of it, they recognized that it had [2)]**gone through** various changes over a period of time. The scientists proposed [3)]**a number of** theories and methods that had inaccurate results [4)]**due to lack of** understanding of the Earth and heavy speculation. As the scientific method and logical reasoning developed within the scientific community, scholars [5)]**were motivated to** [6)]**conduct** more precise and scientific **research**.

2 In 1779, a French scientist, Comte de Buffon, attempted the first calculation of Earth's age by experimentation. [7)]**Based on** Earth's internal heat and rate of cooling, Buffon's approach utilized a small globe-like figure that [8)]**resembled** Earth **in** composition. He measured the cooling rate of the figure tested at his laboratory and calculated the age of Earth to be 75,000 years. The result completely underestimated the age of Earth as Buffon, from his globe figure, mainly [9)]**focused on** the cooling rate of iron, an element which cools much quicker than crystals and other rock components. The true significance of his study, however, was that it [10)]**dared to break away** from previous methods that derived Earth's age without experimentation.

3 Later, others [11)]**attempted to measure** Earth's age, but their methods were just as inadequate. Edmund Halley, for example, based his estimation on the simple concept of the salinity of the ocean. He surmised that since rivers continuously dragged salt components from land to the oceans, increasing their salinity, the time they [12)]**took to** [13)]**reach** present salinity **levels** will give an approximate timeframe for Earth's formation. Just like the previous conjectures, Halley's method was not a viable way of measuring Earth's age, as it oversimplified the complex salinification process and [14)]**failed to** [15)]**take into account** plate tectonics and undersea volcanic eruptions that continuously [16)]**add** salt **to** the ocean.

4 Since then, measurements of physical properties have [17)]**been used to estimate** the age of Earth using the laws of physics. William Thomson, the forerunning supporter of these physical measurements, believed that during Earth's primitive stage, it was a sphere of hot molten rock [18)]**held together** by gravity and the only conceivable source of heat energy was the nebula. By estimating the [19)]**rate at which** heat dissipated from the nebula, scientists could determine the time [20)]**necessary for Earth to cool** from the molten ball of rock to its present state. Through this method, the age of Earth [21)]**was calculated to be** 20 to 40 million years. He had, however, neglected an important variable: the viscous fluid mantle that [22)]**play** an influential **role in** the circulation of heat energy within the Earth.

5 Scientists calculated Earth's age with even more precision after the arrival of the radiometric dating. It [23)]**allowed** them **to derive** the absolute age of rock using its elements. First developed by Ernest Rutherford and enhanced by Arthur Holmes, radiometric dating is a technique **based on** the spontaneous decay of different naturally occurring radioactive isotopes found in rocks. These initial parent isotopes are unstable and break down into more stable daughter isotopes. This break down occurs [24)]**according to** an isotope's individual rate of decay, or "decay constant," regardless of the physical or chemical conditions it is exposed to. Scientists, therefore, do not have to [25)]**be concerned with** other variables since the rate of isotope transformation is almost invariable. Radiometric dating allows scientists to calculate the time that has elapsed since the formation of rocks by measuring the [26)]**ratio of** parent **to** daughter isotopes in them. Radiometric testing shows Earth to be around 4.5 billion years, the most widely accepted age of Earth today.

6 Still, there are [27)]**controversies over** the age of the earth as a minor group of scientists argues that Earth is less than 4.5 billion years. These people believe that the earth is 'young', only about 6,000 to 10,000 years old. Stressing that the **ratio of** parent **to** daughter isotopes when the rock was created is unknown, they challenge the validity of scientifically-accepted radiometric methods. They further claim that some parent or daughter isotopes may be added from external sources. These issues of initial ratio of isotopes spotlight a flaw within radiometric dating method. Although there is evidence for [28)]**variability in** radiometric dating, Arthur Holmes [29)]**used** a variety of isotopes **to** obtain sufficient data and derived a precise result. Therefore, many [30)]**regard** these refutations **to be** implausible and until further scientific research produces a more accurate result, 4.5 billion years will [31)]**continue to be considered** the approximate age of the Earth.

Calculating the Age of Earth

1 Religion was the only source of historical and scientific knowledge, such as the age of Earth, until the mid-eighteenth century. After this time, scientists began more openly questioning the formation of Earth, and while studying the different rock layers of it, they recognized that it had gone through various changes over a period of time. The scientists proposed a number of theories and methods that had inaccurate results due to lack of understanding of the Earth and heavy speculation. As the scientific method and logical reasoning developed within the scientific community, scholars were motivated to conduct more precise and scientific research.

2 In 1779, a French scientist, Comte de Buffon, attempted the first calculation of Earth's age by experimentation. Based on Earth's internal heat and rate of cooling, Buffon's approach utilized a small globe-like figure that resembled Earth in composition. He measured the cooling rate of the figure tested at his laboratory and calculated the age of Earth to be 75,000 years. The result completely underestimated the age of Earth as Buffon, from his globe figure, mainly focused on the cooling rate of iron, an element which cools much quicker than crystals and other rock components. The true significance of his study, however, was that it dared to break away from previous methods that derived Earth's age without experimentation.

3 Later, others attempted to measure Earth's age, but their methods were just as inadequate. Edmund Halley, for example, based his estimation on the simple concept of the salinity of the ocean. He surmised that since rivers continuously dragged salt components from land to the oceans, increasing their salinity, the time they took to reach present salinity-levels will give an approximate timeframe for Earth's formation. Just like the previous conjectures, Halley's method was not a viable way of measuring Earth's age, as it oversimplified the complex salinification process and failed to take into account plate tectonics and undersea volcanic eruptions that continuously add salt to the ocean.

4 Since then, measurements of physical properties have been used to estimate the age of Earth using the laws of physics. William Thomson, the forerunning supporter of these physical measurements, believed that during Earth's primitive stage, it was a sphere of hot molten rock held together by gravity and the only conceivable source of heat energy was the nebula. By estimating the rate at which heat dissipated from the nebula, scientists could determine the time necessary for Earth to cool from the molten ball of rock to its present state. Through this method, the age of Earth was calculated to be 20 to 40 million years. He had, however, neglected an important variable: the viscous fluid mantle that play an influential role in the circulation of heat energy within the Earth.

5 Scientists calculated Earth's age with even more precision after the arrival of the radiometric dating. It allowed them to derive the absolute age of rock using its elements. First developed by Ernest Rutherford and enhanced by Arthur Holmes, radiometric dating is a technique based on the spontaneous decay of different naturally occurring radioactive isotopes found in rocks. These initial parent isotopes are unstable and break down into more stable daughter isotopes. This break down occurs according to an isotope's individual rate of decay, or "decay constant," regardless of the physical or chemical conditions it is exposed to. Scientists, therefore, do not have to be concerned with other variables since the rate of isotope transformation is almost invariable. Radiometric dating allows scientists to calculate the time that has elapsed since the formation of rocks by measuring the ratio of parent to daughter isotopes in them. Radiometric testing shows Earth to be around 4.5 billion years, the most widely accepted age of Earth today.

6 Still, there are controversies over the age of the earth as a minor group of scientists argues that Earth is less than 4.5 billion years. These people believe that the earth is 'young', only about 6,000 to 10,000 years old. Stressing that the ratio of parent to daughter isotopes when the rock was created is unknown, they challenge the validity of scientifically-accepted radiometric methods. They further claim that some parent or daughter isotopes may be added from external sources. These issues of initial ratio of isotopes spotlight a flaw within radiometric dating method. Although there is evidence for variability in radiometric dating, Arthur Holmes used a variety of isotopes to obtain sufficient data and derived a precise result. Therefore, many regard these refutations to be implausible and until further scientific research produces a more accurate result, 4.5 billion years will continue to be considered the approximate age of the Earth.

Identifying Playful Behavior in Children

1 Play, usually **¹⁾associated with** children, comes **²⁾in** many **forms** in both humans and other animals. Even **³⁾with** such **prevalence**, its definition, function and forms are often misunderstood. This may be because play evolves both with age and over time. For example, most people recognize that a toddler's frolicking is play, but not that **⁴⁾engaging in** sport activities by adults is another form. Moreover, the way play has changed **⁵⁾over time** is also ignored. One such major change is the decrease in usage of imagination since computers and video games have **⁶⁾begun to create** virtual worlds for children, when **⁷⁾compared to** the past when they had only wooden toys and dolls with which to play. With such major changes happening, one cannot predict what **⁸⁾form** it will **take** next, only that it will **⁹⁾continue to exist**. **¹⁰⁾Due to** these changes and the lack of an apparent distinction between playful and non-playful behaviors sociologists have continuously **¹¹⁾tried to form** a complete definition of play, with three having **¹²⁾gained** widespread **acceptance**: the functional, the structural, and the criterion approaches.

2 Anthropologist Donald Symons, after observing African monkeys, developed the first of these in 1978. He **¹³⁾defined** play **as** an act that has **¹⁴⁾neither** a clear benefit, **nor** external goal. Following this, acts like learning are not considered play because their benefits are readily noticeable. Similarly, eating and working **¹⁵⁾are not considered** play because their purposes are specific and obvious. Although Symons' definition was intended for the monkeys that he studied, it soon became evident to other scholars that his definition, which **¹⁶⁾came to be known as** the functional approach, could likewise **¹⁷⁾be applied to** play in humans. **Applying** his approach **to** further studies has shown that although there are benefits to playful behavior, its long-term consequences are unclear. An easy **¹⁸⁾way to see** this is to **¹⁹⁾look at** common playground toys, like the jungle gym. While children enjoy climbing, hanging and swinging on the metal labyrinth, the ultimate goal of these activities is not known, and neither is the actions' **²⁰⁾ability to** **²¹⁾supply** the child **with** food, clothing, or shelter. Further, it is unclear whether **²²⁾time spent on** the playground fulfills the child's education, health, or other basic needs **²³⁾at all**, and it **²⁴⁾is**, thus, **considered** playful behavior under this approach.

3 The functional approach, however, does not **²⁵⁾account for** the many non-playful actions without immediately obvious purposes, or for playful behavior that **²⁶⁾seems to** **²⁷⁾serve a purpose**, such as running. While running is often a playful behavior, if a person was running towards shelter to **²⁸⁾hide from** the rain, it would have a clear purpose, and therefore not **²⁹⁾qualify as** functionalistic play. **³⁰⁾In cases** such as this, the structural approach can be used. The structural approach identifies specific behaviors that are associated with play or with the playful execution of actions. When studying an action using this approach, one begins by identifying any characteristics that often only occur during playtime, like laughter or playful squabbling, such as a push or a light punch. Secondly, the structural approach **³¹⁾looks for** repeated, fragmented, exaggerated, and or re-ordered actions. For example, climbing stairs has a clear end and goal, but if the child repeats it by quickly climbing up and down the stairs, fragments the climb by climbing up only half-way, exaggerates it by jumping two stairs **³²⁾at a time**, or re-orders it by climbing them backwards, then under the structural approach the child **is considered to be** performing playful behavior.

4 When studying play, it became evident that the two approaches were not mutually exclusive, but that the factors that they **³³⁾used to identify** behavior were dissimilar. Thus, in 1980, Krasnor and Pepler suggested a third method, called the criterion approach. It combined ideas from the other approaches into four criteria for identifying playful behavior. The first criterion, positive effect, refers to the enjoyment that comes from doing playful behavior. The second, non-literality, is the imaginative aspect of playing, which encompasses acts such as pretending and placing oneself in fictitious perspectives **³⁴⁾for the purpose of** play. The third, intrinsic motivation, means that the behavior is done **³⁵⁾of one's own accord** and not due to social pressure. Finally, flexibility covers the characteristics described by the structural approach. While **³⁶⁾meeting** one **criterion** is sufficient to define a behavior **as** being playful, when the behavior **meets** more than one **criterion**, one may **³⁷⁾be more certain that** the behavior is playful. **³⁸⁾Confusing as it may be**, one must understand that the criterion approach was not developed to create a one-sentence definition for play, as many behaviors that are undoubtedly non-playful will **³⁹⁾fall within** one or more of the criterion. Instead, the approach defines which factors an everyday observer **⁴⁰⁾uses as** a basis for determining if an action is playful. So, while the criterion approach may not **be used to** definitively **distinguish** between activities that are play and **⁴¹⁾those** that are not, it **⁴²⁾plays a** significant **role in** helping sociologists understand how humans recognize play.

Identifying Playful Behavior in Children

1 Play, usually associated with children, comes in many forms in both humans and other animals. Even with such prevalence, its definition, function and forms are often misunderstood. This may be because play evolves both with age and over time. For example, most people recognize that a toddler's frolicking is play, but not that engaging in sport activities by adults is another form. Moreover, the way play has changed over time is also ignored. One such major change is the decrease in usage of imagination since computers and video games have begun to create virtual worlds for children, when compared to the past when they had only wooden toys and dolls with which to play. With such major changes happening, one cannot predict what form it will take next, only that it will continue to exist. Due to these changes and the lack of an apparent distinction between playful and non-playful behaviors sociologists have continuously tried to form a complete definition of play, with three having gained widespread acceptance: the functional, the structural, and the criterion approaches.

2 Anthropologist Donald Symons, after observing African monkeys, developed the first of these in 1978. He defined play as an act that has neither a clear benefit, nor external goal. Following this, acts like learning are not considered play because their benefits are readily noticeable. Similarly, eating and working are not considered play because their purposes are specific and obvious. Although Symons' definition was intended for the monkeys that he studied, it soon became evident to other scholars that his definition, which came to be known as the functional approach, could likewise be applied to play in humans. Applying his approach to further studies has shown that although there are benefits to playful behavior, its long-term consequences are unclear. An easy way to see this is to look at common playground toys, like the jungle gym. While children enjoy climbing, hanging and swinging on the metal labyrinth, the ultimate goal of these activities is not known, and neither is the actions' ability to supply the child with food, clothing, or shelter. Further, it is unclear whether time spent on the playground fulfills the child's education, health, or other basic needs at all, and it is, thus, considered playful behavior under this approach.

3 The functional approach, however, does not account for the many non-playful actions without immediately obvious purposes, or for playful behavior that seems to serve a purpose, such as running. While running is often a playful behavior, if a person was running towards shelter to hide from the rain, it would have a clear purpose, and therefore not qualify as functionalistic play. In cases such as this, the structural approach can be used. The structural approach identifies specific behaviors that are associated with play or with the playful execution of actions. When studying an action using this approach, one begins by identifying any characteristics that often only occur during playtime, like laughter or playful squabbling, such as a push or a light punch. Secondly, the structural approach looks for repeated, fragmented, exaggerated, and or re-ordered actions. For example, climbing stairs has a clear end and goal, but if the child repeats it by quickly climbing up and down the stairs, fragments the climb by climbing up only half-way, exaggerates it by jumping two stairs at a time, or re-orders it by climbing them backwards, then under the structural approach the child is considered to be performing playful behavior.

4 When studying play, it became evident that the two approaches were not mutually exclusive, but that the factors that they used to identify behavior were dissimilar. Thus, in 1980, Krasnor and Pepler suggested a third method, called the criterion approach. It combined ideas from the other approaches into four criteria for identifying playful behavior. The first criterion, positive effect, refers to the enjoyment that comes from doing playful behavior. The second, non-literality, is the imaginative aspect of playing, which encompasses acts such as pretending and placing oneself in fictitious perspectives for the purpose of play. The third, intrinsic motivation, means that the behavior is done of one's own accord and not due to social pressure. Finally, flexibility covers the characteristics described by the structural approach. While meeting one criterion is sufficient to define a behavior as being playful, when the behavior meets more than one criterion, one may be more certain that the behavior is playful. Confusing as it may be, one must understand that the criterion approach was not developed to create a one-sentence definition for play, as many behaviors that are undoubtedly non-playful will fall within one or more of the criterion. Instead, the approach defines which factors an everyday observer uses as a basis for determining if an action is playful. So, while the criterion approach may not be used to definitively distinguish between activities that are play and those that are not, it plays a significant role in helping sociologists understand how humans recognize play.

Sentinel Behavior in Meerkats

1 Meerkats are small, mongoose-like mammals that live in the Kalahari Desert of Southern Africa. Being primarily insectivores, they [1)]**feed on** beetles and scorpions buried underground, which they locate using their strong sense of smell. Unfortunately, when the meerkat lowers its head to [2)]**search out** prey under grasses, it limits its own range of sight by a significant amount. [3)]**As a result** they [4)]**are** extremely **vulnerable to** airborne predators such as hawks and owls. To ensure that they can reach the safety of their bolt-holes before being snatched up by birds, meerkats forage in packs and [5)]**partake in** what [6)]**is known as** sentinel behavior. As the term suggests, one meerkat in the group [7)]**acts as** a sentinel and does not [8)]**look for** food like the rest, but rather stands upright on its hind legs to gain a wider field of view with which it scans the surrounding area for possible predators and other [9)]**threats to** the community. When it senses danger approaching, the sentinel barks loudly to [10)]**warn the others of** the danger. Many scientists questioned this phenomenon because the revealing stance and loud vocalization were thought to [11)]**expose** the meerkat **to** an increased risk of predation.

2 The motivations behind this behavior have [12)]**been attributed to** kin selection, the evolutionary strategy that favors the reproductive success of an organism's relatives over one's own survival. In Belding's ground squirrels, individuals sound an alarm at the approach of a predator, warning its nearby relatives and thereby benefitting the population. This explanation gained credibility because research revealed that, like Belding's squirrels, meerkat communities [13)]**are composed** mostly **of** family members. In a typical community of meerkats, about 70 percent of its members [14)]**are related to** the dominant female. In their authoritarian societies, the alpha female rarely tolerates offspring from anyone [15)]**other than** herself. Therefore, if the sentinel is able to protect one of its siblings, it ensures passing on 50 percent of its own genes, or 25 percent for saving a niece or nephew. This follows the gene selection theory, postulating that individuals are genetically programmed to proliferate their DNA. [16)]**In addition**, if the sentinel [17)]**allows** other group members **to** [18)]**spend** less time **scanning** and more time **foraging**, they will be able to catch more prey, which will also increase the survivability of the group.

3 A variant theory was that [19)]**in order to protect** their kin, meerkats demonstrated reciprocal altruism, an act that benefits another [20)]**at the expense of** one's own interest. If the receiver's benefit outweighs the cost of the altruist, and if the receiver [21)]**is expected to** also **become** the altruist, then evolutionarily the entire group [22)]**profits from** the behavior. This can be seen in various animals such as fish and birds, [23)]**as well as** in close relatives of the meerkat, the banded mongoose. Their pups cooperate in creating annoying chirps to [24)]**beg for** food from their chaperones, which [25)]**are assigned to** individual pups. When one chaperone [26)]**was removed from** the group, the corresponding pup would [27)]**stop crying**. This [28)]**in turn** [29)]**caused** the rest of the pups **to increase** the volume of their crying, which [30)]**induces** the adults **to bring** more food, benefitting the quiet pup. Scientists [31)]**tested for** two conditions that had been [32)]**laid out** by the developed, mature definition of reciprocal altruism to determine [33)]**if this was what the meerkats were** [34)]**in fact** doing: a systematic method of deciding individuals' duty as sentinels, and a unified punishment for those who abandon their duties as a sentinel. But observations substantiated that there was [35)]**neither** a particular order **nor** any sort of punishment. Moreover, the dedication and the length of time that a meerkat displayed sentinel behavior were consistent [36)]**regardless of** the number of non-relatives in the group.

4 Later scientists questioned the theory, proposing that sentinel behavior was a selfish anti-predator behavior. The proposition was that, [37)]**contrary to** popular belief, standing guard would increase the sentinel's own chances for survival. To find evidence for this claim, a team of scientists [38)]**set out to observe** sentinel behavior in lone meerkats. They confirmed that solitary meerkats first [39)]**focused on** foraging, then returned to the sentinel stance once their hunger was satiated. This strengthened the anti-predator hypothesis. The next [40)]**question to answer** was whether sentineling meerkats had better chances of survival [41)]**than those** who were not standing guard when attacked by a predator. Of a total of 2,000 hours of observation, not a single meerkat that was standing guard [42)]**at the moment of** attack was caught because they chose positions that were safer when sentineling than foraging. Further, they never wandered more than five meters away from at least one of their group's bolt-holes. The conclusion was that meerkats stand guard to [43)]**protect** themselves **from** predators, but they forage in groups because then they can invest more time [44)]**hunting for** food and [45)]**put trust in** the sentinels to [46)]**warn** them **of** any signs of danger.

Sentinel Behavior in Meerkats

1 Meerkats are small, mongoose-like mammals that live in the Kalahari Desert of Southern Africa. Being primarily insectivores, they feed on beetles and scorpions buried underground, which they locate using their strong sense of smell. Unfortunately, when the meerkat lowers its head to search out prey under grasses, it limits its own range of sight by a significant amount. As a result they are extremely vulnerable to airborne predators such as hawks and owls. To ensure that they can reach the safety of their bolt-holes before being snatched up by birds, meerkats forage in packs and partake in what is known as sentinel behavior. As the term suggests, one meerkat in the group acts as a sentinel and does not look for food like the rest, but rather stands upright on its hind legs to gain a wider field of view with which it scans the surrounding area for possible predators and other threats to the community. When it senses danger approaching, the sentinel barks loudly to warn the others of the danger. Many scientists questioned this phenomenon because the revealing stance and loud vocalization were thought to expose the meerkat to an increased risk of predation.

2 The motivations behind this behavior have been attributed to kin selection, the evolutionary strategy that favors the reproductive success of an organism's relatives over one's own survival. In Belding's ground squirrels, individuals sound an alarm at the approach of a predator, warning its nearby relatives and thereby benefitting the population. This explanation gained credibility because research revealed that, like Belding's squirrels, meerkat communities are composed mostly of family members. In a typical community of meerkats, about 70 percent of its members are related to the dominant female. In their authoritarian societies, the alpha female rarely tolerates offspring from anyone other than herself. Therefore, if the sentinel is able to protect one of its siblings, it ensures passing on 50 percent of its own genes, or 25 percent for saving a niece or nephew. This follows the gene selection theory, postulating that individuals are genetically programmed to proliferate their DNA. In addition, if the sentinel allows other group members to spend less time scanning and more time foraging, they will be able to catch more prey, which will also increase the survivability of the group.

3 A variant theory was that in order to protect their kin, meerkats demonstrated reciprocal altruism, an act that benefits another at the expense of one's own interest. If the receiver's benefit outweighs the cost of the altruist, and if the receiver is expected to also become the altruist, then evolutionarily the entire group profits from the behavior. This can be seen in various animals such as fish and birds, as well as in close relatives of the meerkat, the banded mongoose. Their pups cooperate in creating annoying chirps to beg for food from their chaperones, which are assigned to individual pups. When one chaperone was removed from the group, the corresponding pup would stop crying. This in turn caused the rest of the pups to increase the volume of their crying, which induces the adults to bring more food, benefitting the quiet pup. Scientists tested for two conditions that had been laid out by the developed, mature definition of reciprocal altruism to determine if this was what the meerkats were in fact doing: a systematic method of deciding individuals' duty as sentinels, and a unified punishment for those who abandon their duties as a sentinel. But observations substantiated that there was neither a particular order nor any sort of punishment. Moreover, the dedication and the length of time that a meerkat displayed sentinel behavior were consistent regardless of the number of non-relatives in the group.

4 Later scientists questioned the theory, proposing that sentinel behavior was a selfish anti-predator behavior. The proposition was that, contrary to popular belief, standing guard would increase the sentinel's own chances for survival. To find evidence for this claim, a team of scientists set out to observe sentinel behavior in lone meerkats. They confirmed that solitary meerkats first focused on foraging, then returned to the sentinel stance once their hunger was satiated. This strengthened the anti-predator hypothesis. The next question to answer was whether sentineling meerkats had better chances of survival than those who were not standing guard when attacked by a predator. Of a total of 2,000 hours of observation, not a single meerkat that was standing guard at the moment of attack was caught because they chose positions that were safer when sentineling than foraging. Further, they never wandered more than five meters away from at least one of their group's bolt-holes. The conclusion was that meerkats stand guard to protect themselves from predators, but they forage in groups because then they can invest more time hunting for food and put trust in the sentinels to warn them of any signs of danger.

usherin.usher.co.kr

USHER

iBT TOEFL
FINAL TEST READING
해설집

USHER

iBT TOEFL

FINAL TEST READING

TEST 1

답안 및 취약 유형 분석표
해석·해설

답안 및 문제 유형 분석표

TEST 1-1

01 (D) Fact
02 (D) Fact
03 (C) Vocabulary
04 (D) Inference
05 (B) Purpose
06 (D) Fact
07 (B) Purpose
08 (D) Highlight
09 3rd ■ Insertion
10 (A), (B), (C) Summary

TEST 1-2

11 (D) Fact
12 (C) Fact
13 (A) Vocabulary
14 (D) Inference
15 (D) Fact
16 (C) Purpose
17 (C) Highlight
18 (C) Fact
19 2nd ■ Insertion
20 (A), (D), (E) Summary

각 문제 유형별 맞춘 개수를 아래에 적어 보세요.

유형	맞춘 답의 개수	정답률	
단어 (Vocabulary)	/ 2	정답률:	%
사실 확인 문제 (Fact)	/ 7	정답률:	%
지시어 찾기 (Reference)	/ 0	정답률:	%
끼워 넣기 (Insertion)	/ 2	정답률:	%
문장 변환문제 (Highlight)	/ 2	정답률:	%
목적 (Purpose)	/ 3	정답률:	%
추론 (Inference)	/ 2	정답률:	%
단락 요약(Summary / Category Chart)	/ 2	정답률:	%
전체	/ 20	정답률:	%

※ 자신이 취약한 유형은 READING STRATEGIES를 통해 다시 한번 점검하시기 바랍니다. (p.31)

TEST 1-1   Method of Measuring Bats' Age 박쥐의 연령 계산 방법

Introduction	단락 1	박쥐 연령 측정의 어려움
Point 1	단락 2	박쥐의 연령 - 생활 연령과 생물학적 연령
Point 2	단락 3	어린 박쥐의 연령 측정 방법
Point 3	단락 4	어른 박쥐의 연령 측정 방법 I
Point 4	단락 5	어른 박쥐의 연령 측정 방법 II

단 락 정 리	지 문	해 석
단락 1 박쥐 연령 측정의 어려움	**1** For many decades, biologists have compiled scores of data on the life spans of various bat species using data obtained by the fortuitous recapture of individuals tagged **at birth**. It has been found that **on average**, bats live **three times longer** than other mammals of similar size and metabolic rate. Determining their exact age is, however, particularly difficult because [Q1]**it is likely that** they display more environmental and physiological variation throughout their lives **than** mammals with shorter lifespans, which may confuse several studied aspects of bat biology.	수십 년 동안, 생물학자들은 태어났을 때 달아놓은 꼬리표가 붙은 박쥐들을 우연히 재포획하여 얻은 많은 정보를 사용하여 다양한 종의 박쥐들의 수명에 대한 정보를 모아오고 있다. 평균적으로, 박쥐들은 비슷한 크기의 몸과 대사율 가진 다른 포유류들에 비해 3배 이상 길게 사는 것으로 알려져 왔다. 그러나, 박쥐들의 정확한 연령을 측정하는 것은 특히 어려운데 이는 박쥐들이 좀 더 짧은 수명을 가진 포유류들에 비해서 [Q1]더 다양한 환경적, 생리적 변화를 평생동안 보여줄 것 같다는 사실이 박쥐 생물학의 다양하게 연구된 측면을 혼란스럽게 할 것이기 때문이다.
단락 2 박쥐의 연령 - 생활 연령과 생물학적 연령	**2** When studying bat lifespans, **it is important to note** the [Q10-A]distinction between chronological and biological age. Chronological age is the interval between the time of birth and the present. Biological or physiological age, **on the other hand**, reflects the life expectancy and **is based on** physical **changes in** the morphology and function of the body, which may not always coincide with chronological age. The only means of knowing a bat's exact chronological age is to permanently mark it at birth, **so that** at any subsequent recaptures, its exact age can be determined. [Q2]This method has drawbacks, as marking bats is time consuming, requiring long-term monitoring, and recapture rates are typically low, **not to mention that** the process itself may disturb the bat.	박쥐의 연령을 연구할 때, [Q10-A]생활 연령과 생물학적 연령 사이의 차이에 주목하는 것이 중요하다. 생활 연령은 출생 시간과 현재 시간 사이의 시간적 간격이다. 반면에 생물학적 혹은 생리학적 연령은 기대수명을 반영하며 몸의 구조와 기능의 신체적인 변화들에 기반하는데, 생물학적 연령이 생활연령과 늘 일치하는 것은 아니다. 박쥐의 정확한 생활 연령을 측정하는 유일한 방법은 박쥐가 태어날 때 영구적으로 유지될 꼬리표를 붙여서 이후의 어떠한 재포획에서도 박쥐의 정확한 연령을 측정할 수 있도록 하는 것이다. [Q2]이 방법은 많은 단점들을 가지는데, 이는 그 과정 자체가 박쥐들의 생활을 방해한다는 것은 말할 것도 없이 박쥐에게 꼬리표를 붙이는 것은 시간이 많이 걸리고, 오랜 기간의 감시가 요구되며 재포획 비율이 보통 낮기 때문이다.

Vocabulary

1단락 lifespan [laifpǽn] n. 수명   biologist [baiálədʒist] n. 생물학자   fortuitous [fɔːrtjúːətəs] a. 우연한
tag [tæg] n. 꼬리표   metabolic [mètəbálik] a. 신진대사의   physiological [fìziəláːdʒikəl] a. 생리학상의
confuse [kənfjúːz] v. 혼동하다

2단락 morphology [mɔːrfálədʒi] n. (생물에 대한) 형태학   subsequent [sʌ́bsikwənt] a. 차후의, 다음의   distinction [distíŋkʃən] n. 구별
chronological [krànəláːdʒikəl] a. 연대순의   expectancy [ikspéktənsi] n. 기대   coincide [kòuinsáid] v. 일치하다
recapture [riːkǽptʃər] v. 탈환하다   subsequent [sʌ́bsikwənt] a. 뒤이은

단락 3
어린 박쥐의 연령 측정 방법

3   Several other methods have been developed to determine the biological age of bats. The first measures the long bones, like the forearm, metacarpals, and digits, which **go through** a phase of rapid linear growth **shortly after** birth. These measurements, especially **that of** the forearm, can **be used to distinguish** juveniles **from** adults. A species-specific reference correlating these measurements with examples of a known-age can provide age estimates [Q10-B] within 1-2 days **with** 95 percent **accuracy**. The advantages of this empirical method are its accuracy, ease of use in the field and laboratory, and lack of invasiveness. Only a caliper or a ruler is **needed to obtain** the measurements, **making this method ideal** for use on both live animals and museum specimens. The major disadvantage is that these bones grow only during the first few weeks of life and the valid time frame varies between species from only 12 days in M. lucifugus to as long as 45 days in R. leschenaulti. Other traits, such as **changes in** the patterns and rates of closure of the cartilaginous epiphyseal growth plates **are**, therefore, **necessary to estimate** the age of older individuals. **In** its simplest **form**, this method **distinguishes between** young bats **and** adults. By transilluminating the wing of a juvenile, a researcher can discern the cartilaginous zone of the long phalanges which **allows** more light **to pass through** and thus appears lighter than bone. [Q4] As the bat **continues to grow**, the epiphyseal plates eventually close and are **no longer visible to** the unaided eye. This method of age categorization requires **no more than** a flashlight and is **ideal for** use in both the field and the laboratory.

단락 4
어른 박쥐의 연령 측정 방법 I

4   Another method of estimating bats' age is to study their teeth. [Q5] Much like puppies that lose their sharp baby teeth before growing **a set of** permanent adult teeth, in most bat species, permanent teeth replace the deciduous ones by the time juveniles are able to fly and feed independently. Once **in place**, these permanent teeth reach full size and **cease to grow**. [Q6] A lifetime of mastication however **wears down** their surfaces and erodes their enamel. The degree of tooth wear can, therefore, **be used to place** bats into relative age categories as this process occurs from weaning until death. [Q7] **Due to differences** in diet, tooth usage in aggressive interactions, and the populations' annual activity periods, species show significant **variation in** tooth wear. Therefore, the development of species-specific reference standards based on a wide-ranging sample of known-age individuals **is critical for** the proper **use of** this method, **as are** investigators with extensive species-specific experience assessing tooth wear.

Vocabulary

3단락
- metacarpal [mètəkáːrpəl] n. 손바닥뼈
- phalanges [fəlǽndʒiːz] n. 지골
- juvenile [dʒúːvənəl] a. 젊은

4단락
- deciduous [disídʒuːəs] a. 떨어지는
- weaning [wíːniŋ] n. 젖떼기
- reference [réfərəns] n. 참조

- caliper [kǽləpər] n. 캘리퍼스, 측정 양각기
- digit [dídʒit] n. 손(발)가락
- transilluminate [trænsilúːmənèit] v. 빛을 통과시키다

- mastication [mæ̀stəkéiʃən] n. 씹음, 저작
- independently [ìndipéndəntli] ad. 독립적으로
- assess [əsés] v. 평가하다

- cartilaginous epiphyseal n. 뼈끝연골
- valid [vǽlid] a. 정당한 근거가 있는
- flashlight [flǽʃlàit] n. 회중전등

- enamel [inǽməl] n. (치아의) 애나맬질
- aggressive [əgrésiv] a. 공격적인

단락 5

어른 박쥐의 연령 측정 방법 II

5 Zoologists Klevezal and Kleinenberg suggested a new method of aging bats using their teeth. They suggested that the number of incremental lines, or annuli, on bat's teeth could be counted to determine its age. The robustness of the incremental lines, however, varies among species **so that** in some the lines may be difficult to count, especially in small species. Another zoologist, C.J. Phillips, examined the incremental lines in two species of bats from known-age specimens. [■] [Q10-C] He found that the number of incremental lines observed **depended on** which tooth was extracted and on the section examined, and suggested that several factors, such as mechanical stress and tooth movement, can alter the patterns of layered growth yielding non-annual cycles of dentin and cementum deposition. [■] Other researchers have found a lack of correlation between age and incremental lines in some species. [■] **Aside from variation in** incremental lines and the questionable accuracy of this method, other disadvantages are that it requires tooth extraction, which can only be done on dead specimens, it is time consuming, and it requires specialized equipment. ◎The problems **associated with** this method highlight the **need to better understand** how and when these incremental lines are deposited and **use** this information **to develop** more accurate reference standards that can **be correlated with** other methods. [■] i) **Notwithstanding**, this method has proven **useful for** ii) **a variety of** behavioral and ecological studies iii) where broad age categories suffice to obtain meaningful results.

동물학자인 클레베잘과 클레이넨버그는 치아를 사용한 박쥐 연령 측정의 새로운 방법을 제안했다. 그들은 박쥐 치아에 있는 발육선 혹은 '섬유'의 숫자로 연령을 측정할 수 있다고 하였다. 하지만 종 사이의 발육선의 강도의 차이가 났기 때문에 특히 작은 종 일부에선 선의 숫자를 헤아리는 것이 어렵다. 또 다른 동물학자인 필립스는 나이가 알려진 표본으로부터의 두 박쥐 종의 발육선을 조사하였다. [■] [Q10-C] 그는 관찰된 발육선의 숫자가 추출된 치아 종류와 검사된 부분에 따라 달라지는 것을 발견했고 기계적인 압박과 치아 움직임과 같은 여러 요소들이 상아질과 백악질의 비연간 최적 순환을 만들어 내는 층자람의 패턴을 변화시킬 수 있다고 주장했다. [■] 다른 조사관들은 일부의 종에서 연령과 발육선의 연관성이 없다고 발견했다. [■] 발육선의 차이와 이러한 방법의 의심스러운 정확성을 제외하고도 그 방법이 죽은 표본에서만 가능한 치아추출이 요구되고 시간이 많이 걸리고 전문 도구가 필요하다는 것이 단점이다. ◎이 방법과 관련된 문제들은 발육선이 어떻게 그리고 언제 퇴적되는지를 더 잘 이해해야 한다는 것과 다른 방법과 연관될 수 있는 정확된 표준 시료들을 믿기 위해 이 정보를 사용해야 한다는 필요들을 강조한다. [■] 그럼에도 불구하고, 이 방법은 iii)폭넓은 연령 범주가 의미있는 결과를 얻기 위해 ii)충분한 다양한 행동학적, 생태학적 연구에서 i)중요 하다고 입증되었다.

Sentence analysis

◎ The problems associated with this method / highlight the need /
이 방법과 관련된 문제점들은   필요성을 대두시킨다

to better understand how and when these incremental lines are deposited / and use this information to develop /
발육선들이 어떻게 그리고 언제 추출되는지 이해하여야 하고   이러한 정보를 통해 발전시켜

more accurate reference standards / that can be correlated with other methods.
더 정확한 참고 기준을   다른 측정법과 연관성이 있도록 해야 하는

Vocabulary

5단락
incremental line n. 발육선
cementum [siméntəm] n. (이의)백악질
extracted [ikstræktid] a. 추출한
robustness [roubʌ́stnes] n. 강건함
dentin [déntin] n. (이의) 상아질
correlate [kɔ́ːrəlèit] v. 연관시키다

01
According to paragraph 1, why is it difficult to calculate the age of bats?

(A) ~~They are dangerous~~ compared to other short-lived mammals.
(B) They are ~~too vulnerable~~ to many transformations they undergo. ★
(C) Age calculation ~~is related to an area of study other than biology~~.
(D) The wide variety of bats' habitats and physical aspects is too broad to cover.

1단락에 의하면 박쥐의 나이는 왜 측정하기 어려운가?

(A) 수명이 짧은 다른 포유류보다 ~~위험하다~~.
(B) 그들이 겪는 많은 변화들에 ~~너무 취약하다~~. ★
(C) 연령 측정법은 생물학 ~~그 이상의 영역과 관련이 있다~~.
(D) 박쥐의 다양한 서식지와 신체적인 측면이 너무 광범위하다.

Fact 문제의 키워드인 Determining their exact age 부분 다음의 부분을 보면 because 이하의 it is likely that they display more environmental and physiological variation (더 다양한 환경적, 생리적 변화를 보여줄 것 같다는 사실) 이라는 내용에 따라 그 변화의 광범위성을 이야기한 (D)가 정답이며 (B)가 오답인 이유는 그들의 체내에서만의 변화만을 언급했기 때문에 오답이 된다.

02
All of the following are mentioned in paragraph 2 as difficulties of marking bats at birth to track their chronological age EXCEPT:

(A) It takes ~~too much time to process~~. ★
(B) ~~A long observation period~~ is required.
(C) ~~Re-trapping bats occurs rarely~~.
(D) The method is disturbed by bats.

다음 중, 2단락에 나와 있는 어린 나이에 꼬리표를 붙여 나이를 측정하는 방법의 단점이 아닌 것은?

(A) ~~처리시간이 오래 걸린다~~. ★
(B) ~~오랜 관찰시간이 필요하다~~.
(C) ~~다시 잡는 경우가 드물다~~.
(D) 박쥐가 실험을 방해한다.

Fact 문제의 키워드인 drawbacks가 있는 문장을 살펴보면 This method has drawbacks, because (A) marking bats is time consuming, (B) requiring long-term monitoring, and (C) recapture rates are typically low, not to mention that the process itself may disturb the bat. (이 방법들은 많은 단점들을 가지는데, 이는 그 과정 자체가 박쥐들의 생활을 방해한다는 것은 말할 것도 없이 박쥐에게 꼬리표를 붙이는 것은 시간이 많이 걸리고, 오랜 기간의 감시가 요구되며 재 포획 비율이 보통 낮기 때문이다.) 문장 속에 (A), (B), (C)가 다 나와있다. 하지만 (D)가 오답인 이유는 실험이 박쥐를 방해하는 것이지 박쥐에 의해서 방해되는 것이 아님으로 오답이다.

03
The word empirical in the passage is closest in meaning to

(A) preliminary
(B) related
(C) observational
(D) reliable ★

지문의 단어 empirical와 가장 유사한 단어는?

(A) 예비의 [prilímənèri]
(B) 관련성이 있는 [riléitid]
(C) 관찰할 수 있는 [àbzərvéiʃənl]
(D) 의지할 수 있는 ★ [riláiəbl]

Vocabulary empirical(경험적인)과 비슷한 뜻을 가지는 observational(관찰할 수 있는)과 정답이며 reliable(의지 할 수 있는)은 대체할 경우에 의미는 통하지만 본문의 단어와 뜻이 다르므로 오답이 된다.

04
What can be inferred from paragraph 3 about the cartilaginous epiphyseal plate?

(A) It is the easiest external physical characteristic for accurately measuring bats' age ~~throughout its lifetime~~.
(B) It is possible to determine ~~the adult bats'~~ age by looking at its ~~mineralized bone tissue~~. ★
(C) Changes in the pattern and rate of closure happen ~~due to linear growth~~ in adult long bones.
(D) Light can no longer penetrate it because it shuts as the bat gets older.

3단락에 언급된 연골로 된 단골 선을 통해 유추할 수 있는 내용은?

(A) ~~정확하게 박쥐와 모든 나이를 측정할 수 있는~~ 가장 쉬운 외관적 특징이다.
(B) ~~광물질을 함유한~~ 뼈 조직을 통해 ~~어른 박쥐의~~ 나이를 추정할 수 있다. ★
(C) 패턴과 닫히는 속도의 변화는 어른의 긴 뼈의 ~~직선적 성장 때문이다~~.
(D) 박쥐가 나이가 들수록 단골 선이 닫히므로 빛이 더 이상 투과되지 않는다.

Inference 문제의 키워드인 the epiphyseal plates의 부분을 살펴보면 As the bat continues to grow, the epiphyseal plates eventually close and are no longer visible to the unaided eyes.(박쥐가 계속 성장하면서 성장판은 결국에는 닫히고 더 이상 육안으로 볼 수 없게 된다) 따라서 닫히게 되어 보이지 않음으로 투과되지 않는다고 표시된 (D)가 정답이 된다. (A)는 모든 나이가 아닌 어린 나이만 가능하므로 오답이고 (B)는 어른 박쥐가 아니고 광물질을 함유한 뼈 조직 또한 언급된 바 없다. (C)는 직선적 성장 때문에 패턴과 닫히는 속도의 변화가 일어나지 않으므로 오답이다.

05

In paragraph 4, why does the author mention the teeth of puppies?

(A) ~~To show~~ that dogs' ages can also be measured through their teeth ★
(B) To show the similarity of the growth of teeth with bats
(C) To illustrate ~~the high degree of accuracy of age measurement using teeth~~
(D) To support the claim that dogs ~~live longer than bats due to~~ their healthy teeth

4단락에서 왜 글쓴이가 강아지의 치아를 언급했는가?

(A) 강아지의 나이도 치아를 통해 측정될 수 있다는 것을 ~~보이기 위해~~ ★
(B) 박쥐의 치아의 성장과 유사함을 보여주기 위해
(C) 치아를 통해 나이를 측정하는 방법의 높은 확률을 설명하기 위해
(D) 강아지의 건강한 치아 ~~때문에 박쥐보다 오래 산다는~~ 주장을 강화하기 위해

Purpose 키워드인 teeth가 언급된 지문을 살펴보면 Much like puppies that lose their sharp baby teeth before growing a set of permanent adult teeth, in most bat species, permanent teeth replace the deciduous ones by the time juveniles are able to fly and feed independently.(강아지가 영구치가 모두 자라기 전에 그들의 날카로운 젖니를 잃는 것처럼 대부분의 박쥐 종에서 어린 박쥐가 혼자 날고 먹을 수 있을 때 영구치가 유치를 대체한다) 지문에서 글쓴이가 강아지를 언급한 이유는 박쥐의 치아의 변화와의 공통점을 보여주기 위함이고 이는 much like를 통해 유추할 수 있음으로 정답은 (B)이다. 나머지 (A), (C), (D)는 모두 의도한 바가 아니므로 오답이다.

06

According to paragraph 4, what is true about bat's teeth?

(A) The age of bats ~~can be determined by the degree at which their teeth are angled~~ regularly. ★
(B) Bats experience ~~continuous~~ tooth growth until death.
(C) ~~Through their size~~, it is possible to know the bat's ~~exact age~~.
(D) When bats become adults, they will have more blunt teeth.

4단락에서 박쥐의 치아에 대해 사실인 것은?

(A) 박쥐의 나이는 ~~규칙적인 치아의 각도를 통하여 추정할 수 있다~~. ★
(B) 박쥐는 죽을 때까지 ~~지속적으로~~ 치아의 성장을 경험한다
(C) ~~사이즈를 통하여 박쥐의 정확한 나이를 추정할 수 있다~~
(D) 박쥐가 어른이 될 경우, 더욱 무딘 치아를 가지게 될 것이다

Fact 본문의 A lifetime of mastication however wears down their surfaces and erodes their enamel.(하지만 일생 동안 씹는 작용을 통해 치아의 표면은 마모되고 에나멜은 부식된다)를 살펴보면 시간이 지나면서 치아가 마모되기 때문에 어른 박쥐가 무딘 치아를 가진다는 것을 알 수 있으므로 정답이다. (A)는 언급되어 있지 않았고 (B) 또한 언급되지 않았다. (C)의 경우 사이즈를 통해 정확한 나이를 알 수 있다는 내용은 나와 있지 않았고 알 수 있다고 하여도 박쥐의 정확한 나이를 아는 것은 불가능하므로 역시 오답이다.

07

Why does the author mention the differences in diet, tooth usage in aggressive interactions, and populations' annual activity periods?

(A) To illustrate the bats' ~~life cycle~~ as they grow older
(B) To give some reasons that a species-specific reference standard was required to determine bats' ages
(C) To provide evidence that ~~adult bats live in wild habitats~~
(D) To show the ~~main seasons~~ in which adult bats' teeth are worn ★

글쓴이가 음식물의 차이, 공격적인 상호작용에서의 치아 사용, 인구의 연간 활동 기간을 언급한 의도는?

(A) 박쥐의 ~~생활주기를~~ 설명하기 위해
(B) 종 특이 표준 시료가 박쥐의 나이를 측정하기 위해 필요한 이유를 제공하기 위해
(C) ~~어른 박쥐는 야생의 서식지에 거주한다는 점을~~ 증거로 보여주기 위해
(D) 박쥐의 치아가 닳는 ~~주요한 계절을~~ 보여주기 위해 ★

Purpose 본문의 키워드가 들어간 문장인 Due to differences in diet, tooth usage in aggressive interactions, and the populations' annual activity periods, species show significant variation in tooth wear.(먹는 음식, 공격적 상호작용에서의 치아 사용, 개체수의 연간 활동 기간에서의 차이 때문에 치아 마모 정도는 종에 따라 상당히 다양하다) 다음에 Therefore 이후 species-specific reference standards(종 특이 표준 시료)가 중요하다는 이야기를 해주고 있다. 그러므로 정답은 (B)이다.

08

Which of the sentences below best expresses the essential information in the highlighted sentence in the passage? Incorrect choices change the meaning in important ways or leave out essential information.

(A) The variety of biological ~~studies gave insight into the methods of using teeth~~ to determine the age of bats. ★

(B) The teeth of bats provided substantial information to the researchers studying methods of ~~determining their age~~.

(C) There was abundant scientific research that gave ~~significant outcomes regardless of the help of a broad reference~~.

(D) In various studies, where an approximate age range is sufficient, scientists have found tooth measurements to be valid forms of age determination in bats.

아래 문장 중 지문 속의 음영된 문장의 핵심 정보를 가장 잘 표현하고 있는 것은 무엇인가? 오답은 문장의 의미를 현저히 왜곡하거나 핵심 정보를 빠트리고 있다.

(A) 다양한 생물학적 ~~연구는 치아를 통해~~ 박쥐의 나이를 추정할 수 있는 방법을 이해시켰다. ★

(B) 박쥐의 치아는 ~~나이를 알아내는~~ 방법을 연구하는 학자들에게 충분한 정보를 제공하였다.

(C) ~~광범위한 참고자료와는 관계없이~~ 중요한 결과를 도출한 과학적 연구가 많았다.

(D) 추정 나이의 범위가 다양한 많은 연구에서는, 과학자들은 치아의 측정이 박쥐의 나이를 측정하는데 타당한 유형이라는 것을 알아냈다.

Highlight 음영된 부분을 보면 i) Notwithstanding, this method has proven useful for ii) a variety of behavioral and ecological studies iii) where broad age categories suffice to obtain meaningful results.(그럼에도 불구하고, 이 방법은 iii) 폭넓은 연령 범주가 의미있는 결과를 얻기 위해 ii) 충분한 다양한 행동학적, 생태학적 연구에서 i) 중요하다고 입증되었다) 치아 측정의 방법이 유용하다는 것을 나타내며 다른 모든 뜻을 아우르는 (D)가 정답이 되며 (A)의 경우 iii)의 where절 내용이 생략되어 있고 (B)의 경우 iii)의 내용이 빠져있다. (C)의 경우에는 iii)의 내용이 반대로 적혀있다.

09

Look at the four squares [■] that indicate where the following sentence could be added to the passage.

Aside from variation in incremental lines and the questionable accuracy of this method, other disadvantages are that it requires tooth extraction, which can only be done on dead specimens, it is time consuming, and it requires specialized equipment.

Where would the sentence best fit? Click on a square [■] to add the sentence to the passage. 3rd

네 개의 네모[■]는 다음 문장이 삽입될 수 있는 부분을 나타내고 있다.

발육선의 차이와 이러한 방법의 의심스러운 정확성을 제외하고도 그 방법이 죽은 표본에서만 가능하며 가능한 치아 추출이 요구되고 시간이 많이 걸리고 전문 도구가 필요하다는 것이 단점이다.

이 문장은 어느 자리에 들어가는 것이 가장 적절한가? 세번째

Insertion 핵심단어는 other disadvantages 이다. 즉 이전에 단점으로서, 3번째 네모 이전의 내용은 incremental line이 나이와 관련없다는 문제점에 관한 얘기이고 그 다음에 다른 문제점들을 언급하는 3번째 네모가 가장 적절하며 그 다음에 자연스럽게 그 문제들을 정리해 주고 있다.

10

Directions: An introductory sentence for a brief summary of the passage is provided below. Complete the summary by selecting the THREE answer choices that express the most important ideas in the passage. Some sentences do not belong in the summary because they express ideas that are not presented in the passage or are minor ideas in the passage. **This question is worth 2 points.**

지시 : 지문 요약을 위한 도입 문장이 아래에 주어져 있다. 지문의 가장 중요한 내용을 나타내는 보기 3개를 골라 요약을 완성하시오. 어떤 문장은 지문에 언급되지 않은 내용이나 사소한 정보를 담고 있으므로 요약에 포함되지 않는다. 이 문제는 2점이다.

Because bats are long-lived animals, it is more difficult to determine their ages because they experience more environmental and physiological variation.

- (A) The age of bats can be categorized in two separate ways which measure different aspects of a bat's life span. - Paragraph 2

- (B) While impractical for most stages of a bat's life, physical measurements and observations in juvenile bats' age can provide reliable calculations of its age. - Paragraph 3

- (C) Many scientists argued that adult bats' age can be measured by their teeth, but there are drawbacks and inaccuracies in the methods. - Paragraph 4, 5

박쥐들은 오래 사는 동물이기 때문에, 그들의 나이를 측정하는 것은 어려운데 이는 박쥐들이 더 많은 환경적, 생리적 변화를 겪기 때문이다.

- (A) 박쥐의 나이는 박쥐의 일생에 따라 다르게 측정되는 두 가지의 다른 종류로 나누어 질 수 있다.

- (B) 박쥐의 일생의 다른 단계에서는 실용적이지 않은 생물학적 측정과 관찰을 통한 어린 박쥐의 나이는 박쥐의 믿을 만한 나이 계산을 제공한다.

- (C) 많은 과학자들은 성인 박쥐의 나이는 그들의 치아를 통해 측정될 수 있다고 주장하나 이 방법에는 많은 단점과 부정확성이 있다.

(D) People ~~can determine puppies' age~~ through examining their teeth, which is the same as a theory that scientists suggested.
 - Minor

(E) Chronological age of juvenile bats is easier to find ~~because their teeth are not eroded like those of adult bats.~~ - Not mentioned

(F) Using long bones and the cartilaginous epiphyseal plates for measuring ages can be done on adult bats ~~with no teeth.~~
 - 틀린정보

(D) 과학자들이 주장한 이론처럼 사람들은 ~~강아지와 나이를~~ 치아를 통해 ~~파악할 수 있다.~~

(E) 어린 박쥐의 생활연령은 ~~어른 박쥐와 달리 치아가 침식되지 않아서~~ 더 파악하기 쉽다.

(F) 긴 뼈나 연골로 된 단골 선을 통해 나이를 측정하는 방법은 ~~치아가 없는~~ 어른 박쥐도 가능하다.

Summary 지문의 내용은 박쥐의 나이를 측정하는 방법이 중점적으로 다루어지고 있다. 2번째 단락의 중점적인 내용은 생물학적 나이와 생활연령을 구분한 내용이므로 (A)가 이에 해당하고 3번째 단락은 어린 박쥐의 나이를 측정하는 방법이 제기되고 이는 (B)가 가장 유사한 문장이다. 4번째 단락과, 5번째 단락은 어른 박쥐의 나이를 측정하는 방법으로 치아를 제기하고 있고 이와 가장 유사한 문장은 (C)라고 볼 수 있다. (D)는 지문의 너무 작은 부분을 요약한 부분이고, (E)는 틀린정보를 제시 하였고 (F)는 긴 뼈나 연골로 된 단골 선을 통한 나이 측정 방법은 어린 박쥐에게만 해당하므로 틀린 문장이다.

usherin.usher.co.kr

TEST 1-2 Tracing Language Diversification 언어의 다양화 추적

Introduction	단락 1	언어학자들의 관심과 언어의 변화
Point 1	단락 2	역재건의 설명과 방법
Point 2	단락 3	윌리엄 존스 경의 기여
Point 3	단락 4	제이콥 그림의 기여
Point 4	단락 5	언어의 공통된 근원지 - 원조 인도 - 유럽어
Point 5	단락 6	언어의 분산
Point 6	단락 7	재건의 어려운 점

단락정리 | 지문 | 해석

단락 1
언어학자들의 관심과 언어의 변화

1 Linguists study language relationships to find their similarities and differences. One **way to find** and chart these is to **look for** inter-language sound shifts **over time**. These are slight alternations in words between related subfamily languages since their origin. From these linguists can deduce a connection between them through sound shifts.

언어학자들은 언어 관계들에서의 유사점과 차이점을 확인하기 위해 연구를 수행한다. 유사점과 차이점을 찾고 기록하는 하나의 방법은 시간의 흐름에 따른 언어간 소리 변화를 찾는 것이다. 이 소리 변화는 그 근원 이래로의 관련된 어파 언어들 사이에서의 단어의 경미한 변화이다. 이 경미한 변화들로부터 언어학자들은 소리 변환을 통한 언어간 관계를 추정할 수 있다.

단락 2
역재건의 설명과 방법

2 The technique **used to** record sound shifts and consonant hardening **is called** backward reconstruction. This technique takes humanity's linguistic family tree back thousands of years. [Q11]Using it, scholars **infer** vocabulary **from** previous languages. It may even be possible **to go further** and re-create the preceding languages.

소리 변화와 된소리를 기록하기 위해 사용된 기법은 역재건이라고 불린다. 이 기법은 인류 언어 가계도를 몇 천년 전까지 확인 할 수 있도록 해준다. [Q11]그 기법을 사용함으로써 학자들은 이전 언어의 단어를 추정한다. 심지어 더 나아가 이전 언어를 재건하는 것도 가능할 수도 있다.

단락 3
윌리엄 존스 경의 기여

3 Linguist Sir William Jones was an early **researcher into** language diversification. °He **made** unrivalled **contributions to** linguistic scholarship, promoting an understanding of and appreciation for Asian languages and cultures. [Q12]Having **arrived in** Calcutta as a Bengal Supreme Court judge, he studied Sanskrit **in order to approach** Muslim and Hindu laws **in** their original **form**. He found grammatical roots **corresponding to** classical European languages. From this, he developed the idea of a common language source. In 'The Sanskrit Language', he wrote of [Q14]Sanskrit's **resemblance to**

언어학자 윌리엄 존스 경은 언어 다양화에 대한 초기 연구자였다. °그는 아시아 언어와 문화에 대한 이해와 평가를 증진시키며 언어학에 대한 타의 추종을 불허하는 공헌을 하였다. [Q12]뱅갈 대법원 판사로 갤커타에 도착하여 그는 무슬림과 힌두법을 그 원본의 형태로 접근하기 위해 산스크리트어를 공부했다. 그는 고대 유럽 언어와 상응하는 문법적인 근원을 발견했다. 이것으로부터 그는 공통 언어 근원의 아이디어를 진전시켰다. '스크리트어'에서 그는 [Q14]그리스와 라틴어에 대한 산스크리트어의 유사점을 기술하며, 그 유사점을 통해 그 언어들이 공통된

Vocabulary

1단락 shift [ʃift] n. 이동   alternation [ɔ̀:ltərnéiʃən] n. 교대   subfamily [sʌbfǽməli] n. 어파   deduce [didjú:s] v. 추정하다

2단락 consonant [kánsənənt] n. 자음   infer [infə́:r] v. 추론하다   preceding [prisí:diŋ] a. 이전의

3단락 diversification [divə̀:rsəfikéiʃən] n. 다양화   unrivalled [ʌnráivəld] a. 타의 추종을 불허하는   corresponding [kɔ̀:rəspándiŋ] a. 상응하는
resemblance [rizémbləns] n. 유사   quote [kwout] v. 인용하다   antiquity [æntíkwəti] n. 고대, 유물
copious [kóupiəs] a. 엄청난, 방대한   exquisitely [ikskwízitəli, kskwizítli] ad. 정교하게, 우아하게   philologist [filálədʒist] n. 문헌학자

Greek and Latin, which **led** him **to suggest** that they **not only** had a common root **but were also related to** other European languages. He stated: The Sanskrit language, **whatever be** its antiquity, **is of** a wonderful structure; more perfect than the Greek, more copious than the Latin, and more exquisitely refined than either, yet bearing to both of them a stronger affinity, both in the roots of verbs and the forms of grammar, than could possibly have been produced **by accident**; **so** strong indeed, [Q14]**that** no philologer could examine them all three, without **believing** them **to have** sprung from some common source, which, perhaps, **no longer** exists.

4 Another major linguistic contributor was Jacob Grimm. During the nineteenth century, he **sought to** scientifically **prove** that sound shifts showed relationships between languages. Grimm sought rare unchanged words throughout the German countryside to clarify the history of the German language. [Q15]Unfortunately, rural Germans presumed that a linguistics researcher' was just a new **way for** the government **to figure out** how much property tax they owed. [■] To **entice** people **to speak** freely, Grimm **asked** them **to tell** him stories, which he faithfully recorded. His primary interest was **not** initially the stories themselves **but** any exotic vocabulary they **happened to use**. [■] What he **ended up with** was a fascinating body of folklore which he and his brother Wilhelm published as Grimms' Fairy Tales. Grimm, however, did get what he wanted word-wise. [■] In the stories, he noticed an evolutionary pattern of Germanic languages which **pointed to** a change that had **taken place** long ago. [■] He explained that related languages have similar, but not identical consonants, [Q16]which had undergone predictable changes **over time**. Hard consonants such as the V and T in German word vater, softened into the Dutch vader and the English father. Using Grimm's theory, linguists realized that consonants would become harder as they went backwards toward the original language.

5 From Jones' and Grimm's theories, linguists **came up with** the first major linguistic hypothesis: the existence of a common ancestral language called Proto-Indo-European which **transformed into** ancient Latin, Greek, and Sanskrit. This single language links modern languages around the world. Study of this language has helped identify that, although

Vocabulary

4단락 presume [prizúːm] v. 여기다
exotic [igzátik] a. 외국의, 이국적인
5단락 ancestral [ænséstrəl] a. 조상의, 원형을 이루는
6단락 divergence [divə́ːrdʒəns] n. 분기

entice [entáis] v. 유도하다
predicate [prédikit] v. 단언하다, 암시하다
hearth [haːrθ] n. 가정, 중심
fragment [frǽgmənt] n. 파편

faithfully [féiθfəli] ad. 정확히
dispersion [dispə́ːrən] n. 분산, 살포
discrete [diskríːt] a. 별개의

they share only a few similarities, both Slavonic and Germanic are sub-branches of a common ancestral language. Several research tasks naturally followed this hypothesis. ⓒFirst, the vocabulary of the proposed ancestral language **needed to be reconstructed**, before the hearth of the language could be located. After this, the routes of dispersion needed to be traced. Finally, the ways of life of those who spoke and spread the language needed to be established.

슬라브어와 독일어 모두 공통 언어의 하위 계열이라는 것을 확인하도록 해주었다. 여러 조사 업무들은 자연스레 이 가정을 따랐다. ⓒ먼저, 제안된 조상어의 단어가 그 언어가 중심을 잡기 이전에서 모습으로 재건될 필요가 있었다. 이 이후에 분산 경로를 추적해야만 했다. 마지막으로, 그 언어를 말하고 퍼트리는 사람들의 생활 방식도 설정해야 했다.

단락 6
언어의 분산

6 Nineteenth century linguist August Schleicher described language families as the branches of a tree. He suggested that new languages form through language divergence, when a language breaks down and **fragments into** dialects and then **into** discrete tongues **due to** separation of speakers. This can be seen in Spanish and Portuguese and is now happening with Quebecois French. Due to geographical separation, Parisian French and Quebecois French **started to differ** after the colonial era. Now the pronunciation and vocabulary use of the two places differ greatly. These new languages become the leaves on the tree. Through backward reconstruction, linguists can find how languages branches fit together. Tracing backward far enough, they can find the hearth of a language.

19세기 언어학자인 아우구스터 슐라이허는 어족을 나뭇가지로 묘사했다. 그는 화자의 분리에 의해 언어가 나뉘어지고 각 방언으로 쪼개지고 그 다음 분리된 말로 될 때 언어 분기를 통해 새로운 언어가 형성 된다고 제안했다. 이것은 스페인어와 포르투갈어 에서 보여질 수 있고 현재 퀘벡식 프랑스어에서 발생하고 있다. 지리적 분리에 의해 파리식 프랑스어와 퀘벡식 프랑스어는 식민지 시대 이후 달라지기 시작 했다. 현재 두 장소에서의 발음과 단어의 사용은 크게 달라진다. 이 새로운 언어들은 나무에서 잎사귀들이 된다. 역재건을 통해 언어학자들은 어떻게 언어 가지들이 서로 조화를 이루는지 알 수 있다. 역으로 충분히 추적하면 언어의 중심을 찾을 수 있다.

단락 7
재건의 어려운점

7 Finding this hearth is a daunting task, as reconstructing even a small branch is complicated. A complicating factor is that i)with human mobility, ii)languages did not merely diffuse through static populations; iii)they also spread by relocation diffusion. [Q18]If people with different languages have consistent spatial interaction, language convergence can **take place**, collapsing two languages into one. This creates problems for researchers because the reconstruction rules sometimes do not apply and can be unreliable.

이러한 중심을 찾는 것은 심지어 작은 가지를 재건하는 일마저도 복잡하기 때문에 힘든 작업이다. 복잡한 요인은 i) 사람의 유동성으로 인해 ii) 언어가 정체 된 인구를 통해서는 단지 퍼져나가지 않고 iii) 이전 확산을 통해서도 또한 퍼져나간다는 것이다. [Q18]만약 다른 언어를 사용하는 사람들이 꾸준한 공간적 상호 작용을 한다면 언어 집합이 발생하고 두 언어를 하나로 만들 것이다. 이것은 조사관들에게 문제를 발생 시키는데 재건 법칙들이 종종 적용되지 않거나 의지할 수 없기 때문이다.

Sentence analysis

◎ He made unrivalled contributions to linguistic scholarship, /
그는 언어학에 타의 추종을 불허하는 기여를 하였고

promoting an understanding of and appreciation for Asian languages and cultures.
촉진시키며 아시아 문화와 언어에 대한 이해와 가치를

◎ First, / the vocabulary of the proposed ancestral language / needed to be reconstructed, /
먼저   과거에 쓰였던 단어들을   재건해야 했다

before the hearth of the language could be located.
언어가 중심을 잡기 이전 모습으로

Vocabulary

5단락 daunting [dɔːntiŋ] a. 위협적인   diffuse [difjúːz] a. 널리 퍼진 / v. 분산시키다   relocation [rìːloukéiʃən] n. 이전, 이주
take place : phr. 발생하다   unreliable [ʌ̀nriláiəbəl] a. 믿을 수 없는

11 According to paragraph 2, which of the following is true about backward reconstruction?

(A) It allows ~~the derivation of new vocabulary~~ from ~~previous~~ language forms. ★
(B) It is a technique that ~~has been used for thousands of years~~.
(C) It ~~is used to create a new language~~ from ancient languages.
(D) It enables revival of pre-existing words.

2단락에 의하면, 역재건에 관해 사실인 것은?

(A) 과거 언어에서 새 단어를 얻을 수 있게 해준다. ★
(B) 몇천 년 동안 쓰여진 기법이다.
(C) 고대 언어에서 새로운 언어를 만들기 위해 쓰였다.
(D) 이미 있었던 단어를 부활할 수 있게 한다.

Fact backward reconstruction 과 관련된 내용을 확인하면 Using it, scholars infer vocabulary from previous languages. (그 기법을 사용함으로써 학자들은 이전 언어의 단어를 추정한다)를 볼 수 있다. 여기서 이것은 backward reconstruction을 뜻하므로 답은 (D)이다. (A)는 과정이 반대로 되었으므로 오답이며, (B)는 지문에 없는 내용이므로 오답이다. 그리고 (C)는 새로운 언어를 만드는 것이 아니므로 오답이다.

12 According to paragraph 3, Muslim and Hindu laws were

(A) ~~only accessible~~ to the Indian people.
(B) similar ~~to that of~~ Greek and Latin. ★
(C) both originally written in Sanskrit.
(D) ~~further developed~~ by William Jones.

3단락에 의하면, 무슬림과 힌두법서는

(A) 오직 인도인들에게만 ~~허용되었다~~.
(B) 그리스와 라틴의 ~~법과~~ 비슷하다. ★
(C) 둘 다 본래 산스크리트어로 적었었다.
(D) 윌리엄 존스에 의해 ~~좀 더 개발되었다~~.

Fact Muslim과 Hindu laws가 언급된 부분을 보면, Having arrived in Calcutta as a Bengal Supreme Court judge, he studied Sanskrit in order to approach Muslim and Hindu laws in their original form. (뱅갈 대법원 판사로 캘커타에 도착하여 그는 무슬림과 힌두 법을 그 원본의 형태로 접근하기 위해 산스크리트어를 공부했다)라고 말한다. 즉, 무슬림과 힌두법서의 원본은 산스크리트어로 읽을 수 있다는 말이다. 그러므로 답은 (C)이다. (A)는 본문에 없는 내용이므로 오답이고, (B)는 그리스와 라틴 법서에 관한 얘기가 아니었으므로 오답이며, (D)는 윌리엄 존스가 법서를 읽으려 했지 그것을 개발하려는 내용은 없으므로 오답이다.

13 The word affinity is closest in meaning to

(A) resemblance
(B) understanding
(C) affection ★
(D) superiority

지문의 단어 affinity와 가장 유사한 것은?

(A) 유사함 [rizémbləns]
(B) 이해 [ʌ̀ndərstǽndiŋ]
(C) 애정 ★ [əfékʃən]
(D) 우월함 [səpìərió(:)rəti]

Vocabulary 지문의 단어 affinity(관련성)은 resemblance(유사함)과 동의어이므로 정답이다.

14 According to paragraph 3, it can be inferred from William Jones's quote that a philologer

(A) would ~~not be able to find the same root~~ for three languages. ★
(B) would not understand ~~why Sanskrit is more advanced~~ than the others.
(C) would not believe the fact that ~~the three languages no longer exist~~.
(D) would not doubt William Jones's hypothesis of language.

3단락에 의하면, 윌리엄 존스의 인용문에서 추론할 수 있듯이 문헌학자들은

(A) 세가지 언어의 ~~공통된 근원을 찾지 못할 것이다~~. ★
(B) 왜 ~~산스크리트어가 다른 것들보다 나은 것인지~~ 이해 못 할 것이다.
(C) ~~세 언어가 더 이상 존재하지 않는다~~는 것을 믿지 못할 것이다.
(D) 윌리엄 존스의 언어가정에 의심을 하지 않을 것이다.

Inference   문제의 키워드인 philologer(문헌학자들)이 나오는 부분을 살펴보면 that no philologer could examine them all three, without believing them to have spring from some common source, which, perhaps, no longer exists. (어떠한 문헌학자들도 그 세 언어가 아마도 더 이상 존재하지 않을 공통의 기원을 가지고 있다는 것을 믿지 않고서야 세 언어 모두를 검토할 수가 없다)라고 말한다. 즉, 이들은 같은 근원에서 나왔다는 것을 믿을 것이라는 것이다. 위에 부분을 보면 존스는 Sanskrit's resemblance to Greek and Latin, which led him to suggest that they not only had a common root but were also related to other European languages. (그리스와 라틴어에 대한 산스크리트어의 유사점을 기술하며, 그 유사점을 통해 그 언어들이 공통된 근원을 가지고 있을 뿐 아니라 다른 유럽어와 연관이 있다는 것을 시사하게 된다) 라고 말했으므로 정답은 (D)이다. (A)는 반대의 뜻이므로 오답이며, (B)는 문헌학자와 관련 없는 내용이므로 오답이다. (C)는 더 이상 존재하지 않는 것이 세 언어가 아니므로 오답이다.

---

15 According to paragraph 4, the rural inhabitants did not welcome Grimm because

(A) he asked them ~~personal questions about their taxes.~~ ★
(B) he ~~was better educated than~~ they were.
(C) he ~~bothered~~ them by requesting to tell him stories.
(D) he was thought to work for the government.

4단락에 의하면, 시골에 사는 사람들은 _____ 때문에 그림을 반기지 않았다.

(A) 그가 세금에 관해 개인적인 것을 물어봤다. ★
(B) 그가 그들보다 더 잘 배웠다.
(C) 그가 이야기를 해달라고 귀찮게 했다.
(D) 그가 정부를 위해 일한다고 생각했다.

Fact   키워드인 rural inhabitants 가 표현된 부분을 살펴보면, Unfortunately, rural Germans presumed that a 'linguistics researcher' was just a new way for the government to figure out how much property tax they owed. (불행하게도, 시골 사람들이 '이 언어학자'를 그들이 빚진 재산세의 양을 알아내기 위한 정부의 단지 새로운 방법이라고 생각했다) 라고 말한다. 즉, 그를 정부 사람이라고 착각한 이유에서 반기지 않았으므로 정답은 (D)이다. (A)는 그가 개인적으로 물어본 것은 사유가 아니므로 오답이며, (B)는 지문에 언급되지 않았으므로 오답이다. 그리고 (C)또한 지문에 귀찮게 했다는 내용이 없으므로 오답이다.

---

16 Why does the author mention the Hard consonants?

(A) To show how the same word can ~~be transformed differently~~
(B) To exemplify ~~the letters shared by languages in the same subfamily~~ ★
(C) To explain the theory of language change that Grimm suggested
(D) To emphasize that ~~softer consonant words are found in old languages~~

글쓴이는 왜 된소리를 언급하는가?

(A) 같은 단어가 ~~다르게 변할 수 있다는~~ 것을 보여주고자
(B) 그림이 같은 ~~어파의 단어가 유사하단~~ 예를 들기 위해서 ★
(C) 그림이 제안한 언어 변화의 이론을 설명하기 위해서
(D) ~~약한 자음의 단어를 오래된 언어에서 찾을 수 있다는~~ 것을 강조하기 위해서

Purpose   Hard consonants가 들어간 부분을 살펴보면, Which had undergone predictable changes over time. Hard consonants such as the V and T in German word vater, softened into the Dutch vader and the English father. (예측 가능한 변화들을 겪었다는 것을 의미 한다고 설명했다. 독일어 vater에서의 V나 T와 같은 거센소리는 네덜란드어 vader와 영어에서 father로 부드러워졌다)라고 말한다. 즉, 그림의 주장 한 이론의 한 예로써 hard consonants를 소개했으므로 답은 (C)이다. (A)는 사실이기는 하지만 그것을 보여주기 위해서가 아니었으므로 오답이며, (B)는 특정 단어를 보여주기 위한 것이 아니었으므로 오답이다. 그리고 (D)는 본문 내용과 반대이므로 오답이다.

---

17 Which of the sentences below best expresses the essential information in the highlighted sentence in the passage? Incorrect choices change the meaning in important ways or leave out essential information.

(A) Because languages were able to be spread by relocation diffusion, it ~~allowed people to freely move to another place~~ with no difficulty.

(B) Relocation diffusion, which is caused by people moving to different places, makes languages complicated to track.

아래 문장 중 지문 속의 음영된 문장의 핵심 정보를 가장 잘 표현하고 있는 것은 무엇인가? 오답은 문장의 의미를 현저히 왜곡하거나 핵심 정보를 빠뜨리고 있다.

(A) 이전 확산을 통해 언어가 퍼트려질 수 있기 때문에, ~~사람들로 하여금 자유롭게 아무 어려움 없이 다른 곳으로 이동할 수 있게 했다.~~

(B) 사람들이 이동하여 생기는 이전 확산은 언어를 추적하기 복잡하게 한다.

(C) Languages do not simply spread by people remaining stationary ; the process is complicated by relocation diffusion, which is done when people move around.

(D) Human mobility has made the study of language difficult for language was diffused ~~not by fixed population but by relocation diffusion.~~ ★

(C) 언어는 움직이지 않는 사람을 통해 퍼진다 ; 이 과정은 사람들이 움직였을 때 이전 확산을 통해 더 복잡해진다.

(D) 언어가 ~~움직이지 않는 사람들이 아니라 이전확산 때문에~~ 사람이 움직이는 것은 언어 연구에 어려움을 주었다. ★

Highlight 문장을 살펴보자. A complicating factor is that i) with human mobility, ii) languages did not merely diffuse through static populations; iii) they also spread by relocation diffusion. (복잡한 요인은 i)사람의 유동성으로 인해 ii)언어가 정체된 인구를 통해서는 단지 퍼져나가지 않고 iii)이전 확산을 통해서도 또한 퍼져나간다는 것이다) 이 내용을 포함하고 있는 보기는 (C)이므로 (C)가 정답이다. (A)는 인과관계가 반대로 돼있으므로 오답이며, (B)는 움직이지 않는 사람들에 대한 언급이 없으므로 오답이다. 그리고 (D)는 이전 확산으로만 된다는 내용이므로 오답이다.

18 According to paragraph 7, convergence makes the study of language difficult because

(A) it changes a language ~~into two different languages~~.
(B) it allows ~~relocation diffusion~~ to take place. ★
(C) it makes an exception to a rule of relocation diffusion.
(D) it ~~uses the unreliable rules~~ of reconstruction.

7단락에 의하면, _____ 때문에 언어집합은 언어 연구를 어렵게 한다.

(A) 한 언어를 ~~다른 두개의 언어로~~ 만든다.
(B) ~~이전 확산~~을 하게 한다. ★
(C) 이전 확산의 법칙에 예외를 만든다.
(D) 재건의 믿지 못할 만한 법칙을 사용한다.

Fact 키워드인 language convergence 부분을 살펴보면, If people with different languages have consistent spatial interaction, language convergence can take place, collapsing two languages into one. This creates problems for researchers because the rules of reconstruction may not apply or may be unreliable. (만약 다른 언어를 사용하는 사람들이 꾸준한 공간적 상호작용을 한다면 언어 집합이 발생하고 두 언어를 하나로 만들 것이다. 이것은 조사관들에게 문제를 발생시키는데 재건 법칙들이 종종 적용되지 않거나 의지할 수 없기 때문이다) 라고 말한다. 즉, 사람이 움직이면서 언어가 집합하게 되고 그것은 언어 재건에 예외를 만들어서 힘들다는 내용인 (C)가 정답이다. (A)는 분산에 관한 내용이므로 오답이며, (B)는 이전 확산과 관련 없으므로 오답이다. 그리고 (D)는 재건의 법칙이 믿지 못할 만한 것이 아니므로 오답이다.

19 Look at the four squares [■] that indicate where the following sentence could be added to the passage.

What he ended up with was a fascinating body of folklore which he and his brother Wilhelm published as Grimms' Fairy Tales.

Where would the sentence best fit? Click on a square [■] to add the sentence to the passage.   2nd

네 개의 네모[■]는 다음 문장이 삽입될 수 있는 부분을 나타내고 있다.

그가 결국 끝낸 것은 그와 그의 동생 월헴이 그림동화로 출간했던 민간 문학의 흥미진진한 이야기 였다.

이 문장은 어느 자리에 들어가는 것이 가장 적절한가?   두번째

Insertion 삽입 문장의 전 문장에서는 His primary interest was not initially the stories themselves but any exotic vocabulary they happened to use. (그의 주요한 관심사는 초기에는 이야기 자체에 있지 않았고 그들이 우연히 사용한 이색적인 단어에 있었다)라고 말한 후 2번째 네모 다음 문장은 Grimm, however, did get what he wanted word-wise. (그러나 그림은 그가 원했던 단어 속성을 확인했다)이라고 했다. 삽입 문장은 그림형제가 출판을 했다는 내용이다. 그것은 그들의 주된 목적이 아니니 2번째 네모 다음 문장에서 설명하듯 그가 원했던 단어 방면에서 얻어낸 것의 반대의 뜻인 삽입문장이 들어와야 한다. 핵심키워드 즉, 동그라미 쳤어야 할 단어는 "tales" 이다. 삽입문장 주변내용은 크게 그들이 해낸 일이 word 관련(목적)과 tale 관련(방법)이라는 사실인데, 끼워넣을 문장은 tale 관련(방법)이다. 그림형제가 원했던 것은 word 관련(목적)이므로, 방법을(tale 관련) 언급 마친 뒤 word 관련 얘기를 진행시켜야 맞는 순서이므로 두번째 네모에 넣고 tale 관련 언급을 마친 뒤 word 관련 언급(2번째 네모 뒤)으로 넘어가야 한다.

20

Directions: An introductory sentence for a brief summary of the passage is provided below. Complete the summary by selecting the THREE answer choices that express the most important ideas in the passage. Some sentences do not belong in the summary because they express ideas that are not presented in the passage or are minor ideas in the passage. **This question is worth 2 points.**

지시 : 지문 요약을 위한 도입 문장이 아래에 주어져 있다. 지문의 가장 중요한 내용을 나타내는 보기 3개를 골라 요약을 완성하시오. 어떤 문장은 지문에 언급되지 않은 내용이나 사소한 정보를 담고 있으므로 요약에 포함되지 않는다. 이 문제는 2점이다.

> **For hundreds of years, linguists have studied languages and tracked their changes.**
>
> - (A) In order to study the language of the past, scholars use a technique to track sound shifts and hardening of consonants. - Paragraph 2
> - (D) The results from different studies on two linguistic hypotheses had similarities which implied the existence of a common source of language. - Paragraph 3, 4
> - (E) The Proto-Indo-European language has split into many languages through the divergence process but convergence has made it hard to find its hearth. - Paragraph 5, 6, 7

> **수백 년 동안, 언어학자들은 언어를 연구해왔고 그 변화를 추적해왔다.**
>
> - (A) 언어의 과거를 연구하고자, 학자들은 소리 변화와 자음의 된소리화를 추적할 수 있는 기법을 사용하였다.
> - (D) 두 가지의 언어학적 가정에 대한 다른 연구로부터의 결과는 언어의 공통 근원의 존재를 암시하는 유사점을 가졌다.
> - (E) 원조 인도-유럽어는 분산을 통해 여러 언어로 나뉘었지만 집합은 그 시작을 찾기 어렵게 하였다.

(B) Linguists use backward reconstruction ~~to infer new words~~ from previous forms of a language. - 틀린정보

(C) Sir William Jones ~~mastered multiple languages at an early age~~ and also mastered Sanskrit in order to learn the law. - 틀린정보

(F) ~~William Jones~~ and Jacob Grimm focused on ~~fairytales~~ to use the resources to decipher the ancient texts. - 틀린정보

(B) 언어학자들은 이전의 언어 형태로부터 ~~새로운 언어를 추론하기~~ 위해서 역재건을 사용한다.

(C) 윌리엄 존스 경은 ~~여러가지 언어를 어린나이에 마스터했고~~ 법을 배우고자 산스크리트어도 마스터했다.

(F) ~~윌리엄 존스와~~ 제이콥 그림은 ~~동화이야기에~~ 집중하여 고대문서를 해독하는데 쓰려고 하였다.

Summary 지문의 중심 내용은 언어에 관해 연구한 학자들의 공통된 의견과 그것의 어려운 점에 관한 것이었다. (A)는 역재건의 내용과 언어학자들의 노력이 주 내용인 1, 2 단락을 요약했으므로 정답이고, (D)는 두 학자의 연구와 결과가 주 내용인 3, 4 단락을 요약했으므로 정답, (E)는 공통된 의견과 그것이 가지고 있는 어려운 점이 주 내용인 5, 6, 7단락을 요약해서 정답이다. (B)는 (A)에 비해 가지고 있는 내용이 적어서 오답이며, (C)는 지문에는 언급되었으나 관련된 내용이 아니므로 오답이다. 그리고 (F)는 지문에 언급되지 않은 내용을 넣어서 오답이다.

참고 이미지

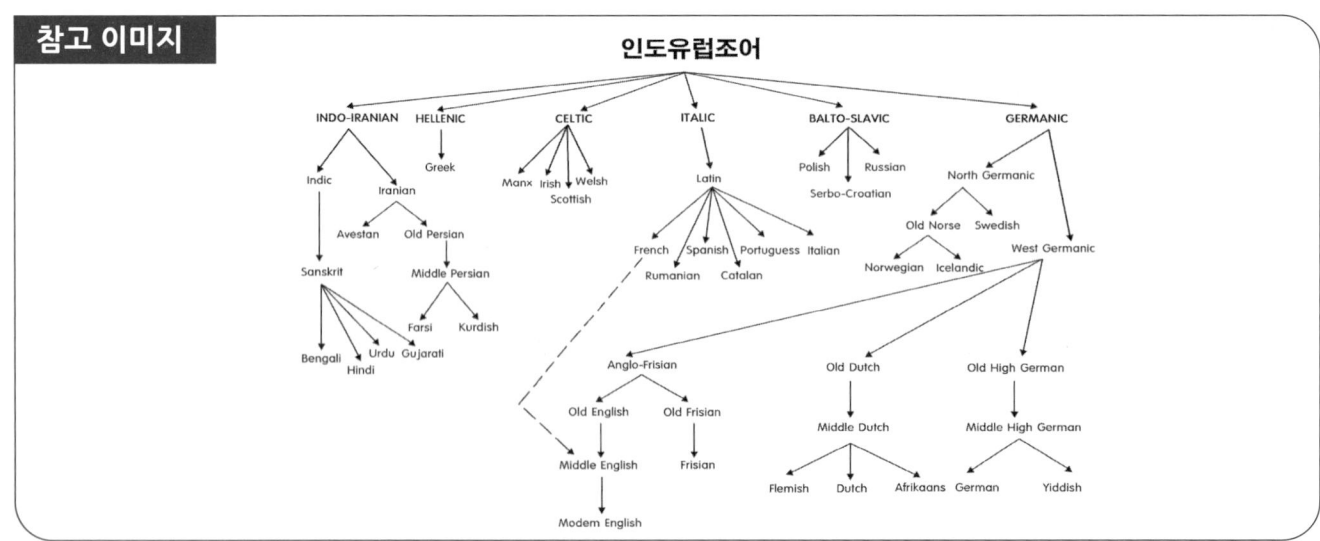

usherin.usher.co.kr

USHER

iBT TOEFL
FINAL TEST READING
TEST 2

답안 및 취약 유형 분석표
해석·해설

답안 및 문제 유형 분석표

TEST 2-1

01 (C) Fact

02 (A) Fact

03 (D) Purpose

04 (B) Vocabulary

05 (A) Inference

06 (C) Highlight

07 (C) Fact

08 (A) Reference

09 4th ■ Insertion

10 (A), (C), (D) Summary

TEST 2-2

11 (A) Inference

12 (B) Highlight

13 (B) Fact

14 (C) Purpose

15 (B) Fact

16 (C) Reference

17 (D) Fact

18 (A) Vocabulary

19 1st ■ Insertion

20 (A), (D), (E) Summary

각 문제 유형별 맞춘 개수를 아래에 적어 보세요.

유형	맞춘 답의 개수	정답률	
단어 (Vocabulary)	/ 2	정답률:	%
사실 확인 문제 (Fact)	/ 6	정답률:	%
지시어 찾기 (Reference)	/ 2	정답률:	%
끼워 넣기 (Insertion)	/ 2	정답률:	%
문장 변환문제 (Highlight)	/ 2	정답률:	%
목적 (Purpose)	/ 2	정답률:	%
추론 (Inference)	/ 2	정답률:	%
단락 요약 (Summary / Category Chart)	/ 2	정답률:	%
전체	/ 20	정답률:	%

※ 자신이 취약한 유형은 READING STRATEGIES를 통해 다시 한번 점검하시기 바랍니다. (p.31)

TEST 2-1　Earth's Atmosphere　지구의 대기층

Introduction	단락 1	지구 대기층과 우주 구성물의 다른점
Point 1	단락 2	지구 대기와 다른 행성의 대기 비교
Point 2	단락 3	지구 대기층에 질소량이 많아진 이유
Point 3	단락 4	가이아 이론
Point 4	단락 5	Planetary Atmosphere Tectonic Machine 이론

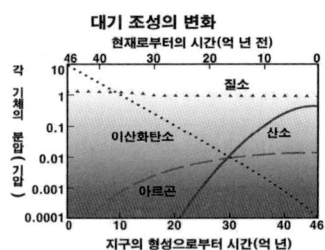

단락 정리	지문	해석
단락 1 지구 대기층과 우주 구성물의 다른점	**1**　[Q21]The Earth's atmosphere **consists** mainly **of** heavy gases like nitrogen, but lacks light gases such as hydrogen and helium. This is odd, because nitrogen **is known to be the seventh most abundant** element in the universe, whereas hydrogen is the most common, which **begs the question** of why hydrogen is **no longer** abundant in Earth's atmosphere. Earth, currently the only planet known to support life, has an atmosphere **distinguishable from** others in the solar system, due to being **composed of** byproducts of life, such as oxygen. This distinction can be seen in the changes observed through studies done by **a series of** scientists, which have ultimately **classified** Earth's atmosphere **into** three stages of evolution: primordial atmosphere, secondary atmosphere, and the addition of oxygen.	[Q21]지구의 대기는 질소 같은 무거운 기체로 주로 구성되어 있지만 수소나 헬륨과 같은 가벼운 기체는 없다. 이것은 특이한 일인데, 수소가 가장 흔한 물질 이라고 알려진 반면에 질소가 7번째로 가장 풍부한 요소로 알려져 있기 때문인데, 이 사실은 왜 수소가 지구 대기에서 더 이상 풍부하지 않는지에 대한 질문을 야기한다. 생명체를 유지하는 유일한 행성으로 알려진 지구는 산소와 같은 생명체의 부산물로 구성된 성질 때문에 태양계에서 다른 행성과는 구별되는 대기를 가진다. 이 차이는 일련의 과학자들에 의해서 행해진 연구를 통하여 관찰된 변화들에서 확인될 수 있으며, 이 사실은 지구 대기를 궁극적으로 3개의 진화 단계로 분류한다: 원시대기, 부대기, 그리고 산소 추가의 대기이다.
단락 2 지구 대기와 다른 행성의 대기 비교	**2**　Initially, light gases were abundant in Earth's primordial atmosphere, but gradually **started to decline**. This can be explained through 'Jeans escape', a classical form of thermal escape **based on** Maxwell's Distribution that prescribes that the kinetic energy distribution of molecules is **dependent on** the mass and velocity of the molecule. ⓒFrom this, one can conclude that **the bigger** the molecule, **the lower** its average velocity **at a** given **temperature**, which makes escape more unlikely. Furthermore, **the greater** the mass of the planet, **the higher** the required escape velocity; which ultimately **results in** less escaping molecules. Thus, giant planets with high gravity possess higher concentrations of light gases such as hydrogen and helium, which are **rare in** the inner	초기에, 가벼운 기체는 지구의 원시대기에서 풍부했다. 하지만 점점 사라지기 시작했다. 이것은 분자의 운동에너지 분포가 분자의 질량과 속도에 의존한다라고 규정하는 맥스웰의 분포에 기초하는 열 방출의 고전 형태인 'Jeans escape'를 통해 설명할 수 있다. ⓒ이것으로부터, 분자가 더 크면 클수록 주어진 온도에서 평균속도가 더 낮아지고, 이것은 탈출의 실행을 더 어렵게 만든다는 것을 결론 지을 수 있다. 게다가, 행성의 질량이 크면 클수록 요구되는 방출 속도가 더 높게 되며, 그것은 결과적으로 더 적은 분자의 방출을 야기한다. 그리하여, 높은 중력을 가지는 거대 행성들에서는 지구형 행성의 대기에는 드물게 있는 수소나 헬륨과 같은 가벼운 기체들의 농도가 높다. [■] 별로부터의 거리는 또한

Vocabulary

1단락
consist of : phr. ~로 이루어지다
classify A into B : phr. A를 B로 분류하다.
due to : phr. ~때문에
be abundant in : phr. ~이 풍부하다
byproduct [báiprádəkt] n. 부산물
a series of : phr. 일련의

2단락
thermal [θə́ːrməl] a. 열의
prescribe [priskráib] v. 규정하다
velocity [vilásəti] n. 속도
result in : phr. ~한 결과를 초래하다.
base A on B : phr. A를 B에 기초시키다
be dependent on : phr. ~에게 의지하다
gravity [grǽvəti] n. 중력
distribution [dìstrəbjúːʃən] n. 분배
molecule [máləkjùːl] n. 분자
lead to : phr. 이끌다, 초래하다

planet's atmospheres. [■] The distance from the star also affects. molecular velocity; **the closer** the planet, **the hotter** the atmosphere becomes, **leading to** higher molecular velocity and higher escape rates. [■] This is how Saturn's relatively small moon, [Q22]Titan, keeps its atmosphere. [■] Even though its gravitational pull is lower than **that of** Earth, its cooler temperature **allows it to hold on to** its atmosphere. [■] Neptune's moon, Triton, **being attached to** the farthest planet from the sun, is also, **in this way**, **able to retain** a non-negligible nitrogenous atmosphere due to the extreme temperatures **at the edge of** the solar system.

단락 3
지구 대기층에 질소량이 많아진 이유

3   [Q23]Scientists believe that as light gases **escaped from Earth's** atmosphere, nitrogen **began constituting** a larger part of it after volcanic eruptions spewed gases, ultimately forming the main component of the secondary atmosphere. Three primary reasons why only nitrogen filled the environment are that it is volatile even **at low temperatures**, **unreactive with** the materials that make up the earth's crust, and very stable **in the presence of** solar radiation. **In contrast to** more abundant elements which are major components of Earth's crust, [Q25]nitrogen is not stable as a part of a crystal lattice, and will not **bond with** the others to form the terrestrial earth; it, instead, remains a gas. Unlike nitrogen, other elements are unstable and easily **react with** each other in the atmosphere **as well as** break down when **exposed to** solar radiation. Thus, **over time**, nitrogen built up in the atmosphere **to a** much greater **extent** than other elements.

단락 4
가이아 이론

4   One theory introducing the presence of atmospheric oxygen is the Gaia theory. It is believed by scientists i) that the primordial atmosphere of Earth did not contain oxygen and ii) that the appearance of this gas required the evolution of photosynthetic life forms, such as early cyanobacteria and later single-celled algae, which emerged as the earth cooled and the gaseous water condensed and formed oceans. **As a result of** photosynthesis, molecular oxygen built up **to** the present **level**, which **appears to** have been relatively stable for several billion years. If this level were even slightly higher, then the earth's biomass would be combustible, leading to extensive explosions and forest fires, severely damaging earth's ecosystem. [Q27]⊙The Gaia theory, thus, suggests that there is a planetary, homeostatic **control over** the oxygen concentration in the atmosphere that balances the **ratio of** organisms producing oxygen **to those** consuming it.

Vocabulary

3단락
- spew [spju:] v. 토하다, 분출하다
- stable [stèibl] a. 안정된
- make up : phr. 이루다. 형성하다.
- lattice [lǽtis] a. 격자모양의
- react with : phr. ~과 반응하다
- in contrast to : phr. ~와 대조적으로
- volatile [válətil / vólətàil] a. 휘발성의
- terrestrial [təréstriəl] a. 지구의, 육생의

4단락
- primordial [praimɔ́ːrdiəl] a. 근원의, 원시의
- combustible [kəmbʌ́stəbəl] a. 타기쉬운, 연소성의
- homeostatic [houmastatic] a. 항상성의
- algae [ǽldgi] n. 해조, 조류
- biomass [báioumæs] n. 생물자원
- condense [kəndéns] v. 응축하다. 농축하다
- convert A into B : phr. A를 B로 전환시키다

USHER

단락 5

Planetary Atmosphere Tectonic Machine 이론

5 However, some argue that the amount of oxygen collected in the Earth's atmosphere cannot be accounted for entirely by cyanobacteria. They believe that the theory is not adequate because it can only **account for** 1 percent to 10 percent concentration levels, while today's atmosphere contains 21 percent. Thus, a second theory called the planetary atmosphere tectonic machine theory was developed. The theory posits that all of earth's oxygen came from not life forms, but the ocean, near the tectonic plates where magma is released and water **comes into contact with** temperatures over 2000 °C. The super-heated water is then **converted into** hydrogen and oxygen. The oxygen bubbles then oxygenate the ocean, and **are released into** the atmosphere when they reach the surface. This oxygen in the atmosphere **is** then **shielded from** being fully **lost to** space by the ozone and the earth's magnetic field.

그러나 일부는 지구 대기에 모아진 산소의 양이 전적으로 시아노박테리아만으로는 생산되었다고는 설명되어 질 수 없다고 주장했다. 그들은 이론이 적합하지 않다고 믿었는데 오늘날의 대기가 21%의 산소를 가지고 있는 반면에 시아노박테리아에 의해 생산된 것은 단지 1%에서 10%까지만 설명할 수 있기 때문이다. 그리하여 Planetary Atmosphere Tectonic Machine 이론이 생겨났다. 그 이론은 지구의 모든 산소는 생명체 형태로부터 온 것이 아니며 마그마가 분출되고 물이 섭씨 2,000도가 넘는 온도와 접촉하는 지각판 근처의 바다로부터 생겨난다고 가정했다. 과열된 물은 그 후 수소와 산소로 변환 된다. 산소 거품이 수면에 도달할 때 바다에 산소를 공급하고 대기로 분출된다. 대기에서의 지구의 이 산소는 오존과 지구의 자기장에 의해 우주로 손실되는 것으로부터 보호된다.

Sentence analysis

◎ From this, / one can conclude that / the bigger the molecule, / the lower its average velocity at a given temperature, /
이것으로부터 우리는 결론 지을 수 있다.   분자가 더 크면 클수록   주어진 온도에서 평균 속도는 더 낮게 된다

which makes escape more unlikely.
이것은 탈출을 더욱 더 일어나지 못하게 만든다

◎ The Gaia theory, thus, suggest that / there is a planetary, homeostatic control over the oxygen concentration in the atmosphere /
가이아 이론은, 그리하여, 나타낸다   대기에서 산소 농도에 대한 행성 항상성 통제가 있다

that balances the ratio of organisms producing oxygen to those consuming it.
그것은 산소를 소비하는 유기체에 대한 산소를 만들어 내는 유기체의 비율의 균형을 맞춘다

Vocabulary

5단락   account for : phr. 설명하다   tectonic [tektˈʌnik] a. 지질 구조의   shield A from B : phr. B로부터 A를 보호하다
oxygenate [ˈɑksidʒəneit / ˈɔks-] v. 산소화 하다.

01

According to paragraph 1, which of the following is true about Earth?

(A) It ~~currently has three different atmospheres~~: the primordial atmosphere, secondary atmosphere and the addition of oxygen. ★
(B) Nitrogen is most dominant in its atmosphere due to ~~it being a byproduct of life~~.
(C) The ratio of the components in its atmosphere is different from that of the universe.
(D) Nitrogen is ~~the seventh most abundant element on Earth~~.

1단락에 따르면, 지구에 대해 사실인 것은?

(A) 이것은 현재 세 개의 다른 대기층을 가진다: 원시 대기층, 두 번째 대기층, 산소층. ★
(B) ~~질소는 생명체의 부산물이기~~ 때문에 대기층에서 가장 우세하다.
(C) 지구의 대기층에서 구성요소의 비율은 우주의 것과 다르다.
(D) 질소는 지구에서 일곱 번째로 가장 흔한 원소이다.

Fact 문제의 키워드인 difference between Earth and other planets를 설명하는 부분을 살펴보면 The Earth's atmosphere consists mainly of heavy gases like nitrogen, but lacks light gases such as hydrogen and helium. This is odd, because nitrogen is known to be the seventh most abundant element in the universe, whereas hydrogen is the most common. (지구의 대기는 질소 같은 무거운 기체로 주로 구성되어 있지만 수소나 헬륨과 같은 가벼운 기체는 없다. 이것은 특이한 일인데, 수소가 가장 흔한 물질이라고 알려진 반면에 질소가 7번째로 가장 풍부한 요소로 알려져 있기 때문이다)와 Earth, currently the only planet known to support life, has an atmosphere distinguishable from others in the solar system, due to being composed of byproducts of life, such as oxygen. (생명체를 유지하는 유일한 행성으로 알려진 지구는 산소와 같은 생명체의 부산물로 구성된 성질 때문에 태양계에서 다른 행성과는 구별되는 대기를 가진다)라는 내용으로 구성되어있다. 즉, 산소를 포함하는 특이한 지구의 대기층과 다른 구성요소의 비율이 다른 행성과 다르다고 설명하는 (C)가 정답이다. (A)가 틀린 이유는 현재 대기는 세 종류로 나뉘어 있는 것이 아니기 때문이다.

02

What is the significance of Titan mentioned in paragraph 2?

(A) It exemplifies how the distance from the Sun affects the atmosphere of an object despite the effects of its gravity.
(B) It is a relatively small moon that is ~~an example of an object that is far from the Sun~~. ★
(C) It is far away from the Sun and ~~hence sustains a ring structure~~ through low temperatures.
(D) It shows that ~~Jeans escape may not be enough to preserve its atmosphere~~.

2단락에서 언급된 Titan의 의미는 무엇인가?

(A) 태양으로부터의 거리가 중력과 상관없이 어떻게 대기층에 영향을 미치는지 예증화 한다.
(B) 태양으로부터 멀리 떨어진 물체의 예시이며 상대적으로 작은 달이다. ★
(C) 태양으로부터 멀리 떨어져 있고 크기서 낮은 온도에서도 링 구조를 유지한다.
(D) 'Jeans escape'가 그 대기를 유지하기에는 불충분하다는 것을 보여준다.

Fact 문제의 키워드인 Titan이 언급된 부분을 살펴보면 Even though its gravitational pull is lower than that of Earth, its cooler temperature allows it to hold on to its atmosphere. (심지어 그 중력이 지구보다 더 낮을지라도, 그것의 더 낮은 온도가 그 대기를 유지할 수 있게 해준다)라고 말한다. 즉, 토성에서부터 태양의 거리가 멀어 온도가 낮음으로써 중력과 관계없이 대기층에 영향을 준다는 내용인 (A)가 정답이 된다. (B)가 틀린이유는 크기와 거리에 대한 내용은 나왔으나 그것이 어떻게 어디에 영향을 준다는 내용이 없어서이다.

03

In paragraph 3, why does the author mention that light gases are not found in Earth's atmosphere?

(A) ~~To emphasize the fact that the gases escaped~~ from the Earth's atmosphere
(B) To point out that hydrogen is the most common element in the universe, but ~~is no longer common in the Earth's atmosphere~~ ★
(C) To support the idea that light gases ~~once existed~~ as a component of the Earth's atmosphere
(D) To point out one of the reasons nitrogen became dominant in the atmosphere

3단락에서, 왜 글쓴이는 가벼운 기체가 지구의 대기층에서 뚜렷하게 보이지 않는다는 것을 언급하는가?

(A) 기체가 지구의 대기층으로부터 ~~방출되었다는~~ 사실을 강조하려고
(B) 수소가 우주에서 가장 흔한 성분이지만, ~~더 이상 지구의 대기층에서는 흔하지 않다는~~ 것을 지적하려고 ★
(C) 가벼운 기체가 지구의 대기층의 성분으로서 ~~존재했었다는~~ 의견을 뒷받침하려고
(D) 질소가 대기층에서 더욱 많아지는 이유를 가리키기 위해

Purpose 문제의 키워드인 hydrogen과 why not apparent in the atmosphere of the Earth가 언급된 부분을 살펴보면 Scientists believe that as light gases escaped from Earth's atmosphere, nitrogen began constituting a larger part of it after volcanic eruptions spewed gases, ultimately forming the main component of the secondary atmosphere. (과학자들은 지구 대기로부터 가벼운 기체들이 탈출하면서, 화산 분출이 기체를 내뿜으면서 질소가 지구 대기의 대부분을 형성하며, 궁극적으로 부대기의 주요 성분을 형성했다고 믿었다)라고 말한다. 즉, 수소량이 줄어들면서 질소량이 늘어날 수 있는 자리를 만들어 줬다는 내용인 (D)가 정답이 된다. 다른 문항들이 틀린 이유는 수소량이 줄어들었다는 내용은 모두 있지만 그것이 무엇을 야기했는지에 대한 내용이 없어서이다.

---

04 The word volatile in the passage is closest in meaning to

(A) flammable ★
(B) evaporable
(C) mixable
(D) condensable

지문의 단어 volatile의 의미와 가장 유사한 것은?

(A) 가연성의 ★ [flǽməbl]
(B) 증발성의 [ivǽpərəbl]
(C) 혼합할 수 있는 [míksəbl]
(D) 응축할 수 있는 [kəndénsəbl]

Vocabulary 지문의 volatile(증발하는)의 동의어는 evaporable(증발성의)로 정답은 (B)이다.

---

05 According to paragraph 3, what can be inferred about nitrogen?

(A) Nitrogen is stable and does not react with other elements easily.
(B) Nitrogen becomes stable as a part of a crystal lattice and doesn't bond with other elements.
(C) Nitrogen is the most common element in the Earth's crust. ★
(D) Nitrogen was originally frozen, but filled the atmosphere after volcanic eruptions caused temperatures to rise.

3단락에 따르면, 질소에 대해 추론할 수 있는 것은 무엇인가?

(A) 질소는 안정적이며 다른 성분과 쉽게 반응하지 않는다.
(B) 질소는 결정격자의 부분으로서 안정적어 되며 다른 성분들과 결합하지 않는다.
(C) 질소는 지구의 지각에서 가장 흔한 성분이다. ★
(D) 질소는 원래 얼려져 있었지만 화산 분출이 온도를 상승시킨 후 대기를 채웠다.

Inference 문제의 키워드인 nitrogen이 언급된 부분을 찾아보면 Unlike nitrogen, other elements are unstable and easily react with each other in the atmosphere as well as break down when exposed to solar radiation. (질소와는 달리 다른 요소들은 불안정하며 방사성에 노출 될 때 붕괴되는 것뿐만 아니라 대기에서 다른 물질들과 쉽게 반응한다)라고 말한다. 즉, 산소와 대조하며 산소가 매우 불안정하고 다른 요소와 쉽게 반응한다는 점을 보여준 (A)가 정답이 된다. (C)가 틀린 이유는 질소가 지구 대기에서 가장 흔한 원소이지 지구의 지각에서 가장 흔한 원소는 아니기 때문에 오답이다.

---

06 Which of the sentences below best expresses the essential information in the highlighted sentence in the passage? Incorrect choices change the meaning in important ways or leave out essential information.

(A) Due to the appearance of photosynthetic life forms, the primordial atmosphere did not contain any oxygen.
(B) Photosynthesis, a crucial process which bacteria and plants use to produce energy from sunlight and water, is the main reason oxygen was not present in the primordial atmosphere. ★
(C) Scientists think that without photosynthetic life forms such as cyanobacteria and algae, the primitive atmosphere could not have acquired oxygen.
(D) Oxygen gas was one of the important compounds which algae and bacteria used to thrive in primordial atmosphere.

아래의 문장 중 지문 속의 음영 표시된 문장의 핵심 정보를 가장 잘 표현하고 있는 것은 무엇인가? 오답은 문장의 의미를 현저히 바꾸거나 핵심정인 정보를 빠뜨리고 있다.

(A) 광합성하는 생명체의 등장 때문에, 원시 대기는 어떤 산소도 포함하지 않았다.
(B) 박테리아와 식물들이 태양과 물로부터 에너지를 생산하는 중대한 과정인 광합성은 산소가 원시 태커에서 존재 하지 않는 중요한 이유이다. ★
(C) 과학자들은 시아노 박테리아와 해조류 같은 광합성하는 생명체없이 원시 대기는 산소를 가지지 못했을 것이라고 믿는다.
(D) 산소는 해조류와 박테라아카 원시 대기에서 번창할 수 있었던 중요한 화합물 중에 하나이다.

Highlight 음영문구를 보면 It is believed by scientists i) that the primordial atmosphere of Earth did not contain oxygen and ii) that the appearance of this gas required the evolution of photosynthetic life forms, such as early cyanobacteria and later single-celled algae. (과학자들은 i) 지구의 원시대기가 산소를 포함하지 않고 ii) 이 기체의 존재는 지구가 식고 기체성 물이 응축되고 바다를 형성하면서 나타난 사이노 박테리아나 이후의 단세포 해조류와 같은 광합성을 하는 생명체의 진화를 필요로 한다고 믿었다) 같이 두 내용으로 나뉘어 진다. 이 두 가지 내용을 모 두 포함하고 인과관계가 정확한 (C)가 정답이 된다. (B)가 틀린 이유는 비슷하게 생긴 단어를 이용해가며 그럴듯한 문장을 만들었지만 음영문구의 핵심적인 내용이 모두 빠져있다.

---

07 According to paragraph 4, which of the following is true according to the Gaia theory?

(A) The oxygen levels of Earth have ~~gone through several fluctuations~~ over the past billions of years.
(B) If ~~nitrogen concentrations in the atmosphere~~ were higher, the earth's biomass would be combustible.
(C) A balance between oxygen producers and consumers controls the amount of atmospheric oxygen.
(D) ~~It explains the evolution of photosynthetic life forms~~ such as cyanobacteria and single-celled algae. ★

4단락에 따르면, 다음 중 가이아 이론에 관해 사실인 것은?

(A) 지구의 산소 레벨은 지난 수십 억년 동안 ~~수많은 변동을 겪었다.~~
(B) ~~만약 대기의 질소 농도가~~ 더 높다면, 지구의 생물량은 가연성이 될 것이다.
(C) 산소 생산자와 소비자 사이에 균형이 대기의 산소의 양을 통제한다.
(D) ~~이론은 시아노 박테리아와 단세포 해조류와 같은 광합성 생물 형태의 진화를~~ 설명한다. ★

Fact 문제의 키워드인 가이아 이론이 언급된 부분을 보면 The Gaia theory, thus, suggest that there is a planetary, homeostatic control over the oxygen concentration in the atmosphere that balances the ratio of organisms producing oxygen to those consuming it. (그래서 가이아 이론은 대기 내의 산소 농축에 대한 행성의 항상성 통제가 존재하고 그것이 산소를 소비하는 유기체에 대한 산소를 생산하는 유기체의 균형해 맞추게 된다고 설명했다)라고 말한다. 즉, 산소의 양에 대한 통제 능력을 가지고 있다는 것을 의미함으로 정답은 (C)이다. (D)가 정답이 되지않는 이유는 생물 상태의 진화 자체를 설명하고 있지는 않기 때문이다.

---

08 The word **it** in paragraph 5 refers to

(A) theory
(B) atmosphere
(C) oxygen ★
(D) earth

5단락에서 **it** 이 언급하는 것은?

(A) 이론
(B) 대기
(C) 산소 ★
(D) 지구

Reference 1~10%를 차지하는 이유 설명만 가능한 건 산소가 아닌 이론이기 때문에 (A)가 되어야 한다.

---

09 Look at the four squares [■] that indicate where the following sentence could be added to the passage.

Neptune's moon, Triton, being attached to the farthest planet from the sun, is (also), (in this way), able to retain a non-negligible nitrogenous atmosphere due to the extreme temperatures at the edge of the solar system.

Where would the sentence best fit? Click on a square [■] to add the sentence to the passage.   4th

네 개의 네모[■]는 다음 문장이 삽입될 수 있는 부분을 나타내고 있다.

태양으로부터 가장 멀리 위치하고 있는 해왕성의 달인 트리톤은 또한 이러한 방식으로 태양계 가장 자리에서 지나친 온도 때문에 무시할 수 없는 양의 질소 대기층을 보존할 수 있다.

이 문장은 어느자리에 들어가는 것이 가장 적절한가?   네 번째

Insertion 핵심키워드는 in this way이다. 이러한 방법이란, 거리가 태양으로부터 멀어서 대기를 가질 수 있는 것을 말하는 것이다. 이는 4번째 네모 전에 위치한 토성의 타이탄의 예와 일치함으로써 답은 네번째 네모이다.

10

Directions: An introductory sentence for a brief summary of the passage is provided below. Complete the summary by selecting the THREE answer choices that express the most important ideas in the passage. Some sentences do not belong in the summary because they express ideas that are not presented in the passage or are minor ideas in the passage. **This question is worth 2 points.**

지시 : 지문 요약을 위한 도입 문장이 아래에 주어져 있다. 지문의 가장 중요한 내용을 나타내는 보기 3개를 골라 요약을 완성하시오. 어떤 문장은 지문에 언급되지 않은 내용이나 사소한 정보를 담고 있으므로 요약에 포함되지 않는다. **이 문제는 2점이다.**

The atmosphere of earth has gone through many different phases.

- (A) Nitrogen was spread through Earth's atmosphere without reacting with other compounds to form compounds, but remained a gas. - Paragraph 3

- (C) Light gases were able to escape from the Earth's atmosphere because its molecular velocity was fast enough to overcome the pull of the Earth's gravity. - Paragraph 2

- (D) A theory explains that under the ocean, at the location of the tectonic plates, tremendously hot magma boils water and releases its oxygen. - Paragraph 5

지구의 대기층은 다양한 현상을 겪어왔다.

- (A) 질소는 화합물을 만들기 위해 다른 화합물들과 결합 없이도 지구의 대기층에 퍼져있지만, 가스로 남는다.

- (C) 가벼운 가스는 그 분자 속도가 지구 중력의 끌어당기 는 힘을 이겨낼 만큼 충분히 빠르기 때문에 지구 대기 부터 탈출할 수 있다.

- (D) 판이 위치하고 있는 바다 아래에서 엄청나게 뜨거운 마그마가 물을 뜨겁게 만들고 물속의 산소를 방출시켰다.

(B) Even though its gravitational force is lower than that of Earth, Titan keeps its atmosphere. - Paragraph 2 detail
(E) According to the Gaia Theory, the appearance of photosynthetic life forms started to ~~consume~~ molecular oxygen in the primordial atmosphere. - 틀린정보
(F) The availability of atmospheric oxygen is ~~a critically important environmental factor~~ for most of Earth's species and for many ecological processes. - 상식

(B) 비록 타이탄의 중력이 지구의 중력보다 작지만, 타이탄은 자신의 대기층을 유지한다.
(E) 가이아 이론에 따르면, 광합성 생물의 출현은 원시대기에서 산소분자를 ~~소비하기~~ 위해 시작되었다.
(F) 대기층 산소의 이용가능성은 대부분의 지구에 ~~중요한 환경적 과정이다.~~

Summary (A)는 질소가 대기층에 널리 퍼져있지만 다른 것들과 섞이지 않는다는 내용인 3단락을 요약한 것이고, (C)는 2단락의 중심내용인 수소가 지구 대기층을 빠져 나갈 수 있었던 이유들을 설명한 것이며 (D)는 4단락에서 다루어지는 산소는 이것이 지구에 어떻게 생기게 되었는지의 대한 이론을 중심내용을 요약한 것이다.

usherin.usher.co.kr

TEST 2-2　The Effects of Light on Flowering 개화에 빛이 미치는 영향

Introduction 단락 1	식물의 성장에서 빛의 중요성
Point 1 단락 2	개화가능성을 높이기 위한 식물의 적응
Point 2 단락 3	낮의 길이에 대한 반응에 따른 식물의 3가지 분류
Point 3 단락 4	식물들이 낮시간과 밤시간을 구별하는 방법
Point 4 단락 5	어두움의 길이에 따른 다른 반응
Point 5 단락 6	신호를 통한 개화

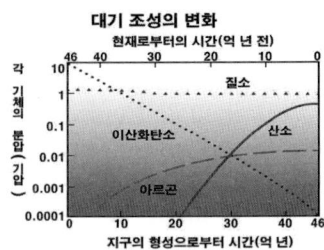

단락 1 — 식물의 성장에서 빛의 중요성

1 °Plant growth and development are controlled by interactions between environmental factors and inner developmental processes. **Amongst** the diverse environmental factors, light **plays** the most essential **role**, affecting plants **in** various **ways**, from their growth and **ability to produce** energy **to** their bloom time. For example, **in the absence of** sufficient light, plants exhibit a unique growth pattern called etiolation. [Q1] These plants will produce thinner and longer stems with longer internodes to reach a faint light source or to find one, in a much more rapid way than those exposed to adequate sunlight. A plant **suffering from** etiolation will also produce fewer leaves.

°식물의 성장과 발달은 환경 요인과 내적 발달 과정간의 상호작용에 지배 받는다. 다양한 환경요인 중 빛은 가장 중요한 역할을 하는데, 성장과 에너지를 생성하는 능력에서부터 개화 시기까지 다양한 방법으로 식물에 영향을 끼친다. 예를 들어, 충분한 빛이 없을 때, 식물은 황화라고 불리는 독특한 성장패턴을 보인다. [Q1]이 식물들은 희미한 빛 자원에 도달하거나 이를 찾기 위해 적절한 햇빛에 노출된 식물들보다 훨씬 빠른 방법으로 더 긴 절간과 함께 더 가늘고 긴 줄기를 만들어 낼 것이다. 황화현상을 겪는 식물은 또한 더 적은 잎을 생산할 것이다.

단락 2 — 개화가능성을 높이기 위한 식물의 적응

2 Perhaps the most interesting influence light has on plants is on their flowering patterns. °The blossoming of flowers in plants is an intricate and delicate process which has evolved to suit plants' different environments. To maximize the probability of their seeds being successfully dispersed, plants **use** environmental factors **to determine** the current season. Some of these factors, like temperature and water availability, can fluctuate heavily. An unusually cool summer or unexpected rain outside the monsoon seasons would confuse the plants. Fortunately, plants can also **use** the length of day **as** a cue. Length of day is perhaps the most reliable indicator of the season because it is controlled by the angle of Earth's rotation, which is unaltered by terrestrial events. Longer days always indicate springtime and the coming of summer while shorter days are only possible during autumn and winter.

빛이 식물들에 대해 갖는 가장 흥미로운 영향은 아마 개화 패턴에 대한 것일 것이다. °꽃의 개화는 식물의 다른 환경에 적응하기 위해 진화되어온 복잡하고 섬세한 과정이다. 씨앗이 성공적으로 퍼뜨려지는 가능성을 극대화하기 위해, 식물은 현재 계절을 확인하는데 환경요인을 사용한다. 온도나 물 이용 가능성과 같은 몇몇 요인들은 격하게 변할 수 있다. 드물게 시원한 여름이나 장마 기간 외 예기치 못한 비는 식물을 혼동시킬 수 있다. 다행히도 식물들은 낮의 길이 또한 단서로 이용할 수 있다. 낮의 길이는 아마 가장 신빙성 있는 계절 지표일 것이다. 왜냐하면 낮의 길이는 지구의 공전 각에 의해 결정되기 때문인데 이는 지구의 사건들에 의해 변동되지 않는다. 긴 낮은 항상 봄과 여름의 도래를 나타내는 반면, 짧은 낮은 오직 가을이나 겨울에만 가능하다.

Vocabulary

1단락
- amongst [əmʌ́ŋst] prep. 중에, 사이에
- stem [stem] n. 줄기
- bloom [blu:m] n. 개화 / v. 꽃이 피다
- internode [íntərnòud] n. 절간
- etiolation [íːtiəlèition] n. 황화
- faint [feint] a. 희미한 / v. 기절하다

2단락
- blossom [blásəm] n. 꽃 / v. 꽃이 피다
- fluctuate [flʌ́ktʃuèit] v. 변동하다
- alter [ɔ́ltər] v. 바꾸다, 교체하다
- intricate [íntrəkit] a. 복잡한, 미묘한
- monsoon [mansúːn] n. 계절풍, 우기
- terrestrial [tərɛ́striəl] a. 지구의, 육생의
- disperse [dispə́ːrs] v. 퍼뜨리다, 전파시키다
- cue [kju:] n. 단서, 신호

단락 3 밤의 길이에 대한 반응에 따른 식물의 3가지 분류	3 **Depending on** their reaction to the length of the day, species of plants are traditionally categorized into three groups: the long-day, the short-day and day-neutral plants. A day-neutral plant produces flowers **as soon as** it has sufficiently grown and developed, [Q3-C] **regardless of** the length of the day. The traditional names of long-day and short-day plants are, however, better **described as** short-night and long-night plants since [Q3-AB]it is the duration of continuous darkness **rather than** the day length which controls flowering. Long-night plants produce flowers during times when there is more than a specified duration of continuous darkness. Conversely, short-night plants **require** periods of darkness **to be** less than a specified period. The threshold for the length of darkness of both long-night and short-night plants differ by species. The duration of this **is called** the critical photoperiod. For example, spinach, [Q3-D]a short-night plant, only produces flowers when **exposed to** less-than-eleven-hour intervals of darkness. Spinach's critical photoperiod is, therefore, eleven hours.	낮의 길이에 대한 반응에 따라 식물 종은 일반적으로 세 가지 그룹으로 분류된다: 장일성, 단일성, 중일성 식물. 중일성 식물은 [Q3-C]낮의 길이와 상관없이 충분히 자라고 성장하면 꽃을 피운다. 하지만, 일반적 장일성, 단일성 식물의 일반적 이름은 단야와 장야 식물로 더 잘 설명된다. 왜냐하면 [Q3-AB]개화를 결정하는 것은 낮의 길이라기 보다는 지속적인 어둠의 길이이기 때문이다. 장야 식물은 특정 길이의 지속적인 어둠이 있을 때 꽃을 만들어낸다. 반대로 단야 식물은 정해진 기간보다 적은 기간의 어둠을 필요로 한다. 장야 식물과 단야 식물 어둠 길이의 기준점은 종마다 다르다. 이것의 기간은 임계광주기라고 불린다. 예를 들어, [Q3-D]단야식물인 시금치는 11시간미만의 어둠에 노출 될 때에만 꽃을 피운다. 시금치의 임계광주기는 따라서 11시간이다.
단락 4 식물들이 낮시간과 밤시간을 구별하는 방법	4 **Compared to** their flowering behavior, the actual method **used** by plants **to distinguish** daytime from nighttime is not well understood. **So far**, botanists have discovered that plants utilize an internal clock and a light-detecting pigment **called** phytochrome **in order to** measure the length of uninterrupted darkness. The internal biological clock **is used to measure** the length of time the plant has spent without light. It **works as** a timer that starts ticking when the light goes out, and resets when it returns. This clock is found in almost all organisms, including humans, yet is poorly understood. There is, however, a better grasp of the phytochrome. Phytochrome is a pigment found in plants which has the **ability to detect** light and **bring about** cellular change when it is present. [Q5]One such cellular change is the resetting of the internal clock that measures the length of continuous darkness.	이들의 개화 활동에 비해 식물들이 실제 낮과 밤을 구별하는 데 이용하는 방법은 잘 이해되지 못한다. 지금까지 식물학자들은 연속적인 어둠 길이를 측정 하기 위해 식물들이 내부 시계와 피토크롬이라는 빛 감지 색소를 이용한다는 것을 발견했다. 내부의 생물 학적 시계는 식물이 빛 없이 보낸 시간을 측정하는 데 쓰인다. 이것은 타이머로서 작용하는데 빛이 없으면 움직이다가 해가 돌아오면 다시 맞춰진다. 이 시계는 사람을 포함한 거의 모든 생물에서 발견되지만 잘 이해되지는 못하고 있다. 하지만 피토크롬에 대해서는 더 잘 알려져 있다. 피토크롬은 식물에서 발견되는 색소인데 빛을 감지하고 이것이 있을 때 세포 변화를 야기시킨다. [Q5]이러한 세포변화의 하나는 지속적인 어둠 길이를 측정하는 내부 시계의 재설정이다.
단락 5 어두움의 길이에 따른 다른 반응	5 This mechanism is quite sensitive; many species of long-night plants that have their darkness interrupted for even a minute or two with **either** sunlight **or** artificial light may not flower. [■] This effect, however, does not occur with all types of light. It was found that red light shone on a plant during	이 체계는 꽤 민감하다; 많은 장야 식물 종이 겨우 1, 2분 동안이라도 햇빛이나 인공 빛이 들어간 어둠을 보내면 꽃을 피우지 않을 것이다. [■] 그러나 이러한 영향은 모든 종류의 빛에 적용되는 것은 아니다. 밤에 식물에게 비치는 적외선은 식물에게 감지되고 식물은 생물학적

Vocabulary

3단락
- neutral [njúːtrəl] n. 중립, 중간
- photoperiod [fòutəpíəriəd] n. 광주기, 명기

4단락
- distinguish [distíŋgwiʃ] v. 구별하다, 분간하다
- phytochrome [fáitəkroum] n. 피토크롬(색소단백질)
- tick [tik] n. 똑딱소리 / v. 작동하다, 똑딱 소리내다

5단락
- interrupt [ìntərʌ́pt] v. 방해하다, 간섭하다

- threshold [θréʃhould] n. 기준점, 한계점
- spinach [spínitʃ] n. 시금치

- botanist [bátənist] n. 식물학자
- uninterrupted [ʌ̀nintərʌ́ptid] a. 연속적인, 끊임없는
- reset [riːsét] v. 다시 맞추다 / n. 고쳐 놓기

- artificial [ὰːrtəfíʃəl] a. 인공적인

- critical [krítikəl] a. 결정적인, 중대한
- interval [íntərvəl] n. 기간, 간격

- pigment [pígmənt] n. 색소
- cellular [séljələr] a. 셀 방식의, 세포의

- wavelength [wéivlèŋkθ] n. 파장, 주파수

the night is perceived by the plant and the plant resets its biological clock. [■] But the same plant does not reset its clock when exposed to far-red light (light with a longer wavelength than red light), and therefore it produces flowers. [■] This is **not** because phytochrome cannot detect far-red light, **but** because it **reacts to** the two types of light differently. [■]

단락 6
개화를 결정짓는 요인

6 The discovery of what internal factors actually signal plants to flower **in response** to light has overarching potential in biology and agriculture, which **makes** it an intriguing topic of study. Experiments conducted on cockleburs, a family of long-night plants that require more than eight hours of darkness **to flower**, revealed that despite their strong **sensitivity to** light exposure, if even a single leaf of the cocklebur experiences a long night, while the rest of the plant is subjected to short nights, it still produced flowers. This experiment suggested that a flowering factor **is sent from** the leaves to the flower buds when the flowering conditions for the plants are met. [Q7]**So far** scientists have not found this factor, but the most widely accepted notion is that interactions **among** multiple, as yet unidentified plant hormones or other compounds, **referred to as** florigen, trigger flowering.

Sentence analysis

◎ Plant growth and development are controlled by interactions /
　　　식물 성장과 발달은 상화 작용에 의해 통제된다
between environmental factors and inner developmental processes.
　　　환경적인 요인과 내부의 발전하는 과정 사이에

◎ The blossoming of flowers in plants　/　is an intricate and delicate process　/
　　　식물의 개화는　　　　　　　　　　　복잡하고 섬세한 과정이다
which has evolved to suit plants' different environments.
　　　식물들의 다른 환경에 맞추기 위해 진화된

Vocabulary

6단락　overarching [òuvərá:rtʃ] a. 모든 것을 포함하는, 무엇보다 중요한　　agriculture [ǽgrikʌltʃər] n. 농업, 축산
　　　　intrigue [intríːg] v. 흥미를 끌다, 호기심을 유발시키다　　　　　　cocklebur [kάklbə̀ːr] n. 도꼬마리, 우엉
　　　　bud [bʌd] n. 싹, 봉오리 / a. 시작하는　　　　　　　　　　　　notion [nóuʃən] n. 생각, 개념
　　　　florigen [flɔ́(ː)rədʒən] n. 화성소　　　　　　　　　　　　　trigger [strígər] v. 유발하다 / n. 방아쇠

11 According to paragraph 1, what can be inferred about slower-growing plants with healthy leaves?

(A) The area in which they are growing is favorable to them.
(B) They ~~receive insufficient levels of energy~~ to initiate photosynthesis. ★
(C) ~~Their thin, long stems~~ are not strong enough to support the entire plant.
(D) Their leaves lack the ability to convert carbon dioxide into organic compounds.

1단락에 따르면 건강한 잎을 갖고 천천히 자라는 식물에 대해 추론할 수 있는 것은?

(A) 이 식물들이 자라는 곳은 이들에게 좋다.
(B) 이 식물들은 광합성을 하기 위한 ~~충분한 수준의 에너지를 받지 못했다.~~ ★
(C) 이 식물들의 ~~가늘고 긴 줄기는~~ 식물 전체를 지탱하기 위해 충분히 튼튼하지 못하다.
(D) 이 식물들의 잎은 이산화탄소를 유기적 혼합물로 전환하는 능력이 없다.

Inference 문제의 내용이 포함된 1단락을 보면 These plants will produce thinner and longer stems with longer internodes to reach a faint light source or to find one, in a much more rapid way than those exposed to adequate sunlight. A plant suffering from etiolation will also produce fewer leaves. (이 식물들은 희미한 빛 자원에 도달하거나 이를 찾기 위해 적절한 햇빛에 노출된 식물들보다 훨씬 빠른 방법으로 더 긴 절간과 함께 더 가늘고 긴 줄기를 만들어 낼 것이다. 황화현상을 겪는 식물은 또한 더 적은 잎을 생산할 것이다) 식물이 길고 얇게 자랄 때는 빛이 부족하다는 의미이므로 B는 반대로 유추가 된 것이다. (C) 또한 반대로 유추가 된 것이며 (D)에 대한 내용은 언급되지 않았다. 식물이 얇게 자라지 않고 건강하게 자란다는 것은 그곳에 충분한 빛이 있다는 의미이므로 정답은 (A)이다.

12 Which of the sentences below best expresses the essential information in the highlighted sentence in the passage? Incorrect choices change the meaning in important ways or leave out essential information.

(A) When exposed to inadequate sunlight, plants grow shorter internodes ~~which have longer and thinner stems~~ to search for sources of light. ★
(B) Sunlight-deprived plants will grow taller stems with longer internodes more quickly than those with adequate sunlight as they search for a new light source.
(C) Plants that are ~~exposed to enough sunlight~~ grow thinner and longer stems with fewer internodes compared to plants that do not have adequate sunlight.
(D) Plants that have not received enough sunlight will continue to rapidly produce longer but thinner and ~~fewer stems~~, that search for light.

아래의 문장 중 지문 속의 음영 표시된 문장의 핵심 정보를 가장 잘 표현하고 있는 것은 무엇인가? 오답은 문장의 의미를 현저하게 바꾸거나 핵심 정보를 빠트리고 있다.

(A) 부적절한 햇빛에 노출되었을 때 식물들은 더 짧은 ~~길고 얇은 줄기를 가진~~ 절간을 찾기 위해 빛 지원을 발달시킨다. ★
(B) 햇빛이 결핍된 식물은 새로운 빛 자원을 찾으면서 충분한 햇빛이 있는 식물보다 큰 줄기와 더 긴 절간을 빠르게 발달시킨다.
(C) ~~충분한 햇빛에 노출된~~ 식물들은 불충분한 햇빛을 받은 식물에 비해 얇고 긴 줄기와 더 적은 절간을 발달시킨다.
(D) 충분한 햇빛을 받지 않은 식물들은 길지만 얇고 ~~적은 빛을 찾는~~ 줄기를 계속해서 빠르게 만들어낼 것이다.

Highlight i) These plants will produce thinner and longer stems with longer internodes ii) to reach a faint light source or to find one, iii) in a much more rapid way than those exposed to adequate sunlight. (iii)그들은 적절한 태양빛에 노출된 식물보다 더 빠른 방법으로 ii)희미한 빛에 도달하거나 그것을 찾아내기 위해 i)더 긴 절간을 가진 보다 얇고 긴 줄기를 계속 만들어 낼 것이다) 본문에 따르면, (A)는 빠르다는 내용이 없으므로 오답이다. (C)는 반대이므로 오답이다. (D)는 절간이 빠졌으므로 오답이다. (B)는 황화 현상과 그것의 특징 모두가 포함됐으므로 정답이다.

13 According to paragraph 3, which of the following is true about the flowering of plants?

(A) The flowering of plants is strictly controlled by their exposure to ~~light~~ in various durations. ★
(B) The flowering of plants, whether short-day or long-day, does not depend on the amount of time that they are exposed to light.
(C) The day-neutral plants flower ~~in response to the length of the daytime~~, hence they mainly flower in the summer.
(D) The spinach, a long-day plant, ~~requires long nights, a minimum of eleven hours of darkness~~, in order to produce flowers.

3단락에 따르면, 꽃의 개화에 대한 것으로 다음 중 알맞은 것은?

(A) 꽃의 개화는 빛에 노출된 시간에 엄격히 규제된다. ★
(B) 단일이든 장일이든 꽃의 개화는 빛에 노출된 시간의 양에 좌우되지 않는다.
(C) 중일성 식물들은 ~~낮시간의 길이에 반응하여~~ 꽃피운다. 따라서 이들은 주로 여름에 꽃피운다.
(D) 장일성 식물인 시금치는 꽃을 피우기 위해 긴 밤을, ~~적어도 11시간의 어둠을 필요로 한다~~.

Fact it is the duration of continuous darkness rather than the day length which controls flowering.(꽃을 피우는 것을 조절하는 것은 낮의 길이보다는 지속되는 어둠의 길이이다) (A)는 모든 종류의 식물에 빛에 노출된 시간에 영향을 받는게 아니므로 오답이다. (C)에 day neutral plant는 지속되는 낮의 길이와는 관계없이 꽃을 피우므로 오답이다. (D)는 시금치에 대한 반대 내용이므로 오답이다. 본문에 보면 꽃을 피우는 것은 낮의 길이와는 관계가 없다고 하기 때문에 (B)가 정답이다.

14 The author mentions humans in the passage in order to

(A) Point out that the biological clock of humans is poorly understood ★
(B) Explain that humans are also organisms and a part of nature
(C) Illustrate how widespread the internal biological clock is in nature
(D) Suggest that plants' ~~light detection methods~~ are similar to those of humans

글쓴이는 왜 humans를 언급하는가?

(A) 인간의 생물학적 시계가 잘 이해되고 있지 않음을 나타내기 위해서 ★
(B) 인간들 또한 생물이고 자연의 일부임을 설명하기 위해서
(C) 내부 생물학적 시계가 자연에서 얼마나 널리 퍼져있는지를 설명하기 위해서
(D) 식물들의 ~~빛 감지 방법~~이 인간들의 것과 유사하다는 것을 제시하기 위해서

Purpose 문제의 키워드인 humans(사람들)가 언급된 부분을 보면, This clock is found in almost all organisms, including humans, yet is poorly understood.(이 생체 시계는 인간을 포함한 거의 모든 생물체에서 발견되지만 이해되지 않고 있다) (A), (B)는 지문에 언급된 사실이지만 목적이 아니다. (D)에서 비슷한 것은 생체시계이지 빛을 인지하는 방법이 아니므로 오답이다. 생체시계가 거의 모든 생물들에게서 발견되고 사람들에게도 발견된다고 했으므로 (C)가 정답이다.

15 According to paragraph 4, what role does phytochrome play in a plant's flowering?

(A) ~~Stimulating growth and development~~ in the plant's leaves
(B) Resetting the biological clock of a plant by way of light detection
(C) Keeping track of the length of nighttime ~~in the absence of external signals~~
(D) ~~Reacting~~ to cellular changes in the plant caused by light ★

4단락에 따르면 식물의 개화에 있어서 피토크롬은 어떤 역할을 하는가?

(A) 식물의 잎에서 ~~성장과 발달을 촉진시킨다~~.
(B) 빛을 감지하는 방법으로 식물의 생물학적 시계를 재설정 한다.
(C) ~~외적인 신호 없이~~ 밤시간의 길이를 알아낼 수 있다.
(D) 빛에 의해 야기된 식물의 세포변화에 ~~반응한다~~. ★

Fact One such cellular change is the resetting of the internal clock that measures the length of continuous darkness.(이러한 세포 변화는 지속되는 어둠의 길이를 측정하는 체내시계를 초기화 하는 것이다) (A)는 사실이 아니므로 오답이다. (C)는 체내 시계와 빛의 표시가 필요하므로 오답이다. (D)는 피토크롬이 세포변화에 반응하는 것은 아니므로 오답이다. (B)는 빛의 발견을 통해 생체 시계를 초기화 한다고 했으므로 정답이다.

16

The word **it** in the passage refers to

(A) ability
(B) phytochrome ★
(C) light
(D) pigment

지문의 단어 **it** 와 가장 근접한 뜻의 단어는?

(A) 능력 [əbíləti]
(B) 피토크롬 ★ [fáitəkroum]
(C) 빛 [lait]
(D) 색소 [pígmənt]

Reference it이 언급된 부분을 살펴보면 Phytochrome is a pigment found in plants which has the ability to detect light and bring about cellular change when it is present (피토크롬은 빛이 있을 때 생기는 세포의 변화와 빛을 발견하는 능력을 가진 식물에서 발견되는 색소이다)이므로 지시어 it에 대입을 하였을 때 정답은 (C)가 된다.

17

According to paragraph 6, all of the following statements about the alleged characteristics of florigen are true EXCEPT

(A) Florigen may be a number of collaborative compounds
(B) Florigen has the ability to travel from one part of a plant to another
(C) The release of florigen stimulates flower buds to begin producing flowers
(D) Scientists' level of understanding of florigen has recently improved to match the understanding of phytochrome

6단락에 따르면 진술된 플로리젠의 특징에 대한 문장 중 사실이 아닌 것은?

(A) 플로리젠은 수많은 협조적인 화합물일 것이다.
(B) 플로리젠은 식물의 한 부분에서 다른 곳으로 넘어갈 수 있는 능력이 있다.
(C) 플로리젠의 방출은 꽃 봉우리가 개화하는 것을 시작하도록 촉진시킨다.
(D) 플로리젠에 대한 과학자들의 이해 수준은 최근 피토크롬에 대한 이해에 못지않게 높아졌다.

Fact So far scientists have not found this factor, but the most widely accepted notion is that interactions among multiple, as yet unidentified plant hormones or other compounds, referred to as florigen, trigger flowering. (아직까지 과학자들은 이 요인을 찾지는 못했지만, 가장 많이 인정되는 개념은, 플로리젠이라고 불리는 확인되지 않은 식물 호르몬이나 다른 혼합물의 상호관계가 꽃을 피우는 것을 유발한다) 피토크롬에 대한 이해도는 이전의 단락에서 언급되었으나 플로리젠에 대하여서는 찾지 못했다고 했으므로 (D)가 정답이 된다.

18

The word **subjected to** in the passage is closest in meaning to

(A) exposed to
(B) removed from ★
(C) uncovered by
(D) weakened by

지문의 단어 **subjected to**와 의미와 가장 유사한 것은?

(A) 노출된
(B) 제거된 ★
(C) 가려지지 않은
(D) 취약해진

Vocabulary 지문의 Subjected to(노출되는)는 exposed to(노출시킨)의 동의어이므로 정답이다.

19

Look at the four squares [■] that indicate where the following sentence could be added to the passage.

This effect, however, does not occur with all types of light.

Where would the sentence best fit? Click on a square [■] to add the sentence to the passage.   1st

네 개의 네모[■]는 다음 문장이 삽입될 수 있는 부분을 나타내고 있다.

하지만 이 효과는 모든 종류의 빛에 적용될 수 없다.

이 문장은 어느 자리에 들어가는 것이 가장 적절한가?

첫번째

Insertion 핵심 키워드인 however는 첫번째 네모 앞부분의 의견에 예외가 되는 부분을 언급하기 위해 나온 것이고, 두번째 네모에 들어갔을 때 두 번째 네모 뒤에 있는 내용에 But이 나오므로 오답이 된다. 그래서 정답은 첫 번째 네모다.

USHER 20

Directions: An introductory sentence for a brief summary of the passage is provided below. Complete the summary by selecting the THREE answer choices that express the most important ideas in the passage. Some sentences do not belong in the summary because they express ideas that are not presented in the passage or are minor ideas in the passage. **This question is worth 2 points.**

지시 : 지문 요약을 위한 도입 문장이 아래에 주어져 있다. 지문의 가장 중요한 내용을 나타내는 보기 3개를 골라 요약을 완성하시오. 어떤 문장은 지문에 언급되지 않은 내용이나 사소한 정보를 담고 있으므로 요약에 포함되지 않는다. 이 문제는 2점이다.

The plants show different reactions to light, which is an essential factor of growth.

- (A) Long-day plants and short-day plants produce flowers depending on the duration of uninterrupted darkness, while day-neutral plants are unaffected by the length of exposure to light and darkness. - Paragraph 3

- (D) Plants use a biological internal clock and the pigment phytochrome, which reacts to specific types of light, to measure the length of time without light. - Paragraph 4

- (E) Although not enough information has been uncovered regarding the internal processes in initiating flower production in plants, it is proposed that the signal can travel from the leaf to the bud. - Paragraph 6

식물은 서로 소통할 때 다양한 화학적이고 물리적인 방법들을 쓴다.

- (A) 장일성 식물과 단일성 식물은 지속되는 어둠의 길이에 따라 꽃을 피우는 반면 중일성 식물은 빛과 어둠에 노출된 시간에 영향을 받지 않는다.

- (D) 식물들은 빛 없이 시간의 길이를 측정하기 위해 생물학적 내부 시계와 특정 종류의 빛에 반응하는 피토크롬 색소를 이용한다.

- (E) 비록 개화를 시작하는데 있어서의 내부과정에 대한 충분한 정보가 밝혀지지 않았지만, 신호가 잎에서 봉우리로 이동할 수 있다는 것이 제안되었다.

(B) Cockleburs are a family of long-night plants which scientists have used to learn about plants' flowering in different lighting conditions. - Paragraph 6 detail

(C) Long-day, short-day and day-neutral plants ~~all~~ require different intervals of continuous darkness while also maintaining certain temperature levels. - 틀린 정보

(F) ~~The ability of a plant's flower to absorb light is influenced by a variety of factors including temperature and water availability.~~ - 틀린정보

(B) 과학자들이 다른 빛 조건에서의 개화에 대해 알기 위해 이용했던 우엉은 장야성 식물의 일종이다.

(C) 장일성과 단일성 그리고 중일성 식물들은 ~~모두~~ 다른 시간의 지속되는 어둠을 필요로 하면서 또한 특정 온도 수준을 유지한다.

(F) ~~빛을 흡수하는 식물 꽃의 능력은 온도와 물 용이성을 포함한 다양한 요인에 영향을 받는다.~~

Summary (A)는 식물의 3가지 분류에 대하여 설명한 3단락을 요약한 것이고, (D)는 식물들이 낮시간과 밤시간을 구별하는 방법에 대하여 설명한 4단락을 요약한 것이고, (E)는 꽃을 피우는 것이 신호를 통하여 이루어진다는 6단락을 요약한 것이다.

usherin.usher.co.kr

USHER

iBT TOEFL
FINAL TEST READING
TEST 3

답안 및 취약 유형 분석표
해석·해설

답안 및 문제 유형 분석표

TEST 3-1

01 (C) Fact
02 (B) Fact
03 (D) Vocabulary
04 (B) Purpose
05 (A) Inference
06 (B) Fact
07 (C) Purpose
08 (D) Highlight
09 2nd ■ Insertion
10 (A),(C),(F) Summary

TEST 3-2

11 (D) Fact
12 (B) Fact
13 (B) Fact
14 (A) Vocabulary
15 (D) Fact
16 (B) Inference
17 (B) Purpose
18 (A) Highlight
19 2nd ■ Insertion
20 Category Chart

Gradualism (A), (E), (G)
Punctuated Equilibrium (C), (D)

각 문제 유형별 맞춘 개수를 아래에 적어 보세요.

유형	맞춘 답의 개수	정답률
단어 (Vocabulary)	/ 2	정답률: %
사실 확인 문제 (Fact)	/ 7	정답률: %
지시어 찾기 (Reference)	/ 0	정답률: %
끼워 넣기 (Insertion)	/ 2	정답률: %
문장 변환문제 (Highlight)	/ 2	정답률: %
목적 (Purpose)	/ 3	정답률: %
추론 (Inference)	/ 2	정답률: %
단락 요약 (Summary / Category Chart)	/ 2	정답률: %
전체	/ 20	정답률: %

※ 자신이 취약한 유형은 READING STRATEGIES를 통해 다시 한번 점검하시기 바랍니다. (p.31)

TEST 3-1 Naturalistic Painting 자연주의 그림

Introduction	단락 1	유럽의 자연주의
Point 1	단락 2	파라시우스와 제욱시스
Point 2	단락 3	자연주의에 대한 의문점
Point 3	단락 4	예술로서의 자연주의

Image by Karl Paul Themistokles von Eckenbrecher(1842-1921)

단락 1 — 유럽의 자연주의

1 The civilization of Ancient Greece, which lasted from the 8th century to the mid-1st century BC, had a lasting cultural influence over such a huge area, and over such powerful empires that it **is** often **considered** the underpinning of Western culture. Historians have discovered that even paintings from Ancient Greece **had a** strong **influence on** art in remote parts of Europe for millennia to come. One such artistic influence was the movement **known as** naturalism. Naturalistic painters **aspire to** depict the world's natural objects, people and unadorned scenery **as** realistically **as possible**. Their paintings are characterized by meticulous detail and near-perfect symmetry. **In** simple **terms**, naturalistic artists **strive to create** realistic paintings hardly **distinguishable from** actual photographs. This movement **originated** in Ancient Greece and spread through Europe to the Netherlands, where it continuously evolved.

8세기부터 1세기 중반까지 지속된 고대 그리스 문명은 매우 광활한 지역과 강력한 제국들에 지속적인 문화적 영향을 끼쳐왔기 때문에 이는 종종 서양문화의 토대라고 여겨진다. 역사가들은 심지어 고대 그리스의 그림이 유럽의 멀리 떨어진 지역까지 천 년의 세월에 걸쳐서 강한 영향력을 가지고 있다는 것을 알아냈다. 이러한 하나의 예술적 영향은 자연주의라고 알려진 운동이다. 자연주의 화가들은 세상의 자연물, 사람들 그리고 꾸밈없는 풍경을 가능한 사실적으로 묘사하기를 갈망했다. 그들의 그림은 섬세한 묘사와 완벽에 가까운 대칭성에 의해 특징지어졌다. 쉽게 말해서, 자연주의 예술가들은 실제 사진과 거의 구별하기 힘든 사실적인 그림들을 창조하기 위해 노력했다. 이 움직임은 고대 그리스에서 기원을 뒀으며, 유럽을 통해 네덜란드로 펴졌고 계속해서 진화해 나갔다.

단락 2 — 파라시우스와 제욱시스

2 In Ancient Greece, the early naturalistic painters **tended to put** more **emphasis on** skill than **on** creativity, and painters of Greece would often compare their works to see which was more realistic. [Q11]While the artists' creativity was largely subjective, a brushstroke was an objective **means of** assessment. [Q20-A] **As a result**, naturalistic painting became a competitive style of painting, as shown by the legendary painting competition of Parrhasius and Zeuxis, two of the greatest painters of the 5th century BC. Parrhasius, who was born in the city of Ephesus and lived in Athens, had **distinguished** himself **as** an extraordinary artist at a young age. [Q12]Often, those who witnessed the initial stages of his paintings **mistook** him **for** a sketch artist, an

고대 그리스에서, 초기 자연주의 화가들은 창의성보다 기술에 중점을 두는 경향이 있었고, 그리스 화가들은 종종 어떤 작품이 더 사실적인지 비교하곤 했다. [Q11]예술가들의 창의성은 거의 주관적인 반면, 붓 놀림은 평가의 객관적인 수단이었다. [Q20-A]결과적으로, 파라시우스와 제욱시스라는 기원전 5세기의 가장 위대한 화가인, 두 사람의 전설적인 그림 경쟁에서 보여지듯이, 자연주의적 그림은 경쟁적인 그림 양식이 되었다. 파라시우스는 에페수스에서 태어났고 아테네에서 자랐는데 어린 시절에 비범한 화가로서의 두각을 나타냈다. [Q12]흔히, 그의 작품의 초기 단계를 본 사람들은 그를 단지 연필과 파스텔만 사용해서

Vocabulary

1단락
- aspire [əspáiər] v. 열망하다
- evolve [iválv] v. 차츰 발전시키다
- meticulous [mətíkjələs] a. 세세한
- depict [dipíkt] v. 묘사하다
- realistic [ríːəlistik] a. 현실주의의
- strive [straiv] v. 분투하다
- distingusable [distíŋgwiʃéibəl] a. 구별할 수 있는
- symmetry [símətri] n. 대칭

2단락
- brushstroke [brʌ́ʃstròuk] n. 붓 놀림
- mural [mjúərəl] a. 벽면의
- confound [kənfáund] v. 어리둥절하게 만들다
- emphasis [émfəsis] n. 강조
- exclaim [ikskléim] v. 외치다
- capitol [kǽpitl] n. 국회 의사당
- competition [kàmpətíʃən] n. 경쟁
- curtain [kə́ːrtn] n. 막

artist who completes his work using only a pencil or pastel. His works were **so great that** they **were preserved as** study **aids for** painters that **came after** him. His rival Zeuxis was born in the Southern Italian city of Heraclea, and was widely renowned in the artistic scene of the time. **At the peak** of their careers, a contest was staged to determine the greater of the two. At the competition, Zeuxis revealed a painting of grapes which was realistic **enough to fool** nearby birds. **Absorbed in** a sense of achievement, he confidently **asked** Parrhasius **to pull aside** the curtains and reveal his painting, **only to be told** that the curtains themselves were his painted work. Zeuxis **was confounded by** this and exclaimed "I have deceived the birds, but Parrhasius has deceived Zeuxis." Parrhasius' painting later **became known as** 'Parrhasius' Curtain' and he attained the title of the best naturalistic painter of the time, **gaining even more fame and respect**. He **was** even **asked to paint** murals for the Capitol of Rome by city officials.

3 Millenniums later, Adriaen van der Spelt and Frans van Mieris, painters from Netherlands, led a movement that challenged the original principles of naturalism. °Their paintings portrayed objects and acts that interested them, **with little regard for** whether they resembled the natural world. For example, they painted a lily in the center of Parrhasius' Curtain with insects around it. [Q14] The lily **served no** naturalistic **purpose**, but with it the painting gained **scores of** symbolic meaning. Critics and fellow artists **were awakened to** the ideas of naturalist painting, surprised and awed **at the same time**. [Q15]The lily represented wealth and property while the insects around the flower illustrated how the flower could **be robbed of** its nectar and **left to die in a matter of days**. The painting **was lauded for** its combination of symbolism and realistic insights. This **led** critics **to begin** questioning whether 'art' **was defined by** how well a natural object is depicted, or by how well it is embellished and enhanced. [■] This became more pronounced as technological progress and development **led to** the emergence of cameras and professional photography. [■] Initially, photography was used to capture and record subjects of scientific interest, but

Vocabulary

3단락
laud [lɔːd] v. 칭찬하다
portray [pɔːrtrei] v. 그림으로 그리다
pronounce [prənáuns] v. (공개적으로) 선언하다, 표명하다
embellish [imbéliʃ] v. 장식하다
lily [líli] n. 백합
principle [prínsəpl] n. 원칙
property [prápərti] n. 재산
intricate [íntrikət] a. 뒤엉킨

it quickly turned into a new art form. Clearly, the new artistic photographs captured naturalistic images much more easily than paintings. [■] While an intricate and time-consuming process in the past, re-creating nature on paper became only a matter of the click of a shutter. [■]

단락 4
예술로서의 자연주의

4 As art entered the modern era, [Q20-C]the common belief became that painting to resemble nature **as closely as possible** is not really art, but rather an act of duplication. There have **not only** been convincing arguments which support this claim, **but also** several credible arguments that oppose it. One modern artist, for instance, **added** his touch **to** Adriaen van der Spelt and Frans van Mieris' painting by coloring the lily bright red. [Q16]The red lily, the artist explained, represented passion and supported the assertion that art should express the artist's mind. **According to** him, an artist must deliberately convey his vision through various methods, such as the use of color and brushstroke. **On the other hand**, the French Neoclassical painter Jean Auguste Dominique Ingres, [Q17]pointed out that **regardless of** what or how an artist paints, the painter unintentionally leaves traces of himself in the work. Ingres believed that the painter would subconsciously make different choices **according to** his mood, such as using harsher brushstrokes when feeling angry, or passionate colors when **in love**, all inadvertently. ○**With all things considered, i) despite the fact that** it was **decreasing in popularity and was occasionally criticized, ii)** [Q20-F]the naturalistic style of painting has **played a major role in** the history of art and iii) will **continue to do** so **in the future**.

곧 새로운 예술 형태로 변모됐다. 명백하게, 그 새로운 예술 사진은 자연적인 이미지를 그림보다 훨씬 수월하게 담아냈다. [■] 과거에는 복잡하고 시간 소모적인 과정이었지만, 종이 위에 자연을 재창조하는 것은 단지 셔터를 한 번 누르는 일에 지나지 않게 되었다. [■]

예술이 근대 시대에 들어서면서, [Q20-C]가능한 자연과 비슷한 그림은 진짜 예술이 아니고 오히려 복제행위 라는 것이 보편적 믿음이 되었다. 이 논의를 뒷받침하는 설득력 있는 주장뿐 아니라 그것에 반대하는 신빙성 있는 주장 또한 생겨났다. 예를 들어, 한 현대예술가는 에이드리안 반 더 스펠드와 프란스 반 미에리스의 그림의 백합을 밝은 붉은 색으로 칠함으로써 그의 손길을 더했다. [Q16]그 붉은 백합은, 화가가 설명하기를, 정열을 상징하고 예술이 화가의 마음을 표현해야 한다는 주장을 뒷받침했다. 그에 따르면, 화가는 반드시 색과 붓 놀림 사용과 같은 다양한 방법을 통해 그의 상상력을 의도적으로 전달해야 한다. 반면, 프랑스의 신고전주의 화가 장 오귀스트 도미니크 앵그르는 [Q17]화가가 무엇을 어떻게 그리는지와 상관없이 그 화가는 의도하지 않게 작품에 그의 흔적을 남긴다고 말했다. 앵그르 화가는, 화가 날 때는 붓놀림을 거칠게 하고, 사랑에 빠졌을 때는 정열적인 색을 의도하지 않게 사용하게 되듯이, 잠재적으로 그의 기분에 따라 다른 선택을 한다고 믿었다. ○모든 것을 고려해볼 때, i) 자연주의 양식의 인기가 떨어지고 때로는 비판된다는 사실에도 불구하고, ii) [Q20-F]자연주의 형식의 그림은 예술사에서 중요한 역할을 했고 iii) 앞으로도 계속 그러할 것이다.

Sentence analysis

◎ Their paintings / portrayed / objects and acts / that interested / them, / with little regard / for whether they /
그들의 그림은 묘사했다 사물과 행동을 흥미를 느끼게 하는 그들이 상관 없이 그들이
resembled the natural world.
자연과 비슷하든 그렇지 않든

◎ With all things considered / despite the fact that / it was / decreasing in popularity and /
모든 것을 고려해볼 때 불구하고 자연주의 양식의 그림이 인기가 하락하고
was occasionally criticized, / the naturalistic style of painting / has played a major role / in the history of art /
때때로 비판됨에도 이것은 주요한 역할을 했고 미술의 역사에
and will continue to do so in the future.
미래에도 계속 그럴 것이다

Vocabulary

4단락
duplication [djùːpləkéiʃən] n. 복제
assertion [əsə́ːrʃən] n. 주장
allude [əlúːd] v. 암시하다

resemble [rizémbl] v. 닮다
mimic [mímik] v. 흉내를 내다

convince [kənvíns] v. 납득시키다
atypical [eitípikəl] a. 이례적인

01

According to paragraph 2, why did naturalistic painting become a competitive style of painting?

(A) There were ~~too many painters of naturalistic style~~ that only those who made a name for themselves could be remembered by the public.
(B) Naturalistic painters ~~started to mimic the painting competition of Parrhasius and Zeuxis~~.
(C) The artistic achievement of naturalistic painting was easier to measure than that of other styles of painting.
(D) The mastery of a brushstroke, which was largely ~~subjective~~, was a criterion for evaluation. ★

2단락에 따르면, 왜 자연주의 그림은 경쟁적인 그림양식이 되었는가?

(A) 너무 많은 자연주의 화가들이 있어서 그 중 오직 유명한 화가들만이 대중들로부터 기억될 수 있었다.
(B) 자연주의 화가들은 파라시우스와 제욱시스의 그림 크리커 경쟁을 모방하기 시작했다.
(C) 자연주의적 그림의 예술적 성취도는 다른 형식의 그림보다 더 쉽게 측정할 수 있었다.
(D) 평가의 기준은 주관적인 붓 놀림의 장악력이었다. ★

Fact 문제의 키워드인 competitive style of painting(경쟁적인 양식의 그림)이 언급된 부분을 살펴보면 While the artists' creativity was largely subjective, a brushstroke was an objective means of assessment.(예술가들의 창의성은 거의 주관적인 반면 붓 놀림은 평가의 객관적인 수단이었다) 그림을 객관적인 잣대로 평가한다는 내용이 나온 후 As a result, naturalistic painting became a competitive style of painting.(결과적으로, 자연주의 그림은 경쟁적인 그림 양식이 되었다) 결과적으로 경쟁적인 그림이 되었다는 것을 알 수 있다. (D)는 subjective(주관적)이 아니라 objective(객관적)이기 때문에 오답이다.

02

Which of the following is true about Parrhasius and his style according to paragraph 2?

(A) Parrhasius' ~~parents started training him~~ to be an artist at an early age.
(B) Parrhasius was known for being attentive to the foundations of his painting.
(C) Parrhasius ~~began his career as a sketch artist~~ but eventually turned to naturalistic painting. ★
(D) Parrhasius was criticized by his rival because ~~the sketches of his paintings were too elaborate~~.

2단락에서 파라시우스와 그의 스타일에 관하여 사실인 것은?

(A) 파라시우스의 부모님은 그를 예술가로 키우기 위해 어렸을 때부터 훈련시키기 시작했다.
(B) 파라시우스는 그림의 윤곽에 주의를 기울인다는 점으로 널리 알려져 있었다.
(C) 파라시우스는 직업을 스케치 화가로 시작했지만 결국에는 자연주의 그림으로 전향했다. ★
(D) 파라시우스의 그림의 커초는 너무 정교했기 때문에 그의 라이벌로부터 비판을 받았다.

Fact 문제의 키워드인 parrhasius's style (파라시우스의 양식)이 언급되는 부분을 살펴 보면 Often, those who witnessed the initial stages of Parrhasius' paintings mistook him for a sketch artist, an artist who completes his work using only a pencil or pastel. (그의 작품의 초기 단계를 본 사람들은 그를 단지 오직 연필과 파스텔을 사용하여 작품을 완성하는 스케치 화가로 오해했다)라는 부분에서 그가 그림 윤곽에 아주 주의를 기울였기 때문에 스케치 화가로 오해 받았다는 것을 알 수 있으므로 답은 (B)이다. (C)는 그가 '스케치 화가로 오해 받았다' 는 내용이 그가 처음에 스케치 화가였다는 것은 말이 되지 않기 때문에 오답이다.

03

The word attained in the passage is closest in meaning to

(A) required ★
(B) retained
(C) awarded
(D) achieved

지문의 단어 attained와 의미상 가장 유사한 것은?

(A) 필요하였다 ★ [rikwáiərd]
(B) 유지했다 [ritéin]
(C) 포상을 받았다 [əwɔ́:rd]
(D) 성취했다 [ətʃíːv]

Vocabulary 지문의 attained(이뤘다)은 achieved(성취했다)와 동의어이므로 정답은 (D)이다.

04 Why does the author mention Netherlands painters Adriaen van der Spelt and Frans van Mieris?

(A) To show that ~~painters in The Netherlands~~ were ~~inherited and developed~~ the ideals of the naturalist movement. ★
(B) To show how naturalist paintings evolved into more symbolic modern paintings
(C) To show that critics were ~~unwilling to accept~~ paintings that displayed symbolism.
(D) To show that ~~later painters had much more talent~~ than the earlier naturalistic painters.

글쓴이는 왜 네덜란드 화가인 에이드리안 반 더 스펠트와 프란스 반 미에리스를 언급했는가?

(A) ~~네덜란드 화가들이 자연주의 운동을 계승발전 시켰다~~는 것을 보여주기 위해 ★
(B) 어떻게 자연주의 화가들이 좀더 상징적인 현대 그림으로 진화했는지를 보여주기 위해
(C) 비평가들이 상징주의를 나타내는 그림들을 ~~받아드리지 않으려고 했다~~는 것을 보여주기 위해
(D) ~~이후 화가들이 초기 자연주의 화가들보다 더 재능이 있었다~~는 것을 보여주기 위해

Purpose 언급된 화가에 대한 내용을 언급 후 the painting gained scores of symbolic meaning(그림은 수많은 상징적인 의미를 얻었다)라는 언급이 나온다. 즉 화가들의 활동에 의해서 상징적인 의미를 얻게 된 것임으로 (B)가 정답이 된다. (A)는 네덜란드 화가 전체가 자연주의 운동에 저항적이었다는 내용은 없으므로 오답이 된다.

05 What do the insects around the flower of Parrhasius' Curtains in paragraph 3 signify?

(A) The beauty and perfection of affluence are easily lost.
(B) Flowers, ~~which make their owners wealthy~~, would be destroyed by insects
(C) ~~Happiness and comfort~~ are associated with the rich. ★
(D) The poverty-stricken members of the society ~~are attracted to the rich~~.

3단락에서 파라시우스의 커튼의 꽃 주변에 있는 곤충이 의미하는 것은?

(A) 부의 미와 완벽함은 일시적이다
(B) ~~소유자를 부자로 만드는~~ 꽃은 곤충에 의해서 파괴될 수 있다
(C) ~~행복과 안락은~~ 부자들과 연관되어 있다 ★
(D) 가난에 시달리는 사회 구성원들은 ~~부자에게서 매력을 느낀다~~

Inference 문제의 키워드인 insects around the flower(꽃 주변에 있는 곤충)이 언급된 부분을 살펴 보면 The lily represented wealth and property and the insects around the flower illustrated how the flower could be robbed of its honey and left to die in a matter of days.(백합은 부와 재산을 의미하는 반면 꽃 주변의 곤충은 어떻게 꽃의 꿀을 빼앗기고 불과 며칠만에 죽은 채로 남겨지는 지를 묘사했다)라는 부분에서 부를 의미한 꽃이 곤충들에 의해 꿀을 금방 빼앗긴다는 내용은 불과 단 며칠만에 사라질 수 있다는 (A)의 내용을 추론할 수 있다. (C)에서 나오는 행복에 관한 내용은 지문에 언급되지 않기 때문에 (C)는 오답이다.

06 According to paragraph 4, what is the significance of coloring the lily in red?

(A) It acts as evidence of the claim that the artist ~~unknowingly puts down his personality~~ into his works. ★
(B) It is an example of a way the artist intentionally expresses himself in the painting.
(C) It was a way for the artist ~~to bring attention to Parrhasius' painting~~ and remind others of the founding philosophy of naturalism.
(D) By painting the lily in its most common color, the painting was ~~improved to better portray the real world~~.

4단락에 따르면, 붉은 백합의 색의 의미는 무엇인가?

(A) 예술가는 ~~자신도 모르게 크와 인격을 작품에 반영한다~~는 주장으로써의 증거로 작용한다. ★
(B) 예술가가 의도적으로 자기 자신을 그림에 표현하는 방법의 예다.
(C) 예술가가 ~~파라시우스의 크림에 관심을 가지고~~ 다른 사람들에게 자연주의 철학의 기초를 상기시켜 주려는 방법이었다.
(D) 가장 흔한 색을 백합에 그림으로써, 그림은 실제 세상을 더욱 잘 묘사하도록 개선됐다.

Fact 문제의 키워드인 coloring lily red(백합을 붉게 칠 하는 것)이 언급된 부분을 살펴 보면 The red lily, the artist explained, represents passion and supported the assertion that art should express the artist's mind.(붉은 백합은 그 화가가 설명하기를, 정열을 상징하고 예술이 화가의 마음을 표현해야 한다는 주장을 뒷받침했다)라는 부분에서 백합을 붉게 칠한 것이 예술가의 생각을 표현한 것이라는 (B)의 내용을 알 수 있으므로 답은 (B)이다. (A)는 unknowingly(자신도 모르게)한 것이 아니므로 오답이다.

07
Why does the author mention Jean Auguste Dominique Ingres in paragraph 4?

(A) To explain the modernized form of the naturalist movement through ~~one of the strongest opponents of naturalism~~.
(B) To ~~indicate the role French painters had~~ in the development of naturalistic painting ★
(C) To describe an argument against the statement that naturalistic paintings do contain the artist's intention
(D) To show that painters can ~~unknowingly make mistakes~~ on their finished works

글쓴이는 4단락에서 왜 장 오귀스트 도미니크 앵그르를 언급하였는가?

(A) 자연주의에 대한 가장 강한 반대자의 하나로서 자연주의 운동에 근대화된 형태를 설명하기 위해서
(B) 자연주의적 그림의 발전에 있어서 프랑스 화가들이 기여했던 역할을 설명하기 위해 ★
(C) 자연주의 그림은 예술가의 의도를 포함한다는 언급에 대항하는 주장을 묘사하기 위해
(D) 화가들은 자신도 모르게 그들의 완성품에 실수를 할 수 있다는 것을 보여주기 위해

Purpose 글쓴이가 장 오귀스트 도미니크 앵그르를 언급한 이유는 고의적으로 백합에 붉은 색을 칠하지 않아도 화가는 자신도 모르게 자신의 생각을 그림에 담는다는 주장이 있었다는 것을 설명하기 위해서이므로 답은 (C)이다. (B)의 내용 '프랑스 화가들이 자연주의 미술에 큰 기여를 했다' 는 것은 지문에 언급되지 않았기 때문에 오답이다.

08
Which of the sentences below best expresses the essential information in the highlighted sentence in the passage? Incorrect choices change the meaning in important ways or leave out essential information.

(A) Because naturalism ~~was not well accepted throughout history~~, it could ~~not play an important part~~ in the past, present, and future of art.
(B) Because naturalism is an essential part of the history of art, ~~it is slowly losing its reputation among critics~~.
(C) The naturalistic style of painting influenced the development of art in the past and will continue to impact artists in the future. ★
(D) There was a growing dissent of naturalism, but the influences of naturalism which span from the past to future are irrefutable.

아래 문장 중 지문 속의 음영된 문장의 핵심 정보를 가장 잘 표현 하고 있는 것은 무엇인가? 오답은 의미를 현저히 왜곡하거나 핵심 정보를 빠뜨리고 있다.

(A) 자연주의는 역사적으로 잘 수용되지 않았기 때문에, 자연주의는 예술의 과거, 현재, 미래에 중요한 역할을 할 수 없었다.
(B) 자연주의는 예술의 역사에서 중요한 부분이기 때문에, ~~이것은 천천히 비평가들 사이에서 명성을 잃어가고 있다~~.
(C) 과거에 자연주의 그림은 예술의 발전에 영향을 미쳤고 미래에도 계속적으로 예술가들에게 영향을 줄 것이다. ★
(D) 자연주의를 반대하는 추세가 점점 생겨났지만, 과거에서부터 미래까지 끼친 자연주의의 영향은 반박할 수 없다.

Highlight 음영문구를 보면 With all things considered, i) despite the fact that it was decreasing in popularity and being occasionally criticized, ii) the naturalistic style of painting has played a major role in the history of art and iii) will continue to do so in the future. (모든 것을 고려해볼 때, i) 자연주의 양식의 인기가 떨어지고 때로는 비판된다는 사실에도 불구하고, ii) 자연주의 형식의 그림은 예술사에서 주요한 역할을 했고 iii) 앞으로도 계속 그럴 것이다)와 같이 세 부분으로 나뉜다. 이 세가지 내용을 모두 포함하고 인과관계가 정확한 (D)가 정답이 된다. (A)는 세 부분 모두 뜻이 바뀌었고, (B)는 틀린 인과관계, (C)는 첫 번째 부분이 빠져있어서 오답이다.

09
Look at the four squares [■] that indicate where the following sentence could be added to the passage.

Initially, photography was used to capture and record subjects of scientific interest, but it quickly turned into a new art form.

Where would the sentence best fit? Click on the square [■] to add the sentence to the passage.

2nd

네 개의 네모 [■]는 다음 문장이 삽입될 수 있는 부분을 나타내고 있다.

처음에, 사진은 과학적으로 흥미를 끄는 사물을 포착하고 기록함으로써 사용됐지만, 그것은 곧 새로운 예술형태로 변모됐다

이 문장은 어느 자리에 들어가는 것이 가장 적절한가?

두번째

Insertion 삽입 문장의 내용은 상위내용에서 하위내용을 설명하기 전에 나와야 하는 것이다. 문장에서 initially라 하며 상위내용과 연결하려는 단서가 있으니 사진과 관련된 언급이 있고 난 후에 있는 2 번째 네모가 정답이 된다.

10

Directions: An introductory sentence for a brief summary of the passage is provided below. Complete the summary by selecting the THREE answer choices that express the most important ideas in the passage. Some sentences do not belong in the summary because they express ideas that are not presented in the passage or are minor ideas in the passage. **This question is worth 2 points.**

지시 : 지문 요약을 위한 도입 문장이 아래에 주어져 있다. 지문의 가장 중요한 내용을 나타내는 보기 3개를 골라 요약을 완성하시오. 어떤 문장은 지문에 언급되지 않은 내용이나 사소한 정보를 담고 있으므로 요약에 포함되지 않는다. 이 문제는 2점이다.

Naturalistic painting is a style of painting in which the artist emulates natural subjects as closely as possible.

- (A) For a certain period of time, naturalism was a competitive art form. - Paragraph 2

- (C) Technological improvements and the movement towards symbolism has led opponents of naturalistic painting to argue that naturalism cannot be considered artistic. - Paragraph 3

- (F) Naturalistic artists have helped shape the history of art and will likely continue to be an essential part of art. - Paragraph 4

자연주의 그림은 예술가가 가능한 근접하게 자연의 사물을 모방하는 그림의 한 종류이다.

- (A) 자연주의그림은 일정기간 동안 경쟁적인 예술형태였다.

- (C) 기술적인 발전과 상징주의를 향한 운동은 반대자들이 자연주의는 예술로써 고려 될 수 없다라는 주장을 하도록 이끌었다.

- (F) 자연주의적 화가들은 예술의 역사를 형성하는데 도움을 주었고 앞으로도 계속 예술의 중요한 부분이 될 것이다.

(B) Naturalism emerged ~~in theater and literature~~ as a reaction to naturalistic painting in the 19th century. - 틀린 정보

(D) In a contest to select the best naturalistic painter, Zeuxis' painting fooled nearby birds and Parrhasius's Curtains fooled Zeuxis. - Paragraph 2 detail

(E) Symbolism in painting was ~~frowned upon~~ by many when it was first introduced in Netherlands. - 틀린 정보

(B) 19세기 초에 자연주의는 자연주의적 그림에 대한 반응으로 ~~극장과 문학에서~~ 생겨났다.

(D) 최고의 자연주의 화가를 선택하는 경쟁에서, 제욱시스의 그림은 근처의 새를 속이고 파라시우스의 커튼은 제욱시스를 속였다.

(E) 그림에서의 상징성이 처음 네덜란드에서 소개되었을 때 많은 사람들은 이것을 ~~싫어했다~~.

Summary   (A)는 2단락에서 다루어지는 자연주의 그림의 경쟁적인 형식에 대해 요약한 것이고, (C)는 예술로서 여겨질 수 없다는 자연주의의 의문점이 중심내용인 3단락을 요약한 것이고, (F)는 자연주의가 미래에 미친 영향을 논한 4단락의 중심내용이다. 따라서 답은 (A), (C), (F)가 된다.

usherin.usher.co.kr

TEST 3-2 Two Types of Evolutionary Theories 두가지 진화이론

Introduction	단락 1	점진진화와 중단평형설의 설명
Point 1	단락 2	과거 점진진화의 예시
Point 2	단락 3	중단평형설이 만들어진 계기
Point 3	단락 4	공통적으로 가지고 있는 환경적응
Point 4	단락 5	항상 변하는 환경과 생물

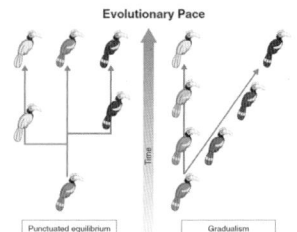

| 단락정리 | 지 문 | 해 석 |

단락 1
점진진화와 중단평형설의 설명

1 Evolution occurs as populations **adjust to** habitat change with **those experiencing** the best genetic adaptations surviving and **passing on** their genes. These phenotypic **changes in** populations **are common to** all organisms and affect every species, **no matter what** ecosystem. There are two prevailing, non-mutually exclusive theories of evolution today, gradualism and punctuated equilibrium, which **differ in the speed at which** evolutionary changes occur.

진화는 어떤 집단이 생존과 그들의 유전자를 전달하는데 있어 가장 최고의 유전적 적응을 경험하면서 서식지의 변화에 맞추어 감에 따라 발생한다. 집단에서의 이런 표현형의 변화는 생태계가 어떠하던 간에, 모든 유기체들에게 공통적이고 모든 종(種)들에게 영향을 미친다. 오늘날에 상호배타적이지 않은 두 가지 보편화된 이론이 있는데, 점진진화이론과 중단평형설이며, 그들은 진화변형 속도에 차이가 있다.

단락 2
과거 점진진화의 예시

2 [Q30-G]One of the early proponents of complete gradualism was Charles Darwin whose [Q21]'Origin of Species' adopted Charles Lyell's 'Principles of Geology' to suggest [Q30-E]gradualism occurs **in a** slow **manner** with only small intergenerational changes. As Lyell proposed, sudden changes cannot **be assumed to occur** as they are not presently observed and thus cannot **be assumed to have occurred** in the past. [Q30-A]Darwin also felt that extreme **deviations from** the usual phenotypic variation would **be more likely to be selected against**. The most famous historical model supporting the idea of complete gradualism was the evolution of the modern horse from the fox-sized, forest-dwelling Hyracotherium. **Over time**, paleozoologists **pieced together** the [Q22]gradual evolution of the horse **in a** more complete **way** than any other modern animal. ⓒThey traced the lineage from early ancestors with splayed toes [Q23]for walking on the soft, moist grounds of primeval forests, to the longer legged, faster species which grazed on the firm grassy steppes and were able to outrun predators and eventually to

[Q30-G]완벽한 점진주의의 초기 지지자 중 한 사람은 '종의 기원' 에서 [Q30-E]점진주의가 세대 간에 약간의 변화와 함께 느린 방식으로 일어난다고 주장하기 위해 [Q21]찰스 라이얼의 '지질학의 원칙' 을 채택한 찰스 다윈이었다. 라이얼이 제안 했듯, 갑작스런 변화는 오늘날에 관찰되지 않기 때문에 발생한다고 추정할 수 없으며, 그리하여 과거에도 발생했다고 추정 될 수 없다. [Q30-A]또한 다윈은 일반적인 표현형에서 극단적인 변형은 선택되지 않을 것이라고 생각했다. 완벽한 점진진화론 사상을 지지하는 가장 유명한 역사적인 예는 오늘날의 말이 여우크기의, 숲에 사는 히라코테륨에서 진화했다는 것이다. 시간이 흐름에 따라, 고동물학자들은 다른 [Q22]어떤 현대 동물보다 말의 점진진화론을 더 완벽한 방식으로 종합했다. ⓒ그들은 부드럽고 습기 찼던 초창기 숲의 지면을 걷기 위해 벌어진 발가락을 가진 조상으로부터, 풀로 덮인 스텝지역에서 방목하고 포식자를 피할 수 있는 더 긴 다리를 가지고, 더 빠른 말까지, 그리고 결국 현대의 발굽 있는 말에 이르기까지의 혈통을 추적했다. 고생물학자 오스닐 마쉬는 말의 점진적 진화이론을 확신하고 1870년에 일련의 화석들을 제시했다.

Vocabulary

1단락
gradualism [grǽdʒuəlìzəm] n. 점진주의
evolutionary [èvəlúːʃənèri] a. 진화론의
deviation [dìːviéiʃən] n. 탈선, 일탈, 편향
branch [bræntʃ] a. 가지, 분지, 분파, 파생물 / v. 파생하다, 분화하다.

adaptation [ædæptéiʃən] n. 적응
punctuated equilibrium theory : n. 중단편형설
phenotype [fíːnətàip] n. 표현형, 육안으로 볼 수 있는 생물의 형질

gene [dʒiːn] n. 유전자

cladogenesis [klædʒiːnsis] n. 분기진화

2단락
Hyracotherium n. 히라코테륨
assume [əsjúːm] v. 가정하다

paleozoologist n. 고동물학자
ancestor [ǽnsestər] n. 조상

intergenerational [ìntərdʒènəréiʃənl] a. 세대간의
predator [prédətər] n. 포식자
splay [splei] v. 넓히다/a. 바깥쪽으로 벌어진

the modern hoofed horse. Paleontologist Othniel C. Marsh **was so sure of** this theory of gradual equine evolution **that** he **put together** a series of fossils showing it in 1870. The fact that these fossils displayed successive adaptations was held as an example of gradualism until 100 years later, when it was shown they [Q23] were not, in fact, even successive members of a single line of descent, let alone stages of an unbroken, gradually evolving lineage.

3   [Q30-C]Scientists studying fossils noted that the evolution of some species was nearly 'mapped out', while others had a few, very different species along the evolutionary course, with few or no intermediary fossils. They envisaged that this second group's evolution must have occurred rapidly to produce a great change over a short period. They reasoned that there had to be another evolutionary method that was quicker and left fewer intermediate species, thus the idea of punctuated equilibrium was formed. [Q28][Q30-D] i) The theory of punctuated equilibrium states that most sexually-reproducing species will remain in an extended state of little evolutionary change between generations, called stasis, ii) which is broken up by rare, rapid events of branching speciation called iii) cladogenesis when they **split into** two distinct species. They pointed out that for most species, there was a sudden appearance in the geologic record with no evidence of substantial, gradual changes. Darwin had noted this problem also, but **ascribed** it **to** imperfections in the fossil record rather than catastrophism and progressive creationism, or supernatural creation, while privately noting on the margin of his essay, "Better **begin with** this: If species really, after catastrophes, created **in showers world over**, my theory false."

4   While these theories vary widely on their methods of evolution, both show major adaptations **over time whereby** a population becomes better **suited to** its habitat. [■] These successive intergenerational changes occur in all species and are one of the basic phenomena of biology. [■] Even creatures which have very simple bodily structures, like internal

Vocabulary

3단락
- steppe [step] n. 스텝, 나무가 없는 시베리아의 대초원
- catastrophism [kətǽstrəfìzm] n. 천변지이설, 격변설
- ascribe [əskráib] v. ~에 돌리다, ~의 탓으로 돌리다.
- substantial [səbstǽnʃəl] a. 상당한
- intermediate [ìntərmíːdiət] a. 중간에 있는
- equine [íːkwain, ék-] a. 말의, 말 같은, 말에 관한
- creationism [kriːéiʃənìzm] n. 창조론, 영혼 창조설
- fossil [fásl] n. 화석
- equilibrium [ìːkwəlíbriəm] n. 균형
- speciation [spìːʃiéiʃən] n. 종분화
- punctuate [pʌ́ŋktʃuèit] v. 중단시키다

4단락
- demise [dimáiz] n. 서거, 사망
- adaptation [ædæptéiʃən] n. 적응
- trait [treit] n. 특징
- habitat [hǽbətæt] n. 서식지

parasites, are highly adapted to their specific environments. From this one can see that adaptation is **not just** a matter of visible traits, complex adaptations to changes can occur during an organism's life. [■] These reactions to habitat change happen **in** three major **ways**, either exclusively or **in succession**. [■] [Q25]The most basic adaptation to change is to simply move to a locale that better suits the organism. [Q26]This response, **typical of** organisms that have wide spheres of movement such as flying insects or sea-dwellers, is called habitat tracking, and is one explanation **put forth** for the periods of apparent stasis in the fossil record. The term genetic change, **on the other hand**, **pertains** to changes in the population when natural selection **acts on** the genetic variations of a population. These mutations, which may be physical features or adjusted physiological activity, create genetic variations that **lead to** differing characteristics in offspring and, consequently, a population better genetically **adapted to** its environment. The third, and most dramatic, change that can occur to resident populations is extinction, or the demise of a population that was **unable to** properly **adapt to** change.

구조를 가진 생물조차도 특정 환경에 아주 잘 적응되어 있다. 이것으로부터 우리는 적응이 단지 가시적인 특징일 뿐 아니라, 복잡한 적응도 역시 유기체 생명주기안에서 발생함을 알 수 있다. [■] 이러한 서식지 적응은 세 가지의 주요한 방법으로 일어나는데, 독점적이거나 혹은 연속적이다: 거주지 추적, 유전자 변형, 혹은 멸종 [■] [Q25]변화에 대한 가장 기본적인 적응은 그 유기체에게 더 적합한 곳으로 단순히 이동하는 것이다. [Q26]이 반응은 날아다니는 곤충이나 혹은 바다생물처럼 넓은 활동범위를 가지고 있는 생물의 전형적인 특성이며, 서식지 추적이라고 불리고, 화석기록에 있어 정지된 기간을 설명해 주기도 한다. 반면에, 유전적 변화라는 용어는 자연 도태가 개체에서 유전자적 다양성을 만들고자 할 때 개체 안에서의 변화와 관련된다. 이 돌연변이는 신체적 형태로 나타나거나 혹은 생리학상의 활동에 적용될 수도 있는데, 자손에게 다른 특성을 가지게 하고 결국, 환경에 유전적으로 더 잘 적응하는 개체를 만드는 유전적 다양성을 야기한다. 세 번째로, 정착한 개체들에게 일어날 수 있는 가장 극적인 변화는 멸종, 혹은 변화에 제대로 적응하지 못하는 개체에서 일어나는 종의 종말이다.

단락 5
항상 변하는 환경과 생물

5   Whether by gradualism or punctuated equilibrium, a species must always **adapt to** its changing habitat, as it is now clear that habitats and biota are constantly changing and the process of adaptation is never complete.

점진적 진화이든 중단평형진화이든, 서식지와 생물군은 끊임없이 변화하고 적응의 과정은 결코 끝나지 않는다는 것이 명백하므로, 종은 항상 그것의 변화하는 서식지에 적응해야만 한다.

Sentence analysis

◎ They traced the lineage / from early ancestors / with splayed toes /
   그들은 혈통을 추적하였다   초창기의 조상들로부터   벌어진 발가락을 가진
for walking on the soft, moist grounds of primeval forests, / to the longer legged, /
          습하고 촉촉했던 초창기의 숲을 걷고자 하는   더 긴 다리를 가진
faster species which grazed on the grassy steppes / and were able to outrun predators /
     풀로 덮인 스텝 지역에 방목된 더 빠른 종들은   그리고 습격자들로부터 도망갈 수 있었다
and eventually to the modern hoofed horse.
     그리고 발굽이 있는 현대의 말이 되었다.

Vocabulary

	sphere [sfiər] n. 영역	stasis [stéisis] n. 균형상태
5단락	biota [baióutə] n. 생물군, 생물상	

11 According to paragraph 2, on what grounds did Darwin insist that an occurrence which cannot be observed today could not have happened in the past?

(A) He theorized that the ~~evolutionary process must occur gradually~~, not abruptly. ★
(B) Cladogenesis, which breaks stasis, ~~cannot be proven scientifically~~.
(C) ~~Phenotypic variation would be selected against from~~ extreme variation.
(D) He thought Lyell's principles of methodology should be adopted to biology as well.

2단락에 따르면, 다윈은 왜 현재 관찰할 수 없는 사건은 과거에 일어나지 않았을 것이라고 주장하였는가?

(A) 그는 ~~진화과정이 급작스럽게 일어나는 것이 아니라 점진적으로 일어나는~~ 것이라고 주장했다. ★
(B) 진화의 정지를 깨는 분기진화는 ~~과학적으로 증명될 수 없다~~.
(C) 극단적인 변이로부터 ~~표현형 변화가 된다~~.
(D) 그는 라이엘의 방법론 원칙이 생물학에도 적용되어야 한다고 생각했다.

Fact 문제의 내용을 포함한 2단락을 살펴보면, 'Origin of Species' adopt Charles Lyell 'Principles of Geology' to suggest gradualism occurs in a slow manner with only small intergenerational changes. As Lyell proposed, saltations cannot be assumed to occur as they are not presently observed and thus cannot be assumed to have occurred in the past'.(찰스 라이엘의 '지질학의 원칙' 을 채택한 찰스 다윈이었다. 라이엘이 제안 했듯, 급격한 변동은 오늘 날에 관찰되지 않기 때문에 발생한다고 추정할 수 없으며, 그리하여 과거에도 발생했다고 추정될 수 없다)라는 부분에서, 다윈이 라이엘의 Principles of Geology(지질학의 원칙)에 근거하여 그의 이론을 완성했다는 것을 알 수 있으므로 답은 (D)이다. (A)가 틀린 이유는 묻는 말에 대답하지 않았기 때문이다. 문제는 왜 현재에 일어날 수 없는 것이 과거에도 일어날 수 없는가를 물었지만 문항은 다윈이 그것을 통해 내린 결과를 얘기해서이다.

12 According to paragraph 2, all of the following affected horses evolution EXCEPT:

(A) The firmer steppe meant they no longer needed wide-toed feet. ★
(B) Early horses migrated from the primeval forest ~~because~~ their feet had evolved into hooves.
(C) Soft, moist grounds gave less pressure to horse's feet.
(D) Adaptations which occurred on the steppes helped early horses to evade predation.

2단락에 따르면, 다음 중 _____을 제외하고는 말의 진화에 영향을 주었다

(A) 단단한 초지는 넓은 발가락이 필요 없다는 것을 의미한다. ★
(B) 초창기 말들은 그들의 발이 말굽으로 진화했기 때문에 원시림으로부터 이주했다.
(C) 부드럽고, 촉촉한 지대는 말의 발에 적은 부담을 주었다.
(D) 스텝지역에서의 적응은 초창기 말들이 포식자들을 피하도록 해 주었다.

Fact 질문의 키워드인 horse evolution을 2단락에서 찾아보면, with sprayed toes for walking on the soft, moist grounds of primeval forests (부드럽고 습기찼던 초창기 숲의 지면을 걷기 위해 벌어진 발가락)라는 부분에서 부드럽고 촉촉한 숲을 지나다니기 위해선 갈라진 발가락이 필요하다고 하니 이것은 진화에 영향을 준 요인이 아니므로 (B)가 정답이다. (A)는 초지로 나오면서 부드러운 바닥을 거닐 때 필요했던 갈라진 발가락이 필요 없어졌으니 진화에 영향을 주었기 때문에 맞고, (C)는 31번 근거문장에 firm grassy stepps라는 말과 soft ground라는 말이 대비되므로 알수 있다.

13 Which of the following statements is true about horses according to paragraph 2?

(A) They are ~~a good example~~ of gradualism. ★
(B) The evolutionary history of horses was inaccurate.
(C) ~~Fossils of the horse's~~ ancestors were abundant.
(D) ~~Their fossils are evidence of punctuated equilibrium.~~

2단락에 따르면, 다음 중 말에 대해서 사실인 것은?

(A) 말은 점진진화의 ~~좋은 예이다~~. ★
(B) 말의 진화 역사는 부정확하다.
(C) 말과 조상의 ~~화석은 많다~~.
(D) ~~말의 화석은 중단평형설의 증거가 된다~~.

Fact 문제의 키워드인 horses가 나오는 부분을 2단락에서 찾아 볼 때, The fact that these fossils displayed successive adaptations was held as an example of gradualism until it was shown they were not, in fact, even successive members of a single line of descent, let alone stages of an unbroken, gradually evolving lineage, nearly 100 years later.(이 화석들이 연속적 적응을 보여준다는 그 사실은 100년 후에 그들이 사실 끊어지지 않고 점진적으로 진화된 혈통은 고사하고, 심지어 하나의 단일 혈통에서 유래된 구성원도 아니라는 것이 밝혀질 때까지 연속적인 적응을 보여주는 점진적 진화의 예로 사용되었다)라는 부분에서 말의 화석이 연속적인 것이 아니라는 것이 밝혀짐으로 점진적 진화가 힘을 잃는다는 내용이 있다. 그러므로 (B)가 정답이 된다. (C)는 화석의 수에 대해 언급한 적이 없기 때문에 오답이다.

14 The word envisaged in the passage is closest in meaning to

(A) visualized
(B) dreamed ★
(C) publicized
(D) confirmed

지문의 단어 envisaged와 의미상 가장 유사한 것은?

(A) 상상했다 [víʒuəlàiz]
(B) 꿈꿨다 ★ [driːm]
(C) 공표했다 [pʌbləsàiz]
(D) 확증했다 [kənfə́ːrmd]

Vocabulary envisaged(예상하다)는 visualize(상상하다)와 동의어이므로 (A)가 답이다.

---

15 According to paragraph 4, how does habitat tracking possibly explain the periods of apparent stasis in the fossil record?

(A) Populations migrate to favorable environments where they can flourish exclusively.
(B) Flying insects or sea-dwellers with limited ranges of movement did not show signs of evolution.
(C) Habitat tracking can only occur in populations that evolve through punctuated equilibrium. ★
(D) Populations are unlikely to change if they keep moving to favorable places for their survival.

4단락에 따르면, 서식지 추적이 어떻게 화석기록에서 정지된 부분을 설명하는가?

(A) 개체들은 그들이 독점적으로 번창할 수 있는 좋은 환경으로 이주했다.
(B) 날아다니는 곤충이나 해양 생물과 같이 좁은 이동범위를 가지고 있는 생물은 많은 진화를 하지 않았다.
(C) 서식지 추적은 중단평형설로 진화한 그룹에만 일어난다. ★
(D) 개체들이 살아남기 위해 지속적으로 좋은 환경으로 이주한다면 진화하지 않을 확률이 높다.

Fact 문제의 키워드인 habitat tracking(서식지 추적)이 있는 부분을 찾아보면, This response, typical of organisms that have wide spheres of movement such as flying insects or sea-dwellers, is called habitat tracking, and is one explanation put forth for the periods of apparent stasis in the fossil record.(이 반응은 날아다니는 곤충이나 혹은 바다 생물처럼 넓은 활동 범위를 가지고 있는 생물의 전형적인 특징이며, 서식지 추적이라고 불리며, 화석기록에 있어 정리된 기간을 설명해주기도 한다) 서식지 추적, 즉 생물이 이동하는 것이 화석 기록에서 정체된 부분을 설명해 준다고 말한다. 이는 즉, 생물이 이동하면 진화를 하지 않기 때문에 화석에 진화한 흔적을 찾을 수 없다는 뜻이므로, 답은 (D)가 된다. (C)가 틀린 이유는 중단평형설이 genetic tracking process와 어떤식으로 연관되어 있어를 설명할 수 있는지 아무런 추가 정보가 없기 때문이다.

---

16 Which of the following claims about habitat tracking can be inferred from paragraph 4?

(A) It is required before evolution or extinction can occur. ★
(B) It is the most common reaction to habitat change in mobile organisms.
(C) Extinction is followed immediately by it most of the time.
(D) Populations usually return to their original environment.

4단락에 따르면, 다음 중 어떤 주장이 서식지 추적에 대하여 추론될 수 있는가?

(A) 서식지 추적은 진화나 멸종 전에 필요한 것이다. ★
(B) 그것은 이동성 있는 생물들의 거주지 변화에 대한 가장 흔한 반응이다.
(C) 멸종은 서식지 추적 직후 일어나는 경우가 많다.
(D) 거주 개체들은 보통 이전 서식지로 돌아온다.

Inference 문제의 키워드인 habitat tracking이 언급된 부분을 살펴보면 The most basic adaptation to change is to simply move to a locale that better suits it.(변화에 대한 가장 기본적인 적응은 그 유기체에서 더 적합한 곳으로 이동하는 것이다)라고 말하면서 habitat tracking(서식지 추적)라 설명한다. 즉, 다른 곳에 가서 적응하여 살수 있다는 (B)가 정답이다. (A)는 3번째 네모 뒤에 exclusively하게 발생할 수 있다 했는데 서식지 추적이 진화나 멸종전에 필요한 것이라는, 없는 인과관계를 만들었기 때문에 오답이다.

17 What is the main purpose of this passage?

(A) To explain why scientists cannot agree on which theory of evolution is the most accurate ★

(B) To compare and contrast two theories of the process of evolution

(C) To emphasize that ~~punctuated equilibrium has rendered gradualism obsolete~~

(D) To show the ~~similarities~~ between two dominant theories.

이 글의 주된 목적은 무엇인가?

(A) 왜 과학자들이 어떤 진화론이 가장 정확한지에 대해 동의하지 않는지 설명하기 위해 ★

(B) 두가지 진화이론을 대조비교하기 위해

(C) ~~평형진행론이 점진진화론을 더 이상 쓸모없는 폐형된 이론이라는~~ 점을 강조하기 위해

(D) 두가지 우세론 사이의 ~~공통점을~~ 보여주기 위해

Purpose 지문은 마지막에 적응력에 대해 설명하였으나, 전체적으로 봤을 때는 진화론에 대해 다루고 있으므로, 두 가지 다른 진화론을 설명했다는 (B)가 답이 된다. (A)가 틀린 이유는 adaptation은 상반되는 이론을 설명하는데 쓰인 예일 뿐이지 그것이 주된 지문의 목적이 아니기 때문이다. (C) 와 (D)는 마이너한 포인트로써 지문 전체를 아우르지 못했다.

18 Which of the sentences below best expresses the essential information in the highlighted sentence in the passage? Incorrect choices change the meaning in important ways or leave out essential information.

(A) Punctuated equilibrium says that evolution happens through cladogenesis in sexually-reproducing species which usually display few changes between generations.

(B) While remaining in an extended state or little evolutionary change between generations is called stasis, splitting into two distinct species with huge change is called cladogenesis. ★

(C) Punctuated equilibrium explains that species evolve through cladogenesis, an uncommon event in which a species splits into two distinct species in a short period of time.

(D) The splitting into two distinct sexually-reproducing species of punctuated equilibrium ~~was a means to explain~~ the lack of change between generations that Darwin mentioned.

아래 문장 중 지문 속의 음영 표시된 문장의 핵심 정보를 가장 잘 표현하고 있는 것은 무엇인가? 오답은 문장의 의미를 현저하게 바꾸거나 핵심정보를 빠뜨리고 있다.

(A) 진화가 유성생식 종들의 분기진화를 통해 일어나고 그것은 세대사이에서 거의 변화를 보이지 않는다고 말한다.

(B) 세대간 작은 진화상태로 오랜기간 머무르는 것을 stasis라고 부르는 반면, 큰 변화와 더불어 두 개의 별 개종으로 나누는 것을 cladogenesis라고 부른다. ★

(C) 중단평형설은 보통 정체상태로 있는 유성생식 생물의 종 분화가 일어나는 이유를 설명한다.

(D) 중단평형설에서의 유성생식 생물의 종분화가 다윈이 언급한 세대간의 변화를 ~~설명한다~~.

Highlight 음영된 문장을 살펴보면 i)The theory of punctuated equilibrium states that most sexually-reproducing species will remain in an extended state of little evolutionary change between generations, called stasis, ii) which is broken up by rare, rapid events of branching speciation called cladogenesis when they split into two distinct species. (i) 중단평형설 이론은 대부분의 성적 교배를 하는 종이 세대간에 미미한 진화만 겪고 정지라는 상태를 유지 한다고 말하는데, ii) 그리고 그것은 그들이 두 개의 구별되는 종으로 나뉠 때, 분기진화라고 불리는 매우 드물고 빠른 분리종형성에 의해 갈리진다)는 정보를 확인할 수 있는데 이 모든 핵심 내용이 들어간 (A)가 정답이 된다. (B)는 종의 변화에 대한 내용을 빠뜨리고 있고, (C)는 abruptly 내용을 빠뜨리고 있고 (D)는 인과 관계가 틀렸다. 답이 안되는 이유, Punctuated equilibrium의 정의에 대해 적혀 있어야 하나, 정작 주절 내용이 전혀 없다.

19 Look at the four squares [■] that indicate where the following sentence could be added to the passage.

(Even) creatures which have very simple bodily structures, like internal parasites, are highly adapted to their specific environments.

Where would the sentence best fit? Click on a square [■] to add the sentence to the passage.

2nd

네 개의 네모[■]는 다음 문장이 삽입될 수 있는 부분을 나타내고 있다.

심지어 내부 기생충처럼, 매우 단순한 신체 구조를 가진 생물조차도 특정 환경에 아주 잘 적응되어 있다.

이 문장은 어느 자리에 들어가는 것이 가장 적절한가?

두번째

Insertion 삽입문장은 환경에 대해 적응하는 동물에 대한 구체적인 예제이다. 앞 문장에서 포괄적인 설명이 나와 있으며, 포괄적인 설명 뒤 예제를 넣는 것이 타당함으로 답은 첫번째 네모이다.

20

Directions: Select the appropriate phrases from the answer choices and match them to the type of evolutionary theory to which they relate. TWO of the answer choices will NOT be used. This question is worth 3 points.

지시: 주어진 선택지에서 적절한 구를 선택하여 관계있는 진화 이론의 종류에 연결시키시오. 선택지 중 2개는 답이 아니다. 이 문제는 3점이다.

(B) Othniel C. Marsh compiled a series of fossils that accurately illustrated its evolutionary steps.
(F) Complex adaptations can occur during an organism's life.

Gradualism
- (A) Radical changes from the usual phenotypic variation are less likely to be passed on.
- (E) Evolution takes place with small changes between successive generations.
- (G) Charles Darwin used theories in 'Principles of Geology' to explain the evolutionary change.

Punctuated Equilibrium
- (C) Evolution leaves few intermediate species.
- (D) Long periods of stasis are interrupted by rare, branching speciation.

(B) 마쉬는 진화 단계를 정확히 알려주는 일련의 화석들을 수집했다.
(F) 복잡한 적응들이 유기체의 삶에서 발생할 수 있다.

점진설
- (A) 일반적인 표현형 변이로부터의 급진적인 변화들이 전달될 것 같지 않다.
- (E) 진화는 연속적인 세대들 사이에서의 작은 변화들과 함께 발생한다.
- (G) 찰스 다윈은 진화적 변화를 설명하기 위해 '지질 학 원리'에서의 이론들을 사용했다.

중단평형설
- (C)진화는 거의 중간 종을 남기지 않는다.
- (D) 희귀한 분기 종분화가 오랜 정체를 중단한다.

Category Chart

Gradualism

보기 (A), (E), (G) 는 점진 주의에 대한 특징으로 모두 2단락에서 확인할 수 있는데,
(A)는 본문 Darwin also felt that extreme deviations from the usual phenotypic variation would be more likely to be selected against. (또한 다윈은 일반적인 표현형에서 극단적인 변형은 선택되지 않을 것이라고 생각했다)의 내용과 일치한다.
(E)는 Gradualism occurs in a slow manner with only small intergenerational changes. (점진주의가 세대간에 약간의 변화와 함께 느린 방식으로 일어난다)와 일치한다.
(G)는 One of the early proponents of complete gradualism was Charles Darwin whose 'Origin of Species' adopted. Charles Lyell's 'Principles of Geology' to suggest gradualism occurs(완벽한 점진주의의 초기 지지자 중 한 사람은 '종의 기원' 에서 점진 주의가 일어난다고 주장하기 위해 찰스 라이열의 '지질학의 원칙' 을 채택한 찰스 다윈이었다)의 내용과 일치한다. (F)는 두가지 이론 모두에 해당된다.

Punctuated Equilibrium

(C), (D)는 중단 평형설 이론에 대한 특징으로 모두 3단락에서 확인할 수 있는데,
(C)는 Scientists studying fossils noted that the evolution of some species was nearly 'mapped out', while others had a few, very different species along the evolutionary course, with few or no intermediary fossils. (화석을 연구하는 과학자들은 어떤 종들의 진화는 거의 '틀을 잡을 수' 있지만, 소수의 매우 다른 종들은 진화단계 중에서 아주 적거나 중재화석이 아예 존재하지 않는다고 언급했다)의 내용과 일치한다.
(D)는 The theory of punctuated equilibrium states that most sexually-reproducing species will remain in an extended state of little evolutionary change between generations, called stasis, which is broken up by rare, rapid events of branching speciation called cladogenesis when they split into two distinct species. (중단 평행설 이론은 대부분의 성적교배를 하는 종들은 세대간의 미비한 진화만 있는 정체라고 불리는 연장된 상태를 유지할 것이라고 말하는데 그리고 그것은 그들이 두 개의 구별되는 종으로 나뉠 때, 분기 진화라 불리는 매우 드물고 빠른 분지종행성에 의해 갈라진다)의 내용에서 확인할 수 있다.

참고 이미지

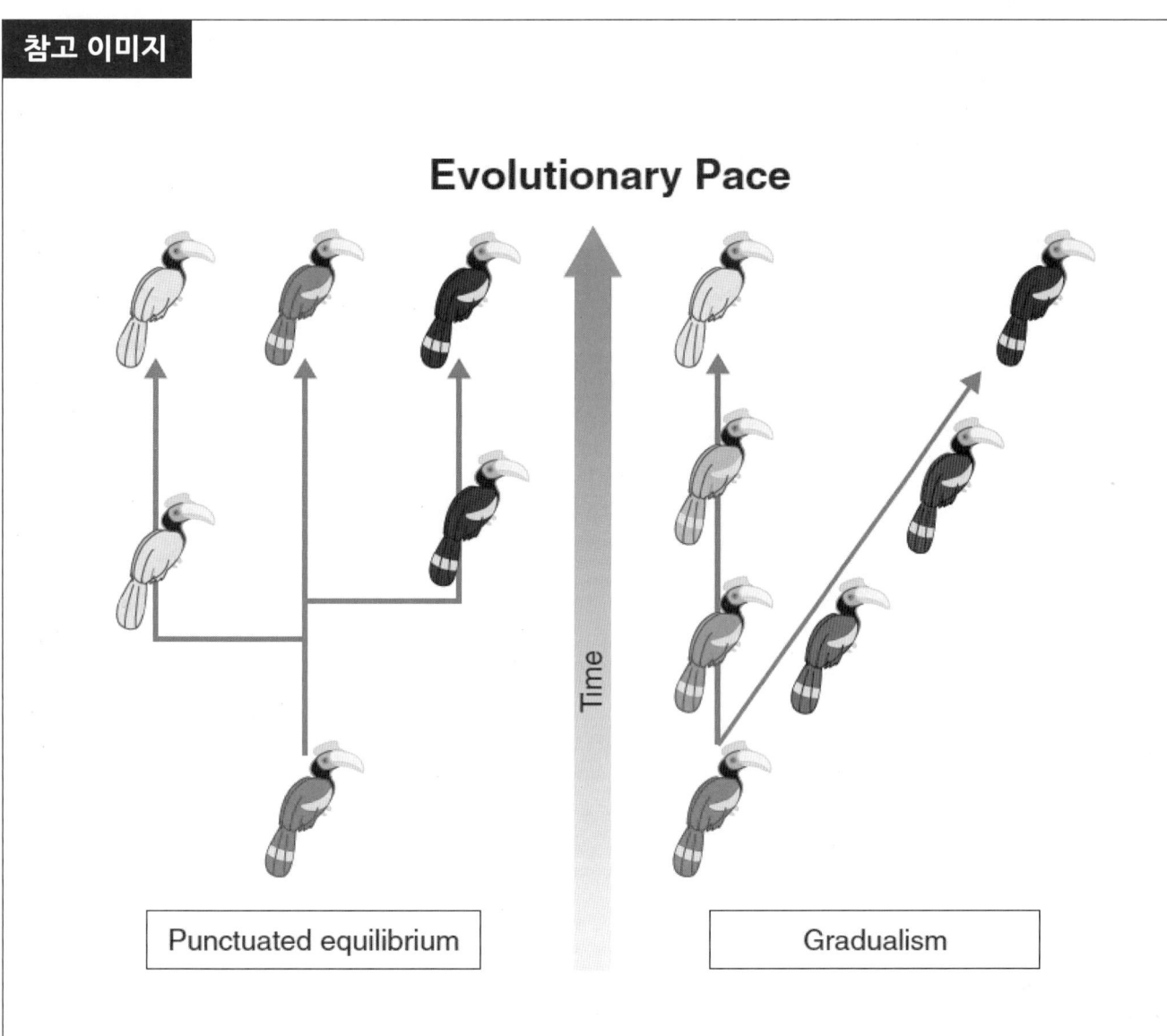

USHER

iBT TOEFL
FINAL TEST READING
TEST 4

답안 및 취약 유형 분석표
해석·해설

답안 및 문제 유형 분석표

TEST 4-1

01 (A) Vocabulary

02 (D) Purpose

03 (C) Fact

04 (C) Inference

05 (A) Highlight

06 (D) Fact

07 (D) Fact

08 (B) Purpose

09 2nd ■ Insertion

10 (B), (C), (E) Summary

TEST 4-2

11 (C) Inference

12 (A) Vocabulary

13 (C) Purpose

14 (C) Reference

15 (D) Fact

16 (C) Fact

17 (B) Highlight

18 (B) Fact

19 3rd ■ Insertion

20 (B),(D),(E) Summary

각 문제 유형별 맞춘 개수를 아래에 적어 보세요.

유형	맞춘 답의 개수	정답률
단어 (Vocabulary)	/ 2	정답률: %
사실 확인 문제 (Fact)	/ 6	정답률: %
지시어 찾기 (Reference)	/ 1	정답률: %
끼워 넣기 (Insertion)	/ 2	정답률: %
문장 변환문제 (Highlight)	/ 2	정답률: %
목적 (Purpose)	/ 3	정답률: %
추론 (Inference)	/ 2	정답률: %
단락 요약(Summary / Category Chart)	/ 2	정답률: %
전체	/ 20	정답률: %

※ 자신이 취약한 유형은 READING STRATEGIES를 통해 다시 한번 점검하시기 바랍니다. (p.31)

TEST 4-1 Griffith and Transformation 두가지 진화이론

Introduction	단락 1	그리피스 실험과 배경
Point 1	단락 2	S 와 R 폐렴균의 특성
Point 2	단락 3	새로 발견된 박테리아의 성질
Point 3	단락 4	전염을 일으키는 원인 분석
Point 4	단락 5	그리피스 실험의 영향

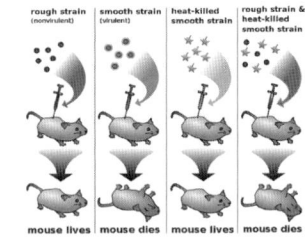

단락 1 — 그리피스 실험과 배경

1 The 19th century Romantic Movement reshaped science by opening new avenues of research that **were unheard of** under the Enlightenment's classical approaches. Major breakthroughs, such as Darwin's theory of evolution, were developed during this period, **along with advances in** physics, non-Euclidean geometry and organic chemistry. During this time, science became a major source for increasing humankind's knowledge. During the 19th and 20th centuries, the practice of science became much more professionally institutionalized than it had been. One of the great breakthroughs in biology **is attributed to** Frederick Griffith of the British Ministry of Health. Griffith undertook one of the most pivotal experiments of the era, which **tried to establish** a more precise scientific understanding by typing, or classifying, pneumococci bacteria samples **in order to find overarching** patterns **so as to clarify** the epidemiology of lobar pneumonia, an infectious lung disorder.

19세기 낭만주의 운동은 계몽운동의 고전적인 접근에서는 들어보지 못한 연구의 새로운 수단에 의해 과학을 다시 개척했다. 다윈의 진화 이론과 같은 주요한 획기적인 발전은 이 시기 동안에 물리학, 비유 클리드 기하학과 유기 화학에서의 진보와 함께 발달 되었다. 이 시기 동안에, 과학은 인류 지식의 증가를 위한 주요한 원천이 되었다. 19세기와 20세기 동안에, 과학 실험은 과거보다 좀 더 전문적으로 제도화 되었다. 생물학에서의 가장 큰 발전은 영국 보건 복지부의 프레데릭 그리피스의 덕분이다. 그리피스는 당대의 가장 중요한 실험에 착수했고, 그것은 전염성 폐질환인 대엽성 폐렴의 병리학을 명확히 하기 위해 중요한 패턴들을 확인하고자 폐렴 박테리아 샘플들을 구분하고 분류함으로써 좀 더 정확한 과학적인 이해를 확고히 하기 위한 시도였다.

단락 2 — S와 R 폐렴균의 특성

2 [Q2]He also **sought to improve** the understanding of the pathology of pneumococci on the individual by testing them on mice. [Q2]Pneumococci generally have two forms, smooth and rough. Smooth pneumococci, denoted by S, are encapsulated and more virulent; this form **was shown to result in** pneumonia and death of the mice within days of being injected. [Q3]Their capsules are slippery polysaccharide coatings that **allow** the bacteria **to evade** phagocytosis **from** the host's immune cells. **On the other hand**, the rough form, R, lacks a capsule and was considered non-infective. In Griffith's experiment, **as expected**, when mice **were injected with** S that had been killed by heat, it **failed to cause** illness

[Q2]그는 또한 폐렴균을 쥐에 실험함으로써 개체에 대한 폐렴균 병리학에 대한 이해를 높이고자 추구하였다. [Q2]폐렴균은 일반적으로 부드럽고 거친 두 가지의 형태를 가진다. S로 표현되는 부드러운 폐렴균은 포로 둘러싸여 있고 독성이 있다: 이 형태는 병균이 주입된 며칠 안에 쥐에게서 폐렴이나 죽음의 형태를 초래하는 것으로 나타나게 된다. [Q3]그들의 캡슐은 미끄러운 다당류의 피복이고 박테리아가 숙주의 면역 세포로부터 식균작용을 피할 수 있도록 해준다. 반면에 거친 형태인 R은 캡슐이 없으며 비 전염적인 것으로 간주된다. 그리피스의 실험에서 예상된 대로 열에 의해서 멸균된 S를 쥐에 주입했을 때 독성이 있는 변종임에도 발병시키는 것에 실패했다. 하지만

Vocabulary

1단락 avenue [ǽvənjùː] n. (나아갈) 길, 방안 / institutionalize [ìns-tətjúʃənəlàiz] v. 제도화하다 / pivotal [pívətl] n. (가장 중요한) 중심 / breakthrough n. 돌파구, 획기적인 발전 / professionally [prəféʃənəli] ad. 전문적으로 / attribute [ətríbjuːt] v. rv의 결과라고 생각하다 / precise [prisáis] a. 정확한 / pneumonia [njumóunjə] n. 폐렴 / infectious [infékʃəs] a. 전염성의 / overarching [òuvəráːrtʃiŋ] a. (많은 것에 관련되므로) 대단히 중요한 / epidemiology [èpidìːmiálədʒi] n. 역학(疫學), 전염병학

2단락 pathology [pəθálədʒi] n. 병리학 / encapsulate [inkǽpsjulèit] v. 캡슐에 싸다 / slippery [slípəri] a. 미끌끌한 / immune [imjúːn] a. 면역의 / denote [dinóut] v. 의미하다, 나타내다 / avirulent [eivírjulənt] a. 〈생물체가〉 독성이 없는, 악성이 아닌

despite being the virulent strain. Surprisingly, however, Griffith observed pneumonia and death when live R were injected alongside large amounts of heat-killed S; this was generally unexpected, since R, the only live bacteria in the experiment, were avirulent. During necropsy, Griffith found that the live R had developed capsules and **morphed into** S, then retained this phenotype over successive generations. Griffith hypothesized that a transforming principle **derived from** the killed S-had helped **transform** the R **into** S. [Q4]He also reported that heavy loads of live R alone could also **transform into** S. Griffith, however, noted that the addition of heat-killed S bacteria made this transformation much more likely.

단락 3
새로 발견된 박테리아의 성질

3 Griffith had previously held, along with most bacteriologists, that bacteria's forms were essentially fixed and unchangeable. They **held that** each strain had **emerged from**, and was genetically **similar to** their progenitor, through an evolutionary lineage determined by Darwinian natural selection **resulting in** the death of unfit bacterial cells. ◎[Q5]i)Besides this implicit belief that bacterial strains could be extinguished through competition, ii)many bacteriologists and physicians believed that any particular strain of bacteria had necessarily multiplied from previous, genetically-related strains. ◎[Q6]Griffith's findings, though generally neglected after the initial contention against them subsided, revealed that his original supposition was incorrect by showing that bacteria **are able to acquire** genes without the need for reproducing **as well**.He summarized his work **as such**: "The results of the **experiments on** enhancement of virulence and **on** transformation of type are discussed and their significance **in regard to** questions of epidemiology is indicated."

단락 4
전염을 일으키는 원인 분석

4 An American medical researcher named Oswald Avery with colleagues Macleod and McCarty furthered Griffith's 1927 findings **regarding** the mysteries of inheritance. [■] **Being driven to prove** Griffith's theory, Avery **continued to work on** adjusting previous techniques even after he retired in 1943. [■] By using techniques to remove bacteria's organic compounds, scientists could observe if the R-strain bacteria still transformed, it would mean that the materials removed were not the carrier of the transformation gene. [Q7] To do this, the cellular structures of the S strain bacteria were first removed, and then their proteins were removed **through the**

Vocabulary

3단락
- necropsy [nékrapsi] n. 검시, 부검
- progenitor [proudʒénətər] n. (사람·동식물의) 조상
- implicit [implísit] a. 절대의
- epidemiology [èpidìːmiálədʒi] n. 역학
- morph [mɔːrf] v. 변하다, 바뀌다; 바꾸다
- previously [príːviəsli] ad. 미리
- supposition [sʌpəzíʃən] n. 가정
- indicate [índikèit] v. 가리키다
- emerge [imə́ːrdʒ] v. (안보이던 것이) 나타나다
- enhancement [inhǽnsmənt] n. 고양
- lineage [líniidʒ] n. 혈통

4단락
- inheritance [inhérətəns] n. 상속재산
- resist [rizíst] v. 저항하다
- enzyme [énzaim] n. 효소
- strain [strein] n. 변종
- deoxyribonuclease [diːáksiráibounjúːklièis] n. DNA 분해 효소
- protein [próutiːn] n. 단백질

use of protease enzyme treatments. [■] Finally, the cellular remainders were placed in a dish containing R strain bacteria. [■] The R strain bacteria transformed, meaning that proteins did not carry the virulent genes. Then the remainder of the S strain bacteria **had** their DNA **removed by being treated with** deoxyribonuclease. When they were treated **in** this **manner**, the R strain bacteria resisted transformation, proving that DNA was the transforming factor of pneumococci.

단락 5
그리피스 실험의 영향

5 [Q8]**Over time**, more advanced discoveries have been made **through the findings of** Griffith and Avery. Joshua Lederberg's discoveries **concerning** genetic recombination and the organization of the bacterial genetic material are a prime example of this continuation. Inspired by previous discoveries, Lederberg, in 1944, **started to think about** genetic **experimentations on** bacteria **despite the fact that** there was still no **consensus on** whether bacteria even had genes or not. He showed that bacteria could reproduce sexually and substantiated the hypothesis by proving that they **are endowed with** genetic systems **akin to** those of higherlevel organisms, thus opening a new realm for scientists to study the genetic basis of life and winning the 1958 Nobel Prize in Physiology or Medicine. During his speech, he stated that former researchers and their laboratories provided the historical platform of modern DNA research.

Sentence analysis

◎ Besides this implicit belief that bacterial strains could be extinguished through competition, /
　　박테리아 변종들이 경쟁을 통해 소멸될 수 있다는 절대적인 믿음 외에도,
many bacteriologists and physicians believed that / any particular strain of bacteria /
　　많은 세균학자들과 의사들은 믿었다　　어떠한 박테리아의 특정한 변종들이
had necessarily multiplied from previous, genetically-related strains.
　　이전의 유전적으로 관련된 변종들로부터 필연적으로 증식되었다는 것을

◎ Griffith's findings / though generally neglected after the initial contention against them subsided /
　그리피스의 발견들은,　　그것들에 적대하는 초기 논쟁이 비록 가라앉은 후에 일반적으로 무시 되었지만,
revealed that his original supposition was incorrect /
　그의 초기 가정이 정확하지 않다는 것을 드러냈다
by showing that bacteria are able to acquire genes without the need for reproducing as well.
　박테리아가 재생산하는 것에 대한 필요없이 유전자를 얻을 수 있다는 것을 보여줌으로써

Vocabulary

5단락　endow [endáu] v. 주다　　　　　　　　　　recombination [rìːkɑmbənéiʃən] n. [유전학] 재조합
　　　　experimentation [ikspèrəmentéiʃən] n. 실험방법　consensus [kənsénsəs] n. 일치　　　akin [əkín] a. 유사한

01

The word **overarching** in the passage is closest in meaning to

(A) encompassing
(B) bending ★
(C) clear
(D) overwhelming

지문의 단어 **overarching** 와 의미상 가장 유사한 것은?

(A) 아우르는 [inkʌ́mpəs]
(B) 구부려진 ★ [bend]
(C) 분명한 [kliər]
(D) 압도적인 [òuvərhwélmiŋ]

Vocabulary 지문의 overching(대단히 중요한)은 그 시대의 모든것을 아우른다는 표현이 됨으로 encompassing(아우르는) (A)가 정답이다

02

What is important about the fact that pneumococci generally have two forms?

(A) It proves Griffith's ~~hypothesis~~ that bacteria of the same species display different phenotypes. ★
(B) It suggests that some forms of bacteria have ~~beneficial effects~~ on organisms.
(C) It is the reason that Griffith ~~refused to experiment~~ on bacteria.
(D) It is a fundamental characteristic that allowed Griffith to produce his significant results.

폐렴균이 일반적으로 두 가지 형태를 가진다는 사실에 대해 중요한 것은?

(A) 같은 종들이 다른 표현형을 보인다는 그리피스의 ~~가설을 증명한다.~~ ★
(B) 박테리아의 어떤 형태는 유기체에게 ~~이로운 효과를 줄~~ 수도 있다는 것을 나타낸다.
(C) 그리피스가 박테리아에 대한 ~~실험을 거절한~~ 이유이다.
(D) 그리피스가 중요한 결과를 만들어내는 기본적인 특징이다.

Purpose 문제의 주요 핵심 내용이 들어간 문장에서 Pneumococci generally have two forms, smooth and rough(폐렴균은 대부분 매끄러운 것과 거친 두 형태가 있다)와 He also sought to improve the understanding of the pathology of pneumococci on the individual by testing them on mice. (그는 또한 폐렴균을 쥐에 실험함으로써 개체에 대한 폐렴균 병리학에 대한 이해를 높이고자 추구하였다)이라 말한다. 또한 전반적인 단락의 내용이 S, R 폐렴균에 관해 독성을 가진 S와 가지지 않은 R을 가지고 실험하였는데, 열로 죽인 S는 더 이상 독성이 없었으나, 죽은 S를 살아있는 R에 넣었더니 R이 S의 독성성질을 가지게 된 것이니 그리피스의 연구에 관해 기본적인 정보를 제공한다. 그러므로 정답은 (D)이다. (A)는 정보는 사실이나 글쓴이가 의도했던 것이 아니라서 오답이다.

03

According to paragraph 2, which of the following statements regarding the R and S pneumococcus is true?

(A) S form of pneumococci usually ~~does not cause any harm~~ in animals because they have smooth exteriors.
(B) The smooth polysaccharide-coated cell wall of S are able ~~to fight~~ the host's immune cells ~~and consume them~~. ★
(C) The immune system is unable to defeat pneumococci because S can effectively slip away from the immune cells.
(D) The R type is known to be the same pneumococci that ~~causes other illnesses in~~ the host's body.

2단락에서 R과 S폐렴균에 관한 내용 중 사실인 것은?

(A) S폐렴균의 형태는 그들이 부드러운 외벽을 가지고 있기 때문에 동물에게 ~~어떠한 해도 입히지 않는다.~~
(B) S폐렴균의 부드러운 다당류로 입혀진 세포벽은 숙주의 면역세포와 ~~싸울 수 있고 그들을 먹어치운다.~~ ★
(C) S폐렴균은 효율적으로 항체를 피할 수 있기 때문에 면역 시스템이 폐렴균에 대항할 수 없다.
(D) R폐렴균은 숙주의 몸체에서 ~~다른 질병을 야기시킬 수 있는~~ 폐렴균과 같은 것으로 알려져 있다.

Fact 문제의 키워드인 R and S pneumococcus를 살펴보면 Their capsules are slippery polysaccharide coatings that allow the cells to evade phagocytosis from the host's immune cells. (그것의 캡슐들의 매끄러운 다당류 피복은 세포로 하여금 숙주의 항체세포의 식작용을 피하게 해준다) 이라 말한다. 즉 S에 관해 말한 주장으로서 S가 어떻게 항체를 피하는가의 (C)가 답이다. (A)는 반대의 내용이고 (B)는 S폐렴균이 숙주의 면역 세포와 싸울 수 있다는 내용이 지문에 없어서 오답이다.

04 Which of the following can be inferred from paragraph 2 about the bacteria used in Griffith's experiments?

다음 중 2단락에서 그리피스의 실험에 관해 추론할 수 있는 것은?

(A) The R pneumococcus ~~can steal~~ the capsule of the dead S ★
(B) The S pneumococcus has slippery cell walls that ~~can destroy~~ immune cells.
(C) Introduction of sufficient loads of either type of pneumococcus bacteria can lead to infection.
(D) An R pneumococcus that has transformed into S remains in its new form ~~until it is surrounded by large amounts of R.~~

(A) R 폐렴균은 죽은 S 폐렴균의 캡슐을 ~~훔칠 수 있다.~~ ★
(B) S 폐렴균은 면역세포를 ~~파괴할 수 있는~~ 매끄러운 세포벽을 가지고 있다.
(C) 각각 폐렴균의 충분히 많은 양의 주입은 감염을 야기시킬 수도 있다.
(D) S 폐렴균으로 변형된 R 폐렴균은 그것이 ~~많은 양의 R 폐렴균으로 둘러싸일 때까지~~ 새로운 형태로 남아있다.

Inference 문제의 키워드인 Griffith's experiments 를 살펴보면 He also reported that heavy loads of live R alone could also transform into S. Griffith, however, noted that the addition of heat-killed S bacteria made this transformation much more likely. (그는 또한 살아있는 R의 수많은 양만으로도 S로 변형될 수 있다고 보고했다. 그러나 그리피스는 열에 의해 죽은 S박테리아의 주입이 이 변형을 좀 더 가능성 있게 한다고 말했다) 이라고 한다. 즉 R폐렴균과 S폐렴균의 충분한 양의 주입이 있으면 폐렴이 발병할 수 있다는 말이므로 (C)가 정답이다. (A)는 내용자체의 언급이 없고 (B)는 면역세포를 파괴할 수 있다는 말이 없으며 (D)는 수많은 R세포로 둘러싸인다는 내용이 없으므로 오답이다.

05 Which of the sentences below best expresses the essential information in the highlighted sentence in the passage? Incorrect choices change the meaning in important ways or leave out essential information.

아래 문장 중 지문 속의 음영된 문장의 핵심 정보를 가장 잘 표현하고 있는 것은 무엇인가? 오답은 문장의 의미를 현저히 왜곡하거나 핵심 정보를 빠뜨리고 있다.

(A) Bacteriologists and physicians thought that unfit bacteria died through competition, and bacteria could, only be replicated through sharing particular genes seen in previous generations.
(B) There was a belief among biologists that bacteria ~~kill each other for better habitats~~ and that they multiplied asexually.
(C) Replication of bacteria was known to occur within pneumococci ~~because they fight each other to multiply.~~
(D) Bacteriologists believed that bacteria come from a previous generation of the same ~~strain which survived massive competition.~~ ★

(A) 세균학자와 내과의는 부적합한 박테리아는 경쟁을 통해 치사하고 따라서 박테리아는 오직 앞선 세대에서 보여진 특정 유전자를 공유함으로서 증가될 수 있다고 생각하였다.
(B) 박테리아는 ~~더 나은 환경과 서식지를 위해 서로 죽이고~~ 무성생식을 했다고 생태학자들 사이에서 믿어져 왔었다.
(C) ~~박테리아는 생식하기 위해 서로 싸우기 때문에~~ 박테리아 복제는 특정 박테리아에게서만 일어난다고 알려져 있었다.
(D) 세균학자들은 박테리아들은 ~~태단한 경쟁을 견디고 살아난~~ 유형의 박테리아는 같은 것에서 비롯됐다고 믿어왔다. ★

Highlight 음영 표시된 문장의 핵심 정보는 i) Besides this implicit belief that bacterial strains could be extinguished through competition, ii) many bacteriologists and physicians believed that any particular strain of bacteria had necessarily multiplied from previous, genetically-related strains.(i) 박테리아 변종이 경쟁을 통해 소멸 될 수 있다는 맹목적인 믿음 외에도 ii) 많은 세균학자들과 의사들은 박테리아의 어떠한 변종도 이전의 유전적으로 관련된 변종으로부터 필연적으로 증가될 수 있다고 믿었다)이다. Besides this implicit belief that bacterial strains could be extinguished through competition(이 함축적인 신념 외에 변종들은 경쟁을 통해 소멸되고)는 unfit bacteria died through competition(부적합한 박테리아는 경쟁을 통해 치사하고)으로 표현되었고, many bacteriologists and physicians believed that any particular strain of bacteria had necessarily multiplied from only that very strain initially acquired (많은 세균학자들과 의사들은 박테리아의 어떠한 변종도 이전의 유전적으로 관련된 변종으로부터 필연적으로 증가될 수 있다고 믿었다)은 Bacteriologists and physicians thought that … only be replicated from the same strain as seen in the previous generation(세균학자와 내과의는 … 박테리아는 오직 앞 선 세대에서 보여진 같은 변종에서만 증가될 수 있다고 생각하였다)으로 요약되었다. 그러므로 정답은 (A)가 된다. (D)가 정답이 틀린 이유는 경쟁을 통해 살아남은 것들에서만 이라는 내용이 음영문장에 없기 때문이다.

06
What was the importance of Griffith's findings according to paragraph 3?

(A) They were ~~accepted by the scientific community~~ soon after Griffith's death.
(B) They proved that ~~unfit bacterial cells face death or even extinction~~.
(C) They showed that ~~bacteria follow Darwinian natural selection~~. ★
(D) They proved that bacteria are one exception that only partially follows lineage determined by Darwinian selection.

다음 중 3단락에서 그리피스의 연구결과의 중요한 점은 무엇인가?

(A) ~~과학자들은 그리피스의 죽음 이후에 안정했다.~~
(B) ~~그들은 부적합한 박테리아 세포가 죽거나 심지어 멸종하는 것을 증명하였다.~~
(C) 그의 결과는 ~~박테리아가 다윈의 자연 도태를 따른다는 것을 보여주었다.~~ ★
(D) 그것들은 박테리아가 다윈 도태에 의한 계보를 부분적으로 따르는 유일한 예외란 것을 증명하였다.

Fact 문제의 키워드인 Griffith's findings를 살펴보면 Griffith's findings, though generally neglected after the initial contention against them subsided, revealed that this initial supposition was incorrect by showing that bacteria are able to acquire genes without the need for reproducing. (그리피스의 발견은 그것에 적대하는 초기 논쟁이 가라 앉으면서 보통 무시되었지만 그의 초기 가정이 박테리아가 또한 번식에 대한 필요없이도 유전자를 얻을 수 있다는 것을 보여줌으로 틀렸다는 것을 나타내었다)이라 한다. 즉 박테리아만이 Darwinian natural selection을 바탕으로 한 기존의 가설을 부분적으로만 따르는 예외라고 주장하는 (D)가 정답이 된다. (C)가 정답이 아닌 이유는 그렇다고 그의 발견이 Darwinian natural selection을 따르지 않기 때문이다.

07
According to paragraph 4, under which of the following circumstances will the phenotype of R pneumococcus most likely change?

(A) ~~DNA-removed S pneumococci~~ are mixed with intact R pneumococci.
(B) The ~~non-infective~~ R type is solely injected
(C) ~~A small amount of live, untreated R pneumococcus~~ are present. ★
(D) Remains after the use of protease enzymes are present.

4단락에 따르면, 다음 중 어떤 환경에서 R 폐렴균의 형질이 변할 확률이 가장 높은가?

(A) ~~DNA가 제거된 S폐렴균이~~ 손대지 않은 R폐렴균과 섞일 때
(B) ~~비~~ 전염적인 R 타입이 단독으로 주입되었을 때
(C) 아무런 처리 하지 않은 소량의 살아있는 ~~R 폐렴균이 있을때~~ ★
(D) 프로테아제 효소가 처리되고 잔재가 있을 때

Fact 문제의 키워드인 phenotype of R pneumococcus change를 지문에서 살펴보면 To do this, the cellular structures of the S strain bacteria were first removed, and then their cells proteins were removed through the use of protease enzyme treatments. Finally, the cellular remainders were placed in a dish containing R strain bacteria. The R strain bacteria transformed.(이것을 위해, S 변종 박테리아의 세포구조는 처음에 제거되고 단백질 분해 효소 처리의 사용을 통해 그 단백질이 제거되었다. 마지막으로, 남겨진 세포들은 R 변종 박테리아가 있는 접시에 놓여졌다. R변종 박테리아는 변형되었다)이라 과정을 설명한다. 즉 프로테아제 효소를 사용하고 세포조직이 제거된 S 박테리아가 R 박테리아 용기에 있을 때 R 박테리아가 변형된다는 지문내용과 겹치는 (D)가 정답이다. (B)가 틀린 이유는 비 전염적인 R 타입은 아무런 변화를 가져오지 못하므로 오답이다.

08
What is the purpose of mentioning Joshua Lederberg in paragraph 5?

(A) To show that ~~Avery's research into bacteria was flawed~~ ★
(B) To illustrate that Griffith's findings led to other experiments with significant results
(C) ~~To show that the Nobel Prize was won~~ through more advanced research on bacteria
(D) To ~~disprove Griffith's findings~~ from his experiments on bacteria

글쓴이가 5단락에서 조슈아 레더버그를 언급한 목적은?

(A) 에이버리 박테리아의 관한 연구가 결점이 있음을 보여주기 위해 ★
(B) 그리피스의 연구결과는 귀중한 결과를 낸 다른 실험들을 야기했다는 것을 설명하기 위해
(C) 박테리아에 대해 더 발전된 연구를 하여 ~~노벨상을 탔다는~~ 것을 보여주기 위해
(D) 박테리아에 대한 그의 실험으로부터 ~~크라피스와~~ 연구결과의 오류를 입증하기 위해

Purpose 5단락에서 Joshua Lederberg가 언급된 부분을 살펴보면 overtime, more advanced discoveries have been made through the findings of Griffith and Avery. Joshua Lederberg's discoveries concerning genetic recombination and the organization of the bacterial genetic material are a prime example of this continuation. (시간이 지나면서 좀더 진화된 발견이 그리피스와 에이버리의 발견을 통해 이뤄졌다. 유전 재조합과 박테리아 유전 물질의 조직에 관한 조슈아 레더버그의 발견은 이러한 연장의 주요한 예시이다)라고 한다. 그러므로 그리피스의 연구 이후 레더버그의 연구는 추가적인 연구를 하여 더 많은 발견했다는 지문내용과 문항 (B)의 내용은 일치한다. (A)가 틀린 이유는 문항의 내용이 사실이나 글쓴이의 목적이 아니었다.

09 Look at the four squares [■] that indicate where the following sentence could be added to the passage.

> **By using techniques to remove bacteria's organic compounds, scientists could observe that if the R-strain bacteria still transformed, it would mean that the materials removed were not the carrier of the transformation gene.**

Where would the sentence best fit? Click on a square [■] to add the sentence to the passage.   2nd

네 개의 네모[■]는 다음 문장이 삽입될 수 있는 부분을 나타내고 있다.

> 박테리아에서 다양한 유기 화학물을 제거할 수 있는 기술이 있었고, 만약에 남아 있는 유기 화학물이 계속 R 유전질 박테리아를 변형하게 한다면 제거된 물질은 유전자를 가지고 있는 것이 아니라는 것이다.

이 문장은 어느 자리에 들어가는 것이 가장 적절한가?   두번째

Insertion 삽입 문장의 내용은 실험방법의 설명이다. 그러므로 문장 이 후에 이와 같은 실험방법을 사용하여 실험을 진행했다는 내용이 나와야 한다. Being given to prove Griffith' theory, Avery continued to work on adjusting previous techniques even after he retired in 1943. (그리피스의 이론을 증명하게 되면서 에이버리는 심지어 1943년 은퇴한 후에도 이전 기술을 조정하는 일을 계속했다)은 전반적인 시험을 했다는 내용이다. 2번째 네모의 다음 문장인 To do this, the cellular structures of the S strain bacteria were first removed, and then their cells proteins were removed through the use of protease enzyme treatments.(이것을 위해, S 변종 박테리아의 세포구조는 처음에 제거되고 단백 질 분해 효소 처리의 사용을 통해 그 단백질이 제거되었다)는 실험을 이같은 방법으로 진행했다는 내용이다. 개념적인 실험방법의 설명이기 때문에 이후에 이 실험방법을 사용하여 실험한 내용이 나와야 하므로 정답은 2번째 네모가 된다.

10 Directions: An introductory sentence for a brief summary of the passage is provided below. Complete the summary by selecting the THREE answer choices that express the most important ideas in the passage. Some sentences do not belong in the summary because they express ideas that are not presented in the passage or are minor ideas in the passage. **This question is worth 2 points.**

지시: 지문 요약을 위한 도입 문장이 아래에 주어져 있다. 지문의 가장 중요한 내용을 나타내는 보기 3개를 골라 요약을 완성하시오. 어떤 문장은 제문에 언급되지 않은 내용이나 사소한 정보를 담고 있으므로 요약에 포함되지 않는다. **이 문제는 2점이다.**

Griffith's work influenced science for years to come.

- (B) The ability of R-type pneumococci to convert to S-type proved that there was a transforming factor that did not follow Darwinian evolution.   - Paragraph 2/3
- (C) Oswald Avery worked subsequently to Griffith in order to find the cause of inheritance and was able to find that DNA was the transforming factor of pneumococci.   - Paragraph 4
- (E) Joshua Lederberg was able to prove that bacteria were equipped with genetic systems due to prior research from former bacteriologists.   - Paragraph 5

(A) ~~All scientific discoveries including areas of~~ chemistry, physics, and biology can be attributed to the Romantic movement of the 19th century. - 틀린정보
(D) Scientists were intrigued by the ability of the ~~R type pneumococci to shed their capsules to become S type, depending on the environment.~~ - 틀린정보
(F) Bacteriologists originally believed that the form of a bacterium was unchangeable and was determined by the ancestral line from which they had descended minor. - Detail

그리피스의 업적은 과학계를 크게 발전시켰다.

- (B) R타입이 S타입으로 바뀌는 능력은 다윈의 진화이론을 따르지 않는 변형요소가 있음을 증명한다.
- (C) Avery는 유전 원인을 찾기 위해 Griffith를 따라 작업했고 폐렴균의 변형 요소가 DNA임을 밝혀낼 수 있었다.
- (E) Joshua는 박테리아가 유전체제를 가지고 있다는 사실을 예전 학자의 연구 때문에 밝혀낼 수 있었다.

(A) 화학, 물리학, 생물학을 ~~포함한 모든~~ 과학적 발견은 19세기의 낭만주의 운동에 출처를 둔다.
(D) 학자들은 ~~R타입 폐렴균이 환경에 따라 캡슐을 허물었고 S 타입이 될 수 있다라는~~ 사실에 흥미로워했다.
(F) 원래 세균학자들은 박테리아가 각기 같은 원종으로부터 비롯되어 형태와 기능은 고정되고 변하지 않는다고 믿어왔다.

Summary 지문의 중심내용은 그리피스의 연구결과와 그것이 끼친 영향이다. (B)는 2번째 단락의 내용인 R 과 S 유형의 폐렴균에 관한 것을 요약한 것이고, (C)는 3번째 단락의 내용인 그리피스의 연구결과가 기존의 이론과 대립한다는 내용을 요약한 것이고, (E)는 4번째와 5번째 단락에서 그리피스 이후의 과학자들이 끼친 영향을 요약한 것이다. 그러므로 정답은 (B), (C), (E)이다.

usherin.usher.co.kr

TEST 3-2 Maximilian Weber and His Influence 막스밀리안 베버와 그의 영향력

Introduction	단락 1	막스베버의 권력의 정의
Point 1	단락 2	사회에 따른 권력의 세가지 종류
Point 2	단락 3	베버의 권력정의에 대한 비판
Point 3	단락 4	세가지 리더십으로 발전된 베버의 이론
Point 4	단락 5	베버의 이론의 실제 중요성

Image by Charles Auguste Guillaume Steuben

단락정리	지문	해석
단락 1 막스베버의 권력의 정의	1 Authority can **be defined as** the forceful domination of a group of people who have the underlying condition of being absolutely obedient. The German sociologist Maximilian Weber, **on the other hand**, **defined** authority **as 'the chance' of** commands being obeyed **according to** distinct justifications by a specifiable group of people. [Q11]Pointing out that Germany's political fiasco during WWI was essentially a problem of leadership, Weber proposed a theory of authority that **classified** it **into** three types, **each differing in** its justifications to compel acquiescence and its **influences on** the public.	권력은 절대적으로 순종적이라는 기본적인 조건을 가지고 있는 사람들의 그룹의 강제적인 지배로써 정의 내려질 수 있다. 독일 사회학자 베버는 반면에 권위를 특정 그룹에 의한 구별되는 정당화에 따라 복종되어질 수 있는 명령의 가능성으로 정의했다. [Q11]1차 세계 대전 동안의 독일의 정치적인 대실패는 본질적으로 리더십의 문제였다라고 지적하면서 베버는 권력을 각각 묵인을 강제하는 정당화와 공공에 대한 그것의 영향력이라는 측면에서 서로 달라지는 3가지의 종류로 분류할 수 있는 권력 이론을 제안했다.
단락 2 사회에 따른 권력의 세가지 종류	2 In a society that is governed by a system of 'traditional' authority, social status **plays a** vital **role in** determining the sovereign power. The leaders of these types of societies are a ruling elite with an inheritable leadership role **based on** factors **such as** age, bloodline, or social connections, which shows that there is an inequality in the society. ⓒThe disadvantage of this system is that it **is vulnerable to** change, **as is** evident when **looking at** the challenges faced by the Russian Empire as it encountered a more complex **division of labor** and wider population diversity **due to** Industrialization in the early 20th century. The helplessness of the traditional authority against the rise of the bourgeois and proletariat classes ultimately **brought about** the introduction of 'rational legal' authority in Russia. 'Rational-legal' authority is a system in which an individual, or institution, exercises power through the socially accepted set of rules and the right of those **elevated to**	'전통적' 권력의 체계에 의해서 통제되는 사회 내에서 사회적 지위는 주권을 결정하는데 중요한 역할을 한다. 이러한 종류의 사회의 리더들은 사회 내에서 불평등이 있다는 것을 보여주는 나이, 혈통, 사회적 관계와 같은 요소들에 기반을 둔 세습적인 리더십을 소유한 통치 엘리트이다. ⓒ이러한 체계의 단점은 러시아 제국이 20세기 초기 산업화로 인한 좀 더 복잡한 분업화와 폭넓은 인구 다양성에 부딪힐 때, 러시아 제국의 의해 직면된 과제들을 볼 때 명백해 지듯이, 그 체계가 변화에 취약하다는 것이다. 부르주아와 프롤레타리아 계층의 상승에 맞선 전통적 권력의 무기력함은 결국에는 '합리적-법적' 권력의 도입을 초래 하였다. '합리적-법적' 권력은 개인이나 기관이 사회적으로 용인된 일련의 규칙들과 그러한 명령들을 내리기 위한 권력의 지위들까지 상승한 그들의 권리를 통하여 힘을 행사하는 체계이다. [■]

Vocabulary

1단락
domination [dàmənéiʃən] n. 우세, 지배
specifiable [spisifaiéibəl] a. 특정할 수 있는
obedient [oubí:diənt] a. 순종적인
fiasco [fiǽskou] n. 대실패
justification [dʒʌ̀stəfikéiʃən] n. 정당화
acquiescence [æ̀kwiésəns] n. 묵인

2단락
sovereign [sávərin] n. 주권
helplessness [hélplisnis] n. 무력함
codify [kádəfài] v. 성문화하다
volatile [válətil] a. 변덕스러운
inheritable [inhéritəbl] a. 유전되는
bourgeois [buərʒwá:] n. 부르주아
sanctity [sǽŋktəti] v. 신성화하다
feat [fi:t] n. 업적
vulnerable [vʌ́lnərəbl] a. 취약한
proletariat [pròulitɛ́əriət] n. 프롤레타리아
exemplary [igzémpləri] a. 전형적인
consolidate [kənsálədèit] v. 공고히하다
exile [ègzail] n. 국외추방

positions of authority to **issue** such **commands**. [■] [Q13]Power is held by the office itself, with no regard to the personal attributes of the office holder, and it is limited by the official codified rules which state the extent of the office's power. [■] Rational-Legal authority fosters financial stability and technological development because the rights of individuals **act as** the law, guaranteeing their property and investments. [■] It, however, does not automatically **lead to** economic stability or scientific development . 'Charismatic' authority can exist under 'traditional' or 'rational-legal' authorities **systems** when power is gained through widespread **devotion to** the exceptional sanctity, heroism, or a specific exemplary characteristic of a person. [■] [Q15]**According to** Weber, this form of authority is extremely volatile and dynamic as charisma eventually recedes after it has entered the permanent routine of social interaction, which can **result in** the sudden collapse of its power. For example, Napoleon Bonaparte **gained** his **fame** through his military feats, immediately consolidating absolute political power over France and reforming the country. His defeat during the Napoleonic Wars, however, **resulted in** the abrupt end of his reign as emperor and the beginning of his exile.

단락 3
베버의 권력 정의에 대한 비판

3   Although Weber's theory has strongly influenced the aspects of sociology that **deal with** leadership, scholars have pointed out two flaws in it. First, they believed that the standardization of **a variety of** concepts of authority and Weber's theoretical notion of an iron cage, in which the increased rationalization of modern life **causes** individuals **to be driven** purely by objective, **rather than** by values, was an oversimplified, limited idea of authority. Furthermore, they posit that he **failed to distinguish** between reigning and governing, with governing requiring a positive change in society whereas reigning does not.

단락 4
세가지 리더십으로 발전된 베버의 이론

4   Despite these objections, Weber's theory of authority influenced modern sociology and **brought about** the development of three new models of leadership in the late 20th century. The theory behind 'transformational' leadership is that [Q16]leaders can make radical **changes in** their followers'

Vocabulary

3단락
- deal with : phr 다루다
- notion [nóuʃən] n. 개념
- oversimplify [òuvərsímpləfài] v. 너무 간략화하다
- flaw [flɔː] n. 결점
- rationalization [ræʃənlizèiʃʌn] n. 합리화
- distinguish [distíŋgwiʃ] v. 구별하다
- confine [kənfáin] v. 국한시키다
- theoretical [θìːərétikl] a. 이론적인
- objective [əbdʒéktiv] n. 목적

4단락
- radical [rædikəl] a. 급진적인
- mutual [mjúːtʃuəl] a. 상호간의
- anarchy [ǽnərki] n. 무정부 상태
- satisfy [sǽtisfài] v. 만족시키다
- gratify [grǽtəfài] v. 만족시키다
- exploit [iksplɔ́it] v. 이용하다
- intrinsic [intrínsik] a. 내면의
- aligned [əláind] a. 나란히

thoughts and actions and exploit the order of their needs and aims to **satisfy** the greater **need**, which is, in turn, closely **aligned with** the followers' internal motivational factors. The leaders who Weber would have **classified as** having charismatic authority are, therefore, transformational, since they approach things **from** entirely different **perspectives**. **In contrast**, individuals that can **be described as** 'rational-legal' leaders can also **be seen as** [Q18] 'transactional' leaders, as they are **effective in** using their knowledge to achieve results, based on the hypothesis that followers are motivated through a system of 'quid pro quo' or 'give and take'. i)The differing qualities of the two leaership types can **be** simply **stated as**: 'transactional leaders' form mutual **bonds with** people through reward and punishment, while, ii) **in contrast**, 'transformational leaders' **seek to gratify** the intrinsic **needs of** the individual. The third form, 'laissez-faire' leadership, is characterized by a completely permissive leader who does not **contribute to making decisions**, which produces groups that often lack direction, and may **lead to** anarchy, but offer their followers many **opportunities to make** their own decisions.

단락 5 — 베버의 이론의 실제 중요성

5   Weber **stressed that** the importance of theories of authority is not to label, or classify, **prevalent** forms of leadership in history, but rather to show how the state of authority transitions from one type to another. His precise intention led to scholars **viewing** his theory **as** a hierarchical development order, and it is now **considered** more of a **theory on** social evolution.

Sentence analysis

◎ The disadvantage of this system is / that it is vulnerable to change, / as is evident when looking at the challenges faced by /
 이 시스템의 단점은   변화에 취약하고   직면했던 문제에서 분명하게 볼 수 있듯이
the Russian Empire as it encountered a more complex division of labor and wider population diversity /
 분업화가 더 복잡해지고 인구가 다양해진 러시아제국이
due to Industrialization in the early 20th century.
 20세기 초 산업화로 인해

◎ The third form,' laissez-faire'leadership / is characterized /
 무간섭주의인 리더쉽인 세 번째 형태는   특징지어진다
by a completely permissive leader who does not contribute to making decisions /
 의사결정에 아무런 기여를 하지 않는 완전히 수동적인 리더들에 의해
which produces groups that often lack direction / and may lead to anarchy /
 그것은 방향이 결여된 그룹들을 생산하며   아마도 무정부 상태로 이끌 것이다
but offer their followers many opportunities to make their own decisions.
 하지만 그들의 추종자들에게 그들 자신의 의사 결정을 내릴 수 있는 많은 기회들을 제공한다.

Vocabulary

5단락   prevalent [prévələnt] a. 널리 퍼진   intention [inténʃən] n. 목적   hierarchical [hàiərá:rkikəl / -kik] a. 계급에 따른

11
According to paragraph 1, what can be inferred about the background of the development of Weber's theory?

(A) He found the systematic classification termed by leaders around the world in terms of succession and transition of country with regards to authority.
(B) He argued against the fact that the traditional definition of authority be further categorized in three ways. ★
(C) He realized the importance of authority and its immense effects on society.
(D) He wanted to find a way to take over Germany's leadership after WWI.

베버 이론의 발달 배경에 관하여 1단락에서 추론할 수 있는것은?

(A) 그는 권력에 관해 국가의 승계와 이행에 있어 전세계 러더들에의해 이름 붙여진 체계적 구별을 발견했다.
(B) 그는 전통적인 권위의 개념이 3가지로 나뉘는 것을 주장하는 것을 반대했다. ★
(C) 그는 권위의 중요성과 이것이 사회에 끼치는 영향에 대해 깨달았다.
(D) 그는 세계1차대전이 끝난 후 독일에 러더쉽을 장악할 방법을 찾고 싶었다.

Inference 첫 번째 단락에서 볼 수 있듯이 베버는 pointing out that Germany's political problems during WWI were essentially a problem of leadership.(1차 세계 대전 동안의 독일의 정치적인 대실패는 본질적으로 리더십의 문제였다)이라 말했다. 이것은 즉 권위가 얼마나 중요한지를 보여주고 사회에 지대한 영향을 미친다는 (C)가 정답이다.

12
The word sovereign in the passage is closest in meaning to

(A) reigning
(B) dependent ★
(C) minimal
(D) coarse

지문의 단어 sovereign과 의미상 가장 유사한 것은?

(A) 군림하는 [réiniŋ]
(B) 의존적인 ★ [dipéndənt]
(C) 아주 적은 [mínəməl]
(D) 거친 [kɔːrs]

Vocabulary 지문의 sovereign(권력을 지닌)은 reigning(군림하는)과 동의어이므로 정답은 (A)이다.

13
The author mentions with no regard to personal attributes in order to

(A) demonstrate that an office holder must impose influence on the office.
(B) show that once the office holder loses power they leave office. ★
(C) explain that the extent of power of an office holder is limited by the rules.
(D) highlight that the authority acquires its power due to individual characteristics.

글쓴이가 with no regards to personal attributes를 다음을 위해 언급하였다.

(A) 공직자가 공직에 영향을 행사해야 한다는 것을 보여주고자
(B) 공직자가 일단 힘을 잃으면 공직을 떠난다는 걸 보여주기 위해 ★
(C) 공직자가 서류상과 공직에서만 권력이 제한된다는 것을 설명하고자
(D) 개인적 특성 때문에 권력이 힘을 얻는다는 것을 강조하고자

Purpose 음영문구 with no regards to personal attributes(개인의 능력과는 관련이 없고)를 살펴보면 Authority is held by the office itself, with no regards to the personal attributes of the office holder, and it is limited by the official codified rules which state the extent of the office's power. (권력은 공직자 개인의 능력을 고려하지 않고 공직 그 자체 안에 있으며 이 범위는 국가 공식 편성된 법에 의거하여 제한된다) 라고 언급했다. 즉, with no regards to personal attributes(개인의 능력과는 관련이 없고)는 공직자는 오직 공직에만 한정되어 있는 권력을 행사 할 수 있다는 걸 보여주기 위한 것이다. 따라서 답은 (C)이다.

14 In paragraph 2, it refers to

(A) The office holder
(B) The office ★
(C) The power
(D) The character

2단락 지문의 단어 it 이 가리키는 것은?

(A) 공직자
(B) 공직 ★
(C) 권위
(D) 인성

Reference 음영 처리된 지시어 it 자리에 the authority(권위)를 대입해 보면, 가장 자연스러운 단어가 authority라는걸 알 수 있다.

---

15 Why is Napoleon Bonaparte a good example of a charismatic leader according to paragraph 2?

(A) He brought dramatic changes to his followers ★
(B) His authority lasted longer than the other types.
(C) He took over a complex country with a strong division of labor.
(D) His authority fell at an unexpected rate.

2단락에서 왜 나폴레옹 1세가 카리스마 리더의 좋은 예인가?

(A) 그는 추종들에게 인상적인 변화를 가져다 주었다. ★
(B) 그의 권위는 다른 종류의 권위보다 오래 지속 되었다.
(C) 강력한 분업과 함께 복잡한 나라를 떠맡다.
(D) 카리스마 권위가 예상하지 못한 속도로 몰락될 수 있다.

Fact Napoleon Bonaparte가 언급되기 전 문장을 살펴보면 According to Weber, this form of authority is extremely volatile and dynamic as charisma eventually recedes after it has entered the permanent routine of social interaction, which can result in the sudden collapse of its power(베버에 따르면, 이러한 형태의 권력은 권력이 사회적인 상호작용의 영국적인 일상으로 들어간 후에 결국에는 약해지기 때문에 극단적으로 불안정하고 역동적일 수 있는데 그 권력의 갑작스러운 붕괴로 이어질 수 있다)라고 언급됐다. 즉 나폴레옹 1세는 카리스마 리더의 예이며 그의 권력행보를 보면 급작스럽게 붕괴된 그의 권력을 볼 수 있다. 따라서 답은 (D)이다.

---

16 According to paragraph 4, in what aspect does charismatic authority resemble transformational leaders?

(A) They both derive their power from a foundation of social standings such as age, class, experience, and gender.
(B) They are ideal leaders who follow long-established obligations and deal with their citizens according to the law. ★
(C) They both have different points-of-view and are extremely influential to their followers.
(D) They are both based on the fact that the leader changes to adapt to the followers' needs and social systems.

4단락에 따르면, 어떠한 카리스마 권위 특징들이 변형적 리더와 유사한가?

(A) 둘 다 나이, 계층, 경험, 성별과 같은 사회적 위치에서부터 권력을 얻는다.
(B) 그들은 오랫동안 따라왔던 의무감과 법의 의거하는 성질을 가지고 있다. ★
(C) 둘 다 다른 관점을 가지고 있고 추종자들에게 영향이 상당히 강하다.
(D) 둘 다 추종자들의 욕구와 사회적 시스템에 의해 변화되고 적응한다.

Fact 문제의 키워드인 charismatic authority(카리스마 권위)와 transformational leaders(변형적 리더들)의 공통되는 부분을 살펴보면 since they approach things from entirely different perspectives.(그들이 완전히 다른 관점으로부터 일에 접근하기 때문에)와 leaders can make radical changes in their followers.(리더들이 추종자에게 급격한 변화를 만들 수 있고)를 말하며 그들이 다른 관점을 통해보는 것과 변화에 민감하다는 부분이 나온다. 따라서 답은 (C)가 된다.

17 Which of the sentences below best expresses the essential information in the highlighted sentence in the passage? Incorrect choices change the meaning in important ways or leave out essential information.

(A) Transactional leaders ~~formulate closer relationships~~ based on rewards and punishment creating a ~~more intimate bond than transformational leaders.~~

(B) Transactional leaders negotiate with those being led while transformational leaders emphasize the individual needs.

(C) Transactional leaders ~~aim to satisfy the needs of individuals,~~ whereas transformational leaders ~~control people with rewards and punishment.~~ ★

(D) Transactional and transformational leaders ~~both create strong bonds~~ with their followers to gratify their intrinsic needs.

아래 문장 중 지문 속의 음영된 문장의 핵심 정보를 가장 잘 표현하고 있는 것은 무엇인가? 오답은 문장의 의미를 현저히 왜곡하거나 핵심 정보를 빠뜨리고 있다.

(A) '거래적' 리더들은 '변형적' 리더들보다 상벌을 통해 더 친밀한 결속을 만든다.

(B) '거래적' 리더들은 따르는 이들과 협상하고 '변형적' 리더들은 개인의 욕구를 강조한다.

(C) '거래적' 리더들은 개개인의 욕구를 채워주려 하고 반면에 '변형적' 리더들은 상벌로 사람들을 지배하려 한다. ★

(D) '거래적' 리더와 '변형적' 리더 둘 다 추종자들의 욕구를 채워주며 그들과 강한 유대를 만든다.

Highlight 음영 표시된 문장의 핵심 정보는 i) the differing qualities of the two leadership types transactional leaders form mutual bonds with people through reward and punishment, while, ii) in contrast, transformational leaders seek to gratify the intrinsic needs of the individual. (i) 두 종류의 리더십의 서로 다른 질들은 단지 다음과 같이 진술 될 수 있는데: '거래적 리더들은' 보상과 벌을 통해 사람들과 공통의 유대관계를 형성하는, ii)대조적으로 '변형적' 리더들은 개인의 내재적인 필요들은 충족시키기 위해 추구한다고 생각했다)이다. the differing qualities of the two leadership types(두 종류의 리더십)을 creating a divergence in leadership styles(두개의 다른 리더십 유형)으로, transactional leaders form mutual bonds with people through reward and punishment (거래적 리더는 상벌이 있는 관계를 형성하고)를 Transactional leaders make deals with those being led(거래적 리더들은 따르는 이들과 거래하고)으로, transformational leaders seek to gratify the intrinsic needs of the individual(변형적 리더는 내면의 욕구를 채워주고 싶어한다)를 transformational leaders emphasize the individual needs.('변형적' 리더들은 개인의 욕구를 강조하여)으로 간략하게 표현한 (B)가 정답이다.

18 What is true about the characteristics of the transactional leaders?

(A) Transactional leaders rest their ideology on satisfying ~~follower's needs.~~

(B) They are in power because their followers accept the validity of their leadership based on the mutual benefits.

(C) They are ~~those that permit the decisions to be carried out by the followers.~~ ★

(D) They are proactive and ~~form new expectations in their followers.~~

거래적 리더들의 특징에 관해 사실인 것은?

(A) 거래적 리더들은 그들의 이론을 추종자들의 ~~욕구에~~ 기초한다.

(B) 그들은 상호 이익에 근거한 리더십의 타당성과 추종자들의 받아들임에 의해 권력을 얻는다.

(C) 거래적 리더들은 ~~추종자들이 원하는 결정을 따르는 이들이다.~~ ★

(D) 거래적 리더들은 상황에 앞서 주도하며 ~~추종자들에게 새로운 기대를 형성한다.~~

Fact Fact 단락의 키워드인 transactional leaders(거래적 리더들)가 언급된 부분을 살펴보면 as they are effective in using their knowledge to achieve results, based on the hypothesis that followers are motivated through a system of 'quid pro quo' or 'give and take'(결과를 얻기 위해 그들의 지식을 이용하는 것에 효과적임으로 '거래적' 리더로 간주될 수 있다, 이것은 '주고 받는' 체계를 통해 따르는 사람들이 동기부여를 받는다는 가정에 근거한다)이라 한다. 즉 추종자들이 중심이 되어 그들이 받아 들이냐 안받아 들이냐에 따라 권위가 부여된다고 논하니 답은 (B)가 된다.

19 Look at the four squares [■] that indicate where the following sentence could be added to the passage.

It, (however,) does not automatically lead to economic stability or scientific development.

Where would the sentence best fit? Click on a square [■] to add the sentence to the passage.

네 개의 네모[■]는 다음 문장이 삽입될 수 있는 부분을 나타내고 있다.

하지만 그것이 자동적으로 경제적 안정성과 과학적인 발전을 이끄는 것은 아니다.

이 문장은 어느 자리에 들어가는 것이 가장 적절한가?

3rd

세번째

USHER

Insertion 삽입 문장의 단서는 however(반면에)이다. However(반면에)는 무엇과 반대될 때 쓰이는 것이므로 삽입 문장 앞에는 economic stability(경제 안정)와 scientific development(과학 발전)에 관한 내용이 나와야 한다는 것이다. 3번째 네모의 전 문장에 Rational-Legal authority fosters financial stability and technological development because the rights of individuals act as the law, guaranteeing their property and investments.(개인의 권리가 법의 역할을 하기 때문에 '합리적-법적' 권력은 금융 안정성과 기술적 발전을 조성하고 그들의 재산과 투자를 보장한다)가 나오며 기술 발전과 금융적 안전에 대해 논한다. 또한 3번째 네모 다음 문장은 카리스마 리더를 논하며 카리스마 리더의 단점이 나오니 정답은 3번째 네모가 된다.

20

Directions: An introductory sentence for a brief summary of the passage is provided below. Complete the summary by selecting the THREE answer choices that express the most important ideas in the passage. Some sentences do not belong in the summary because they express ideas that are not presented in the passage or are minor ideas in the passage. **This question is worth 2 points.**

지시: 지문 요약을 위한 도입 문장이 아래에 주어져 있다. 지문의 가장 중요한 내용을 나타내는 보기 3개를 골라 요약을 완성하시오. 어떤 문장은 지문에 언급되지 않은 내용이나 사소한 정보를 담고 있으므로 요약에 포함되지 않는다. 이 문제는 2점이다.

Weber came up with a theory that states different reasons and motivations for obedience to authority, having subsequent influence.

- (B) Weber categorized leadership based on how authority was gained and held in a society. - Paragraph 2

- (D) Weber's theory on authority influenced the development of three styles of leadership, which differ based upon the leaders' relationship formed with the followers. - Paragraph 4

- (E) Critics of Weber's theory argue that it limits the variables in society and does not have a clear measure to discern reigning from governing. - Paragraph 3

베버는 권력의 순종에 따른 각기 서로 다른 이유나 동기 설명하는 이론을 제시했고, 그것은 계속되는 영향력을 가지고 있다.

- (B) 베버는 리더십을 권위가 어떻게 얻어지고 사회에 느껴지는지에 따라 분류하였다.

- (D) 베버의 권위 이론은 3가지 형태의 각기 다른 추종자들과의 관계를 가진 리더십을 만드는데 영향을 줬다.

- (E) 베버의 비판자들은 사회의 변할 수 있는 점을 제한하고 군림과 통치를 분리하지 못하는 점을 비판한다.

(A) Weber's theory discusses ~~the inept leaders around the world in order to categorize~~ them into his theory. - 틀린 정보
(C) Laissez-faire leaders are those that exercise the minimum influence on the group that the person imposes control of. - Detail
(F) Weber wanted to emphasize ~~the role of values~~ in individuals' actions in the increased rationalization of modern life by developing the concept of 'iron cage'. - 반/반

(A) 베버의 이론은 ~~세계의 서투른 리더들의 특징별로 크와 이론에 맞춰 논한다.~~
(C) 무간섭 리더는 최소의 영향력을 추종자들에게 행하는 리더이다.
(F) 베버는 iron cage라는 이론을 만듦으로써 현대 삶의 증가된 합리화에서 개인들의 행동이 카치에 의해 영향을 받는다는 것을 강조하였다.

Summary 지문의 중심 내용은 권위에 관한 베버의 이론이다. (B)는 두번째 단락의 중심내용인 각각의 권위의 성격을 요약한 것과 일치하고, (D)는 네 번째 단락의 중심내용인 베버의 이론이 현대 3가지 리더십을 파생시킨 것과 일치하고, (E)는 세 번째 단락의 중심내용인 이론의 결점들과 일치한다. 따라서 답은 (B), (D), (E)이다.

usherin.usher.co.kr

USHER

iBT TOEFL
FINAL TEST READING
TEST 5

답안 및 취약 유형 분석표
해석·해설

답안 및 문제 유형 분석표

TEST 5-1

01 (B) Vocabulary

02 (C) Purpose

03 (D) Highlight

04 (C) Fact

05 (A) Inference

06 (B) Fact

07 (D) Fact

08 (C) Fact

09 2nd ■ Insertion

10 (A), (C), (F) Summary

TEST 5-2

11 (B) Inference

12 (A) Fact

13 (D) Purpose

14 (A) Vocabulary

15 (C) Highlight

16 (D) Fact

17 (A) Purpose

18 (C) Fact

19 3rd ■ Insertion

20 (A), (B), (D) Summary

각 문제 유형별 맞춘 개수를 아래에 적어 보세요.

유형	맞춘 답의 개수	정답률	
단어 (Vocabulary)	/ 2	정답률:	%
사실 확인 문제 (Fact)	/ 7	정답률:	%
지시어 찾기 (Reference)	/ 0	정답률:	%
끼워 넣기 (Insertion)	/ 2	정답률:	%
문장 변환문제 (Highlight)	/ 2	정답률:	%
목적 (Purpose)	/ 3	정답률:	%
추론 (Inference)	/ 2	정답률:	%
단락 요약(Summary / Category Chart)	/ 2	정답률:	%
전체	/ 20	정답률:	%

※ 자신이 취약한 유형은 READING STRATEGIES를 통해 다시 한번 점검하시기 바랍니다. (p.31)

TEST 5-1 Pasteur and The Origin of Life 파스퇴르와 생명의 기원

Introduction	단락 1	오랫동안 믿어졌던 설을 반박한 파스퇴르의 이론
Point 1	단락 2	파스퇴르의 실험 과정
Point 2	단락 3	오파린의 반박하는 이론
Point 3	단락 4	밀러와 유리의 실험

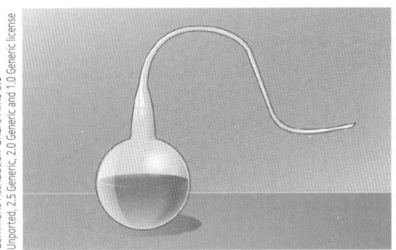

단락 1
오랫동안 믿어졌던 설을 반박한 파스퇴르의 이론

1 Logical and methodical scientists sometimes, ironically, blindly **adhere to** spuriously hypothesized assertions. For instance, Aristotle hypothesized that flies were the result of spontaneous generation in rotting materials and that microorganisms could appear naturally. Scientists believed these theories for nearly two millennia. These errant theories **led** them **to believe** that the bacteria required for fermentation were naturally generated without any external stimuli. [Q22] Scientist Louis Pasteur, however, **skeptical of** spontaneous generation, successfully falsified the long-held theory.

단락 2
파스퇴르의 실험 과정

2 i) Pasteur proposed the new theory of biogenesis, ii) claiming that the natural generation of bacteria was preposterous, iii) and that fermentation required the introduction of the necessary bacteria. In **order to prove** this, he **conducted** two **experiments**. In the first, a glass **filled with** meat broth, which would have fermented in open air, was placed in a sealed box that was completely sterile and had a filter over its opening. This did not **allow** anything **to enter** the glass and **as a result** there were no signs of fermentation in the glass. This, however, did not convince scientists **at the time**, because they thought that **even if** organisms were generated in the glass, they **would have expired due to lack of** oxygen. Therefore, he conducted a second experiment, the 'swan-neck duct' experiment. In this experiment, he put the broth into a spherical glass with a long curved tube atop it. With this structure, **nothing but** weightless air could enter. This also yielded no fermentation. [Q24] In 1864, Pasteur finally announced the results of these and further experiments, demonstrating that life cannot spontaneously arise in areas that have not **been exposed to** existing life.

Vocabulary

1단락
- methodical [məθάdikəl] a. 체계적인
- hypothesize [haipάθəsàiz] v. ~의 거짓임을 증명하다
- errant [érənt] a. 잘못된, 벗어난
- stimuli [stímjulài] n. 1. 자극제, 자극(이 되는 것) 2. (생물에게서 반응을 유발하는) 자극
- adhere to : phr. ~을 고수하다[충실히 지키다]
- assertion [əsə́ːrʃən] n. 주장, 단언
- fermentation [fə̀ːmentéiʃən] n. 발효(작용)
- spuriously [spjúrisli] ad. 거짓으로
- spontaneous [spantéiniəs] a. 자발적인
- falsify [fɔ́ːlsəfài] v. (문서를) 위조하다

2단락
- preposterous [pripάstərəs] a. 말도 안 되는, 터무니없는, 가당찮은
- duct [dʌkt] n. (물, 가스, 전선 등의) (배)관
- yield [jiːld] v. 산출하다, 생산하다
- broth [brɔ(ː)θ] n. (걸쭉한) 수프, 죽
- expire [ikspáiər] v. 끝나다
- spontaneously [spantéiniəsli] ad. 저절로 일어나는, 자연스러운
- sterile [stèril] a. 살균한, 소독한
- spherical [sférikəl] a. 구 모양의, 구체의

단락 3
오파린의
반박하는 이론

3 Unsurprisingly, Pasteur's experiments were eye-openers, having definitively disproved the antiquated theory of spontaneous generation and **giving birth to** biogenesis. Even though he was the first to empirically prove this, he was not the first scientist to propose this type of theory. Scientists Girolamo Fracastoro, Agostino Bassi, and Friedrich Henle had previously suggested various theories which influenced Pasteur's work later. The development of biogenesis, however, [Q25]left a vacuum **in the understanding of** how life first arose. As it requires previous forms of life, biogenesis alone could not ultimately explain the origin of life on the early, barren Earth. [Q26]No notable related theories, however, appeared until 1924, when Alexander Oparin surmised that the presence of oxygen in the atmosphere prevents the synthesis of certain organic compounds that are **necessary for** the evolution of life. In 'The Origin of Life', he proffered that the type of abiogenesis that Pasteur's attacked had in fact occurred once, but **no longer** could because the conditions found on the early earth had changed. Oparin felt that an organic 'primeval soup' could be created in an oxygen-free atmosphere due to the effects of sunlight. He hypothesized that 4 billion years ago, the earth's environment **met** these **criteria** after volcanic eruptions filled the environment with carbon dioxide, nitrogen, and other gases. Originally he thought that the early atmosphere, **in contrast to** the Earth's current atmosphere, contained mostly ammonia and methane, but **it is likely that** most of the atmospheric carbon was carbon dioxide with perhaps some carbon monoxide and nitrogen. In practice these mixtures have many of **the same properties as** those containing ammonia and methane **as long as** free oxygen molecules are not present.

단락 4
밀러와
유리의 실험

4 [■] These theories were tested in the Miller and Urey experiment which **attempted to recreate** these hypothetical conditions, and **tested for** the occurrence of the chemical origins of life. [■] Specifically, the experiment tested Oparin's hypothesis that conditions on the primitive Earth favored chemical reactions that synthesized organic compounds from inorganic precursors. [Q28]**In order to** test for the generation of the amino acids, required for protein generation in living cells **under** primitive Earth's **conditions**, they required a less hydrogen-rich mixture than the current environment.

Vocabulary

3단락
antiquated [æntikwéitid] a. 오래된, 구식의
surmise [sərmáiz] v. 추측하다
synthesis [sínθəsis] n. (생물체의 체내에서 일어나는) 합성
hypothesize [haipáθəsàiz] v. 가설을 세우다

4단락
hypothetical [hàipəθétikəl | -ik] a. 가설상의
evaporation [ivæpəréiʃən] n. 증발

empirically [empírikəlli] ad. 실증적으로
compound [kámpaund, kɔm-] n. 합성물
property [prápərti] n. 재산, 소유물
electrode [iléktroud] n. 전극
simulate [símjəlèit] v. 모의실험을 하다

ultimately [ʌltəmətli] ad. 최후로, 마침내
proffer [práfər] v. (충고, 설명 등을) 해 주다

[■] Their experiments used water, methane, ammonia, and hydrogen, sealed inside interconnected sterile glass tubes and beakers, with one half filled with water and another holding two electrodes. [■] ◎The water was boiled to produce evaporation, then the electrodes were fired to simulate lightning through the atmosphere and water vapor, and then it was cooled again to condense the water back into the first beaker in a repetitive cycle. After one week, they observed that 10-15 percent of the carbon was **in the form of** organic compounds. Two percent of the carbon had formed amino acids, with glycine being the most plentiful. Although nucleic acids were not formed, the 20 common amino acids were formed in various concentrations. This was interesting because amino acids can potentially create the most basic component of most living creatures, namely DNA.

[■] 그들의 실험들은 한 쪽 유리관은 물로 반쯤 채워지고 다른 것은 두개의 전극을 가지고 있는 서로 연결된 멸균 유리관과 비커 안에 밀봉된 곳에서 물, 메탄, 암모니아, 그리고 수소를 사용했다. [■]◎물은 증발 시키기 위해 끓여졌고 전극은 대기와 증기를 통해 번개를 모의로 만들기 위해 점화되고 그리고 나서 반복되는 사이클 안에서 첫 번째 비커 안으로 물을 다시 응축시키기 위해 차갑게 했다. 1주 후, 그들은 1~15%의 탄소가 유기 화합물의 형태를 띤다는 것을 관찰했다. 2%의 탄소는 가장 풍부한 글리신을 가진 아미노산을 형성했다. 비록 핵산이 생기지는 않았지만 20개의 흔한 아미노산은 다양한 농도에서 형성됐다. 이것은 아미노산이 대부분의 살아있는 생명체의 가장 기본적인 구성요소 즉, DNA를 잠재적으로 만들 수 있다는 점에서 흥미롭다.

Sentence analysis

◎ Logical and methodical scientists sometimes, / ironically, / blindly adhere to / spuriously hypothesized assertions. /
논리적이고 체계적인 과학자들은, 가끔씩, 아이러니하게도 고수합니다 가설로 세워진
Pasteur proposed the new theory of biogenesis, / claiming that the natural generation of bacteria was preposterous, /
파스퇴르는 생물 발생설의 새로운 이론을 제안했는데 박테리아의 자연발생은 터무니없는 일이라고 주장하고
and that / fermentation required the introduction of the bacteria necessary.
그리고 발효에는 도입이 필요하다고 했다

◎ The water was boiled to produce evaporation, /
물은 증발시키고자 끓여졌고
then the electrodes were fired to simulate lightning through the atmosphere and water vapor /
전극들은 대기와 수증기 사이의 번개를 가장하기 위해 불에 태워졌고
and then it was cooled again / to condense the water / back into the first beaker / in a repetitive cycle.
다시 식혀져서 물을 다시 응결시켜서 첫 번째 비커로 돌아가게 하는 반복적인 순환이었다.

Vocabulary

repetitive [ripétətiv] a. 되풀이 되는
condense [kəndéns] v. (액체가) 농축되다
concentration [kánsəntréiʃən] n. 농축

01
The word spuriously in the passage is closest in meaning to

(A) genuinely
(B) inaccurately
(C) quickly
(D) meticulously ★

지문의 단어 spuriously 과 의미상 가장 유사한 것은?

(A) 성실하게 [dʒénjuinli]
(B) 부정확하게 [inækjəritli]
(C) 빠르게 [kwíkli]
(D) 꼼꼼하게 ★[mətíʃjuləsli]

> **Vocabulary** 지문의 spuriously(가짜의) 의미랑 가장 유사한 것은 정확하지 않다는 의미를 가지는 inaccurately, (부정확하게) 즉 (B)가 정답이다.

02
Why did author mention spontaneous generation in the first paragraph?

(A) ~~To indicate~~ there were many significant discoveries over two millennia
(B) ~~To show~~ that Aristotle's theories were often wrong. ★
(C) To propose Pasteur's new theory and state how it refuted a long held misconception
(D) ~~To criticize scientists~~ who believed in spontaneous bacterial generation during the previous two millennia

첫 번째 단락에서 글쓴이는 왜 자연발생을 언급하는가?

(A) 이천 년 동안 많은 중요한 발견들이 있었다는 것을 ~~보여 주기 위해서~~
(B) 아리스토텔레스의 이론이 종종 틀리다는 것을 ~~보여주기 위해~~ ★
(C) 파스퇴르의 새로운 이론을 제시하고 이것이 어떻게 오랫동안 지속되었던 오해를 반박했는지 진술하기 위해서
(D) 그 지난 이천 년 동안 박테리아의 자연발생을 믿었던 ~~과학자들을~~ ~~비판하기 위해서~~

> **Purpose** 음영문구 spontaneous generation가 나오는 부분을 살펴보면 However, scientist Louis Pasteur, skeptical of spontaneous generation, successfully falsified the long-held theory.(하지만 자연 발생에 회의적인 과학자인 루이 파스퇴르는 오래 유지된 이 이론이 잘못되었다고 성공적으로 증명했다)라고 한다. 즉, 파스퇴르는 새로운 이론을 제기하면서 잘못된 설인 자연발생을 반박했으므로 (C)가 정답이다. (B)가 틀린 이유는 글쓴이가 의도한 목적이 아니기 때문이다.

03
Which of the sentences below best expresses the essential information in the highlighted sentence in the passage? Incorrect choices change the meaning in important ways or leave out essential information.

(A) Biogenesis opposed spontaneous generation, and supported the idea that only living things can give life to other living organisms. ★
(B) An influx of bacteria is required as evidence of Pasteur's new theory on ~~natural generation of bacteria~~, which is required in fermentation.
(C) ~~Without bacteria~~, fermentation cannot occur, and thereby ~~no natural generation is possible~~.
(D) Pasteur's new theory of biogenesis states that the bacteria that play an important role in fermentation can only be derived from other living organisms, not spontaneous generation.

아래 문장 중 지문 속의 음영 표시된 문장의 핵심 정보를 가장 잘 표현하고 있는 것은 무엇인가? 오답은 문장의 의미를 현저하게 바꾸거나 핵심 정보를 빠뜨리고 있다.

(A) 생물 발생설은 자연발생설에 반대했고, 오직 살아있는 생물만이 다른 살아있는 생물에게 생명을 줄 수 있다는 설을 지지했다. ★
(B) 박테리아의 유입은 발효에 필요한 박테리아의 자연적인 발생에 관한 파스퇴르의 새로운 이론의 증거로써 필요하다.
(C) ~~박테리아 없이는~~ 발효가 진행될 수 없고, 그럼으로써 그 어떤 자연적인 발생도 가능하지 않다.
(D) 파스퇴르의 생물발생에 관한 새로운 이론에서 발효에 중요한 역할을 하는 박테리아는 다른 살아있는 생명체로부터만 얻을 수 있다고 진술한다.

> **Highlight** 음영 표시된 문장의 핵심 정보는 i) Pasteur proposed the new theory of biogenesis, ii) claiming that natural generation of bacteria is preposterous, iii) and that fermentation required the introduction of the bacteria necessary for fermentation (ii) 파스퇴르는 박테리아의 자연 발생이 터무니 없는 것이며 iii) 발효는 박테리아의 유입이 당연히 필요하다는 것을 주장하며 i) 생물 발생설의 새로운 이론을 제안 했다)이다. Pasteur proposed the new theory of biogenesis(파스퇴르는 생물 발생설의 새로운 이론을 제안했는데)를 pasteur's new theory of biogenesis(파스퇴르의 생물발생에 관한 새로운 이론)으로 하고 발효를 위해선 박테리아가 필요하다는 구성이 모두 들어가므로 (D)가 정답이 된다. (A)와 (C)가 틀린 이유는 파스퇴르가 새로운 이론를 제시했다는 내용이 빠져있기 때문이다.

04 According to paragraph 2, what did Pasteur prove?

(A) ~~Spontaneous generation of bacteria~~ may occur through the addition of substances.★
(B) Biogenesis ~~was the cause of spontaneous generation~~ in the fermenting process.
(C) Generation of bacteria cannot be natural and an external source must exist.
(D) Bacteria generation ~~is not the major cause of fermentation.~~

2단락에 따르면, 파스퇴르가 증명한 것은?

(A) ~~박테리아와 자연발생은 물질을 추가함으로써 발생할 수 있다.~~ ★
(B) 생물 발생설은 발효과정에서 ~~자연발생의 원인이 된다.~~
(C) 박테리아의 생성은 자연적일 수 없고 반드시 외적인 근원이 존재해야 한다.
(D) 박테리아는 ~~발효의 주된 원인이 아니다.~~

Fact 단락의 주된 내용인 부분을 살펴보면 In 1864, Pasteur finally announcd the results of these and further experiments, demonstrating that life cannot spontaneously arise in areas that have not been exposed to existing life (1864년에 파스퇴르는 결국에 생명체는 현존하는 생명체에 노출되지 않은 지역에서는 자연적으로 발생할 수 없다는 것을 증명하는 이 실험들과 추가 실험에 대한 결과들을 발표했다)고 한다. 즉, 박테리아가 만들어지려면 외부에서부터 와야 한다는 내용인 (C)가 정답이 된다. (A)가 아닌 이유는 파스퇴르가 자연발생을 증명한 것이 아니기 때문이다.

05 According to paragraph 3, what can be inferred about Pasteur's experiment?

(A) Although it explained a natural phenomenon at the time, it failed to do the same for the initial rise of life.
(B) Scientists were shocked and ~~wanted to prove that spontaneous generation~~ of life ~~was not possible.~~★
(C) Biogenesis is automatically established when life forms ~~are exposed to a natural environment.~~
(D) Scientists' rebuttal of the first experiment was ~~weaker~~ than their rebuttal of the second experiment.

3단락에 따르면, 파스퇴르의 실험에 대해서 추론할 수 있는 것은?

(A) 그 당시에는 자연적인 현상들을 설명할 수 있었지만, 생명의 처음 시작에 대해서는 그러지 못했다.
(B) 과학자들은 충격을 받았고 ~~자연발생설이 불가능하다는 것을 증명하길 원했다.~~ ★
(C) 생물 발생은 생명이 ~~자연 생태계에 노출될 때~~ 성공적으로 확립될 수 있었다.
(D) 첫 번째 실험에 관한 과학자들의 반박은 두 번째 실험에 대한 반박보다 ~~약했다.~~

Inference 문제의 키워드인 Pasteru's experiments가 언급된 부분을 살펴보면 left a vacuum in the understanding of how life first arose. As it requires previous forms of life, biogenesis alone could not ultimately explain the origin of life on the early, barren Earth. (어떻게 생명체가 처음으로 생겨났는지에 대한 이해의 공백을 남겼다. 그것은 생명체의 이전의 형태가 필요하기 때문에 생물 발생설만으로는 궁극적으로는 초기의 황폐한 지구에서의 생명체의 기원을 설명할 수 없었다)라고 했다. 즉, 초기의 생명이 어떻게 생겼는지 모른다는 내용인 (A)가 정답이 된다. (B)가 틀린 이유는 파스퇴르의 이론이 과학자들이 자연발생설이 가능하다는 것을 증명하고 싶었기 때문이다. 즉 내용이 반대로 되었다.

06 Which of the following is true about biogenesis and abiogenesis according to paragraph 2 and 3?

(A) They contradict each other, but ~~have to be combined to explain spontaneous generation~~★
(B) They both mention oxygen in different ways to either support life or prevent synthesis of certain organic compounds.
(C) ~~Pasteur thought~~ that they complement each other because abiogenesis theory suggests the possible origin of life and biogenesis supports the reproductive cycle of life.
(D) They are both attributed to the swan neck duct experiments in a way that the experiment showed how life ~~cannot be generated with only oxygen.~~

2단락과 3단락에서 생물 발생과 무생물 발생 이론에 관해 사실인 것은?

(A) 서로를 반박하지만 ~~결합되어야 자연발생설을 설명할 수 있다.~~★
(B) 양쪽 모두 산소가 다른 방법으로 생명을 지지하거나 특정 유기 화합물의 합성을 저지한다고 언급한다.
(C) 무생물 발생 이론은 생명의 기원을 설명하고 생물 발생 이론은 생식주기를 설명하기 때문에 서로를 보완한다고 ~~파스퇴르가 생각했다.~~
(D) 양쪽 모두 어떻게 생명이 ~~산소만으로는 생성될 수 없다는~~ 것을 보여준, 백조목형관을 사용한 실험에 덕을 봤다.

Fact 문제의 키워드인 biogenesis and abiogenesis in terms of genesis가 언급된 부분을 살펴보면 No notable related theories, however, appeared until 1924, When Alexandr Oparin surmised that the presence of oxygen in the atmosphere prevents the synthesis fo certain organic compounds that are necessary for the evolution of lie. (하지만 알렉산더 오파린이 대기중의 산소의 존재가 생명 진화에 필요한 특정 유기 화합물의 합성을 막는다는 것을 추정했던 1924년까지는 어떠한 주목할 만한 관련된 이론이 나오지 않았다)라고 한다. 즉, 다시 설명하면 오파린이 특정 유기물의 합성을 지지하는 이론을 제시했고 그것이 주목을 받았다는 의미로 확인됨으로 정답이 (B)가 된다. (A)가 틀린 이유는 서로 보완되어야 한다는 부분이 지문의 내용과 상반되기 때문이다.

07

What is the importance of the 'primeval soup' theory mentioned in paragraph 3?

(A) It attempts to explain the Earth's atmosphere and conditions 4 billion years ago. ★
(B) It was a theory by Alexander Oparin which attacked Pasteur's findings.
(C) It explains why the Earth's current atmosphere is so different from the past.
(D) It indicates that abiogenesis was possible in the past.

3단락에 언급된 '원시수프' 이론이 중요한 것은?

(A) 40억 년 전의 지구 대기와 상태에 대해서 설명하려 노력했다. ★
(B) 알렉산더 오파린이 그의 이론을 통해서 어떻게 파스퇴르의 발견들을 공격했는지 언급한다.
(C) 지구의 현대 대기가 왜 과거의 것과 이렇게 다른지 설명한다.
(D) 자연 발생이 어떻게 과거에 가능하였다고 보여준다.

Fact 문제의 키워드인 'primeval soup'가 언급된 부분을 살펴보면 These theories were tested in the Miller and Urey experiment which attempted to recreate these hypothetical conditions, and tested for the occurrence of the chemical origins of life. (이 이론은 이러한 가설 조건들을 재창조하려고 시도하고 생명체의 화학적 기원의 발생을 실험하려고 시도했던 밀러와 유리의 실험에서 테스트 되었다)라고 했다. 즉, 밀러의 실험이 다음 단락에서 나오는 자연발생이 어떻게 가능했었는지 보여주므로 (D)가 정답이 된다. (A)가 틀린 이유는 지문에서 나온 것이 맞으나 문제에서 묻는 내용이 아니기 때문이다.

08

According to paragraph 4, why was it necessary to experiment using gases sealed inside interconnected sterile glass tubes and beakers?

(A) It was very complicated to recreate an environment resembling early Earth's for Miller's experiment.
(B) They hypothesis by Oparin had clear instructions as to how to conduct the experiment. ★
(C) It was essential that Miller and Urey mimic earth's early environment as closely as possible.
(D) The array was the only way to show each process and chemical reaction of earth's atmosphere in its early stages.

4단락에 따르면, 소독한 유리관과 비커를 설치하는 것이 필요했던 이유는?

(A) 밀러의 실험을 위해 초기 지구와 유사한 환경을 만드는 것은 매우 복잡했다.
(B) 오파린의 가설은 실험절차에 대해 자세하게 설명했었다. ★
(C) 밀러와 유리가 초기 지구의 환경을 최대한 똑같이 모방하는 것은 중요했다.
(D) 그 배열만이 지구 초기의 대기의 각 화학반응을 보여줄 수 있는 유일한 방법이었다.

Fact 문제의 키워드인 a sterile array of glass tubes and flasks가 언급된 부분을 살펴보면 in order to test the generation of aromatic amino acids, which are required for protein generation in living cells, under primitive Earth's conditions they required a less hydrogen-rich mixture. (원시 지구 조건들에서 살아 있는 세포에서의 단백질 발생에 필요한 아미노산의 발생에 대한 실험을 하기 위해 그들은 현재의 환경보다 더 수소 함유량이 낮은 화합물을 필요했다)라고 했다. 즉, 실험을 하기 위해서 환경을 최대한 똑같이 모방해야 했으므로 (C)가 정답이 된다. (B)가 틀린 이유는 명확한 지시사항이 있었다는 내용이 지문에 없기 때문이다.

09

Look at the four squares [■] that indicate where the following sentence could be added to the passage.

> (Specifically,) the experiment tested Oparin's hypothesis that conditions on the primitive Earth favored chemical reactions that synthesized organic compounds from inorganic precursors.

Where would the sentence best fit. Click on a square [■] to add the sentence to the passage
2nd

네 개의 네모[■]는 다음 문장이 삽입될 수 있는 부분을 나타내고 있다.

> 특별히, 그 실험은 원시 지구의 조건들이 비유기적인 선조로부터 유기적인 화합물을 합성하는 화학적인 반응들을 선호한다는 오파린의 가설들을 테스트했다.

이 문장은 어느 자리에 들어가는 것이 가장 적절한가?
두번째

Insertion 삽입 문장에서 정답의 단서는 specifically인데, 첫 번째 문장을 보면 밀러가 실험을 주관했다고 나온다. 여기서, 다음 문장으로 넘어가 보면 실험의 절차가 나오므로 삽입 문장을 두번째 칸에 넣었을 때 실험에 대해 더 자세하게 설명하므로 글의 흐름이 자연스럽다. 또한 오래된 정설화된 theory를 보기 좋게 실험을 통해 반박했다는 내용이니 정답은 두 번째 네모가 된다.

10

Directions: An introductory sentence for a brief summary of the passage is provided below. Complete the summary by selecting the THREE answer choices that express the most important ideas in the passage. Some sentences do not belong in the passage or they express ideas that are not presented in the passage or are minor ideas in the passage. **This question is worth 2 points.**

지시: 지문 요약을 위한 도입 문장이 아래에 주어져있다. 지문의 가장 중요한 내용을 나타내는 보기 3개를 골라 요약을 완성하시오. 어떤 문장은 지문에 언급되지 않은 내용이나 사소한 정보를 담고 있으므로 요약에 포함되지 않는다. 이 문제는 2점이다.

> In the 19th century, Pasteur questioned Aristotle's long-held assertion on spontaneous generation as he proposed an alternative hypothesis, later leading to more research concerning the origin of life.
>
> - (A) In order to overcome the criticism after his first experiment, Pasteur conducted another experiment, to verify his theory. - Paragraph 2
> - (C) After Pasteur's experiments proving biogenesis, a theory was suggested to explain the initial appearance of living organisms on Earth from inorganic matter. - Paragraph 3
> - (F) The Miller and Urey experiment helped the 'primordial soup' theory gain credibility by succeeding in creating common amino acids. - Paragraph 4

> 19세기에 파스퇴르는 대안론을 제시하면서 아리스토텔레스의 오랫동안 유지되었던 주장, 자연 발생에 의문을 제시했고 후에는 생명의 기원에 관련해서 더 많은 발견들을 이뤄냈다.
>
> - (A) 첫 실험에서 받은 비판을 극복하기 위해, 파스퇴르는 그의 이론을 증명하고자 또 다른 실험을 진행했다.
> - (C) 파스퇴르의 실험이 생물 발생을 증명하고 난 후, 무생물로부터 나온 살아있는 생물들의 초기 발생을 설명하기 위한 이론이 제시되었다.
> - (F) 밀러와 유리의 실험은 아미노산을 만드는데 성공하여 '원시 수프' 가설에 신뢰성을 주었다.

(B) Swan-neck duct was ~~one of the most significant discoveries of the era~~ due to its help in Pasteur's experiment. - 반/반
(D) ~~Due to Pasteur's experiments,~~ Oparin was able to successfully prove that living organisms could spontaneously form from inorganic matter. - 반/반
(E) The dominance of ammonia and methane released into the atmosphere made it a favorable place for abiogenesis to occur 4 billion years ago. - Paragraph 3 detail

(B) 백조목형 관은 파스퇴르의 실험에서 도움이 되었기 때문에 ~~시대에서 가장 최고의 발명 중 하나였다.~~
(D) ~~파스퇴르의 실험 때문에~~ 오파린은 살아있는 생물들이 자연적 으로 무생물에서 생성될 수 있었다는 것을 성공적으로 증명할 수 있었다.
(E) 대기로 방출된 암모니아와 메탄의 압도하는 양은 40억년 전에 자연 발생이 일어나기에 이상적인 장소로 만들어주었다.

Summary 지문의 중심내용은 파스퇴르의 실험을 통해 알게 된 생명 발생론이다. (A)는 2단락의 중심 내용인 파스퇴르의 실험 과정을 설명한것과 일치하고, (C)는 3단락의 중심 내용인 무생물로부터 생물이 나올 수 있다는 새로운 생물 발생론을 설명하는 것과 일치하고, (F)는 4단락의 중심 내용인 밀러의 실험의 결과와 일치한다. 따라서 정답은 (A), (C), (F)이다.

usherin.usher.co.kr

TEST 5-2 Early Research on Air 공기에 대한 초기연구

Introduction	단락 1	공기 성분에 대한 초기 이해와 연구
Point 1	단락 2	보일의 공기에 대한 기초 연구와 성과
Point 2	단락 3	새로운 연구 장비의 결여로 진전되지 않은 공기 연구
Point 3	단락 4	공기에 대한 연구를 하는데 큰 기여를 한 장치와 그 성과
Point 4	단락 5	새로운 실험 기구를 토대로 후에 거둔 연구 성과

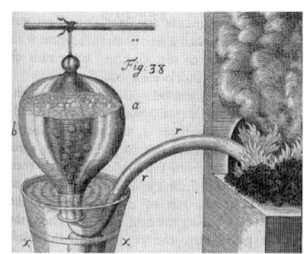

Image by Stephen Hales

단락 1 — 공기 성분에 대한 초기 이해와 연구

1 The composition of air has fascinated scientists since early times. **According to** the ancient Greeks, air **was regarded as** one of the four elements, which also included fire, earth, and water. It was not, however, precisely studied or correctly understood by many scholars. [Q1]They generally thought that the air people breathe had the same composition as the gases found in any other part of the universe. Eventually, a few analytical scientists **began to question** its properties and **conducted research** to define them, but their studies were limited **by the fact that** they only **sought to study** air **in the perspective of** their specialties. **Prior to** the seventeenth century, chemists believed that gases **were** not **involved in** chemical reactions, and **focused on** matter **in** its solid or liquid **states: according to** them, gases were **in the domain of** physicists. This trend significantly impeded progress on the study of air.

공기의 성분은 예전부터 많은 과학자들의 관심을 끌었다. 고대 그리스인에 따르면, 공기는 불, 흙 그리고 물을 포함하는 네 가지 원소들 중 하나로 여겨졌다. 하지만, 이것은 많은 학자들에 의해 정확히 연구되거나 바르게 이해되지는 않았다. [Q1]그들은 일반적으로 사람들이 숨쉬는 공기는 우주의 다른 부분에서도 발견되는 기체들과 같은 성분을 가지고 있다고 생각했다. 마침내, 몇 몇의 과학자들이 공기의 성질에 대해 의문을 가지기 시작했고, 그것들을 정의하기 위해 연구를 했지만, 그들의 연구는 그들이 그저 자신의 전문분야의 관점에서 공기를 연구했다는 것에 의해 한계가 있었다. 17세기 이전, 화학자들은 기체들이 화학적 반응과는 연관이 없다고 믿었고, 그것의 고체나 액체 상태에만 초점을 맞췄다: 그들에 따르면, 기체는 물리학자들의 영역이었다. 이러한 경향은 공기에 대한 연구 진행을 상당히 지연시켰다.

단락 2 — 보일의 공기에 대한 기초 연구와 성과

2 **It was not until** the seventeenth century that the understanding of air was seriously pursued by scientists. However, **due to the lack of** scientific instruments and the need for those beyond the usual tools, their experiments soon faced limitations. For example, Robert Boyle, a British scientist **known for** Boyle's Law, began a series of experiments to find out the composition of air through combustion. Boyle vacuumed the air out of a jar and showed that **neither** charcoal **nor** sulfur burned in the vacuum. Boyle had discovered the very first property of air stating that it **is required for a fire to burn.** His finding was not, however, recognized by the scientific community **of the day** because his definition of the component of air **responsible for** combustion was vague.

17세기가 되어서야 공기에 대한 이해가 과학자들에 의해 진지하게 추구되었다. 그러나, 과학 기기들의 부족과 일상 도구들을 능가하는 것들이 필요해서, 그들의 실험은 곧 한계에 부딪혔다. 예를 들어, 보일의 법칙으로 유명한 영국 과학자 로버트 보일은 연소를 통해 공기의 성분을 알아내기 위해 여러 가지 실험을 시작했다. 보일은 병에서 공기를 빼내고 숯이나 황이 진공상태에서는 타지 않는다는 것을 보여줬다. 보일은 불이 타기 위해서는 공기가 필요하다는 공기의 첫 번째 특성을 발견했다. 하지만, 연소에 필요한 공기 성분의 그의 정의가 모호했기 때문에, 그의 발견은 그 시대 과학계에서 인정받지 못했다.

Vocabulary

1단락
fascinate [fǽsənèit] v. 매혹하다
analytical [æ̀nəlítikəl] a. 분석의
precisely [prisáisli] ad. 정확하게
prior to : phr. 이전의
domain [douméin] n. 범위
composition [kàmpəzíʃən] n. 구성, 조직
impede [impíːd] v. (진행을) 지연시키다

2단락
pursue [pərsúː] v. 뒤쫓다, 추적하다
charcoal [tʃáːrkòul] n. 숯; 목탄
revise [riváiz] v. 개정하다, 수정하다
combustion [kəmbʌ́stʃən] n. 연소
sulfur [sʌ́lfər] n. (유)황 (비금속 원소; 기호 S, 원자 번호 16)
credit [krèdit] v. 공적을 인정하다
vacuum [vǽkjuəm] v. 진공으로 만들다
vague [veig] a. 막연한
persistence [pəːrsístəns] n. 고집, 인내, 지속성

In addition, most scientists **were** reportedly more **interested in** finding the chemical composition of air than in its physical characteristics. Thus, he **shifted** the focus of his research **to** air's chemical aspects and in 1659, **with** continuous **effort**, discovered that both hydrogen and nitric oxide gases were **present in** air. Boyle also **tried to revise** misconceptions **regarding** air, such as the popular belief that air had no weight. Years later, Einstein **credited** Boyle **for** having a holy curiosity in poorly understood phenomena that [Q2]others simply **accepted as** 'natural'. **As a result of** his persistence, he **is** now **known as** the father of chemistry.

3   Even with all of Boyle's achievements, people's understanding of air was still elementary and [Q3,6-B]more study using advanced laboratory equipment was required. [■] Scientists still **struggled to uncover** the many unknown properties of air, which were exemplified by the rudimentary definition of air as 'the elastic, invisible mixture of gases that surround the earth' from an eighteenth century encyclopedia. [■] [Q5][Q6-C]Its invisibility meant that it i)could not be observed **under** a microscope and [Q6-A] its ii)**ability to diffuse** quickly **proved to be** an irritable characteristic to scientists, iii)for it complicated calculations measuring the amount of air being experimented upon. [■] Additionally, chemists thought that air was out of their scope of research. ⓒTherefore, many prominent physicists investigated air **wishing to further** their understanding, but they showed little noticeable progress; **having no success in** isolating even one of the many compounds in air. [■]

4   Luckily, the **research on** air was significantly advanced by Stephen Hales, an English physiologist and chemist, in the late eighteenth century. **In search of** the various properties of air and **anxious to** clearly define it, he **gave birth to** a new branch in chemistry called pneumatic chemistry. He invented the pneumatic trough to study the physical properties of air and their **relation to** chemical reactions. The trough **was made from** household objects such as a hunting gun and a glass vessel. ⓒThe device measured the amount of gas produced when a substance was heated by measuring the amount of water displaced in the vessel. Hales' pneumatic trough became the basis for experimental instruments that are widely used today. [Q8]The creativity demonstrated through his improvisation of turning common tools into useful scientific

Vocabulary

3단락
- exemplify [igzémpləfài] v. ~을 예증하다
- diffuse [difjúːz] v. 퍼지다, 보급하다
- rudimentary [rùːdəméntəri] a. 근본의
- irritable [írətəbl] a. 성급한, 화를 잘 내는
- elastic [ilǽstik] a. 신축성 있는
- isolate [áisəlèit] v. 격리하다

4단락
- pneumatic [njumǽtik] a. 공기가 가득한
- improvisation [imprávəzéiʃən imprəvi-] n. 즉석에서 하기
- recognition [rèkəgníʃən] n. 인식
- trough [trɔ(ː)f] n. 구유, 여물통
- displace [displéis] v. 추방하다, 옮기다
- deserve [dizə́ːrv] v. 받을 만하다

		instruments was recognized by, and won the praise of, fellow scientists. **According to** the scientific community, however, Hales deserves more recognition than he received in the past as experiments **regarding** air were actively held by scientists of various fields using his invention.	그러나 과학계에 의하면, 헤일즈는 다양한 분야의 과학자들이 그의 발명을 이용해 공기에 대한 실험을 활발히 했다는 점에서 과거에 그가 받았던 것보다 더 많은 인정을 받아야 마땅하다.
	단락 5 새로운 실험 기구를 토대로 후에 거둔 연구 성과	**5** Despite his tremendous **contributions to** pneumatic chemistry, Hales **passed up** the **opportunity to study** the chemical properties of the various gases, as he was solely interested in studying their concentrations. Scientists that **came after** him revised his pneumatic trough and proceeded with further experiments. **With the efforts** of these scientists, the properties of the air have been gradually unveiled. They have even successfully broken down all of the components of atmospheric air and calculated their proportions.	기체 화학에 대한 그의 지대한 공헌에도 불구하고, 헤일즈는 오직 공기의 농도를 연구하는 것에 흥미가 있었으므로, 다양한 가스들의 화학적 특성에 관한 연구기회를 포기했다. 그를 뒤따르는 과학자들은 그의 기체수조를 수정했고 추가적인 실험을 진행했다. 이런 과학자들의 노력으로, 공기의 특성은 점차적으로 밝혀졌다. 그들은 심지어 대기 공기 중 모든 성분을 성공적으로 분석하고 그것들의 비율을 계산했다.

Sentence analysis

◎ Therefore, many prominent physicists / investigated air wishing to further their understanding, /
   그러하여, 많은 유명한 물리학자들은   더 나은 이해를 바라면서 공기를 조사했지만
   but they showed little noticeable progress; / having no success in isolating even one of the many compounds in air.
   그들은 크게 눈에 띄지 않는 진척만을 보여줬다.   공기의 많은 성분 중에서 단 하나도 구분시키지 못하고

◎ The device measured / the amount of gas produced when a substance was heated /
   이 장치는 측정했다   물질에 열이 가해졌을 때 만들어지는 기체의 양을
   by measuring the amount of water displaced in the vessel.
         그릇 안에서 대체되는 물의 양을 측정하여

Vocabulary

5단락   contribution [kάntrəbjúːʃən / kɔn-] n. 공헌, 기부   concentration [kάnsəntréiʃən] n. 집중, 농축
         proceed [prousíːd] v. 나아가다   unveil [ʌnvéil] v. 베일을 벗기다

11 What can be inferred from paragraph 1 about why air was not studied carefully by scholars in earlier times?

(A) Scholars working on the research on air attempted to study many other subjects, resulting in the lack of specialization.
(B) Scientists did not consider studying doing research on the components of air important and only made false assumptions.
(C) Scholars working on individual aspects of the research on air had difficulty unifying air with fire, earth, and water.
(D) Early people had limited skills in breaking down the composition of air. ★

1단락에서 공기가 이전에는 학자들에 의해 신중하게 연구되지 않았던 이유에 대해 무엇을 추측할 수 있는가?

(A) 공기에 대한 연구하는 학자들은 많은 다른 과목 공부에 전념하여 결과적으로 전문성이 결여되었다.
(B) 과학자들은 공기의 성분 연구가 중요하다고 생각하지 않았고 오직 잘못된 가정만을 만들었다.
(C) 자신의 전공에 한해서 공기에 대한 연구하는 학자들은 공기를 불, 흙, 물과 통합하는데 어려움을 겪었다.
(D) 초기 사람들은 공기의 성분을 밝혀내는데 제한된 능력을 가지고 있었다. ★

Inference 문제의 키워드인 air가 언급된 부분을 살펴보면 It was not precisely studied or correctly understood by many scholars.(이것은 많은 학자들에 의해 정확하게 연구되거나 바르게 이해되지 않았다)라고 되어 있어 문제가 묻고 있는 내용과 연관되어 있는 부분을 찾을 수 있다. 이 문장 바로 다음으로 오는 They generally thought that the air people breathe had the same composition as the gases found in any other part of the universe.(그들은 일반적으로 사람들이 숨쉬는 공기는 우주의 다른 부분에서 발견되는 기체들과 같은 성분을 가지고 있다고 생각 했다)이란 문장에서 과학자들이 공기의 성분을 별로 중요하게 생각하지 않았다는 내용을 추론할 수 있다. (A)는 왜곡된 내용이며, (C)는 unifying air with fire, earth, and water(공기를 불, 흙, 물과 통합하는데), (D)는 limited skills(제한된 능력)에 관한 내용이 언급되지 않았기 때문에 오답이다.

12 According to paragraph 2, what is Einstein's opinion about Boyle?

(A) He commended Boyle for his meticulous inquisitiveness that never overlooked 'natural' phenomena.
(B) He felt that Boyle's accomplishment in the combustion experiment were no longer valid. ★
(C) He thought that his theories were unnatural.
(D) He thought that Boyle accepted holy phenomena as natural.

2단락에 따르면 보일에 대한 아인슈타인의 생각은 무엇인가?

(A) 그는 보일을 '자연스런' 현상을 간과하지 않는 세심한 호기심때문에 칭찬했다.
(B) 보일의 연소 실험에 대한 성과가 더 이상 유효하지 않다고 생각했다. ★
(C) 그의 이론이 부자연스럽다고 생각했다.
(D) 보일이 신성한 현상을 자연적인 것으로 받아들였다고 생각했다.

Fact 문제의 키워드인 Einstein과 보일의 대한 평가를 하게 된 원인이 나와 있는 부분을 살펴보면 with continuous effort, discovered that both hydrogen and nitric oxide gases were present in air. Boyle also tried to revise misconceptions regarding air, such as the popular belief that air had no weight.(끊임없는 노력으로 수소와 산화질소가스 두 가지가 공기 중에 존재한다는 것을 발견했다. 보일은 또한 공기는 무게가 없다는 보편적인 믿음과 같은 공기에 대한 오해를 수정하려고 애썼다.)라고 언급되어 있다. 즉 이것에 대한 평가로 아인슈타인이 보일을 당연한 것을 새롭게 본 신성한 호기심으로 평가했다고 지속적인 노력으로 당대의 지배적이론의 오류를 수정하려고 했다는 부분으로 보아 정답은 (A)가 된다. (B)는 비슷한 내용이나 글쓴이의 목적은 업적보다 노력 그 자체를 강조한 내용임으로 문제와의 연관성이 부족하여 오답이 된다.

13 In paragraph 3, why does the author mention the definition of air as is exemplified in the encyclopedia?

(A) To indicate that scientists were never able to collect the gases in the air due to its invisibility. ★
(B) To illustrate that they could not precisely understand what people wanted to know about air.
(C) To argue that physicists and chemists could not agree on the definition of air due to their different points of view.
(D) To show that they could not draw in-depth conclusions about the properties of air.

3문단에서 백과사전에서 예시되어 있는 공기의 정의를 저자는 왜 언급했는가?

(A) 과학자들은 이것의 비가시성 때문에 공기 중에서 기체들을 모을 수 없었다는 사실을 가리키기 위해. ★
(B) 그들은 사람들이 공기에 대해서 무엇을 알고 싶어하는지 정확하게 이해할 수 없었다는 사실을 예를 들기 위해.
(C) 물리학자들과 화학자들은 그들의 관점의 차이 때문에 공기에 대한 한 정의를 지을 수 없었다는 사실을 주장하기 위해.
(D) 그들은 공기의 특성에 대해 깊이있는 결론을 도출할 수 없었다는 사실을 보여주기 위해.

Purpose 문제의 키워드인 defining air(공기의 정의)가 언급되는 부분을 살펴보면 more study using advanced laboratory equipment was required.(진보된 실험 장치를 이용한 보다 많은 연구가 필요했다)라는 내용을 통해 장비가 없어 실험을 하지 못해 자료가 없었다는 점을 알 수 있으므로 (D)가 답이 된다. (A)는 앞서 보일이 기체를 모아 실험을 했기에 오답이다. (B)는 what people wanted(사람들이 원하는 것)라는 내용이, (C)역시 different points of view(다른 관점)에 관한 내용이 언급되지 않아 오답이다.

14
The word **rudimentary** in the passage is closest in meaning to

(A) primitive
(B) vague
(C) straightforward
(D) ancient ★

지문의 단어 **rudimentary** 와 가장 유사한 것은?

(A) 근본의 [prímətiv]
(B) 모호한 [veig]
(C) 직접의 [streitfɔ́:rwərd]
(D) 고대의 ★ [éinʃənt]

Vocabulary rudimentary(근본의)와 동의어인 primitive(근본의) (A)가 정답이다.

15
Which of the sentences below best expresses the essential information in the highlighted sentence in the passage? Incorrect choices change the meaning in important ways or leave out essential information.

(A) ~~Irritable characteristics of air, such as its ability to diffuse,~~ complicated scientists' measurements of the amount of air used in experiments and other scrutiny of it. ★
(B) The complicated calculation associated with the amount of air ~~irritated scientists~~ who were ~~exploring the invisibility of air~~ and its ability to diffuse.
(C) Scholars had difficulty seeing air due to its transparency while its propensity to spread made it difficult to determine the amount of air upon which they were experimenting.
(D) Since air cannot be observed through the microscope, scientists could not calculate the amount of air.

아래의 문장 중 어떤 문장이 이 글 속 강조된 문장의 핵심을 잘 표현하는가? 오답은 문장의 의미를 현저히 바꾸거나 핵심 정보를 빠뜨리고 있다.

(A) ~~빨리 분산되는 능력과 같아 공기와 거슬리는~~ 특성은 과학자의 실험에 사용된 공기의 양 측정과 다른 정밀성 측정을 복잡하게 만들었다. ★
(B) 공기의 양과 관련된 복잡한 계산은 ~~공기와 비카시성과~~ 그것의 분산되는 능력을 ~~탐구하고 있는 과학자들을 거슬리게 했다.~~
(C) 과학자들은 공기의 분산되는 성향이 그들이 실험하는 공기의 양을 결정하는 것을 어렵게 하는 동안 그것의 투명도 때문에 공기를 가시화하는데 어려움을 겪었다.
(D) 공기는 현미경을 통해서 관찰될 수 없기 때문에, 과학자들은 공기의 양을 계산할 수 없었다.

Highlight 음영이 표시된 문장의 핵심 내용인 air in experiment(공기 실험), irritable characteristics of air(공기의 화를 돋구는 특성) 그리고 complicating calculation(계산을 복잡하게 하는)가 모두 들어간 문장은 (C)임으로 (C)가 답이다. (A)가 틀린 이유는 invisibilty(불가시성)이 빠져있기 때문이다. (B)는 내용상 exploring the invisibility of air(공기의 비가시성을 연구하는)이 틀리다. (D)는 characteristics of air(공기의 특성)에 관한 내용이 없다.

16
According to paragraph 3, all of the following are mentioned as a difficulty of a successful research on air EXCEPT:

(A) Its rapid rate of dispersal
(B) Physicists' lack of proper equipment ★
(C) Its transparent nature
(D) Its ability ~~to mix with other gases~~

3단락에 따르면, 다음 중 공기에 대한 성공적인 조사의 어려움으로써 언급되지 않은 것은?

(A) 공기의 급속한 분산 속도
(B) 물리학자들의 적절할 도구의 부족 ★
(C) 공기의 투명한 본질
(D) 공기의 다른 가스들과 혼합되는 능력

Fact 문제의 키워드인 difficulty of research on air(공기 연구의 어려운점)이 언급된 부분을 살펴보면 (A) its rapid rate of dispersal(공기의 급속한 분산 속도), (B) physicists' lack of proper equipment(물리학자들의 적절한 도구의 부족), (C) Its transparent nature(공기의 투명한 본질) 이 전부 나와 있는 반면 (D)는 나와 있지 않으므로 (D)가 답이다.

17 What is the main purpose of paragraph 3?

(A) To show that the discoveries mentioned in paragraph 2 did not satisfy researchers' curiosity
(B) To explain that the eighteenth century encyclopedia ~~had an incorrect definition of air~~
(C) To ~~differentiate the intention of studies on air done~~ by scientists of different fields
(D) To give a reason for Hales ~~not gaining more recognition~~ ★

3단락의 주 목적은 무엇인가?

(A) 2단락에서 언급된 발견된 사실들은 연구자들의 호기심을 만족시키지 못했다는 것을 보여주기 위해
(B) 18세기 백과사전에 있는 ~~공기의 뜻이 틀렸다는 것을~~ 설명하기 위해
(C) 공기에 대한 연구 ~~의도가~~ 다른 분야의 과학자들에 따라 ~~다르다는~~ 것을 보여주려고
(D) 헤일즈가 더 많은 인정을 받지 못한 이유를 설명하기 위해 ★

Purpose 3단락의 주 목적은 연구자들이 아직 더 많은 연구자료를 요구했다는 점을 설명하기 위함이기에 답은 (A)이다. (D)는 내용이 지문과 일치하지만 주체를 헤일즈의 인지도로 한다면 의도에서 벗어나게 된다.

---

18 What is true about Hales and his invention according to paragraph 4?

(A) The inspiration in constructing the pneumatic trough ~~came from Boyle's vacuum device~~.
(B) His pneumatic trough guided other scholars who were ~~interested in making experimental tools~~. ★
(C) His ingenuity and originality were precursors of the success of pneumatic chemistry.
(D) His research was ~~a basis for the respect~~ physicists had for chemists.

4단락에서 헤일즈와 그의 발명에 관해 사실인 것은?

(A) 기체 수조를 만들기 위한 영감은 ~~보일의 진공장치로부터 왔다~~.
(B) 그의 기체 수조는 ~~실험 도구들을 만드는데 흥미가 있는~~ 다른 학자들에게 도움이 되었다. ★
(C) 그의 재주와 독창성은 기체화학 성공의 선도자였다.
(D) 그의 연구는 물리학자들이 화학자들에게 갖고 있는 ~~존경심의 바탕이다~~.

Fact 문제의 키워드인 Hales와 invention(발명품)이 언급된 부분을 살펴보면 Hales deserves more recognition than he received in the past as experiments regarding air were actively held by scientists of various fields using his invention.(헤일즈는 다양한 분야의 과학자들이 그의 발명품을 이용해 공기에 대한 활발한 연구를 했다는 점에서 과거에 그가 받은 것보다 더 많은 인정을 받아야 마땅하다)라는 내용으로 그의 독창성이 기체화학에 큰 기여를 했다는 것을 알 수 있으므로 (C)가 답이다. 다른 도구들을 만드는데 도움이 된게 아니라, 다른 실험들을 할 때 도움이 되었기 때문에 (B)는 오답이다.

---

19 Look at the four squares [■] that indicate where the following sentence could be added to the passage.

(Additionally,) chemists thought that air was out of their scope of research.

Where would the sentence best fit? Click on a square [■] to add the sentence to the passage.

3nd

네 개의 네모[■]는 다음 문장이 삽입될 수 있는 부분을 나타내고 있다.

게다가, 화학자들은 공기가 그들의 연구 영역 밖이라고 생각했다.

이 문장은 어느 자리에 들어가는 것이 가장 적절한가?

세번째

Insertion Therefore, many prominent physicists(그러므로, 많은 유명한 물리학자들은)로 시작하는 문장이 뒤에 나오므로 이 문장이 앞에서 physicists들이 떠맡게 된 이유 즉, chemist의 생각을 설명해 주어야 한다. 그리고 앞에는 limitation에 관한 내용이 언급되어야 하므로 정답은 세번째 네모이다.

20

Directions: An introductory sentence for a brief summary of the passage is provided below. Complete the summary by selecting the THREE answer choices that express the most important ideas in the passage. Some sentences do not belong in the summary because they express ideas that are not presented in the passage or are minor ideas in the passage. **This question is worth 2 points.**

Early research on air was rarely done by many scientists of any field because of their misunderstanding of its composition.	공기에 대한 초기연구는 그들의 공기의 성분에 대한 오해 때문에 그 어떤 분야의 많은 과학자들에 의해서도 매우 드물게 행해졌다.

- (A) Research on air as a new area of scientific study progressed modestly because researchers were uninterested in others' field of studies regarding the subject matter. - Paragraph 1

- (B) By the mid-seventeenth century, experiments that were designed to satiate the scientific communities' specific interests were able to unveil a few properties of air. - Paragraph 2

- (D) The pneumatic trough enabled scientists to study air more effectively and precisely define its properties for others. - Paragraph 4/5

- (A) 과학적인 연구의 새로운 분야로서의 공기에 대한 연구는 천천히 진행되었다, 왜냐하면 조사관들이 주제와 관련된 다른 분야에 무관심 했기 때문이다.

- (B) 17세기 중반까지, 과학 공동체의 구체적인 흥미를 만족시키기 위해 고안된 실험들은 공기의 몇몇의 특성들을 드러낼 수 있었다.

- (D) 가스 채취용 수조는 과학자들에게 공기를 좀 더 효율적으로 연구하는 것과 다른 사람들을 위해 그것의 정의를 더 정확하게 해주는 것을 가능하게 해주었다.

(C) Robert Boyle's experiment related to combustion ~~led him to invent a trough~~ that was used by other scientists. - 틀린정보

(E) As one of the most renowned scholars of his time, Stephen Hales ~~shed light on the chemical properties~~ of various gases. - 반/반

(F) Boyle's vacuum jar experiment ~~was able to prove that air had no weight~~, in addition to answering some of the most questioned chemical properties of air - 틀린정보

(C) 로버트 보일의 연소와 관련된 실험은 다른 과학자들이 사용하는 ~~수조 개발을 야기했다~~.

(E) 그의 시대에 가장 잘 알려진 학자 중 하나인 스티븐 헤일즈는 다양한 공기의 ~~화학적 특성을 밝히는데~~ 공헌을 했다.

(F) 보일의 진공 병 실험은 공기는, 가장 많이 질문된 공기의 화학적 특성에 관한 답과 함께 ~~무게가 없다는 주장이 옳았음을 증명했다~~.

Summary (A)는 3단락에 언급되어 있듯, 연구자들이 서로 다른 영역만 연구해 진전이 느렸다는 점과 일치하고, (D)는 4단락에서 헤일즈가 발명품을 통해 공기에 대한 이해를 넓혔다는 것과 일치하며 (B)는 2단락에서 보일이 다른 연구자들이 원한 기체화학적 공기에 대한 다른 연구와 이해를 진보 시켰다는 것과 일치한다. 그러므로 정답은 (A), (B), (D)이다.

usherin.usher.co.kr

USHER

iBT TOEFL
FINAL TEST READING
TEST 6

답안 및 취약 유형 분석표
해석·해설

답안 및 문제 유형 분석표

TEST 6-1

01 (C) Fact
02 (B) Fact
03 (B) Vocabulary
04 (B) Fact
05 (C) Highlight
06 (A) Purpose
07 (D) Reference
08 (B) Inference
09 1st ■ Insertion
10 (A), (C), (F) Summary

TEST 6-2

11 (A) Inference
12 (A) Vocabulary
13 (A) Fact
14 (C) Purpose
15 (A) Highlight
16 (D) Fact
17 (B) Fact
18 (C) Fact
19 3rd ■ Insertion
20 (A), (E), (F) Summary

각 문제 유형별 맞춘 개수를 아래에 적어 보세요.

유형	맞춘 답의 개수	정답률
단어 (Vocabulary)	/ 2	정답률: %
사실 확인 문제 (Fact)	/ 7	정답률: %
지시어 찾기 (Reference)	/ 1	정답률: %
끼워 넣기 (Insertion)	/ 2	정답률: %
문장 변환문제 (Highlight)	/ 2	정답률: %
목적 (Purpose)	/ 2	정답률: %
추론 (Inference)	/ 2	정답률: %
단락 요약(Summary / Category Chart)	/ 2	정답률: %
전체	/ 20	정답률: %

※ 자신이 취약한 유형은 READING STRATEGIES를 통해 다시 한번 점검하시기 바랍니다. (p.31)

TEST 6-1 — Photography as an Art 예술로서의 사진술

Introduction	단락 1	사진이 예술인가에 대한 논쟁
Point 1	단락 2	사진가들의 노력
Point 2	단락 3	픽토리얼리즘의 탄생배경과 설명
Point 3	단락 4	예술로 인정받고자 나온 결과
Point 4	단락 5	사실적 사진이 예술계에 미친 영향
Point 5	단락 6	지금의 사진 활용법과 위치

Image by Charles Emile Joachim Constant Puyo (1857-1933)

단락 1 — 사진이 예술인가에 대한 논쟁

1 Three components are required **for a work to be considered** artistic: [Q11]artist, medium, and artwork, the idea being that an artist manifests artwork through the medium. [Q20-A]Since the camera's invention, photography has **struggled to convince many that** it **falls within** this definition. [Q15-D] The opposition **recognizes** the medium and work **as** artful, but not the photographers' role as artist. [Q11 A-B]They **see** them **as** technicians who operate the medium' to produce works **instead of** as artists, who, they claim, **take time to complete** works, **poring over** them. The photographer's **ability to capture** an image with a simple click was thus unequal, and photography was a process **unequal to** art. Photographer Mark Chamberlain **disagreed with** this, stating that [Q12] "**in the hands of** an artist, the camera is only another tool," which can become an extension of the eye **if** properly **utilized**, but is a lifeless piece of metal **otherwise**. He **contended that** releasing the shutter may only **take a second**, but timing and framing are crucial, and the photographer **has to find** perfect lighting and conditions.

하나의 작품이 예술로서 인정받기 위해서는 세가지 요소가 충족되어야 한다: [Q11]예술가, 수단, 그리고 작품으로, 이는 예술가가 수단을 통해서 작품을 보여 준다는 생각이다. [Q20-A]카메라의 발명 이래로, 사진은 많은 사람들로 하여금 사진이 이 정의에 부합한다고 확신시키려고 애써왔다. [Q15-D]이에 반대하는 사람들은 그 수단과 작품은 예술적이라고 인정하지만, 예술가로서 사진작가의 역할은 예술적이지 않다고 하였다. [Q11 A-B]그들은 사진작가들을, 그들이 주장하듯이, 완벽한 작품을 위해 시간을 들이고 모든 것을 쏟아 붓는 예술가라기 보다 작품을 생산하기 위해 '수단을 조작하는' 기술자라고 보았다. 따라서 간단한 클릭 한번으로 이미지를 포착하는 사진작가의 능력은 예술가의 능력과 비교될 수 없고, 사진술은 예술과 비교될 수 없는 과정이었다. 사진작가, 마크 체임벌린은 [Q12]"카메라는 예술가가 사용하는, 단지 또 다른 도구일 뿐이다." 라고 말하며, 카메라는 적절히 사용 된다면 또 다른 관점이 될 수 있지만, 그렇지 않다면 하나의 고철 덩어리에 불과하다며 이 의견에 동의하지 않았다. 그는 셔터를 누르는 것은 단지 1초밖에 걸리지 않을지 모르지만, 타이밍과 구도가 매우 중요하며, 사진 작가는 최적의 빛과 조건을 찾아야 한다고 주장했다.

단락 2 — 사진가들의 노력

2 Chamberlain was not the only photographer to fight denigration of photography. Earlier, between 1851 and 1862, [Q20-C]famous photographers such as Antoine Claudet, Andre Disderi, and William Lake Price published articles in professional journals **attempting to analyze** the aesthetic similarities and differences between graphic works and

체임벌린은 사진의 명예훼손에 맞선 유일한 사진작가는 아니었다. 그 이전인 1851년과 1862년 사이, [Q20-C]안토니 클라우뎃, 안드레 디스데리, 그리고 윌리엄 레이크 프라이스 같은 유명한 사진작가들이 그림과 사진의 미적 유사점과 차이점을 분석하고 독자들에게 사진이 진짜 예술이라는 것을 설득하려고 전문 잡지에 기사를 발표했다.

Vocabulary

1단락
- component [kəmpóunənt] n. 구성성분
- opposition [ɑ̀pəzíʃən] n. 반대, 저항
- manifest [mǽnəfèst] v. 분명히 나타내다
- extension [iksténʃən] n. 확장
- struggle [strʌ́gl] v. 투쟁하다, 힘겹게 나아가다
- contend [kənténd] v. 다투다, 강력히 주장하다

2단락
- analyze [ǽnəlàiz] v. 분석하다
- per se [pər séi] : phr. 본질적으로, 말 그대로
- convince [kənvíns] v. 확신시키다
- echo [ékou] n. 울림, 메아리, 반향
- exposition [èkspəzíʃən] n. 전시회, 해설, 설명

3단락
- in an effort to : phr. to do 하기 위한 노력으로
- still-life n. 정물화
- allegorical [æ̀ligɔ́(:)rikəl] a. 우화적인

photographs and to convince readers that photography was actually an art. Their **points of view** were summed up in a piece in the 1862 Photographic Journal addressing whether photography should be hung in the Fine Arts or Industrial Section of the International Exposition. The author observed that the question is not whether photography is fine art **per se**, but whether it **is capable of** artistic expression in the hands of an artist. Their **point - of - view** was echoed in the Catalogue of the 1859 Salon of Photography by French naturalist Louis Figuier. He and other scientists **were convinced that** artistic expression and taste would be improved by photography, just as the general quality of life **benefits from applied science**. They, like Chamberlain, **considered the lens a new tool**, like the pencil or brush, which conveys the feelings of the photographer, and photography is, therefore, an art.

단락 3 — 픽토리얼리즘의 탄생배경과 설명

3   Later, photographers, **in an effort to compete with** high art, **focused on** still-lifes, allegorical costumes, genre scenes and composite images. However, as the novel idea of capturing images **began to wear off**, people **began to question** whether the camera's images were too accurate and detailed. To overcome this literalism, photographers used inferior optical elements, smeared lenses, kicked tripods, or blurred their black-and-white prints. [Q14] **As a result**, pictorialism, an aesthetic movement imitating contemporary painting styles and techniques, was born. This movement which originated in Britain **reached its height** in the 20th century and **had a strong influence on** American photography **in its later phases**. i) **One of** the most important promoters of this movement was the journal 'Camera Work' ii) published by Alfred Stieglitz, whose sale of fifteen photographs to the Albright Gallery iii) **solidified** photography's **status as** an art in the United States.

단락 4 — 예술로 인정받고자 나온 결과

4   With the **rise and fall** of pictorialism, **struggles over** artistic nature and the quest to determine what truly constituted art **raged on** for over a century. **In hindsight**, many conclude that photographic art is at its best when capturing the real world, and least inspiring when emulating other art forms. The unique power of photography is its **disposition to form** the varies of textural experience and the **contrasts in** lighting, rather than narrative content, **regardless of** whether the images **were considered** documents or art.

Vocabulary

composite [kampázit] n. 합성물
blur [bləːr] v. 흐리게 하다

inferior [infíəriər] a. 하위의, 열등한
solidify [səlídəfài] v. 응결시키다

smear [smiər] v. 마구 바르다, 더럽히다

4단락   rage [reidʒ] n. 격노, 분노
disposition [dìspəzíʃən] n. 성향, 경향

inspiring [inspáiəriŋ] a. 고무하는, 감동시키는
regardless of : phr. ~에 관계 없이

emulate [émjəlèit] v. 모방하다

5단락   masterpiece [mǽstərpìːs] n. 명작, 걸작

artifact [áːrtəfǽkt] n. 인공물

revolutionize [rèvəlúːʃənàiz] v. 혁명을 일으키다

단락 5 사실적 사진이 예술계에 미친 영향	**5** Recognizing this, some photographers **began producing** prints of artistic masterpieces **for** both their commercial and the general population's cultural **benefit**. Since then, photographs have been the most significant supplier of visual artifacts to the masses, revolutionizing public **access to** the art heritage of the world. ◎[Q16] What was once rejected as being too real had become indispensable in terms of historical preservation. This was a welcomed advantage of photography since it was believed that familiarity with classical art would **not only** lift people's spirit, **but also** improve their taste.	이것을 인식한 몇몇 사진작가들은 그들의 상업적 목적과 대중의 문화적 혜택 두 가지 모두를 위한 명작의 복제품을 만들어내기 시작했다. 그 이후로, 사진은 세계 예술 유산에 대한 대중의 접근성을 개혁하면서, 대중을 위한 시각적 산물의 가장 중요한 제공자가 되었다. ◎[Q16] 한때 너무 사실적이어서 거부되었던 것은 이제 역사적 보존을 위해 필수적인 것이 되었다. 고전미술과의 친근함은 사람들의 정신을 고양시킬 뿐 아니라 그들의 취향도 개선시킨다고 믿어졌기에 이것은 사진의 이점으로 환영 받았다.
단락 6 지금의 사진 활용법과 위치	**6** Today, there is little doubt that photography is a fine art. [■] Every well-known, respected fine-art museum has a section **dedicated** solely **to** photographic art; and there are a number of museums and galleries dedicated specifically to photography. This shows that photography has **stood its ground** and found its place in the art world. [■] In recent decades, photography's potential has radically expanded. [■] **Aside from** the traditional two-dimensional, modest-sized black-and-white photographs, photographs now display various shapes, colors, and formats, to provide information, **make statements**, sell products, or analyze events. [■] [Q18] ◎The development of new technology and aesthetic theories **combined with** the enhanced role of photography as a marketable commodity has influenced the way the medium is now used and perceived. This expanded role of photography is the result of a rich history **tied to** developments in technology, art, and society.	현대에는 사진이 과연 미술인가에 대한 의혹은 남아 있지 않다. [■] 모든 유명하고 존경 받는 미술관에는 오직 사진 예술을 위한 구역이 따로 있다; 그리고 특히 사진만을 위한 박물관과 미술관도 존재한다. 이것은 사진이 예술세계에 기초를 두고 자리잡았다는 것을 보여준다. [■] 최근 수십 년 동안, 사진의 가능성은 급진적으로 확장되었다. [■] 전통적인 평면의, 작은 흑백사진 외에도, 오늘날의 사진은 정보를 제공하고, 물건을 팔고 혹은 사건을 분석하기 위해 다양한 모양, 색깔, 그리고 형태로 표현된다. [■] [Q18] ◎시장 상품으로서 강화된 사진의 역할이 결합된 신기술의 발전과 심미학적 이론의 발달은 오늘날 매체가 사용되고 인식되는 방식에 영향을 미쳤다. 이러한 사진의 확장된 역할은 기술의 발전, 예술, 그리고 사회와 깊이 관련된 풍부한 역사적 산물이다.

Sentence analysis

◎ What was once rejected as too real / had become indispensable / in terms of historical preservation. /
한때 너무 사실적이어서 거부당했던 것은   필수적인 것이 되었다   역사적 보존을 위해

◎ The development of new technology / and aesthetic theories /
　　새로운 기술의 발전과　　　　　　그리고 미술적 이론
combined with the enhanced role of photography as a marketable commodity /
시장의 상품으로서의 강화된 사진의 역할과 결합된
has influenced the way the medium is now used and perceived.
오늘날 사진의 용도와 그에 대한 인식에 영향을 미쳤다

Vocabulary

heritage [héritidʒ] n. 유산　　　reject [ridʒékt] v. 거절하다　　　preservation [prèzərvéiʃən] n. 보존

6단락　doubt [daut] n. 의심　　　discipline [dísəplin] n 규율, 훈련법　　　aside from : phr. 무엇을 제외하고
　　　　dimensional [diménʃənəl, dai-] a. 치수의, 규모의, 차원의　　　aesthetic [esθétik] a. 미의
　　　　enhance [enhǽns] v. 높이다, 강화하다

01 According to paragraph 1, the following were the ideas of those opposing photography as art EXCEPT

(A) It was too simple a process compared to real art, such as drawings. ★
(B) Photographers were seen as technicians who operated the camera to make pictures.
(C) A camera is just a lifeless piece of metal until a photographer uses it.
(D) It did not satisfy all three components needed to be considered art.

1단락에 따르면, 다음 중 사진이 예술이라는 것에 대한 반대 의견이 아닌 것은?

(A) 그림 그리기와 같은 실제 예술에 비해 너무 간단한 과정이다. ★
(B) 사진작가들은 사진을 찍기 위해 카메라를 작동시키는 기술자로 간주되었다.
(C) 카메라는 사진작가가 사용하기 전까지는 사사한 고철덩어리일 뿐이다.
(D) 예술로 간주되기 위한 세가지 요소를 모두 만족시키지 못했다.

Fact 문제의 키워드인 ideas of those opposing photography as art가 언급된 부분을 살펴보면 the opposition recognizes the medium and work as artful, but not the photographer's role as artist. They see them as technicians who 'operate the medium' to produce works instead of as artists, who, they claim, take time to complete works, pouring themselves into it. The photographers ability to capture an image with a simple click was thus unequal, and photography was a process unequal to art.(이에 반대하는 사람들은 그 수단과 작품을 예술적이라고 인정하지만, 예술가로서 사진 작가의 역할은 예술적이 아니라고 하였다. 그들은 사진작가들은, 그들이 주장하듯이, 완벽한 작품을 위해 시간을 들이고 모든 것을 쏟아 붓는 예술가라기 보다 작품을 생산하기 위해 '수단을 조작하는' 기술자로 보았다. 따라서 간단한 클릭 한번으로 이미지를 표현하는 사진작가의 능력은 예술가의 능력과는 같지않고 사진 찍는 것은 예술과는 동등할 수 없는 과정이었다.)라고 한다. 즉, the opposition recognizes the medium and work as artful, but not the photographer's role as artist.(이에 반대하는 사람들은 사진의 매체와 작품은 예술적이라고 인정하지만 사진작가는 예술가의 역할에 부합하지 않는다고 주장한다)라는 부분은 (D)에서 언급된 three components needed to be considered art (예술로 간주되기 위한 세가지 요소)를 충족하지 못하다는 내용이고 They see them as technicians who 'operate the medium' to produce works.(그들은 사진을 찍는 사람들을 작품을 완성하기 위해 자신을 쏟아 붓고 시간을 투자하는 예술가들이 아닌, 작품을 만들기 위해 '매체를 작동시키는' 기술자로 간주한다)라는 부분은 (B)에서 언급된 photographers seen as technicians(사진작가가 기술자로 간주)된다는 부분과 일치한다. The photographer's ability to capture an image with a simple click(사진작가가 단순한 찰칵 소리로 이미지를 포착하는 능력)라는 부분은 (A)에서 언급된 too simple process(너무 단순한 과정)과 일치한다. 그리하여 언급되지 않은 (C)가 정답이다.

02 What is the importance of Mark Chamberlain's views according to paragraph 1?

(A) They demonstrate a view of an artist from back when photography was first discovered. ★
(B) They exemplify how a camera can be seen as just a tool, like a paintbrush.
(C) They show many artists viewed the camera in relation to art.
(D) They explain what was meant by photographers being technicians who produced artwork.

1단락에서 Mark Chamberlain의 관점의 중요성은 무엇인가?

(A) 사진이 처음 발견되었을 때 예술가의 관점을 예시한다. ★
(B) 페인트 브러쉬처럼 어떻게 카메라가 하나의 도구로 간주되어짐을 예로 보여준다.
(C) 어떻게 어떤 사진작가들이 카메라를 예술과 연관하여 바라봤다는 것을 제시한다.
(D) 사진작가들이 작품을 만드는 기술자라는 것이 무슨 의미인지를 설명한다.

Fact 음영문구인 Mark Chamberlain이 언급된 부분을 살펴보면 Photographer Mark Chamberlain disagreed with this, stating that "In the hands of an artist, the camera is only another tool,"(사진작가, 마크 체임벌린은 "카메라는 예술가가 사용하는, 단지 또다른 도구일 뿐이다.")라고 말한다. 즉, 카메라가 붓과 같이 다른 도구로 여겨지는 예를 들고 싶어서인 (B)가 정답이 된다. (A)가 틀린 이유는 과거의 예술가의 관점을 보여준 사실은 맞으나 문제가 의도한 것이 아니기 때문이다.

03

The word novel in the passage is closest in meaning to

(A) fiction ★
(B) innovative
(C) chronicle
(D) peculiar

지문에 있는 novel 과 가장 유사한 것은?

(A) 소설 ★ [fíkʃən]
(B) 혁신적인 [ínəvèitiv]
(C) 연대기 [krɑnikl]
(D) 독특한 [pikjúːljər]

Vocabulary novel(새로운)은 innovative(혁신적인)와 fiction(소설)과도 동의어지만 문맥상 뜻에 따라 정답은 (B)이다.

04

According to paragraph 3, pictorialism

(A) was popular amongst artists in the 20th century, ~~when photography was first invented~~.
(B) imitated the styles of paintings of that time to be more art-like.
(C) was ~~later also termed fine art photography~~, which then later played an important role in advancing causes.
(D) was a series of procedures for making pictures ~~look less familiar~~. ★

3단락에 따르면, 픽토리얼리즘은

(A) ~~사진이 처음 발명되었을 때~~ 20세기 예술가들 사이에서 인기가 있었다.
(B) 좀 더 예술에 가까워지기 위해 동시대의 화법을 모방했다.
(C) 이후 발전에 중요한 역할을 한 ~~예술 사진이라고 불리었다~~.
(D) 사진을 덜 ~~익숙히~~ 보이게 만드는 방법이다. ★

Fact 문제의 키워드인 pictorialism이 언급된 부분을 살펴보면 pictorialism, or photographs imitating contemporary painting styles and techniques.(픽토리얼리즘이라는 사진으로 현대 미술의 스타일과 기술을 모방하는)라고 한다. 즉, 픽토리얼리즘이 사진을 이용하여 현대미술을 따라하는 운동이라 설명하는 (B)가 정답이 된다. (D)가 틀린 이유는 결과적으로 사진이 덜 자세히 보이게 되었으나 그것이 운동의 정의는 아니기 때문이다.

05

Which of the sentences below best expresses the essential information in the highlighted sentence in the passage? Incorrect choices change the meaning in important ways or leave out essential information.

(A) Alfred Stieglitz ~~produced a series of fifteen photographs~~ called 'Camera Work' to help promote Pictorialism, and this helped make photography an art.
(B) 'Camera Work' ~~began the movement~~ of Pictorialism, and when all fifteen of Stieglitz's photographs were ~~sold by~~ Albright Gallery, photography officially became accepted by artists as an art. ★
(C) 'Camera Work' by Alfred Stieglitz helped further progress the movement, and when a gallery bought fifteen photographs, photography could be more confidently called art.
(D) Alfred Stieglitz's 'Camera Work' played the biggest role in promoting the movement, when the Albright Gallery bought its fifteen photographs in order to use it ~~as an example of artistic photography~~.

아래 문장 중 지문 속의 음영된 문장의 핵심 정보를 가장 잘 표현하고 있는 것은 무엇인가? 오답은 문장의 의미를 현저히 왜곡하거나 핵심 정보를 빠뜨리고 있다.

(A) 픽토리얼리즘을 촉진시키기 위해 ~~15점의~~ '카메라 작품' 이라 불리는 ~~작품~~을 만들었다, 그리고 사진이 아트라 불리도록 도왔다.
(B) '카메라 작품' 은 픽토리얼리즘 ~~운동을 시작한 것으로~~, 스티글리츠의 15개 작품이 모두 올브라이트 갤러리에 ~~의해~~ 팔리고 나자 사진은 비로소 예술가들에게 예술로 인정 받았다. ★
(C) 알프레드 스티글리츠의 '카메라 작품'은 운동을 더욱 진전시키는데 도움을 주었고, 갤러리가 15개의 작품을 모두 구입하자 사진은 더욱 더 자신있게 예술이라고 불릴 수 있게 되었다.
(D) 알프레드 스티글리츠의 '카메라 작품' 은 올브라이트 갤러리가 ~~예술적 사진의 예로써~~ 그것을 사용하기 위해 15개의 작품을 구입했을 때 운동을 진전시키는데 가장 큰 역할을 하였다.

Highlight 음영 표시된 문장은 i) One of the most important promoters of this movement was the journal 'Camera Work' ii)and its publisher Alfred Stieglitz whose sale of fifteen photographs to the Albright Gallery, iii)solidified photography's status as an art in the United States (i) 이 동향을 장려하는데 가장 중요한 역할을 할 것 중 하나는 '카메라 작품' 이라는 잡지와 ii) 올브라이트 갤러리에 15개의 사진 작품을 팔며 iii) 미국에서 사진이 예술로서의 지위를 확고하게 한 출판자 알프레드 스티글리츠였다) 이렇게 세가지 내용으로 나뉜다. 이 내용을 모두 포함한 (C)가 정답이 된다. (B)가 틀린 이유는 camera work가 pictorialism을 시작했다는 언급되지 않은 내용 때문이다.

06

In paragraph 5, what is the author's purpose of mentioning that what was once rejected as being too real had become indispensable in terms of historical preservation?

(A) To explain an ironic situation regarding photography
(B) To point out the photographers who adamantly fought for photography as an art form
(C) To support the idea that fine art can be enjoyed by an exclusive group of people
(D) To stress photography's profound ability to resemble reality ★

5단락에서 한때 너무 사실적이어서 거부되었던 것은 이제 역사적 보존을 위해 필수적인 것이 되었다는 정보를 제시한 글쓴이의 의도는 무엇인가?

(A) 사진에 대한 아이러니한 상황을 설명하기 위해
(B) 사진을 예술행위로 인정받기 위해 끝까지 싸운 사진작가들을 가리키기 위해
(C) 예술은 오직 독점적인 무리의 사람들만이 즐길 수 있었다는 점을 뒷받침하기 위해
(D) 사진의 현실을 유사할 수 있는 기능을 강조하기 위해 ★

Purpose 음영 문구는 what was once rejected as being too real had become indispensable in terms of historical preservation(한때 너무 사실적이어서 거부되었던 것은 이제 역사적 보존을 위해 필수적인 것이 되었다)라고 말한다. 즉, 한때 예술이라 칭하지 못하게 했던 사실적임이 미래에는 작품을 배포하는데 필수적인 아이러니한 상황을 보여준다는 (A)가 정답이다. (D)가 틀린 이유는 사진이 유사할 수 있다는 점은 사실이나 작가가 그런 의도로 음영 문구를 삽입한 것은 아니어서이다.

07

The word This in the passage refers to

(A) art
(B) photography ★
(C) heritage
(D) preservation

지문의 단어 이것이 가리키는 것은?

(A) 예술 [aːrt]
(B) 사진 ★ [fətágrəfi]
(C) 유산 [héritidʒ]
(D) 보존 [prèzərvéiʃən]

Reference 음영 처리된 지시어 this 자리에 preservation(보존)를 대입해 보면, 가장 자연스러운 단어가 (D) preservation이라는 걸 알 수 있다.

08

What can be inferred from paragraph 6 about photography's radical expansion?

(A) The radical expansion is attributed solely to artistic photographers who fought for the name 'artists' about two decades ago. ★
(B) Photography is now accepted as art, but has transcended it to influence other aspects of people's life and society as a whole.
(C) The radical expansion of photography has led to privacy concerns.
(D) Photography has gone from not being considered an art form to dominating the art world.

6단락에서 사진의 급진적 확장에 대하여 추론할 수 있는 것은?

(A) 급진적 확장은 20년 전 예술가라는 명칭을 얻기 위해 분투하던 오로지 사진작가들 덕분이다. ★
(B) 오늘날 사진은 예술로 인정받지만 그보다도 사람들의 일상에서의 다른 면과 사회 전체에 영향을 끼친다는 점에서 예술을 뛰어 넘는다.
(C) 사진의 급진적 확장은 사생활침해 문제를 일으켰다.
(D) 사진은 예술로 인정받지 못하다가 예술 세계를 지배하게 되었다.

Inference 문제의 키워드인 photography's expansion이 소개된 지문을 보면 the development of new technology and aesthetic theories combined with the enhanced role of photography as a marketable commodity has influenced the way the medium is now used and perceived.(시장의 상품으로서의 강화된 사진의 역할과 결합된 신기술의 발전과 심미학적인 이론의 발달은 오늘날 매체가 사용되고 인식되는 방식에 영향을 미쳤다)라고 한다. 즉, 사진의 지대한 영향력을 요약한 (B)가 정답이 된다. (A)는 사실이긴 하나 6단락에서 추론해내기에는 너무 비약적인면이 크기 때문에 오답이다. (D)도 비약이다.

09 Look at the four squares [■] that indicate where the following sentence could be added to the passage.

Every well-known, respected fine-art museum has a section dedicated solely to photographic art; and there are a number of museums and galleries dedicated specifically to photography.

Where would the sentence best fit? Click on a square [■] to add the sentence to the passage.   1st

네 개의 네모[■]는 다음 문장이 삽입될 수 있는 부분을 나타내고 있다.

모든 유명하고 존경 받는 미술관에는 오직 사진 예술을 위한 구역이 따로 있다; 그리고 특히 사진만을 위한 박물관과 미술관도 존재한다.

이 문장은 어느 자리에 들어가는 것이 가장 적절한가?   첫번째

Insertion 삽입문장은 사진이 현재 얼마나 예술로서 인정을 받는가에 대한 구체적인 예제이다. 앞 문장에서 사진이 예술로서 인정을 받는다는 내용이 포괄적으로 나와 있으며, 포괄적인 설명 뒤 뒷받침을 하기 위해 상세한 예제를 넣는 것이니 가장 타당함으로 답은 1번째 네모이다. 첫번째 네모 뒤의 This를 받은 내용이 끼워 넣을 문장이다. 끼워 넣을 문장이 빠지면 This가 받는 것이 없다.

---

10 **Directions:** An introductory sentence for a brief summary of the passage is provided below. Complete the summary by selecting the THREE answer choices that express the most important ideas in the passage. Some sentences do not belong in the summary because they express ideas that are not presented in the passage or are minor ideas in the passage. **This question is worth 2 points.**

지시: 지문 요약을 위한 도입 문장이 아래에 주어져 있다. 지문의 가장 중요한 내용을 나타내는 보기 3개를 골라 요약을 완성하시오. 어떤 문장은 지문에 언급되지 않은 내용이나 사소한 정보를 담고 있으므로 요약에 포함되지 않는다. 이 문제는 2점이다.

The status of photography as an art form has been debated for hundreds of years.

- (A) With the invention of the camera, the debate about photography being considered an art came into question. - Paragraph 1

- (C) Photographers in the 19th century worked to formalize their status as artists, not mere practitioners of cameras who only push the shutter button. - Paragraph 2

- (F) Photographic art is best at producing lifelike images and its power has allowed it to change and expand its role in society. - Paragraph 4,5

미술로써의 사진의 입장은 몇백 년 동안 논의되었다.

- (A) 카메라의 발명과 함께 사진이 과연 예술인가에 대한 논쟁이 일어났다.

- (C) 19세기의 사진작가들은 단지 카메라의 셔터를 누르는 기술자가 아닌 예술가로서의 지위를 얻기 위해 일했다.

- (F) 사진 예술은 실제와 똑같은 이미지를 만드는데 적합했고 사진의 능력은 이것으로 하여금 사회에서 자신의 역할을 변화시키고 확장시키도록 허락했다.

(B) Mark Chamberlain is a photographer that supported the view that photographers should be considered artists and ~~foresaw that photography holds greater good for mankind just like applied sciences.~~ - 반/반

(D) Pictorialism is ~~still considered predominant~~ in the area of art up to day because of its superiority. - 틀린정보

(E) The Pictorialism movement emerged as photographers continued to struggle to have the idea that taking photographs was a process that ~~was as demanding as creating pieces of fine art~~ accepted. - 틀린정보

(B) 마크 체임벌린은 사진작가들은 예술가로 인정받아야 하고 ~~사진은 응용과학처럼 인류에게 큰 도움이 된다고 예견했던~~ 사진작가이다.

(D) 픽토리얼리즘은 우월성 덕분에 ~~여전히 오늘날까지~~ 예술 영역에서 지배적인 것으로 간주됩니다.

(E) 픽토리얼리즘은 사진작가들이 사진을 찍는 것이 ~~예술 작품을 만드는 것만큼 노력을 요한다는 것을~~ 알리기 위해 노력하면서 생겨났다.

Summary (A)는 사진기의 발명으로 인해 사진이 예술로서 받아들여져야 하는 논쟁이 있었다는 내용인 1단락을 요약한 것이고, (C)는 19세기부터 사진가들이 예술가로서의 지위를 얻기 위해 노력한 것과 다르게 기술자로써 멸시를 받았다는 2단락의 중심 내용이며 (F)는 4, 5단락에서 다루는 사진의 자세힘이 사회에 미치는 역할을 증가시켰다는 중심내용이다.

usherin.usher.co.kr

TEST 6-2 How and Why Birds Learn to Sing
새는 어떻게, 그리고 왜 노래하는 것을 배우는가

Introduction	단락 1	새소리 연구의 발단
Point 1	단락 2	새소리의 용도 - 짝짓기와 영역 표시
Point 2	단락 3	새소리를 배우는 과정과 환경
Point 3	단락 4	새소리의 습득과정

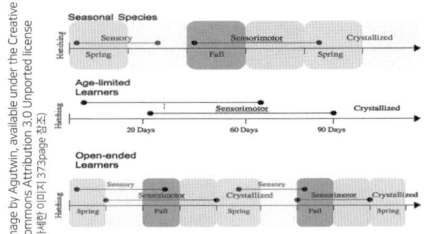

Image by Agutwin available under the Creative Commons Attribution 3.0 Unported license (자세한 이미지 373page 참조)

단락 1 — 새소리 연구의 발단

1 Beautifully complex birdsongs have inspired our greatest poets and composers, and aroused the curiosity of biologists. They wondered how and why such an **elaborate** communication form developed among birds. One of the many who **struggled to answer** these questions was Darwin who was clearly influenced by these intricate songs as he developed the theory of sexual selection. Since then biologists from many disciplines have **found** birdsongs **to be** fascinating and productive research subjects.

아름답도록 복잡한 새소리들은 우리의 가장 위대한 시인과 작곡가들의 영감을 고취시켰고, 생물학자들의 호기심을 불러 일으켰다. 그들은 어떻게, 그리고 왜 이러한 **정교한** 통신 수단이 새들 사이에서 발달했는지 궁금해왔다. 이 질문들에 답을 하기 위해 노력했던 많은 이들 중 하나는 자웅선택의 이론을 발전시키면서 이 복잡한 노래들에 의해 분명히 영향을 받았던 다윈이었다. 그 이후로, 많은 지식 분야의 생물학자들은 새소리를 대단히 흥미롭고 생산적인 연구 주제라고 생각했다.

단락 2 — 새소리의 용도 - 짝짓기와 영역 표시

2 Birdsongs, generally **regarded as** an attribute of males, are in some rare species produced by females with complexity **comparable to** those of males. **In general** though, male songbirds are the sources of these complex songs. Darwin suggested that this was the result of [Q21]sexual selection because females choose mates with more complex songs. ⓒAlthough this **ability** of birdsongs **to attract** females is frequently cited, there is little experimental evidence to support this assertion because field experiments proving that female **attraction to** the male's territory is **in direct response to** his singing are nearly impossible. One experiment on pair formation of flycatchers, however, **came close to doing** so. Male dummies were positioned near nest-boxes with automatic traps; some played a tape-recorded song from loudspeakers, while others remained silent. Even when their positions were switched to control external variables, 90 percent of females were caught in nest-box traps of singing' dummies, showing that a male's song attracts mates.

일반적으로 수컷의 속성이라고 여겨지는 새소리는 몇몇 희귀 종에서 수컷의 소리와 견줄만한 복잡성을 가지고 암컷에 의해서도 만들어진다. 그러나 일반적으로는, 수컷 새소리가 이 복잡한 노래들의 근원이다. 다윈은 이것이 암컷이 더 복잡한 노래를 부르는 수컷을 선택했기 때문에 [Q21]자웅선택의 결과라고 주장했다. ⓒ비록 이 암컷을 유혹하는 새소리의 능력은 흔히 언급되지만, 수컷의 영역으로 암컷이 끌리는 것이 그의 노래에 대한 직접적인 반응이라는 것을 증명하는 현장 실험은 거의 불가능 하기 때문에 이 주장을 뒷받침하는 실험적 증거는 희박하다. 그러나 딱새류의 짝을 만드는 한 실험은 거의 성공을 거두었다. 수컷 모형들이 자동 덫이 설치된 둥지 상자 근처에 세워졌고, 몇몇은 확성기로 테이프에 녹음된 노래를 틀었고, 나머지는 조용히 있었다. 심지어 외부 변수를 조절하기 위해 그들의 위치가 변경되었을 때도, 90%의 암컷들이 '노래하는' 모형의 둥지상자 덫에 걸렸다는 것은 수컷의 노래가 암컷을 유혹한다는 것을 보여준다.

Vocabulary

1단락
- inspire [inspáiər] v. 영감을 주다
- elaborate [ilǽbərèit] a. 정교한
- intricate [íntrəkiət] a. 복잡한
- sexual selection n. 자웅 선택 : 생물의 암, 수컷이 상대를 선택할 때 색채, 행동, 울음소리 등의 상대를 끄는 특징에 의한다는 다윈의 학설
- discipline [dísəplin] n. 지식 분야; 학과목
- fascinate [fǽsənèit] v. 매료시키다

2단락
- attribute [ətríbjuːt] n. 속성
- assertion [əsəːrʃən] n. 주장
- flycatcher [fláikætʃər] n. 딱새류
- repertoire [répərtwàːr] n. 연주 목록, 레퍼토리
- assortment [əsɔːrtmənt] n. 분류
- indicate [índikèit] v. 나타내다, 가리키다
- longevity [landʒévəti] n. 장수, 오래 지속됨
- act as : phr. ~ 로서 역할을 하다

Further, females of some species prefer males with more varied songs, so these males quickly **add to** their repertoires. The diverse assortments of songs may indicate an older male with access to better resources or proven longevity and survival skills, both good traits to **pass on to** offspring. Experiments have also shown that songs **act as** [Q21]territorial markers. House Wrens, for example, **respond** aggressively **to** recordings of other males' songs, sometimes even attacking the speaker. Researchers have also shown that removing male birds from their territories but broadcasting their songs [Q23]**prevented** neighboring males **from entering** their territories, showing that the songs **warned** others **to keep out**.

3   Just as their reasons for singing vary, so do the ways that songbirds **learn to sing**. Some are **born with** an innate knowledge of the songs, while others learn them from older birds then add to them to create personalized songs, and still others **incorporate** auditory stimuli **into** their repertoire and eventually **end up with** thousands of variations. Unlike birds **with** innate **abilities to sing**, some **are** extremely **susceptible to** external sound stimuli when learning songs. Studies of the White-crowned Sparrow show that nestlings raised alone in a laboratory develop an abnormal song. [Q24]If they are housed with a tutor adult White-crowned Sparrow, however, they will learn proper songs from it. If they are only housed with a Song Sparrow, however, they may **learn to sing** as a Song Sparrow. i) Scientists have also **taught** baby sparrows to sing a complete song ii) by **exposing** them **to** overlapping segments of a tune iii) rather than a full melody. This means that the sparrows reassembled segments of a song which were imprinted in their brains, showing that they have the **ability to identify and utilize** the different song parts presented in the experiment. Other birds, such as Northern Mockingbirds and Brown Thrashers, **are adept at** mimicking the calls of other species and add to their repertoires throughout their lives, learning around 200 and 2,000 different songs, **respectively**.

4   An interesting fact is that birds acquire most of these songs during critical periods of brain development. To do this, they **rely on** the specialized frontal cortex section of the brain **known as** the basal ganglia.

This section of the brain internalizes sensory experiences and then **shapes** them **into** vocal output through sensorimotor learning and integration. [■] This innate disposition for 'language acquisition' **is similar to** humans. [■] ◎Humans have critical periods when sensorimotor functions and regions in the frontal cortex, like the basal ganglia in birds, allow accelerated learning and vocal output shaping. [■] Similarly, most songbirds **seem to have what is called** a 'sensitive period' for song learning. [Q26] It is during these brief periods that birds are best equipped to memorize details of a tutor's song. [■] For the White-crowned Sparrow, this age is between 15 and 50 days, after which learning becomes more difficult. They, therefore, begin practicing singing **shortly after** leaving the nest, at about three weeks of age. Recalling the sounds they heard during the sensitive period, they match it in their practice singing called the subsong. The subsong becomes louder, more persistent, and structured **over time**. These corrections eventually **result in** a perfect copy of the remembered song, which **goes through** 'crystallization,' after which there is little variation. Evidence, however, suggests that auditory feedback is actively used in adulthood to maintain the song's structure. [Q27] It can be shown that disturbing auditory feedback during adult Zebra Finches' singing **caused** their song **to** deteriorate. This 'decrystallization' is a marked loss of the temporal and spectral stereotypy seen in crystallized songs. [Q28] Once normal feedback is restored, these deviations gradually disappear and the original song returns. Thus, adult birds that do not **seem to learn** new songs still retain a significant amount of plasticity in their brains.

Sentence analysis

◎ Although this ability of birdsongs / to attract females is frequently cited, / there is little experimental evidence to support this assertion, / because field experiments proving that / female attraction to the male's territory / is in direct response to his singing / are nearly impossible.

◎ Humans have similar critical periods / when / sensorimotor functions / and regions in the frontal cortex, / like the basal ganglia in birds, / allow / accelerated learning / and vocal output shaping.

Vocabulary

stereotypy [stériətàipi, stíər-] n. 상동증: 같은 행동, 말을 무의미하게 끊임없이 반복하는 증세
plasticity [plæstísəti] n. 가소성: (신경계 연구) 기억, 학습 등 뇌기능의 유연한 적응능력을 일컬음

11 According to paragraph 2, What can be inferred about birdsongs being generally regarded as an attribute of males?

(A) The songs play an important role in songbird reproduction and social interactions.
(B) The number of songs a male learns correlates to their ~~territorial range~~.
(C) ~~Only~~ male songbirds ~~are born with an ability to sing complex songs~~. ★
(D) Female songbirds are ~~unable~~ to learn songs.

2단락에 따르면, 일반적으로 수컷의 특성으로 간주되는 새 노래에 관해 추론할 수 있는 것은?

(A) 새소리는 노래하는 새들에게 번식과 사회적 교류에 중요한 역할을 한다.
(B) 수컷이 배우는 노래의 수는 그들의 ~~영역범위와~~ 상관관계가 있다.
(C) ~~오직 수컷 새만이 복잡한 노래를 부를 수 있는 능력을 타고 난다~~. ★
(D) 암컷 노래 새들은 노래를 ~~배울 수 없다~~.

Inference 지문에서 키워드인 Birdsong부분을 살펴보면 Darwin suggested that this was the result of sexual selection because females choose mates with more complex songs. (다윈은 이것이 암컷들이 더 복잡한 노래를 부르는 수컷을 선택했기 때문에 자웅선택의 결과라고 제안했다) 라고 했다. 종의 번식과 사회적 지위에 있어 새노래가 중요한 역할을 한다는 것을 알 수 있다. (B) 는 영역과의 상관관계에 대한 특정한 언급이 없고 (C)는 수컷은 복잡한 노래를 부르는 능력을 타고났다는 얘기가 없으며 (D)는 암컷은 노래를 습득할 수 없다는 내용이 없어서 오답이다.

12 The word **assortment** in the passage is closest in meaning to

(A) collection
(B) segment ★
(C) style
(D) adaptation

지문의 단어 **assortment** 와 가장 유사한 것은?

(A) 수집 [kəlékʃən]
(B) 부분 ★ [ségmənt]
(C) 방식 [stail]
(D) 적응 [ædəptéiʃən]

Vocabulary 지문의 assortment(모음)은 collection(수집)과 동의어이므로 정답이다. (B)는 문맥상 어울리지만 부분을 칭하는 것이 아니므로 오답이다.

13 According to paragraph 2, which of the following responses occurs in male birds of the surrounding territory when a male bird is removed and a pre-recorded song is played in a territory?

(A) They are discouraged from encroaching on the territory by the singing.
(B) They ~~place territorial markers~~ in the vacated territory.
(C) They are ~~more frightened~~ by the pre-recorded song than by the real one.
(D) They ~~sing louder~~ to compete with the recorded song. ★

2단락에 의하면, 다음 보기 중 수컷 새가 옮겨지고 미리 녹음된 노래가 한 영역에서 재생될 때 주위 영역의 수컷 새들에게 어떤 일이 일어나는가?

(A) 그들은 노래 때문에 영역을 침해하는 것에 대해 좌절된다.
(B) 그들은 비어있는 ~~영역에 영역표시를 한다~~.
(C) 그들은 진짜 것 보다 미리 녹음된 노래에 ~~더 겁을 먹는다~~.
(D) 그들은 녹음된 노래와 경쟁하기 위해서 ~~더 크게 노래를 부른다~~. ★

Fact 지문에서 살펴보면, 새소리를 틀어놓는 것은 다른 새들로 하여금 prevented neighboring males from entering their territories. (다른 이웃 수컷들로 하여금 그들의 영토에 들어오는 것을 못하게 한다는 것)이라고 써있다. 따라서 침해하는 것을 좌절 당한 (A)가 정답이다. (B), (C), (D)는 지문에서 언급된 적이 없으므로 오답이다.

14 Why does the author mention the **tutor adult White-crowned Sparrow** in paragraph 3?

(A) To describe the ~~steps in the rearing~~ of White-crowned Sparrows
(B) ~~To explain why~~ some White-crowned Sparrow nestlings developed abnormal songs
(C) To introduce a song-learning characteristic of one type of birdsong learning
(D) To demonstrate how nestlings of a bird species can be ~~raised by adults of different species~~ ★

3단락에서 글쓴이는 왜 **가정교사인 어른 노랑턱멧새를** 언급하는가?

(A) 노랑턱멧새를 ~~사육하는~~ 과정을 설명하기 위해서
(B) 몇몇 노랑턱멧새의 새끼들이 왜 비정상적인 노래를 발달시키는지 설명하기 위해서
(C) 한 종류의 새소리 학습의 노래학습 특성을 배우는 특성을 소개하기 위해서
(D) 어떻게 한 종의 ~~새끼가 다른 종의 성년에 의해서 길러질 수 있는지~~ 증명하기 위해서 ★

Purpose 음영의 뒷부분을 살펴보면, they will learn proper songs from them. If they are only housed with a Song Sparrow, however, they may learn to sing as a Song Sparrow.(그들은 그들로부터 제대로 된 노래를 배울 것이다. 그러나 만약 그들이 오직 노래참새와 같이 머물게 되면, 그들은 노래참새같이 노래하는 법을 배우게 될 것이다) 라고 제시되면서 노래를 배우는 특성에 대해 나와있다. 가르치는 성년인 새에 따라서 새끼 새의 노래가 바뀌는 점으로 보아서 (C)가 정답이다. (A)는 언급되지 않은 양육에 대한 설명이고, (B)는 지문에는 언급이 된 사항이지만 질문의 의도와 맞지 않으므로 오답이다. 그리고 (D)는 핵심이 잘못 맞춰져 있기 때문에 오답이다.

---

15 Which of the sentences below best expresses the essential information in the highlighted sentence in the passage? Incorrect choices change the meaning in important ways or leave out essential information.

(A) Sparrow nestlings were trained to learn a song in its entirety even though scientists only played short overlapping sections of it to them.
(B) Scientists have taught young sparrows to sing complete songs by overlapping segment of different adult sparrows, which was more effective than playing the entire song.
(C) The overlapping segments of a tune were placed in the incorrect melodic order by the baby sparrows that the scientists had trained.
(D) The sparrows that were exposed to many segments of adult sparrows' songs could be taught by scientists to learn a full melody. ★

아래 문장 중 지문 속의 음영된 문장의 핵심 정보를 가장 잘 표현하고 있는 것은 무엇인가? 오답은 문장의 의미를 현저히 왜곡하거나 핵심 정보를 빠뜨리고 있다.

(A) 참새 새끼들은 과학자들이 노래의 짧은 겹치는 부분들만 틀어주었음에도 불구하고 노래의 전체를 배우도록 훈련 받았다.
(B) 과학자들은 다른 어른 참새들의 부분을 겹침으로써 어린 참새들에게 완전한 노래를 부르도록 가르쳤는데, 이것은 전체적인 노래를 틀어주는 것보다 효과적이었다.
(C) 한 곡조의 겹치는 부분들은 과학자들이 교육한 새끼 참새에 의해서 올바르지 않은 선율의 순서로 놓여졌다.
(D) 어른 참새들의 노래의 많은 부분들에 노출된 참새들은 과학자들에 의해서 완전한 선율을 배우도록 학습되어질 수 있었다. ★

Highlight 문장을 살펴보자. i) Scientists have also taught baby sparrows to sing a complete song ii) by exposing them to overlapping segments of a tune iii) rather than a full melody. (i) 과학자들은 iii) 전체 멜로디보다 ii) 한 곡조의 겹쳐지는 부분들에 어린 참새들을 노출함으로써 i) 완전한 노래를 부르도록 가르쳤다.) 이 내용을 포함하고 있는 보기는 (A)이므로 정답이다. (B)는 성년인 새들이 노래를 부르지 않았기 때문에 오답이고, (C)는 언급되지 않은 내용이므로 오답이며, (D)는 overlapping 언급되지 않았으므로 오답이다.

---

16 According to paragraph 4, which of the following occurs in the basal ganglia after the critical period?

(A) It changes and therefore has a different function than that of humans.
(B) It becomes unable to recognize or integrates different melodies the bird hears. ★
(C) It is best timely for it to learn and retain the details of a teacher's song.
(D) It becomes relatively less sensitive to perceive and memorize details of a tutor's song.

4단락에 의하면, 다음 중 임계기 이후에 기저핵에서 일어나는 현상은?

(A) 그것은 변화하고, 따라서 사람의 그것과는 다른 기능을 가진다.
(B) 그것은 알아볼 수 없게 변하거나 새가 듣는 각각 다른 선율을 통합시킨다. ★
(C) 그것이 강사의 노래 세부 사항을 배우고 유지하는 것이 가장 적절해진다.
(D) 그것은 강사의 노래의 세부사항을 인지하고 외우는데 비교적 덜 민감해진다.

Fact 지문을 살펴보면, These corrections eventually result in a perfect copy of the remembered song, which goes through 'crystallization,' after which there is little variation.(이 수정들은 마침내 기억된 노래의 완벽한 복제품으로 완성되고, 이것은 '결정화' 되는데, 나중에는 거의 변하지 않는다)라고 써 있다. 지문의 앞 내용을 살펴보면, acquire most of these songs during critical periods (새들은 대부분의 노래들을 뇌가 발달하는 임계기에 습득한다)라는 내용으로 보아 노래의 습득은 임계기 도중에 이뤄지고, 후에는 변화가 적은 것으로 보인다. 따라서 (D)가 정답이다. (C)는 임계기 이후가 아닌 도중에 일어나는 현상이므로 오답이고, (A)는 사람도 비슷한 기능을 할 수 있다고 제시되어 있으므로 오답이다.

17 The experiment mentioned in paragraph 4 suggest that birds whose auditory systems were disturbed

(A) could ~~acquire and develop a new song even in their adulthoods.~~
(B) developed distortions as well as inaccuracies in their songs.
(C) were able to ~~maintain the perfect version~~ of their songs.
(D) ~~forget their original songs~~ should their plasticity return. ★

4단락에 언급된 실험은 다음을 나타낸다. 청각 시스템이 방해된 새들은

(A) ~~성년이 된 후에도 새로운 노래를 습득하고 발달시킬 수 있었다.~~
(B) 그들의 노래에서 일그러짐과 부정확함을 발달시켰다.
(C) 그들의 ~~노래와 완벽한 버전을~~ 유지할 수 있었다.
(D) ~~그들의 가소성이 돌아올 시에 원래의 노래를 잊어버린다.~~ ★

Fact 지문의 내용을 봤을 때, It can be shown that disturbing auditory feedback during adult Zebra Finches singing caused their song to deteriorate.(성년인 금화조가 노래를 부를 때 청각적 피드백을 방해하는 것이 그들의 노래를 악화시킨다는 것으로 보여질 수 있다)라고 제시되어 있으므로 inaccuracy가 일어난다는 것을 알 수 있다. 따라서 답은 (B)이다. (A)는 없는 내용이므로 오답이고, (C)는 노래가 방해됐을 때 유지가 되지 않으므로 오답이다. 그리고 (D)는 노래가 다시 원상복귀 되기 때문에 오답이다.

18 In paragraph 4, which of the following plays the most significant role in maintaining the song the bird has acquired?

(A) subsong ★
(B) sensitive period
(C) auditory feedback
(D) spectral variation

4단락에서, 다음 중 새가 습득한 노래를 유지시키는 일에 가장 중요한 역할을 하는 것은?

(A) 서브송 ★
(B) 민감기
(C) 청각적 피드백
(D) 스펙트럼 변동

Fact 지문에 살펴보면, Evidence, however, suggests that auditory feedback is actively used in adulthood to maintain the song's structure. (그러나 노래의 구조를 유지하기 위해서 어른일 때 청각적 피드백이 활동적으로 사용된다는 것을 보여주는 증거가 있다) 라고 제시되어 있기 때문에 피드백이 꾸준히 사용된다는 것을 알 수 있다. 따라서 정답은 (C)이다. (A)는 노래의 유지가 아닌 만들어지는 단계를 일컫기 때문에 오답이다.

19 Look at the four squares [■] that indicate where the following sentence could be added to the passage.

Similarly, most songbirds seem to have what is called a 'sensitive period' for song learning.

Where would the sentence best fit? Click on a square [■] to add the sentence to the passage. 3rd

네 개의 네모[■]는 다음 문장이 삽입될 수 있는 부분을 나타내고 있다.

유사하게, 대부분의 명금들은 노래를 배우기 위해 소위 '민감기' 라는 것을 가지고 있는 듯 하다.

이 문장은 어느 자리에 들어가는 것이 가장 적절한가? 세번째

Insertion 삽입 문장에서 정답의 단서는 Similarly(비슷하게도)라는 연결어로, 전 문장에서는 Humans have similar critical periods. (사람도 비슷한 임계기를 가진다)와 It is during these brief periods that birds are best equipped to memorize details of a tutor's song. (이 짧은 기간 동안이 새들이 교사의 노래의 세부 사항들을 외우는데 가장 적합한 시기이다)을 살펴보면 먼저 인간의 임계기의 내용이 언급되고 후에는 새들의 외우는 적합한 시기가 나오기 때문에 중간에 전환점이 필요하다는 걸 알 수 있으므로 세번째 네모가 정답이다. (B)는 Similarity은 설명할 수 있으나 'period' 에 관해서는 설명할 수 없다.

20

Directions: An introductory sentence for a brief summary of the passage is provided below. Complete the summary by selecting the THREE answer choices that express the most important ideas in the passage. Some sentences do not belong in the summary because they express ideas that are not presented in the passage or are minor ideas in the passage. **This question is worth 2 points.**

지시: 지문 요약을 위한 도입 문장이 아래에 주어져 있다. 지문의 가장 중요한 내용을 나타내는 보기 3개를 골라 요약을 완성하시오. 어떤 문장은 지문에 언급되지 않은 내용이나 사소한 정보를 담고 있으므로 요약에 포함되지 않는다. **이 문제는 2점이다.**

Biologists have developed various theories explaining how and why songbirds sing.

- (A) Bird songs have many communicative functions and have been proven to be used as mating calls and territorial markers. - **Paragraph 2**

- (E) The process of learning songs may differ significantly depending on the birds' species and environment. - **Paragraph 3**

- (F) Nestlings, like humans, are likely to utilize auditory input more effectively than adults whose song development has been finalized. - **Paragraph 4**

생물학자들은 노래를 부르는 새들이 어떻게, 왜 노래를 부르는지를 설명하는 이론을 발달시켜 왔다.

- (A) 새들의 소리는 많은 의사소통의 기능이 있고, 짝짓기 울음소리와 영역 표시의 기능으로 쓰이는 것으로 증명되었다.

- (E) 노래를 배우는 것의 과정은 새의 종과 환경에 따라 현저하게 다를 수 있다.

- (F) 사람과 마찬가지로, 새끼들은 노래의 발달이 끝난 성년보다 청각의 투입을 더 효과적으로 사용할 것으로 예상된다.

(B) ~~Primitive birds learned to sing through an intuitive ability~~, and have evolved since to the point where some species can copy the songs of other birds. - 틀린정보

(C) Female birds are attracted to male birds with the ability to sing a variety of songs, as they are reliable indicators of strong survival abilities. - Paragraph 2 detail

(D) ~~Through the process of crystallization~~, birds obtain a collection of subsongs during the critical periods, which occurs in early childhood. - 틀린정보

(B) 원시 새들은 직감적 능력을 통하여 노래를 배우거나 다른 새들이 노래를 일부의 종이 복제할 수 있는 지점까지 배운이래로 진화시켜 온다.

(C) 암컷들은 다양한 노래를 부를 수 있는 능력을 가진 수컷에게 끌리는데, 이는 이것이 신뢰할 수 있는 강한 생존 능력의 지표이기 때문이다.

(D) 결정화의 과정을 통해서, 이른 새끼 시절에 일어나는 임계기동안 새들은 subsong의 모음집을 습득한다.

Summary 지문의 중심 내용은 새가 어떻게, 왜 노래를 하는지에 대한 다양한 이론이다. 보기 (A)는 2단락의 중심내용인 새소리의 용도를 설명하기 때문에 정답이고, (E)는 3단락에서 새끼 새가 노래를 배우는 과정을 설명하는 것과 일치한다. (F)는 새끼 새들이 subsong을 형성하는 내용의 설명이므로 정답이다. (B)는 지문에서 예로 든 내용을 설명해서 중심에서 빗겨난 내용이기 때문에 오답이며 (C)는 2단락에서 언급된 미미한 내용을 설명했으므로 오답이다. 그리고 (D)는 지문에서 언급된 핵심 단어들을 사용해서 만든 틀린 보기이기 때문에 오답이다.

참고 이미지

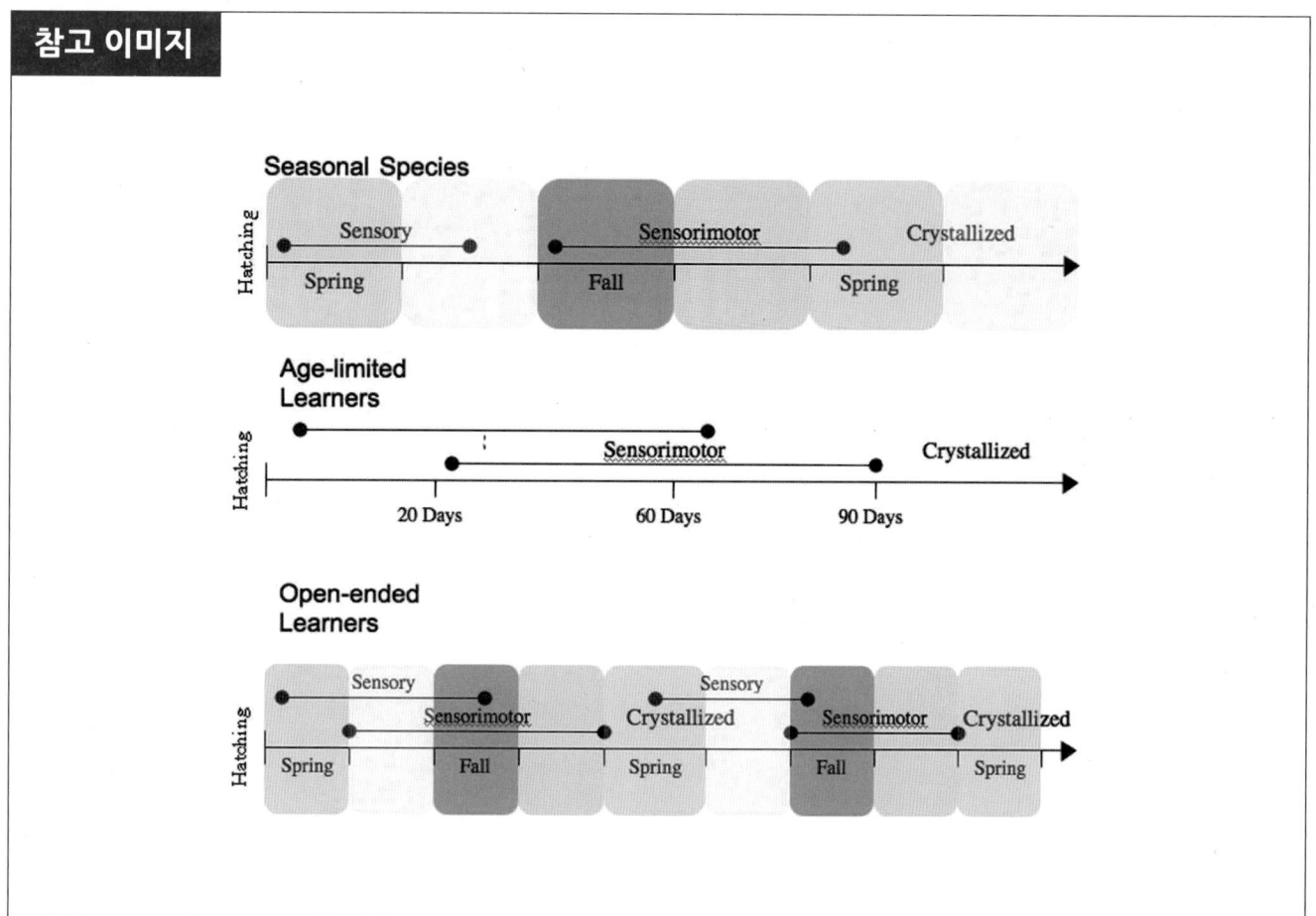

USHER

iBT TOEFL
FINAL TEST READING
TEST 7

답안 및 취약 유형 분석표
해석·해설

답안 및 문제 유형 분석표

TEST 7-1

01 (C) Purpose

02 (C) Fact

03 (C) Highlight

04 (A) Inference

05 (B) Vocabulary

06 (B) Fact

07 (D) Purpose

08 (C) Fact

09 2nd ■ Insertion

10 (A), (E), (F) Summary

TEST 7-2

11 (D) Reference

12 (B) Fact

13 (B) Highlight

14 (A) Fact

15 (C) Inference

16 (D) Fact

17 (A) Vocabulary

18 (B) Fact

19 4th ■ Insertion

20 (A), (E), (F) Summary

각 문제 유형별 맞춘 개수를 아래에 적어 보세요.

유형	맞춘 답의 개수	정답률
단어 (Vocabulary)	/ 2	정답률: %
사실 확인 문제 (Fact)	/ 7	정답률: %
지시어 찾기 (Reference)	/ 1	정답률: %
끼워 넣기 (Insertion)	/ 2	정답률: %
문장 변환문제 (Highlight)	/ 2	정답률: %
목적 (Purpose)	/ 2	정답률: %
추론 (Inference)	/ 2	정답률: %
단락 요약(Summary / Category Chart)	/ 2	정답률: %
전체	/ 20	정답률: %

※ 자신이 취약한 유형은 READING STRATEGIES를 통해 다시 한번 점검하시기 바랍니다. (p.31)

TEST 7-1　Functions of Roots 뿌리의 기능

Introduction	단락 1	뿌리의 주요 기능
Point 1	단락 2	주요 기능의 예시
Point 2	단락 3	열악한 환경 - 망그로브 나무
Point 3	단락 4	경쟁을 피하는 방법
Point 4	단락 5	뿌리의 화학물질 분비

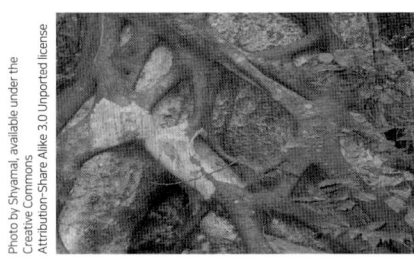

Photo by Shyamal, available under the Creative Commons Attribution-Share Alike 3.0 Unported license

단락 정리 / 지문 / 해석

단락 1 — 뿌리의 주요 기능

1 Roots, the water-absorbing organs of a plant, are present on essentially all vascular plants and **serve** three primary **functions**: to anchor the plant to a substrate, to absorb nutrients through osmosis, and to store food reserves. [Q10-A]They can **adapt to carry out** these primary **functions in ways** optimized for different environments.

물을 흡수하는 식물의 기관인 뿌리는 본질적으로 모든 관다발 식물에 존재하고 3가지 주요한 기능을 수행한다: 식물을 지지층에 고정시키기, 삼투작용을 통해 영양분 흡수하기, 음식 저장물들을 저장하기. [Q10-A]뿌리는 다른 환경에서 최적화된 방법으로 이러한 주요 기능들을 실행하기 위해 조정될 수 있다.

단락 2 — 주요 기능의 예시

2 One of the most important functions of root networks is to provide a stable footing for plants so they do not **fall over** or get swept away. This also provides the secondary benefit of controlling soil erosion around the plant's base. **In addition to** this, many plants like the carrot and turnip also store nutrients in modified roots. [Q1]Roots of plants such as the bluebell store **so** much energy **that** they **act as** perennating organs **allowing** the plant **to survive** harsh conditions such as drought, frigid winters, or light deficiency. They do this by **allowing** the exposed part of the plant **to** die down and storing **as** much energy **as possible** for regrowth when conditions improve.

뿌리 망의 가장 중요한 기능 중의 하나는 식물에게 안정적인 기반을 제공하여 식물이 넘어지거나 쓸려 가지 않도록 한다. 뿌리는 또한 식물 기반 주위의 토양 침식을 통제하는 부차적인 혜택도 제공한다. 이것 에 더해서, 당근과 순무와 같은 많은 식물들은 또한 변형된 뿌리에 영양분을 저장한다. [Q1]Bluebell과 같은 식물의 뿌리들은 너무 많은 에너지를 저장하여 다년생 기관의 역할을 하면서 가뭄, 추운 겨울이나 빛의 결핍과 같은 가혹한 환경에서 살아남을 수 있도록 한다. 뿌리들은 이것을 위해 식물의 노출된 부분은 죽게 내버려 두고 조건이 개선되면 재성장을 위해 가능한 한 많은 에너지를 저장한다.

단락 3 — 열악한 환경 - 망그로브 나무

3 For plants which **are** constantly **exposed to** harsh environments, such as salt water swamps, survival is more challenging **due to** the lack of basic necessities. The deeper roots of most plants die because of the lack of oxygen under the waterlogged soil, **leading to** the plant's slow death. Mangrove roots, however, are well-suited to the region. ⓒThe red mangrove, a tropical tree which colonizes coastlines and brackish water between the northern and southern latitudes of 25 degrees, can often be found on the water's edge.

해수 늪지대와 같은 가혹한 환경에 끊임없이 노출된 식물들에게, 생존은 기본적인 필수 요소의 부족 때문에 좀 더 어려운 일이다. 물에 잠긴 토양 아래에서 산소의 부족 때문에 대부분의 식물들 뿌리의 깊은 부분은 이로 인해 식물들은 서서히 죽게 된다. 하지만 맹그로브 뿌리들은 그 환경에 잘 적응한다. ⓒ붉은 맹그로브는 북위, 남위 25도 사이에 있는 해안과 염분이 있는 물에 대량 서식하는 열대 나무로서 종종 물가에서 발견된다.

Vocabulary

1단락
- vascular [vǽskjulər] a. (혈관 등의) 관의
- anchor [ǽŋkər] n. 닻 / v. 고정시키다
- nutrient [njú:triənt] a. 영양이 되는 / n. 영양분
- substrate [sʌ́bstreit] n. 기질
- primary [práiméri] a. 주요한
- osmosis [azmóusis] n. 삼투(현상)
- optimize [áptəmàiz] v. 낙관하다

2단락
- erosion [iróuʒən] n. 부식, 침식
- turnip [tə́:rnip] n. 순무
- perennating a. 다년생의
- harsh [ha:rʃ] a. 거친
- frigid [fríd,id] a. 몹시 추운
- deficiency [difíʃənsi] n. 결핍
- stable [stèibl] a. 안정된
- drought [draut] n. 가뭄

3단락
- waterlogged [wɔ́:tərlɔ(:)gd] a. 물에 잠긴
- brackish [brǽkiʃ] a. 염분이 섞인
- saline [séili:n] a. 소금이 든

These **are distinguished from** other mangroves by the prominent prop roots extending into the water from high up on their stems. They thrive in the highly saline habitats by not **relying on** traditional roots growing under the substrate. [Q2]Instead, it is assumed, lenticels, or pores, on their prop roots **act as** conduits for supplying oxygen for respiration to the subterranean roots. Unlike most plants, their roots also **enable** them **to obtain** freshwater from highly saline water sources through non-metabolic ultra-filtration, using negative pressure inside the root to draw freshwater in through a membrane **too fine for salt to pass through**, **in a process** called reverse-osmosis.

4 Unlike the mangroves, however, most plants exist in environments **filled with** other plants **leading to** a competition-filled bio-diverse habitat. To **triumph over** competition, plants use various methods such as root adaptations to attain the necessary nutrients, water, sunlight, and territory. i)If the plants are grown **in close proximity**, ii)there may be a limited amount of these essential nutrients, iii)**resulting in** a head-to-head **competition for as large a share as possible**. One of the ways they do this is by adapting. One example of this is the dark, competition-filled forest floor where strangler figs have adapted roots that snake down the trunk of a host tree or dangle from its branches as aerial roots **enabling** it **to live** in the tree branches. [Q4]When they reach the ground, however, they dig in and grow more rapidly, fighting the host for nutrients. This root network surrounds the host and intertwines around it. As they grow thicker they squeeze the trunk of the host and **cut off** its flow of nutrients. Eventually the host **dies from** strangulation, insufficient sunlight and root competition, and the strangler fig **stands on its own**.

5 Some plants also compete using chemical methods. The roots of these plants secrete chemical compounds **known as** root exudates. [Q6]Through the exudation of **a variety of** compounds, they regulate the microbial content of nearby soil, **cope with** herbivores, alter the physical and chemical make-up of the soil, and inhibit the growth of competing plants. [■] Chemical-mediated plant-plant interference, or allelopathy, is one mechanism plants use to **gain an advantage over** their

Vocabulary

- subterranean [sʌbtəréiniən] a. 지하의
- tropical [trápikəl] a. 열대의
- prominent [prámənənt] a. 눈에 띄는
- non-metabolic [nan-mètəbálik] a. 신진대사가 아닌
- substrate [sʌbstreit] n. 기질
- swamp [swamp] n. 습지
- membrane [mémbrein] n. 막

4단락
- aerial [ɛəriəl] a. 공중의
- intertwine [intərtwáin] v. 엮다
- proximity [praksíməti] n. 근접
- strangulation [stræŋgjuléiʃən] n. 교살
- insufficient [ìnsəfíʃənt] a. 부족한

5단락
- exudation [èksjudéiʃən] n. 삼출물
- herbicide [ə́ːrbəsàid] n. 제초제
- leptospermone [léptəspəːmʌn] n. 렙토스퍼몬 뿌리 삼출물 중 하나
- secrete [sikríːt] v. 분비하다
- compound [kámpaund] n. 합성물

competitors. [■] It also has important **implications for** agriculture where its effects may be beneficial, as **in the case of** natural weed control, or detrimental, when chemicals produced by plants affect the growth of crops. [Q7]In research conducted by biologists from a chemical company, it was found that a plant called lemon bottlebrush excreted an allelopathic chemical called leptospermone. [■] One day, [Q8]they noted that under certain bushes, such as lemon bottlebrush, other plants only rarely grew. By collecting samples of the soil under the bush, they were able to **extract** many chemicals **from** the plants, one of which **was identified as** an herbicide. [■]◎While it did have herbicidal effects, the amount required for effective crop coverage was **too** high **to** be practical. Leptospermone **was**, therefore, **reworked into** thousands of compounds, with several being effective but too toxic, environmentally persistent or non-selective. Mesotrione, the final compound they created could, however, **be used as** a selective herbicide for corn crops.

[■] 그것은 또한 농업에서 중요한 영향을 가지는데, 자연적인 잡초 통제와 같은 경우에서처럼 유용할 수도 있고 식물에 의해 만들어진 화학물질이 곡식의 성장에 영향을 끼칠 때는 해로울수도 있다. [Q7]한 화학 회사의 생물학자들이 시행한 조사에서, 병솔나무라고 불리는 식물은 렙토스퍼몬 이라는 타감작용을 하는 화학 물질을 분비한다고 발견됐다.
[■] 어느 날, [Q8]생물학자들은 병솔나무와 같은 특정한 관목 아래에서 거의 자라지 못한다는 것을 알아차렸다. 관목아래에 있는 토양 샘플들을 수집함으로, 그들은 식물로부터 많은 화학 물질들을 추출할 수 있었고 그 중 하나가 제초제라는 것을 확인하였다. [■] ◎이것은 제초효과를 가지고 있는 반면, 효과적인 곡식 수확량을 위해 필요되어지는 양이 너무 높아서 실용적일 수 없다. 렙토스퍼몬은 수천 개의 화합물로 재가공 되고, 그 중 일부는 효과적이지만 독성이 강하거나, 환경에 오래 잔류하거나 무차별적이었다. 하지만 그들이 만든 마지막 화합물인 메소트리온은 곡류작물에서 선택적 제초제로 사용될수 있었다.

Sentence analysis

◎ The red mangrove, / a tropical tree / which colonizes coastlines and brackish water /
붉은 맹그로브는   열대 나무로서   바닷가나 소금물 속에 서식하는
between the northern and southern latitudes of 25 degrees, / can often be found on the water's edge.
북쪽과 남쪽 위도 25도 사이에   주로 물가에서 발견된다

◎ While it did have herbicidal effects, / the amount required for effective crop coverage /
이 삼출물은 제초제의 효과를 가지고 있는 반면에   효율적인 곡식 범위를 위해 필요한 양이
was too high to be practical.
실용적이기에는 너무 높았다.

Vocabulary

competitor [kəmpétətər] v. 경쟁자   interference [ìntərfíərəns] n. 방해   allelopathy [ɔːlləpéiθai] n. 타감작용
implication [ìmpləkéiʃən] n. 영향

01

Why does the author mention bluebells in paragraph 2?

(A) To show how plant footing also prevents erosion

(B) To give an example of a harsh environment in which modified roots store nutrients.

(C) To show one of the crucial functions plants roots have

(D) To illustrate that plants regrow when conditions improve ★

글쓴이는 왜 2단락에서 bluebells를 언급하는가?

(A) 어떻게 식물이 고정하는 것이 침식되는 것을 예방하는지 보여주기 위해서

(B) 뿌리가 영양분을 저장하는 극한 환경의 예시를 제시하고자

(C) 식물 뿌리가 가지고 있는 중요한 기능 중 하나를 보여주기 위해

(D) 식물들이 상황이 좋아지면 다시 자란다는 것을 보여주고자 ★

Purpose 지문에서 bluebells가 나온 부분을 살펴보면, store so much energy that they act s perennating organs allowing the planet to survive harsh conditions such as drought, frigid winters, or light deficiency. (너무 많은 에너지를 저장하여 다년생 기관의 역할을 하면서 가뭄, 추운 겨울이나 빛의 결핍과 같은 가혹한 환경에서 살아남을 수 있도록 한다)라고 말한다. 즉, 뿌리가 어떻게 식물을 오래 살 수 있게 해주는지를 말하는 (C)가 정답이다. (D)는 상황에 따른 식물의 성장에 대한 이야기랑은 관계가 없음으로 오답이다.

02

According to paragraph 3, how do red mangroves survive in their environment?

(A) The roots of the mangrove are able to expel the salt it has absorbed.

(B) The mangrove has roots that separately absorb water and salt. ★

(C) Lenticels on the prop roots provide oxygen to the subterranean roots.

(D) The salinity of water lessens as it passes through a strainer in the stem.

3단락에 따르면, 붉은 맹그로브는 어떻게 그것의 환경에서 살아 남는가?

(A) 맹그로브의 뿌리는 그것이 흡수한 염분을 배출할 수 있다.

(B) 맹그로브는 물과 소금을 따로 흡수하는 뿌리가 있다. ★

(C) 지지근에 있는 피목들은 지하뿌리에게 산소를 공급한다.

(D) 물의 염도는 줄기에 있는 여과기를 거치면서 줄어든다.

Fact 지문에서 red mangroves가 언급된 부분을 살펴보면, They thrive in the highly saline habitats by not relying on traditional roots growing under the substrate. Instead, it is assumed, lenticels, or pores, on their prop roots act as conduits for supplying oxygen for respiration to the subterranean roots. (그들은 지지층 아래에서 성장하는 전통적인 뿌리에 의존하지 않으며 염분이 높은 서식지에서 번영한다)라고 말한다. 즉, 피목을 통해 산소공급을 받아 살 수 있다는 (C)가 정답이다. (A)는 지문에 없는 빼낸다는 내용이 있어서 오답이고, (B)는 따로 흡수하는 뿌리가 있다고 말해서 오답이며, (D)는 줄기와 관련이 없으므로 오답이다.

03

Which of the sentences below best expresses the essential information in the highlighted sentence in the passage? Incorrect choices change the meaning in important ways or leave out essential information.

(A) The restricted amount of nutrients plants need results in a direct competition between plants to take as many nutrients as they can.

(B) When there is a scarcity of nutrients, plants grow near each other, competing for limited nutrients. ★

(C) The amount of plant necessities may be limited if plants grow too close to one another, leading to competition between the plants.

(D) Plants save the limited amount of nutrients through a fierce competition with other plants that are located near them.

아래 문장 중 지문 속의 음영된 문장의 핵심 정보를 가장 잘 표현하고 있는 것은 무엇인가? 오답은 문장의 의미를 현저히 왜곡하거나 핵심 정보를 빠트리고 있다.

(A) 식물이 필요한 제한된 양분의 양은 식물간의 얻을 수 있을 만큼 얻으려 하는 직접적인 경쟁을 야기한다.

(B) 양분이 부족할때, 제한된 양분을 위해 경쟁하려고, 식물은 서로 가까이 산다. ★

(C) 만약 식물이 너무 가까이 살면 식물들끼리 경쟁이 생겨 필요요소들의 제한적이게 된다.

(D) 식물들은 근처에 있는 다른 식물들과의 경쟁을 통해 제한된 양분을 아껴둔다.

Highlight 주어진 문장을 살펴보면 i) If the plants are grown in close proximity, ii) there may be a limited amount of these essential nutrients, iii) resulting in a head-to-head competition for as large a share as possible. (i) 만약 식물들끼리 서로 근접하여 자란다면 iii) 가능한 커다란 몫에 대한 직접 경쟁이 가득하여 ii) 이러한 영양분에 대한 제한이 있게 될 것이다) 라는 내용을 찾을 수 있다. (A)는 가까운 거리라는 내용이 없으므로 오답이고, (B)는 인과 관계가 틀려서 오답이며, (D) 문장에 없는 내용을 포함해서 오답이다. 전반적으로 내용을 다 포함하는 (C)가 정답이다.

04
According to paragraph 4, what can be inferred about the strangler figs?

(A) It grows relatively slowly until it begins competing with its host.
(B) It penetrates the host tree to find the nutrients it requires.
(C) It harms the host plant in the process of growing downward to reach the soil. ★
(D) It steals the host's nutrients by strangling its trunk.

4단락에 의하면, 교살목에 관해 추론할 수 있는 것은?

(A) 숙주와 경쟁할 때까지 비교적 천천히 자란다.
(B) 숙주을 뚫고 들어가 필요한 양분을 찾는다.
(C) 토양을 향해 밑으로 자랄 때 숙주에게 해를 입힌다. ★
(D) 숙주의 몸통을 졸라 양분을 훔친다.

Inference 키워드인 교살목이 언급된 부분을 살펴보면 When they reach the ground, however, they dig in and grow more rapidly, fighting the host for nutrients.(하지만 뿌리가 지면에 도달할 때, 땅속으로 파고들어 재빠르게 성장하며 영양분을 위해 숙주와 경쟁한다) 라고 말한다. 즉, 숙주와 경쟁할 수 있기 전에는 상대적으로 느리게 자랐다는 것을 말하므로 답은 (A)이다. (B)는 뚫는다는 내용이 없으므로 오답이며 (C)는 밑으로 자랄 때 해를 입힌다는 내용이 없으므로 오답이다. 그리고 (D)는 훔친다는 내용이 없으므로 오답이다.

05
The word secrete in the passage is closest in meaning to

(A) promote ★
(B) discharge
(C) conceal
(D) exploit

지문의 단어 secrete 와 가장 유사한 것은?

(A) 촉진시키다 ★ [prəmóut]
(B) 배출하다 [distʃɑ́:rdʒ]
(C) 숨기다 [kənsíːl]
(D) 이용하다 [ikspló it]

Vocabulary 지문의 secrete(분비하다)는 discharge(배출하다)와 동의어이므로 정답은 (B)이다.

06
According to paragraph 5, which of the following is NOT a characteristic of exudates?

(A) They can cause changes in the soil conditions. ★
(B) They encourage competitiveness with other species.
(C) They can hinder the growth of other plants.
(D) They control nearby microorganism colonies.

5단락에 의하면, 다음 중 분출물의 성질이 아닌 것은?

(A) 토양 상태를 바꿀 수 있다. ★
(B) 다른 식물과 경쟁을 조장한다.
(C) 다른 식물 성장을 방해한다.
(D) 근처 미생물 사회를 제어한다.

Fact 문제의 키워드인 exudates 와 관련된 지문을 살펴보면 Through the exudation of a variety of compounds, they regulate the microbial content of nearby soil, cope with herbivores, alter the physical and chemical make-up of the soil, and inhibit the growth of competing plants.(다양한 혼합물의 분비를 통해 그들은 근처 토양의 미생물량을 조절하고 초식동물에 대처하고 토양의 물리적, 화학적 구성 성분을 바꾸고 경쟁 식물의 성장을 방해한다) 즉, 경쟁을 조장한다는 (B)의 내용은 없으므로 정답이다.

07 According to paragraph 5, why does the author mention the research conducted by biologists from a chemical company?

(A) ~~To prove the existence~~ of the herbicidal compound ★

(B) To ~~describe how~~ allelopathy can affect bushes and nearby plants

(C) ~~To explain why~~ lemon bottlebrush excretes leptospermone

(D) To provide an example of a plant that use allelopathy

5단락에 따르면, 글쓴이는 왜 한 화학회사의 실험을 언급하는가?

(A) 제초제의 화합물이 존재한다는 것을 증명하기 위해서 ★

(B) 어떻게 타감작용이 덤불과 근처 식물에 영향을 미치는지 설명하고자

(C) 왜 병솔나무가 렙토스퍼몬을 분출하는지 설명하고자

(D) 타감작용을 쓰는 식물의 예를 제시하고자

Purpose 음영된 부분이 포함된 문장을 보면 In research conducted by biologists from a chemical company, it was found that a plant called lemon bottlebrush excreted an allelopathic chemical called leptospermone.(한 화학 회사의 생물학자들이 시행한 조사에서, 병솔나무 라고 불리는 식물은 렙토스퍼몬이라는 타감작용을 하는 화학 물질을 분비한다고 발견됐다) 라고 말한다. 병솔나무를 언급하며 그것이 타감작용을 쓰고 있는 것이 연구를 언급한 글쓴이 목적이므로 답은 (D)이다. (A)는 연구의 결과를 논하는 것이므로 오답이며, (B)는 타감작용이 식물에 어떻게 영향을 끼치는지 설명하는 것이 목적이 아니므로 오답이다. 그리고 (C)는 이유 설명이 목적이 아니므로 오답이다.

08 What is true about lemon bottlebrush bushes according to paragraph 5?

(A) Lemon bottlebrush bush exudates are not practically useable ~~because of their strong herbicidal effect~~. ★

(B) ~~Usually many plants can live under the bushes~~ despite their allelopathy.

(C) The soil surrounding them is much different than the soil under nearby bushes.

(D) Lemon bottlebrush bushes in ~~their original form~~ can be used as a selective herbicide for corn crops.

5단락에서 병솔나무에 관해 사실인 것은?

(A) 병솔나무 삼출물은 너무 강한 제초제 효과로 인해 실용적으로 사용될 수 없다.★

(B) 타감작용에도 불구하고 많은 식물들이 덤불밑에서 자랄 수 있다.

(C) 병솔나무 근처 토양은 근처 다른 덤불 밑의 토양과 매우 다르다.

(D) 원래 형태의 병솔나무는 옥수수 작물에 선택성 제초제로 쓰일수 있다.

Fact 문제의 키워드인 lemon bottlebrush 가 언급된 부분을 보면, they noted that under certain bushes, such as lemon bottlebrush, other plants only rarely grew. By collecting samples of the soil under the bush, they were able to extract many chemicals from the plants, one of which was identified as an herbicide. (생물학자들은 병솔나무와 같은 특정 관목 아래에서 거의 자라지 못한다는 것을 알아차렸다. 관목아래에 있는 토양 샘플들을 수집함으로, 그들은 식물로부터 많은 화학 물질들을 추출할 수 있었고 그 중 하나가 제초제라는 것을 확인하였다) 라고 말한다. 즉, 주위 토양에서 제초제 역할을 하는 물질을 추출해냈으므로 다른 곳과 토양이 다르다는 것을 알 수 있으므로 (C)가 정답이다. (A)는 지문에는 강하지 못해 실용적이지 못한 것이라 말하니 반대의 뜻이어서 오답이며, (B)는 타감작용은 존재하므로 오답이다. 그리고 (D)는 원래 형태의 병솔나무가 선택성 제초제로 쓰일 수 없기 때문에 오답이다.

09 Look at the four squares [■] that indicate where the following sentence could be added to the passage.

> It (also) has important implications for agriculture where its effects may be beneficial, as in the case of natural weed control, or detrimental, when chemicals produced by plants affect the growth of crops.

Where would the sentence best fit? Click on a square [■] to add the sentence to the passage.

2nd

네 개의 네모[■]는 다음 문장이 삽입될 수 있는 부분을 나타내고 있다.

> 그것은 또한 농업에서 중요한 영향을 가지는데, 자연적인 잡초 통제와 같은 경우에서처럼 유용할 수도 있고 식물에 의해 만들어진 화학물질이 곡식의 성장에 영향을 끼칠 때는 해로울 수도 있다.

이 문장은 어느 자리에 들어가는 것이 가장 적절한가?

두번째

USHER

Insertion 답을 잡을 수 있는 핵심 단어는 agriculture이다. 삽입 문장의 전 문장인 Chemical-mediated plant-plant interference, or allelopathy, is one mechanism plants use to gain an advantage over their competitors(타감 작용이라고 불리는 화학 매개 식물간 방해는 다른 경쟁자들에 비해 이점을 얻기 위해 식물이 사용하는 하나의 장치이다)라고 경쟁과 우월에 관해 말한다. 삽입 문장은 다른 식물들과의 경쟁이 농업과 관련 있다고 말하므로 2번째 네모가 정답이다. 정답 B일 경우에는 문장의 it이 가리키는 것을 allelopathy 이어야 하지만 오답 D일 경우에 it은 herbicide 가리키며 이때 삽입문장 when 절에 chemical 과 중복되게 되어 D는 될 수 없다.

10

Directions: An introductory sentence for a brief summary of the passage is provided below. Complete the summary by selecting the THREE answer choices that express the most important ideas in the passage. Some sentences do not belong in the summary because they express ideas that are not presented in the passage or are minor ideas in the passage. **This question is worth 2 points.**

지시: 지문 요약을 위한 도입 문장이 아래에 주어져 있다. 지문의 가장 중요한 내용을 나타내는 보기 3개를 골라 요약을 완성하시오. 어떤 문장은 지문에 언급되지 않은 내용이나 사소한 정보를 담고 있으므로 요약에 포함되지 않는다. 이 문제는 2점이다.

Plants are able to adapt to harsh environments when their roots can carry out primary roles through specialization.

- (A) Plants that are subjected to unfavorable conditions develop unique roots that help the plant overcome such circumstances. - Paragraph 3

- (E) To physically compete against nearby plants for nutrients, plants utilize their roots. - Paragraph 4

- (F) Chemicals exuded by some plants can affect the growth of other plants and are used by humans. - Paragraph 5

식물들은 그들의 뿌리가 특수화를 통해 주요 기능을 수행 할 수 있을 때 열악한 환경에 적응 할 수 있다.

- (A) 열악한 환경에 지배를 받는 식물은 그러한 환경들을 이겨낼 수 있도록 도와주는 특별한 뿌리를 발달시킨다.

- (E) 근처의 식물들과 영양분을 위해 물리적으로 경쟁하기 위해 식물은 그들의 뿌리를 사용한다.

- (F) 일부 식물에 의해 분비되는 화학물은 다른 식물의 성장에 영향을 줄 수 있으며 인간에 의해 사용될 수 있다.

(B) When roots are exposed to unfavorable environments, such as saline water, ~~they utilize nutrients that they have stored in the roots.~~ - 틀린정보

(C) Some plants produce chemical compounds ~~that are too toxic~~ for other plants and herbivores that feed on the plants. - 반/반

(D) Some plants like the strangler fig grows on other trees with roots exposed in the air. - Detail

(B) ~~뿌리가 염수와 같이 열악한 환경에 노출되면, 그들은 뿌리에 저장해 두었던 영양분을 사용한다.~~

(C) 몇몇 식물들은 식물을 먹고 사는 초식동물과 다른 식물에게 ~~너무 독성이~~ 강한 화학물질을 만든다.

(D) 교살목 같은 몇몇 식물들은 뿌리를 공중에 내놓고 다른 나무 위에서 자란다.

Summary 지문의 중심 내용은 식물이 뿌리를 사용하는 여러 가지 방법과 예시였다. (A)는 3단락의 중심내용을, (E)는 4단락의 중심 내용을, (F)는 5단락의 중심내용을 각각 잡았다. (B)는 틀린 내용이기 때문에 오답이고, (C)는 초식동물 내용과 너무 독성이 강하다는 부분이 아니므로 오답이다. (D)는 정답으로 하기엔 너무 비중이 적어서 오답이다.

usherin.usher.co.kr

TEST 7-2 History of The Patent Law 특허법의 역사

Introduction	단락 1	특허권 부재
Point 1	단락 2	르네상스시대에 특허권 발생
Point 2	단락 3	영국에서의 특허권과 인식변화
Point 3	단락 4	미국에서의 특허권의 헌법화
Point 4	단락 5	특허권의 사회공헌 기조 유지

단락정리	지문	해석
단락 1 특허권 부재	1 ⓞThe State's protection of a person's **right to utilize and control** the utilization of an [Q11]invention, **be it** a machine or a unique method of production, was not prevalent until the Renaissance period. **As a result**, in the Middle Ages, one would have had to hide the fact that one had invented a novel product **in order to keep** it. [Q12]This lack of **protection from** the state has **been attributed to** rigid social structures and hierarchies that ignored the talent of the individual inventor.	ⓞ기계이든 독자적인 방법이든 [Q11]발명의 활용을 사용하고 통제하는 개인의 권리에 대한 국가의 보호는 르네상스 시기까지 일반적이지 않았다. 결과적으로, 중세 시대에서는 새로운 것을 유지하기 위해서는 그것을 발명한 사실을 숨겨야만 했을 것이다. [Q12]국가에 의한 보호 부족은 개인 발명가의 재능을 무시했던 엄격한 사회구조와 지배구조 탓이었다.
단락 2 르네상스시대에 특허권 발생	2 i)This changed when the first systemic mechanism for protecting an inventor's rights to monopoly was introduced by a 1474 Act of the Venetian Senate, ii)which prohibited the production of a device **conforming to** a patented one without the authorization of the inventor for 10 years, iii)**provided** the inventor had recorded the innovation with the council. [Q14]This system **differed from** the modern one **in that** it required the inventor **to produce** a completed, working device. **In other words**, the inventor **had to report** a device that could be used immediately and was societally useful. However, it still **laid out** all the major features of modern patent law, **such as** requiring the device to be officially registered, 'useful' to the society, 'not previously made in this state', and providing a fixed term of exclusivity.	i) 이것은 Venetian Senate의 1474 법령에 의해서 발명가의 독점에 대한 권리를 보호하는 첫 번째 체계적인 장치가 도입됐을 때 변화했는데, iii) 이 법령은 만약 발명가가 의회에 발명을 등록한다면 ii) 10년 동안 발명가의 허가 없이는 특허 받은 제품과 일치 하는 도구의 생산을 금지하는 것이었다. [Q14]이 체계는 당시 발명가에게 완전하게 작동하는 도구를 생산하는 것을 요구했다는 점에서 현대의 체계와는 다르다. 즉, 발명가는 바로 이용할 수 있고 사회적으로 유용한 장치들을 신고해야만 했다. 그러나 그것은 여전히 모든 장치가 공식적으로 등록되어야 하고, 사회에 유용하며, 같은 국가에서 이전에는 만들어진 적이 없고, 배타적인 고정된 용어를 제공하는 것과 같은 현대 특허법의 모든 주요 특징들을 제시했다.
단락 3 영국에서의 특허권과 인식변화	3 Even before the Venetian Senate's act of 1474, isolated monopolies were granted in Europe. For example, in England the monarchs would grant letters patent, or 'letters that **lie open**', to people **in their graces, granting them a monopoly** to produce or provide specific goods and services. This tradition of granting monopolies eventually **led to** the	심지어 1474년 Venetian Senate의 법령 이전에도 유럽에서는 배타적인 독점이 주어졌다. 예를 들면, 영국에서 군주는 왕의 은총으로 특정한 제품과 서비스를 생산하고 제공하는 독점을 줌으로써 사람들에게 특허증, 즉 모두에게 열려있는 증서를 수여했다.

Vocabulary

1단락 hierarchy [háiərɑːrki] n. 계급, 지배층, 체계   utilize [júːtəlàiz] v. 활용하다   prevalent [prévələnt] a. 널리퍼진
attribute [ətríbjuːt] v. (B를 A의) 결과라고 생각하다

2단락 council [káunsəl] n. 의회   systemic [sistémik] a. 체계의   monopoly [mənápəli] n. 독점   prohibit [prouhíbit] v. 금지하다
authorization [ɔ̀ːθərizéiʃən] n. 권한부여   innovation [ìnəvéiʃən] n. 혁신   device [diváis] n. 장치   register [rédʒistər] v. 기록하다
exclusivity [èksklusívəti] n. 배타성

3단락 Implement [ímpləmənt] v. 시행하다   ale-house [èilhus] n. 술집   corruption [kərʌpʃən] n. 부패, 오염, 변질

term 'patents' we use today. **It** was **not**, however, **until** the Venetian Act **that** the standardized process of granting patents occurred. [Q15]Britain, influenced by this new concept, eventually implemented such a system as a kind of mercantilist instrument to attract emigrants with skills that could possibly aid British industry with the guarantee of exclusive monopoly, after the significant economic drain caused by the War of the Roses. **By** the early 17th century, patents had become royal favors to subjects of loyalty or wealth, with **monopolies being granted on** products and services **such as** running ale-houses. ⓒThis **led to** inefficiency and **left room for** the corruption that **brought about** the Statute of Monopolies of 1624, which **required courts to outlaw** all monopolies but **those based on** true inventive intentions. When the Industrial Revolution spurred an explosive number of new inventions, patents became an increasingly important component of the socioeconomic machine. This era marks a **change in** the perception of the role of patents in society, **in that** they were **no longer** given only for the introduction of a new finished product, but also for the introduction of technological know-how or processes.

단락 4
미국에서의 특허권의 헌법화

4 **Along with** many other British legal concepts, the patent system was introduced in the United States during the colonial period between 1640 and 1776. Initially, each of the 13 colonies formed their own patent systems, which led to disputes, **such as** identifying the true inventor of the steamboat, as different inventors were registered in the patent archives of two colonies. These problems **continued to arise** even after the United States' independence. The government, therefore, **sought to solve this problem** and [Q16]the 1789 Constitutional Convention imbedded a national patent system in the constitution itself. [■] The result was Article I, Section 8 of the Constitution which **authorized** Congress **to** selectively **endow** individual authors and inventors **with** 'exclusive rights **to** their writings and discoveries'. [■] Samuel Hopkins received the first United States federal patent in 1790 for a process that **derived** potash **from** wood ashes. [■][Q18]The United States patent system **grew to** its full, modern **status** with the 1836 revision that introduced a formal system of examination by appointed, professional examiners. [■] Therefore, **not only** was the patent law nationalized, **but also** the process of granting patents standardized. [Q16-A]Since then, patents have

Vocabulary

grant [grænt] v. 승인하다, 인정하다
emigrant [émigrənt] n. 이민자

4단락
endow [endáu] v. 기부하다
colony [káləni] n. 식민지
selectively [siléktivli] ad. 선별하여

spurred [spə:rd] a. 독촉을 받은
explosive [iksplóusiv] a. 폭발성의

potash [pátæʃ] n. 탄산칼륨
constitutional [kànstətjúːʃənl] a. 구성상의
derive [diráiv] v. 이끌어 내다

socioeconomic [sòusiouèkənámik] a. 사회 경제적인
revolution [rèvəlúːʃən] n. 혁명

thread [θred] n. 실, 가닥

fabric [fǽbrik] n. 직물

| 단락 5
특허권의
사회공헌 기조
유지 | rapidly become an important thread of the American economic fabric, **despite the fact that** the process' effectiveness is still debated.

5 Throughout history the concept of protecting one's rights to one's own creations has advanced **along with** the burgeoning capitalist, industrial world economy, which is increasingly **dependent on** new technological advancements. Despite **changes in** the patent systems **over time**, the principal idea that the inventor must **contribute** in some way **to** the state, or society, through novel, useful inventions has remained. | 역사 내내, 고유 창작의 고유 권리를 보호하는 개념은 새로운 기술적 진보에 점점 더 의존적인 산업적 세계 경제인 급성장하는 자본주의와 함께 진보해왔다. 시간이 지나며 발생한 특허 체계의 변화에도 불구하고, 발명가가 새롭고도 유용한 발명을 통해 여러 방법에서 국가 또는 사회에 공헌해야만 한다는 주된 생각은 여전히 남아있다. |

Sentence analysis

◎ The States' protection of a person's right / to utilize and control the utilization of an invention /
　개인의 권리에 대한 국가의 보호는　　　　　발명품의 이용과 사용 통제에 관해
　be it a machine or a unique method of production / was not prevalent until the Renaissance period.
　기계이던 독특한 생산 방식이던 간에　　　　르네상스 시대 전까지는 일반적이지 않다.

◎ This led to inefficiency and left room for corruption / that brought about the Statute of Monopolies of 1624 /
　이것은 비능률을 야기시켰으며 부패에 대한 여지를 남겨　　1624년의 the Statute of Monopolies를 초래하였다
　which required courts to outlaw all monopolies but those based on true inventive intentions.
　　　법원이 진실된 창의적인 의도에 기초되지 않은 모든 독점을 불법화 하게 하는

Vocabulary

5단락　　capitalist [kǽpətəlist] n. 자본주의자, 자본가

11
What does the word it in paragraph 1 refer to

(A) individual
(B) state
(C) idea ★
(D) invention

1단락에서 it 이 가리키는 단어는 무엇인가?

(A) 개인 [ìndəvídʒəl]
(B) 국가 [steit]
(C) 생각 ★ [aidíːə]
(D) 발명품 [invénʃən]

Reference 보기 중에 'it' 에 넣었을 때 의미가 맞는 것은 (D) Invention이다. (C)가 되지 않는 이유는 invention(발명)이 언제나 '생각' 이 아니기 때문에 오답이다. 보기 중에 'it' 에 넣었을 때 의미가 맞는 것은 (D) Invention이다.

12
Which of the following is true about the Renaissance period according to paragraph 1?

(A) There were ~~many more talented inventors~~ worth protecting in the ~~Renaissance period.~~ ★
(B) During the Renaissance period people started to recognize the importance of the talent and achievements of the individual.
(C) Because of rigid structures and hierarchies of the Renaissance period, ~~people decided to utilize more inventions.~~
(D) Talented inventors of the Renaissance period were ~~eager to share their novel products.~~

1단락에서 르네상스 시대에 관해서 사실인 것은?

(A) ~~르네상스 시대에 보호할 가치가 있는 많은 재능 있는~~ 발명가들이 있었다. ★
(B) 르네상스 기간은 개인의 재능과 업적의 중요성을 알아가기 시작한 시기였다.
(C) 르네상스 시대의 엄격한 구조와 계층으로 인해 사람들이 더 많은 발명품을 사용하기로 했다.
(D) 르네상스 시대의 재능있는 발명가들은 그들의 새로운 발명품을 나누고 싶어했다.

Fact 문제의 키워드인 Renaissance(르네상스)가 언급된 부분을 살펴 보면 ignored the talent or well-being of the individual inventor in favor of the whole of society.(개인 발명가의 재능을 무시했던 엄격한 사회구조와 지배층 탓이었다)라는 부분에서 이전에는 재능과 복지가 무시되었지만 특허권이 생긴 르네상스에서는 그렇지 않았다는 것을 알 수 있다. (A)가 답이 되지 않는 이유는 르네상스시대에 특허권이 생겼다고 해서 재능있는 발명가가 더욱 많다는 주장은 비약이기 때문이다.

13
Which of the sentences below best expresses the essential information in the highlighted sentence in the passage? Incorrect choices change the meaning in important ways or leave out essential information.

(A) Efforts in making a systemized way of protecting inventors' rights started with the Venetian Senate's 1474 Act, which ~~took 10 years to establish this prohibition of~~ producing devices similar to an already invented one, because each inventor had to report his device to the council.

(B) The Venetian Senate's 1474 Act is the first standardized implementation of a patent law in that as long as an original, completed device was reported to the council, it prohibited anyone from producing a device similar to the patented one without the consent of the inventor for a given period.

(C) The inventors reported their products to the council, ~~prompting~~ the Venetian Senate's 1474 Act which prohibited reproduction of such devices without authorization by the inventor. ★

(D) The systemized protection of inventors' rights is considered to have started with the Venetian Senate's 1474 Act, which required that ~~anyone who~~ produces a device similar to a patented one ~~report it to the council.~~

아래 문장 중 지문 속의 음영된 문장의 핵심 정보를 가장 잘 표현 하고 있는 것은 무엇인가? 오답은 의미를 현저히 왜곡하거나 핵심 정보를 빠뜨리고 있다.

(A) 발명가 권리를 보호하는 체계화된 방법을 만들기 위한 노력은 1474년 Venetian Senate's 법령과 함께 시작되었는데, 각각의 발명가는 장비를 의회에 보고해야 했기 때문에 이 법령은 이미 발명된 것과 유사한 장비 생산하는 것을 금지하는 ~~이 법령을 제정하는데 10년이 걸렸다.~~

(B) Venetian Senate의 1474년 법령은 처음으로 체계화된 특허법이 이행됐는데 있어 원래의 완성된 장비가 의회에 보고돼있는 한 그 어떤 이로 하여금 주어진 기간동안 발명가의 동의없이 특허된 장비와 비슷한 장비를 만드는 것을 금지하였다.

(C) 발명가들은 그들의 상품을 의회에 보고하여, 이는 발명가의 허가 없이 장치를 복제할 수 없게 하는 Venetian Senate의 1474년 법령을 ~~촉진시켰다.~~ ★

(D) 체계화 된 발명가의 권리 보호는 Venetian Senate's의 1474년 법령과 함께 시작했다고 여기며, 이것은 특허권 장치를 받은 유사한 장비를 생산하는 ~~그 누구도 의회에 보고하도록 했다.~~

Highlight i) This changed when the first systemic mechanism for protecting an inventor's rights to monopoly was introduced by a 1474 act of the Venetian Senate (i) 이것은 Venetian Senate의 1474 법령에 의해서 발명가의 독점에 대한 권리를 보호하는 첫 번째 체계적인 장치가 도입됐을 때 변화했는데) ii), which prohibited the production of a device conforming to a patented one without the authorization of the inventor for 10 years,(ii) 10년 동안 발명가의 허가 없이는 특허 받은 제품과 일치하는 도구의 생산을 금지하는 것이었다) i) provided the inventor had recorded the innovation with the council. (iii) 이 법령은 (만약 발명가가 의회에 발명을 등록한다면) 본문에 따르면 i), ii), iii)내용을 모두 포함한 것은 (B)이기 때문에 답이 되며 (C)는 그들의 권리가 침해되고 있기 때문에 의회에 등록하는 것이 아니기 때문에 인과가 바뀐 내용이므로 오답이다.

14
Which statement regarding modern patent systems is supported by paragraph 2?

현대 특허권 시스템과 관련된 언급 중에 2단락에 의해 지지될 수 있는 것은?

(A) The modern system allows for the registration of devices that may not yet be suitable for real life use.
(B) The first patent system allowed for the endowment of patents to ~~the same kind of inventions~~ as the modern system. ★
(C) The modern system ~~does not appreciate 'complete' and 'perfect' devices~~ that are ready for use right away.
(D) The modern system ~~allows monopolization of 10 years~~ for inventions.

(A) 이것은 실제 사용에 아직 적합하지 않을지도 모르는 장치의 등록을 허용한다.
(B) 첫 특허 시스템은 현대 시스템은 ~~같은 유형의 발명품에~~ 특허권 수여를 허용했다. ★
(C) 현대 시스템은 당장 사용할 수 있는 '완성'되고 '완벽한' 장치를 ~~평가하지 않는다.~~
(D) 현대시스템은 발명에 대해서 ~~10년간 독점을 허용했다.~~

Fact 문제의 키워드인 Modern patent systems(현대 특허권 시스템)이 언급된 부분을 살펴보면 In other words, the inventor had to report a device that could be used immediately and was societally useful. (즉, 발명가는 바로 이용할 수 있고 사회적으로 유용한 장치들을 보고해야만 했다)라는 부분에서 예전에는 바로 사용 가능해야 했지만 현재는 그렇지 않아도 된다는 점을 알 수 있으므로 답은 (A)이다.

15
What is implied in paragraph 3 about Britain at around the time a patent system was introduced?

3단락에서 체계화 된 특허권 시스템이 도입될 시기쯤에 영국에 관해서 추론할 수 있는 것은 무엇인가?

(A) Britain was one of the ~~most attractive~~ states for emigrants to go to due to the invention ~~of the first patent system~~.
(B) The increased rate of immigration caused by the introduction of the patent system ~~improved England's faltering economy.~~ ★
(C) Britain did not have a population skilled and technically proficient enough to develop as fast as the government wanted.
(D) The patent system, as a mercantilist instrument, significantly ~~drained England's economy~~ as many emigrants flooded in.

(A) 영국은 ~~특허권 시스템을 처음으로~~ 이행하기 때문에 이민자들에게 ~~가장 매력적인~~ 나라였다.
(B) 특허권 시스템의 도입으로 인해 증가된 이민자의 수는 ~~영국의 흔들리는 경제를 향상시켰다.~~ ★
(C) 영국은 국가정부가 원하는 만큼 나라를 발전시킬 충분히 숙달되고 기술적으로 능숙한 인구가 없었다.
(D) 중상주의 수단으로써, 특허권 시스템은 많은 이민자들이 쇄도하게 하여 영국의 경제가 ~~나빠지게 했다.~~

Inference 문제의 키워드인 systemized patent(체계화된 특허권)이 언급된 부분을 살펴보면 Britain, influenced by this new concept, eventually implemented such a system as a kind of mercantilist instrument to attract emigrants with skills that could possibly aid Britain's industry with the guarantee of exclusive monopoly, due to the significant economic drain caused by the War of the Roses. (이러한 새로운 개념에 영향 받은 영국은 장미 전쟁에 의해 야기된 상당한 경제 손실 이후에 아마도 배타적인 독점의 보장으로 영국 산업에 도움을 줄 기술을 가진 이민자들을 끌어당기기 위해 일종의 상업 도구와 같은 체계를 결국에는 시행했다) 라는 부분에서 전쟁 이후 인재들이 부족했다는 것을 알 수 있으므로 답은 (C)가 된다. (B)는 본문엔 뒤쳐진 영국경제가 형성되었다는 결론이 언급되지 않았다.

16 According to paragraph 4, why was the patent law an important aspect of the Constitutional Convention of 1789?

(A) It allowed each of the 13 states to enact its own patent law.
(B) It classified the steamboat to have been invented by two different people.
(C) It added an American characteristic to a legal concept imported from Great Britain. ★
(D) It made a national patent system so as to avoid confusion between states.

4단락에 따르면 왜 특허권 법은 1789년의 헌법제정 회의의 중요한 면이 되었는가?

(A) 13개의 주가 그들 자신의 법을 제정할 수 있게 해주었다.
(B) 증기선이 두 사람에 의해 발명 됐다고 했다.
(C) 영국으로부터 들어온 법적 개념에 미국 특징을 추가하였다. ★
(D) 주들 간의 혼란을 피하기 위해 국가적으로 특허권 법을 만들었다.

Fact 문제의 키워드인 Constitutional Convention(헌법제정)가 언급된 부분을 살펴 보면 Due to this there were common disputes, such as who was the true inventor of the steamboat, as different inventors were registered in the patent archives of two colonies.(그러한 이유로 서로 다른 발명가가 등록이 되면서 증기선에 대한 실제 발명가가 누구인지를 확인하는 것 같은 논쟁으로 이어지게 되었다)라는 내용을 통해 주들 사이에 혼란을 막기 위해 헌법을 제정한 것을 알 수 있음으로 정답은(D)이다. (C)는 그럴듯 하지만 전혀 언급되지 않은 관계없는 내용이다.

17 The word exclusive in the passage is closest in meaning to

(A) unshared
(B) partial
(C) noble
(D) unprecedented ★

지문의 단어 exclusive 와 의미상 가장 유사한 것은?

(A) 분배되지 않은 [ʌnʃɛərd]
(B) 부분적인 [pɑːrʃəl]
(C) 고결한 [nóubl]
(D) 전례가 없는 ★[ʌnprésidentid]

Vocabulary 지문의 exclusive (독점적인)은 unshared(분배되지 않은)과 동의어이므로 답은 (A)이다. (D)는 문맥상 이전에 없던 권리를 가질 수 있었다는 내용으로 말은 되지만 exclusive와 동의어가 아니기에 오답이다.

18 Why is the United States patent system considered to have reached full maturity in 1836 according to paragraph 4?

(A) Because the patent system had evolved from an already efficient mechanism. ★
(B) Because an established protocol of examination was introduced.
(C) Because the patent system did not have an important impact on the economic system of America any more.
(D) Because the system was revised so that the government could appoint certain inventors.

4단락에 따르면 왜 미국 특허권 시스템이 1836년에 완전히 완성되었다고 고려하는가?

(A) 특허권 시스템은 이미 효과적인 방법으로부터 발달했기 때문이다. ★
(B) 설립된 조사 협약이 도입되어졌기 때문이다.
(C) 특허권 시스템이 더 이상 미국경제시스템에 중요한 영향을 끼치지 못했기 때문이다.
(D) 정부가 일정한 발명가를 지정할 수 있게 시스템이 개정되었기 때문이다.

Fact 문제의 키워드인 full maturity in 1836(1836년에 완전히 완성)가 언급되는 부분을 살펴 보면 introducing a formal system of examination by appointed, professional examiners(미국의 특허 체계는 임명된 전문적인 검사관에 의해 공식 조사 체계를 도입하는) 전문 시험관이 특허권 시스템에 참여하여 특허권이 완성될 수 있음을 알 수 있음으로 정답은 (B)이다. (A)는 예전에도 효율적인 특허권에서 진화했기 때문에 특허권이 완성되었다는 내용이 없기 때문에 오답이다.

19

Look at the four squares [■] that indicate where the following sentence could be added to the passage.

Therefore, not only was the patent law nationalized, but also the process of granting patents standardized.

Where would the sentence best fit? Click on the square [■] to add the sentence to the passage.   **4th**

네 개의 네모[■]는 다음 문장이 삽입될 수 있는 부분을 나타내고 있다.

그리하여 특허법이 국유화되었을 뿐만 아니라 특허를 수여하는 과정이 표준화 되었다.

이 문장은 어느 자리에 들어가는 것이 가장 적절한가?   네번째

> **Insertion** 네번째 네모 앞에 introducing a formal system of examination by appointed, professional examiners (미국의 특허 체계는 임명된 전문적인 검사관에 의해 공식 조사 체계를 도입하는)라는 부분이 특허권이 nationalized(국영화)되었고 standardized(표준화)되었다는 내용과 연결되므로 답은 4번째 네모이다.

20

Directions: introductory sentence for a brief summary of the passage is provided below. Complete the summary by selecting the THREE answer choices that express the most important ideas in the passage. Some sentences do not belong in the summary because they express ideas that are not presented in the passage or are minor ideas in the passage. **This question is worth 2 points.**

지시: 지문 요약을 위한 도입 문장이 아래에 주어져 있다. 지문의 가장 중요한 내용을 나타내는 보기 3개를 골라 요약을 완성하시오. 어떤 문장은 지문에 언급되지 않은 내용이나 사소한 정보를 담고 있으므로 요약에 포함되지 않는다. 이 문제는 2점이다.

The law of patents has gone through dramatic changes.

- **(A)** The first patent law to properly protect an individual's right to manufacture a newly established invention was enacted in 1474 by the Venetian Senate. - Paragraph 2

- **(E)** The Industrial Revolution marked a major change in the patent system, as the British patent office began issuing patents from both products and technological knowledge. - Paragraph 3

- **(F)** The American patent law was nationalized and the process of granting patents standardized when the principles of individuals' rights to their creations was included and revised in the constitution. - Paragraph 4

특허법은 많은 변화를 겪었다.

- **(A)** 발명자에게 발명품을 제조할 수 있는 특권을 주는 첫 특허법은 1474년 Venetian Senate가 제정하였다.

- **(E)** 산업혁명은 사람들이 완성된 상품 이외에도 기술적 노하우의 도입에 대해 지지하기 시작한 특허법의 큰 변화를 일으킨 시기이다.

- **(F)** 헌법에 발명품에 대한 개인의 원칙이 포함되고, 개정되었을때, 미국 특허법은 전국화 되었고, 특허 주는 과정은 표준화 되었다.

(B) The Venetian Senate's 1474 Act allowed the monopolization of a device for 10 years. - Paragraph 2 detail
(C) ~~Letters patent was~~ issued before the Venetian Senate's Act of 1474 and ~~influenced the systemized implementation of patent law.~~ - 틀린정보
(D) The United States patent law matured ~~because monarchs granted patent holder a monopoly to produce or provide specific goods and services.~~ - 틀린정보

(B) 1474년 The Venetian Senate의 법령은 10년 동안 장비의 독점권을 허용했다.
(C) ~~특허장은~~ 1474년 the Venetian Senate'의 법령 전에 발행 되었고 ~~체계화된 특허법 이행에 영향을 주었다.~~
(D) ~~군주가 특허권 보유자에게 특정한 제품과 서비스를 생산하고 제공하는~~ 독점권을 부여 ~~했기 때문에~~ 미국의 특허 제도가 완성되었다.

> **Summary** (A)는 1단락에서의 특허 시스템의 발전이 필요했다는 분분에서 확인할 수 있으며, (E)는 3단락에서 완성된 제품뿐만 아니라 아이디어도 특허가 필요했다는 부분에서, 그리고 (F)는 4단락에서 헌법에서 창작물의 대한 개인의 권리가 인정되었을 때 특허권이 국영화된 내용을 확인할 수 있다.

usherin.usher.co.kr

USHER

iBT TOEFL

FINAL TEST READING

TEST 8

답안 및 취약 유형 분석표
해석·해설

답안 및 문제 유형 분석표

TEST 8-1

01 (A) Inference
02 (B) Fact
03 (A) Purpose
04 (D) Highlight
05 (C) Fact
06 (B) Purpose
07 (A) Fact
08 (C) Vocabulary
09 4th ■ Insertion
10 (A), (E), (F) Summary

TEST 8-2

11 (A) Highlight
12 (A) Reference
13 (C) Fact
14 (B) Vocabulary
15 (D) Fact
16 (D) Inference
17 (C) Fact
18 (B) Purpose
19 4th ■ Insertion
20 (B), (C), (E) Summary

각 문제 유형별 맞춘 개수를 아래에 적어 보세요.

유형	맞춘 답의 개수	정답률
단어 (Vocabulary)	/ 2	정답률: %
사실 확인 문제 (Fact)	/ 6	정답률: %
지시어 찾기 (Reference)	/ 1	정답률: %
끼워 넣기 (Insertion)	/ 2	정답률: %
문장 변환문제 (Highlight)	/ 2	정답률: %
목적 (Purpose)	/ 3	정답률: %
추론 (Inference)	/ 2	정답률: %
단락 요약 (Summary / Category Chart)	/ 2	정답률: %
전체	/ 20	정답률: %

※ 자신이 취약한 유형은 READING STRATEGIES를 통해 다시 한번 점검하시기 바랍니다. (p.31)

TEST 8-1 Communication of Ants 개미들의 의사소통

Introduction	단락 1	개미의 의사소통과 이점들
Point 1	단락 2	독샘과 배끝마디샘이 만드는 각기 다른 페로몬
Point 2	단락 3	파라오 개미의 페로몬 사용법
Point 3	단락 4	마찰음을 이용한 의사소통
Point 4	단락 5	꿀벌과 개미의 의사소통의 다른 점

단락 정리 / 지문 / 해석

단락 1 — 개미의 의사소통과 이점들

1 Ants **have** several **advantages over** solitary insects such as increased system reliability and **division of labor**. The major advantage, however, is the communication among members. This **allows** the colony **to regulate** its foraging activity and retain a memory of previously rewarding locations. To do this, ants **rely on** chemical signals called pheromones. When foragers find a successful foraging site, they deposit a trail of pheromones on their return to the nest. This trail **gains strength** as more and more workers **add** more pheromones **to** it.

개미들은 군집 생활을 하지 않는 곤충들에 비해서 강화된 체계 신뢰도와 분업과 같은 여러 장점들을 가지고 있다. 하지만 주요 장점은 구성원들간의 의사 소통이다. 이것은 군집이 먹이 채집 행동을 규제하고 이전에 먹이가 수집된 장소에 대한 기억을 간직하는 것을 가능하게 한다. 이것을 위해, 개미들은 페로몬이라고 불리는 화학적 신호들에 의존한다. 채취자가 풍부한 채집 장소를 찾을 때, 그들은 둥지로 돌아오는 길에 페로몬 흔적을 남긴다. 이 흔적은 좀 더 많은 일개미들이 그 흔적에 좀 더 많은 페로몬을 더하면서 뚜렷해진다.

단락 2 — 독샘과 배끝마디샘이 만드는 각기 다른 페로몬

2 [Q21]⊙Unlike the traditional **views on** ant pheromone trails, recent studies have shown that distinct roles **are assigned to** different pheromones, **as** can be illustrated by the differences in the pheromones produced by the poison and pygidial glands of Malaysian ponerine army ants. The poison glands of these ants contain two pheromone components, one eliciting a strong, short-term attraction to prey targets and another guiding workers from foraging sites back to the colony. These pheromone trails are highly volatile, [Q22]lasting only a few minutes, to ensure that ants are not attracted to sites **long after** the prey has been collected. The pygidial gland, **on the other hand**, produces a longer-lasting trail pheromone that guides workers back to the trail network of the colony. These pheromones **act as** the bread crumbs' in the tale of 'Hansel and Gretel', **allowing the ants to maintain** their spatial organization and **helping** them **forage in an** organized **manner** which enables the rapid transport of food to the colony.

[Q21]⊙개미 페로몬에 흔적에 대한 전통적인 관점과는 달리, 최근 연구는 각각의 다른 페로몬에 대해 각기 독특한 역할이 지정되었다는 것을 보여주는데, 이것은 Malaysian ponerine army 개미의 독샘과 배끝 마디샘의 차이에서 보여진다. 이 개미들의 독샘은 두 가지 페로몬 구성요소를 가지는데, 하나는 사냥감에 대해 강하고 짧은 유인물질을 끌어내고 다른 하나는 일개미들 먹이 채집 장소에서 군집으로 돌아가는 길을 안내하는 역할을 한다. 이런 페로몬의 흔적들은 [Q22]사냥감이 포획되고 오랜 후에도 개미들이 같은 장소에 끌리지 않도록 매우 빨리 사라지고 몇 분 정도만 지속된다. 반면에 배끝마디샘은 길게 지속되는 추적 페로몬을 남기는데, 이것은 일개미들은 군집의 추적망에 다시 돌아올 수 있게 해준다. 이러한 페로몬은 '헨젤과 그레텔' 의 이야기에서의 빵 부스러기와 같은 역할을 하는데, 개미가 그들의 공간 조직을 유지하게 하고 먹이의 재빠른 군집으로의 수송을 가능하게 하는 조직화된 방식으로 먹이를 사냥하게끔 한다.

Vocabulary

1단락
- solitary [sálitèri] a. 혼자하는, 독단적인
- regulate [régjəlèit] v. 규제하다
- trail [treil] n. 흔적, 자취
- reliability [rilàiəbíləti] n. 신뢰할 수 있음
- forage [fɔ́ːridʒ] v. 먹이를 찾다
- output [áutpùt] n. 산출량
- division of labor : phr. 분업
- reward [riwɔ́ːrd] n. 보상, 수익

2단락
- elicit [ilísit] v. 끌어내다, 유인하다
- crumb [krʌm] n. 부스러기
- volatile [válətil] a. 변덕스러운
- spatial [spéiʃəl] a. 공간의, 공간적인
- act as : phr. ,-로서 역할을 하다
- transport [trænspɔ́ːrt] v. 수송하다

| 단락 3 파라오 개미의 페로몬 사용법 | 3 [■] Furthermore, in Pharaoh's ant, research has shown distinct, short-lived and long-lived attractive-trail pheromone effects, **as well as** a short-lived repellent pheromone. [■] **In contrast to** most ant pheromones, the long-lived trails of Pharaoh's ants can persist **for** several days, **allowing** the trail network **to be explored** for a longer period of time. [■] Sections of the network **leading to** food are reinforced with the short-lived trail pheromone, and the repellent pheromone is placed immediately after non-rewarding trails. [■] **In other words**, the long-lived attractive pheromone acts as a memory, the short-lived attractive pheromone marks out routes to current food sources, and the short-lived repellent pheromone is a no entry signal to unrewarding branches of rewarding trail sections. These three scents **seem to work** complementarily. | [■] 게다가, 파라오개미에선, 조사는 단기간 기피 페로몬뿐 아니라 선명한 단기와 장기 유인-추적 페로몬이 있음을 나타낸다. [■] 대부분의 개미 페로몬과는 대조적으로, 파라오 개미의 장기 흔적은 며칠이나 유지되어 흔적 망이 오랜 기간 탐색될 수 있도록 해준다. [■] 먹이로 이어지는 흔적 망의 부분들은 단기 흔적 페로몬에 의해 강화되며 기피 페로몬은 먹이를 찾을 수 없었던 흔적 이후에 즉시 그 장소에 뿌려진다. [■] 즉, 장기 유인 페로몬은 기억이며, 단기 유인 페로몬은 최신의 먹이 소스로의 길을 표시하며, 단기 기피 페로몬은 음식으로 가는 흔적 부분에서 먹이가 없는 곳으로 가는 지점에 대해 출입 불가 흔적이 된다. 이러한 세가지 향은 상호 보완적으로 작용하는 것으로 보인다. |
| 단락 4 마찰음을 이용한 의사소통 | 4 [Q30-A]Foraging ants also utilize tactile communication methods, such as vibration to communicate a wider repertoire of messages that promote the organization of the colony's foraging system. Desert ants, for example, rub their abdominal areas together to make sounds. Although ants do not have auditory organs, they can still perceive these messages by sensing the vibration of the ground with their legs. i) When a worker locates a large prey item, such as a dead insect, it makes sharp sounds ii) to attract workers in the area, through a process called stridulating, that **encourages** nearby workers **to release** pheromones over longer distances, iii) causing rapid recruitment to the prey item, thereby retrieving it significantly faster. Furthermore, in leaf-cutting ants, recruitment behavior changes **in relation to** the quality of food. **In order to test** what **causes** different levels of sound **to be created**, researchers **presented** ants **with** leaves of different qualities - tender leaves, tough leaves, sugar-coated tough leaves, and acid-coated leaves and then noted the proportion of workers that stridulated as they cut through the different leaves. [Q25]The results clearly showed that the workers stridulated most strongly when cutting through leaves of a good quality or attractiveness, with the most stridulation occurring while cutting tender or sugar-coated leaves **as opposed to** the other leaves. | [Q30-A]채집 개미는 또한 군집의 채집 체계를 조직을 진척시키는 폭넓은 메시지 레퍼토리를 전달하기 위해 진동과 같은 촉감 의사소통 방법을 사용한다. 예를 들면, 사막 개미는 소리를 내기 위해 자신의 배를 비빈다. 비록 개미들이 청각 기관은 없지만 여전히 자신의 다리로 지면의 진동을 감지함으로 이러한 메시지를 인지할 수 있다. i) 일개미들은 죽은 곤충과 같은 커다란 먹이를 발견할 때, ii) 주변의 주변동료 들을 끌어당기기 위해 날카로운 소리를 낸다, 이것은 '울기' 라고 불리는 과정을 통하는데 근처에 있는 일개미들이 원거리에 페로몬을 분비하도록 하며 iii) 먹이가 있는 지역으로 빠르게 동료를 모집하여 상당히 재빠르게 수거한다. 게다가. 가위개미의 모집행동은 먹이의 질과 관계해서 변한다. 무엇이 소리의 다른 레벨을 만들어내는지를 실험하기 위해 조사관들은 개미에게 부드러운 잎, 거친 잎, 설탕이 발린 거친 잎, 산이 발라진 잎과 같은 다른 종류의 잎을 제공하고 각기 다른 잎들을 자르면서 우는 일개미의 비율을 기록했다. [Q25]그 결과는 명확히 일개미들이 좋은 질을 가졌거나 개미들의 이목을 끄는 잎을 자를 때 강하게 운다는 것을 보여주며 다른 잎들과는 대조적 으로 부드럽거나 설탕이 발린 잎을 자를 때 가장 심하게 운다는 것을 보여주었다. |

Vocabulary

3단락
repellent [ripélənt] a. 격퇴하는
complementarily [kàmpləméntərili] ad. 보완하여
persist [pərsíst] v. 지속하다
reinforce [rìːinfɔ́ːrs] v. 강화하다

4단락
tactile [tǽktil] a. 촉감이 있는
abdominal [æbdámənəl] a. 복부의
stridulate [strídʒəlèit] v. 울다, 소리내다
repertoire [répərtwàːr] n. 레퍼토리, 연주(목록)
auditory [ɔ́ːditɔ̀ːri] a. 청각의
tender [téndər] a. 부드러운
recruitment [rikrúːtmənt] n. 신병 모집, 신규 모집
perceive [pərsíːv] v. 감지하다

USHER

단락 5
꿀벌과 개미의 의사소통의 다른 점

5 [Q30-E]This pheromone system may seem unique, but other communal insects, such as honeybees, have also developed advanced communication systems. Unlike ants honeybees use discernible movements like the 'waggle dances' to communicate complex concepts such as the approximate distance and directions to food sources. Returning foragers also **perform** tremble **dances** to recruit receiver bees to collect their nectar. A further difference is that honeybees individually remember their rewarding foraging sites and return to them. [Q27] 'Trail-following' ants, **on the other hand, are bound to** the externally encoded group memory of their pheromone trails. These trails ensure that a channel of communication is always open and **allows** them **to** continually **react** and exchange information whilst foraging without **needing to return** to their nest, unlike the honeybees. This **ability to** constantly **locate** productive foraging sites is probably the most important reason **for insects to communicate**.

[Q30-E]이러한 페로몬 시스템은 유일해 보이지만, 꿀벌과 같은 다른 집단 곤충들 또한 의사소통 방법을 발전시켜왔다. 개미와 달리 꿀벌들은 'waggle dance' 와 같은 식별 가능한 움직임을 사용해 먹이 출처로의 근접거리나 방향 등의 복잡한 개념들을 의사 소통한다. 돌아오는 채집 곤충들은 역시 그들의 과즙을 모을 수 있도록 다른 채집 벌들을 모집하려고 진동 춤을 춘다. 더욱 다른점은 꿀벌은 개별적으로 먹이를 찾은 지역을 기억하여 되돌아 오는 것이다. [Q27]반면에 '흔적을 추적하는' 개미들은 그들의 페로몬 흔적에 대해 외부적으로 기록된 기록 기억에 묶여 있다. 이러한 흔적들은 의사소통 통로가 늘 열려있고 그들에게 계속해서 반응하고 벌과는 달리 둥지로 돌아올 필요 없이 먹이를 찾는 동안에 정보를 교환하는 것을 가능하게 한다. 끊임없이 생산적인 먹이 장소를 찾는 능력은 아마도 곤충이 의사소통을 하기 위한 가장 중요한 이유일 것이다.

Sentence analysis

◎ Unlike the traditional views on ant pheromone trails / recent studies have shown that /
  개미 페로몬 흔적에 대한 전통적인 관점과는 다르게   최근 연구는 보여준다
  distinct roles are assigned to different pheromones /
  다른 역할들이 각 다른 페로몬에게 할당되어 있다
  as can be illustrated by the differences in the pheromones /
  이것은 호르몬의 차이에서 증명되어 질 수 있다
  produced by the poison and pygidial glands of Malaysian ponerine army ants Malaysian ponerine army ants.
  독이나 개미의 독샘과 배끝마디샘에서 분비되는

◎ Another discernible movement is the 'waggle dance' / which summons others to the 'dance floor'
  다른 식별할 수 있는 움직임은 '꼬리춤' 이다   그것은 다른 개미들을 '춤추는 무대'로 모은다.
  where returning foragers perform tremble dances, recruiting receiver bees to collect their nectar.
  그곳에서 돌아오는 채집꾼들이 진동춤을 수행하며 그들의 과즙을 모으기 위해 수집 벌들을 모집한다.

Vocabulary

5단락
approximate [əpráksəmət -rák-] a. 인접한, 대강의
tremble [trémbl] v. 떨다
encode [enkóud] v. 암호로 바꾸다
discernible [disə́ːrnəbl] a. 알아볼 수 있는
constantly [kánstəntli] ad. 끊임없이

01

According to paragraph 2, what can be inferred about the traditional view of ant pheromone trails?

(A) The communicational methods of ants were thought to be simple.
(B) The long-lasting and short-lasting attraction pheromones were believed to attract nearby ants ~~for a long period of time.~~ ★
(C) The trail pheromones were thought to be secretions from a single gland that ~~poisoned and repelled other insects.~~
(D) The pygidial and poison glands were believed to secrete harmful pheromones ~~that capture prey.~~

2단락에 따르면, 개미 페로몬 흔적에 가졌던 기존의 견해에 관해 추론할 수 있는 것은?

(A) 개미의 의사소통 방법은 간단하다고 생각해져 왔다.
(B) 장기간과 단기간 유인 페로몬은 오랜 기간 동안 근처의 개미를 유인한다고 믿어져 왔다. ★
(C) 흔적 페로몬은 하나의 샘에서 분비물로 ~~다른 곤충을 독으로 해치고 쫓아낸다고~~ 생각해져 왔다.
(D) 배끝마디와 독샘은 ~~먹이를 잡을 수 있는~~ 해로운 페로몬을 분비한다고 믿어져 왔다.

Inference 두 번째 단락에서 unlike traditional view(기존의 가졌던 견해와 달리)라 말하며 recent studies have shown that distinct roles are assigned to different pheromones, as can be illustrated by the differences in the pheromones produced by the poison and pygidial glands of Malaysian ponerine army ants.(최근 연구는 각각의 다른 페로몬에 대해 각기 독특한 역할이 지정되었다는 것을 보여주는데, 이것은 Malaysian ponerine army 개미의 독샘과 배끝마디샘의 차이에서 보여진다)라고 한다. 즉, 그전과 달리 현재는 독샘과 배끝마디샘의 차이점을 알아냈으니 그전에는 한가지의 종류만 있었다고 생각했다는 (A)가 답이 된다.

02

According to paragraph 2, why does the 'attraction pheromone' last only for a short period of time?

(A) ~~To provide protection~~ from predators to ants when foraging
(B) To prevent foragers from going to sites after prey is completely acquired
(C) ~~To guide~~ the foragers ~~back to their colony~~
(D) ~~To attract as many foragers~~ as possible to capture certain prey ★

2단락에 의하면, 왜 '유인 페로몬'은 단기간만 지속 되는가?

(A) 개미가 먹이 채취를 할 때 포식자로부터 ~~보호 받기 위해~~
(B) 먹이를 완전히 습득했을 때 채취자가 현장으로 가는 것을 막기 위해서
(C) 채취자를 ~~집단으로 인도하기 위해~~
(D) 특정 먹이를 잡고자 최대한 많은 ~~채취자를 유인하기 위해~~ ★

Fact 문제의 키워드인 attraction pheromone(유인 페로몬)과 short period of time(단기간)을 보면 ensuring that ants are not attracted long after the prey has been captured.(사냥감이 잡히고 난 뒤 오랜 뒤에 개미가 유인되지 않게 하기 위해)이라 말한다. 즉, 먹이가 잡힌 후 개미가 유인되지 않기 위해 쫓아내고 단기간만 지속된다는 (B)가 정답이다.

03

In paragraph 2, the author mentioned the tale of 'Hansel and Gretel' in order to

(A) provide an analogy to explain a phenomenon that occurs in ants.
(B) show how ~~ants foraged for bread crumbs~~ in the tale.
(C) demonstrate that ~~pheromones are as volatile~~ as Hansel and Gretel's situation.
(D) show that ants enable the rapid transport of food to the colony. ★

2단락에서 글쓴이는 다음 중 '헨젤과 그레텔' 의 이야기를 _____ 을 위해서 언급하였다.

(A) 개미들에게서 일어나는 현상을 설명하는 비유를 제공하고자
(B) 이야기에서 어떻게 ~~캐머가 빵가루를 채집하는지~~ 보여주고자
(C) 헨젤과 그레텔의 상태와 같이 ~~페로몬이 변하기 쉽다는~~ 것을 증명하고자
(D) 개미가 음식을 빨리 가져올 수 있다는 것을 보여주기 위해 ★

Purpose 문제의 키워드인 tale of 'Hansel and Gretel' ('헨젤과 그레텔')이 언급된 부분을 살펴보면 These pheromones act as the 'bread crumbs' in the tale of 'Hansel and Gretel'allowing the ants to maintain their spatial organization and helping them forage in an organized manner which enables the rapid transport of food to the colony.(이러한 페로몬은 '헨젤과 그레텔' 의 이야기에서의 빵 부스러기와 같은 역할을 하는데, 개미가 그들의 공간 조직을 유지하게 하고 먹이의 재빠른 군집으로의 수송을 가능하게 하는 조직된 방식으로 먹이를 사냥하게끔 한다)이라 한다. 즉, 이야기를 통해 페로몬 사용을 통한 개미의 음식 채취 과정을 비교 및 이해시키고자 사용한 것이므로 정답은 (A)가 된다.

04

Which of the sentences below best expresses the essential information in the highlighted sentence in the passage? Incorrect choices change the meaning in important ways or leave out essential information.

(A) A forager ~~uses an extensive amount of pheromones when locating prey which attracts nearby foragers~~ to help it when returning to its colony.
(B) Foragers release a large amount of pheromones when they detect another forager that has located prey, ~~attracting other by stridulating, which in turn causes the poison gland to produce a pheromone trail.~~ ★
(C) Ants ~~return to the colony rapidly~~ when they detect stridulation and pheromones, creating clear trailing system to the prey.
(D) By stridulating when it has found prey, a foraging ant draws in other members in the area which leads to an increase in the pheromone markers, allowing rapid collection.

아래 문장 중 지문 속의 음영된 문장의 핵심 정보를 가장 잘표현하고 있는 것은 무엇인가? 오답은 문장의 의미를 현저히 왜곡하거나 핵심 정보를 빠뜨리고 있다.

(A) 채취자는 먹이의 위치를 알아내면 많은 양의 페로몬을 사용하여 근처 채취자를 유인하고 집단에 돌아오는 것을 도와준다.
(B) 채취자들은 먹이를 찾은 채취자를 발견하면 많은 양의 페로몬을 내뿜고 다른 채취자를 ~~마찰음을 통해 유인하여 페로몬 흔적을 생산하도록 만든다.~~ ★
(C) ~~캐미는~~ 마찰음과 페로몬을 인지하면 ~~집단에 빠르게 돌아오면서~~ 먹이까지 명확한 흔적 체계를 남긴다.
(D) 먹이를 찾은 개미는 마찰음을 내어 근처의 다른 구성원을 불러오고 그러면서 페로몬의흔적을 명확하게 만들어 빠르게 채집을 할 수 있게 해준다.

Highlight 음영 표시된 문장의 정보는 i) When a worker locates a large prey item, such as a dead insect, it makes sharp sounds ii) to attract workers in the area, through a process called stridulating, that encourages nearby workers to release pheromones over longer distances, iii) causing rapid recruitment to the prey item, thereby retrieving it significantly faster.(i) 일개미들은 죽은 곤충과 같은 커다란 먹이를 발견할 때, ii) 지역의 주변동료들을 끌어당기기 위해 날카로운 소리를 낸다, 이것은 '울기' 라고 불리는 과성을 통하는데 근처에 있는 일개미들이 긴 지역에 페로몬을 분비하도록 하며 iii) 먹이가 있는 지역으로 빠르게 동료를 모집하여 상당히 재빠르게 수거한다)이다. 이 모든 내용을 표현한 (D)가 정답이다.

05

According to paragraph 4, what is true about stridulating by ants?

(A) The sounds they produced by stridulating deters other ~~foraging insects from approaching their prey items.~~
(B) Ants begin stridulating when they find a prey item so that ants in the area ~~can hear~~ it and join them in bringing the prey item back to the nest. ★
(C) The volume of the stridulating is determined by the quality of the food item the ants are foraging.
(D) Stridulating ~~in the nest~~ gives the worker ants information about nearby prey items.

4단락에 의하면, 개미가 내는 마찰음에 대해 사실인 것은?

(A) 마찰에 의해 그들이 내는 소리는 ~~먹이를 찾는 다른 곤충 들이 그들의 먹이에 접근하는 것을 막아준다.~~
(B) 개미는 먹이를 발견했을 때 그 지역에 있는 개미가 ~~소리를 듣고~~ 그것을 집으로 가져가는데 도울 수 있도록 마찰음을 내기 시작한다. ★
(C) 마찰음의 크기는 개미가 채취하고 있는 먹이의 양질에 의해 결정된다.
(D) ~~둥지에서의~~ 마찰음은 일개미들에게 근처에 있는 먹이의 정보를 알려준다.

Fact 지문에서 마찰음에 관해 언급한 내용을 보면 The results clearly showed that the workers stridulated most strongly when cutting through leaves of good quality or attractiveness, with the most stridulation occurring while cutting tender or sugar-coated leaves as opposed to the other leaves. (그 결과는 명확히 일개미들이 좋은 질을 가졌거나 개미들의 이목을 끄는 잎을 자를 때 강하게 운다는 것을 보여주며 다른 잎들과는 대조적으로 부드럽거나 설탕이 발린 잎을 자를 때 가장 심하게 운다는 것을 보여주었다)라고 했다. 먹이의 상태나 질에 따라 마찰의 강도가 달라진다는 것을 알 수 있기 때문에 정답은 (C)이다. (B)는 개미는 청각 기관이 없다고 했는데 소리를 들을 수 있다고 했기 때문에 오답이다.

06

In paragraph 5, the author mentions the 'waggle dances' in order to

(A) show that honeybees have one of the ~~most sophisticated forms of communication.~~ ★
(B) contrast the ant's communication methods with that of another communal insect.
(C) explain how animals which cannot produce pheromones can use ~~chemical~~ methods of communications.
(D) provide an example of how the ~~ant's~~ communication methods are more based on the physical methods.

5단락에서 글쓴이가 '꼬리춤' 을 언급한 이유는 무엇인가?

(A) 꿀벌이 가장 복잡한 소통방법을 가지고 있다는 것을 보여주기 위해 ★
(B) 개미의 소통방법을 다른 곤충의 소통방법과 비교하기 위해
(C) 페로몬을 분비하지 못하는 동물은 어떻게 소통의 화학적 방법을 사용하는지 설명하기 위해.
(D) 캐머와 소통방법은 물리적인 방법으로 이루어진다는 점의 예를 들기 위해

Purpose 문제의 키워드인 waggle dance(꼬리춤) 을 보면 개미와 어떻게 다른지 설명을 하는 단락이다. 따라서 (B)가 정답이다.

07

What is true about ants according to paragraph 5?

(A) They increase the efficiency of their foraging by allowing themselves to share information collectively.
(B) There are ~~many undiscovered communication movements~~ that they use to communicate with one another.
(C) Their ability to remember rewarding foraging sites ~~is similar~~ to that of honeybees. ★
(D) Ants ~~individually~~ recall the sites where their prey objects have been detected and return to them.

5단락에서 개미에 관해 사실인 것은?

(A) 개미는 집합적으로 공유할 수 있도록 함으로써 먹이 수집의 효율성을 증가시킨다.
(B) ~~아직 발견되지 못한~~ 개미가 서로 소통하기 위해 쓰는 많은 소통하는 움직임이 있다.
(C) 먹이를 찾는 장소를 기억할 수 있는 개미의 능력은 꿀벌의 것과 ~~비슷하다.~~ ★
(D) 개미는 ~~개별적으로~~ 먹이를 찾은 지역을 기억하여 되돌아온다.

Fact 지문에서 개미가 언급되는 부분을 보면 'Trail-following' ants, on the other hand, are bound to the externally encoded group memory of their pheromone trails. These trail ensure that a channel of communication is always open and allows them to continually react and exchange information while foraging without needing to return to their nest, unlike the honeybees. (반면에 '흔적을 추적하는' 개미들은 그들의 페로몬 흔적에 대해 외부적으로 기록된 기록 기억에 묶여 있다. 이러한 흔적들은 의사소통 통로가 늘 열려있고 그들에게 계속 해서 반응하고 벌과는 달리 둥지로 돌아올 필요 없이 먹이를 찾는 동안에 정보를 교환하는 것을 가능하게 한다.) 라고 한다. 개미는 벌과 달리 둥지로 돌아올 필요가 없다고 나오기 때문에 정보 교류와 먹이 수집에 있어 벌보다 효율적임을 알 수 있음으로 답은 (A)이다. (D)에서 개별적으로 먹이를 찾은 지역을 기억하는 건 개미가 아니라 꿀벌이므로 오답이다.

08

The word discernible in the passage is closest in meaning to

(A) meaningful★
(B) creative
(C) perceptible
(D) predictable

지문의 단어 discernible 과 의미상 가장 유사한 것은?

(A) 뜻 깊은 ★[míːninfəl]
(B) 창의적인 [kriéitiv]
(C) 지각되는 [pərséptəbl]
(D) 예상되는 [pridíktəbl]

Vocabulary 지문의 discernible(인식되는)은 perceptible(지각되는)과 동의어이므로 정답은 (C)이다.

09

Look at the four squares [■] that indicate where the following sentence could be added to the passage.

> (In other words,) the long-lived attractive pheromone acts as a memory, the short-lived attractive pheromone marks out routes to current food sources, and the short-lived repellent pheromone is a no entry signal to unrewarding branches of rewarding trail sections.

Where would the sentence best fit? Click on the square [■] to add the sentence to the passage.   4th

네 개의 네모[■]는 다음 문장이 삽입될 수 있는 부분을 나타내고 있다.

> 즉, 장기 유인 페로몬은 기억이며, 단기 유인 페로몬은 현재 음식 소스로의 길을 표시하며, 단기 기피 페로몬은 음식으로 가는 흔적 부분에서 음식이 없는 곳으로 가는 지점에 대해 출입 불가 흔적이 된다.

이 문장은 어느 자리에 들어가는 것이 가장 적절한가?   네번째

Insertion 삽입 문장의 첫 단어는 in other words(다른 말로)이다. 이것은 모든 내용이 나온 후 정리할 때 쓰이는 말이므로 문장에서 말하는 세가지 페로몬의 설명 뒤에 나와야 한다. 그러므로 모든 내용이 설명되고 나서 나오는 네 번째 네모가 가장 알맞은 답이 된다.

10

Directions: An introductory sentence for a brief summary of the passage is provided below. Complete the summary by selecting the THREE answer choices that express the most important ideas in the passage. Some sentences do not belong in the summary because they express ideas that are not presented in the passage or are minor ideas in the passage. **This question is worth 2 points.**

지시: 지문 요약을 위한 도입 문장이 아래에 주어져 있다. 지문의 가장 중요한 내용을 나타내는 보기 3개를 골라 요약을 완성하시오. 어떤 문장은 지문에 언급되지 않은 내용이나 사소한 정보를 담고 있으므로 요약에 포함되지 않는다. **이 문제는 2점이다.**

Ants employ various chemical and physical methods when communicating with each other.	**개미는 서로 소통할 때 다양한 화학적이고 물리적인 방법들을 쓴다.**
• (A) Ants utilize tactile methods of communication to complement the wide range of messages that they communicate through their chemical trails. - Paragraph 4	• (A) 개미는 그들의 화학적 흔적을 통해서 소통하는 넓은 범위의 메시지를 보완하기 위해 촉각적 의사소통 방법을 사용한다.
• (E) Other communal insects have physical methods of communicating information which differ from those of ants. - Paragraph 5	• (E) 다른 의사사통 곤충들은 개미와는 다르게 정보를 소통하는 물리적인 방법을 가지고 있다.
• (F) Ants have glands that secrete chemical pheromones for the purpose of communicating with one another during foraging activities. - Paragraph 2	• (F) 개미는 먹이 채집을 하는 동안 서로 소통하기 위해 페로몬을 분비하는 샘이 있다.

(B) The poison gland of ants secretes a short-term pheromone, which plays significant roles of attracting foragers from its colony ~~while repelling those of other species.~~   - 반/반
(C) Foraging involves wide varieties of pheromones and stridulations in order ~~to communicate both direction and distance of food sources.~~   - 반/반
(D) ~~Ants~~ can communicate through ~~hearing the sounds~~ created by using their abdominal body parts while foraging   - 반/반

(B) poison gland는 ~~다른 종의 forager를 못오게 하는~~ 반면 자신들의 foreger와는 담기는데 중요한 역할을 하는 단기 페로몬을 분비한다.
(C) 먹이 채집은 ~~먹이 수집 장소의 방향과 거리 둘 다~~ 소통하고자 여러 페로몬과 마찰음을 수반한다.
(D) ~~개미는~~ 먹이를 채집할 때 복부부분에서 만드는 ~~소리를 들음으로써~~ 소통한다.

Summary   지문의 중심내용은 개미의 의사소통이다. (A)는 4번째 단락의 중심내용인 개미의 마찰음을 이용한 다양한 의사소통 방식을 요약한 것과 일치하고, (E)는 마지막 단락의 중심내용인 꿀벌과의 비교한 점을 요약한 것과 같다. (F)는 두번째 단락의 중심내용인 개미의 독샘과 배끝마디샘에서 분비되는 페로몬 사용에 관한 것을 요약한 것과 일치하므로 정답은 (A), (E), (F)이다.

usherin.usher.co.kr

TEST 8-2 Calculating the Age of Earth 지구 나이 계산

Introduction	단락 1	지구 나이 계산에 대한 관심과 많은 연구들
Point 1	단락 2	Comte de Buffon의 실험과 그의 실수
Point 2	단락 3	Edmund Halley의 가설과 실험
Point 3	단락 4	물리학 법칙을 이용한 가설과 실험
Point 4	단락 5	방사성 연대 측정법 도입
Point 5	단락 6	방사성 연대 측정법의 인정

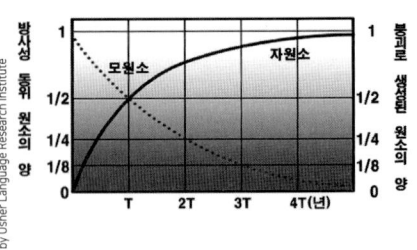

문단주제	본문내용	해석
단락 1 지구 나이 계산에 대한 관심과 많은 연구들	**1** Religion was the only source of historical and scientific knowledge, such as the age of Earth, until the mid-eighteenth century. After this time, scientists **began** more openly **questioning** the formation of Earth, and while studying the different rock layers of it, they recognized that it had **gone through** various changes over a period of time. The scientists proposed **a number of** theories and methods that had inaccurate results **due to lack of** understanding of the Earth and heavy speculation. As the scientific method and logical reasoning developed within the scientific community, scholars **were motivated to conduct** more precise and scientific **research**.	종교만이 18세기 중반 전 까지 지구의 나이와 같은 역사적 그리고 과학적 지식에 대한 유일한 원천이었다. 이 시대 이후, 과학자들은 지구의 형성에 대해 좀 더 의문을 갖기 시작했고, 지구의 암석층을 연구하는 동안 지구가 오랜시간에 걸쳐 다양한 변화를 겪었다는 것을 알아냈다. 그 과학자들은 지구에 대한 이해의 부족과 과도한 추측 때문에 부정확한 결과를 가진 많은 이론과 방법들을 제안했다. 과학계 내에서 과학적 방법과 논리적 사고가 발달함에 따라, 학자들은 더 정확하고 과학적인 조사를 수행하기 위한 자극을 받았다.
단락 2 Comte de Buffon의 실험과 그의 실수	**2** In 1779, a French scientist, Comte de Buffon, attempted the first calculation of Earth's age by experimentation. **Based on** Earth's internal heat and rate of cooling, Buffon's approach utilized a small globe-like figure that **resembled** Earth **in** composition. He measured the cooling rate of the figure tested at his laboratory and calculated the age of Earth to be 75,000 years. i) The result completely underestimated the age of Earth as ii) Buffon, from his globe figure, mainly **focused on** the cooling rate of iron, iii) an element which cools much quicker than crystals and other rock components. The true significance of his study, however, was that it **dared to break away** from previous methods that derived Earth's age without experimentation.	1779년, 프랑스 과학자 Comte de Buffon은 실험을 통해 지구나이의 첫 번째 계산을 시도했다. 지구의 내부 열과 냉각 속도에 근거한 Buffon의 접근은 구성에 있어 지구와 비슷한 작은 구 모형을 사용했다. 그는 그의 실험실에서 실험 대상인 모형의 냉각 속도를 측정했고, 지구 나이를 75,000년이라고 계산했다. ii) Buffon은 그의 구 모형에서 iii) 냉각 속도가 수정과 다른 돌 성분보다 더 빠른 성분인 철의 냉각속도에 주로 초점을 맞췄기 때문에 i) 그 결과 지구의 나이를 완전히 과소평가했다. 그러나, 그의 연구의 진짜 중요성은 실험없이 지구의 나이를 도출해낸 이전의 방법을 과감히 타파했다는데 의의가 있다.

Vocabulary

1단락 christianity [krìstʃiǽnəti] n. 기독교 questioning [kwéstʃəniŋ] a. 묻고 싶은 듯한 propose [prəpóuz] v. 제의하다
inaccurate [inǽkjərit] a. 정확하지 않은 motivate [móutəvèit] v. 동기를 주다 conduct [kándʌkt / kón-] v. 수행하다

2단락 derive [diráiv] v. 끌어내다, 얻다 calculation [kælkjuléiʃən] n. 계산 experimentation [ikspèrəmentéiʃən] n. 실험작업
resemble [rizémbl] v. 닮다 figure [fígjər] n. 모습다 component [kəmpóunənt] a. 구성하는 significance [signífikəns] n. 중요성

3단락 estimation [èstəméiʃən] n. 판단, 평가 inadequate [inǽdikwət] a. 부적절한 approximate [əpráksəmèit] a. 대략의
oversimplify [òuvərsímpləfài] v. 지나치게 단순화하다 plate tectonics : phr. 판구조론 attempt [ətémpt] v. 시도하다

단락 3
Edmund Halley 의 가설과 실험

3   Later, others **attempted to measure** Earth's age, but their methods were just as inadequate. Edmund Halley, for example, based his estimation on the simple concept of the salinity of the ocean. ◎He surmised that since rivers continuously dragged salt components from land to the oceans, increasing their salinity, [Q3]the time they took to reach present salinity-levels will give an approximate timeframe for Earth's formation. Just like the previous conjectures, Halley's method was not a viable way of measuring Earth's age, as it oversimplified the complex salinification process and **failed to take into account** plate tectonics and undersea volcanic eruptions that continuously **add** salt **to** the ocean.

단락 4
물리학 법칙을 이용한 가설과 실험

4   Since then, measurements of physical properties have **been used to estimate** the age of Earth using the laws of physics. ◎William Thomson, the forerunning supporter of these physical measurements, believed that during Earth's primitive stage, it was a sphere of hot molten rock **held together** by gravity and the only conceivable source of heat energy was the nebula. By estimating the **rate at which** heat dissipated from the nebula, scientists could determine the time **necessary for Earth to cool** from the molten ball of rock to its present state. Through this method, the age of Earth **was calculated to be** 20 to 40 million years. [Q5]He had, however, neglected an important variable: the viscous fluid mantle that **play** an influential **role in** the circulation of heat energy within the Earth.

단락 5
방사성 연대 측정법 도입

5   Scientists calculated Earth's age with even more precision after the arrival of radiometric dating. It **allowed** them **to derive** the absolute age of rock using its components. First developed by Ernest Rutherford and enhanced by Arthur Holmes, [Q6]radiometric dating is a technique **based on** the spontaneous decay of different naturally occurring radioactive isotopes found in rocks. These initial parent isotopes are unstable and break down into more stable daughter isotopes. This break down occurs **according to** an isotope's individual rate of decay, or 'decay constant', regardless of the physical or chemical conditions it is exposed to. [Q6, 7]Scientists, therefore, do not have to **be concerned with** other variables since the rate of isotope transformation is almost invariable. Radiometric dating **allows** scientists **to calculate** the time that has elapsed since the formation of rocks by measuring the

---

Vocabulary

4단락
- surmise [sərmáiz] v. 추측하다
- property [prápərti] n. 특성
- variable [vέəriəbl] n. 변수
- drag [dræg] v. 끌다
- primitive [prímətiv] a. 원시의, 초기의
- viscous [vískəs] a. 점성있는
- conjecture [kəndʒéktʃər] n. 억측
- nebula [nébjələ] n. 성운
- fluid [flùːid] a. 유동성의
- dissipate [dísəpèit] v. 흩뜨리다
- circulation [səːrkjuléiʃən] n. 순환

5단락
- spontaneous [spantéiniəs] a. 자발적인, 임의의
- predictable [pridíktéibl] a. 예언할 수 있는
- invariable [invέəriəbl] a. 일정하다
- isotope [áisətòup] n. 동위원소
- transformation [trænsfərméiʃən] n. 변화
- elapse [ilǽps] v. 경과하다, 지나다
- radiometric [rèidiámitrik] a. 탄소연대측정의

USHER

단락 6
방사성 연대 측정법의 인정

ratio of parent to daughter isotopes in them. [■] Radiometric testing shows Earth to be around 4.5 billion years, the most widely accepted age of Earth today.

6 [■] Still, there are **controversies over** the age of the earth as a minor group of scientists argues that Earth is less than 4.5 billion years. These people believe that the earth is 'young', only about 6,000 to 10,000 years old. [■] Stressing that the **ratio of** parent **to** daughter isotopes when the rock was created is unknown, they challenge the validity of scientifically-accepted radiometric methods. They further claim that some parent or daughter isotopes may be added from external sources. [■] These issues of initial ratio of isotopes spotlight a flaw within radiometric dating method. Although there is evidence for **variability in** radiometric dating, Arthur Holmes **used** a variety of isotopes **to** obtain sufficient data and derived a precise result. [Q8]Therefore, many **regard** these refutations **to be** implausible and until further scientific research produces a more accurate result, 4.5 billion years will **continue to be considered** the approximate age of the Earth.

[■] 방사성 연대측정법은 지구의 나이를 대략 45억년으로 계산했고, 오늘날 지구의 가장 널리 인정된 나이이다.

[■] 여전히, 45억년보다 적다고 주장하는 소수의 과학자들 때문에 지구의 나이에 관한 논란들이 많다. 이 사람들은 지구가 '어린', 단지 6,000년에서 10,000년 사이의 나이라고 믿는다. [■] 암석이 형성 될 때의 자원소에 대한 모원소의 비율이 확실하지 않다는 것을 강조하면서, 그들은 과학적으로 받아들여진 방사성 탄소 연대 측정법의 타당성에 이의를 제기한다. 그들은 약간의 모원소와 자원소 일부가 외부 근원으로부터 더해졌을지도 모른다고 한층 나아가 주장한다. [■] 이 초기 동위원소 비율에 관한 이슈들은 방사성 연대 측정법이 가지고 있는 문제점에 주목하게 한다. 비록 방사성 탄소 연대 측정법의 타당성에 증거가 있을 지라도, Arthur Holmes는 충분한 자료를 얻기 위해 다양한 동위 원소를 사용했고, 정확한 결과를 도출했다. [Q8]따라서, 많은 이들은 이러한 반박들은 받아들이기 힘들다고 보고, 좀 더 과학적인 조사가 한층 정확한 결과를 도출할 때까지, 45억 년은 지구의 대략적인 나이로 계속 간주될 것이다.

Sentence analysis

◎ He surmised / that since rivers continuously dragged salt components from land to the oceans, /
그는 추측하였다 　　　　　강이 끊임없이 육지에서 바다로 소금 성분을 끌어내린 것이
increasing their salinity, / the time they took to reach present salinity-levels /
염분을 증가시키면서 　　　현재의 염도에 도달하는 시간은
will give an approximate timeframe for Earth's formation.
지구의 형성에 관한 대략적인 기간을 줄 것이라고

◎ William Thomson, the forerunning supporter of these physical measurements, believed /
이러한 물리적 특징의 선구적 지지자인 William Thomson은 믿었다
that during Earth's primitive stage, / it was a sphere of hot molten rock / held together by gravity /
지구의 원시 단계 동안　　　뜨거운 용암의 구형이고　　　중력에 의해 유지된
and the only conceivable source of heat energy was the nebula.
오직 열 에너지를 생각할 수 있는 근원은 성운이라고

Vocabulary

6단락
controversy [kántrəvə̀ːrsi] n. 논쟁, 논의
implausible [implɔ́ːzəbl] a. 받아들이기 어려운
approximate [əpráksəmət, -rɔ́k-] a. 대체로 정확한

validity [vəlídəti] n. 정당함, 타당성
ratio [réiʃou] n. 비율

refutation [rèfjutéiʃən] n. 논박
evidence [évidəns] n. 증거

11 Which of the sentences below best expresses the essential information in the highlighted sentence in the passage? Incorrect choices change the meaning in important ways or leave out essential information.

(A) Buffon's experiment underestimated Earth's age since iron, which was the major component he used to make his figure, cooled much faster than crystals and other rock components.
(B) The age of Earth was not what Buffon calculated as his research using the globe model was limited to one of the many constituents of Earth. ★
(C) As crystals and other rock components cool relatively faster than iron, experiment that Buffon conducted with globe-like figure underestimated the age of Earth.
(D) Buffon miscalculated the age of Earth with his globe-figure and then focused on the cooling rate of iron.

아래 문장 중 지문 속의 음영 표시된 문장의 핵심 정보를 가장 잘 표현하고 있는 것은 무엇인가? 오답은 문장의 의미를 현저하게 바꾸거나 핵심 정보를 빠트리고 있다.

(A) Buffon의 실험은 지구의 주요 요소인 철이 크리스탈과 다른 돌 요소보다 빨리 식기 때문에 지구의 나이를 너무 적게 계산했다.
(B) 지구의 나이는 공 모델을 사용한 그의 조사에서 계산한 Buffon는 지구의 많은 구성 중에서 가장 제한적인 것 중 하나가 아니다. ★
(C) 수정들과 다른 암석 성분들은 철보다 상대적으로 더 빠르게 냉각했기 때문에 공 같은 모양을 가지고 수행한 Buffon의 실험은 지구의 나이를 과소평가했다.
(D) Buffon은 그의 공 모양을 가지고 지구의 나이를 잘못 계산했고, 크리고 철의 냉각 속도에 초점을 맞추었다.

Highlight 음영된 부분의 핵심 내용을 크게 나누어 보면 i) The result completely underestimated the age of Earth as ii) Buffon, from his globe figure, mainly focused on the cooling rate of iron, iii) an element which cools much quicker than crystals and other rock components. (ii)Buffon은 그의 구 모형에서 iii) 냉각 속도가 수정과 다른 돌 성분보다 더 빠른 요소인 철의 냉각 속도에 주로 초점을 맞췄기 때문에 i) 그 결과는 지구의 나이를 완전히 과소평가하였다)이다 여기서 핵심 내용 중에 (B)는 냉각속도에 관련된 내용이 없다. (C)는 철이 다른 암석 성분보다 빨리 식는다는 사실을 뒤집었으며 (D)는 철이 다른 암석 물질보다 빨리 냉각된다는 내용이 빠져있다. 그러므로 정답은 모든 핵심 정보를 보유한 (A)가 된다.

12 The word they in paragraph 3 refers to

(A) oceans
(B) rivers ★
(C) salts
(D) methods

3단락에서 they 가 언급하는 것은?

(A) 대양
(B) 강 ★
(C) 소금
(D) 방법

Reference 내용을 보면 현재의 염분 정도에 도달해야 할 것은 ocean이므로 they이 지칭하는 것은 oceans(대양), 그러므로 정답은 (A)이다.

13 According to paragraph 3, how did Edmund Halley determine the age of Earth?

(A) He calculated the salinity of the ocean water at his time and compared it with that of the rivers.
(B) He constructed a model of the complex systems of rivers and oceans to precisely show the age of Earth.
(C) He computed a formula which showed how long it takes for the salinity of the oceans to reach the present levels.
(D) He complicated the simple courses of the ocean's salinity and used his understanding of the structure in determining the age. ★

3단락에 따르면 어떻게 Edmund Halley가 지구의 나이를 결정했는가?

(A) 그는 현재 바닷물의 염분성을 계산했고 그것을 강의 염분성과 비교했다.
(B) 그는 지구의 나이를 정확하게 보여주기 위해 강과 바다의 복잡한 시스템의 모델을 만들었다.
(C) 그는 바다의 염분성이 현재의 정도에 도달하는데 얼마나 오래 걸리는지 공식을 계산했다.
(D) 그는 바다의 소금화의 단순한 과정을 복잡하게 했고 나이를 결정함에 있어 구조의 그의 이해를 사용했다. ★

Fact 지문에서는 reach present salinity-levels will give an approximate timeframe for Earth's formation.(현재의 염분 정도에 도달하는데 걸린 시간은 지구의 형성에 관한 대략적인 시간을 줄 것)이라고 언급 하였기 때문에, 처음 소금기가 없는 바다가 지금의 소금기를 가지기 위해 강을 통해 소금이 바다로 흘러 들어오는 시간을 계산한다는 내용인 (C)가 답이 되며, (A)는 강의 염분과 바다의 염분을 비교한 것이 아니기에 오답이고, (B)와 (D)는 지문에서 it oversimplified the complex salinification process(복잡한 염분화 과정을 너무 단순화 하였고)라는 내용과 반대가 되기 때문에 오답이다.

14 The word viscous in the passage is closest in meaning to

(A) scorching
(B) thick
(C) overflowing
(D) salient ★

지문의 단어 viscous 과 의미상 유사한 것은?

(A) 뜨거운 [skɔ́:rtʃiŋ]
(B) 액체가 걸죽한 [θik]
(C) 넘쳐 흐르는 [òuvərflóuiŋ]
(D) 중요한 ★[séiliənt]

> **Vocabulary** 지문의 viscous(점성의)와 가장 유사한 의미를 가지는 것은 (B) thick(액체가 걸쭉한)이다.

15 According to paragraph 4, what was the problem with William Thomson's calculations?

(A) The law of physics he used in the calculation had fundamental flaws which distorted the results. ★
(B) He neglected the fact that the core of Earth was the main energy source during the primitive stage of Earth.
(C) The rate of cooling that is seen in Earth's core and the nebula is different.
(D) Thomson was not aware of a variable that affected the temperature of the Earth.

4단락에 따르면, William Thomson의 계산의 문제점은 무엇인가?

(A) 계산에서 그가 사용한 물리학의 법칙은 결과를 왜곡한 근본적인 약점을 갖고 있었다. ★
(B) 그는 지구의 원시단계 동안 지구의 핵이 주요 에너지 근원이었다는 사실을 무시했다.
(C) 지구의 핵과 성운의 식는 속도는 다르다.
(D) Thomson은 지구의 온도에 영향을 끼칠 수 있는 다른 변수를 알아채지 못했다.

> **Fact** 지문에서 언급된 He had, however, neglected an important variable: the viscous fluid mantle that played an influential role in the circulation of heat energy within the Earth.(그러나 그는 중요한 변수, 즉 지구 내에서 열에너지 순환의 영향력 있는 역할을 하는 끈적하고 유동적인 맨틀을 간과하였다)와 같은 내용은 (D)임으로 (D)가 답이다. (A)는 언급 되지 않은 내용이며 (B), (C) 역시 지문의 내용과 맞지 않는 내용임으로 오답이다.

16 According to paragraph 5, what can be inferred about the process of isotopes decaying in rocks?

(A) When a large number of parent isotopes are present in a rock, it indicates that there will be more rapid decay.
(B) After an isotope breaks down, daughter isotopes are removed from the rock.
(C) All isotopes decay at the same rate, known as the decay constant. ★
(D) Rocks with more parent isotopes are relatively younger than those with more daughter isotopes.

5단락에 의하면, 암석에서의 동위원소 붕괴에 대해 추론할 수 있는 것은 무엇인가?

(A) 많은 수의 모원소가 바위에 존재한다면, 그것은 더 빠른 붕괴가 있을 것이라는 것을 나타낸다.
(B) 동위원소가 붕괴된 후에, 자원소는 바위로부터 제거된다.
(C) 모든 동위원소는 붕괴 항수라고 알려진 동일한 속도로 붕괴된다. ★
(D) 더 많은 모원소를 함유한 바위는 더 많은 자원소를 가진 바위보다 상대적으로 어리다.

> **Inference** 지문에서 암석에서의 동위원소 붕괴과정에 대한 부분을 살펴보면 radiometric dating is a technique based on the spontaneous decay of different naturally occurring radioactive isotopes found in rocks. These initial parent isotopes are unstable and break down into more stable daughter isotopes. This break down occurs according to an isotope's individual rate of decay, or 'decay constant,' regardless of the physical or chemical conditions it is exposed to.(방사성 연대측정법은 암석에서 발견된 자연적으로 일어나는 방사성 원자의 자연스러운 붕괴에 근거를 둔 기술이다. 이들 초기 모원소는 불안정 하지만, 후에 더 안정적인 자원소로 분해된다. 이 붕괴는 노출된 물리적 혹은 화학적 환경에 상관없이 원자 각각의 붕괴률 혹은 '붕괴 항수' 에 따라 발생한다) 라고 했다. 모원소가 붕괴되어 안정적인 자원소로 변하는 것이기 때문에 모원소가 많은 바위는 자원소가 많은 바위보다 상대적으로 어리다는 것을 알 수 있으므로 답은 (D)이다.

17 According to paragraph 5, which of the following is true about the radiometric dating method?

(A) Despite its accuracy in dating, it is not regarded as a useful method for determining Earth's age.
(B) It ~~makes use of rock elements that remain relatively constant over a long period of time.~~★
(C) It measures a property that behaves in a predictable manner, deriving reliable results.
(D) Because their rates of decay are invariable, ~~isotopes cannot be used as a variable~~.

5단락에 따르면 방사성 탄소 연대측정법에 대해 옳은 것은?

(A) 탄소 연대 측정법의 정확성에도 불구하고, 지구의 나이를 결정하는데 유용한 방법으로써 여겨지지 않았다.
(B) 그것은 오랜 기간에 걸쳐 ~~상태적으로 꾸준히 남아있는 암석 물질을 이용한다.~~★
(C) 그것은 예측할 수 있는 방법으로 행동하는 특성을 측정하고, 신뢰할 수 있는 결과들을 도출한다.
(D) ~~동위원소~~의 붕괴 속도는 변하지 않아서 방사성 탄소 연대 측정에서 ~~하나의 변수로 사용될 수 없다.~~

Fact 문제의 키워드인 탄소 연대 측정법에 대한 부분을 살펴보면 This process happens according to a more or less constant and predictable internal clock regardless of physical or chemical conditions.(이것은 물리적이나 화학적인 조건에 관계 없이 다소 꾸준하고 예측 할 수 있는 내부시계에 따라 일어난다)와 Scientists, therefore, do not have to be concerned with other variables since the rate of isotope transformation is almost invariable. Radiometric dating allows scientists to calculate the time that has elapsed since the formation of rocks by measuring the ratio of parent to daughter isotopes in them. (동위원소 변형 속도가 거의 변하지 않기 때문에 과학자들은 다른 변수들을 고려하지 않는다. 방사성 연대측정법은 과학자들로 하여금 암석 안에서 모원소와 자원소의 비율을 측정함으로써 암석 형성 이후 경과한 시간을 계산할 수 있게 하였다)의 내용에서 변수 자체가 예측 가능하고 비율이 일정함으로 정확한 결과를 낼 수 있다는 (C)가 정답이 된다. (B)의 경우에는 오랜 기간 유지되는 암석 물질을 이용한 것이 아니라 쉴 새 없이 붕괴하는 동위원소를 이용하는 것이다.

18 What is the author's main argument in paragraph 6?

(A) To ~~refute~~ the accuracy of radiometric dating method with the support from a group of scientists
(B) To defend radiometric dating as the most precise method of determining the earth's age at present
(C) To point out that the radiometric dating method ~~should be enhanced by other scientific research~~
(D) ~~To suggest that there are some controversies on the validity of radiometric dating method~~ ★

6단락에서 글쓴이의 중심적인 주장은 무엇인가?

(A) 과학자들의 집단으로부터 방사성 탄소연대 지지의 정확성을 ~~부인하기~~ 위해
(B) 방사성 탄소연대 측정법이 현재 지구의 나이를 측정하는 데 가장 정확한 방법이라고 주장하기 위해
(C) 방사성 탄소연대 측정법이 ~~다른 과학적 조사에 의해 강화되어야~~ 한다고 나타내기 위해
(D) 방사성 탄소연대 측정법의 ~~타당성에 몇몇 논란이 있다고 시사하기~~ 위해 ★

Purpose 문제의 키워드인 방사성 탄소 연대 측정법과 관련된 핵심 내용을 살펴보면 Although there is evidence for variability in radiometric dating, Arthur Holmes used a variety of isotopes to obtain sufficient data and derived a precise result.(비록 방사성 탄소연대 측정법의 타당성에 증거가 있을지라도, Arthur Holmes는 충분한 자료를 얻기 위해 다양한 동위원소를 사용했고, 정확한 결과를 도출했다)라고 얘기하며 타당하다는 증거에 더해서 다양한 동위원소를 시작함으로 정확한 결과를 도출했다는 내용이 나옴으로 방사성 탄소 연대 측정법이 가장 현존하는 가장 정확한 방법이라고 언급된 (B)가 정답이다.

19

Look at the four squares [■] that indicate where the following sentence could be added to the passage.

> (These) issues of initial ratio of isotopes spotlight a flaw within radiometric dating method.

Where would the sentence best fit? Click on the square [■] to add the sentence to the passage.

네 개의 네모[■]는 다음 문장이 삽입될 수 있는 부분을 나타내고 있다.

이 초기 동위원소의 비율에 관한 이슈들은 방사성 연대 측정법이 가지고 있는 문제점을 비춰준다.

이 문장은 어느 자리에 들어가는 것이 가장 적절한가?

4th / 네번째

Insertion 이러한 이슈들을 얘기하는 이야기가 앞에서 먼저 나오고 문제점이 있다고 삽입 문장으로 얘기한 다음 그 뒤에 그럼에도 다양한 동위원소를 사용함으로써 정확한 결과를 이끌어냈다는 글을 흐름이 가장 자연스럽기 때문에 4번째 네모가 정답이 된다.

20

Directions: An introductory sentence for a brief summary of the passage is provided below. Complete the summary by selecting the THREE answer choices that express the most important ideas in the passage. Some sentences do not belong in the summary because they express ideas that are not presented in the passage or are minor ideas in the passage. **This question is worth 2 points.**

지시: 지문 요약을 위한 도입 문장이 아래에 주어져 있다. 지문의 가장 중요한 내용을 나타내는 보기 3개를 골라 요약을 완성하시오. 어떤 문장은 지문에 언급되지 않은 내용이나 사소한 정보를 담고 있으므로 요약에 포함되지 않는다. 이 문제는 2점이다.

The challenge of figuring out the age of Earth has been undertaken by many scientists since the nineteenth century.

- (B) Early attempts to calculate the age of Earth were thwarted by inaccurate understandings of its physical composition and environmental systems - Paragraph 2,3

- (C) The law of thermodynamics was utilized by Thomson, but he neglected a major area of thermodynamic heat circulation. - Paragraph 4

- (E) Radiometric dating through counting the parent and daughter isotopes present is the most accurate method of age determination known to scientists. - Paragraph 5

지구의 나이를 계산하는 일은 19세기 부터 많은 과학자들이 도전해왔다.

- (B) 지구의 나이를 계산하기 위한 초기 시도는 물리적 성분과 환경적 시스템에 관한 부정확한 이해 때문에 좌절되었다.

- (C) 열역학법칙은 톰슨에 의해 이용되었지만, 열역학적 열순환의 주요한 부분에 대해 부정적이었다.

- (E) 현재 모원소와 자원소 계산을 통한 방사성 탄소연대 측정법은 과학자들에게 알려진 나이를 결정하는데 가장 정확한 방법이다.

(A) Using a small globe figure, Buffon ~~was able to obtain a reasonable age of Earth.~~ - 틀린정보

(D) William Thomson's attempt to apply the laws of physics to calculate Earth's age was ~~widely accepted by~~ scientists despite its limitations. - 반/반

(F) As radioactive isotopes decay at different rates, radiometric dating method ~~is not the best means~~ to determine the age of Earth. - 반/반

(A) 작은 둥근 물체를 통해 Buffon은 ~~합리적인 결과를 얻을 수 있었다.~~

(D) William Thomson이 지구의 나이를 측정하는데 있어 물리적 법칙을 적용한 시도는 한계점이 있었는데도 불구하고 과학자들에 의해 ~~널리 받아들여졌다.~~

(F) 다른 비율로 방사성 동위원소가 붕괴함에 따라, 방사성 탄소연대 측정은 지구의 나이를 결정하는데 ~~가장 좋은 수단은 아니다.~~

Summary (B)는 2, 3단락에서 예전에 지구의 나이를 측정하려고 했던 시도는 부정확했다는 점에서 확인할 수 있으며, (D)는 4문단에서 폭넓게 받아들여졌다는 내용이 없어서 오답이다. 그리고 (E)는 5단락에서 동위 원소를 이용한 방사성 연대 측정법이 가장 정확하다는 것을 확인할 수 있다. 그럼으로 정답은 (B), (C), (E)이다.

usherin.usher.co.kr

USHER

iBT TOEFL
FINAL TEST READING
TEST 9

답안 및 취약 유형 분석표
해석·해설

답안 및 문제 유형 분석표

TEST 9-1

01 (C) Fact

02 (A) Purpose

03 (B) Highlight

04 (A) Fact

05 (D) Fact

06 (A) Purpose

07 (C) Vocabulary

08 (C) Inference

09 3rd ■ Insertion

10 (A), (C), (E) Summary

TEST 9-2

11 (A) Purpose

12 (A), (D) Fact

13 (B) Highlight

14 (C) Fact

15 (C) Fact

16 (D) Vocabulary

17 (B) Purpose

18 (B) Fact

19 4th ■ Insertion

20 (A), (D), (E) Summary

각 문제 유형별 맞춘 개수를 아래에 적어 보세요.

유형	맞춘 답의 개수	정답률	
단어 (Vocabulary)	/ 2	정답률:	%
사실 확인 문제 (Fact)	/ 7	정답률:	%
지시어 찾기 (Reference)	/ 0	정답률:	%
끼워 넣기 (Insertion)	/ 2	정답률:	%
문장 변환문제 (Highlight)	/ 2	정답률:	%
목적 (Purpose)	/ 4	정답률:	%
추론 (Inference)	/ 1	정답률:	%
단락 요약 (Summary / Category Chart)	/ 2	정답률:	%
전체	/ 20	정답률:	%

※ 자신이 취약한 유형은 READING STRATEGIES를 통해 다시 한번 점검하시기 바랍니다. (p.31)

TEST 9-1　Identifying Playful Behavior in Children 놀이구별

Introduction	단락 1	유희적 행동 정의의 어려움
Point 1	단락 2	기능 접근법 정의
Point 2	단락 3	구조 접근법 정의
Point 3	단락 4	기준 접근법 정의

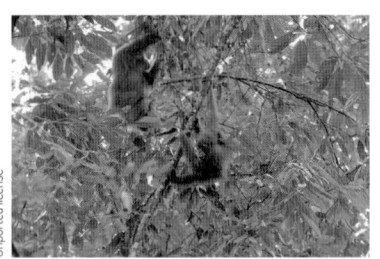

photo by Nomo michael hoefner, available under the Creative Commons Attribution-Share Alike 3.0 Unported license

단락 1 — 유희적 행동 정의의 어려움

1　Play, usually **associated with** children, comes **in** many **forms** [Q11]**in** both humans and other animals. Even **with** such **prevalence**, its definition, function and forms are often misunderstood. This may be because play evolves both with age and over time. [Q11-D]For example, most people recognize that a toddler's frolicking is play, but not that **engaging in** sport activities by adults is another form. Moreover, the way play has changed **over time** is also ignored. [Q11-B]One such major change is the decrease in usage of imagination since computers and video games have **begun to create** virtual worlds for children, when **compared to** the past when they had only wooden toys and dolls with which to play. With such major changes happening, [Q12]one cannot predict what **form** it will **take** next, only that it will **continue to exist**. **Due to** these changes and the lack of an apparent distinction between playful and non-playful behaviors sociologists have continuously **tried to form** a complete definition of play, with three having **gained** widespread **acceptance**: the functional, the structural, and the criterion approaches.

일반적으로 아이들과 연관이 있는 놀이는, [Q11]인간이나 다른 동물 모두에게서 다양한 형태로 나타난다. 이렇게 널리 퍼져있음에도 불구하고, 그것의 정의와 기능 그리고 형태는 흔히 잘못 이해되고 있다. 이것은 아마도 놀이가 나이와 시간의 흐름에 따라 발달하기 때문일 것이다. [Q11-D]예를 들면, 대부분의 사람들은 아이들이 뛰어노는 것을 놀이라고 생각하지만, 어른들이 스포츠 활동에 참여하는 것은 다른 형태의 놀이라고 인지하고 있지 않다. 게다가, 놀이가 시간이 지남에 따라 변화하는 방식도 역시 무시되고 있다. [Q11-B]이러한 중요한 변화 한가지는 아이들이 나무로 만든 장난감이나 인형만 가지고 놀던 과거와 비교해 볼 때, [Q11-B]컴퓨터와 비디오 게임이 아이들에게 가상 현실을 만들어 줌으로써 인해 상상력의 사용이 감소했다는 것이다. 이러한 주요한 변화들이 일어남으로써, [Q12]놀이가 앞으로 어떤 형태를 가질 것이라는 것은 예상할 수 없고 단지 계속 존재할 것이라는 것만 예상할 뿐이다. 이런 변화와 유희적이거나 비유희적인 행동의 명확한 구분이 없어서, 사회학자들은 널리 받아들여지는 놀이의 세가지 정의법인 기능 접근법, 구조 접근법, 그리고 기준 접근법을 통해 계속해서 놀이에 대해 완벽한 정의를 내리려고 노력했다.

단락 2 — 기능 접근법 정의

2　Anthropologist Donald Symons, after observing African monkeys, developed the first of these in 1978. He **defined** play **as** an act that has **neither** a clear benefit, **nor** external goal. Following this, acts like learning **are not considered** play because their benefits are readily noticeable. Similarly, eating and working are not considered play because their purposes are specific and obvious. ⓞ i) Although Symons' definition was intended for the monkeys that he studied, ii) it soon became

인류학자 도날드 사이먼스는, 1978년 아프리카 원숭이를 관찰한 후, 이들중 첫 번째 것을 만들었다. 그는 놀이를 확실한 혜택도 없고 외부적 목적도 없는 행동으로 정의했다. 이에 따르면, 학습과 같은 역할들은 그들의 혜택이 쉽게 눈에 띄기 때문에 놀이라고 할 수 없다. 비슷하게, 먹거나 일하는 것도 특정하고 분명한 목표가 있기 때문에 놀이가 아니다. ⓞ i) 사이먼스의 정의는 본래 그가 연구하던 원숭이를 위해 내려진것이었지만,

Vocabulary

1단락
- associate A with B : phr. A를 B에 연관시키다.
- misunderstand [mìsəndərstǽnd] v. 오해하다
- engage in : phr. ~에 참여하다.
- due to : phr. ~ 때문에
- prevalence [prév(ə)ləns] n. 널리 퍼짐, 유행, 보급
- toddler [tádlər] n. 아장아장 걷는 아기
- virtual [və́ːrtʃuəl] a. 사실상의
- sociologist [sòusiálədʒist] n. 사회학자
- definition [dèfəníʃən] n. 정의
- frolic(frolicking) [frálik] v. 즐겁게 뛰어놀다 / n. 놀이
- predict [pridíkt] v. 예언하다
- criterion [kraitíəriən] n. 기준

2단락
- anthropologist [ænθrəpálədʒist] n. 인류학자
- inherent [inhíərənt] a. 본래의, 고유의
- neither A nor B : phr. A도 아니고 B도 아닌
- external [ikstə́ːrnl] a. 외부의
- duration [djuréiʃən] n. 지속, 지속기간

evident to other scholars that his definition, which **came to be known as** the functional approach, iii) **could likewise be applied to** play in humans. **Applying** his approach **to** further studies has shown that although there are benefits to playful behavior, its long-term consequences are unclear. An easy **way to see** this is to **look at** common playground toys, like the jungle gym. While children enjoy climbing, hanging and swinging on the metal labyrinth, the ultimate goal of these activities is not known, and neither is the actions' **ability to supply** the child **with** food, clothing, or shelter. Further, it is unclear whether **time spent on** the playground fulfills the child's education, health, or other basic needs **at all**, and it is, thus, **considered** playful behavior under this approach.

단락 3 구조 접근법 정의

3 [Q14]The functional approach, however, does not **account for** the many non-playful actions without immediately obvious purposes, or for playful behavior that **seems to serve a purpose**, such as running. While running is often a playful behavior, if a person was running towards shelter to **hide from** the rain, it would have a clear purpose, and therefore not **qualify as** functionalistic play. **In cases** such as this, the structural approach can be used. The structural approach identifies specific behaviors that are **associated with** play or with the playful execution of actions. [Q15]When studying an action using this approach, one begins by identifying any characteristics that often only occur during playtime, like laughter or playful squabbling, such as a push or a light punch. Secondly, the structural approach **looks for** repeated, fragmented, exaggerated, and or re-ordered actions. For example, climbing stairs has a clear end and goal, but if the child repeats it by quickly climbing up and down the stairs, fragments the climb by climbing up only half-way, exaggerates it by jumping two stairs **at a time**, or [Q15]re-orders it by climbing them backwards, then under the structural approach the child **is considered to be** performing playful behavior.

단락 4 기준 접근법 정의

4 [Q16]When studying play, it became evident that the two approaches were not mutually exclusive, but that the factors that they **used to identify** behavior were dissimilar. Thus, in 1980, Krasnor and Pepler suggested a third method, called the criterion approach. It combined ideas from the other

Vocabulary

specific [spisífik] a. 구체적인, 상세한
shelter [ʃéltər] n. 보금자리

3단락 account for : phr. 설명하다
execution [èksikjúːʃən] n. 수행
fragmented [frǽgməntid] a. 단편적인

4단락 mutually [mjúːtʃuəli] ad. 상호간에, 공통으로

consequence [kánsəkwèns] n. 결과
fulfill [fulfíl] v. 충족시키다
functionalistic [fʌ̀ŋkʃənəlístik] a. 기능주의적
characteristic [kæ̀riktərístik] n. 특징
exaggerated [igzǽdʒərèitid] a. 과장된
exclusive [iksklúːsiv] a. 배타적인

labyrinth [lǽbərìnθ] n. 미로
identify [aidéntəfài] v. 확인하다
squabble [skwábl] v. (하찮은 일로) 옥신각신하다.
dissimilar [dissímələr] a. 다른   refer to : phr. 언급하다

approaches into four criteria for identifying playful behavior. The first criterion, positive effect, refers to the enjoyment that comes from doing playful behavior. The second, nonliterality, is the imaginative aspect of playing, which encompasses acts such as pretending and placing oneself in fictitious perspectives **for the purpose of** play. The third, intrinsic motivation, means that the behavior is done **of one's own accord** and not due to social pressure. Finally, flexibility covers the characteristics described by the structural approach. [■] ◎While **meeting** one **criterion** is sufficient to **define** a behavior **as** being playful, when the behavior **meets** more than one **criteria**, one may **be more certain that** the behavior is playful. [■] [Q18]**Confusing as it may be**, one must understand that the criterion approach was not developed to create a one-sentence definition for play, as many behaviors that are undoubtedly non-playful will **fall within** one or more of the criterion. [■] Instead, the approach defines which factors an everyday observer **uses as** a basis for determining if an action is playful. So, while the criterion approach may not **be used to** definitively **distinguish** between activities that are play and **those** that are not, it **plays a** significant **role in** helping sociologists understand how humans recognize play. [■]

이것은 다른 접근법들의 개념을 합쳐 유희적 행동을 규정하기 위해 네 가지 기준으로 만든 것이다. 첫 번째 기준은, 긍정적인 효과로써, 유희적 행동으로부터 얻는 즐거움을 뜻한다. 두 번째는 비실제성으로써, 놀이의 상상적 측면인데, 놀기 위해서 연기하거나 자신을 허구적 상황에 놓는 것과 같은 행동을 포함한다. 세 번째는 내적 동기로써, 사회적 압력 때문이 아닌, 자발적으로 되는 행동을 의미한다. 마지막으로, 유연성은 구조 접근법에 의해 설명된 특징들을 포함한다. [■] ◎한가지 기준을 충족시키는 것으로도 유희적 행동으로 정의하기에 충분하지만, 한 행동이 하나 혹은 그 이상의 기준을 충족시킨다면 그것은 더욱 확실한 유희적 행동이 된다. [■] [Q18]의심할 여지없이 비유희적 행동들이 한 가지 혹은 그 이상의 기준을 맞추기 때문에 기준 접근법이 혼동될 수 있으나, 이것은 놀이를 한 문장으로 정의하려고 만들어진 것이 아니라는 것을 이해해야만 한다. [■] 대신, 접근법은 일반 사람들이 어떤 행동이 유희적인지 아닌지 결정하는 근거로서 사용하는 요소가 무엇인지 정의한다. 따라서, 기준 접근법은 유희적 행동과 비유희적 행동을 구별하는데 확실하게 사용될 수는 없지만, 그것은 사회학자들이 인간이 어떻게 놀이를 인식하는지 이해하는데 중요한 역할을 했다. [■]

Sentence analysis

◎ Although Symons' definition was intended for the monkeys that he studied, /
　　사이먼스가 내린 정의는 본래 원숭이를 위해 만들어진 것이지만
it soon became evident to other scholars that his definition, / which came to be known as the functional approach, /
　　곧 다른 학자들로부터 그의 정의는 명확해졌다　　　　　　　　기능 접근법이라고 알려지게 된
could likewise be applied to play in humans.
　　인간의 놀이에게도 적용될 수 있다고

◎ While meeting one criterion is sufficient to define a behavior as being playful, /
　　하나의 기준만 맞아도 행동이 놀이라 할 수 있으나
when the behavior meets more than one criteria, / one can be more certain that the behavior is playful.
　　만약에 한 행동이 하나 이상의 기준에 맞는다면　　　　더 확실한 유희적 행동이 된다.

Vocabulary

nonliterality [nɑnlìtərǽləti] n. 비실제성
pretend [priténd] v. ~인체하다
perspective [pərspéktiv] n. 관점, 시각

encompass [inkʌ́mpəs] v. 포함하다, 에워싸다
fictitious [fiktíʃəs] a. 허구의, 자아낸
intrinsic [intrínsik, -zik] a. 고유한, 본질적인

01 According to paragraph 1, all of the following statements are true of playful behavior EXCEPT:

(A) Members of species other than humans also partake in playful behavior.
(B) Children today are less obliged to use their imagination in play because of technology.
(C) Wooden toys are no longer played with, because ~~only video games are considered to be fun playthings now.~~
(D) Although their perception of play is different from that of children, adults also enjoy playful behavior. ★

1단락에 따르면, 다음 중 유희적 행동에 대한 설명이 아닌 것은?

(A) 사람이 아닌 다른 동식물도 유희적 행동을 범한다.
(B) 오늘날 아이들은 기술의 발전으로 인하여 상상력이 줄어들었다.
(C) ~~비디오 게임만 재미있다고 생각하기~~ 때문에 나무로 만든 장난감을 더 이상 가지고 놀지 않는다.
(D) 유희적 행동으로 판단되는 행위가 어른들 또한 유희적 행동을 즐긴다. ★

Fact (A)는 지문의 comes in many form in both humans and other animals.(인간이나 다른 동물들 모두에게서 다양한 형태로 나타난다)와 일치한다. (B)는 지문의 decrease in usage of imagination since computers and video games have begun to create virtual worlds.(컴퓨터나 비디오 게임이 아이들에게 가상현실을 만들어 줌으로써 상상력 사용이 감소했다는 것이다)와 일치한다. (D)는 지문의 but not that engaging in sports activities by adults is another form.(어른들이 스포츠 활동에 참여하는 것은 다른 형태의 놀이라고 인지하고 있지는 않다) 따라서 (A), (B), —(D)는 지문의 내용과 일치하므로 오답이다. 그러나 (C)는 지문에 언급되지 않은 내용이므로 정답이다.

02 Why does the author mention that one cannot predict what form it will take next, only that it will continue to exist?

(A) To suggest that the evolution of play will continue in unknown ways in the future
(B) To suggest the ~~futility~~ of people's attempts at predicting the future
(C) To suggest that humans' preference for types of play is ~~predictable~~
(D) To illustrate that the distinction between play and non-play ~~will get more obscure in the future~~ ★

1단락에서 글쓴이는 왜 놀이가 지속될 것이라고 확신할 수 있으나 어떤 형태로 변화될 것인지는 예상할 수는 없다라고 언급하는가?

(A) 놀이의 발전은 알 수 없는 방법으로 계속될 것이라는 것을 제안하기 위해
(B) 사람들이 미래를 예상하려는 시도들의 무용성을 제안하기 위해
(C) 인간이 원하는 놀이의 종류는 ~~예상할 수 있다는~~ 것을 보여주기 위해
(D) 놀이와 비놀이의 차이점이 ~~미래에는 더 불투명해질 것이라고~~ 설명하기 위해 ★

Purpose 음영 절이 언급된 앞 문장을 살펴보면, with such major changes happening(이 같은 주요한 변화들이 일어남으로써)라고 언급하며 변화가 이루어 진다는 것을 의미한다. 뒷부분을 살펴보면, sociologists have continuously tried to form a complete definition of play.(사회학자들은 계속해서 놀이에 대한 완벽한 정의를 내리려고 노력했다)라고 언급했다. 또한 앞부분에 미리 the way play has changed over time is also ignored.(놀이가 시간이 지남에 따라 변화하는 방식도 역시 무시되고 있다)이라 말했으니 변화는 계속 되나 변화 형태를 예상할 수 없다는 것을 언급한 것이다. 따라서 정답은 (A)이다. (D)가 틀린 이유는 미래에 더 불투명해질 것이라는 내용이 지문에 없는 내용이기 때문이다.

03 Which of the sentences below best expresses the essential information in the highlighted sentence in the passage? Incorrect choices change the meaning in important ways or leave out essential information.

(A) ~~After the similarity was discovered between humans and monkeys,~~ sociologists believed that Symons' functional approach could be applied to humans. ★
(B) Scientists agreed that the functional approach could also be applied to humans even though Symons produced the definition for monkeys.
(C) Because his peers thought that the functional approach for monkeys was exceptional, Symons was ~~encouraged to create a definition for humans as well.~~
(D) Even though Symons' definition would be ~~inadequate to be applied to humans,~~ other scholars believed that it worked just as well for monkeys.

아래 문장 중 지문 속의 음영 된 문장의 핵심 정보를 가장 잘 표현하고 있는 것은 무엇인가? 오답은 문장의 의미를 현저히 왜곡하거나 핵심 정보를 빠뜨리고 있다.

(A) 인간과 원숭이의 ~~공통점이 발견된 후,~~ 사회학자들은 사이먼스의 기능 접근법이 사람에게도 적용될 수 있다고 생각했다. ★
(B) 과학자들은 기능 접근법이란 사이먼스가 원숭이를 대상으로 정의한 것임에도 불구하고 이것은 사람에게도 적용 될 수 있다고 동의했다.
(C) 그의 친구들이 원숭이의 기능 접근법이 예외적이라고 생각했기 때문에, 사이먼스는 ~~사람들 또한 정의하려고 했다.~~
(D) 사이먼스의 정의는 ~~사람에게 적용하기에는 부적당하지만,~~ 다른 학자들은 이것이 원숭이에게 또한 적용될 수 있다고 생각했다.

> **Highlight** 음영 표시된 문장 전체가 핵심 정보로서 i) Although Symons' definition was intended for the monkeys that he studied (사이먼스가 내린 정의는 본래 그가 연구하던 원숭이를 위해 만들어진 것이었지만), ii) it soon became evident to other scholars that his definition, which came to be known as the functional approach, iii) could likewise be applied to play in humans(ii)기능 접근법으로 알려지게 된 그것은 곧 다른 학자들로부터 iii) 인간에게도 적용될 수 있다고 인정을 받았다)를 accurately applied to humans(사람에게도 적용될 수 있다)로 간략하게 바꾸어 표현한 (B)가 정답이다. (A)가 틀린 이유는 인과에 있어 사람과 원숭이의 유사점이 발견된 후 과학자들이 기능 접근법을 사람에게 적용한 것이 아니기 때문이다.

04 What is the main problem with the functional approach according to paragraph 3?

(A) It will wrongly categorize many acts because it does not consider the conditions under which the action was performed.
(B) Its definition of playful behavior ~~is at odds with that of the structural approach.~~
(C) It does not take into account that sometimes ~~play occurs without laughter.~~
(D) It disregards the fact that ~~individuals of different ages have varying views on what they consider to be playful.~~ ★

3단락에 따르면, 기능 접근법의 가장 큰 문제점은 무엇인가?

(A) 기능 접근법은 어떤 조건 하에 행동들이 행해지는지 설명하지 않기 때문에 여러 행동들을 잘못 분류할 수 있다.
(B) 기능 접근법과 ~~구조 접근법이~~ 내린 놀이적 행동의 정의는 ~~일치하지 않는다.~~
(C) 기능 접근법은 가끔씩 ~~웃음소리없이 놀아가 행해진다는~~ 것을 설명하지 않는다.
(D) 기능 접근법은 ~~다른 나이의 개개인이 놀이적에 대한 개인적인 의견에 따라 다른 견해를 가지고 있다는 사실을 무시한다.~~ ★

> **Fact** 문제의 키워드 main problem with the functional approach(기능 접근법의 큰 문제점)이 언급된 부분의 주변을 지문에서 살펴보면, The functional approach, however, does not account for ~ as running.(그러나 기능 접근법은 즉각적으로 명확한 목적이 없는 비유희적 행동들이나, 달리는 것과 같이 목적이 있는 것처럼 보이는 유희적 행동을 설명하지 않는다)라는 것을 알 수 있다. 따라서 (A)는 지문의 내용과 일치하므로 정답이다. (D)가 틀린 이유는 나이에 따라 다른 견해를 가진다는 것이 기능 접근법의 주된 문제점이 아니어서이다.

05 According to paragraph 3, all of the following are identified as playful behavior by the structural approach EXCEPT:

(A) Laughing while running with friends towards a tree on a hill
(B) Climbing up the slippery slope and then walking down the stairs of a slide ★
(C) Kicking and splashing large amounts of water in a shallow pool
(D) Punching and pushing other children ~~to take their toys~~

3단락에 따르면, 다음 중 구조 접근법에 의해서 유희적 행동이라고 생각되지 않는 것은?

(A) 친구와 함께 웃으면서 언덕 위에 나무로 뛰어가는 행동
(B) 미끄러운 경사를 올라가고 경사에 있는 계단으로 내려 오는 행동 ★
(C) 얕은 수영장에서 많은 양의 물을 차고 튀는 행동
(D) 장난감을 뺏으려고 한 아이를 때리고 미는 행동

Fact 문제의 키워드 structural approach(구조 접근법)가 언급된 부분의 주변을 살펴보면 다음을 알 수 있다.
(A)는 지문의 exaggerates it by jumping two stairs at a time(한번에 두 계단을 과장되어 뛰어오르거나)와 일치한다.
(B)는 지문의 re-orders it by climbing them backwards.(뒤돌아서 올라가며 그것을 재배치한다)와 일치한다.
(C)는 (A)의 이유와 같이 exaggerates it by jumping two stairs at a time(한번에 두 계단을 과장되어 뛰어오르거나)와 일치한다.
(D)를 제외하고 다른 보기들은 지문에 나온 내용과 일치하다. 때리고 미는 행동이 유희적 행동으로 고려되는 상황은 무엇을 뺏기 위해가 아니라 playful squabbling일 때다.

---

06 By stating that the approaches are not mutually exclusive, the author means that

(A) Some actions covered by one approach might also be covered by the other.
(B) If one theory is true, then ~~the other must be false.~~
(C) ~~Children's actions are~~ covered by one or two of the approaches. ★
(D) ~~The two approaches are similar~~ in the way they classify behavior.

기능 접근법과 구조 접근법이 상호 배타적이지 않은의 의미는?

(A) 기능 접근법에 적용되는 행동들이 구조 접근법에 적용될 수 있다.
(B) 하나의 접근법이 진실이라면 ~~다른 접근법은 무조건 거짓이다.~~
(C) ~~아이들의 행동들은~~ 하나 혹의 두 개의 접근법에 적용된다. ★
(D) ~~기능 접근법과 구조 접근법은 행동을~~ 분류하는데 있어 ~~유사하다.~~

Purpose 음영 문구 not mutually exclusive(상호 배타적이지 않는)가 언급된 부분의 뒷문장을 살펴보면, but that the factors that they used to identify behavior were dissimilar.(행동을 구별하는 요인들이 서로 다르다는 점)라고 언급했다. 따라서 두 유희에 적용되는 행동들은 다르기 때문에 한 접근법에 적용되어도 다른 접근법에 적용 될 수 없다는 것을 뜻하는 것이니 (A)가 정답이다. (C)가 틀린 이유는 둘 다 틀릴 경우를 mutually exclusive가 설명하지 못하기 때문이다.

---

07 The word intrinsic is closest in meaning to

(A) intriguing ★
(B) intricate
(C) innate
(D) integral

지문의 단어 intrinsic 과 의미상 가장 유사한 것은?

(A) 흥미로운 ★ [intríːgiŋ]
(B) 복잡한 [íntrikət]
(C) 선천적인 [inéit]
(D) 필수의 [íntigrəl]

Vocabulary 지문의 intrinsic(본질적인)은 innate(선천적인)과 동의어이므로 정답은 (C)이다.

---

08 What can be inferred from paragraph 4 about the methods of identifying playful behavior?

(A) The structural approach ~~is the method that the majority of sociologists agree is most reliable.~~
(B) Krasnor and Pepler were successful in making ~~an absolute definition~~ of playful behavior by establishing the criterion approach.
(C) The criterion approach is liable to misclassify many non-play activities as play.
(D) If an act is classified as play by one or more of the criteria, then one ~~must consider~~ the act as playful. ★

유희적 행동을 판정하는 방법에 대해 4단락으로부터 추론할 수 있는 것은?

(A) ~~구조 접근법은 대부분의 사회학자들이 가장 신뢰성이 있다고 동의하는 방법이다.~~
(B) Kransor과 Pepler은 기준 접근법을 만들면서 유희적 행동의 ~~절대적 정의를~~ 내렸다.
(C) 기준 접근법은 많은 비유희적 행동들을 유희적으로 잘못 분류할수 있다.
(D) 만약 행동이 하나 혹은 더 많은 기준으로부터 놀이라고 분류 된다면, 한 사람은 그 행동이 유희적이라고 ~~확신할수 있다.~~ ★

Inference 4단락에서 문제의 키워드 methods of identifying playful behavior(놀이적 행동을 판정하는 방법)이 언급된 지문에서 criterion approach(기준 접근법) 부분을 살펴보면, as many behaviors ~ will fall within one or more ~ criterion(비유희적 행동들이 한가지 혹은 한가지 이상의 기준을 맞추기 때문에 기준 접근법이 혼동될 수 있으나) 즉, 잘못 분류시킬 수 있다는 것을 추론할 수 있다. 따라서 정답은 (C)이다. (D)가 틀린 이유는 지문에서 분류가 되어도 문제가 계속 된다고 나와서이다.

09

Look at the four squares [■] that indicate where the following sentence could be added to the passage.

(Instead,) the approach defines which factors an everyday observer uses as a basis for determining if an action is playful.

Where would the sentence best fit? Click on the square [■] to add the sentence to the passage.

3rd

네 개의 네모[■]는 다음 문장이 삽입될 수 있는 부분을 나타내고 있다.

대신, 접근법은 일반 사람들이 어떤 행동이 유희적인지 아닌지 결정하는 근거로서 사용하는 요소가 무엇인지 정의한다.

이 문장은 어느 자리에 들어가는 것이 가장 적절한가?

세번째

Insertion 삽입 문장에서 정답의 단서는 instead(대신에)라는 연결어로 determining the playful action(놀이적 행동을 결정하는)에 대한 내용을 찾아 그 후에 넣으면 된다. 세 번째 네모에 넣어보면, 구조적 접근이 왜 놀이적과 비놀이적 행동을 구별하는데 쓰일 수 없는지 자연스럽게 설명하게 된다.

10

Directions: An introductory sentence for a brief summary of the passage is provided below. Complete the summary by selecting the THREE answer choices that express the most important ideas in the passage. Some sentences do not belong in the summary because they express ideas that are not presented in the passage or are minor ideas in the passage. **This question is worth 2 points.**

지시: 지문 요약을 위한 도입 문장이 아래에 주어져 있다. 지문의 가장 중요한 내용을 나타내는 보기 3개를 골라 요약을 완성하시오. 어떤 문장은 지문에 언급되지 않은 내용이나 사소한 정보를 담고 있으므로 요약에 포함되지 않는다. 이 문제는 2점이다.

> **Studies of playful behavior have yielded different approaches to understand its characteristics.**
>
> - (A) The criterion approach helps explain how playful behavior is detected, but it is still incomplete in terms of defining play itself - Paragraph 4
> - (C) The functional approach, established by Donald Symons, proposes that all activities without apparent reason or obvious end should be considered playful - Paragraph 2
> - (E) An activity can be scanned for specific characteristics which the structural approach lists to determine the nature of the activity - Paragraph 3

> **유희적 행동의 연구들은 그 특성을 이해하기 위해 다른 접근들을 만들어 왔다.**
>
> - (A) 기준 접근법은 유희적 행동이 어떻게 발견되는지 설명하지만, 이것은 놀이 자체를 설명하기에는 불완전하다.
> - (C) Donald Symons가 만든 기능 접근법은 특정한 이유나 명확한 결말이 없는 행동들은 유희적 행동이라고 생각되어야 한다고 제안했다.
> - (E) 행동은 구조 접근법이 행동의 특성을 결정하려고 만든 상세한 특징으로 조사될 수 있다.

(B) Even after several promising attempts throughout history, ~~sociologists agreed that an exact definition for playful behavior is unachievable.~~ - 비약

(D) The criterion approach borrows ideas used in the structural approach and improves it to ~~directly oppose the functional approach.~~ - 반/반

(F) A child using the equipment found on a playground exemplifies playful behavior described by the functional approach
- Paragraph 2 detail

(B) 역사를 통틀어 여러 번의 가망 있는 시도에도불구하고, 불구하고, ~~사회학자들은 유희적 행동의 명확한 정의는 성취될 수 없다고 동의했다.~~

(D) 기준 접근법은 구조 접근법에서 사용된 개념을 사용하고 ~~기능 접근법을 직접 반대하려고 개선한다.~~

(F) 놀이터에 있는 기구들을 사용하는 아이는 유희적 행동이 기능 접근법으로부터 나타내 질 수 있다고 전형적으로 보여준다.

Summary 지문의 중심 내용은 놀이적 행동을 구별하는 여러 가지의 접근법에 대한 특징이다. (A)는 4단락의 중심 내용인 기준 접근법이 놀이적 행동을 설명을 하나 완전하지 못하다는 것과 일치하고, (C)는 2단락의 중심 내용인 분명한 이유와 끝이 없는 기능 접근법과 일치하고, (E)는 3단락의 중심 내용인 구조 접근법의 특징과 일치한다. 따라서 정답은 (A), (C), (E)이다. (F)가 틀린 이유는 중심내용이 아닌 마이너한 부분이기 때문이다.

usherin.usher.co.kr

TEST 9-2 Sentinel Behavior in Meerkats 미어캣의 보초 행동

Introduction	단락 1	보초 행동의 대한 소개와 배경
Point 1	단락 2	혈연 선택의 소개와 설명
Point 2	단락 3	상호간 이타주의의 소개와 설명
Point 3	단락 4	보초 행동설에 관한 의문과 반론제기

단락 1 — 보초 행동의 대한 소개와 배경

1 Meerkats are small, mongoose-like mammals that live in the Kalahari Desert of Southern Africa. Being primarily insectivores, they **feed on** beetles and scorpions buried underground, which they locate using their strong sense of smell. [Q21]Unfortunately, when the meerkat lowers its head to **search out** prey under grasses, it limits its own range of sight by a significant amount. **As a result** they **are** extremely **vulnerable to** airborne predators such as hawks and owls. [Q22-A]To ensure that they can reach the safety of their bolt-holes before being snatched up by birds, meerkats [Q22-D]forage in packs and **partake in** what **is known as** sentinel behavior. As the term suggests, i) one meerkat in the group **acts as** a sentinel and does not **look for** food like the rest, ii) but rather stands upright on its hind legs to gain a wider field of view with which it scans the surrounding area for possible predators and other **threats to** the community. When it senses danger approaching, the sentinel barks loudly to **warn** the others **of** the danger. Many scientists [Q24]questioned this phenomenon because the revealing stance and loud vocalization were thought to **expose** the meerkat **to** an increased risk of predation.

미어캣은 남부 아프리카의 칼라하이 사막에 사는 작은 몽구스와 같은 포유동물이다. 주로 식충동물인 그들은 지하에 묻혀있는 곤충과 전갈을 먹고 사는데, 그들은 그들의 강력한 후각을 사용하여 위치를 추적한다.[Q21]불행하게도, 미어캣이 수풀 아래에 있는 먹이를 찾기 위해 고개를 숙이면, 그것은 자신의 가시 거리의 상당한 범위를 현저하게 제한하게 된다. 결과적으로 그들은 매와 독수리 같은 공중 포식자들에게 극도로 취약하다. 그들이 새들에게 낚아 채이기 전에 [Q22-A]볼트 구멍에 안전하게 도착하는 것을 확실히 하기 위해, 미어캣은 [Q22-D]무리지어 사냥하고 보초 행동이라 알려진 것에 동참한다. 그 용어가 말해주듯이 i) 무리 중에 한 마리 미어캣은 보초로 활동하고 나머지처럼 식량을 찾지는 않지만, ii) 오히려 더 넓은 시야를 얻기 위해 뒷다리로 꼿꼿이 서서 혹시 모를 포식자와 무리에 위협이 될 다른 것들을 찾아 주변을 둘러본다. 보초가 위험이 다가오는 것을 감지하면, 그것은 다른 무리들에게 위험을 경고하기 위해 크게 짖는다. 많은 과학자들이 [Q24]이 노출되는 자세와 큰 발성이 미어캣을 증가된 포식의 위험에 노출 시킨다고 생각되어졌기 때문에 이 현상에 의문을 가졌다.

단락 2 — 혈연 선택의 소개와 설명

2 The motivations behind this behavior have **been attributed to** kin selection, the evolutionary strategy that favors the reproductive success of an organism's relatives over one's own survival. In Belding's ground squirrels, individuals sound an alarm at the approach of a predator, warning its nearby relatives and thereby benefitting the population. This explanation gained credibility because research revealed that, like Belding's squirrels, [Q25-A]meerkat communities are

이 행동 뒤의 동기부여는 자기 자신의 생존보다 개체의 친족들의 번식 성공에 기여하는 진화 전략인 혈연 선택의 결과인 것으로 보인다. 벨딩 땅다람쥐의 경우, 포식자가 다가오면 각각은 경고음을 울리는데, 이것은 근처 친족들에게 경고를 줌으로서 무리에게 도움이 된다. 조사가 밝혀냈듯이, 벨딩의 다람쥐와 마찬가지로 [Q25-A]미어캣 무리는 대게 가족 멤버로 구성되어

Vocabulary

1단락
- insectivores [inséktəvɔ̀r] n. 식충 동물
- mammal [mǽməl] n. 포유동물
- snatch [snætʃ] v. 잡아채려하다
- airborne [ɛərbɔ̀rn] a. 공기로 운반되는, 하늘 높이 뜬
- prey [prei] n. 먹이
- predator [prédətər] n. 포식자
- stance [stæns] n. 자세, 태세
- significant [signífikənt] a. 중대한

2단락
- kin selection n. 혈연 선택: 가까운 친척에게 애타적 경향을 보이는 자연 선택의 한 유형
- Belding's ground squirrel n. 미국 서부의 산에 서식하는 다람쥐의 종류
- authoritarian [əθɔ̀ːrətɛəriən, əθàr-] a. 권위주의적인, 독재적인
- credibility [krèdəbíləti] n. 진실성, 신뢰성
- postulate [pástʃulèit / pɔ́s-] v. ~을 가정하다, 주장하다

composed mostly of family members. In a typical community of meerkats, about 70 percent of its members are related to the dominant female. [Q25-B]In their authoritarian societies, the alpha female rarely tolerates offspring from anyone other than herself. Therefore, if the sentinel is able to protect one of its siblings, it ensures passing on 50 percent of its own genes, or 25 percent for saving a niece or nephew. This follows the gene selection theory, postulating that individuals are genetically programmed to proliferate their DNA. In addition, if the sentinel allows other group members to spend less time scanning and more time foraging, they will be able to catch more prey, which will also increase the survivability of the group.

단락 3
상호간 이타주의의 소개와 설명

3   [Q27-i]A variant theory was that in order to protect their kin, meerkats demonstrated reciprocal altruism, an act that benefits another at the expense of one's own interest. If the receiver's benefit outweighs the cost of the altruist, and if the receiver is expected to also become the altruist, then evolutionarily the entire group profits from the behavior. This can be seen in various animals such as fish and birds, as well as in close relatives of the meerkat, the banded mongoose. Their pups cooperate in creating annoying chirps to beg for food from their chaperones, which are assigned to individual pups. When one chaperone was removed from the group, the corresponding pup would stop crying. This in turn caused the rest of the pups to increase the volume of their crying, which induces the adults to bring more food, benefitting the quiet pup. Scientists tested for two conditions that had been laid out by the developed, mature definition of reciprocal altruism to determine if this was what the meerkats were in fact doing: a systematic method of deciding individuals' duty as sentinels, and a unified punishment for those who abandon their duties as a sentinel. But observations substantiated that there was neither a particular order nor any sort of punishment. Moreover, the dedication and the length of time that a meerkat displayed sentinel behavior were consistent regardless of the number of non-relatives in the group.

Vocabulary

motivation [mòutəvéiʃən] n. 자극
offspring [ɔ́(ː)fspriŋ, áf-] n. 자손

evolutionary [èvəlúːʃənèri] a. 발전의
survivability [sərvàivəbíləti] n. 생존가능성

strategy [strǽtədʒi] n. 전략

3단락
reciprocal [risíprəkəl] a. 상호간의
chaperone [ʃǽpəròun] n. 감독하는 사람, 샤프롱: 사교계에 나오는 미혼 여성을 따라다니며 돌봐주는 부인
substantiate [səbstǽnʃièit] v. ~을 확증하다, 입증하다   variant [véəriənt] a. 갖가지의   demonstrate [démvnstrèit] v. 논증하다
altruist [ǽltruːst] n. 이타주의자   cooperate [kouápərèit] v. 협력하다

altruism [ǽltruìzəm] n. 애타심, 이타주의   outweigh [àutwèi] v. ~보다 뛰어나다, 중대하다

USHER

단락 4
보초 행동설에 관한 의문과 반론제기

4 [Q27-ii]Later scientists questioned the theory, proposing that sentinel behavior was actually a selfish anti-predator behavior. The proposition was that, **contrary to** popular belief, [Q28]standing guard would increase the sentinel's own chances for survival. To find evidence for this claim, a team of scientists **set out to observe** sentinel behavior in lone meerkats. They confirmed that solitary meerkats first **focused on** foraging, then returned to the sentinel stance once their hunger was satiated. [■] This strengthened the anti-predator hypothesis. [■] The next **question to answer** was whether sentineling meerkats had better chances of survival **than those** who were not standing guard when attacked by a predator. [■] Of a total of 2,000 hours of observation, not a single meerkat that was standing guard **at the moment of** attack was caught because they chose positions that were safer when sentineling than foraging. [■] Further, they never wandered more than five meters away from at least one of their group's bolt-holes. [Q28]The conclusion was that meerkats stand guard to **protect** themselves **from** predators, but they forage in groups because then they can invest more time **hunting for** food and **put trust in** the sentinels to **warn** them **of** any signs of danger.

[Q27-ii]그 이후 과학자들은 보초를 서는 행동은 실제로는 이기적인 반포식자의 행동이라 제안하면서 이 이론에 의문을 가졌다. 그 제안은 일반적 믿음과 반대로, [Q28]보초를 서는 것은 보초 개인의 생존 가능성만을 증가시킨다는 것이다. 이 주장에 대한 증거를 찾기 위해, 과학자 한 팀이 혼자 있는 미어캣의 보초 행동을 관찰하기 시작했다. 그들은 혼자 있는 미어 캣이 처음에는 사냥에 집중하지만, 일단 배고픔이 채워지고 나면 보초 자리로 돌아온다는 것을 확신했다. [■] 이것은 반 포식자 가설을 뒷받침했다. [■] 그 다음 남아있는 질문은 포식자로부터 공격받았을 때 보초를 서고 있는 미어캣이 서지 않은 미어캣보다 더 나은 생존 기회를 가지고 있는지 아닌지였다. [■] 총 2000 시간의 관찰에서, 미어캣들은 사냥을 할 때보다 보초를 설 때 더 안전한 위치를 선택하기 때문에 공격받는 순간에 보초를 서는 미어캣은 단 한 마리도 잡히지 않았다. [■] 게다가, 그들은 그들의 그룹의 볼트 구멍 중 적어도 한 개로부터 5미터 이상은 배회하지 않았다. [Q28]결론은 미어캣은 포식자로부터 그들 자신을 보호하기 위해 보초를 서지만, 먹이를 사냥하는 것에 더 많은 시간을 투자할 수 있고, 그 어떤 위험 신호에도 그들에게 경고를 할 수 있도록 보초들에게 신뢰를 줄 수 있기 때문에 무리지어 수렵한다.

Sentence analysis

◎ Scientists tested for two conditions / that had been laid out by / the developed, mature definition of reciprocal altruism /
과학자들은 두 가지 조건을 실험했다   ~에 의해서 깔린   상호적 이타주의의 고도로 발달하고 공들인 정의에
to determine / if this was what the meerkats were in fact doing: / a systematic method /
확정 짓기 위해서   이것이 미어캣이 사실상 하고 있는 것인지   체계적인 방법
of deciding individuals' duty as sentinels, / and a unified punishment /
보초로써의 개인의 의무를 결정하는   그리고 공통된 벌
for those who abandon their duties as a sentinel.
보초로써 의무를 버린 이들을 위한

Vocabulary

4단락
satiate [sèiʃiéit] v. ~을 배부르게 하다, ~을 충분히 만족시키다
proposition [prɑ̀pəzíʃən -prɔp-] n. 제안
lone [loun] a. 홀로 있는, 혼자의
solitary [sɑ́litèri] a. 고독한
sentinel [séntənəl] n. 파수꾼
forage [fɔ́:ridʒ] n. 먹이

11 In paragraph 1, why does the author mention that they feed on beetles and scorpions buried underground?

(A) To explain the reason for their vulnerability against predators

(B) To show how they survive in a hazardous and arid environment

(C) To provide an example of a type of prey available in Southern Africa ★

(D) To point out an adaptation that has emerged as a response to airborne predation

1단락에서, 글쓴이는 왜 미어캣이 지하에 묻혀있는 곤충과 전갈을 먹고산다고 언급하는가?

(A) 포식자에 대하여 그들이 취약한 이유를 설명하기 위해서

(B) 그들이 어떻게 위험하고 건조한 기후에서 생존하는지 보여주기 위해

(C) 남부 아프리카에서 사용할 수 있는 먹이의 한 종류의 예를 들기 위해서 ★

(D) 공중 포식에 대한 응답으로 나타난 적응을 보여주기 위해

> **Purpose** 음영의 다음 부분을 살펴보면, Unfortunately, when the meerkat lowers its head to search out prey under grasses, it significantly limits its own range of sight by a significant amount. (불행히도, 미어캣이 수풀 아래에 있는 먹이를 찾기 위해서 고개를 숙이면, 그것은 자신의 가시거리의 상당한 양을 현저하게 제한하게 된다)라고 쓰여있는 걸로 보아, 시야가 땅으로 떨어지면 볼 수 있는 것이 한정되는 것을 알 수 있다. 시야 확보가 안되면 위험에 노출되기 때문에, 답은 (A)이다. (B)는 언급되지 않았기 때문에 오답이며 (C)는 사실이지만 의도와는 다른 대답이므로 오답이다. 이 문제는 purpose 스타일이지만, 답 근거가 '앞' 이 아닌 '뒤' 에 있다는 점에서 어려운 스타일로 드물게 나오는 유형이다.

12 Select the TWO answer choices According to paragraph 1, what are the methods utilized by meerkats to avoid predation?
To receive credit, you must select TWO answers.

(A) They utilize bolt-holes to hide from predators.

(B) They stay under the grass to hide from birds.

(C) They bark loudly to scare away the oncoming predator. ★

(D) They form groups when hunting for prey.

1단락에 의하면, 다음 중 미어캣이 포식을 피하기 위해서 사용하는 방법중에 보기 두개를 고르시오
점수를 얻으려면, 답 두개를 선택해야 한다.

(A) 그들은 포식자로부터 숨기 위해 볼트 구멍을 사용한다.

(B) 그들은 새로부터 숨기 위해 수풀 밑에 머무른다.

(C) 그들은 다가오는 포식자를 겁주기 위해 크게 짓는다. ★

(D) 그들은 먹이를 사냥할 때 무리를 형성한다.

> **Fact** 지문에서 살펴보면 두 가지 근거: 1. To ensure that they can reach the safety of their bolt-holes(그들이 새에게 낚아 채이기 전에 볼트구멍의 안전하게 도착하는 것을 확실하게 하기 위해) 2. forage in packs(무리 지어 사냥)가 나온다. 구멍을 활용하고, 무리 지어 다니는 것이 포식을 피하는 방법이기 때문에 (A)와 (D)가 답이다. (B)는 수풀에 숨는 언급은 없으므로 오답이며, (C)는 겁주기 위해 크게 소리를 낸다는 내용이 없기 때문에 오답이다.

13 Which of the sentences below best expresses the essential information in the highlighted sentence in the passage? Incorrect choices change the meaning in important ways or leave out essential information.

(A) A sentineling meerkat stands upright to gain a panoramic view of its environment, so it can forage for prey more easily and anticipate predators and other threats more accurately.

(B) A meerkat scans the surrounding area more keenly in order to spot danger, by getting up on its back legs and acting as a sentinel, rather than looking for food with the rest of the group.

(C) Because of the dangers of predators, a meerkat stands on its back legs, which allows it a better view of the surrounding area, so it can forage faster while the rest do not. ★

(D) When a meerkat has finished foraging for food, it begins to act as the sentinel to protect its community, getting up on its hind legs and scanning the area for predators.

아래 문장 중 지문 속의 음영된 문장의 핵심 정보를 가장 잘표현하고 있는 것은 무엇인가? 오답은 문장의 의미를 현저히 왜곡하거나 핵심 정보를 빠트리고 있다.

(A) 보초서는 미어캣은 그것의 환경의 파노라마 식의 시야를 확보하기 위해 꼿꼿이 서서 식량을 더 쉽게 사냥하고 포식자와 다른 위협들을 더 정확하게 예상할 수 있게 한다.

(B) 미어캣은 다른 그룹원들이 식량을 찾는 대신, 보초로 활동할 때 뒷다리로 서서 위험을 알아채기 위해 주위를 빈틈없이 바라볼 수 있다.

(C) 포식자의 위험 때문에 미어캣은 그것의 뒷다리로 서있는데, 이것은 주위의 더 나은 시야를 확보하기 때문에 그는 나머지가 하지 못할 때 더 빨라 사냥할 수 있다. ★

(D) 미어캣이 식량을 사냥하는 것이 끝났을 때, 그는 뒷다리로 서서 포식자를 찾아 주변을 탐색하면서 그것의 무리를 보호하기 위해서 보초로서 일하기 시작한다.

Highlight 주어진 문장의 요소들을 보면, i) one meerkat in the group acts as a sentinel and does not look for food like the rest(무리중의 한 마리의 미어캣은 보초로 활동하고 나머지처럼 식량을 찾지 않는다), ii) but rather stands upright on its hind legs to gain a wider field of view with which it scans the surrounding area for possible predators and other threats to the community(오히려 더 넓은 시야를 얻기 위해서 뒷다리로 꼿꼿이 서서 혹시 모를 포식자와 무리에 위협이 될 만한 요소들을 찾아 주변을 둘러본다)라는 내용을 찾을 수 있다. (A)는 더 수렵이 쉽다는 내용이 없으므로 정답이 아니며, (C)는 나머지 그룹과 먹이 찾는 속도를 비교적이 없기에 오답이다. 그리고 (D)는 전반적인 순서가 틀리므로 오답이다. 전반적으로 내용을 다 포함하는 (B)가 정답이다.

14
According to paragraph 1, why was sentinel behavior thought to be disadvantageous?

(A) It warns the predator of where the meerkat group is. ★

(B) It allows the meerkat to sense danger and warn the group.

(C) It helps the predators locate the sentinel meerkat.

(D) It encourages the predator to prey on meerkats over other species.

1단락에 의하면, 보초 행동은 왜 불리하다고 생각되었는가?

(A) 그것은 미어캣 무리가 어디에 있는지 포식자에게 경고를 준다. ★

(B) 그것은 미어캣이 위험을 감지하고 무리에게 경고하도록 도와준다.

(C) 그것은 포식자로 하여금 보초 미어캣의 위치를 파악할 수 있도록 도와준다.

(D) 그것은 포식자가 다른 종들보다 미어캣을 더 잡아먹도록 장려한다.

Fact 문제의 키워드인 sentinel behavior(보초 행동)이 언급된 부분을 살펴보면, because the revealing stance and loud vocalization was thought to expose the meerkat to an increased risk of predation. (노출되는 자세와 큰 발성이 미어캣을 증가된 포식의 위험에 노출시키기 때문에) 라는 점에서, 보초를 서는 중 큰 소리를 내면 포식의 위험에 노출시키기 때문에 (C)가 정답이다. (A)는 반대되는 내용이므로 오답이다.

15
According to paragraph 2, all of the following statements are true of a meerkat community EXCEPT:

(A) The relatives of a single meerkat comprises the majority of the community.
(B) It is usually headed by one individual.
(C) About a quarter of nieces and nephews remain in the community until death.
(D) Meerkats of a community benefit from one another. ★

2단락에 의하면, 다음 중 미어캣의 무리에 대해 옳지 않은 것은?

(A) 한 미어캣의 친척들은 그 무리의 대부분을 포함한다.
(B) 그것은 주로 한 개인에 의해서 지도된다.
(C) 조카의 사분의 일 정도가 죽을 때까지 무리에 머무른다.
(D) 한 무리의 미어캣들은 서로서로 이익을 본다. ★

Fact 지문에서 살펴보면, (A) meerkat communities are composed mostly of family members(미어캣 무리는 대게 가족 구성원으로 구성) (B)In their authoritarian societies(그들의 권위주의적인 사회에서) (D) if the sentinel allows other group members to spend less time scanning and more time foraging, they will be able to catch more prey, which will also increase the survivability of the group(만약 보초병이 다른 구성원들이 살펴보는데 더 적은 시간을 보내고 수렵하는데 더 많은 시간을 보내도록 허락한다면, 그들은 더 많은 먹이를 잡을 것이고, 또한 무리의 생존 가능성을 높일 것이다)와 같이 사실이 언급되므로 답은 (C)이다.

16
The word substantiated in the passage is closest in meaning to

(A) argued ★
(B) disproved
(C) authorized
(D) confirmed

지문의 단어 substantiated 와 의미상 가장 유사한 것은?

(A) 논했다 ★ [áːrgjuː]
(B) 논박했다 [disprúːv]
(C) 권한을 줬다 [ɔ́ːθəràizd]
(D) 굳었다 [kənfɔ́ːrmd]

Vocabulary 지문의 substantiated(구체화됐다)는 confirmed(굳었다)와 동의어이므로 정답이다.

17 What is the main purpose of paragraph 3?

(A) To give examples of studies conducted in an attempt to support ~~the hypothesis mentioned in the previous paragraph~~ ★
(B) To introduce a theory that is related to the one mentioned in the previous paragraph, which is then challenged in the next paragraph
(C) To point out evidence for the proposition that is ~~described in the following paragraph~~
(D) To provide an explanation of ~~how a behavior mentioned in the previous paragraph is carried out~~

3단락의 주된 목적은 무엇인가?

(A) 전 단락에서 언급된 가설을 지지하려는 시도로 시행된 연구의 예를 들기 위해서 ★
(B) 전 단락에서 언급된 이론과 연관되었고, 다음 단락에서 설명이 요구된 이론을 소개하기 위해서
(C) ~~어어지는 단락에서 설명된 제안에 대한 증거를~~ 가리키기 위해서
(D) ~~이전의 단락에서 언급된 행동이 어떻게~~ 시행되었는지에 대한 설명을 제공하기 위해서

Purpose   지문에서는 답을 두 부분으로 나눠 찾을 수 있다: (39-i)A variant theory was that in order to protect their kin, meerkats demonstrated reciprocal altruism.(다른 변형된 이론은 그들의 친척을 보호하기 위해 미어캣은 상호간 이타주의를 취한다는 것이다)와 (39-ii) Later scientists questioned the theory, proposing that sentinel behavior was a selfish anti-predator behavior.(그 이후 과학자들은 보초를 서는 행동은 실제로는 이기적인 반포식자의 행동이라 제안하면서 이 이론에 의문을 가졌다) 이전 단락의 내용과는 다른 가설이 주어지고, 다음 단락에서 과학자들이 의문을 제기했기 때문에 정답은 (B)이다.

18 According to paragraph 4, why were lone meerkats observed?

(A) To demonstrate that they were ~~just as likely to flee~~ from predators as meerkats in communities ★
(B) To confirm that sentinel behavior was performed for the protection of the meerkat's own interest
(C) To study sentinel behavior ~~more closely~~ than could be done with a large group of meerkats
(D) To prove that ~~they have more time to spend foraging~~ compared to meerkats in a group

4단락에 의하면, 혼자 있는 미어캣은 왜 관찰되었는가?

(A) 그들이 무리에 있는 미어캣과 ~~마찬가지로 포식자로부터~~ 도망칠 가능성이 있다는 것을 증명하기 위해서 ★
(B) 보초 행동이 미어캣 스스로의 이익을 지키기 위해 행해졌다고 확증하기 위해서
(C) 큰 무리의 미어캣들과 할 수 있는 연구보다 보초 행동을 ~~더 자세히~~ 연구하기 위해서
(D) 무리에 있는 미어캣보다 ~~큰들이 수렵에 투자할 수 있는 시간이 더 많다는~~ 것을 증명하기 위해서

Fact   지문에서 보이듯이, standing guard would increase the sentinel's own chances for survival. To find evidence for this claim, a team of scientists set out to observe sentinel behavior in lone meerkats. (보초를 서는 것은 보초 개인의 생존 가능성만을 증가시킨다는 것이다. 이 주장에 대해 증거를 찾으려고 한 팀의 과학자가 혼자 있는 미어캣의 보초 행동을 관찰하기 위해 떠났다) 과학자들이 연구한 이유는 보초 미어캣이 개인 혼자만 살아남으려고 하는 습성을 가졌다고 의심했기 때문이다. 따라서 정답은 (B)이다.

19 Look at the four squares [■] that indicate where the following sentence could be added to the passage.

(Further,) they never wandered more than five meters away from at least one of their group's bolt-holes.

Where would the sentence best fit? Click on the square [■] to add the sentence to the passage.   4th

네 개의 네모[■]는 다음 문장이 삽입될 수 있는 부분을 나타내고 있다.

게다가 그들은 최소한 그들의 무리의 볼트 구멍 중 적어도 한개로부터 5미터 이상의 거리로는 배회하지 않았다.

이 문장은 어느 자리에 들어가는 것이 가장 적절한가?
네번째

Insertion   삽입 문장의 전 문장인 Of a total of 2,000 hours of observation, not a single meerkat that was standing guard at the moment of attack was caught because they chose positions that were safer when sentineling than foraging.(총 2,000시간의 관찰 동안, 미어캣은 수렵을 할 때보다 보초를 설 때 더 안전한 장소를 골랐기 때문에 공격받는 순간에 보초를 서고 있던 미어캣 중 단 한 마리도 공격받지 않았다) 안전한 곳에서 보초를 서는 내용이 나온다. 그리고 삽입 다음 문장에는 결론이 나오므로, 4번째 네모가 답인 것을 알 수 있다.

20

Directions: An introductory sentence for a brief summary of the passage is provided below. Complete the summary by selecting the THREE answer choices that express the most important ideas in the passage. Some sentences do not belong in the summary because they express ideas that are not presented in the passage or are minor ideas in the passage. **This question is worth 2 points.**

지시: 지문 요약을 위한 도입 문장이 아래에 주어져 있다. 지문의 가장 중요한 내용을 나타내는 보기 3개를 골라 요약을 완성하시오. 어떤 문장은 지문에 언급되지 않은 내용이나 사소한 정보를 담고 있으므로 요약에 포함되지 않는다. 이 문제는 2점이다.

Meerkats are known to exhibit sentinel behavior to increase their communitys' chance of escape from predators.

- (A) Sentinelling is thought to be the result of evolution, which selected the meerkat behavior that allowed improved proliferation of their DNA. - Paragraph 2

- (D) Research on the studies of meerkat behavior demonstrated their unselfish devotion to the welfare of others. - Paragraph 3

- (E) Backed up by research results, proponents of the selfish anti-predator theory asserted that meerkats were acting as sentinels on their own behalf. - Paragraph 4

미어캣은 포식자로부터 그들의 무리의 탈출 확률을 증가시키기 위해서 보초 행동을 나타내는 것으로 알려져 있다.

- (A) 보초를 서는 것은 진화의 결과라고 생각되어지는데, 이것은 그들의 DNA의 개선된 확산을 허용하는 미어캣의 행동을 선택한다.

- (D) 미어캣 행동의 대한 연구는 다른 사람의 복지에 대한 그들의 사심 없는 헌신을 보여주었다.

- (E) 연구 결과에 의해 뒷받침되어, 이기적인 반포식자 이론의 지지자들은 미어캣이 스스로의 이익을 위해서 보초로 활동한다고 주장했다

(B) Meerkats are thought to be the ~~only animal~~ to partake in actions that put the interests of their relatives ahead of its own, like the Belding's ground squirrels. - 틀린정보

(C) Scientists deducted that, despite being a close relative of the meerkats, the banded mongoose's sentinel behavior could ~~not~~ be explained by reciprocal altruism. - 틀린정보

(F) During the 2,000-hour observation, ~~scientists could not figure why~~ not a single meerkat that was standing guard at the moment of attack was caught - 틀린정보

(B) 미어캣은 벨딩의 땅 다람쥐처럼 그들 친척의 이익을 스스로의 것보다 우선 순위에 놓는 활동에 참가한 ~~유일한 동물인~~것으로 생각되었다.

(C) 과학자들은 미어캣의 친척인 몽구스를 보초행동이 상호이타주의로 설명될 수 ~~없음을~~ 추론했다.

(F) 2,000 시간의 관찰 중, 과학자들은 왜 공격의 순간에 보초를 서는 단 한 마리의 미어캣도 잡히지 않는 걸 ~~이해할 수 없었다.~~

Summary 지문의 중심 내용은 포식자로부터의 피해를 줄이기 위해서 보초를 세우는 미어캣의 행동에 관한 내용이다. (A)는 그들의 증식을 위한 행동의 선택이라는 내용이 담긴 2단락과 관련 내용이며, (D)와 (E)는 각각 3, 4단락이 중심내용인 내용을 요약 했으므로 정답이다. (B)는 중대하지 않은 내용이기 때문에 오답이며 (C)는 banded mongoose의 행동도 reciprocal altruism이다. (F)는 틀린 정보이므로 오답이다.

usherin.usher.co.kr

USHER

iBT TOEFL
FINAL TEST READING
부록

다음내용은, 부록으로
앞선 지문들에 있는 내용으로 풀 수 있는 보너스 문제입니다.

"문제는 많이 풀수록 좋다는거 아시죠?"

TEST 1 - 1
Method of Measuring Bats' Age

▶ 47페이지 1문단을 참고하세요.

01 The word scores of in the passage is closest in meaning to

(A) recorded
(B) copious
(C) aggressive
(D) temporary

1 → For many decades, biologists have compiled scores of data on the life spans of various bat species using data obtained by the fortuitous recapture of individuals tagged at birth. It has been found that on average, bats live three times longer than other mammals of similar size and metabolic rate.

▶ 47페이지 2문단을 참고하세요.

02 The word coincide in the passage is closest in meaning to

(A) coexist
(B) correspond
(C) disagree
(D) incorporate

Biological or physiological age, on the other hand, reflects the life expectancy and is based on physical changes in the morphology and function of the body, which may not always coincide with chronological age.

▶ 47페이지 3문단을 참고하세요.

03 According to paragraph 3, what is the reason that techniques other than measuring long bones are necessary?

(A) Juvenile bats can live only 12 days in M. lucifugus and 45 days in R. leschenaultia.
(B) Some species do not have long-bones in their juvenile period.
(C) The long-bones only grow during a limited period of development.
(D) The patterns and rates of closure of the long-bones gradually decrease after 45 days.

paragraph 3 is marked with an arrow [→].

3 → Several other methods have been developed to determine the biological age of bats. The first measures the long bones, like the forearm, metacarpals, and digits, which go through a phase of rapid linear growth shortly after birth. These measurements, especially that of the forearm, can be used to distinguish juveniles from adults. A species-specific reference correlating these measurements with examples of a known-age can provide age estimates within 1-2 days with 95 percent accuracy.

▶ 49페이지 5문단을 참고하세요.

04 What is true about Phillips' examination of incremental lines in two species of bats?

(A) It explains how incremental lines are formed in bats' teeth.
(B) It offers a different method of measuring bats' age not using their teeth which counters the drawbacks of the former.
(C) It provides an example of experimentation which contradicts the theory of Klevezal and Kleinenberg.
(D) It supports the claim that 'annuli' in teeth can be used to estimate the bats' ages.

Another zoologist, C.J. Phillips, examined the incremental lines in two species of bats from known-age specimens. [■] He found that the number of incremental lines observed depended on which tooth was extracted and on the section examined, and suggested that several factors, such as mechanical stress and tooth movement, can alter the patterns of layered growth yielding non-annual cycles of dentin and cementum deposition. [■] Other researchers have found a lack of correlation between age and incremental lines in some species.

TEST 1 - 2
Tracing Language Diversification

▶ 52페이지 5문단을 참고하세요.

01 According to paragraph 5, what is true about Slavonic and Germanic?

(A) They are older than the Proto-Indo-European language.
(B) They should be learned prior to studying Latin or Greek.
(C) They have common descendent languages.
(D) They shared ancestors with Latin and Greek.

paragraph 5 is marked with an arrow [→].

This single language links modern languages around the world. Study of this language has helped identify that, although they share only a few similarities, both Slavonic and Germanic are sub-branches of a common ancestral language. Several research tasks naturally followed this hypothesis.

▶ 52페이지 5문단을 참고하세요.

02 The word dispersion is closest in meaning to

(A) scattering
(B) change
(C) Interference
(D) disapproval

First, the vocabulary of the proposed ancestral language needed to be reconstructed, before the hearth of the language could be located. After this, the routes of dispersion needed to be traced.

▶ 53페이지 6문단을 참고하세요.

03 According to paragraph 6, what is true about Quebecois French?

(A) It is a relatively modern example of language divergence.
(B) Its evolution does not fit the language divergence process.
(C) It does not qualify as an example of language divergence because it has been separate from French for so long.
(D) It has diverged to the point of being unrecognizable by native-French speakers.

paragraph 6 is marked with an arrow [→].

He suggested that new languages form through language divergence, when a language breaks down and fragments into dialects and then into discrete tongues due to separation of speakers. This can be seen in Spanish and Portuguese and is now happening with Quebecois French. Due to geographical separation, Parisian French and Quebecois French started to differ after the colonial era. Now the pronunciation and vocabulary use of the two places differ greatly.

▶ 53페이지 7문단을 참고하세요.

04 The word daunting is closest in meaning to

(A) intimidating
(B) timid
(C) urgent
(D) doubtful

7 → Finding this hearth is a daunting task, as reconstructing even a small branch is complicated. A complicating factor is that with human mobility, languages did not merely diffuse through static populations; they also spread by relocation diffusion.

TEST 2 - 1
Earth's Atmosphere

▶ 61페이지 2문단을 참고하세요.

01 According to paragraph 2, all of the following are true about molecules' escape velocities EXCEPT:

(A) Higher velocities are required in larger planets, which in turn results in more escaping molecules.
(B) A molecule's velocity and mass are some of the features that determine its existence in an atmosphere.
(C) Shorter distances between planets and stars result in hotter atmospheres which result in higher molecular velocities.
(D) Larger molecules have slower velocities at given temperatures.

paragraph 2 is marked with an arrow [→].

2 → Initially, light gases were abundant in Earth's primordial atmosphere, but gradually started to decline. This can be explained through 'Jeans escape', a classical form of thermal escape based on Maxwell's Distribution that prescribes that the kinetic energy distribution of molecules is dependent on the mass and velocity of the molecule. From this, one can conclude that the bigger the molecule, the lower its average velocity at a given temperature, which makes escape more unlikely.

▶ 62페이지 3문단을 참고하세요.

02 The word primary in the passage is closest in meaning to

(A) first
(B) main
(C) elementary
(D) latest

Three primary reasons why only nitrogen filled the environment are that it is volatile even at low temperatures, unreactive with the materials that make up the earth's crust, and very stable in the presence of solar radiation.

▶ 62페이지 3문단을 참고하세요.

03 What is the author's primary purpose of paragraph 3?

(A) To describe how long it took nitrogen to occupy the majority of the atmosphere
(B) To explain how nitrogen filled the Earth's atmosphere through volcanic activities
(C) To provide reasons why nitrogen prevailed in the atmosphere
(D) To show that oxygen is a major component of the solid earth

3 → Scientists believe that as light gases escaped from Earth's atmosphere, nitrogen began constituting a larger part of it after volcanic eruptions spewed gases, ultimately forming the main component of the secondary atmosphere. Three primary reasons why only nitrogen filled the environment are that it is volatile even at low temperatures, unreactive with the materials that make up the earth's crust, and very stable in the presence of solar radiation.

▶ 62페이지 5문단을 참고하세요.

04 The word adequate in the passage is closest in meaning to

(A) sufficient
(B) surprising
(C) absolute
(D) near

5 However, some argue that the amount of oxygen collected in the Earth's atmosphere cannot be accounted for entirely by cyanobacteria. They believe that the theory is not adequate because it can only account for 1 percent to 10 percent concentration levels, while today's atmosphere contains 21 percent.

TEST 2 - 2
The Effects of Light on Flowering

▶ 65페이지 2문단을 참고하세요.

01 The word dispersed in the passage is closest in meaning to

(A) diffused
(B) germinated
(C) protected
(D) scattered

The blossoming of flowers in plants is an intricate and delicate process which has evolved to suit plants' different environments. To maximize the probability of their seeds being successfully dispersed, plants use environmental factors to determine the current season.

▶ 66페이지 3문단을 참고하세요.

02 The author provides spinach as an example of a short-night plant in paragraph 3 in order to

(A) Clarify the concept of the critical photoperiod and how it is different for each species
(B) Explain that spinach has a critical photoperiod of less than eleven hours
(C) Provide an example of a plant that exhibits characteristics that do not correspond to short-night plants
(D) Contrast spinach with other types of plants mentioned in the paragraph

The threshold for the length of darkness of both long-night and short-night plants differ by species. The duration of this is called the critical photoperiod. For example, spinach, a short-night plant, only produces flowers when exposed to less-than-eleven-hour intervals of darkness. Spinach's critical photoperiod is, therefore, eleven hours.

▶ 66페이지 5문단을 참고하세요.

03 According to paragraph 5, which of the following types of light will NOT reset a plant's biological clock?

(A) Artificial light
(B) Red light
(C) Sunlight
(D) Far-red light

paragraph 5 is marked with an arrow [→].

5 → This mechanism is quite sensitive; many species of long-night plants that have their darkness interrupted for even a minute or two with either sunlight or artificial light may not flower. [■] It was found that red light shone on a plant during the night is perceived by the plant and the plant resets its biological clock.

▶ 67페이지 6문단을 참고하세요.

04 According to paragraph 6, what has been revealed about the flowering process through experiments conducted on cockleburs?

(A) The plant initiates flowering through the use of a single hormone.
(B) Every part of the plant must experience the same length of uninterrupted darkness in order to flower.
(C) A signal triggered in a leaf can induce flower production of the plant.
(D) Exposing different parts of the plant to varying lengths of darkness will always inhibit flower production.

paragraph 6 is marked with an arrow [→].

6 → The discovery of what internal factors actually signal plants to flower in response to light has overarching potential in biology and agriculture, which makes it an intriguing topic of study. Experiments conducted on cockleburs, a family of long-night plants that require more than eight hours of darkness to flower, revealed that despite their strong sensitivity to light exposure, if even a single leaf of the cocklebur experiences a long night, while the rest of the plant is subjected to short nights, it still produced flowers.

TEST 3 - 1
Naturalistic Painting

▶ 75페이지 1문단을 참고하세요.

01 The word underpinning in the passage is closest in meaning to

(A) basis
(B) column
(C) center
(D) evidence

1 → The civilization of Ancient Greece, which lasted from the 8th century to the mid-1st century BC, had a lasting cultural influence over such a huge area, and over such powerful empires that it is often considered the underpinning of Western culture.

▶ 75페이지 1문단을 참고하세요.

02 According to paragraph 1, all of the following statements are true of naturalistic painters EXCEPT:

(A) They are more concerned with capturing the level of detail in an object than with capturing its beauty.
(B) Their primary goal is to create as accurate a portrayal of what is perceived as possible.
(C) Many consider the Ancient Greeks to be the best naturalistic painters to this day.
(D) The subjects of their paintings more often tend to be naturally occurring events and rarely man-made constructions.

paragraph 1 is marked with an arrow [→].

1 → The civilization of Ancient Greece, which lasted from the 8th century to the mid-1st century BC, had a lasting cultural influence over such a huge area, and over such powerful empires that it is often considered the underpinning of Western culture. Historians have discovered that even paintings from Ancient Greece had a strong influence on art in remote parts of Europe for millennia to come.
One such artistic influence was the movement known as naturalism.

▶ 75페이지 2문단을 참고하세요.

03 Which of the following is true of the contest mentioned in paragraph 2?

(A) The contest was held as a means to determine which of the two painters was better.
(B) Parrhasius won the contest without ever showing his painting behind the curtain to Zeuxis.
(C) Even after losing the contest, Zeuxis became more popular thanks to its publicity.
(D) Parrhasius' winning painting was displayed in the Capitol of Rome.

2 → In Ancient Greece, the early naturalistic painters tended to put more emphasis on skill than on creativity, and painters of Greece would often compare their works to see which was more 'realistic'. While the artists' creativity was largely subjective, a brushstroke was an objective means of assessment.

▶ 77페이지 4문단을 참고하세요.

04 The word duplication in the passage is closest in meaning to

(A) multiplication
(B) conformation
(C) imitation
(D) germination

belief became that painting to resemble nature as closely as possible is not really art, but rather an act of duplication. There have not only been convincing arguments which support this claim, but also several credible arguments that oppose it.

TEST 3 - 2
Two Types of Evolutionary Theories

▶ 79페이지 2문단을 참고하세요.

01 The phrase successive adaptations in the passage is closest in meaning to

(A) Adaptations that are advantageous
(B) Adaptations that come one after another
(C) Adaptations that occur gradually
(D) Adaptations that occur at the same time

The fact that these fossils displayed successive adaptations was held as an example of gradualism until 100 years later, when it was shown they were not, in fact, even successive members of a single line of descent, let alone stages of an unbroken, gradually evolving lineage.

▶ 80페이지 3문단을 참고하세요.

02 According to paragraph 3, which of the following statements is most accurate about punctuated equilibrium?

(A) Unlike gradualism, it required an external factor to set the changes in motion.
(B) It was introduced by Darwin after he announced his well known work the 'Origin of Species'.
(C) It is a theory made to explain the lack of fossils of intermediate organisms.
(D) It insists that organisms took very little time to evolve, through an extended state of little evolutionary change between generations.

paragraph 3 is marked with an arrow [→].

3 → Scientists studying fossils noted that the evolution of some species was nearly 'mapped out,' while others had a few, very different species along the evolutionary course, with few or no intermediary fossils. They envisaged that this second group's evolution must have occurred rapidly to produce a great change over a short period. They reasoned that there had to be another evolutionary method that was quicker and left fewer intermediate species, thus the idea of punctuated equilibrium was formed.

▶ 80페이지 3문단을 참고하세요.

03 According to paragraph 3, how did Darwin feel about his gradualism theory?

(A) He thought that it was not good enough to cover every missing link.
(B) He thought that the prevailing influences of progressive creationism could invalidate gradualism after Darwin's death.
(C) He was afraid that catastrophism and progressive creationism could threaten its prestige.
(D) He thought that his theory can disprove catastrophism through arguments made in 'Origin of Species'.

3 → Scientists studying fossils noted that the evolution of some species was nearly 'mapped out,' while others had a few, very different species along the evolutionary course, with few or no intermediary fossils. They envisaged that this second group's evolution must have occurred rapidly to produce a great change over a short period. They reasoned that there had to be another evolutionary method that was quicker and left fewer intermediate species, thus the idea of punctuated equilibrium was formed.

▶ 81페이지 4문단을 참고하세요.

04 The word pertains in the passage is closest in meaning to

(A) varies
(B) points
(C) responds
(D) refers

for the periods of apparent stasis in the fossil record. The term genetic change, on the other hand, pertains to changes in the population when natural selection acts on the genetic variations of a population.

TEST 4 - 1
Griffith and Transformation

▶ 89페이지 1문단을 참고하세요.

01 In paragraph 1, what point does the author make about Frederick Griffith and the era he was in?

(A) Griffith undertook one of the most pivotal experiments of the Enlightenment.
(B) Griffith's findings corresponded with the era he was living in, which was a time of great scientific advancements.
(C) Theories of Darwin and Griffith played a crucial role in the transition from Enlightenment to Romanticism.
(D) Griffith was lucky to have the technology and education he needed in order to conduct experiments on pneumococci.

1 The 19th century Romantic Movement reshaped science by opening new avenues of research that were unheard of under the Enlightenment's classical approaches. Major breakthroughs, such as Darwin's theory of evolution, were developed during this period, along with advances in physics, non-Euclidean geometry and organic chemistry. During this time, science became a major source for increasing humankind's knowledge.

▶ 90페이지 3문단을 참고하세요.

02 The word progenitor in the passage is closest in meaning to

(A) protagonist
(B) ancestor
(C) descendent
(D) prototype

They held that each strain had emerged from, and was genetically similar to their progenitor, through an evolutionary lineage determined by Darwinian natural selection resulting in the death of unfit bacterial cells.

▶ 90페이지 3문단을 참고하세요.

03 The word contention in the passage is closest in meaning to

(A) acclaim
(B) competition
(C) convention
(D) dispute

Griffith's findings, though generally neglected after the initial contention against them subsided, revealed that his original supposition was incorrect by showing that bacteria are able to acquire genes without the need for reproducing as well.

▶ 91페이지 5문단을 참고하세요.

04 The phrase akin to in paragraph 5 is closest in meaning to

(A) similar to
(B) applicable to
(C) contrary to
(D) unknown to

He showed that bacteria could reproduce sexually and substantiated the hypothesis by proving that they are endowed with genetic systems akin to those of higher-level organisms, thus opening a new realm for scientists to study the genetic basis of life and winning the 1958 Nobel Prize in Physiology or Medicine.

TEST 4 - 2
Maximilian Weber and His Influence

▶ 94페이지 2문단을 참고하세요.

01 The word consolidating in the passage is closest in meaning to

(A) actualizing
(B) solidifying
(C) compacting
(D) defeating

For example, Napoleon Bonaparte gained his fame through his military feats, immediately consolidating absolute political power over France and reforming the country. His defeat during the Napoleonic Wars, however, resulted in the abrupt end of his reign as emperor and the beginning of his exile.

▶ 94페이지 3문단을 참고하세요.

02 What is the true characteristic of iron cage?

(A) It is a phenomenon of a growing number of people acting for definite aims in their social lives.
(B) It is an imaginary cage proposed by Weber's critics that suggests that his theories have many limitations.
(C) It is the idea created by Weber in order to argue against the criticisms of detractors.
(D) It forces the governments to work to fulfill the ideal values of every member of the society.

First, they believed that the standardization of a variety of concepts of authority and Weber's theoretical notion of an 'iron cage', in which the increased rationalization of modern life causes individuals to be driven purely by objective, rather than by values, was an oversimplified, limited idea of authority.

▶ 94페이지 3문단을 참고하세요.

03 According to paragraph 3, Which of the following is NOT the drawback of Weber's theory that was criticized?

(A) It defined authority to be too objective driven and unconcerned with values.
(B) It homogenized the concepts and characteristics of authority.
(C) It failed to differentiate between reigning and governing.
(D) It supported the notion of 'iron cage' which helped defining reigning and governing.

paragraph 3 is marked with an arrow [→].

3 Although Weber's theory has strongly influenced the aspects of sociology that deal with leadership, scholars have pointed out two flaws in it. First, they believed that the standardization of a variety of concepts of authority and Weber's theoretical notion of an 'iron cage', in which the increased rationalization of modern life causes individuals to be driven purely by objective, rather than by values, was an oversimplified, limited idea of authority.

▶ 95페이지 5문단을 참고하세요.

04 The word prevalent in the passage is closest in meaning to

(A) potential
(B) rare
(C) existing
(D) common

5 Weber stressed that the importance of theories of authority is not to label, or classify, prevalent forms of leadership in history, but rather to show how the state of authority transits from one type to another.

TEST 5 - 1
Pasteur and the The Origin of Life

▶ 103페이지 2문단을 참고하세요.

01 The word sterile in the passage is closest in meaning to

(A) normal
(B) controlled
(C) fine
(D) clean

In the first, a glass filled with meat broth, which would have fermented in open air, was placed in a sealed box that was completely sterile and had a filter over its opening.

▶ 103페이지 3문단을 참고하세요.

02 According to paragraph 3, which of the following is true about biogenesis?

(A) The fundamental concept of biogenesis was first suggested by Louis Pasteur.
(B) Biogenesis was suggested due to spontaneous generation being proven false.
(C) Spontaneous generation used to be a minor theory in the past.
(D) Predecessors of Pasteur failed to empirically prove biogenesis.

paragraph 3 is marked with an arrow [→].

3 → Unsurprisingly, Pasteur's experiments were eye-openers, having definitively disproved the antiquated theory of spontaneous generation and giving birth to biogenesis. Even though he was the first to empirically prove this, he was not the first scientist to propose this type of theory.

▶ 105페이지 4문단을 참고하세요.

03 The word simulate in the passage is closest in meaning to

(A) stimulate
(B) imitate
(C) reflect
(D) define

The water was boiled to produce evaporation, then the electrodes were fired to simulate lightning through the atmosphere and water vapor, and then it was cooled again to condense the water back into the first beaker in a repetitive cycle.

▶ 105페이지 4문단을 참고하세요.

04 The word namely in the passage is closest in meaning to

(A) that is
(B) especially
(C) obviously
(D) generally

Although nucleic acids were not formed, the 20 common amino acids were formed in various concentrations. This was interesting because amino acids can potentially create the most basic component of most living creatures, namely DNA.

TEST 5 - 2
Early Research on Air

▶ 107페이지 2문단을 참고하세요.

01 According to paragraph 2, why did Boyle burn the substances in a vacuum?

(A) To illustrate what happens when air is removed from earth
(B) To provide evidence for a previously undiscovered feature of air
(C) To show the characteristics of oxygen in relation to combustible other substances
(D) To explain how air can destroy certain substances

paragraph 2 is marked with an arrow [→].

2 → It was not until the seventeenth century that the understanding of air was seriously pursued by scientists. However, due to the lack of scientific instruments and the need for those beyond the usual tools, their experiments soon faced limitations. For example, Robert Boyle, a British scientist known for Boyle's Law, began a series of experiments to find out the composition of air through combustion.

▶ 107페이지 2문단을 참고하세요.

02 The word vague in the passage is closest in meaning to

(A) obscure
(B) comprehensive
(C) invisible
(D) specific

His finding was not, however, recognized by the scientific community of the day because his definition of the component of air responsible for combustion was vague. In addition, most scientists were reportedly more interested in finding the chemical composition of air than in its physical characteristics.

▶ 107페이지 2문단을 참고하세요.

03 In paragraph 2, Boyle's experiment on the properties of air could not receive attention from other scientists at that time because

(A) He lacked the ability to clarify his purpose and progress in the experiment.
(B) He successfully identified two compounds of which air is comprised.
(C) Other scientists did not appreciate the invention of a vacuum.
(D) Scientists demanded conclusions from a chemical perspective.

His finding was not, however, recognized by the scientific community of the day because his definition of the component of air responsible for combustion was vague. In addition, most scientists were reportedly more interested in finding the chemical composition of air than in its physical characteristics. Thus, he shifted the focus of his research to air's chemical aspects and in 1659, with continuous effort, discovered that both hydrogen and nitric oxide gases were present in air.

▶ 109페이지 5문단을 참고하세요.

04 The word unveiled in the passage is closest in meaning to

(A) concealed
(B) deviated
(C) revealed
(D) disproved

With the efforts of these scientists, the properties of the air have been gradually unveiled. They have even successfully broken down all of the components of atmospheric air and calculated their proportions.

TEST 6 - 1
Photography as an Art

▶ 117페이지 2문단을 참고하세요.

01 According to paragraph 2, which of the following is true about Figuier?

(A) Apart from the argument that focuses on whether photographers are artists or not, he foresaw a bigger paradigm and thought that photography would bring bigger, positive influence on the artistic taste of the general public.
(B) He thought that with the help of the lens, the quality of life improved just as they did with applied science.
(C) He insisted that photographers should stand up for themselves to be treated as equally as artists, because lens is an instrument superior to the pencil and dye brush.
(D) He believed that applied science benefited quality of life, although it was not enough to improve artistic expression and taste.

paragraph 2 is marked with an arrow [→].

2 → Chamberlain was not the only photographer to fight denigration of photography. Earlier, between 1851 and 1862, famous photographers such as Antoine Claudet, Andre Disderi, and William Lake Price published articles in professional journals attempting to analyze the aesthetic similarities and differences between graphic works and photographs and to convince readers that photography was actually an art.

▶ 118페이지 3문단을 참고하세요.

02 According to paragraph 3, why did some people begin to question the camera?

(A) The images produced were not as clear as previously thought.
(B) The pictures that were produced were too much like art to be called a mechanical process.
(C) The photographs produced were too detailed and too accurate in capturing images.
(D) The photographs produced were too much like 'high art' still lifes, genre scenes and allegorical costumes.

paragraph 3 is marked with an arrow [→].

3 → Later, photographers, in an effort to compete with high art, focused on still-lifes, allegorical costumes, genre scenes and composite images. However, as the novel idea of capturing images began to wear off, people began to question whether the camera's images were too accurate and detailed.

▶ 118페이지 4문단을 참고하세요.

03 The word quest in the passage is closest in meaning to

(A) argument
(B) search
(C) question
(D) experiment

4 With the rise and fall of pictorialism, struggles over artistic nature and the quest to determine what truly constituted art raged on for over a century.

▶ 118페이지 4문단을 참고하세요.

04 The word narrative in the passage is closest in meaning to

(A) fictional
(B) story-like
(C) natural
(D) artistic

The unique power of photography is its disposition to form the varies of textural experience and the contrasts in lighting, rather than narrative content, regardless of whether the images were considered documents or art.

TEST 6 - 2
How and Why Birds Learn to Sing

▶ 121페이지 1문단을 참고하세요.

01 The word elaborate in the passage is closest in meaning to

(A) simple
(B) effective
(C) complicated
(D) laborious

1 Beautifully complex birdsongs have inspired our greatest poets and composers, and aroused the curiosity of biologists. They wondered how and why such an elaborate communication form developed among birds.

▶ 121페이지 2문단을 참고하세요.

02 Which of the following can be supported about female flycatchers by the dummy experiment in paragraph 2?

(A) They are more attracted to natural songs than recordings.
(B) They have poor eyesight and thus depend heavily on their hearing.
(C) The probability that they will sing depends on multiple external factors.
(D) They were trapped in nest-boxes in a way that supported Darwin's proposal.

2 → Birdsongs, generally regarded as an attribute of males, are in some rare species produced by females with complexity comparable to those of males. In general though, male songbirds are the sources of these complex songs. Darwin suggested that this was the result of sexual selection because females choose mates with more complex songs.

▶ 122페이지 3문단을 참고하세요.

03 According to paragraph 3 how do birds with innate ability to sing react to the introduction of new singing styles?

(A) They modify their songs by including the sounds that they hear.
(B) They are not very susceptible to adaptations when exposed to songs.
(C) They learn the new song and store it in their memory.
(D) They replace the old song with the newly introduced song.

paragraph 3 is marked with an arrow [→].

3 → Just as their reasons for singing vary, so do the ways that songbirds learn to sing. Some are born with an innate knowledge of the songs, while others learn them from older birds then add to them to create personalized songs, and still others incorporate auditory stimuli into their repertoire and eventually end up with thousands of variations.

▶ 123페이지 4문단을 참고하세요.

04 The word temporal in the passage is closest in meaning to

(A) fundamental
(B) tonal
(C) immaterial
(D) time-related

It can be shown that disturbing auditory feedback during adult Zebra Finches' singing caused their song to deteriorate. This 'decrystallization' is a marked loss of the temporal and spectral stereotypy seen in crystallized songs.

TEST 7 - 1
Functions of Roots

▶ 131페이지 1문단을 참고하세요.

01 The word anchor is closest in meaning to

(A) control
(B) fasten
(C) speed
(D) damper

1 Roots, the water-absorbing organs of a plant, are present on essentially all vascular plants and serve three primary functions: to anchor the plant to a substrate, to absorb nutrients through osmosis, and to store food reserves.

▶ 131페이지 3문단을 참고하세요.

02 Which of the following is true about the habitats of the red mangrove?

(A) They are inland areas of the northern and southern hemisphere.
(B) They are favorable places in which a variety of plants grow and adapt.
(C) They are devoid of plant life due to their high temperatures.
(D) They lack what other plants essentially need.

Mangrove roots, however, are well-suited to the region. The red mangrove, a tropical tree which colonizes coastlines and brackish water between the northern and southern latitudes of 25 degrees, can often be found on the water's edge.

▶ 131페이지 3문단을 참고하세요.

03 The word prominent is closest in meaning to

(A) tall
(B) conspicuous
(C) practical
(D) insignificant

These are distinguished from other mangroves by the prominent prop roots extending into the water from high up on their stems. They thrive in the highly saline habitats by not relying on traditional roots growing under the substrate. Instead, it is assumed, lenticels, or pores, on their prop roots act as conduits for supplying oxygen for respiration to the subterranean roots.

▶ 131페이지 3문단을 참고하세요.

04 According to paragraph 3, reverse osmosis, allows plants to

(A) obtain freshwater using negative pressure.
(B) absorb the salt necessary for ultra-filtration.
(C) be drained of their freshwater.
(D) draw water from the leaves to the roots.

3 → For plants which are constantly exposed to harsh environments, such as salt water swamps, survival is more challenging due to the lack of basic necessities. The deeper roots of most plants die because of the lack of oxygen under the waterlogged soil, leading to the plant's slow death. Mangrove roots, however, are well-suited to the region.

TEST 7 - 2
History of The Patent Law

▶ 135페이지 3문단을 참고하세요.

01 Why does the author mention the letters patent system in paragraph 3?

(A) To explain the etymology of the word 'patent'
(B) To show that patents used to be granted to persons favored by the monarchy
(C) To place the Venetian Senate's Act in the context of the history of patent law
(D) To prove that the British started the idea of a standardized patent system

3 Even before the Venetian Senate's act of 1474, isolated monopolies were granted in Europe. For example, in England the monarchs would grant letters patent, or 'letters that lie open', to people in their graces, granting them a monopoly to produce or provide specific goods and services.

▶ 136페이지 3문단을 참고하세요.

02 Why does the author mention Industrial Revolution in paragraph 3?

(A) To prove that the establishment of a patent system brought about the Industrial Revolution
(B) To show that the Industrial Revolution was an important component of the socioeconomic development of Great Britain
(C) To demonstrate an example of how patents have changed people's perceptions of the role of the Industrial Revolution
(D) To show that the increased rate of invention of the time required major changes in the patent system

This led to inefficiency and left room for the corruption that brought about the Statute of Monopolies of 1624, which required courts to outlaw all monopolies but those based on true inventive intentions. When the Industrial Revolution spurred an explosive number of new inventions, patents became an increasingly important component of the socioeconomic machine.

▶ 136페이지 4문단을 참고하세요.

03 The word disputes in the passage is closest in meaning to?

(A) arguments
(B) grants
(C) confusions
(D) investigations

Initially, each of the 13 colonies formed their own patent systems, which led to disputes, such as identifying the true inventor of the steamboat, as different inventors were registered in the patent archives of two colonies.

▶ 137페이지 5문단을 참고하세요.

04 The word burgeoning in the passage is closest in meaning to

(A) coincidental
(B) moderating
(C) flourishing
(D) troublesome

5 Throughout history the concept of protecting one's rights to one's own creations has advanced along with the burgeoning capitalist, industrial world economy, which is increasingly dependent on new technological advancements.

TEST 8 - 1
Communication of Ants

▶ 145페이지 1문단을 참고하세요.

01 Which of the following is NOT an advantage of communal insects like ants stated in paragraph 1?

(A) Assignment of specific duties to members
(B) Systematic stability in the colony
(C) Positive influence on the neighboring ecosystem
(D) Better foraging through communication

1 Ants have several advantages over solitary insects such as increased system reliability and division of labor. The major advantage, however, is the communication among members.

▶ 145페이지 1문단을 참고하세요.

02 The word retain in the passage is closest in meaning to

(A) discard
(B) stimulate
(C) keep
(D) encourage

This allows the colony to regulate its foraging activity and retain a memory of previously rewarding locations. To do this, ants rely on chemical signals called pheromones. When foragers find a successful foraging site, they deposit a trail of pheromones on their return to the nest.

▶ 145페이지 3문단을 참고하세요.

03 According to paragraph 3, what is unique about the pheromones of Pharaoh's ants?

(A) They allow the ants to live a longer period of time by working complementarily while foraging.
(B) They are short-lived pheromones which guide them back to the colony.
(C) They allow them to return to their forage sites for a longer period of time.
(D) They can repel ants that are near the foraging spot in order to protect their prey items from others.

paragraph 3 is marked with an arrow [→].

3 → [■] Furthermore, in Pharaoh's ant, research has shown distinct, short-lived and long-lived attractive-trail pheromone effects, as well as a short-lived repellent pheromone. [■] In contrast to most ant pheromones, the long-lived trails of Pharaoh's ants can persist for several days, allowing the trail network to be explored for a longer period of time. [■]

▶ 145페이지 3문단을 참고하세요.

04 The word reinforced in the passage is closest in meaning to

(A) strengthened
(B) explored
(C) reconstructed
(D) followed

Sections of the network leading to food are reinforced with the short-lived trail pheromone, and the repellent pheromone is placed immediately after non-rewarding trails. [■] These three scents seem to work complementarily.

TEST 8 - 2
Calculating the Age of Earth

▶ 149페이지 1문단을 참고하세요.

01 According to paragraph 1, which of the following can be inferred about scientists before the eighteenth century?

(A) Scientists generally avoided conforming to the ideas regarding the age of Earth established by religious leaders.
(B) Scientific facts were not the dominant sources of information used to calculate the age of the earth prior to the mid - 1700s.
(C) Prior to the mid-1700s, evidence indicating the true age of Earth did not exist.
(D) They believed that rock layers of Earth had remained uniform throughout the ages. paragraph 1 is marked with an arrow [→].

1 → Religion was the only source of historical and scientific knowledge, such as the age of Earth, until the mid-eighteenth century. After this time, scientists began more openly questioning the formation of Earth, and while studying the different rock layers of it, they recognized that it had gone through various changes over a period of time.

▶ 149페이지 2문단을 참고하세요.

02 In paragraph 2, what was the importance of Buffon's experiment?

(A) It became the grounds for further research that used heavy metals.
(B) It was the first scientific experiment to calculate the earth's age.
(C) It demonstrated how early attempts to determine the age of Earth were scientifically unreasonable.
(D) It showed that the globe-figure was appropriate for calculating the age of the earth.

2 In 1779, a French scientist, Comte de Buffon, attempted the first calculation of Earth's age by experimentation. Based on Earth's internal heat and rate of cooling, Buffon's approach utilized a small globe-like figure that resembled Earth in composition.

▶ 150페이지 4문단을 참고하세요.

03 The word conceivable in the passage is closest in meaning to

(A) questionable
(B) plausible
(C) powerful
(D) influential

William Thomson, the forerunning supporter of these physical measurements, believed that during Earth's primitive stage, it was a sphere of hot molten rock held together by gravity and the only conceivable source of heat energy was the nebula.

▶ 150페이지 4문단을 참고하세요.

04 The word dissipated in the passage is closest in meaning to

(A) dispersed
(B) gathered
(C) exploited
(D) generated

By estimating the rate at which heat dissipated from the nebula, scientists could determine the time necessary for Earth to cool from the molten ball of rock to its present state. Through this method, the age of Earth was calculated to be 20 to 40 million years.

TEST 9 - 1
Identifying Playful Behavior in Children

▶ 159페이지 1문단을 참고하세요.

01 The word apparent is closest in meaning to

(A) obvious
(B) large
(C) accepted
(D) sufficient

Due to these changes and the lack of an apparent distinction between playful and non-playful behaviors sociologists have continuously tried to form a complete definition of play, with three having gained widespread acceptance: the functional, the structural, and the criterion approaches.

▶ 159페이지 2문단을 참고하세요.

02 Which of the following is true of the functional approach mentioned in paragraph 2?

(A) Because the approach was developed to explain play in monkeys, it had to be revised before it could be applied to humans.
(B) It identifies playful behavior as acts that have benefits whatsoever to the performer.
(C) The majority of Symons' fellow sociologists disapproved of his approach.
(D) It identifies playful behavior as acts that do not have a clear purpose.

Paragraph 2 is marked with an arrow [→].

2 → Anthropologist Donald Symons, after observing African monkeys, developed the first of these in 1978. He defined play as an act that has neither a clear benefit, nor external goal. Following this, acts like learning are not considered play because their benefits are readily noticeable. Similarly, eating and working are not considered play because their purposes are specific and obvious.

▶ 160페이지 3문단을 참고하세요.

03 The word execution is closest in meaning to

(A) punishment
(B) understanding
(C) performance
(D) analysis

In cases such as this, the structural approach can be used. The structural approach identifies specific behaviors that are associated with play or with the playful execution of actions.

▶ 160페이지 3문단을 참고하세요.

04 Why does the author mention a push or a light punch?

(A) To show that for those who enjoy violence, fighting can also be a form of playful behavior
(B) To point out that an insignificant disagreement can be exaggerated to hateful aggression
(C) To illustrate an example of an act which is inherently repetitive and fragmented
(D) To clarify what the author means by squabble, through examples

The structural approach identifies specific behaviors that are associated with play or with the playful execution of actions. When studying an action using this approach, one begins by identifying any characteristics that often only occur during playtime, like laughter or playful squabbling, such as a push or a light punch.

TEST 9 - 2
Sentinel Behavior in Meerkats

▶ 163페이지 2문단을 참고하세요.

01 According to paragraph 2, what can be inferred about Belding's ground squirrels?

(A) They were named after the discoverer of their evolutionary behavior.
(B) Their feeding habits are closely related to that of meerkats.
(C) Squirrel sentinels warn their neighbors of a danger after they have secured safety.
(D) The squirrels that warn others of dangers run a higher risk of being preyed upon.

2 → The motivations behind this behavior have been attributed to kin selection, the evolutionary strategy that favors the reproductive success of an organism's relatives over one's own survival. In Belding's ground squirrels, individuals sound an alarm at the approach of a predator, warning its nearby relatives and thereby benefitting the population.

▶ 163페이지 2문단을 참고하세요.

02 The word credibility in the passage is closest in meaning to

(A) notoriety
(B) revenue
(C) plausibility
(D) certainty

This explanation gained credibility because research revealed that, like Belding's squirrels, meerkat communities are composed mostly of family members.

▶ 164페이지 2문단을 참고하세요.

03 The word postulating in the passage is closest in meaning to

(A) explaining
(B) speculating
(C) signifying
(D) uncovering

This follows the gene selection theory, postulating that individuals are genetically programmed to proliferate their DNA.

▶ 164페이지 3문단을 참고하세요.

04 What is true about reciprocal altruism according to paragraph 3?

(A) Unlike the scientists' assumptions, meerkats do not have designated responsibilities.
(B) Meerkats will stop displaying reciprocal altruism should another animal outside their kin appear among them.
(C) The banded mongoose's cooperative begging behavior is not an example of reciprocal altruism.
(D) It is a type of behavior that characterizes a family of species related to the meerkats.

3 A variant theory was that in order to protect their kin, meerkats demonstrated reciprocal altruism, an act that benefits another at the expense of one's own interest. If the receiver's benefit outweighs the cost of the altruist, and if the receiver is expected to also become the altruist, then evolutionarily the entire group profits from the behavior.

USHER

iBT TOEFL
FINAL TEST READING
부록 해설집

TEST 1 - 1
Method of Measuring Bats' Age

01 The word **scores of** in the passage is closest in meaning to

(A) recorded ★
(B) copious
(C) aggressive
(D) temporary

지문의 단어 **scores of**와 가장 유사한 것은?

(A) 기록된 [rikɔ́:rd] ★
(B) 많은 [kóupiəs]
(C) 공격적인 [əgrésiv]
(D) 일시적인 [témpərèri]

Vocabulary 지문의 scores of(다수)은 copious(많은)과 동의어이므로 (B)가 정답이다.

02 The word **coincide** in the passage is closest in meaning to

(A) coexist ★
(B) correspond
(C) disagree
(D) incorporate

지문의 단어 **coincide**와 가장 유사한 단어는?

(A) 동시에 같은 곳에 있다 ★ [kòuigzíst]
(B) 일치하다 [kɔ̀:rəspánd]
(C) 반대하다 [dìsəgrí:]
(D) 무형의 [inkɔ́:rpərèit]

Vocabulary 문제에 coincide가 나온 문장을 보면 which may not always coincide with chronological age.(이는 생활 연령과 늘 일치하는 것은 아니다)에서 일치하다 뜻으로 쓰였으며 동의어인 correspond가 정답이며 나머지 단어는 뜻이 일치하지 않아 오답이 된다.

03 According to paragraph 3, what is the reason that techniques other than measuring long bones are necessary?

(A) Juvenile bats ~~can live only~~ 12 days in M. lucifugus and 45 days in R. leschenaultia.
(B) ~~Some species do not have long-bones~~ in their juvenile period.
(C) The long-bones only grow during a limited period of development.
(D) The ~~patterns and rates of closure~~ of the long-bones ~~gradually decrease~~ after 45 days. ★

3단락에 의하면, 긴 뼈를 측정하는 방법 외에 다른 방법이 필요한 이유는?

(A) 어린 박쥐는 루시푸거스의 경우 12일 밖에 못살고 레스 체놀티의 경우 45일 밖에 살지 못한다.
(B) 몇몇 종들은 어린 나이에도 긴 뼈가 존재하지 않는다.
(C) 긴 뼈는 제한된 기간 동안에만 자란다.
(D) 긴뼈가 닫히는 패턴이나 속도가 45일 이후에는 점점 느려진다. ★

Fact 다음의 문장의 단점들 때문에 다른 방법이 필요하게 된다. The major disadvantage is that these bones grow only during the first few weeks of life and the valid time frame varies between species from only 12 days in M. lucifugus to as long as 45 days in R. leschenaultia.(가장 큰 단점은 이러한 뼈들은 출생 후 초반 몇 주 동안에 자라고 측정을 위한 유효 시간이 루시푸구스는 12일, 라첸날티의 경우에는 45일 정도로 달라진다는 것이다) 지문에서 살펴보면 (A)의 경우 12일~45일까지만 사는 게 아니라 뼈가 그 기간까지만 자라는 내용이므로 오답이고 (B)와 (D)의 경우 언급된 내용이 아니다. 따라서 지문에 언급된 긴 뼈는 제한된 기간 동안에만 자란다는 (C)가 정답이다.

04 What is true about Phillips' examination of incremental lines in two species of bats?

(A) ~~It explains~~ how incremental lines are formed in bats' teeth.
(B) It offers a different method of measuring bats' age ~~not~~ using their teeth which counters the drawbacks of the former. ★
(C) It provides an example of experimentation which contradicts the theory of Klevezal and Kleinenberg.
(D) ~~It supports the claim~~ that 'annuli' in teeth can be used to estimate the bats' ages.

글쓴이가 두 종의 박쥐의 발육 선을 연구한 필립스의 실험에 관해 사실인 것은?

(A) 박쥐의 치아에서 발육 선이 나타나는 ~~과정을 설명한다~~.
(B) 전 실험의 결점을 보완한 치아를 통하지 ~~않은~~ 또 다른 측정법을 제안한다. ★
(C) 클레베잘과 클레이넨버그의 이론을 반박하는 실험의 예를 제공한다.
(D) ~~치아의 '고리'를~~ 통해 박쥐의 나이를 추정할 수 있다는 주장을 강화한다.

Fact 필립스의 이론을 살펴보면 He found that the number of incremental lines observed depended on which tooth was extracted and on the section examined, and suggested that several factors, such as mechanical stress and tooth movement, can alter the patterns of layered growth yielding non- annual cycles of dentin and cementum deposition.(그는 관찰된 발육선의 숫자가 추출된 치아 종류와 검사된 부분에 따라 달라지는 것을 발견했고 기계적인 압박과 치아 움직임과 같은 여러 요소들이 상아질과 백악질의 비연간 최적 순환을 만들어 내는 층자람의 패턴을 변화시킬 수 있다고 주장했다) 특정 요소에 따라 다른 결과가 나올 수 있다고 언급함으로, 발육 선을 통한 박쥐의 나이 측정법을 연구한 클레베잘과 클레이넨버그의 이론을 반박하는 예시를 든다고 볼 수 있다. 따라서 답은 (C)이다. (B)는 치아를 통해 실험이 진행되었으므로 오답이다.

TEST 1 - 2
Tracing Language Diversification

01 According to paragraph 5, what is true about Slavonic and Germanic?

(A) They are older than the Proto-Indo-European language. ★
(B) They should be learned prior to studying Latin or Greek.
(C) They have common descendent languages.
(D) They shared ancestors with Latin and Greek.

5단락에 의하면, 슬라브어와 독어에 관해 사실인 것은?

(A) 그들은 원조 인도-유럽어보다 오래됐다. ★
(B) 그들은 라틴어나 그리스어를 배우기 전에 알아야 한다.
(C) 그들은 같은 파생언어를 가지고 있다.
(D) 그들은 라틴어와 그리스어와 같은 원형을 공유한다.

Fact 지문에서 슬라브어와 독어가 나온 부분을 살펴보면 Proto-Indo-European, which transformed into ancient Latin, Greek, and Sanskrit. (고대 라틴어, 그리스어, 산스크리트어로 변형된 인도 게르만 공통 조어라 불리는)라고 하고 although they share few similarities, both Slavonic and Germanic are sub-branches of a common ancestral language. (비록 라틴어, 그리스어, 산스크리트어가 단지 몇 유사점을 가질 뿐이지 만 슬라브어와 독일어 모두 공통 언어의 하위 계열이라는 것을 확인하도록)라고 말한다. 먼저 원조 인도-유럽어의 파생물이 라틴어와 그리스어라고 말한다. 그리고 나서 이들 또한 같은 파생물이라 말한다. 그러므로 답은 (D)이다. (A)는 오래된 것은 아니므로 오답이며, (B)는 그전에 배워야하는 연관성이 없으므로 오답이고, (C)는 파생언어가 아니므로 오답이다.

02 The word dispersion is closest in meaning to

(A) scattering
(B) change
(C) interference ★
(D) disapproval

지문의 단어 dispersion과 가장 근접한 의미의 단어는?

(A) 산란 [skǽtəriŋ]
(B) 변화 [tʃeindʒ]
(C) 방해 ★ [ìntərfíərəns]
(D) 불허가 [dìsəprúːvəl]

Vocabulary 지문의 단어 dispersion(분산)은 scattering(산란)과 동의어이므로 정답이다.

03 According to paragraph 6, what is true about Quebecois French?

(A) It is a relatively modern example of language divergence.
(B) Its evolution does not fit the language divergence process. ★
(C) It does not qualify as an example of language divergence because it has been separate from French for so long.
(D) It has diverged to the point of being unrecognizable by native-French speakers.

6단락에 의하면, 퀘벡식 불어에 대해 사실인 것은?

(A) 언어 분산의 비교적 현대 예이다.
(B) 그것의 진화는 언어 분산 과정에 맞지 않는다. ★
(C) 오랫동안 프랑스로부터 분리되어 있었기 때문에 언어분기의 예로 맞지 않는다.
(D) 프랑스 원어민이 알아들을 수 없을 정도까지 분기되었다.

Fact Quebecois French이 언급된 부분을 보면 This can be seen in Spanish and Portuguese and is now happening with Quebecois French. (이것은 스페인어와 포르투갈어에서 보여질 수 있고 현재 퀘벡식 프랑스어에서 발생하고 있다) 즉, 지금 분산되어지는 예시를 보여주려했다는 (A)가 정답이다. (B)는 분산과정이 맞으므로 오답이며, (C)는 오래되었다고 해서 예시가 안되는 것은 아니므로 오답이다. 그리고 (D)는 달라진 것은 사실이나 프랑스인들이 알아듣지 못한다는 내용은 없으므로 오답이다.

04 The word daunting is closest in meaning to

(A) intimidating
(B) timid ★
(C) urgent
(D) doubtful

지문의 단어 daunting과 가장 근접한 뜻의 단어는?

(A) 겁을 주는 [intímədèitiŋ]
(B) 소심한 ★ [tímid]
(C) 급한 [ə́ːrdʒənt]
(D) 의심스러운 [dáutfəl]

Vocabulary 지문의 단어 daunting(벅찬, 위협적인)은 intimidating(겁을 주는)과 동의어이므로 정답이다.

TEST 2 - 1
Earth's Atmosphere

01 According to paragraph 2, all of the following are true about molecules' escape velocities EXCEPT:

(A) Higher velocities are required in larger planets, which in turn ~~results in more escaping~~ molecules.
(B) A molecule's velocity and mass are some of the features that determine its existence in an atmosphere. ★
(C) Shorter distances between planets and stars result in hotter atmospheres which result in higher molecular velocities.
(D) Larger molecules have slower velocities at given temperatures.

2단락에 따르면, 대기층으로부터 방출되는 분자에 대한 것 중에 사실이 아닌 것은?

(A) 큰 행성들에게 결국 많은 분자방출을 이끌어 내는 더 높은 속도가 요구된다.
(B) 분자속도와 질량은 대기층의 존재를 결정하는 특징 중에 하나이다. ★
(C) 행성들과 별들의 거리가 가까울수록 분자속도를 빠르게 만드는 대기층의 온도가 더욱 올라간다.
(D) 주어진 온도에서 분자가 클수록 낮은 속도를 갖는다.

Fact 문제의 키워드인 molecule escaping the atmosphere (대기층에서 방출되는 분자)가 언급되는 부분을 살펴 보면 the greater the mass of the planet, the higher the required escape velocity; which ultimately results in less escaping molecules. (행성의 질량이 크면 클수록 요구되는 방출 속도가 더 높게 되며, 그것은 궁극적으로 더 적은 분자의 방출을 야기 한다)라는 내용에서 (A)의 내용은 지문과 반대된다는 것을 알 수 있으므로 답은 (A)이다.

---

02 The word primary in the passage is closest in meaning to

(A) first ★
(B) main
(C) elementary
(D) latest

지문의 단어 primary의 의미와 가장 유사한 것은?

(A) 첫째의 ★ [fəːrst]
(B) 주요한 [mein]
(C) 기본적인 [èləméntəri]
(D) 최근의 [léitist]

Vocabulary 지문의 primary(주된)은 main(주요한)과 first(첫째의)의 동의어이다. 하지만 정답은 (B)이다. (A)가 틀린 이유는 비록 동의어이긴 하나, 지문에서 쓰인 뜻은 아니기 때문이다.

---

03 What is the author's primary purpose of paragraph 3?

(A) ~~To describe how long it took~~ nitrogen to occupy the majority of the atmosphere
(B) To explain how nitrogen filled the Earth's atmosphere ~~through volcanic activities~~ ★
(C) To provide reasons why nitrogen prevailed in the atmosphere
(D) To show that ~~oxygen is a major component~~ of the solid earth

3단락에서 글쓴이가 주요하게 말하고자 하는 것은?

(A) 질소가 대기층의 대부분을 차지하는데 ~~얼마나 걸렸는지 보여주려고~~
(B) 어떻게 질소가 ~~화산활동을 통해~~ 지구의 대기층을 채웠는지 설명하려고 ★
(C) 질소가 다양한 원인을 통해 대기층에서 많아졌다는 요소 를 제공하려고
(D) ~~산소가~~ 지구지면의 ~~주요한 성분임을~~ 보여주려고

Purpose 단락의 주요 내용은 어떻게 질소량이 지구 대기층을 지배하게 되었는지에 대한 전반적인 원인 분석이다. 즉, (C)에서 말하는 어떠한 요소와 이유들로 인하여 대기층에 질소가 많아졌는지가 정답이 된다. (B)가 틀린 이유는 지구 대기층을 채웠다는 사실은 맞으나 이것이 어떠한 이유를 통해서 되었는지에 대한 설명이 부족해서이다.

---

04 The word adequate in the passage is closest in meaning to

(A) sufficient
(B) surprising
(C) absolute
(D) near ★

지문의 단어 adequate 의 의미와 가장 유사한 것은?

(A) 충분한 [səfíʃənt]
(B) 놀라운 [sərpráiziŋ]
(C) 전적인 [ǽbsəlùːt]
(D) 거의 ★ [niər]

Vocabulary 지문의 adequate(적합한)은 sufficient(충분한)와 동의어이므로 정답은 (A)이다. (D)가 틀린 이유는 문장 대입했을 때 말은 되나 동의어는 아니다.

TEST 2 - 2
The Effects of Light on Flowering

01 The word dispersed in the passage is closest in meaning to

(A) diffused ★
(B) germinated
(C) protected
(D) scattered

이 지문의 단어 dispersed와 의미상 유사한 것은?

(A) 방산된 ★ [difjú:zd]
(B) 발아된 [dʒɔ́:rmənèit]
(C) 보호된 [prətékt]
(D) 퍼뜨려진 [skǽtərd]

Vocabulary 지문의 dispersed(흩어진)는 scattered(퍼뜨려진)의 동의어이므로 정답은 (D)이다. (A)가 틀린 이유는 동의어 이기는 하나 지문에서 쓰인 뜻과는 다르기 때문이다.

02 The author provides spinach as an example of a short-night plant in paragraph 3 in order to

(A) Clarify the concept of the critical photoperiod and how it is different for each species.
(B) Explain that spinach has a critical photoperiod of less than eleven hours. ★
(C) Provide an example of a plant that exhibits characteristics that do not correspond to short-night plants.
(D) Contrast spinach with other types of plants mentioned in the paragraph.

글쓴이는 왜 3단락에서 spinach를 단야 식물의 한 예로써 언급하는가?

(A) 임계일장의 개념과 각각 종마다 이것이 어떻게 다른지를 명료하게 하기 위해서
(B) 시금치가 11시간미만의 임계일장을 갖고 있음을 설명하기 위해서 ★
(C) 단야식물에 상응하지 않는 특징을 보이는 식물의 한 예를 제공하기 위해서
(D) 시금치를 이 글에서 언급되었던 다른 식물과 대조시키기 위해서

Purpose 문제의 키워드인 spinach(시금치)가 언급이 되는 부분을 보면, The duration of this is called the critical photoperiod. For example, spinach, a short-night plant, only produces flowers when exposed to less-than-eleven-hour intervals of darkness. (그 기간은 임계일장 이라고 불린다. 예를 들어 단야식물인 시금치는 11시간 이하의 간격으로 어두움에 노출 되었을 때만 꽃을 피운다) (B)는 사실이지만 시금치를 언급한 목적이 아니다. (C)는 지문에서 언급된 사실과 다르다. (D)는 시금치를 언급한 목적이 아니다. 지문에 시금치가 11시간이하의 간격으로 어두움에 노출되었을 때만 꽃을 피운다고 하였으므로 답은 (A)이다.

03 According to paragraph 5, which of the following types of light will NOT reset a plant's biological clock?

(A) Artificial light ★
(B) Red light
(C) Sunlight
(D) Far-red light

5단락에 따르면 다음 중 어떤 종류의 빛이 식물의 생물학적 시계를 재설정하지 않는가?

(A) 인공적인 빛 ★
(B) 적외선
(C) 햇빛
(D) 원적외선

Fact But the same plant does not reset its clock when exposed to far-red light (그러나 같은 식물은 토적광에 노출되었을때 초기화 되지 않는다) 토적광에 노출될 때 초기화 되지 않는다고 언급하였으므로 (D)가 정답이다.

04 According to paragraph 6, what has been revealed about the flowering process through experiments conducted on cockleburs?

(A) The plant initiates flowering through the use of a single hormone. ★
(B) Every part of the plant must experience the same length of uninterrupted darkness in order to flower.
(C) A signal triggered in a leaf can induce flower production of the plant.
(D) Exposing different parts of the plant to varying lengths of darkness will always inhibit flower production.

6단락에 따르면 우엉에 대한 실험을 통해 개화 과정에서 밝혀진 것은 무엇인가?

(A) 식물은 하나의 호르몬을 이용함으로써 개화를 시작한다. ★
(B) 개화하기 위해서는 식물의 모든 부분이 같은 길이의 지속적인 어둠을 보내야 한다.
(C) 잎에서 촉발된 신호는 식물의 개화를 유발시킬 수 있다.
(D) 식물의 다른 부분을 다양한 어둠의 길이에 노출시키는 것은 개화하는 것을 항상 억제할 것이다.

Fact This experiment suggested that a flowering factor is sent from the leaves to the flower buds when the flowering conditions for the plants are met. (이 실험은 꽃이 피는 요인이 식물의 꽃을 피우는 조건이 맞을 때에 잎에서 꽃망울로 보내진다고 제안하였다) (A)는 한 개인지 여러 개인지 알 수가 없으므로 오답이다. (B)는 본문 내용과 반대되므로 오답이다. (D)는 다르다고 해서 항상 억제 시키는 것은 아니기 때문에 오답이다. 지문에서 꽃이 피는 신호가 잎에서부터 시작된다고 하였으므로 정답은 (C)이다.

TEST 3 - 1
Naturalistic Painting

01 The word **underpinning** in the passage is closest in meaning to

(A) basis
(B) column
(C) center ★
(D) evidence

지문의 단어 **underpinning**과 의미상 가장 유사한 것은?

(A) 기본 [béisis]
(B) 기둥 [káləm]
(C) 중앙 ★ [séntər]
(D) 증거 [évədəns]

Vocabulary 지문의 underpinning(토대)은 basis(기본)와 동의어이므로 정답은 (A)이다. (C)가 틀린 이유는 문장을 대입했을 때 말은 되나 지문에서 쓰인 뜻이 아니기 때문이다.

02 According to paragraph 1, all of the following statements are true of naturalistic painters EXCEPT:

(A) They are more concerned with capturing the level of detail in an object than with capturing its beauty.
(B) Their primary goal is to create as accurate a portrayal of what is perceived as possible.
(C) Many consider the Ancient Greeks to be ~~the best naturalistic painters~~ to this day.
(D) The subjects of their paintings more often tend to be naturally occurring events and rarely man-made constructions. ★

1단락에 따르면, 다음 중 자연주의 화가들에 대해 사실이 아닌 것은?

(A) 그들은 각각의 사물의 아름다움보다 세부 정도에 대해서 더욱 관심이 있다.
(B) 그들의 주요한 목표는 가능한 보여지는 것 그대로 정확한 묘사를 만들어내는 것이다.
(C) 많은 사람들은 오늘날까지 고대 그리스인들이 ~~최고의 자연주의 화가~~라고 생각한다.
(D) 그들의 그림의 주제는 대체적으로 자연적으로 발생한 사건을 다루는 경향이 있고 사람이 만든 구조물은 거의 다루지 않는 경향이 있다. ★

Fact 문제의 naturalistic painters (자연주의 화가)가 언급된 부분을 살펴보면 (A)의 내용 realistically as possible (가능한 한 사실적으로) (B)의 내용 meticulous detail and near-perfect symmetry (섬세한 묘사와 완벽에 가까운 대칭성) (D)의 내용 world's natural objects, people and unadorned scenery (세상의 자연물, 사람들 그리고 꾸밈없는 풍경) 모두 언급되어 있지만 (C)에서 그리스인의 최고의 자연주의 화가라는 내용은 언급되지 않았기 때문에 답은 (C)이다.

03 Which of the following is true of the contest mentioned in paragraph 2?

(A) The contest was held as a means to determine which of the two painters was better.
(B) Parrhasius won the contest without ever showing his painting ~~behind the curtain to Zeuxis~~.
(C) Even after losing the contest, ~~Zeuxis became more popular~~ thanks to its publicity.
(D) Parrhasius' winning painting ~~was displayed~~ in the Capitol of Rome. ★

다음 중 2단락에서 언급한 시합에 관련된 것 중 사실인 것은 무엇인가?

(A) 시합은 두 명의 화가 중에 누가 더 실력 있는지를 가리기 위한 방법으로써 개최되었다.
(B) 파라시우스는 ~~제욱시스에게 커튼 뒤에 있는~~ 그의 그림을 단 한번도 보여주지 않고 시합에서 이겼다.
(C) 시합에서 진 ~~제욱시스는~~ 대중의 관심 덕분에 ~~더욱 인기를 얻었다.~~
(D) 시합에서 이긴 파라시우스의 그림은 로마의 의사당에 ~~전시되었다.~~ ★

Fact 문제의 키워드인 contest (시합)이 언급된 부분을 살펴 보면 At the peak of their careers, a contest was staged to identify the greater of the two artists. (그들의 활동이 정점에 이르렀을 때, 둘 중 누가 더 위대한지 구별 하기 위해 대회가 열렸다)라는 부분에서 두 명의 화가 중 더 뛰어난 사람을 가려내기 위한 시합이었음을 알 수 있으므로 답은 (A)이다. (D)는 의사당에 전시해 달라는 요청을 받았지만 지문의 내용만으로 전시가 되었는지는 알 수 없기 때문에 답이 될 수 없다.

04 The word **duplication** in the passage is closest in meaning to

(A) multiplication ★
(B) conformation
(C) imitation
(D) germination

지문의 단어 **duplication**과 의미상 가장 유사한 것은?

(A) 증식 ★[mʌltəplikéiʃən]
(B) 형태 [kànfɔːrméiʃən]
(C) 모방 [ìmitéiʃən]
(D) 발아 [dʒɔ́ːrmənèiʃən]

Vocabulary 지문의 duplication(복제)은 imitation(모방)과 동의어이므로 정답은 (C)이다.

TEST 3 - 2
Two Types of Evolutionary Theories

01 The phrase **successive adaptations** in the passage is closest in meaning to

(A) Adaptations that are advantageous
(B) Adaptations that come one after another
(C) Adaptations that occur gradually ★
(D) Adaptations that occur at the same time

지문의 **successive adaptations**와 의미상 가장 유사한 단어는?

(A) 유리한 적응
(B) 지속적인 적응
(C) 점차적으로 발생하는 적응 ★
(D) 동시에 발생하는 적응

Vocabulary 지문의 successive(연속적)와의 동의어인 come one after another(지속적인)가 가장 유사함으로 (B)가 정답이 된다.

---

02 According to paragraph 3, which of the following statements is most accurate about punctuated equilibrium?

(A) Unlike gradualism, it required an external factor to set the changes in motion.
(B) It was introduced by Darwin after he announced his well known work the 'Origin of Species'.
(C) It is a theory made to explain the lack of fossils of intermediate organisms.
(D) It insists that organisms took very little time to evolve, through an extended state of little evolutionary change between generations. ★

3단락에 따르면, 다음 중 중단평형설에 관하여 가장 정확한 것은?

(A) 점진적 진화와 다르게 외부적 요인이 있어야 실행된다.
(B) 이는 다윈이 그의 유명한 저서 '종의 기원'을 발표한 후에 다윈에 의해 알려졌다.
(C) 이는 생물 사이사이 비어있는 화석기록을 설명하기 위해 만들어진 이론이다.
(D) 이는 세대간 진화의 변화가 거의 없는 확장된 상태를 통해 생물이 진화를 아주 짧은 시간에 할 수 있다는 것을 주장하였다. ★

Fact 문제의 키워드인 punctuated equilibrium(중단 평행설)이 있는 부분을 살펴보면, They reasoned that there had to be another evolutionary method that was quicker and left fewer intermediate species, thus the idea of punctuated equilibrium was formed.(그들은 더 빠르고 적은 종을 남기는 다른 진화방법이 있어야 한다고 추론했고, 결과적으로 중단 평형설이 만들어 졌다)라는 부분이 있다. 그러므로 부족했던 부분을 채워주려는 중단평형론의 목표를 설명하고 있는 (C)가 정답이 된다. (D)가 틀린 이유는 중단 평행론의 요지는 중간 중간 화석기록이 없는 부분을 설명하려는 것이지 생물이 단기간에 진화를 하는 것을 증명하려는 이론이 아니어서이다.

---

03 According to paragraph 3, how did Darwin feel about his gradualism theory?

(A) He thought that it was not good enough to cover every missing link.
(B) He thought that the prevailing influences of progressive creationism could invalidate gradualism after Darwin's death.
(C) He was afraid that catastrophism and progressive creationism could threaten its prestige.
(D) He thought that his theory can disprove catastrophism through arguments made in 'Origin of Species'. ★

3단락에 따르면, 다윈은 그의 점진 진화론에 대해 어떻게 생각하는가?

(A) 그는 그것이 빠진 연결고리를 다 포함할 수 없었다고 생각했다.
(B) 그는 다윈이 죽고 나서 우세했던 진보 천지창조론이 점진 진화론이 틀렸다는 것을 입증할 수 있다고 생각했다.
(C) 그는 진보 천지창조론과 격변설이 자신의 명성에 해를 줄 것을 두려워했다.
(D) 그는 그의 이론이 '종의 기원'에서 나온 주장을 통해서 격변론을 무효화할 수 있다고 생각했다. ★

Fact 3단락의 핵심은 점진적 진화론의 문제점을 제기하는 것이며, 마지막 부분에서 다윈 자신도 문제점을 인식하고 있었다는 내용이 나온다. "Better begin with this: If species really, after catastrophes, created in showers world over, my theory false."(이렇게 시작 하는게 나은 것이다: 만약 종들이 정말 재앙 후에 모든 것에 걸쳐 급격히 생성됐다면, 내 가설은 틀린 것이다)는 다윈이 자신의 이론으로는 문제점을 설명할 수 없다는 것을 인정하는 부분이기에 답은 (A)이다. (C)는 단락 어디에서도 다윈이 자신의 명성에 해가 되어 무서워했다는 내용이 없기 때문에 오답이다.

04 The word pertains in the passage is closest in meaning to

(A) varies
(B) points ★
(C) responds
(D) refers

지문의 단어 pertains 와 의미상 가장 유사한 것은?

(A) 다르다 [vέəri]
(B) 지적하다 ★ [pɔint]
(C) 공표했다 [rispá:nd]
(D) 확증했다 [rifɔ́:r]

Vocabulary 단어 pertains(관련되다)는 refers(연관되다)와 동의어이므로 (D)가 답이다

TEST 4 - 1
Griffith and Transformation

01 In paragraph 1, what point does the author make about Frederick Griffith and the era he was in?

(A) Griffith undertook one of the most pivotal experiments of the Enlightenment.
(B) Griffith's findings corresponded with the era he was living in, which was a time of great scientific advancements.
(C) Theories of Darwin and Griffith played a crucial role in the transition from Enlightenment to Romanticism. ★
(D) Griffith was lucky to have the technology and education he needed in order to conduct experiments on pneumococci.

1단락에 따르면, 프레드릭 그리피스와 그가 살았던 시대에 대해 글쓴이가 주장하는 것은?

(A) 그리피스의 실험은 계몽시대에서 가장 중요한 실험 중 하나였다.
(B) 그리피스의 연구결과는 그가 살고 있던 과학이 대단히 발전한 시대와 연관되었다.
(C) 다윈과 그리피스의 이론들은 계몽시대에서 낭만주의로 전환하는데 중요한 역할을 하였다. ★
(D) 그리피스는 폐렴균에 실험을 할 수 있는 기술과 지식이 있어 운이 좋았었다.

Fact 문제의 키워드인 Fred Griffith와 the era가 언급된 부분을 1단락에서 찾으면 During the 19th and 20th centuries, the practice of science became much more professionally institutionalized than it had been. One of the great breakthroughs in biology is attributed to Fred Griffith of the British Ministry of Health. (19세기와 20세기 동안에, 과학 실험은 과거 보다 좀 더 전문적으로 제도화되었다. 생물학에서의 가장 큰 발전은 영국 보건복지부의 프레데릭 그리피스의 덕분이다)이라 한다. 즉 프레드 그리피스의 업적은 19세기와 20세기 과학발전과 연관되어 있다는 것을 볼 수 있다. 그러므로 정답은 (B)이다.

02 The word progenitor in the passage is closest in meaning to

(A) protagonist ★
(B) ancestor
(C) descendent
(D) prototype

지문의 단어 progenitor과 의미상 가장 유사한 것은?

(A) 주인공 ★ [proutǽgənist]
(B) 선조 [ǽnsestər]
(C) 후손 [diséndənt]
(D) 원형 [próutətaɪp]

Vocabulary 지문의 progenitor(조상)은 ancestor(선조)과 동의어이므로 정답은 (B)이다.

03 The word contention in the passage is closest in meaning to

(A) acclaim
(B) competition ★
(C) convention
(D) dispute

지문의 단어 contention과 의미상 가장 유사한 것은?

(A) 칭송 [əkléim]
(B) 경쟁 ★ [kəmpətíʃən]
(C) 집회 [kənvénʃən]
(D) 논쟁 [dispjú:t]

Vocabulary 지문의 contention (논쟁)은 dispute (논쟁)와 동의어이므로 정답은 (D)이다.

04 The phrase akin to in paragraph 5 is closest in meaning to

(A) similar to
(B) applicable to
(C) contrary to ★
(D) unknown to

지문의 단어 akin to와 의미상 가장 유사한 것은?

(A) 유사한
(B) 응용할 수 있는
(C) 반대로 ★
(D) 알려지지 않은

Vocabulary 지문의 akin to(유사한)과 동의어인 similar to(유사한)가 정답이 된다.

TEST 4 - 2
Maximilian Weber and His Influence

01 The word consolidating in the passage is closest in meaning to

(A) actualizing
(B) solidifying
(C) compacting ★
(D) defeating

지문의 단어 consolidating과 의미상 가장 유사한 것은?

(A) 실현하는
(B) 굳히는
(C) 압축하는 ★
(D) 패배시키는

Vocabulary 지문의 consolidating(통합하는)은 solidifying(굳히는)과 동의어이므로 정답은 (B)이다.

02 What is the true characteristic of iron cage?

(A) It is a phenomenon of a growing number of people acting for definite aims in their social lives.
(B) It is an imaginary cage proposed by Weber's ~~critics~~ that suggests that his theories have many limitations. ★
(C) It is the idea created by Weber ~~in order to argue against~~ the criticisms of detractors.
(D) It forces the ~~governments~~ to work to fulfill the ~~ideal values~~ of every member of the society.

iron cage 의 참 특징은 무엇인가?

(A) 그것은 점점 많은 수의 사람들이 명확한 목표를 가지고 사회를 살아가는 현상이다.
(B) 그것은 베버의 이론이 많은 제한을 가지고 있다며 베버의 ~~비판자들이~~ 제시한 허상의 새장이다. ★
(C) 그것은 비판자들의 비난을 ~~논박하고자~~ 베버가 만든 발상이다.
(D) 이것은 ~~정부로~~ 하여금 사회의 모든 멤버에 ~~이상적인~~ 가치를 충족시키도록 강요한다.

Fact 문제의 키워드인 iron cage가 언급된 단락을 살펴보면 'iron cage', Weber's theoretical notion that the increased rationalization of modern life causes individuals to be driven purely by objective, rather than by values.('iron cage'의 이론적인 개념의 표준화가 권력의 과도하게 단순화되고 제한된 사상이라고 믿었다)라고 논한다. 그러므로 점점 많은 사람이 명확한 목표의식만으로 사회를 살아간다는 (A)가 정답이다.

03 According to paragraph 3, Which of the following is NOT the drawback of Weber's theory that was criticized?

(A) It defined authority to be too objective driven and unconcerned with values.
(B) It homogenized the concepts and characteristics of authority.
(C) It failed to differentiate between reigning and governing. ★
(D) ~~It supported the notion of 'iron cage'~~ which helped defining reigning and governing.

3단락에서 다음 중 베버의 이론이 비판받은 문제점이 아닌 것은?

(A) 그것은 권위가 가치에 대해 걱정하기보단 너무 목적에 의해 움직이게 만들었다.
(B) 그것은 전 세계 권위의 개념과 특징들을 균질화하였다.
(C) 그것은 군림하는 것과 통치하는 것의 차이점을 두는데 실패하였다. ★
(D) 그것은 군림하는 것과 통치하는 것의 정의를 내려주는데 도와주는 ~~'iron cage' 의 개념을 뒷받침했다.~~

Fact 문제의 키워드인 Weber's theory와 단점을 보면 그것은 It caused authority to be too objective driven, rather than worrying about values.(현대 삶의 증가된 합리화가 개인을 가치 대신 오직 목적에 의해만 움직이게 한다)와 standardized the concepts and characteristics of authority around the world.(단순히 여러개념들을 표준화했다), 그리고 failed to differentiate between reigning and governing.(군림하는 것과 통치하는 것의 차이점을 두지 못했다) 했다는 점을 알 수 있다. 따라서 답은 관련없는 (D)이다.

04 The word prevalent in the passage is closest in meaning to

(A) potential
(B) rare
(C) existing ★
(D) common

지문의 단어 prevalent과 의미상 가장 유사한 것은?

(A) 잠재적인 [pouténʃəl]
(B) 드문 [rɛər]
(C) 존재하는 ★[igzístiŋ]
(D) 일반적인 [kámən]

Vocabulary 지문의 prevalent(널리 분포된)은 common(일반적인)과 동의어이므로 정답은 (D)이다.

TEST 5 - 1
Pasteur and the The Origin of Life

01 The word sterile in the passage is closest in meaning to

(A) normal
(B) controlled ★
(C) fine
(D) clean

지문의 단어 sterile과 의미상 가장 유사한 것은?

(A) 보통의 [nɔ́ːrməl]
(B) 관리된★ [kəntróuld]
(C) 좋은 [fain]
(D) 깨끗한 [kliːn]

Vocabulary 지문의 sterile(소독한)은 clean(깨끗한)과 동의어이므로 정답은 (D)이다. (B)가 틀린 이유는 말은 되나 단어와 의미가 다르기 때문이다.

02 According to paragraph 3, which of the following is true about biogenesis?

(A) The fundamental concept of biogenesis was first suggested by Louis Pasteur. ★
(B) Biogenesis was suggested due to spontaneous generation being proven false.
(C) Spontaneous generation used to be a minor theory in the past.
(D) Predecessors of Pasteur failed to empirically prove biogenesis.

3단락에 따르면, 다음 중 생물 발생에 관해 사실인 것은?

(A) 생물 발생의 근본적인 개념은 루이스 파스퇴르에 의해서 처음으로 제기되었다. ★
(B) 생물 발생은 자연발생이 거짓으로 증명되었기 때문에 제시되었다.
(C) 자연발생은 과거에 별로 중요하지 않은 이론이었다.
(D) 파스퇴르의 전임자들은 생물 발생을 실증적으로 증명하는데 실패했다.

Fact 문제의 키워드인 biogenesis가 언급된 부분을 살펴보면 Even though he was the first to empirically pove this, he was not the first scientist to propose this type of theory. (비록 그가 실증적으로 이것을 증명한 첫 번째 과학자였지만, 이러한 종류의 이론을 처음으로 제안한 것은 아니었다)라고 한다. 즉, 파스퇴르 그 전에 있던 사람들은 생물 발생을 과학적으로 증명한 첫 과학자이므로 (D)가 정답이 된다. (A)가 틀린 이유는 생물 발생은 파스퇴르가 처음으로 제기한 것이 아니기 때문이다. (B)는 생물발생설이 거짓으로 증명된 자연발생의 대안으로서 제시된 것이 아니기 때문에 오답이다.

03 The word simulate in the passage is closest in meaning to

(A) stimulate ★
(B) imitate
(C) reflect
(D) define

지문의 단어 simulate 와 의미상 가장 유사한 것은?

(A) 자극하다★ [stímjulèit]
(B) 모방하다 [ímətèit]
(C) 반사하다 [riflékt]
(D) 정의하다 [difáin]

Vocabulary 지문의 simulate(가장하다)는 imitate(모방하다)와 동의어이므로 정답은 (B)이다. (A)가 틀린 이유는 단어와 철자는 비슷하나 뜻이 달라서이다.

04 The word namely in the passage is closest in meaning to

(A) that is
(B) especially★
(C) obviously
(D) generally

지문에 있는 namely 와 의미상 가장 유사한 것은?

(A) 즉
(B) 특별히★ [ímətèit]
(C) 분명히 [ábviəsli]
(D) 보편적으로 [dʒénərəli]

Vocabulary 지문의 단어 namely(즉)는 that is(즉)와 동의어이므로 정답은 (A)이다.

TEST 5 - 2
Early Research on Air

01 According to paragraph 2, why did Boyle burn the substances in a vacuum?

(A) To illustrate what happens when air is removed from earth
(B) To provide evidence for a previously undiscovered feature of air
(C) To show the characteristics of oxygen in relation to combustible other substances ★
(D) To explain how air can destroy certain substances

2단락에 따르면, 왜 보일은 진공상태에서 물질들을 연소시켰는가?

(A) 공기가 지구에서 사라졌을 때 무슨 일이 일어나는지 설명하려고
(B) 이전에 발견되지 않은 공기의 특징에 대한 증거를 보여주려고
(C) 가연성의 다른 물질과 관련된 산소의 특징을 보여주려고 ★
(D) 어떻게 공기가 특정 물질들을 파괴하는지 설명하려고

Fact 문제의 키워드인 burn(combustion:연소)가 언급된 부분을 살펴보면 Boyle had discovered the very first property of air stating that air is required for a fire to burn.(보일은 불이 타오르기 위해선 공기가 필요하다는 공기의 첫 번째 특성을 발견했다)이라는 내용을 찾을 수 있는데 공기의 특성을 발견한 내용임으로 문제의 why(이유)를 대답하는 가장 적절한 답은 (B)가 된다. (A)는 전혀 언급되지 않은 내용이며, (C)는 combustible other substances(가연성의 다른 물질)에 대한 언급이 없고 (D)는 destroy(파괴)라는 지문과 연관없는 내용이기에 오답이다.

---

02 The word vague in the passage is closest in meaning to

(A) obscure
(B) comprehensive
(C) invisible ★
(D) specific

지문의 단어 vague 와 가장 유사한 것은?

(A) 모호한 [əbskjúər]
(B) 포괄적인 [kamprihénsiv]
(C) 보이지 않는 ★[invízəbl]
(D) 구체적인 [spisífik]

Vocabulary 지문의 단어 vague(뚜렷하지 않은)은 obscure(모호한)과 동의어이므로 (A)가 답이다.

---

03 In paragraph 2, Boyle's experiment on the properties of air could not receive attention from other scientists at that time because

(A) He lacked the ability to clarify his purpose and progress in the experiment. ★
(B) He successfully identified two compounds of which air is comprised.
(C) Other scientists did not appreciate the invention of a vacuum.
(D) Scientists demanded conclusions from a chemical perspective.

2단락에서 ____ 때문에 공기의 특성에 대한 보일의 실험은 그 시대 다른 과학자들로부터 관심을 받지 못했다.

(A) 보일은 실험에서 그의 목적과 과정을 명확히 하는 능력이 부족했다. ★
(B) 보일이 성공적으로 공기를 구성하는 두가지 요소를 확인했다.
(C) 다른 과학자들은 진공의 발명을 인정하지 않았다.
(D) 과학자들은 화학적 관점으로부터의 결론을 요구했다.

Fact 문제의 키워드인 scientist가 언급된 부분을 살펴보면 In addition, most scientists were reportedly more interested in finding the chemical composition of air than in its physical characteristics.(게다가, 기록에 의하면 대부분의 과학자들이 공기의 물리적 특성보다 화학적 성분을 알아내는데 더 흥미가 있었다) 라고 제시되었다. 이 과학자들이 화학 영역에 더 관심이 많았다는 것을 알 수 있으므로 답은 (D)가 된다. (A)는 언급되지 않은 사실이며, (B)는 인정 받지 못한 이유가 successfully(성공적으로)라는 긍정적인 말로 받고 있어 오답이다. (C) 역시 vacuum(진공)에 대한 다른 과학자들의 의견은 언급되어 있지 않기 대문에 오답이다.

---

04 The word unveiled in the passage is closest in meaning to

(A) concealed
(B) deviated
(C) revealed
(D) disproved★

지문에 있는 unveiled 와 의미상 가장 유사한 것은?

(A) 숨겨진 [kənsí:l]
(B) 벗어난 [dí:vièit]
(C) 드러난 [rivíːl]
(D) 틀렸음이 입증된 ★ [disprúːv]

Vocabulary unveiled(밝혀진)은 revealed(드러난)과 동의어이므로 (C)가 답이다.

TEST 6 - 1
Photography as an Art

01 According to paragraph 2, which of the following is true about Figuier?

(A) Apart from the argument that focuses on whether photographers are artists or not, he foresaw a bigger paradigm and thought that photography would bring bigger, positive influence on the artistic taste of the general public.
(B) He thought that with the help of the lens, the quality of life improved just as they did with applied science. ★
(C) He insisted that photographers should stand up for themselves to be treated as equally as artists, because lens is an instrument superior to the pencil and dye brush.
(D) He believed that applied science benefited quality of life, although it was not enough to improve artistic expression and taste.

2단락에서 피기에에 관해 사실인 것은?

(A) 사진작가들이 예술가냐 아니냐는 논쟁에서 떠나, 그는 더 큰 패러다임을 예견하고 사진이 사회에 더크고 긍정 적인 영향을 미치게 될 것이라고 예견했다.
(B) 그는 새로운 도구인 렌즈의 도움이 응용과학처럼 삶의 질을 개선시켰다고 생각했다. ★
(C) 그는 사진작가들이 예술가와 동등하게 대접 받기 위해 스스로 피력해야 한다고 주장하는데 왜냐하면 렌즈는 연필과 물감 붓보다 더 발전된 도구이기 때문이다.
(D) 그는 응용과학이 예술적 표현과 감각을 향상시킬 수 없음에도 삶의 질에 도움을 주었다고 믿었다.

Fact 문제의 키워드인 Figuier가 언급된 부분을 살펴보면 Their point-of-view was echoed in the Catalogue of the 1859 Salon of Photography by French naturalist Louis Figuier. He and other scientists were convinced that artistic expression and taste would be improved by photography, just as the general quality of life benefits from applied science. (그들의 관점은 프랑스 자연주의자 루이 피기에 의해 1859년 사진 전람회의 책자에 되풀이 되었다. 그와 다른 과학자들은 전반적인 삶의 질이 응용과학의 혜택을 본 것처럼 예술적 표현과 취향은 사진에 의해 향상될 것이라고 믿었다.)라고 말한다. 즉, 사진을 통해 나온 예술적 표현과 감각이 사회에 긍정적인 영향을 미친다는 (A)가 정답이 된다. (B)가 틀린 이유는 사진가의 삶을 개선시킨다는 내용이 지문에 없기 때문이다.

02 According to paragraph 3, why did some people begin to question the camera?

(A) The images produced were not as clear as previously thought.
(B) The pictures that were produced were too much like art to be called a mechanical process.
(C) The photographs produced were too detailed and too accurate in capturing images.
(D) The photographs produced were too much like 'high art' still lifes, genre scenes and allegorical costumes. ★

3단락에 따르면, 왜 사람들은 카메라에 대하여 의구심을 품기 시작하였는가?

(A) 과거에 생각했던 것에 비해 사진이 선명하게 나오지 않았다.
(B) 기계적인 과정에 의해서 나왔다고 하기엔 사진들이 너무 미술 작품 같았다.
(C) 사진들은 너무나도 정확하고 세세하게 이미지를 포착했다.
(D) 사진들은 정물화, 장르 광경, 그리고 우화 의상과 같이 매우 수준 높은 예술 같았다. ★

Fact 문제의 키워드인 questioning camera가 언급된 부분을 살펴보면 people began to question whether the camera's images were too accurate and detailed.(사람들은 카메라의 이미지가 너무나 정확하고 세밀한 것이 아닌가에 대한 의문을 갖기 시작했다)라고 말한다. 즉, 너무 정확하고 세세한 이미지를 포착하는 카메라 때문에 의구심을 품게 됐으므로 (C)가 정답이 된다. (D)는 지문에서 사진이 수준 높은 예술 같다는 내용이 의구심을 가지게 한 인과에 없었기 때문에 오답이다.

03 The word quest in the passage is closest in meaning to

(A) argument ★
(B) search
(C) question
(D) experiment

지문의 단어 quest 와 가장 유사한 것은?

(A) 논쟁 ★ [á:rgjəmənt]
(B) 수색 [sə:rtʃ]
(C) 의문 [kwéstʃən]
(D) 실험 [ikspérəmənt]

Vocabulary 지문의 quest(조사)는 search(수색)와 동의어이므로 정답은 (B)이다.

04 The word narrative in the passage is closest in meaning to

(A) fictional ★
(B) story-like
(C) natural
(D) artistic

지문의 단어 narrative 과 가장 유사한 것은?

(A) 소설의 ★ [fíkʃənl]
(B) 이야기같은
(C) 자연스러운 [nætʃərəl]
(D) 미적인 [a:rtístik]

Vocabulary 지문의 narrative(서술적인)은 story-like(이야기같은)과 동의어이므로 정답은 (B)이다.

TEST 6 - 2
How and Why Birds Learn to Sing

01 The word elaborate in the passage is closest in meaning to

(A) simple
(B) effective ★
(C) complicated
(D) laborious

지문의 단어 elaborate 와 가장 유사한 것은?

(A) 간단한 [símpl]
(B) 효과적인 ★ [iféktiv]
(C) 복잡한 [kámpləkèitid]
(D) 힘든 [ləbɔ́ːriəs]

Vocabulary 지문의 elaborate(정교한)은 complicated(복잡한)과 동의어이므로 (C)가 정답이다. (B)는 문맥상 어울리나 뜻이 맞지 않으므로 오답이다

02 Which of the following can be supported about female flycatchers by the dummy experiment in paragraph 2?

(A) They are more attracted to natural songs than recordings.
(B) They have poor eyesight and thus depend heavily on their hearing.
(C) The probability that they will sing depends on multiple external factors. ★
(D) They were trapped in nest-boxes in a way that supported Darwin's proposal.

다음 중 2단락의 모형 실험에 의해서 암컷 딱새류에 대해서 뒷받침 할 수 있는 것은?

(A) 그들은 녹음된 노래보다 자연적인 노래에 더 끌린다.
(B) 그들은 나쁜 시력을 가지고 있고 따라서 그들의 청력에 크게 의존한다.
(C) 그들이 노래를 부를 확률은 복합적인 외부적 요소에 의존한다. ★
(D) 그들은 다윈의 제의를 지지하는 방식으로 둥지상자에 갇혀 있었다.

Fact 지문에서 살펴보면, 90 percent of females were caught in nest-box traps of 'singing' dummies, showing that a male's song attracts mates. (90%의 암컷들은 '노래하는' 모형의 둥지상자 덫에 걸렸다는 것은 수컷의 노래가 암컷을 유혹한다는 걸 보여준다)라고 써있는데, 앞서서 지문의 내용에 다윈은 suggested that this was the result of sexual selection because females choose mates with more complex songs.(다윈은 이것이 암컷들이 더 복잡한 노래를 부르는 짝을 선택했기 때문에 자웅 선택의 결과라고 제의했다)라고 제시했기 때문에 (D)가 정답이다. (A), (B), (C)는 언급된 적이 없으므로 오답이다.

03 According to paragraph 3 how do birds with innate ability to sing react to the introduction of new singing styles?

(A) They modify their songs by including the sounds that they hear. ★
(B) They are not very susceptible to adaptations when exposed to songs.
(C) They learn the new song and store it in their memory.
(D) They replace the old song with the newly introduced song.

3단락에 의하면, 노래 부르기에 타고난 능력을 가진 새들은 새로운 노래 부르는 스타일의 소개에 대해 어떻게 반응하는가?

(A) 그들은 그들이 듣는 소리를 추가함으로써 그들의 노래를 수정한다. ★
(B) 그들은 그들이 노출되어 있는 노래에 민감하게 반응하지 않는다.
(C) 그들은 새로운 노래를 배워서 그들의 기억에 저장한다.
(D) 그들은 예전 노래를 새롭게 소개된 노래로 대체한다.

Fact 지문에서 살펴보면, Unlike birds with innate abilities to sing, some are extremely susceptible to external sound stimuli when learning songs.(노래를 부르는 타고난 능력을 가진 새들과는 다르게, 어떤 새들은 노래를 배울 때 외부의 자극에 극도로 민감하다)라고 써있다. 타고난 능력을 가지지 않은 새들이 자극에 민감하다고 하고, unlike라고 제시되어 있기 때문에 타고난 능력을 가진 새라면 외부 환경에 영향을 받지 않는다는 걸 알 수 있다. 따라서 답은 (B)이다. (A)에서 명시된 modify는 사실이 아니므로 오답이다.

04 The word temporal in the passage is closest in meaning to

(A) fundamental
(B) tonal ★
(C) immaterial
(D) time - related

지문의 단어 temporal 과 가장 유사한 것은?

(A) 근본적인 [fʌndəméntl]
(B) 음색의 ★ [tónul]
(C) 무형의 [ìmətíəriəl]
(D) 시간 관련된

Vocabulary 지문의 단어 temporal(시간적)은 durational(지속적인)과 동의어이므로 정답이다.

TEST 7 - 1
Functions of Roots

01 The word anchor is closest in meaning to

(A) control ★
(B) fasten
(C) speed
(D) damper

지문의 단어 anchor 와 가장 유사한 것은?

(A) 제어하다 ★ [kəntróul]
(B) 매다 [fǽsnːsən]
(C) 빠르게하다 [spiːd]
(D) 멈추다 [dǽmpər]

Vocabulary 지문의 anchor(고정시키다)은 fasten(매다)과 동의어이므로 정답은 (B)이다.

---

02 Which of the following is true about the habitats of the red mangrove?

(A) They are inland areas of the northern and southern hemisphere.
(B) They are favorable places in which a variety of plants grow and adapt. ★
(C) They are devoid of plant life due to their high temperatures.
(D) They lack what other plants essentially need.

다음 중 붉은 맹그로브의 서식지에 관해 사실인 것은?

(A) 그곳은 북쪽과 남쪽 반구의 내륙 지역이다.
(B) 그곳은 여러 종류의 식물이 자라고 적응하기에 좋은 곳이다. ★
(C) 그곳은 높은 온도로 인해 많은 식물이 없는 지역이다.
(D) 그들은 다른 식물들이 필수적으로 필요로 하는 것들을 가지고 있지 않다.

Fact 지문에서 보이듯이, salt water swamps, survival is more challenging due to the lack of basic necessities (해수 늪지대와 같은 가혹한 환경에, 생존은 기본적인 필수 요소의 부족에 때문에 좀 더 어려운 일이다)라고 말한다. 즉, 필요 요소가 없다는 곳이니 (D)가 정답이다. (A)는 내륙 지방이 아니므로 오답이며, (B)는 여러 종류의 식물이 살기 좋은 곳이 아니므로 오답이다. 그리고 (C)는 언급이 안된 내용이 있으므로 오답이다.

---

03 The word prominent is closest in meaning to

(A) tall ★
(B) conspicuous
(C) practical
(D) insignificant

지문의 단어 prominent 와 가장 유사한 것은?

(A) 키 큰 ★ [tɔːl]
(B) 눈에 튀는 [kənspíkjuəs]
(C) 실용적인 [prǽktikəl]
(D) 하찮은 [insignífikənt]

Vocabulary 지문의 prominent(눈에 잘 띄는)은 conspicuous(눈에 튀는)과 동의어이므로 정답은 (B)이다.

---

04 According to paragraph 3, reverse osmosis, allows plants to

(A) obtain fresh water using negative pressure.
(B) absorb the salt necessary for ultra-filtration.
(C) be drained of their freshwater. ★
(D) draw water from the leaves to the roots.

3단락에 따르면, 역삼투는 식물들로 하여금

(A) 부압을 이용해 담수를 얻게 해준다.
(B) 초여과를 위해 필요한 염분을 흡수하게 해준다.
(C) 담수를 빼내게 해준다. ★
(D) 잎사귀에서 뿌리로 물을 가져오게 해준다.

Fact 지문의 키워드인 reverse-osmosis가 있는 지문에서 보이듯, its roots also enable it to obtain freshwater from highly saline water sources through non-metabolic ultra-filtration, using negative pressure inside the stem to draw freshwater water in through a membrane too fine for salt to pass through, in a process called reverse-osmosis. (그들의 뿌리는 비-신진대사 초-여과를 통해 높은 염도를 가진 해수로부터 담수를 얻을 수 있게 하는데 역 삼투압이라고 불리는 과정에서 염분이 통과하기에는 너무 미세한 세포막을 통해 담수를 끌어 당기기 위해 줄기 안에서 부압을 이용한다)라고 말한다. 즉, 역삼투를 통해 담수를 얻는다는 걸 알 수 있으므로 답은 (A)이다. (B)는 염분을 흡수하는 것이 아니므로 오답이며, (C)는 사실과 반대이므로 오답이다. 그리고 (D)는 역삼투합과 관련 없는 것이므로 오답이다.

TEST 7 - 2
History of The Patent Law

01 Why does the author mention the letters patent system in paragraph 3?

(A) To explain the etymology of the word 'patent' ★
(B) To show that patents used to be granted to persons favored by the monarchy
(C) To place the Venetian Senate's Act in the context of the history of patent law
(D) To prove that the British started the idea of a standardized patent system

왜 글쓴이는 3단락에서 특허장을 언급했는가?

(A) '특허권'의 어원에 대해서 설명하기 위해 ★
(B) 군주의 은총을 받은 사람들만이 수여했다는 것을 보여주기 위해
(C) 특허권 역사의 맥락에서 Venetian Senate's Act 를 놓기위해
(D) 영국이 보편화된 시스템 개념을 시작했다는 것을 증명하기 위해

Purpose 글쓴이가 'letters patent' (특허권)을 언급한 이유는 Venetian Senate's Act 이전 특허권을 언급함으로 Venetian Senate's Act에 관한 내용을 다루기 위함이다. 그리고 그것을 특허권의 역사적 맥락에서 다루어 그 중요성을 찾으려 하므로 정답은 (C)이다.

02 Why does the author mention Industrial Revolution in paragraph 3?

(A) To prove that the establishment of a patent system brought about the Industrial Revolution
(B) To show that the Industrial Revolution was an important component of the socioeconomic development of Great Britain
(C) To demonstrate an example of how patents have changed people's perceptions of the role of the Industrial Revolution ★
(D) To show that the increased rate of invention of the time required major changes in the patent system

왜 글쓴이는 3단락에서 산업혁명을 언급 하였는가?

(A) 특허권 시스템의 설립이 산업 혁명을 야기했다는 것을 증명하기 위해
(B) 산업 혁명이 영국의 사회경제 개발에 중요한 요소였다는 것을 보여 주기 위해
(C) 어떻게 특허권이 산업 혁명의 역할에 대한 인식을 바꿨는지에 대한 예를 입증하기 위해 ★
(D) 그 시대의 증가한 발명품의 양은 특허권 시스템에서의 주요한 변화가 필요했다는 것을 보여주기 위해

Purpose 글쓴이가 Industrial Revolution(산업혁명)을 언급한 이유는 산업혁명과 같이 수많은 발명품이 나오던 시기를 언급하여 특허권 제도가 바뀌어야 한다는 의도임으로 정답은 (D)이다. (C)는 perception of the role of industrial revolution(산업 혁명의 역할을 바라보는 시각)을 바꾸었다는 내용이므로 오답이다.

03 The word disputes in the passage is closest in meaning to

(A) arguments
(B) grants
(C) confusions
(D) investigations ★

지문의 단어 disputes 과 의미상 가장 유사한 것은?

(A) 논쟁 [àːrgjumənt]
(B) 승인 [grænt]
(C) 혼동 [kənfjúːʒən]
(D) 조사 ★[invèstəgéiʃən]

Vocabulary 지문의 dispute(분쟁)은 argument(논쟁)과 동의어이므로 답은 (A)이다. (D) Collision(충돌)은 문맥상 말이 되기는 하지만 '논쟁, 반박하다' 라는 뜻을 가진 dispute과는 동의어가 아니기에 오답이다.

04 The word burgeoning in the passage is closest in meaning to

(A) coincidental
(B) moderating ★
(C) flourishing
(D) troublesome

지문의 단어 burgeoning 과 의미상 가장 유사한 것은?

(A) 우연의 [kouìnsidéntl]
(B) 완화중인 ★ [mɑdərət]
(C) 번영하는 [fləːriʃ]
(D) 골칫거리인 [trʌblsəm]

Vocabulary Burgeoning(급성장하는)은 flourishing(번영하는)과 동의어이므로 (C)가 답이다.

TEST 8 - 1
Communication of Ants

01 Which of the following is NOT an advantage of communal insects like ants stated in paragraph 1?

(A) Assignment of specific duties to members
(B) Systematic stability in the colony
(C) Positive influence on the ~~neighboring ecosystem~~
(D) Better foraging through communication ★

다음 중 1단락에서 주장된 개미와 같은 소통하는 곤충의 이점이 아닌 것은?

(A) 각 구성원에게 구체적인 의무의 배분
(B) 집단에서 체계적인 안정성
(C) 주변환경에 미치는 긍정적인 영향
(D) 의사 소통을 통한 더 나은 먹이수집 ★

Fact 문제의 키워드인 advantage of communal insect like ants(개미와 같이 소통하는 곤충의 이점)를 보면 increased system reliability(높아진 체계의 신뢰도)와 division of labor and task partitioning(작업의 분할)이라고 한다. 또한 the major advantage, however, is the communication.(가장 큰 이점은 구성원들간의 의사소통이다)라는 것을 알 수 있다. 따라서 답은 지문에서 직접적으로 언급되지 않는 내용이므로 오답이다.

---

02 The word retain in the passage is closest in meaning to

(A) discard
(B) stimulate ★
(C) keep
(D) encourage

지문의 단어 retain 과 의미상 가장 유사한 것은?

(A) 폐기하다 [diskáːrd]
(B) 자극하다 ★[stímjuleit]
(C) 유지하다 [kiːp]
(D) 격려하다 [inkɔ́ːridʒ]

Vocabulary 지문의 retain(보유하다)은 keep(유지하다)과 동의어이므로 정답은 (C)이다.

---

03 According to paragraph 3, what is unique about the pheromones of Pharaoh's ants?

(A) They allow the ants ~~to live a longer period of time~~ by working complementarily while foraging.
(B) They are short-lived pheromones which ~~guide them back to the colony~~.
(C) They allow them to return to their forage sites for a longer period of time.
(D) They can repel ants that are near the foraging spot in order to protect ~~their prey items from others.~~ ★

3단락에 따르면, 무엇이 파라오 개미들의 페로몬의 특징인가?

(A) 그것은 개미들이 먹이를 채집하는 동안 상호보완적으로 일하게 함으로써 ~~더 오래 살 수 있게 해준다.~~
(B) 그것은 개미들을 무리로 ~~다시 돌아오도록~~ 하는 단시간 지속되는 페로몬이다.
(C) 그것은 개미들이 채집장소로 더 오랜 시간 동안 돌아올 수 있게 해준다.
(D) 그것은 ~~다른 아들로부터 먹이를 보호하고자~~ 채집장소부근의 개미를 쫓아내도록 한다. ★

Fact 문제의 키워드인 Pharaoh's ant(파라오 개미)를 다른 개미들과 비교하는 곳을 살펴보면 the long-lived trails of Pharaoh's ants can persist for several days, allowing the trail network to be explored for a longer period of time.(파라오 개미의 장기 흔적은 며칠이나 유지되어 흔적 망이 오랜 기간 탐구될 수 있도록 해준다)이라 언급한다. 즉 다른 개미들은 할 수 없지만 파라오 개미는 며칠동안 흔적을 찾을 수 있으므로 정답은 (C)이다.

---

04 The word reinforced in the passage is closest in meaning to

(A) strengthened
(B) explored ★
(C) reconstructed
(D) followed

지문의 단어 reinforced 과 의미상 가장 유사한 것은?

(A) 강화된
(B) 탐험된★
(C) 재건된
(D) 따라진

Vocabulary 지문의 reinforced(강화되는)은 strengthened(강화되는)과 동의어이므로 정답은 (A)이다.

TEST 8 - 2
Calculating the Age of Earth

01 According to paragraph 1 which of the following can be inferred about scientists before the eighteenth century?

(A) Scientists generally avoided conforming to the ideas regarding the age of Earth established by religious leaders. ★
(B) Scientific facts were not the dominant sources of information used to calculate the age of the earth prior to the mid - 1700s.
(C) Prior to the mid-1700s, evidence indicating the true age of Earth did not exist.
(D) They believed that rock layers of Earth had remained uniform throughout the ages.

1단락에 따르면, 18세기 이전의 과학자들에 관해 추론할 수 있는 것은?

(A) 과학자들은 일반적으로 종교 지도자들에 의해 설립된 지구의 나이에 대한 아이디어에 부합하는 것을 꺼려했다. ★
(B) 과학적 사실은 1700년 중반 이전에 지구나이 계산에 사용되어지는 정보의 중요한 소스는 아니었다.
(C) 1700년대 중반 이전에, 진짜 지구나이를 가리키는 증거가 존재하지 않았다.
(D) 그들은 지구의 암석층이 오랫동안 일정한 형태를 유지했다고 믿었다.

> **Inference** 1단락에서 only source of historical and scientific knowledge, such as the age of Earth, until the mid-eighteenth century(18세기 중반전까지 지구 나이와 같은 역사적 그리고 과학적 지식에 대한 유일한 원천이었다)고 서술되어있다. 이를 근거로 과학적 주장이 받아 들여지지 않았다는 것을 추론할 수 있다.

02 In paragraph 2, what was the importance of Buffon's experiment?

(A) It became the grounds for further research that used heavy metals. ★
(B) It was the first scientific experiment to calculate the earth's age.
(C) It demonstrated how early attempts to determine the age of Earth were scientifically unreasonable.
(D) It showed that the globe-figure was appropriate for calculating the age of the earth.

2단락에서, Buffon의 실험의 중요성은 무엇인가?

(A) 중금속을 사용한 더 많은 조사에 대한 근거가 되었다. ★
(B) 지구의 나이를 계산하기 위해 초기 과학적인 실험이었다.
(C) 어떻게 지구의 나이를 결정하는 초기 시도들이 과학적으로 비합리적인지를 증명했다.
(D) 실험에서 사용된 둥근 모양이 지구 나이 계산에 적절했다고 보여줬다.

> **Fact** 문제의 키워드인 Buffon이 언급된 부분을 보면 In 1779, a French scientist, Comte de Buffon, attempted the first calculation of Earth's age by experimentation.(1779년에, 프랑스 과학자인 Comte de Buffon는 실험으로 지구나이의 첫 번째 계산을 시도했다) 라고 언급되어 있다. 즉 그의 첫 번째 과학적인 실험이 또 다른 과학적인 실험으로 이어지는 계기가 됨으로 그 중요성이 있다고 할 수 있다.

03 The word conceivable in the passage is closest in meaning to

(A) questionable
(B) plausible
(C) powerful ★
(D) influential

지문의 단어 conceivable 과 의미상 유사한 것은?

(A) 의심나는 [kwéstʃənəbəl]
(B) 그럴듯한 [plɔ́:zəbl]
(C) 강력한 ★[páuərfəl]
(D) 영향력 있는 [ìnfluénʃəl]

> **Vocabulary** 지문의 conceivable(생각할 수 있는)은 plausible(그럴듯한)과 동의어이므로 답은 (B)이다.

04 The word dissipated in the passage is closest in meaning to

(A) dispersed
(B) gathered
(C) exploited
(D) generated ★

지문의 단어 dissipated 과 의미상 유사한 것은?

(A) 흩어졌다 [dispɔ́:rst]
(B) 모았다 [gǽðərd]
(C) 이용했다 [iksplɔ́it]
(D) 일으켰다 ★ [dʒénərèit]

> **Vocabulary** 지문의 dissipated(흩어져 사라진)은 disperse(흩어지다)와 동의어이므로 답은 (A)이다.

TEST 9 - 1
Identifying Playful Behavior in Children

01 The word apparent is closest in meaning to

(A) obvious
(B) large
(C) accepted ★
(D) sufficient

지문의 단어 apparent 와 의미상 유사한 것은?

(A) 분명한 [ábviəs]
(B) 큰 [la:rdʒ]
(C) 인정된 ★[ækséptid]
(D) 충분한 [səfíʃənt]

Vocabulary 지문의 apparent는 명확한 뜻이므로 정답은 (A)이다.

---

02 Which of the following is true of the functional approach mentioned in paragraph 2?

(A) Because the approach was developed to explain play in monkeys, it had to be revised before it could be applied to humans. ★
(B) It identifies playful behavior as acts that have benefits whatsoever to the performer.
(C) The majority of Symons' fellow sociologists disapproved of his approach.
(D) It identifies playful behavior as acts that do not have a clear purpose.

다음 중 기능 접근법에 대한 설명으로 2단락에 언급된 것은?

(A) 기능 접근법은 본래 원숭이의 놀이를 설명하려고 전개되었기 때문에 인간의 놀이를 설명하기 위해선 수정되어야 했다. ★
(B) 기능 접근법은 놀이가 행위자에게 어떠한 이득도 안겨 주는 행동이라고 정의한다.
(C) 사이몬스 외 대부분의 다른 사회학자들은 기능 접근법을 반대하였다.
(D) 기능 접근법은 놀이적 행동은 명확한 목적이 없는 행동이라고 정의한다.

Fact 문제의 키워드 functional approach(기능 접근법)가 언급된 부분의 주변을 지문에서 살펴보면, defined play ~ act that has neither an inherent end, nor external goal.(그는 놀이를 내재적 목적도 없고 외부적 목적도 없는 행동으로 정의했다)라는 것을 알 수 있다. 따라서 (D)는 지문의 내용과 일치하므로 정답이다. (A)가 틀린 이유는 수정해야 했다는 내용이 지문에 없었기 때문이다.

---

03 The word execution is closest in meaning to

(A) punishment ★
(B) understanding
(C) performance
(D) analysis

지문의 단어 execution 와 의미상 가장 유사한 것은?

(A) 벌 ★ [pʌníʃmənt]
(B) 이해 [ʌndərstǽndiŋ]
(C) 행동 [pərfɔ́:rməns]
(D) 분석 [ənǽləsis]

Vocabulary 지문의 execution(실행)은 performance(행동)과 동의어이므로 정답은 (C)이다.

---

04 Why does the author mention a push or a light punch?

(A) To show that for those who enjoy violence, fighting can also be a form of playful behavior
(B) To point out that an insignificant disagreement can be exaggerated to hateful aggression
(C) To illustrate an example of an act which is inherently repetitive and fragmented ★
(D) To clarify what the author means by squabble, through examples

3단락에서 글쓴이가 밀거나 살살 때리는을 언급한 이유는?

(A) 폭력을 좋아하는 사람들에게 싸움은 놀이적 행동의 한 형태라고 보여주기 위해서
(B) 사소한 논쟁이 증오에 찬 표현으로 과장될 수 있다는 것을 보여주기 위해서
(C) 내재적으로 반복되고 단편적인 행동의 예를 보여주기 위해서 ★
(D) 글쓴이가 예를 들음으로써 시시한 표현을 어떤 의미로 사용했는지 분명하기 위해서

Purpose 음영 문구 a push or a light punch(밀거나 살살 때리는)이 언급된 부분의 앞 문장을 살펴보면, like laughter or playful squabbling (웃음소리나 시시한 다툼들과 같은)라고 언급한다. 즉 a push or a light punch는 시시한 다툼의 예로 제시했으므로 답은 (D)이다. (C)가 틀린 이유는 내재적으로 반복되고 단편적인 행동의 예로 제시한 것이 아니어서이다.

TEST 9 - 2
Sentinel Behavior in Meerkats

01 According to paragraph 2, what can be inferred about Belding's ground squirrels?

(A) They were named after the discoverer of their evolutionary behavior.
(B) Their feeding habits are closely related to that of meerkats. ★
(C) Squirrel sentinels warn their neighbors of a danger after they have secured safety.
(D) The squirrels that warn others of dangers run a higher risk of being preyed upon.

2단락에 의하면, 다음 중 벨딩의 땅다람쥐로부터 유추할 수 있는 것은?

(A) 그들은 그들의 진화적인 행동의 발견자를 따서 이름 지어졌다.
(B) 그들의 식습관은 미어캣의 그것과 밀접하게 연관되어 있다. ★
(C) 다람쥐 보초는 그들의 안전을 확보한 뒤에 그들의 이웃 에게 경고한다.
(D) 다른 이들에게 위험을 알리는 다람쥐는 포식될 위험이 더 크다.

Inference 지문에서 땅다람쥐가 나오기 전의 내용이 the evolutionary strategy that favors the reproductive success of an organism's relatives over one's own survival(자신의 생존보다는 한 개체의 친족들의 번식 성공에 기여하는 진화전략), 즉 혈연 선택에 대한 내용인 것으로 보아 희생이 뒤따르는 것으로 유추할 수 있다. 따라서 (D)가 정답이다. (C)는 반대되는 내용이므로 오답, (A), (B)는 없는 내용이므로 오답이다.

02 The word credibility in the passage is closest in meaning to

(A) notoriety
(B) revenue
(C) plausibility
(D) certainty ★

지문의 단어 credibility 과 의미상 가장 유사한 것은?

(A) 악평 [nòutəráiəti]
(D) 수입 [révənjùː]
(C) 그럴듯함 [plɔ̀ːzəbíləti]
(D) 확실성 ★[sə́ːrtnti]

Vocabulary 지문의 credibility(신뢰성)은 plausibility(그럴듯함)과 동의어이므로 정답은 (C)이다.

03 The word postulating in the passage is closest in meaning to

(A) explaining
(B) speculating
(C) signifying ★
(D) uncovering

지문의 단어 postulating 와 의미상 가장 유사한 것은?

(A) 설명하는 [ikspléin]
(B) 추측하는 [spékjulèit]
(C) 의미하는 ★ [sígnəfaiiŋ]
(D) 폭로하는 [ənkʌ́vər]

Vocabulary 지문의 postulating(가정하는)은 speculating(추측하는)과 동의어이므로 정답은 (B)이다. 가정하는 것과 의미하는 것은 다르므로 (C)는 오답이다.

04 What is true about reciprocal altruism according to paragraph 3?

(A) Unlike the scientists' assumptions, meerkats do not have designated responsibilities.
(B) Meerkats will stop displaying reciprocal altruism should another animal outside their kin appear among them. ★
(C) The banded mongoose's cooperative begging behavior is not an example of reciprocal altruism.
(D) It is a type of behavior that characterizes a family of species related to the meerkats.

3단락에 의하면 상호적 이타주의에 대해서 다음 중 사실인것은?

(A) 학자들의 추측과 달리, 미어캣은 지정된 책임이 없다.
(B) 만약 그들 사이에서 친족외의 미어캣이 보인다면, 미어캣은 상호 이타주의를 보이는 것을 멈출 것이다. ★
(C) 줄무늬 몽구스의 협력적인 조르는 행동은 상호적 이타주의의 예가 아니다.
(D) 그것은 미어캣과 연관된 종의 무리를 특징화하는 행동의 한 종류이다.

Fact 문제의 키워드인 reciprocal altruism(상호적 이타주의)가 언급된 부분을 살펴보면 two conditions that had been laid out by the developed, mature definition of reciprocal altruism(상호간 이타주의의 발달하고 완성된 정의에 의해 깔린 두 가지 조건)라고 언급하는데, 여기서 이 이론이 쉽게 만들어진 이론이 아니라는 것을 유추할 수 있으므로 (A)가 정답이다. (B)는 관찰을 통해서 얻을 수 있는 정보를 셀 수 있다고 했으므로 오답이다.

usherin.usher.co.kr

별도 구매 서비스 소개

usherin.usher.co.kr

1. USHER **단어암기** 프로그램 소개
2. **첨삭권** 소개
3. **인강**
4. **모의토플**
5. 토플 Reading 공부방법
6. 토플 Listening 공부방법
7. 수강 후기

1 USHER 단어암기 프로그램 소개
usherin.usher.co.kr

1. **듣고 - 아직도 눈으로만 외우나요?**
   어셔단어 프로그램에서는 듣고, 쓰고, 품사외우고, 동의어까지 한번에 진행합니다.
2. **말하고 - 아직도 발음을 못하나요?**
   발음 연습을 정확하게 프로그램이 읽어, 단어 외우면서 발음까지 한번에 준비할 수 있습니다.
3. **집중 암기하고 - 천천히 성장 VS 고성장**
   90일 동안 외울 단어를 13일 안에 끝내므로 반복효과 및 고성장을 이루어 낼수있습니다.
4. **internet based test** - 즉시채점+틀린것만 계속 테스트
   틀린 단어들만 다시 시험보기가 가능합니다.
5. **기분좋은 성취 확인 - 향상 기록 personal trainer**
   본인이 본 시험 기록 내용이 누적 확인되어 본인에 성취를 확인 할수있습니다.

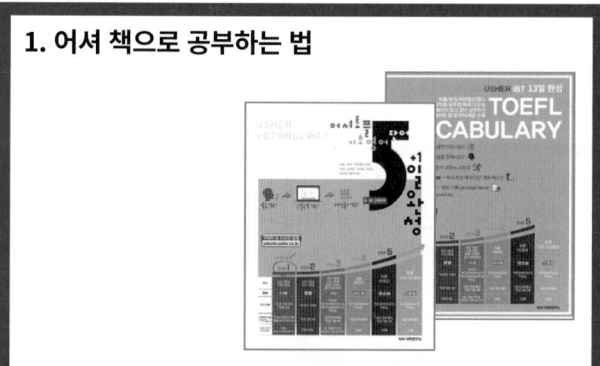

1. 어셔 책으로 공부하는 법

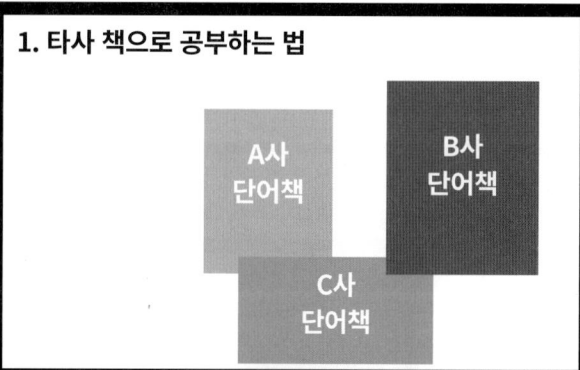

1. 타사 책으로 공부하는 법

2. 발음을 먼저 듣고

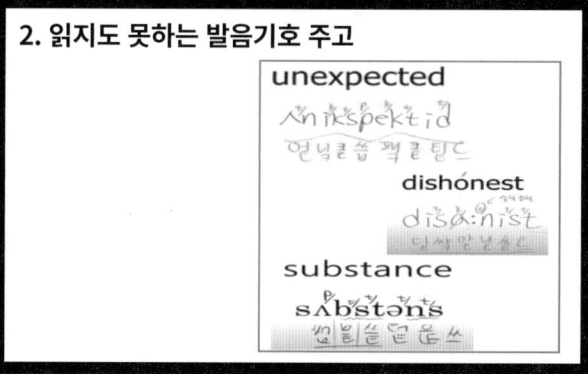

2. 읽지도 못하는 발음기호 주고

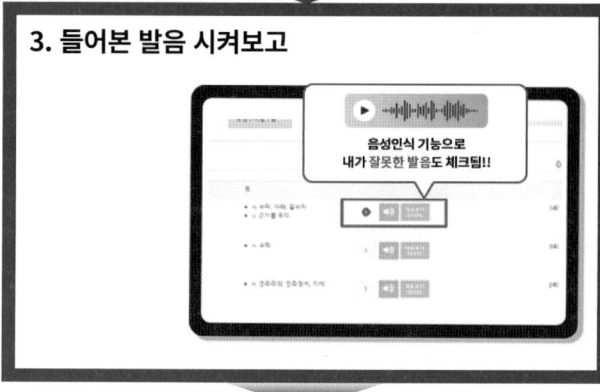

3. 들어본 발음 시켜보고

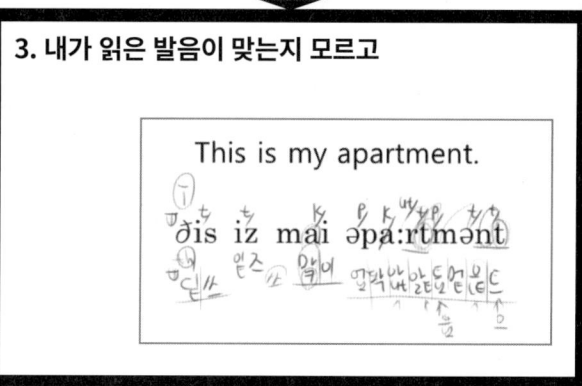

3. 내가 읽은 발음이 맞는지 모르고

4. 인터벌

4. 빽빽이 써가면서 단어 외워야하는데

5. 분량을 나눠서 모의시험
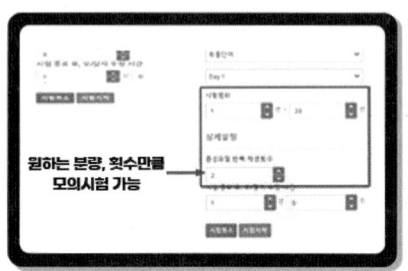

원하는 분량, 횟수만큼 모의시험 가능

5. 빽빽이 써가면서 단어 외워야하는데

6. 준비되면 시전시험!
듣고 → 스펠링 → 품사 → 뜻 순으로 적기
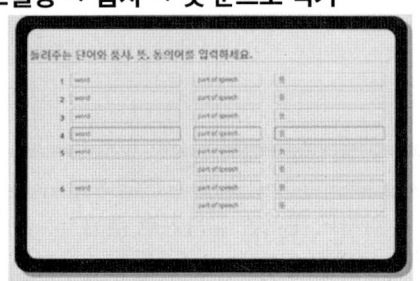

6. 학교 or 학원가서 종이에
한글 또는 스펠링 중 하나만 시험
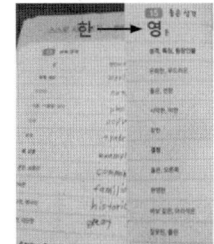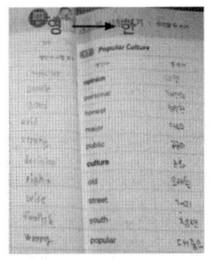

7. 하나라도 틀리면 오답처리
시험결과 자동체크

제출하기 누르면 즉시채점 ~

7. 채점을 내가 하면 잘못 외운 스펠링체크 못해주고
친구가 해주면 우정으로 틀린 것도 맞다고 해주고
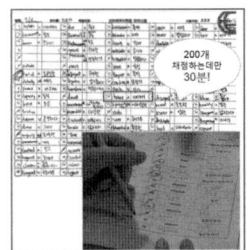

200개 채점하는데만 30분!

8. 틀린 단어 묶음으로 즉시 오답노트 만들어줌

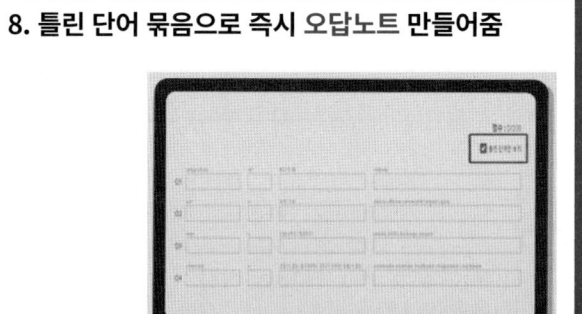

8. 내가 뭘 틀렸는지 일일히 추려내야 하지만... 보통은 보지도 않고 그냥 버리게 됨

9. 틀린 개수 0으로 만들기 틀린 단어만 재시험

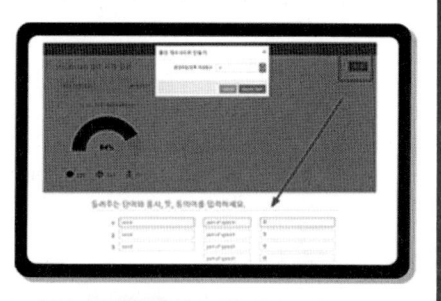

9. 틀린 단어가 뭔지 보지도 않고

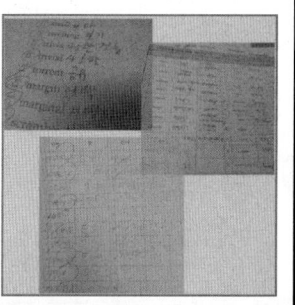

10. 한달 동안 시험 본 모든 기록 체크해주며 자극주는 시스템

10. 종이가 너덜너덜해지면 그냥 버림

단어 프로그램 가격 소개

📱 카카오톡으로 문의하기

	1개월 사용	3개월 사용	6개월 사용
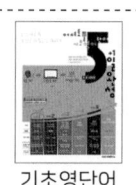 기초영단어	25,000원	~~75,000원~~ 60,000원 (1개월당 20,000원, 20% DC)	~~150,000원~~ 84,000원 (1개월당 7,000원, 44% DC)
 토플단어	25,000원	~~75,000원~~ 60,000원 (1개월당 20,000원, 20% DC)	~~150,000원~~ 84,000원 (1개월당 7,000원, 44% DC)
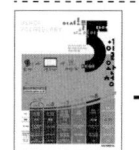 기초영단어 + 토플단어	40,000원	~~120,000원~~ 90,000원 (1개월당 30,000원, 25% DC)	~~240,000원~~ 108,000원 (1개월당 9,000원, 55% DC)

2. 첨삭권 소개
usherin.usher.co.kr

01 스피킹/라이팅 첨삭이 필요한 이유?

대체로 독학을 할 수 있다고 생각하는 리딩, 리스닝과는 달리 스피킹 라이팅은 독학이 힘듭니다.

이유는? "내가 뭘 틀렸는지 모르니까!!!"

대안은?? 독학이라고 했으니, 과외나, 학원은 빼고, 남는 건 첨삭이나, 그냥 혼자 틀린 걸 계속 보거나….

그런데, 첨삭을 받으러 검색을 해보면 가격이 라이팅 한편 당 23,000…원…?

한편만 첨삭 받으면 끝날 것 같진 않은 내 실력을 봐서는…

비용 감당 안됨. 어쩌지?

02 학원까지 다니고 싶진 않은데
스피킹/라이팅 첨삭만 받을 순 없나요?

▼ 라이팅 첨삭   *10회권은 어셔수강생에게만 제공됩니다*
(2024.08. 현재)

1회권	어셔	1회 첨삭권 25,000원	최저가 1회당 25,000원
	해**	1회권 없음 2회 첨삭권 54,000원	1회당 27,000원
	영**	1회 첨삭(1일 소요)권 28,000원	1회당(1일 소요)권 28,000원
5회권	어셔	5회 첨삭권 100,000원	최저가 1회당 20,000원
	해**	5회권 없음	5회권 없음
	영**	5회 첨삭(1일 소요)권 119,000원	1회당(1일 소요)권 23,800원
10회권 *어셔 수강생 한정	어셔	10회 첨삭권 150,000원	최저가 1회당 15,000원
	해**	10회권 없음	10회권 없음
	영**	10회권 없음	10회권 없음

▼ 스피킹 첨삭
(2024.08. 현재)

1회권	어셔	1회 첨삭권 15,000원	최저가 1회당 15,000원
	해**	1회권 없음 2회 첨삭권 54,000원	1회당 27,000원
	영**	1회 첨삭(1일 소요)권 16,000원	1회당(1일 소요)권 16,000원
5회권	어셔	5회 첨삭권 60,000원	최저가 1회당 12,000원
	해**	5회권 없음	5회권 없음
	영**	5회 첨삭(1일 소요)권 68,000원	1회당(1일소요)권 13,600원
10회권 *어셔 수강생 한정	어셔	10회 첨삭권 110,000원	최저가 1회당 11,000원
	해**	10회권 없음	10회권 없음
	영**	10회권 없음	10회권 없음

구매처 및 자세한 설명 usherin.usher.co.kr

03 첨삭 구성은 어떻게 되나요?

▼ 스피킹 첨삭

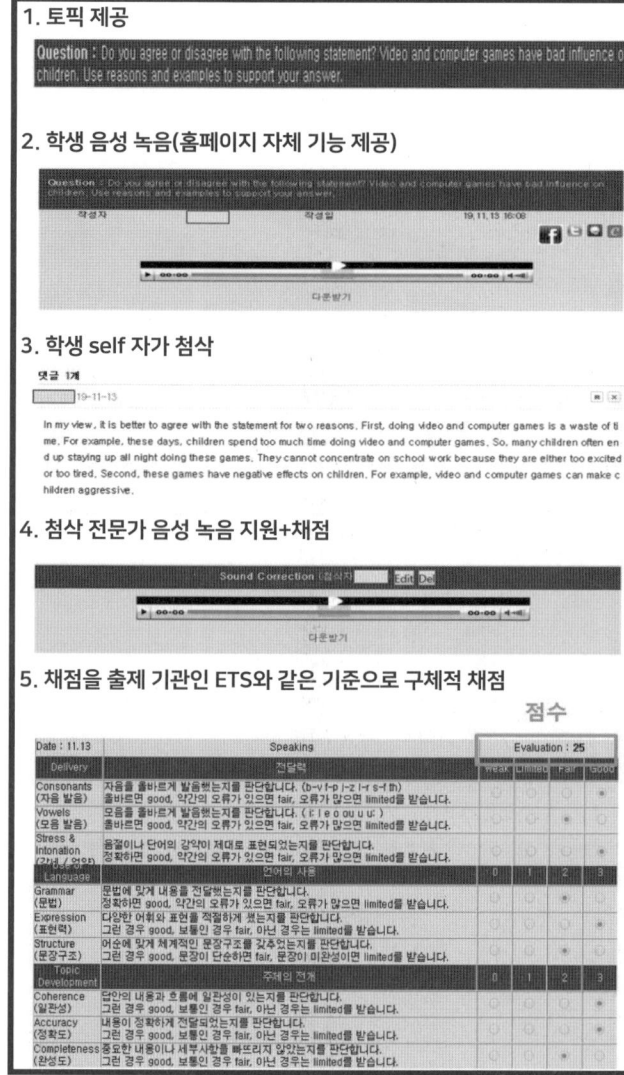

▼ 라이팅 첨삭

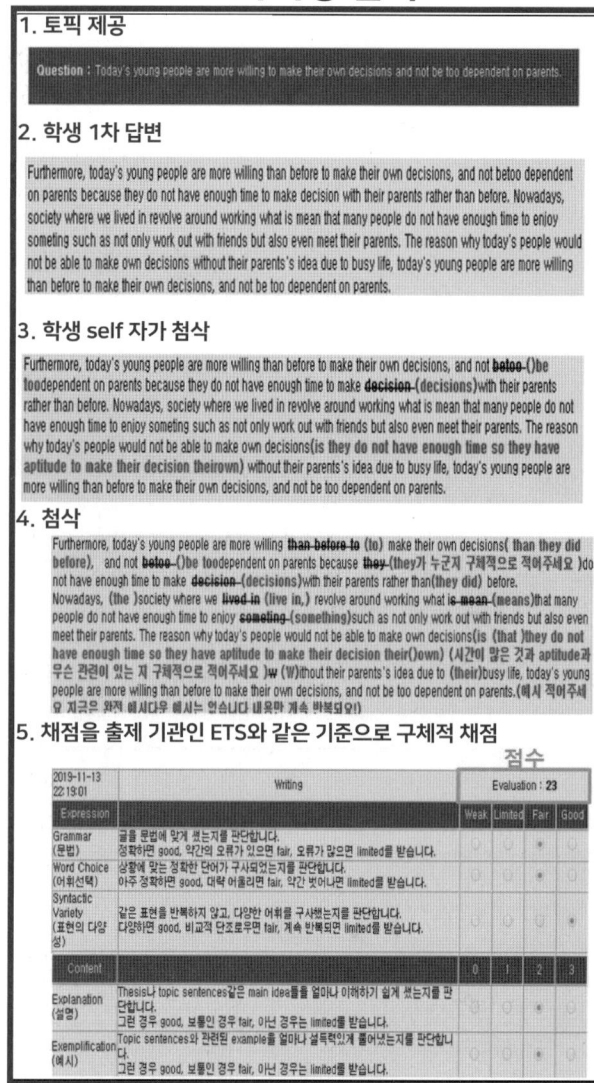

04 첨삭 신청하기

라이팅 첨삭권

10회권은 어셔수강생에게만 제공됩니다

1회 첨삭권	5회 첨삭권	10회 첨삭권
사용기간 15일	사용기간 30일	사용기간 60일
25,000원	~~125,000원~~ → 100,000원	~~250,000원~~ → 150,000원

스피킹 첨삭권

10회권은 어셔수강생에게만 제공됩니다

1회 첨삭권	5회 첨삭권	10회 첨삭권
사용기간 15일	사용기간 30일	사용기간 60일
15,000원	~~75,000원~~ → 60,000원	~~150,000원~~ → 110,000원

첨삭은 근무일 기준(평일)으로 진행되며, 주말 또는 휴일은 익일 평일에 진행됩니다.

3 인강-리딩
usherin.usher.co.kr

	STEP 1	STEP 2	STEP 3 (이 책 수준)	STEP 4	STEP 5	STEP 6
목표	내신 1등급 수능 1등급	내신 1등급 수능 1등급	내신 1등급 수능 1등급 토플 70점대 토익 800점대	토플 80점대	토플 90점대	토플 100~120점대
과목	단어	문법	리딩	라이팅	리스닝	스피킹
책의 종류	①초·중·고등 단어 ②토플 단어	①어셔인 그래머	①BASIC ②INTERMEDIATE 01 ③INTERMEDIATE 02 ④FINAL	①INTERMEDIATE ②FINAL	①INTERMEDIATE ②FINAL	①INTERMEDIATE ②FINAL
USHER어플 Study Tool	①단어시험프로그램 ②발음 체크(모든 단어)	①프로그램 4종	①실전 문제 풀이, ②프로그램 3종	①실전 문제 풀이	①실전 문제 풀이, ②프로그램 2종	①실전 문제 풀이
소요 시간 (1회 독해)	13일 (하루 200개 단어관리)	5일+10일	15~18일/각 권 (BASIC 1지문/1일 기준)	20일	20일	20일

나의 성격 PERSONALITY
INTP 미래 지향, 긍정

핵심 가치 CORE VALUE
성장 # 자조(스스로 돕는다) # 착함 # 긍정 # 정확함 # 결과 # 책임감 # 도전

나의 강점 STRENGTH
관리력 # 집중력 # 기획력 # 체계적 개발능력 # 집요함 # 속도

"할 얘기 많은" "멋진" 삶!!

수업 특징
- 단순화
- 긴장감
- 바뀔때까지

USHER
이덕호

나의 성격 PERSONALITY

ENTP
저는 유연성과 적응력을 가진 사람입니다.
성공의 길과 개인적 성장은 순식간에 이루어지는 것이 아닙니다.
하지만 저는 작은 발전의 단계를 거듭하면서
성장하고자 합니다. 저는 변화하는 세상에 꾸준히 적응하고,
그것을 통해 계속해서 성장하려고 합니다.

핵심 가치 CORE VALUE

저의 주된 가치는 꾸준함입니다. 어떤 일이든지 지속성이
있으면 결국 목표를 달성할 수 있다고 믿습니다.

나의 강점 STRENGTH

저는 변화하는 환경에 잘 적응하고,
다양한 상황에서 필요한
해결책을 발견하는 것을 잘합니다.

This Too Shall Pass
이 또한 지나가리라

VISION BIG5

건강한 삶 저는 몸과 마음이 건강한 삶을 추구합니다.
항상 배우기 저는 세상이 계속 변하고 발전하는 것처럼,
자신도 항상 새로운 것을 배우며 성장하고자 합니다.
긍정적인 삶 저는 긍정의 힘을 믿습니다. 긍정적인 태도를 가지고 삶을 대하고자 합니다.
인내심 저는 어려움을 겪을 때에도 인내심을 잃지 않고 목표를 향해 나아갑니다.
감사함 저는 삶의 모든 것에 감사의 마음을 가지고 그 감사의 마음을 통해
더 많은 긍정적인 에너지를 발산하고자 합니다.

USHER
김채운 부원장

나의 성격 PERSONALITY

ISTJ 현실주의자. 모든 일을 꾸준히 체계적으로

핵심 가치 CORE VALUE

#희망 #긍정 #재미

나의 강점 STRENGTH

#성실함 #솔직함 #원칙적 #긍정적 #체계적

하루아침에
되는것은 없다

VISION BIG5

1. 발전하는 하루   2. 건강한 신체   3. 활기찬 분위기
4. 겸손한 마음   5. 간결한 수업

USHER
김석균

4 모의토플

usherin.usher.co.kr

01 모의토플? 왜 봐야 하지?

Q1. 토플 시험 초보자
난 토플이 뭔지, 이름도 겨우 들었거나, 토플 공부를 해야한다는걸 겨우 알았는데, 일단, 내 실력이나 좀 보고, 대충 시험 구성부터 잡아 보고 싶다면?

A. 27만원짜리 진짜 토플 덜컥 잡고, 돈 날리지 말고, 일단 5만원짜리 모의 토플로, 어찌 생겼는지 파악하는 기회로 사용 바랍니다.

Q2. 영어 실력 충분히 있는 분?

A. 나는 영어 실력은 충분히 있는데, 그냥 시험 유형정도나 파악하고, 바로 시험 보면 되지 않을까? 라는 자신감이 있을 때, 실제 시험 전 몸풀기로 활용 바랍니다.

Q3. 토플 공부를 하면서, 본인의 실력 향상이 궁금하신 분

A. 이제 한달 공부 했는데, 내 공부 한 것이 얼마나 나아졌을지 궁금하다면, 실력 점검용으로 활용 바랍니다.

Q4. 실제 시험전에 최종 확인을 원하시는 분

A. 실제 시험장을 가야 하는데, 계속 종이로만 공부해서, 실제 토플시험장에서 모니터 적응과, 라이팅에서의 타이핑 적응등이 부족하다는걸 안다면, 미리 시험장 분위기를 확인용이 활용 바랍니다.

02 왜 모의토플? 을 봐야 하는가?

▼상세설명

Reading
가. 종이 보는것과 컴퓨터로 보는 것 만으로도 심한경우 리딩 점수 30점 만점중, 5점 차이까지 나므로, 별도로 준비 해야합니다.
나. 밑줄치면 시험 보거나, 연필로 위치를 가리키며 시험을 보는것과, 마우스를 움직여 가며 보는 것을 다르게 느끼는 경우, 시험장 환경에 적응하기 위해
다. 시험장의 엄격한 시간 관리를 미리 준비해야 하므로
라. 내가 많이 틀린 문제 분석을 통해 어느 유형이 약한지 파악하기 위해
마. (선택: 내가 어느유형이 약한지 파악후, 추가 관련 문제의 인강을 통해 미진한 부분에 대한 설명을 듣기 위해)

Listening
가. 스피커를 통해 시험을 보는게 아닌, 헤드셋을 통해 나오는 소리에서의 차이를 어색해 하는 경우가 있다.
나. 시험장 화면에서, 가장 조심 해야 하는 것은, 리딩은 한번 본 화면도 다시 되돌아 와서 체크 할수있지만, 리스닝의 경우, 한번 진행한 문제는 되돌아 가서 수정이 안되는데, 연습 없는 학생들이 가장 어이없게 많이 하는 실수이므로, 실수를 방지하기 위해
다. 시험장의 엄격한 시간 관리를 미리 준비해야 하므로
라. 내가 많이 틀린 문제 분석을 통해 어느 유형이 약한지 파악하기 위해
마. (선택: 내가 어느유형이 약한지 파악후, 추가 관련 문제의 인강을 통해 미진한 부분에 대한 설명을 듣기 위해)

Speaking
가. 시험장에서 마이크에 대고 말하는 것은, 무조건 소리를 크게 내야하는데, 학생들의 경우, 옆에 잘 하는 학생들이 있을경우, 기가 죽어 목소리를 작게 내서, 본인 실력보다 낮은 점수를 받는 경우가 있으므로, 미리 연습해서 본인의 목소리가 얼마나 작게 녹음 되는지 확인 해볼 기회
나. 1번부터 4번까지 네 개의 문제 순서에 적응하여, 실제 시험당일 문제 순서에 당황할일 없게 하기 위해
다. 내가 어느 유형이 약한지 파악하기 위해
라. (선택: 시험 본 것을 "**첨삭**"으로 이어져, 내 실력의 문제를 점검하기 위해) - **별도서비스**
마. (선택: 내가 어느유형이 약한지 파악후, 추가 관련 문제의 인강을 통해 미진한 부분에 대한 설명을 듣기 위해)

Writing
가. 시험장에서 라이팅 시험은 모두 타이핑 시험인데, 시험장 갈때까지도 독수리 타자를 쳐야 할만큼 준비 없는 것을 막기 위해
나. (선택: 시험 본 것을 "**첨삭**"으로 이어져, 내 실력의 문제를 점검하기 위해) - **별도서비스**
다. (선택: 내가 어느유형이 약한지 파악후, 추가 관련 문제의 인강을 통해 미진한 부분에 대한 설명을 듣기 위해)

03 토플의 평가 영역 (리딩, 리스닝, 스피킹, 라이팅) 및 어셔 모의토플 소개

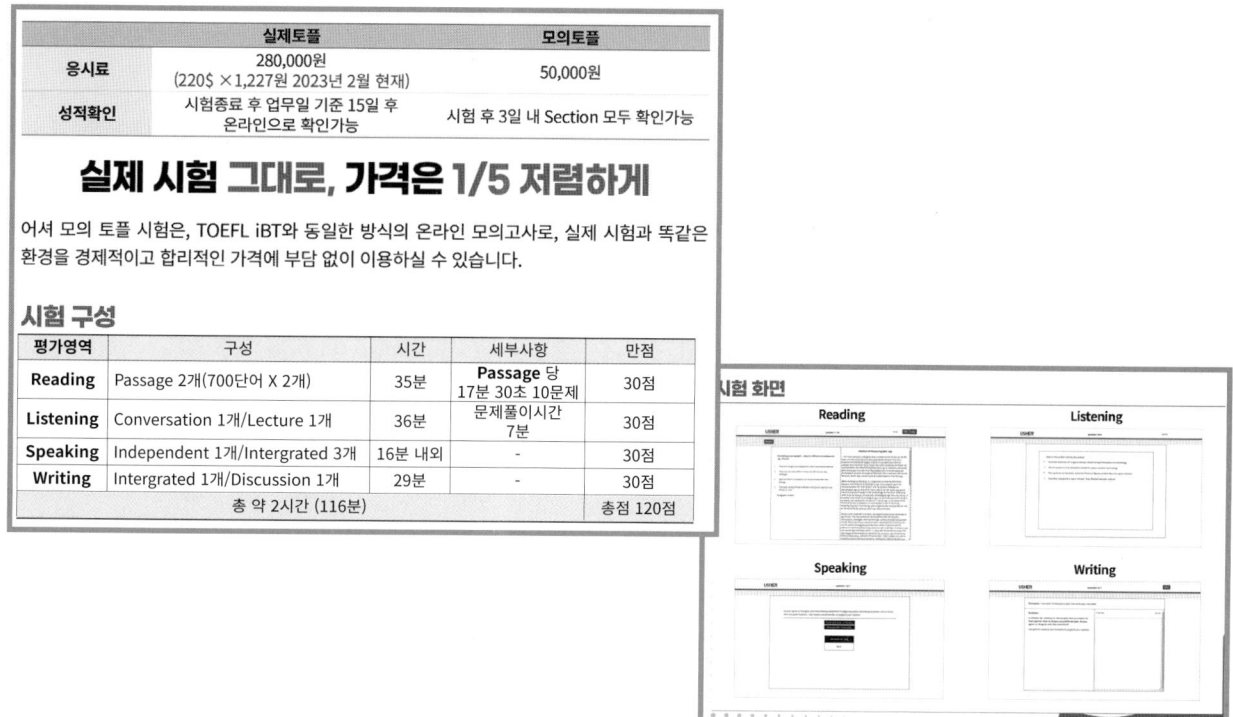

	실제토플	모의토플
응시료	280,000원 (220$ ×1,227원 2023년 2월 현재)	50,000원
성적확인	시험종료 후 업무일 기준 15일 후 온라인으로 확인가능	시험 후 3일 내 Section 모두 확인가능

실제 시험 그대로, 가격은 1/5 저렴하게

어셔 모의 토플 시험은, TOEFL iBT와 동일한 방식의 온라인 모의고사로, 실제 시험과 똑같은 환경을 경제적이고 합리적인 가격에 부담 없이 이용하실 수 있습니다.

시험 구성

평가영역	구성	시간	세부사항	만점
Reading	Passage 2개(700단어 X 2개)	35분	Passage 당 17분 30초 10문제	30점
Listening	Conversation 1개/Lecture 1개	36분	문제풀이시간 7분	30점
Speaking	Independent 1개/Intergrated 3개	16분 내외	-	30점
Writing	Intergrated 1개/Discussion 1개	29분	-	30점
총 약 2시간 (116분)				총점 120점

시험 화면: Reading, Listening, Speaking, Writing

04 구매하기 (개별 과목 별도)

시험명	사용기간	가격
USHER 공식 토플모의고사 Full TEST	1년	50,000원
USHER 공식 토플모의고사 Half(R/L) TEST	1년	27,000원
USHER 공식 토플모의고사 Half(S/W) TEST	1년	27,000원
개별 과목	1년	15,000원

5 토플 Reading 공부방법
usherin.usher.co.kr

리딩 점수에 따라서

- 20점 미만이라면, 리스닝에는 너무 많은 힘을 쓰지 말고, 단어와 리딩에 집중 바랍니다.
  둘 다 하려다 하나도 못 할 수 있습니다.
- 20점 이상이라면, **1.** 단어 **2.** 구문 **3.** 묶기 **4.** 열번읽기 까지 꼼꼼히 처리 바랍니다.
- 25점 이상이면, 단어, 구문은 거의 알 겁니다.
  대략 틀린 것 정도 간단히 마무리 하고 **묶기 및 오답 패턴 확인**에 집중하면 됩니다.

각각의 과정을 적으면 다음과 같습니다.

Step 1. 문제풀이
Step 2. TAGGING
Step 3. 구문 / 단어시험
Step 4. 묶기
Step 5. 타이핑
Step 6. 별지
Step 7. 접속사 암기

과정 순서대로 공부를 해야하는 구체적인 이유와 방법을 적어보겠습니다.

Step 1. 문제 풀이

- 문제 풀이는 실전 화면처럼 컴퓨터로 직접 풀면서 익숙해지는게 좋습니다.

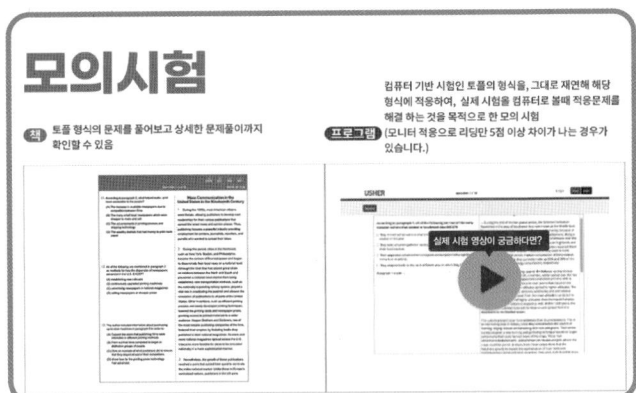

Step 2. TAGGING

- 문제 풀이 직후, 잊기 전에, 문제 풀면서 가장 짜증 났던 부분 = 즉, 이해하기 힘들었던 부분을 체크해 둬야 합니다.

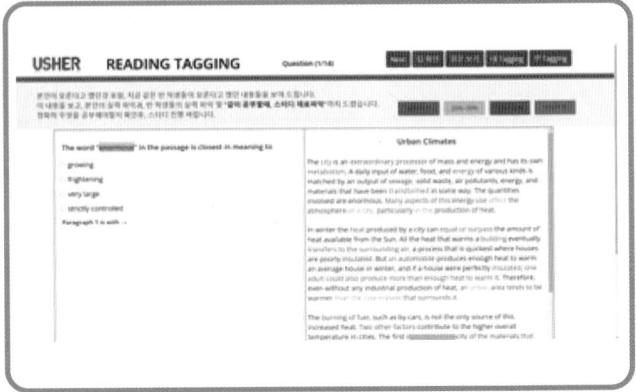

Step 3. 구문 / 단어 시험

- 귀찮은 거 압니다. 그래도 해두시기 바랍니다. 리딩 20점 미만은 실력 없어서 하기 싫어도 해야 하고, 리딩 25점 넘는 분들은 별로 할 것도 없겠지만, 그래도 다 챙겨 두시기 바랍니다.

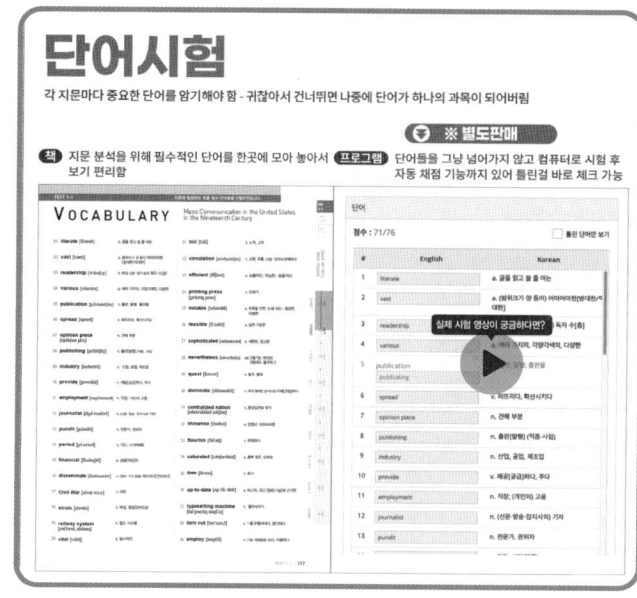

Step 4. 묶기

- 리딩 20점 미만은 실력이 없으니, 파악+ 실력 자체를 늘리기 위해 필요합니다.
- 리딩 25점 이상은 만점 받기 위해서, 본인이 어느 부분이 약한지 "샅샅이 훑어야 할 때", 가장 강력한 툴입니다.
  "30점의 절박함과 귀찮음 중", 더 강한 것이 여러분의 행동을 바꿀겁니다.

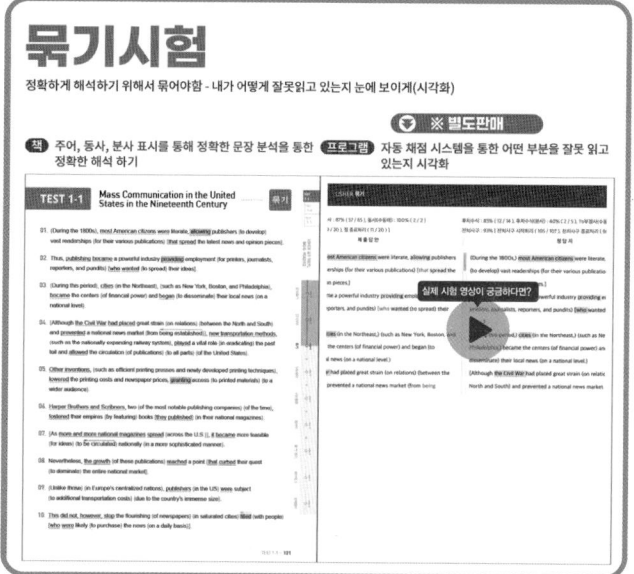

Step 5. 열번읽기(내 발음 체크 = 말 할 수 있으면 들린다)

- 리딩 20점 미만의 학생들에게 가장 중요한 점은 "말 할 수 없으면, 들을 수 없다!!!" 입니다.
- 본인만 아는 이상한 발음으로 기억하면, 절대 못듣습니다.
  이그제그레이션? Exaggeration을 이렇게 읽는 학생. 답 없습니다.
- 말 할 수 있는지는, 학원 프로그램이 모두 파악해 줍니다. 채점까지.
  여러분은 성실함만 있으면 됩니다.

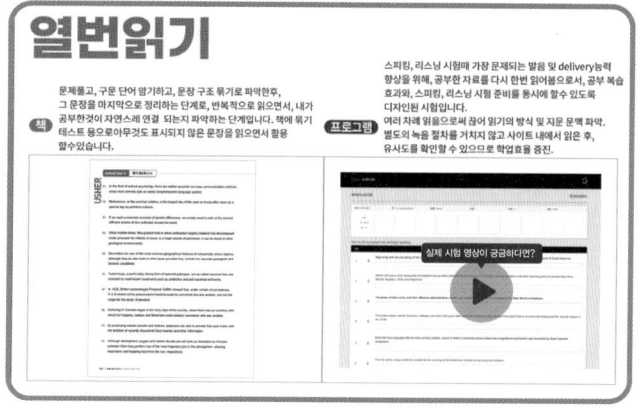

Step 6. 타이핑

- 라이팅 시험은 영타가 기본인데, 이를 따로 준비하는것이 아닌, 공부한 자료를 반복 연습함을서, 영타와 복습을 동시에 진행 가능케 하는 시험
- 주어진 문장을 따라 써 보며 정확도와 속도를 올려, 문맥 파악과 더불어 컴퓨터 기반 시험인 토플에서 고득점 하기 위한 필수 역량을 증진

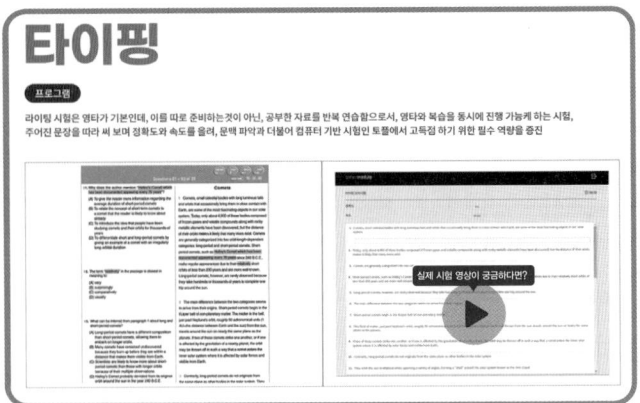

Step 7. 별지

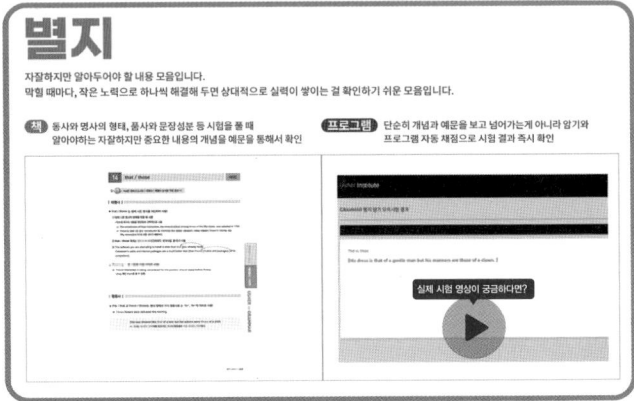

Step 8. 접속사 암기

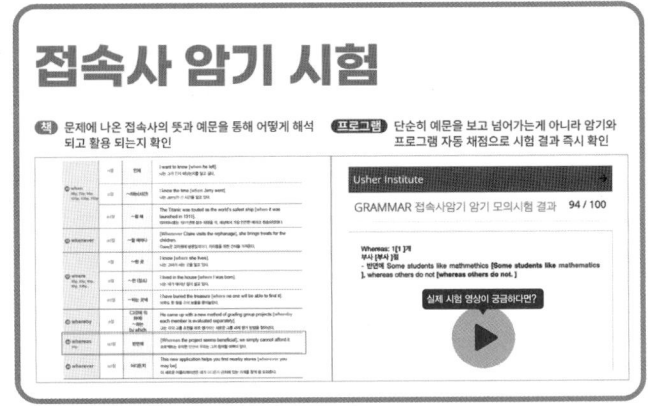

어셔어학원을 다니면,

어셔어학원을 다니면, 이 과정을 모두 스터디 시간에 **무료**로 합니다.

하지만, 사정이 있어서 **인강을 듣거나 프로그램만 구매하시는 분들은**

반드시, 위 내용들을 기억하고, 실행하면, 실력 향상에 큰 도움 되실겁니다.

6 토플 Listening 공부방법
usherin.usher.co.kr

리스닝 점수에 따라서

- 20점 미만이라면, 리스닝에는 너무 많은 힘을 쓰지 말고, 단어와 리딩에 집중 바랍니다.
  둘 다 하려다 하나도 못 할 수 있습니다.

- 20점 이상이라면, **1.** 단어 **2.** 구문 **3.** 딕테이션 **4.** 열번읽기 까지 꼼꼼히 처리 바랍니다.

- 25점 이상이면, 단어, 구문은 거의 알 겁니다.
  대략 틀린 것 정도 간단히 마무리 하고 **딕테이션 및 오답 패턴 확인**에 집중하면 됩니다.

각각의 과정을 적으면 다음과 같습니다.

Step 1. 문제풀이
Step 2. TAGGING
Step 3. 구문 / 단어시험
Step 4. 딕테이션
Step 5. 열번읽기 (내 발음 체크 = 말 할 수 있으면 들린다)
Step 6. 타이핑

과정 순서대로 공부를 해야하는 구체적인 이유와 방법을 적어보겠습니다.

Step 1. 문제 풀이

- 문제 풀이는 실전 화면처럼 컴퓨터로 직접 풀면서 익숙해지는게 좋습니다.

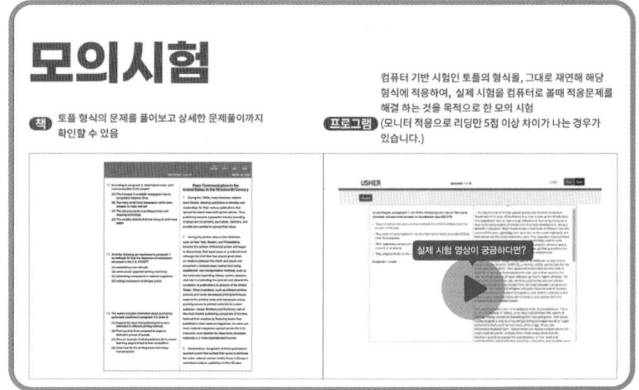

Step 2. TAGGING

- 문제 풀이 직후, 잊기 전에, 문제 풀면서 가장 짜증 났던 부분 = 즉, 이해하기 힘들었던 부분을 체크해 둬야 합니다.

Step 3. 구문 / 단어 시험

- 귀찮은 거 압니다. 그래도 해두시기 바랍니다.

Step 4. 딕테이션

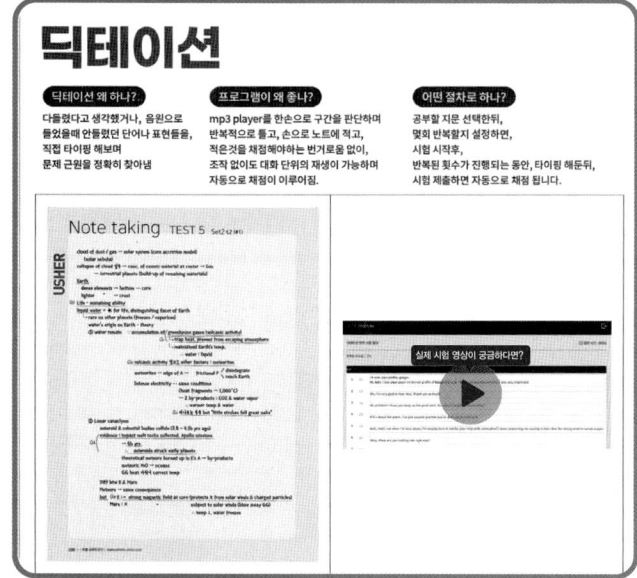

Step 5. 열번읽기(내 발음 체크 = 말 할 수 있으면 들린다)

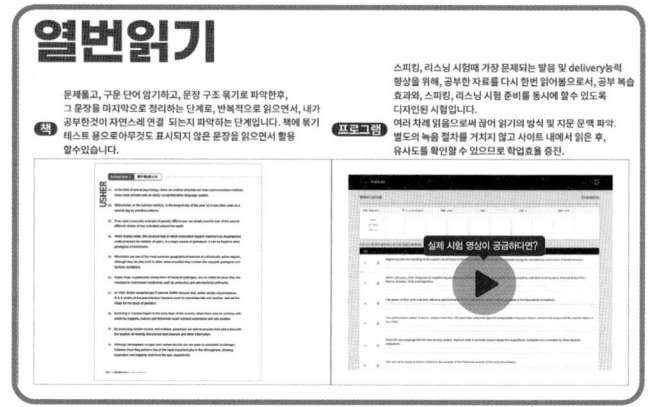

Step 6. 타이핑

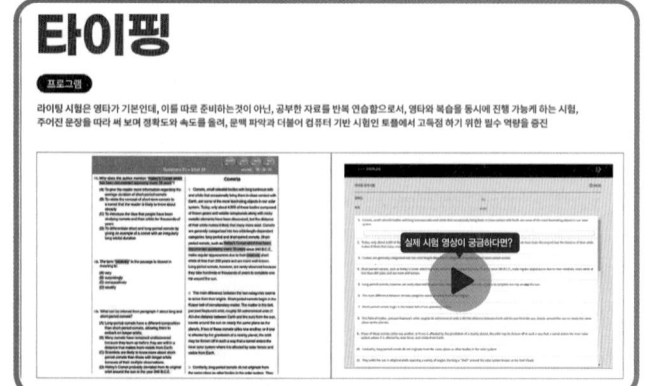

7 수강 후기
usherin.usher.co.kr

김유석
97점 두달간 토플 시험에서의 승리: 훌륭한 교사진, 함께 노력한 학원 동료들에게 감사를

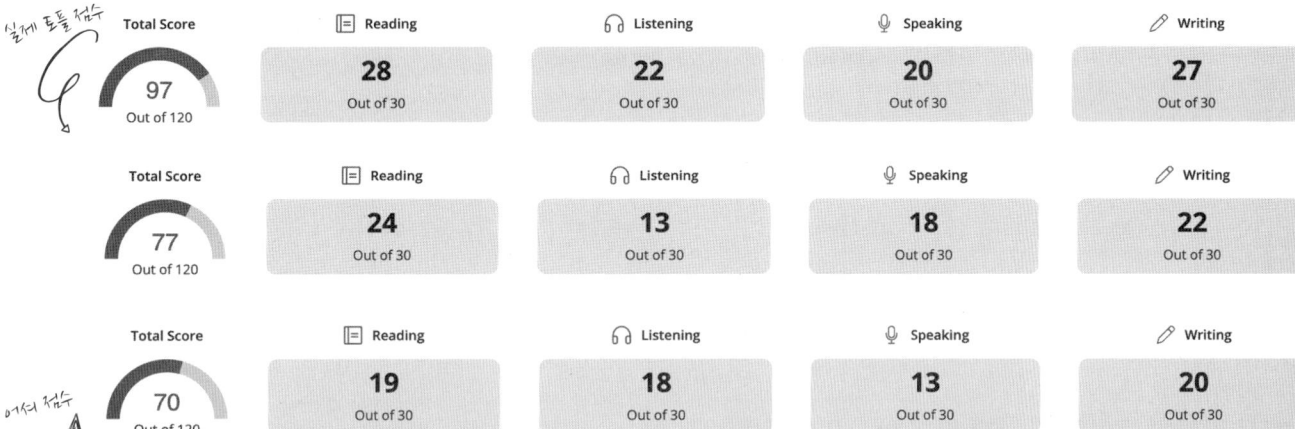

반배치고사						
일자	반	GR			RC	LC
		SW1	SW2	SW1+SW2		
2024-03-29	성인 정규 Intermediate반	10	18	28	32	23
2024-02-29	성인 정규 Intermediate반	11	11	22	28	22
2024-01-23	신규	9	13	22	25	

모의토플					
일자	RC	LC	SP	WR	합계
2024-03-15	17	25	19	20	81
2024-02-16	22	19	0	0	41

2024.03 성인교육중급반 김유석 성취표

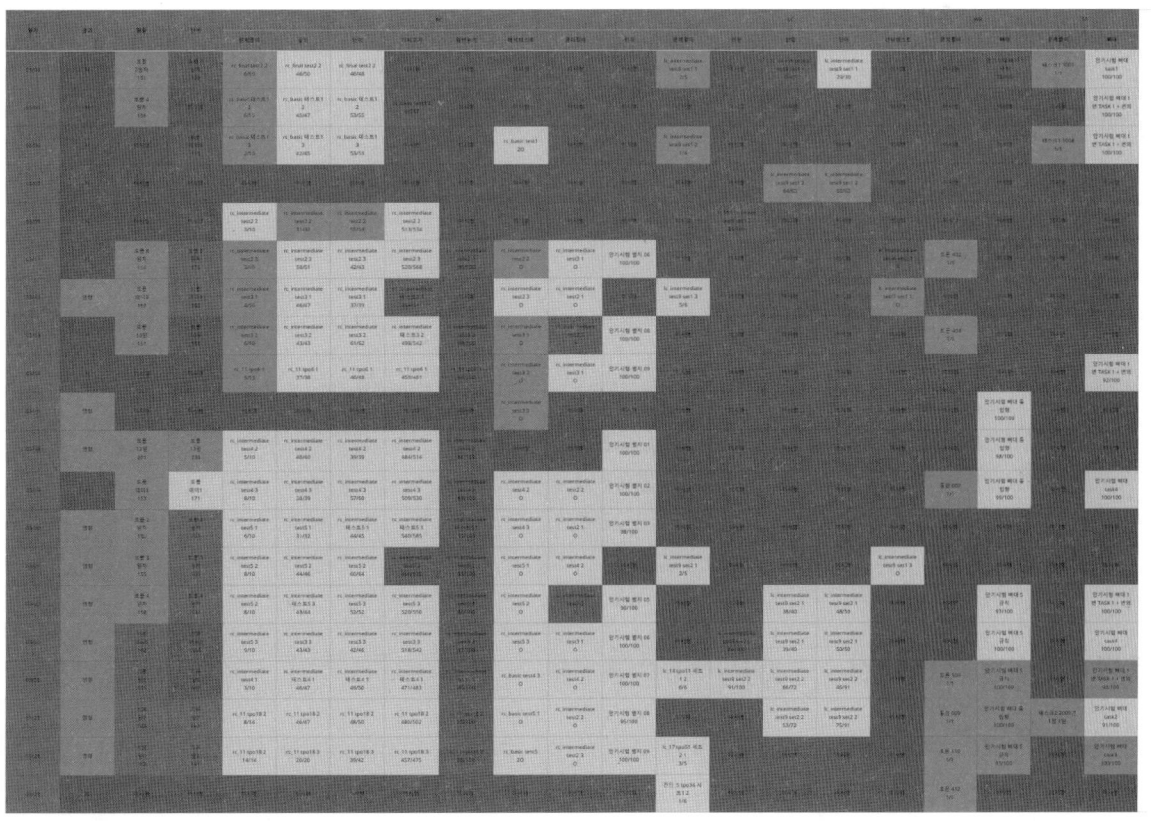

마이페이지 MYPAGE

배치고사 신청/결과확인	예습공지 게시판	수강증 확인	교재 확인하기	증명서 발급
사물함 안내	무료교재 mp3/부록	토익특강 성적표	쿠폰함	사물함 신청

김유석님 반갑습니다 회원정보수정

수강중인 강의 / 반별게시판	결제 진행중인 강의	결제내역	장바구니	교재확인 / 배송조회
0건	0건	20건	0건	0건
자세히 보기	자세히 보기	자세히 보기	자세히 보기	자세히 보기

▌처음 학원에 들어올 때 시작 했던 반
2024년 02월 성인 정규 Intermediate반

▌수강 했던반 / 총 개월수
2024년 02월 성인 정규 Intermediate반
2024년 03월 성인 정규 Intermediate반
2024년 04월 성인 정규 K1반

▌학원에 오기전에 가지고 있었던 점수 (파트별)
- 토익점수_ 합계 : 0 RC : 0 LC : 0
- 토플점수_ 합계 : 70 RC : 19 LC : 18 SP : 13 WR : 20

▌목표했던 토플 점수
100점

▌취득한 토플 점수
RC: 28 LC: 22 SP: 20 WR: 27

▌최초/중간/ 최종
- 최초_ 합계 : 70 RC : 19 LC : 18 SP : 13 WR : 20
- 중간_ 2024-01-23 배치고사 SW:22, RC:25, LC:0
  2024-02-16 모의고사 RC:22, LC:19, SP:0, WR:0
  2024-02-29 배치고사 SW:22, RC:28, LC:22
  2024-03-15 모의고사 RC:17, LC:25, SP:19, WR:20
  2024-03-29 배치고사 SW:28, RC:32, LC:23
- 최종_ RC: 0 LC: 0 SP: 0 WR: 0

▌토플 공부한 이유(학업 이유)
일본유학(EJU)

파트별 상세 설명

• Reading

제가 가장 나댈수 있는 영역입니다.

저는 한 달동안 삼지문 -> 인터 -> K반 까지 승반했었던 유일한 사람이기에, 현재 인터반 학생들이 주의깊게 봤으면 합니다. 다만 한가지 전제조건은, 저는 원래 문해력으로 승부보는 사람이었다는 점입니다. 즉 지문 이해력은 높으나, 영어해석능력이 부족해서 RC영역에서 고생했다는 점을 말해두고 싶습니다.

우선 첫 달은, 영어를 읽고 푸는데에 대한 '자신감', 그리고 긴 문장을 만났을때 '익숙함' 에 중요성에 대해서 배웠습니다. 혜성쌤 께서 강조하신 '오늘 푼 지문 10번 읽기' 과제를 다 하진 못했었으나, 세번씩이라도 읽다보니, 모르는 단어가 나오거나, 긴 문장을 봤을때 느끼는 자신감이 상당히 올라갔고, 정답률 또한 올라갔습니다. 그러나, 아직 이 시기에서는, 문장 직독직해의 수준이 낮은상태였으며, 주어진 시간안에 한 지문을 읽는것이 불안했습니다.

두 번째 달에는, 사실상 제 RC영역에 가장 큰 영향을 주신 김석균 선생님의 수업을 들었습니다.

선생님의 가르침 하에서 선생님이 강조하시는, 그리고 제가 느끼는 중요성의 순서는 다음과 같습니다.

1. 수업시간에 선생님께서 워드에 정리하고, 수업 후에 올려주시는 메모를 빠르게 기억하고 넘어가기 입니다.

>> 각 지문 테마 별, 자주 나오는 단어나 표현들이 익숙해지기 때문에, 다음 번, 비슷한 지문을 만났을 때, 읽는 속도와 정확성, 자신감이 매우 다릅니다.

2. 묶기 빠르게 할 것***

묶기를 연구해가며 하지마세요. 묶기는 하나의 시험입니다. 문장 내에서, 본인이 약한 문법의 영역을 파악할 수 있는 부분이기 때문에, 빠르게 풀 되, 묶기의 결과를 잘 살펴보고, 메모를 남겨둡시다. 특히 토플 RC에서 등위접속사 and, or 과 같은 문법을 다르게 읽는다면, 해석이 전혀 다른 내용이 되기 때문에 지문 이해에 큰 방해가 될 것 입니다.

3. 해석테스트

토플의 RC는 사실 이해를 하지 못한다고 해도, 70프로의 정답률을 보장할 수 있는 시험이라고 생각합니다.

그 이유로는, 어차피 문제에서 물어보는것은 지문의 특정 부분에 관해서 이고, 지문을 한번 읽었을때 기억을 살려, 빠르게 문제에서 요구하는 부분을 지문에서 찾기만 한다면, 정답률 또한 상당히 올라갈 것 입니다.

다만, 지문을 읽고 기억하는데에 있어서, 중요한 능력이 직독직해라고 생각합니다. 토플은 영어단어 바꿔넣기의 시험. 즉 영어를 잘한다는 느낌보다, 유의어 단어나 표현을 얼마나 알고있는지를 묻기에, 기계적인 암기능력을 요구한다고 생각합니다.

그렇기 때문에, 직독직해가 된다면, 유의어가 페러프라이징 된 선지를 고를수 있기때문에, 정답률이 올라갑니다.

또한, 결정적으로 직독직해를 잘 하게 된다면, 영어문장을 빠르게 읽게 되기 때문에, 시간안에 문제를 다 읽고 푸는것이 가능해 진다고 생각합니다. 이런 직독직해능력을 기를 수 있고, 내 상태를 점검할 수 있는 해석테스트를 열심히 준비합시다.

4. 네 번째로 제가 생각하는 석균쌤의 RC포인트 + 어셔에서 가장 중요하게 강요하는 부분인 단어 입니다.

어셔를 다니면서 단어시험은 가장 큰 스트레스중 하나라고 생각합니다. 우선 학원측에서 단어암기를 하라고 과제를 내주면, 암기조차 안하는 학생들이 있기 때문에, 인터반 기준 200개중 180개의 빡센 목표를 요구하는 것 같습니다.

다만 제 생각으론, 단어를 암기하는데에 있어 가장 중요한것은 200개중 180개로 통과해서 초록불을 띄우는 것이 아니라, 내가 한번 본 단어의 뉘앙스를 얼마나 파악했는지 입니다.

아마 저와 수업을 들어보신 분들은 공감하시겠지만, 석균쌤이 수업중에 나온 단어에 대해 동의어를 물어보실 때, 가장 대답을 잘하는 학생이 저 였을 것입니다. 하지만, 반면에 3월달 VOCA 성취율이 가장 낮은 학생도 저라고 생각합니다. 매번 160~170개로 180개를 통과하지 못한적이 허다했거든요.

하지만 그렇다고해서 저는 단어공부의 시간을 줄인적이 없습니다. 대신 낯선 단어가 갖고있는 의미, 그리고 동의어, 이 단어가 어떤 주제의 지문에서 나오는가 에 초점을 맞췄습니다.

그와 반대로, 단어시험 통과율이 엄청 높으신 분들 혹은, 학원을 오랫동안 다니신 분들에게 있어, RC의 점수를 큰 폭으로 향상시키는 대에 방해되는것이 바로 180개 제한 통과방식인것 같습니다. 160개에서 180개로 단어시험 정답률을 높이기 위해선, 한글뜻에 초점을 맞추게 되고, 그러다보면, RC지문에서 만난 낯선 단어를 빠르게 의미를 떠올리는데에 딜레이가 생길 것 입니다. 물론 우선 단어의 익숙함을 줄이고, RC지문에서 만났을 때, 자신감 있게 한글로 해석할 수 있다면, RC의 한 지문을 읽는데에 유의미한 정답률 상승이 있다고 생각합니다. 그렇기 때문에, 단어를 열심히 외우시고, 통과를 잘하는 분들이라면, 지문에서 모르는 단어가 나왔을때는, 남들도 모르는 단어라고 생각하고 일단 자신감 있게 읽고 넘어가셔야 한 지문을 넘어 RC, RC를 넘어 LC, SPK, WRT까지,, 나머지 영역에도 전반적인 영향을 주는 자신감을 잃지 않을 수 있습니다. 그렇기에 본인의 자신감을 유지하는데에 가장 중요한 단어를 소홀히 하시지 마시길 바랍니다.

마지막으로 제 어셔에서의 토플 기간동안 가장 중요했던 3월달 첫 주 "삼지문 반" 입니다.

삼지문반을 수강함으로써, RC에서의 제 단점을 확실히 파악하는것이 가능했습니다.

수강후기 Reading 영역 첫 문두 에서도 말했다시피, 저는 상대적으로 감각적인 문해력을 가진 반면에, 영어를 한국말로 옮기는 부분에 대해서 많이 부족했었습니다. 그러다보니 제가 이해를 할 수 있는 지문들에 대해서는 70% 까지의 정답률을 보장했으나, 이해가 되지 않는 주제에 관해서는 그야말로 처참했었죠..

그러다 원장님이 삼지문반 승반테스트를 진행하시고, RC영역에 대해서 설명해주실때, 그야말로 광명을 찾았습니다.

RC = R+C, 즉, Reading + comprehension 이라는 말, Reading 이 7, Comprehension이 3의 비율을 갖는다는 것을 듣고 나서야 비로소, 그때서야 제 단점이 Reading (직독직해) 라는 점에 대해 확신할 수 있었습니다.

그 이후로는, 인터반 -> 삼지문반으로 하반당했다는 압박을 머금고 친한 동료들 경선이와 건우형과 함께 세가지 지문 부수기에 목숨 걸었습니다. 저의 지문 이해력과 설명 + 경선, 건우의 직독직해 설명이 서로에게 큰 시너지를 주었습니다. 3월의 첫 주에 삼지문 반을 경험한 것이, 지속적인 제 RC점수의 상승에 포문을 열었다고 생각합니다.

그렇게 터프하게 학원 불 꺼져도 11시 반까지 공부하다가 보니 한 가지 재미있는 일화도 남겼던것이 기억에 남내요 ㅋㅋㅋ
원장님이 퇴근하시다가 어둠속에서 공부하던 저와 소연, 경선의 공부하는 동영상을 찍어가신것, 채운쌤께서도 퇴근 하시다가 저희를 발견하시고 기분좋아하셨던 그런것들이 저희에게도 큰 원동력이 되었던 것 같습니다.

다시 궤도로 돌아와서 정리하자면, 삼지문 반을 거쳐, 3월 모의토플 이전까지 문제풀이및 석균쌤의 수업에 익숙해졌고, 3월 셋째 주부터 RC점수가 팍 뛰더니 변동기에 들어오기 시작한 것 같습니다. 그리고 3월 이후 어셔에서의 생활을 마무리 하려던 찰나, 석균쌤과 채운쌤의 설득과 조언에 못이겨 4/2, 4/3의 수업도 듣게 되었고, 이 기간에 RC 고득점 평탄화가 이뤄져, 저를 하여금 어셔에서 졸업을 하도록 만들어 준 것 같습니다.

마무리로, 쌤들 말 안듣는 친구들에게도 한마디 하자면, 자기 멋대로 공부를 하려면 우선 쌤들이 시킨것부터 끝내고 하는것은 어떨까요? 석균쌤의 말씀대로, 제 RC점수가 상승하고 안정된 시기는, 어셔의 syllabus를 다 채우는데 성공한 시점부터라는 점을 알아주셨음 합니다.

- Listening

저에게 있어서, 시험 한번한번의 변동이 가장 큰 과목입니다.
모의토플 에서는 25점도 맞아보았고, 수업시간에 풀었던 문제는 컨버 렉쳐 렉쳐 다 맞은 적도 있었던것을 비추어 볼 때,
듣기의 고점 자체를 한번 끌어올리는데에는 성공했다고 생각됩니다.
먼저 그렇게 끌어올리는데 성공했던 이유를 생각해 보면

첫째. 채운쌤의 세뇌.
질문과 답변 위주로 들어라, 고유명사 연도 는 꼭 적어라, 동사위주로 들어라, 예시는 예시가 나온이유, 그것에 대한 결과를 들어야 한다,, 노트테이킹은 왼쪽에서 오른쪽으로 해라.
사실 더 많은데,, 신입분들은 수업료 내고 들으시라고 여기까지만 !! / 기존 학생들은 본인들이 메모했던 내용들을 한번 정리한다음, WRT통합형의 파이브룰즈 처럼 달달 외우는 것을 추천합니다.

둘째. 디스커버리 유튜브채널의 영상 "마지막 알레스카인" 반복 청취.
1시간 46분짜리 몰아보기 영상을 매 대중교통에서, 집안일 할때, 밥먹을때 반복해서 들었을 시기가 LC점수가 가장 잘 나왔던 시기입니다. 저는 시골출신에, 서바이벌에 관심이 많아 재밌게 봤던 영상인데, 토플 bio지문에 나오는 단어들을 귀로 반복해서 들었던것이 상당히 고무적 이었습니다. 시각을 이용해서 공부하지 않는 시간에는 꼭 귀라도 영어로 채워두길 바랍니다.

셋째. 딕테이션을 단어 단어 단어 적고, 중간에 비었던 부분을 다시 매꾸는 것이 아니라, 영어를 한 뭉탱이 단위로 듣고 적었을 때, 내용이 가장 잘 들렸고, 그러다 보니 노트의 위에도 적어야 하는 내용만 적을 수 있어서, 정답률이 높았던 것 같습니다. 채운쌤이 말하시는 딕테이션의 방식 1단계 2단계 3단계를 잘 수행하시길 바랍니다.

다만, 더 높은 점수를 내지 못한 이유에는
첫째. 어셔에 있는 도중, 리스닝 자습에 시간을 많이 쓰지 못한것.
RC와 LC는 몇번 고점을 찍는것이 가능하다면, 그 이후에는 점수의 변동을 잡아주는것이 중요하다고 생각하는데, 이 변동을 잡는것에 시간을 투자하지 못한것 같아서 아쉽습니다.

둘째. 노트테이킹을 점점 많이 적게 된 것.
노트테이킹의 양에 대해서도, 선생님들마다 다르지만, 저는 적게 적었을때가 오히려 더 정답률이 높았습니다.
단순하게 내용을 많이 적은것은, 디테일을 놓칠 확률이 큽니다.

셋째. 단기기억 기르는 연습을 게을리 함.
영어는 한국말처럼 단어만 투욱 툭 던져서는 의미가 만들어지지 않는다고 선생님들이 많이 말씀하십니다.
그렇다면 영어를 잘 듣기위해선, 언어 하나의 덩어리가 어디부터 어디까지인지 인식을 하고, 기억을 하고있어야 합니다.
청취테스트 연습을 부지런히 한다면, 본인이 들은 한 덩어리 덩어리가, 잘 기억에 남고, LC정답률 상향에 크게 기여할 것 같습니다.

LC영역에서 저의 결론은 "문제풀이 방식에 시간을 쏟지 맙시다" 라는 것입니다. 토플 리스닝 특성 상, 내용이 잘 들리고, 디테일을 기억하거나 노트에 옮겨적는다면 문제는 어지간히 다 맞을 것 이라 생각합니다.

- Speaking

4과목 중 가장 낮은 점수를 맞아서 가장 할말이 적습니다. 뼈대 잘 외우고, 12간지 잘 외우고, 리스닝영역 문장단위로 적고!! 이 삼박자가 맞지 않고서는 의미있는 점수를 낼 수 없다고 생각합니다. 토플이 단과시험이 아니고, 여러 영역을 요구하는 만큼, 전체의 성적을 끌어올리기 위해선, 무리를 해서라도 하루에 스피킹 하나정도 녹음하는것을 추천드립니다.

두번째로 스피킹 1번과 같은경우 암기가 끝이 아니고, 주어진 주제문에 대해 뼈대와 12간지를 변형시키는 유연함 도 길러야한다는 점 잊지 말아주세요.

저 같은 경우, 솔직히 유연하게 대처하는 연습이 소홀했기 때문에, 걍 논리 안맞는 문장나와도 자신있게 어거지로 밀고 들어갔습니다. 그래서 20점이라도 나오지 않았나 싶어요..
자신있게 어거지로 밀고가서 20점이라도 확보하려면 뼈대 + 12간지를 반드시 외워야 할 것입니다.

- **Writing**

4과목중 가장 의외인 점수를 가져다준 고마운 과목입니다. 사실 WRT이 고맙기보단 당연히 채운쌤께 너무 감사드립니다..
스피킹과 더불어 공부량이 적었던 과목인데, 왜 27점이 나왔을까요??...
바로 제 WRT점수가 12간지와 파이브룰즈에 위대함을 다시금 증명했다고 생각합니다.
물론 저도 작전을 세우긴 했는데,, 그게 12간지의 위대함과 더불어 잘 들어맞았네요.
제 작전은, 제가 많은 내용을 생산할 수록, 문법과 스펠링 미스가 많아져서, WRT의 총점을 깎을것이라 예상해서, 안전빵 문장들만 가져다 적었습니다. 절때 어렵게 쓰려고 하지 마시고, 본인만의 예시 뼈대를 만들고, 12간지에 기대어 최대한 문장을 간단하게 쓰는것을 추천드립니다.

- **어셔의 관리 프로그램 (asap프로그램) 관련 사용 팁**

점수 취득 후 얻게된 결과
1) 한번 실패를 맛 보았던 토플에서 성공을 거둔것.
매번 꿈에 나오던 학창시절 담당일진을 길에서 만나 뚜드려 팬것과 동일한 기분이지 않을까요??
2) 자신감
내 인생에 있어서 가장 높았던 벽 '토플'을 넘었기 때문에,, 앞으로 못할건 하나도 없을것 같다는 근자감

저는 ○○스에서 1년 이상의 시간과 돈을 쓰며 영어의 5형식부터 공부했었습니다. ○○스의 기본문법 교실은 to부정사가 뭔지 모르는 저에게는 꽤나 재미있고 이해가 잘 갔던 수업이었죠.
그러나 문제는 ○○스 토플 커리큘럼에 들어가면서 시작입니다. 제가 생각한 ○○스 토플의 문제를 순서대로 나열하자면,
1) 영어 기초반에서 토플 기초반으로 넘어갈 때, 간극이 꽤 크다.
>> 단어 요구량이 너무 차이나기 때문에, 영어 기초반에서 공부한 뒤 바로 토플 기초반수업 못따라갑니다.
2) 영어실력의 "근본"을 경시한다.
>> 이게 가장 큰 문제라고 생각합니다. 특히, 만약 이글을 보는 본인의 목표가 80점 이상이라면.
제 생각으론, ○○스의 '입문+인터미디엇' 반의 수준이, 어셔의 '완초 1~2반' 이랑 비슷합니다.
근데 차이점이 있다면, ○○스에서는 딱 그정도의 영어수준을 지닌 학생들이 그 상태에서 점수를 잘 내도록 교과과정이 맞춰져 있습니다. 그말은 즉, 더 높은 점수대로 도전하는 "근본"을 쌓는데에 아 무 런 도움이 되지 않는 다는 점입니다.
본인이 영어가 안읽히고, 안들려도.. 그 상태에서 점수를 내게 알려주는 방법이 ○○스식 입니다.
이 방식으로는 저같이 영어의 "근본"이 없는 학생들에게 있어서 90점대의 아성에 도전할수가 없습니다.
3) 각 과목 선생님들이 다르고, 같은 과목의 선생님들도 너무 많다.
>> 템플릿 다 난리납니다. 같은 과목의 선생님들 마다 말이 아 다르고 어 다릅니다.
각 과목의 선생님들의 목소리가 너무 큽니다. 수업시간 40~50분의 짧은 시간에 수업을 듣기 위해서, 하루 과목당 4~5시간 정도의 자습량을 요구합니다. 즉, 토플 4과목의 과제를 마치지 않는다면, 수업을 듣는 의미가 없습니다.
○○스 다녀보신 분들 수업 1주차 부터 같은 교실에 사람들이 적어지는것을 경험했거나, 혹은 본인이 점점 수업에 참여를 못하게 되는 학생이셨죠?
그~러~니, 어셔를 토플 학원에 안중을 넣고 계신 분이라면, 혹은 지금 다니고 계신 분이라면 영어의 "근본" 을 쌓기위해서 어떻게 해야하나 열심히 고민해보세요. 공부법에 최첨단 방식은 없습니다.
암기, 반복, 직독직해 이런 무식하다고 여겨지는 공부가 아직도 사용 되는 이유는 '전통적' 이기 때문입니다. 전통이 전통으로 이어져 온 것에는 그것이 최선책 이어왔기 때문입니다.
학생분들의 뇌는 그저, 때려 넣는것만 생각하시고, 학원에서 시키는것에 대해 의문을 가지지좀 마세요.
그렇게 본인이 학원보다 좋은방법을 알고 있었다면, 지금 이 후기를 볼 일도 없을 테니까요.
뇌의 사용량을 다른데 투자할 것 없이, 내용을 집어넣는 것에만 집중한다는것이 얼마나 효율적입니까?
대신, 학원이 이걸 왜 시키는걸까? 에 대해서만 '고민' 수준에서 머물도록 하는것을 추천합니다..
어셔 어학원에서의 시간들을 돌이켜보며...
어셔에서의 두 달은 제 수명 1~2년을 끌어쓴다는 느낌으로 지냈습니다.
1) 수면은 두달동안 평균 5시간 안넘을거라 생각하구요,,
2) 점심또한 편의점 삼각김밥만 먹어서 소화장애 심각했었죠..
같이 공부했던 친구들은 알겠지만 제 말버릇 중 하나가 소화안되서 죽을것같다..
위생천/까스활명수 마셔야겠다 아마 지겹도록 들었을 것입니다
근데 할만했습니다.. 어셔에서 토플은 공부라기 보단, 하나의 팀 스포츠라고 생각합니다. 매일같이 남아서 동료들과 훈련을 하고, 스스로의 한계를 극복하고, 결과로써 증명한다. 이렇게 생각했기 때문에 어셔에서 상당히 즐거운 시간을 보낼 수 있었습니다.
인생에서 무언가를 위해 몰두하는 경험을 쌓기위해 최적의 환경을 잘 조성해주신 원장님, 그리고 채운쌤과 석균쌤, 해성쌤과 같이 교사진들의 엄청난 하드워킹.. 어셔에서의 두 달은 진정한 낙수효과에 대해서도 느끼게 해준 것 같습니다.
저는 두 달하고 빠질생각으로 다녔기 때문에 제가 열심히 해야하는건 당연했구요..
그런데도 불구하고 나를 가르치는 선생님들은 몇년씩 이 생활을 반복하고 있다는 사실을 생각해 본다면,, 적어도 본인이 어셔에 있는 동안은 그들보다 열심히 해야한다는걸 잊지마세요.

▌어셔생활백서

[1] 밥집:
1) 먹고싶은것 없으면 "감미옥" - 시간은 금입니다. 가장 가까운 복합 한식 분식집이며, 맛 또한 일대에서 상위권입니다. 만약 사장님께 아양을 잘 떤다면, 공짜 밥 무한리필도 가능합니다.
2) 먹고싶은것 없고, 감미옥이 질린다면 "KFC" (도보 왕복 약 8분)
3) 학원 MZ세대들이 아마,, 제일 좋아할 김치볶음밥&돈까스 "하트타임" (KFC 근처)
4) 든든한 국밥 "장터순대국" (KFC 아랫층)
5) "뉴코아 킴스클럽" 푸드코드: 가지마세요 시간 다 뺏깁니다. (도보 왕복 약 16분)
>> 참고로 점심은 빠르게 편의점에서 드시고 구문/단어, 묶기 하세요.. 시간은 금입니다.

[2] 자습실 (=학원 오픈시간)
1) 평일: 매일 아침 7시 30분 안에 열리고, 오후 11시 ~ 11시 30분에 닫힙니다.
2) 주말: 주 마다 쌤들께 여쭤보세요. 열릴때도, 안 열릴때도 있습니다.
>> 토플 학원의 학원비는 결코 싸지 않습니다. 최대한 학원의 전기, 수도, 난방 비용을 털어간다는 생각으로 남으세요.

[3] 대인관계:
제 생각으로 어셔에서 공부 다음으로 중요한 영역같습니다. 얼굴을 본 기억이 있는 사람과 마주친다면 정중히 인사부터 나눕시다. 특히, 열심히 하는 학생이 있다면, 혹은 점수를 잘 내는 친구가 있다면 잘 보고 배웁시다.

▌Thanks to

1) 경선.. 어셔가 나에게 선물한 가장 친한 친구.. 덕분에 어셔 너무 재미있게 다녔다... 나도 가끔 너무힘들고 맨탈 흔들릴때 있었는데, 그때마다 경선이의 활기랑 에너지가 나아갈 힘을 계속해서 준것같아.. 진짜 너 없었으면 쉽게 졸업하기 힘들었을것 같아 너무고맙다 경선아. 빠르게 졸업하고 서로 남은 한국에서의 목표한 바를 완수한 다음에 또 신나게 놀아보자

2) 소연.. 아마 본인은 모르실 것 같은데, 소연님이 제 점수가 오르는데 1등 공신이십니다.. 소연님 분석을 꽤 했거든요 ㅋㅋㅋ 소연님 같은 분이랑 수업을 들을수 있었던것이 진짜 엄청난 행운이었습니다. 그리고 왜 또 공부는 그렇게 열심히 하시는지.. 서로 각자의 위치로 돌아간다음에도 잊지말고 자주 연락해요. (콩고물 얻어먹을라니까)

3) 환준.. 같은 일유생의 키즈나.. 인터에서 K반으로 넘어간 동료이자 산책 나카마... 뭐 우리는 일본에서 끈덕지게 볼것같으니 짧게 씀

4) 건우.. 건우햄 행동력 하나는 진짜 끝내줍니다.. 사실 저도 제 친구들 사이에서 미친행동력으로 비난과 감탄 둘다 받는데 형은 그 이상인 것 같아요.. F-k ng 트래블러 건우형. 저도 여행 좋아하니까 아프리카 정도 아니면 한번 같이 가는것도 좋을지도 ..?

5) 혜성.. 경선, 건우와 더불어 삼지문 -> 인터반의 동료.. 혜성님 힘들어 하시다가 저랑 경선이가 혜성님 웃게 만들었을때 상당히 성취감 있었습니다. 그리고 제가 생각하는 가장 빨리 졸업할 것 같은 멤버 3명중 한 분이십니다. 자신감 잃지마시고 토플 부수기 기원합니다.

6) 인터반 친구들
졸업하고 하느라 교실의 분위기도 많이 달라졌지만,, 다들 함께 할 수 있었기 때문에 토플이라는 거대한 압박 안에서 나름 즐겁게 보냈던것 같습니다.. 2월달에 인터반의 화목하고 재미난 분위기를 만들어두고 가신 하륜이형, 동훈이형도 너무 감사드리고,, 수업시간에 저랑 경선이가 어떻게보면 수업을 방해할 수도 있을 수준에 헛소리를 해도 다들 웃고 넘어가주셔서 감사합니다. 모두 목표한 바를 이루시길 기원합니다.

김유석 어셔졸업 일등공신 채운쌤:
처음에 상담할 시기부터 제 토플공부에 가장 크게 기여해주셨다는 점 알아주셨음 합니다 ㅋㅋㅋ
선생님만 믿고 다른생각 안한 덕에, 기대하지 않은 좋은 점수를 만들 수 있었던 것 같아요.. 비록 처음 반 배치가 완초 2반으로 떨어졌지만, 쌤 께서 2달안에 졸업하려면, 힘들더라도 인터반이 좋을수 있다고 조언해주신 덕에, 인터반에서 기분좋은 시작을 할 수 있었습니다. 그리고 또 가끔 제 기강이 해이해질 타이밍에 완벽히, 교실 전체에 기강 다져주신것도 큰 도움이 되었습니다 ㅋㅋㅋㅋㅋ
12간지야 뭐 말하는거 입아프구요.. 저는 선생님께서 단순히 '선생님'이라는 직책을 빼고도 '김채운'이라는 훌륭한 사람을 만난것에 대해 좋은 경험한 것 같습니다. 하지만 건강도 잘 챙기셔서 롱런하셨음 좋겠어요 ㅋㅋ 채운쌤 너무 감사합니다 !!

석균쌤:
가끔 편한길 찾고싶어서 쌤한테 시도할때마다 본전도 못찾고 깨진 기억들이 떠오르네요.. 덕분에 정신차리고 공부했습니다 쌤. ㅋㅋㅋ 어셔 한달 더 다니고 싶었던 가장 큰 이유가 바로 석균쌤의 수업이었는데,, 다행히도 금방 졸업을 했네요...
그리고 리딩 테마별로 지문 별 문제풀이 순서를 직접 고안하셨는지는 모르겠지만,, 테마별 리딩 문제풀이 순서가 너무 도움됐습니다.. 딱 우주에 대해 잊어먹었을 즈음에 복습시키고,, 슬슬 적응되던 테마에서 벗어나서 낯선거 풀게시키고.. 그 외에도 쌤께 고마운거 많지만 이만 줄이겠습니다. 쌤은 쿨하시니까요 ~

조교쌤들도 너무 감사했습니다 !! 특히 예림쌤, 유하쌤, 명준쌤,, 매번 해태할때마다 답답하셨을텐데,, 저였으면 좀 화났을수도 있었을 것 같은데, 친절하게 질문받아주시고 너무 감사했습니다 !!!